Columbian
Consequences

A Contribution from the Society for American Archaeology
in Recognition of the Columbian Quincentenary
1492–1992

Columbian Consequences

Volume 2

**Archaeological and Historical Perspectives
on the Spanish Borderlands East**

Edited by David Hurst Thomas

Smithsonian Institution Press, Washington and London

Copyright © 1990 by Smithsonian Institution
All rights reserved
Editor: Vicky Macintyre
Designer: Janice Wheeler

Library of Congress Cataloging-in-Publication Data
Archaeological and historical perspectives on the Spanish borderlands
　　east / edited by David Hurst Thomas.
　　　　p. cm.– (Columbian consequences : v. 2)
　　　Includes bibliographical references.
　　　ISBN 0–87474–390–7
　　　1. Spaniards—Southern States—History.　2. Spaniards—Caribbean
　　Area—History.　3. Southern States—History—Colonial period, ca.
　　1600–1775.　4. Caribbean Area—History To 1810.
　　5. Ethnoarchaeology—Southern States.　6. Ethnoarchaeology—Caribbean Area.
　　7. Southern States—Antiquities.　　8. Caribbean Area—Antiquities.
　　9. Indians of North America—Southern States—First
　　contact with Occidental civilization.　10. Indians of the
　　West Indies—First contact with Occidental civilization.
　　I. Thomas, David Hurst.　II. Series.
　　F799.C66　　　1990 vol. 2
　　[F212]
　　979 s–dc20
　　[979'.01]　　　　　　　　　　　　　　　　　　　　　　　　　89–29510

British Library Cataloguing-in-Publication Data available

Manufactured in the United States of America

10　9　8　7　6　5　4　3　2
98　97　96　95　94　93

⊗ The paper used in this publication meets the minimum requirements of the American
National Standard for Permanence of Paper for Printed Library Materials Z39.48–1984.

To Gary Shapiro

Gary Shapiro's premature passing created an emptiness in American archaeology. Not only were we robbed of his distinctive flair for investigation, but all who knew him miss the spontaneous goodwill of his character.

Had he lived, Gary would have played a significant role in *Columbian Consequences*. But his impact remains formidable even in death, and derivatives of his research appear posthumously in two chapters herein. We sincerely hope that our individual and collective efforts measure up to Gary Shapiro's unrelenting standards.

We respectfully dedicate this volume of *Columbian Consequences* to his memory.

Columbian Consequences

Contents

List of Illustrations

David Hurst Thomas

Columbian Consequences: Probing the Spanish Borderlands East

In the *Columbian Consequences* seminars, we attempt to explore the range of contemporary thought about New World encounters and to provide an interested public with an accurate and factual assessment of what did—and what did not—happen as a result of the Columbian encounter. Specifically, we probe the social, demographic, ecological, ideological, and human repercussions of European–Native American encounters across the Spanish Borderlands. Although initiated and cosponsored by the Society of American Archaeology, this inquiry moves beyond the traditional scope of archaeological investigations, drawing together a diverse assortment of perspectives. More than one hundred scholars are contributing to the nine symposia published in this three-volume series.

The first installment, published last year, addressed the European–Native American interface along the western Spanish Borderlands—from the Pacific Slope across the Southwestern heartland to East Texas, from Russian Fort Ross to southern Baja California (Thomas 1989). The participants brought to the project a wide range of backgrounds, inspecting the Spanish Borderlands from numerous angles. Many are practicing archaeologists; their essays treat the surviving material evidence relating to the sociopolitics, economics, iconography, and physical environment of the contact period in the Spanish Borderlands West. Other participants provide a critical balance from the disciplines of American history, art history, ethnohistory, physical anthropology, and geography. Two Native American scholars discuss the survival strategies employed by their ancestors in coping with the European newcomers.

This, the second contribution in the *Columbian Consequences* series, takes up a similar agenda in the context of the Spanish Borderlands East, concentrating on La Florida (modern Florida, Georgia, and South Carolina), the greater Southeast, and the Caribbean. Forty-five scholars dissect the Hispanic–Native American interactions that resulted from the militant entradas into the eastern borderlands, the stubborn colonies, and the durable missions that held sway over the Southeastern landscape for more than a century. In these pages, archaeologists present fresh (and at times contentious) evidence that is reshaping our perception of where early explorers like de Soto went and who they encountered along the way. Other archaeologists present up-to-date interpretations, fleshing out our knowledge of demography, economics, architecture, and social dynamics that characterized the frontier towns and missions that sprang up in the second wave of interaction. Several borderlands historians contribute insights derived from documents handed down by the Spaniards themselves. One Franciscan friar reflects on why contemporary Catholics are keeping up with the fast-breaking archaeological news now available from Spanish Florida.

The third volume of *Columbian Consequences* sheds all geographic constraints, seeking to understand the processes behind the borderlands experience by looking at past, present, and future research directions. We begin with a retrospective look at the impact of previous Columbus-related "celebrations," such as the Columbian Quatrocentenary (held at the Chicago World's Fair of 1893), which shaped the directions of scholarly research for the next century. We also put the Spanish Borderlands into a Pan-American perspective by investigating the mission strategies employed beyond the borderlands, where rather different survival strategies were played out. Finally, we assess the recent, revolutionary breakthroughs in our understanding of the demographics of European contact and project how this radically changed picture may alter the approaches and assumptions of disciplines like archaeology, ethnology, history, and geography in the years to come.

The format of *Columbian Consequences* is designed to bring the fruits of this inquiry both to the scholarly community and to the public at large. To render these specialized presentations palatable to a more general audience, several leading scholars in the field have prepared overviews designed to make the rest of the text comprehensible to nonspecialists. Each overview synthesizes current thinking about the specific geographical setting, the Native American context, a history of European involvement, and a history of scholarly research. Each overview also contains a concise chronological table of salient events and extensive suggestions for additional reading.

Acknowledgments

I am especially grateful to the officers of the Society for American Archaeology (SAA) for interest in and support of the *Columbian Consequences* enterprise: Presidents Dena Dincauze, Don Fowler, Prudence Rice, and Jerry Sabloff, Keith Kvamme, program chair for the 1989 annual meetings in Atlanta, and SAA Executive Committee members Robert Bettinger, Kathleen Deagan, and Bruce Smith.

Kathleen Deagan, Jerald Milanich, and Jeffrey Mitchem made up the Advisory Board for this second volume, and I thank each for invaluable assistance in organizing the symposia, helping to chair the sessions, reviewing draft manuscripts, and preparing the synthetic overviews that introduce each geographic subdivision.

I also thank the staff of the Smithsonian Institution Press for sticking with this ambitious project, particularly Daniel Goodwin, Vicky Macintyre, and Ruth Spiegel.

The proceeds from *Columbian Consequences* will be donated as scholarships to assist Native Americans seeking higher educational opportunities. We are at present finalizing the specifics of these scholarships, and all funding will be administered by the Executive Committee of the Society of American Archaeology.

Dennis O'Brien prepared the graphics throughout the volume, and I also thank my staff at the American Museum of Natural History—Margot Dembo, Todd Himstead, and Lorann S. A. Pendleton; each helped out in dozens of ways.

References

Thomas, David Hurst (editor)
    1989 *Columbian Consequences*. Vol. 1: *Archaeological and Historical Perspectives on the Spanish Borderlands West*. Smithsonian Institution Press, Washington, D.C.

Part 1■

Spanish Entrada into the American Southeast

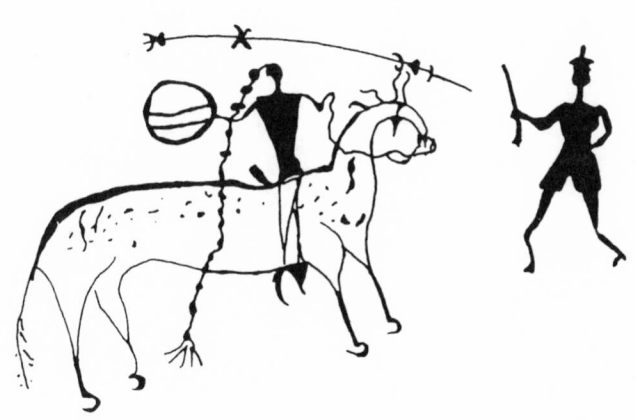

Chapter 1 ■

Jerald T. Milanich

The European Entrada into La Florida: An Overview

Women and even boys of four years of age fought with the [Spaniards]; and Indian boys hanged themselves not to fall into [our] hands, and others jumped into the fire of their own accord. . . . The arrow shots were tremendous, and sent with such a will and force that the lance of one [knight] . . . was pierced by an arrow. . . . [We] killed three thousand of the vagabonds without counting many others who were wounded and whom [we] afterwards found dead. . . . After the end of the battle [we] rested there until November 14, . . . and [we] burned over much of the country [*Rodrigo Ranjel describing the de Soto expedition's battle at Mabila, October 18, 1540, and the aftermath; in Bourne 1904:2:127–128*].

For four years following their landing on the Gulf coast of Florida in May 1539, the members of Hernando de Soto's expedition traveled through the land they called La Florida. There they encountered the ancestors of the Creek, Cherokee, Seminole, Choctaw, and other Native Americans who today still live in parts of the Southeast and Oklahoma.

On the one hand, that initial entrada was an incredible odyssey. The Spanish conquistadors saw, experienced, and survived aboriginal societies and lands

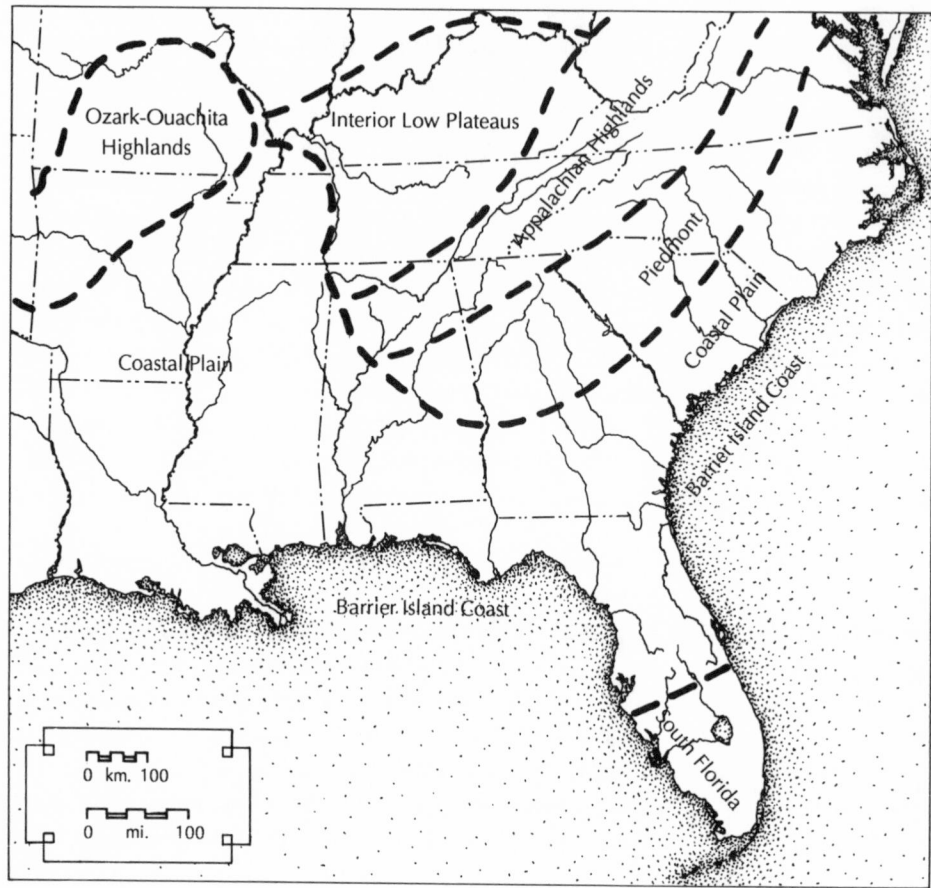

Figure 1-1. La Florida, with major natural zones (adapted from Hudson 1976:16–17).

that had never been seen by Europeans before. Their descriptions fill us with awe. But that same encounter contained the seeds of destruction of hundreds of thousands, perhaps millions, of people and the collapse of aboriginal political systems. It is a horrible irony that, although the firsthand accounts of several members of the de Soto expedition provide our only documentary data on many of the early sixteenth-century native societies in the Southeast, it was that expedition that helped to initiate the decimation of those societies through brute military force and introduced diseases. It is a sobering thought that our nation is built atop the bones of millions of native peoples. Certainly there are lessons to be learned by studying those first sixteenth-century encounters between Spaniards and Native Americans in the southeastern United States.

The Setting

Geographically, the Southeast United States includes Florida, Georgia, Alabama, Mississippi, Tennessee, and North and South Carolina—an environmentally diverse area east of the Mississippi River and south of the Midwest and Middle Atlantic regions. This geographical definition, however, fails to encompass all of the native peoples that shared somewhat similar culture traits at the time of European contact. The region based on ethnographic (Swanton 1946) and archaeological patterns (Smith 1986) would include these states as well as Louisiana and Kentucky and parts of Texas, Oklahoma, Arkansas, Missouri, Illinois, Indiana, Ohio, Virginia, West Virginia, and Maryland (see Figure 1-1). I employ the term *La Florida* to refer to this larger region. La Florida was the name Juan Ponce de León gave to the land whose coasts he explored in 1513. Spaniards soon used the term to designate all the area north and east of New Spain (Mexico) as far as knowledge extended (Sturtevant 1962:43). By the 1530s the eastern coast of La Florida had been explored to Labrador (see Castañeda, Cuesta, and Hernández 1983:371–378). As Spain explored northward from Mexico and as other European powers settled the eastern seaboard, La Florida became more restricted in extent, approximating the southeastern United States.

In the late Holocene period La Florida exhibited differences in elevation, rainfall, temperature, vegetation, and geology (Delcourt and Delcourt 1981; Espenshade 1984; Gagliano 1984; Hudson 1976:14–21; Larson 1980; Shelford 1963:56–119, 474–485). As a result, it can be divided into several distinct physiographic zones: South Florida, the salt-marsh/barrier island coasts, coastal plain, piedmont, Appalachian Highlands, Ozark-Ouachita Highlands, and interior low plateaus (see Figure 1-1). Large and small river systems flowed from the interior mountains and piedmont across the coastal plain to the sea and provided fish and other riverine foods. Rivers also annually deposited soils well suited to aboriginal agriculture.

Native settlements in the interior tended to cluster within the valleys of these rivers, some of which, like the Mississippi, were vast. The rivers also provided a network for transportation (by canoe), as did overland trails. Food and other resources were also extracted from the hardwood or mixed pine and hardwood forests of the interior (Hudson 1976:289–299, 313–316; Meyer 1928; Smith 1985:64–68; Swanton 1946:589–598).

Along the coasts of La Florida settlements were situated adjacent to oak-magnolia forests and the protein-rich waters of the marsh-lagoon-estuarine system. Because there were few large tracts of fertile soils, coastal populations did not rely on agriculture as heavily as did the peoples who lived in the interior river valleys, where soils were richer. However, coastal peoples had ready access to marine resources (Larson 1980:6–22, 206–209).

Exceptions to these general interior and coastal patterns occurred here and there, notably in peninsular Florida, where agriculture was less important or absent altogether. Again this was due to environmental factors; peninsular Florida does not have rivers that flow from the piedmont and annually deposit fertile silts. In the southern two-thirds of the peninsula the native peoples instead relied on the resources that could be hunted, fished, or collected from a mosaic of forests, wetlands, and lakes, and from coastal waters.

According to archaeological evidence, the late prehistoric culture pattern known as Mississippian was present over most of La Florida in 1539, the year that Hernando de Soto set out on his expedition. Mississippian societies were typical of the interior river valleys and first developed during the two centuries from A.D. 750 to 950. By A.D. 1000 they were widespread and, as Bruce D. Smith (1986:53) has noted, represented a pattern "far different from those that existed in A.D. 750" and exhibited new "technology, subsistence, settlement patterns, sociopolitical integrations, and ideology." Mississippian peoples were farmers who grew maize and other crops and built large towns with plazas surrounded by special buildings on constructed earthen mounds.

The people within individual polities were ruled by a permanent sociopolitical and religious elite who were at the apex of a ranked sociopolitical system, or chiefdom, which was associated with a well-defined territory. The political offices in chiefdoms are filled by persons selected on the basis of social ranking ascribed by birth. Some lineages were ranked much higher than others, and these produced the individuals who served as major and minor chiefs and other officials. Each office had certain duties, obligations, and accoutrements associated with it. Among the native chiefdoms of La Florida, such offices were probably both secular and sacred.

Some of the chiefdoms were simple. That is, they had a single chief, whereas others were very complex, with a higher-ranking chief controlling lesser chiefs, each of whom governed villages and territory. A simple chiefdom might contain only a few villages answering to the chief, whereas a complex chiefdom might include many villages and subordinate chiefs, a system of tribute, and, perhaps, redistribution of certain resources.

Archaeologists have found thousands of objects displaying art and symbols that reflect the ideological system behind the social and political structures of the chiefdoms of La Florida. Some of these artifacts were the accoutrements of chiefly officials and other members of the ruling elite. The rich and complex Mississippian iconography was also entwined with agricultural practices and fertility rites (Brown 1985). Although full-blown Mississippian societies did not occur where extensive agriculture was not practiced, some Mississippian culture traits were present even in those areas. One such area was peninsular Florida, which had simple chiefdoms.

Great changes occurred in the native societies as a result of European contact. Nonetheless, there were many similarities—some would say great similarities—among the aboriginal societies of the seventeenth and eighteenth centuries. These similarities have been described as a southeastern culture pattern (Hudson 1976; Swanton 1946). We might attribute the presence of this pattern to long contact among peoples inhabiting the same geographically contiguous region over a period of 14,000 years and to the similar environments in much of the interior, which elicited similar cultural adjustments. At the same time, differences did exist. Some of these, such as the life-styles of the peninsular Florida peoples or the peoples of coastal Georgia, can be traced to differing environments. But others, such as languages from very different linguistic families, must have been the result of other factors.

Native Americans and Their Interactions with Europeans

Much of our information about the native peoples of sixteenth-century La Florida comes from the entradas of the early Spanish explorers. When first encountered by Europeans, the native peoples of interior La Florida must have been incredible to behold. Mississippian chiefs, costumed in magnificent feather cloaks and skillfully crafted accoutrements reflecting their high status, were carried in canopied litters on the shoulders of their principal subjects to meet the Europeans. Diplomacy, political alliances, and military force resulted in complex chiefdoms that integrated large territories under a hierarchy of rulers and chiefs. Large populations allowed polities to develop and rise and fall as the ties that bound them were forged or broken. Those ties would be permanently destroyed with the coming of the Europeans. Although the end result was the same for the native peoples—political collapse and, in many instances, genocide—cultural changes apparently did not occur at the same rate across La Florida.

Spain's Emerging New World Empire

Spain's exploration of the land that came to be known as La Florida was part of an effort to expand its New World empire. By the time of Columbus's second voyage, a colonizing expedition in September 1493 that included 17 ships and more than 1,000 people, other European powers were also sending ships to the New World (Harrisse 1961:662–700; Deagan, this volume). Spain's initial settlements were on the Caribbean island of Hispaniola, but voyages of exploration quickly reached out to other islands and the adjacent mainland of Central and South America. As geographical knowledge increased, it became clear that the Caribbean Basin was only a small part of the New World; vast uncharted lands lay to the west, south, and north. In these lands, as in the Caribbean, the Spaniards would seek wealth—native slaves, land and its products, and precious metals and stones. Between 1520 and 1540 the Spanish empire expanded into Mexico, Central America, and Peru. Settlements were also established along the northern coast of Brazil. A permanent Hispanic presence was established, and the wealth of the Inca, Aztec, and other native societies was shipped to Spain.

Initial Attempts to Explore and Settle La Florida's Coasts

As Spain's empire spread outward from Hispaniola, the early explorers probably learned something about the northerly lands from the Indians captured in the Bahamas or the Caribbean for forced labor. Clandestine voyages (voyages not sanctioned by the Crown, which would have claimed a share of profits) to the coasts of La Florida to capture slaves might also have provided information. If the 1502 Cantino map does indeed show the Florida peninsula, then sailors had undoubtedly reached the U.S. coast by that early date (see Cumming, Skelton, and Quinn 1972:56–57).

The first officially sanctioned voyage to La Florida was that of Juan Ponce de León, the ex-governor of the island colony of San Juan (today Puerto Rico) (see

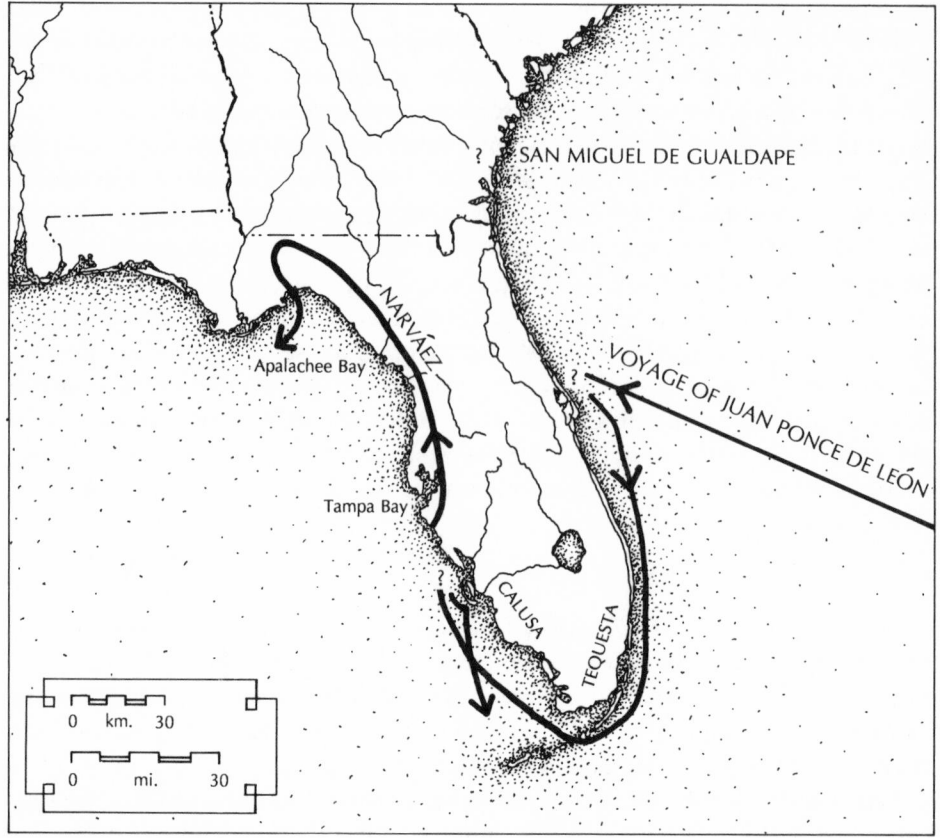

Figure 1-2. La Florida, showing the exploration routes of Juan Ponce de León and Pánfilo de Narváez, the possible location of Ayllón's colony, and the native groups of South Florida.

Davis 1935; Weddle 1985:38–53). The Spanish Crown granted Ponce a three-year contract giving him the sole right to search for and settle Bimini, an island rumored to lie to the north of the Lucayos (Bahama Islands). He set sail from Puerto Rico on March 3, 1513 (or 1512—the year is disputed) on a northwesterly heading that took him up the outer edge of the Bahama island chain past the Caicos, Mayaguana, and several other islands before reaching the island of Guanahani, where Columbus first landed in 1492. He continued northwest, eventually making landfall on the Atlantic coast of Florida north of Cape Canaveral at an unknown location, where he saw the huts of native peoples. He then sailed southward down the peninsular coast, occasionally landing to refill his water casks. The Spaniards had at least two hostile encounters with native peoples, in one instance kidnapping an individual to obtain information.

Ponce's ships sailed south past Miami and then west along the Florida Keys before turning northeasterly to the Florida Gulf coast (Figure 1-2). Sailing south along the coast, they found and entered a harbor. During the nine days they stayed there the Spaniards engaged in several battles with the native peoples, whose chief was Carlos. These people were certainly the Calusa, well known from later sixteenth- (as well as seventeenth-) century encounters with the Spanish. One native "understood the Spaniards," and spoke to them (Davis 1935:20). It was thought he was from Hispaniola or another Spanish island.

The exact location of Ponce's landing is uncertain; he did locate Charlotte Harbor, which, on early maps and the Chaves derrotero (pre-1530; see Castañeda, Cuesta, and Hernández 1983:366), is named the Bahía de Juan Ponce. But his encounter with the Calusa may have occurred at a more southerly location (Weddle 1985:51–52, 62).

From later sixteenth-century documents, including materials related to a Spanish garrison and Jesuit mission established in 1566 in Calos, the principal Calusa town, it is clear that the Calusa formed a nonagricultural chiefdom whose political influence reached across South Florida (Goggin and Sturtevant 1964; Marquardt 1987, 1988; Zubillaga 1946). Their economic base was the fish and shellfish taken from the rich, nearshore tropical waters of the Gulf (Widmer 1988:221–260).

The Spanish garrison and mission among the Calusa, originally founded as a part of Pedro Menéndez de Avilés's plan to settle La Florida (Lyon 1976, 1988), were withdrawn in 1570. The Calusa political structure seems to have been little affected by Spanish contact, and at the end of the seventeenth century the chiefdom was still intact (Hann 1989). After that time the population apparently declined rapidly and by 1742 only remnants of the Calusa were gathered at a short-lived mission at Miami (Sturtevant 1978:147).

Why did the Calusa chiefdom survive for more than a century and a half after European contact? Possibly any disease epidemics they experienced were few at first. We have more than 600 printed pages of documents about Jesuit mission efforts in the 1560s in La Florida, and there are no references to epidemics among the Calusa (Zubillaga 1946). This is in stark contrast to contemporary Jesuit accounts from Brazil (Hemming 1978:139–146). We have much to learn about the consequences of European diseases by comparing groups like the Calusa with the chiefdoms of the southeastern interior.

Juan Ponce would return to La Florida in 1521 to try to establish a settlement, possibly among the Calusa, but that effort failed and he died of a wound suffered in the attempt (Davis 1935:50–64). The Spaniards never were able to establish a long-term mission or settlement among any of the native peoples in southern Florida, despite several efforts to do so. Perhaps this failure was somehow related to the nonagricultural economies of the region, all of which subsisted on fishing, hunting, and gathering (Stahl 1986).

Other Spaniards continued to explore the Gulf and Atlantic coasts of La Florida. Diego Miruelo possibly reached as far north as Apalachee Bay in the big bend area of Florida in 1516, Francisco Hernández de Cordoba reached the southwest Florida coast in 1517, and Alonzo Alvarez de Pineda sailed the entire Gulf coast in 1519 (Weddle 1985:55–65, 95–108). It is doubtful that any of these voyages had sustained contact with the native peoples, but they did greatly increase Spanish knowledge of the coastal geography of La Florida.

In 1521 Pedro de Quexo and Francisco Gordillo sailed into the Santee River in South Carolina on a slaving expedition and encountered a native group or town called Chicora. Historian Paul Hoffman (1984) has carefully documented how the stories told by the sailors and their financial backers spread, reaching Peter Martyr, a contemporary historian who also spoke with Francisco Chicorano, a native brought back to Santo Domingo as a servant. In 1530, Martyr's description of Chicora was published, and Chicora rapidly became known throughout Europe. "Abounding in timber, vines, native olive trees, Indians, pearls, and, . . . perhaps gold and silver" (Hoffman 1984:419), the illusionary Chicora would, over the next half century, lure Spaniards and Frenchmen alike to the Carolina coasts, greatly influencing European attempts to settle La Florida in the sixteenth century.

The first colonizing expedition to the Atlantic coast took place in 1526, probably on Sapelo Sound on the Georgia coast (Hoffman 1984:423, n. 13). Lucas Vásquez de Ayllón, who had been the backer of Francisco Gordillo and who had also sponsored another voyage to the region to gather information, accepted a royal charter to colonize Chicora, establishing forts and settlements at his own cost. Ayllón, royal judge in Santo Domingo in Hispaniola, tried to establish a base settlement (San Miguel de Gualdape) of about 600 persons (Figure 1-2). The colony was an abject failure, lasting only three months. When the Spaniards withdrew, they may have abandoned a number of Africans they had brought as slaves (Wood 1974:3–4).

Native Americans and Spaniards in the Interior of La Florida

The peoples of South Florida and those of the coastal regions of La Florida—the first people that encountered Europeans in the Southeast—were not full participants in the Mississippian culture pattern found in northwest Florida and in the interior river valleys. Thus none of the early Spanish expeditions observed true Mississippian societies. The first to do so was Pánfilo de Narváez, who landed on the Florida Gulf coast near Tampa Bay in 1528 with an army of 400 men and 40 horses (Weddle 1985:185–207; see also Marrinan et al., this volume). Narváez's task was to explore La Florida from the Florida peninsula around the Gulf of Mexico to northern Mexico, and to supplement information from the coastal surveys already completed. The relation of Álvar Núñez de Cabeza de Vaca (Bandelier 1905), a survivor of the ill-fated expedition, provides a firsthand account of the events, although it was written nearly a decade afterward.

After landing, the army reconnoitered the region and found Tampa Bay, where they met Indians who had gold that was said to have come from Apalachee. A ship was sent north (probably to Apalachee Bay) to rendezvous with the expedition at a later date, and Narváez and 350 men set out overland toward Apalachee. They reached the Withlacoochee River before encountering any native peoples. Possibly they were moving through the low-lying, wet woods near the coast, which are not well suited to occupation. The cruelty Narváez showed toward the aborigines near his landing site might also have encouraged people to stay out of his path.

Proceeding north, the Spaniards crossed the Suwannee River and eventually reached Apalachee, where they stayed for 25 days before departing and traveling 9 days to reach the aboriginal town of Aute on the Gulf coast (Figure 1-2; see also Marrinan et al., this volume). Their rendezvous with the ship was never kept. In Aute, illness struck the army and attempts to travel westward toward Mexico were unsuccessful. Finally the Spaniards built several boats and tried to follow the coastline to Mexico, but most of them were either swept out into the Gulf or washed ashore. Four people, including Cabeza de Vaca, were captured on the Texas coast by native peoples. After nearly eight years, they escaped and made their way westward into the Southwest or northern Mexico, where they were found by Spanish slavers. Their stories of wealthy Pueblo towns on the northern Rio Grande River would later lead to the 1539 Fray Marcos de Niza and the 1540–1542 Francisco Vásquez de Coronado expeditions into that region (Cordell 1989:25).

Unfortunately, Cabeza de Vaca's narrative provides little information about the Apalachee peoples (associated with the Fort Walton Mississippian culture). Were it not for later documents (Hann 1988) and the archaeological record (Jones 1982; Scarry 1984; Willey 1949:452–470), we would know nothing of Fort Walton political structure. However, Cabeza de Vaca's narrative does offer important information on the hunter-gatherer peoples of the Texas Gulf coastal region (e.g., Aten 1983:24–25, 28–29; Newcomb 1961).

The Narváez expedition, a dismal failure, did establish that gold was present in La Florida (although it was most likely gold from Central or South America salvaged by the Tampa Bay aborigines from Spanish ships wrecked along the coast). That and the Chicora legend were apparently enough to draw an even larger overland expedition to La Florida, the entrada of the conquistador Hernando de Soto. De Soto had made a fortune while serving as Pizarro's chief military adviser in Peru in the early 1530s and he funded the La Florida expedition with Peruvian gold and silver (Swanton 1985:71–75). His royal charter was very similar to that of Narváez; he was to conquer, pacify, and settle 200 leagues of La Florida's coast, taking with him 500 men and supplies for 18 months (Swanton 1985:76–79). He was also required to build three stone forts. In return, de Soto was to receive titles, lands, and a share of the new colony's profits.

The expedition was well planned and outfitted. While gathering supplies in Cuba, he sent his chief pilot ahead to reconnoiter the landing site, Bahía Honda (Tampa Bay), the same bay Narváez had visited. It is clear de Soto knew where he wished to land on the Gulf coast of Florida and that he wanted to move northward into the interior of the Southeast. Three extant accounts of the expedition, and a recently discovered fragment of a fourth, provide extensive information on de Soto's route (Bourne 1904; Lyon 1982; and see Hudson, DePratter, and Smith 1989). A secondhand account, less accurate than the others, is also available (Varner and Varner 1951).

De Soto and his army went ashore at Tampa Bay in late May 1539, established a camp, and off-loaded their horses and supplies. Not long after, the Spaniards found Juan Ortiz, who, left behind by a ship looking for Narváez in 1528, had lived among the Florida Indians for 11 years. After scouting the surrounding

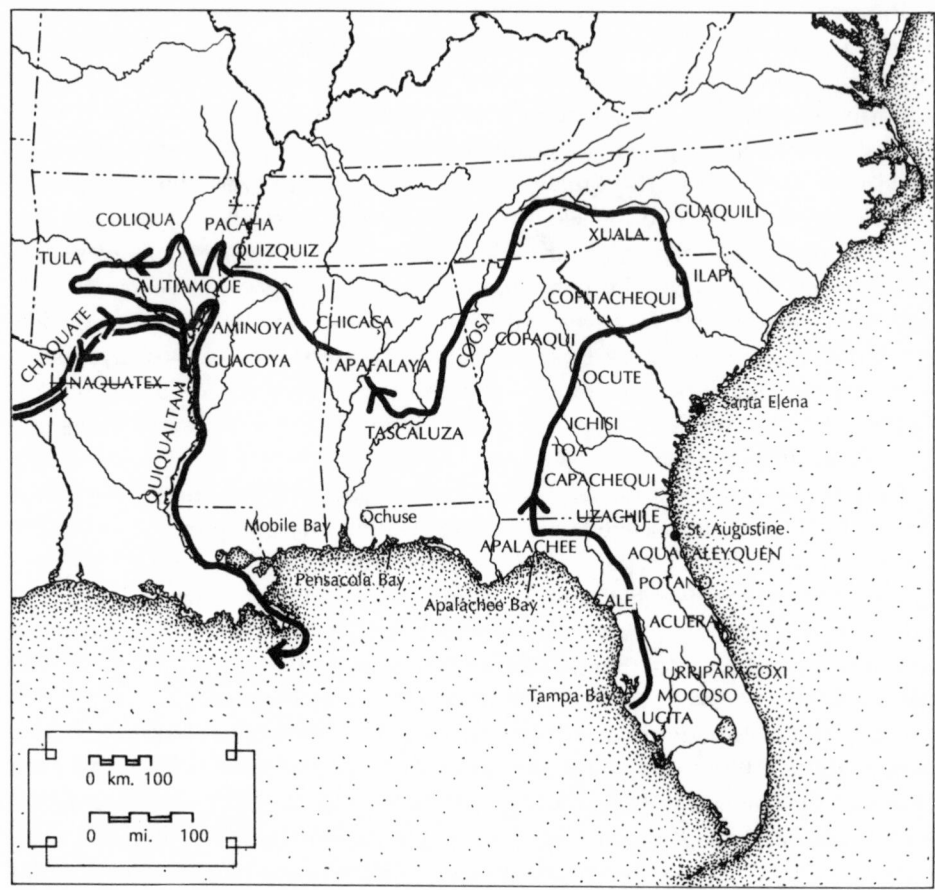

Figure 1-3. Route of Hernando de Soto's expedition and the native chiefdoms encountered (based on Hudson et al. 1989). Also shown are the settlements of de Luna and Menéndez.

territory for six weeks and gathering information from various aboriginal groups, de Soto, about 500 people (including craftsmen, two women, and friars), and perhaps hundreds of captive Indian bearers moved inland, heading northward toward the province of Apalachee, in the vicinity of modern Tallahassee (Figure 1-3).

The expedition spent the winter of 1539–40 at Anhaica, the principal town of the Apalachee Indians. Anhaica, the Martin site, has been located and excavated by B. Calvin Jones and Charles Ewen and provides our most dramatic evidence of the presence of de Soto's expedition in the Southeast (Ewen 1989; see also this volume).

In the spring the army broke camp and moved north across Georgia and the Carolinas, crossing the Appalachian Mountains into Tennessee. Perhaps the discovery of wealth in the highlands of Peru and Mexico stimulated de Soto to seek the mountains. Once across the Appalachians, de Soto followed the Tennessee River Valley southwest into central or southern Alabama, to the town of Mabila (in the chiefdom of Tascaluza) where a major battle was fought (see Little and Curren, this volume). The army then turned northwest, crossing Alabama into Mississippi, where they again wintered (1540–1541). Their route took them to the Mississippi River, which they crossed on rafts into Arkansas. The journey to the river, reached in May 1541, had taken nearly two years. The next year was spent in Arkansas, visiting aboriginal villages and searching for wealth that was never to be found (see Morse and Morse, this volume).

Finally the army returned to the Mississippi River, where de Soto, sick with a fever, died on June 20, 1542. The expedition, now led by Luis de Moscoso, then attempted to walk westerly across Texas to reach New Spain (Mexico). After traveling hundreds of miles, Moscoso decided it was futile to continue without supplies of food. The army retraced its steps to the Mississippi, arriving in December. During the first six months of 1543, they labored to build boats in which they could float down the river to the Gulf of Mexico and to New Spain. The expedition set out down the river in late June 1543, and reached the Gulf 20 days later. On September 10, the 311 survivors reached a Spanish settlement on the River of Panuco (near present-day Tampico, Mexico), ending their journey.

The information on native societies contained in the de Soto expedition narratives is responsible for much of our present view of sixteenth-century La Florida. Around Tampa Bay the Spaniards encountered two groups, the Uçita and Mocoso, both apparently small chiefdoms whose rulers each controlled several villages and about 20–25 km of bay coastline. The Spaniards could march from one polity to the territory of the other in a day. Neither Uçita nor Mocoso grew maize (de Soto's main army was there from late May into early July), and both Tampa Bay chiefs, as well as others nearby, paid tribute (gifts? political homage?) to a chief whose people were agriculturists and who controlled territory about 20–30 leagues (roughly 130 km) away in the interior of the peninsula. That chief (Urriparacoxi, or Iriparascusi, which means "war-prince" in Timucuan; see Granberry 1987:109, 117) probably controlled the central lake district from Lake Apopka southward into Osceola County (Hudson and Milanich 1989). This same pattern of inland agriculturists with military and some political control over small chiefdoms is also mentioned in sixteenth-century French and Spanish descriptions of the central St. Johns River drainage (see Hudson and Milanich 1989).

On the journey northward from Tampa Bay through peninsular Florida, the de Soto expedition encountered many native peoples, but it was not until the Spaniards were four days, or about 75 km, north of Tampa Bay that they first saw maize fields. On the remainder of their journey across La Florida, they encountered agriculturists, whose stored crops would feed de Soto's army. In north peninsular Florida these agriculturists were organized into simple chiefdoms, for example, the Cale and probably the Potano and Acuera.

After crossing the Santa Fe River in northern Florida, the expedition found itself in the territory of Chief Aguacaleyquen, who controlled a region about 80 km long (delineated on the west by the Suwannee River). Many villages and people were vassals of the chief. Archaeology in the region of Aguacaleyquen

(Milanich et al. 1984:14) has shown that although a large chiefdom was present in the sixteenth century, a Mississippian archaeological pattern was not. Apparently—perhaps because of geographical proximity to the Fort Walton (Apalachee) Mississippian system to the west—certain social and political Mississippian traits, but not the entire complex, were present.

A second chiefdom, Uzachile, was encountered immediately to the west of the Suwannee River and, like Aguacaleyquen, it was not associated with the Mississippian culture pattern. The chief of Aguacaleyquen was said to be a kinsman of the chief of Uzachile (Elvas in Bourne 1904:1–41). Even before de Soto and his army left the Aguacaleyquen's territory, flute-playing representatives of Uzachile, "a great chief," came to ask de Soto to aid them against Apalachee, "a mighty province hostile to [them]" (Ranjel in Bourne 1904:2:73).

Once the expedition left Uzachile (where there was "much maize, beans, and pumpkins" [Elvas in Bourne 1904:1:45]) and crossed the Aucilla River into Apalachee, the Spaniards entered the realm of Mississippian societies. That same small river, the Aucilla, was also a linguistic boundary between Timucuan-speaking groups, who had extended north to that point from Tampa Bay, and the Muskogean language-speakers like the Apalachee and many other Mississippian peoples, whose populations dominated La Florida. Not all Mississippian peoples spoke a Muskogean language, however (Muskogean languages include Choctaw-Chickasaw, Alabama-Koasati, Mikasuki-Hitchiti, and Muskogee-Seminole, as well as Apalachee; see Hudson 1976:22–24). Some Mississippian peoples may have spoken Algonkian, Iroquoian, Siouan, or Caddoan languages, all of which are quite different from either the Muskogean languages or from Timucuan. There is much to be learned about possible correlations between ethnic and political affiliations and language.

Apalachee was "well inhabited, producing much corn . . . [and with] many habitations." Towns contained "much maize, pumpkins, beans, and dried plums" (Elvas in Bourne 1904:1:47). Within Apalachee, archaeologists have defined a Mississippian settlement system with multiple- and single-mound villages and outlying farmsteads (Payne 1981), as well as examples of Mississippian iconography (Jones 1982). The Apalachee of de Soto's time formed a complex Mississippian chiefdom. What is uncertain is what effect contact with Narváez (and European diseases) may have already had on the Apalachee by 1539. None of the de Soto narratives mention mounds at Anhaica and none have been found by archaeologists. Could the Fort Walton/Apalachee chiefdom, which was responsible for large multimound sites like Lake Jackson, already have undergone large changes by 1539?

Beyond the Apalachee, the de Soto expedition encountered a number of Mississippian chiefdoms (Figure 1-3). The participants of the de Soto expedition were perhaps the only nonnative people to observe these Mississippian societies before they began to experience depopulation and change (although some believe that epidemics had already penetrated the interior of La Florida; see Dobyns 1983:24–25).

None of the firsthand de Soto narratives provide a complete picture of any one native chiefdom. We only have bits and pieces from many different groups.

But when we put them together an extraordinary picture of the Mississippian societies that inhabited La Florida begins to emerge.

[*Toa*, southwest Georgia, March 1539]—The houses of this town were different from those behind, which were covered with dry grass; thenceforward they were roofed with cane, after the fashion of tile . . . ; some have their sides so made of clay as to look like tapia. Throughout the cold country every Indian has a winter home, plastered inside and out, with a very small door, which is closed at dark, and a fire being made within, it remains heated like an oven. . . . He has likewise a house for summer, and near it a kitchen, where a fire is made and bread baked. Maize is kept in a barbacoa, which is a house with wooden sides, like a room, raised aloft on four posts, and has a floor of cane. The difference between the houses of the masters, or principal men, and those of the common people is, besides being larger than the others, they have deep balconies on the front side, with cane seats, like benches; and about are many barbacoas, in which they bring together the tribute their people give them of maize, skins of deer, and blankets [Elvas in Bourne 1904:1:53].

[*Cofitachequi*, South Carolina, April-May, 1540]—[T]he chief Indians came with gifts and the woman chief, lady of that land whom Indians of rank bore on their shoulders with much respect, in a litter covered with delicate white linen . . . she took off a string of pearls which she wore on her neck, and put it on the Governor [de Soto] as a necklace to show her favor . . . and [the Spaniards] received many presents of skins well tanned and blankets of the country, and blankets of sable fur and others of the skin of wild cats. . . . They took away from [the temple] some two hundred pounds of pearls. . . . In [the temple] of Talimeco there were breastplates like corselets [light half-armor] and headpieces made of rawhide, . . . and also very fine shields. This Talimeco was a village holding extensive sway, and this house of worship was on a high mound and much revered [Ranjel in Bourne 1904:2:98–99, 100–101].

[*Coosa*, a chiefdom extending for more than 300 km through eastern Tennessee, northwest Georgia, into Alabama, July-September, 1540]—This chief is a powerful one and a ruler of a wide territory, one of the best and most abundant that they found in [La] Florida. And the chief came out to receive the Governor in a litter covered with the white mantles of the country, . . . borne on the shoulders of sixty or seventy of his principal subjects. . . . [T]hey came to an old village that had two fences [palisaded walls] and good towers, and these walls are after this fashion: They drive many thick stakes tall and straight close to one another. These are then interlaced with long withes [wattles], and then overlaid with clay within and without. They make loopholes at intervals and they make their towers and turrets separated by the curtain and parts of the wall as seems best. And at a distance it looks like a fine wall or rampart and such stockades are very strong [Ranjel in Bourne 1904:2:112, 115].

[*Tascaluza*, central Alabama, October 1540]—The Cacique was at home, in a piazza. Before his dwelling, on a high place, was spread a mat for him, upon which two cushions were placed, one above another, to which he went and sat down, his men placing themselves around, some way removed, so that an open circle was formed about him, the Indians of the highest rank being nearest to his person. One of them shaded him from the sun with a circular umbrella, spread wide, the size of a target, with a small stem, and having deerskin extended over cross-sticks quartered with red and white, which at a distance made it look of taffeta, the colors were so very perfect. It formed the standard of the Chief, which he carried into battle. His appearance was full of dignity: He was tall of person, muscular, lean, and symmetrical. He was the suzerain of many territories, and of a numerous people, being equally feared by his vassals and the neighboring nations [Elvas in Bourne 1904:1:87–88].

[*Near the territory of Pacaha*, Mississippi River, May 1541]—On the other side of the river about seven thousand Indians had got together, with about two hundred canoes, to defend the passage. All of them had shields made of canes so strong and so closely interwoven with such thread that a crossbow could hardly pierce them. The arrows came raining down so that the air was full of them, and their yells were something fearful [Ranjel in Bourne 1904:2:137–138].

They [the natives] were painted with ochre, wearing great bunches of white and other plumes of many colors, having feathered shields in their hands, with which they sheltered the oarsmen on either side, the warriors standing erect from bow to stern, holding bows and arrows. The barge in which the Cacique came had an awning at the poop, under which he sat; and the like had the barges of the other chiefs: and there, from under the canopy, where the chief man was, the course was directed and orders issued to the rest [Elvas in Bourne 1904:1:113].

[*Pacaha*, eastern Arkansas, June 1541]—On Wednesday [the Spaniards] came to the village of Pacaha, a village and lord of wide repute and highly thought of in that country. The town was a very good one, thoroughly well stockaded; and the walls were furnished with towers and a ditch round about, for the most part full of water which flows in by a canal from the river; and this ditch was full of excellent fish of divers kinds [Ranjel in Bourne 1904:2:139].

[*Message from Cacique of Quiqualtam to de Soto*, Mississippi River, March-April 1542]—As to what you say of your being the son of the Sun, if you will cause him to dry up the great river [the Mississippi], I will believe you: As to the rest, it is not my custom to visit any one, but rather all, of whom I have ever heard, have come to visit me, to serve and obey me, and pay me tribute, either voluntarily or by force: If you desire to see me, come where I am, if for peace, I will receive you with special goodwill; if for war, I will await you in my town; but neither for you, nor for any other man, will I set back one foot [recorded by Ranjel in Bourne 1904:2:154–155).

The Mississippian chiefdoms of interior La Florida were indeed something to behold.

Although the Ponce de León, Ayllón, Narváez, and de Soto expeditions failed to accomplish their objectives, the Spanish crown continued to try to colonize La Florida. Spain needed Gulf coast settlements to help protect her shipping lanes (Weddle 1985:253–255), and missions were sought to minister to the natives (Hoffman 1984:429). The Spaniards also wished to establish an overland road from the Atlantic coast of La Florida to New Spain. Such a road would have one end in South Carolina and would extend westerly to the Gulf coast near modern Pensacola and on to New Spain. It would be used to transport goods to Santa Elena, and then put them on board ships from Spain; too many ships were being wrecked on the coasts of La Florida. A third objective was to thwart growing French interest in La Florida, especially the Atlantic coast. To fulfill these objectives the Spanish planned to have both Gulf and Atlantic settlements, the latter at Santa Elena (Hoffman 1984:428–429). A settlement was also to be started in Coosa, the rich native province that de Soto's army had traveled through earlier.

A new colonization effort was organized, funded by the Viceroy of New Spain and led by Tristán de Luna y Arellano. Fifteen hundred people, including Mexican Indians, and 13 ships set sail from New Spain in the summer of 1559 for the Gulf coast of La Florida.

The expedition first landed at Mobile Bay before finding its objective, Ochuse (at Pensacola Bay, see Figure 1-3; also see Hudson et al. 1989; Priestley 1928). De Luna sent soldiers into the adjacent mainland to reconnoiter, but the men observed few native settlements that could supply the colony with food. The situation grew more desperate when a hurricane struck and sank several of de Luna's ships that had not yet been unloaded, destroying the supplies. In order to feed his colonists, de Luna decided to send most of them into the interior to native towns where they would find food. A large town, Nanipacana, was located 40 leagues inland, and the colonists moved to it (Hudson et al. 1989:126–129). A party was sent northward to relocate Coosa, and found it greatly changed from the province visited by de Soto.

De Luna was unable to maintain the colony. Many of the colonists rebelled and returned to New Spain. In March 1561 Ángel de Villafañe arrived with orders to move the colony to Santa Elena on the coast of South Carolina. But Villafañe lost three of his four ships in storms and apparently never found Santa Elena, and thus aborted his effort (Hoffman 1984:430–431).

Four years later, Pedro Menéndez de Avilés would finally accomplish what those who preceded him had not: establish a Spanish settlement in La Florida. With royal backing, Menéndez ousted short-lived French settlements on the Atlantic coast and founded St. Augustine, as well as a settlement at Santa Elena (Figure 1-3; see also Lyon, this volume). Garrisons, some with missions, were placed along the Gulf and Atlantic coasts (Lyon 1988). But only St. Augustine survived. The garrisons failed in a matter of years and Santa Elena was finally abandoned in 1587. A new period of Spanish–Native American interaction would begin, centered on the Franciscan missions.

The Consequences: Recent Research

The narratives of the de Soto expedition—those of Biedma, Elvas, and Ranjel—are filled with information about the native chiefdoms of La Florida as they were when first encountered by people from the Old World. Four and a half centuries after the Spaniards first saw these magnificent native societies, their descriptions still cause us to marvel. They tell of one chief who ruled 90 vassal villages and another who could summon thousands of warriors to oppose the Spaniards. They repeatedly refer to chiefs who could order hundreds of native bearers and female consorts to serve de Soto's army and they describe large fortified villages that housed huge stores of agricultural produce and wealth, such as skins and blankets routinely paid as tribute. The political relationships that gave rise to chiefly alliances, some of which covered hundreds of kilometers, were maintained by military force or by threat of force. Chiefs were quick to recognize the military prowess of the Spaniards and tried to enlist de Soto's army to help punish recalcitrant vassals or to help release them from the military hold of more powerful chiefs.

By the time of de Luna and Menéndez, great changes had apparently taken place in the interior of La Florida. Evidently the military actions of the de Soto expedition and the impact of introduced diseases had caused depopulation and helped to undo the fragile ties that held together the vast complex chiefdom of Coosa. Similarly, in South Carolina the chiefdom of Cofitachequi described in the de Soto accounts was greatly diminished when it was again seen by Juan Pardo and his men, sent into the interior of La Florida by Pedro Menéndez in 1566–1568 (DePratter, Hudson, and Smith 1983).

Many of the native societies that existed in the early sixteenth century soon disappeared. Others changed and continued to change in an effort to adapt to the new conditions brought about by depopulation and a European presence.

To understand the nature of the native societies of La Florida at the time of European contact and the subsequent changes that occurred, we must rely on data from historical studies, ethnology, firsthand accounts recorded by the European explorers, and archaeology. Important background historical information on Spain in the New World and the context of its initiatives to explore and settle La Florida, including cartographic information, can be found in a variety of histories (e.g., Alexander 1976; Crosby 1972; Cumming, Skelton, and Quinn 1972; Haring 1963; Morison 1971; Quinn 1971, 1977, 1988; Sauer 1966, 1971). The historical studies of noted historian Eugene Lyon are particularly pertinent to La Florida (1976, 1984, 1988), as are those of Robert S. Weddle (1985) and Paul Hoffman (1984).

A voluminous literature on the ethnography of La Florida's native peoples exists. Basic works include those of anthropologists James Mooney and John R. Swanton. Citations for these and other pertinent sources can be found in Charles Hudson's excellent *The Southeastern Indians* (1976). All of these, however, focus on the native peoples of the post–sixteenth century; at the time they were written we simply did not have the information on the chiefdoms of the de Soto era that is emerging today.

It is also widely recognized that the direct historical method is difficult to apply to the sixteenth-century native societies of La Florida (Dobyns 1983:25–26, 337–338; Ramenofsky 1987:173–174; Smith 1987:7–8). In the past archaeologists have used information on, for instance, the various Creek peoples of the seventeenth and eighteenth centuries, to aid in their interpretations of prehistoric archaeological sites. It was assumed that many aspects of the culture of the later Creek peoples (for whom ethnographic descriptions were available) resembled that of the prehistoric peoples because there was a direct historical link between the two groups. But it is now known that because of demographic devastation and the resultant culture changes that occurred in the sixteenth century, the native groups observed in those later centuries were in many instances much different from those that existed at the time of initial European exploration and settlement. The Creek confederacy, for example, is a later phenomenon that bears little resemblance to the polities that existed in the same region two centuries earlier.

Firsthand documents—narratives, letters, and reports—from the various

Spanish expeditions to La Florida are a basic source of information. Many of the documents have been translated and published in English. Others remain untranscribed or translated and must be studied by historians who can locate and read the documents, as well as interpret them within their historical contexts.

Translated accounts from the early expeditions include: Juan Ponce de León (Davis 1935); Pánfilo de Narváez (Bandelier 1904); Hernando de Soto (Bourne 1904; Lyon 1982; Varner and Varner 1951; but see Henige 1986, for a discussion of the reliability of Garcilaso de la Vega), Tristán de Luna (Davila 1922; Priestley 1928), Fernando d'Escalante Fontaneda (shipwrecked in south Florida in the mid-1500s, True 1945); Pedro Menéndez de Avilés (Barrientos 1965; Solís de Merás 1964); and Juan Pardo (Hudson 1989b:part II; Ketchem 1954). The French accounts of their La Florida colony are particularly informative about the Florida Timucuan peoples and the Guale and other groups of the Atlantic coast (Bennett 1964, 1968; Laudonnière 1975; Lorant 1946; Ribault 1964). A number of pertinent documents, some duplicates of the above, have been published in David B. Quinn's five-volume *New American World: A Documentary History of North America to 1612* (1979).

With historical and ethnographic information as background and with the firsthand European accounts, we can begin to interpret the routes and locations of the various sixteenth-century entradas and to better understand the late Mississippian societies and the impact of European contact. But the task is not easy; if it were, it would have been done decades ago. One large problem has been to identify (and prove) that specific archaeological sites are truly associated with the sixteenth-century Spanish expeditions. We must be able to acurately identify and date sites and the materials in them. How can it be determined that an aboriginal site dates from 1540, as opposed to 1440 or 1640, and was visited by de Soto's army and not by a Franciscan missionary? Such precision is necessary if we are to understand, for instance, the impact of disease.

The best tool for providing this precise identification and chronology is European artifacts, items that were brought to La Florida by de Soto and the other Spaniards and were either given to the native peoples, lost, or discarded. Some European-made artifacts changed through time and can be dated to relatively short periods. This line of inquiry is still new and we have a great deal to learn. But archaeology has come a long way since John Goggin (1954) published his article, "Are There De Soto Relics in Florida?"

Much of the work was pioneered by Goggin (ceramics, 1960, 1968), Charles Fairbanks (beads, 1968a, 1968b), Jeffrey Brain (hawk-bells and other artifacts, 1975), and Ian Brown (bells, 1979). Their collective work has laid the basis for a number of new studies of those and other artifacts (Deagan 1987; Mitchem and McEwan 1988; Smith 1982, 1983, 1987:31–44; Smith and Good 1982; South, Skowronek, and Johnson 1988).

Chronologies based on these studies have enabled archaeologists to date components at a number of sixteenth-century sites (see Smith 1987:48–51, for a long list of such sites with citations; also, Curren 1987:7–11; Ewen 1988, 1989, this volume; Fairbanks 1985:129–132; Little and Curren 1981; Mitchem 1989a, 1989b:436–468, 509–518, this volume; Mitchem and Hutchinson 1987; Mitchem and Leader 1988; Mitchem et al. 1985; Mitchem and Weisman 1984; Morse 1981; Ramenofsky 1987:193–196; Scarry, this volume; Smith 1984).

Archaeology has done more than simply provide tools to date sites. Using old documents and new tools and data, archaeologists are now rethinking the first La Florida encounters. Increased research has prompted publishers to reissue John Swanton's 1939 de Soto commission report (1985, with an introduction by Jeffrey Brain; 1985a) and a host of new interpretations of the various entradas— for example, on Narváez (Marrinan, Scarry, and Majors, this volume; Mitchem 1989a); on de Soto (Blake 1987a, 1987b, 1988; Brain 1985b; Curren 1986, 1987; DePratter, Hudson, and Smith 1985; Hudson 1989a; Hudson, DePratter, and Smith 1984, 1989; Hudson and Milanich 1989; Hudson, Worth, and DePratter, this volume; Jones 1988; Lankford 1977; Milanich 1988; Tesar 1980:275–346; for some methodological considerations see Hudson 1987c and Knight 1988); on de Luna (Hudson, DePratter, and Smith 1988, Hudson et al. 1989); and on Juan Pardo (DePratter and Smith 1980; DePratter, Hudson, and Smith 1983; Hudson 1987b, 1989b).

Studies of these specific Spanish–Native American encounters provide the interpretations that give reality to names like the chiefdom of Coosa and allow researchers to correlate historically documented villages and actual archaeological sites. We can derive what Charles Hudson has called a social geography of La Florida (in Hudson, DePratter, and Smith 1989:96), as well as information on, for example, political relationships among known sites (Hudson 1987a).

With these chronological and social-geographical data we can begin to interpret the cultural changes that began in the sixteenth century. Such studies include Marvin Smith's (1987) analysis of the impact of European contact on chiefdoms in the interior of La Florida in parts of Alabama, Tennessee, and Georgia; Jeffrey Mitchem's (1989b) study of the Safety Harbor culture in west-central Florida; and studies of the province of Coosa (Hudson et al. 1985; Hally, Smith, and Langford, this volume; Smith 1989).

Gradually we are assembling the data we need to document archaeologically the biological consequences of the Native American–Spanish interaction (see Dobyns 1983; Milner 1980). Ann F. Ramenofsky's (1987) comparative modeling of the Lower Mississippi Valley versus the Middle Missouri River Valley and Central New York supports the contention that there were epidemics rather than continent-sweeping pandemics and that the timing of disease-caused depopulation varied across North America. Robert Blakely and his associates at Georgia State University are advancing this inquiry even further with their comparative research on skeletal populations from the late prehistoric Etowah site and the King site (including battle casualties), thought to be a village in direct contact with either the de Soto or de Luna expeditions (Blakely 1988, Blakely and Detweiler-Blakely 1989; Detweiler-Blakely 1988; Mathews 1988). The casualties from the King site are a grisly reminder that sixteenth-century encounters between Native Americans and Spaniards were based on military interaction, not diplomacy.

Similar battle casualties have been found at the Tatham Mound, a site near de Soto's route in west-central Florida. Interments in the mound offer strong evidence of a fatal epidemic (Hutchinson, this volume; Mitchem and Hutchinson 1987; Mitchem 1989b:483–498). If we are ever to fully undertand the events of the sixteenth century, we will need more such research that draws on archaeological, biological, and historical evidence.

The native chiefdoms of La Florida have long disappeared. But they were of such stature that not even 450 years have been able to totally obliterate them, although much has been lost under our modern world. Today, five centuries after Christopher Columbus's first voyage, is a fitting time for focused studies of the first Native American–European encounters and their consequences. This is a task that historians and archaeologists must address. All that will ever be known abut sixteenth-century La Florida can only come from documents and from the ground.

Chronology: Key Dates in Sixteenth-Century La Florida

1513 (1512?)	Juan Ponce de León explores the coasts of La Florida.
1516	Diego Miruelo sails to the Gulf coast, possibly Apalachee Bay.
1519	Francisco Hernándo de Cordoba sails to southwest Florida.
1519	Alvarez de Pineda sails the Gulf coast from Florida to Yucatan.
1521	Pedro de Quexo and Francisco Gordilla explore the Atlantic coast.
1526	Lucas Vásquez de Ayllón establishes a short-lived colony on the Atlantic coast.
1528	Pánfilo de Narváez leads an ill-fated expedition from Tampa Bay to Apalachee.
1539	Hernando de Soto and his army land at Tampa Bay and march northward to Apalachee, where they winter.
1540	De Soto's army marches through Georgia, the Carolinas, Tennessee, and Alabama, reaching Mississippi by the end of the year.
1541 (May)	De Soto reaches the Mississippi River and crosses into Arkansas.
1542 (June)	De Soto dies near the Mississippi River; the expedition turns from exploration to survival.
1543 (June)	The remnants of the expedition begin a journey in boats down the Mississippi River to the Gulf of Mexico.
1543	Six months later, the survivors reach New Spain.
1559	Tristán de Luna y Arellano lands at Ochuse (Pensacola Bay), intending to establish a colony.
1561	De Luna's colony is withdrawn; some survivors are to be taken to Santa Elena by Ángel de Villafañe, but the attempt also fails.
1562–1565	France attempts to establish an Atlantic colony, settling first at Santa Elena and then at the mouth of the St. Johns River.
1565	Pedro Menéndez de Avilés ousts the French and establishes settlements at St. Augustine and, later, Santa Elena; shortly, outposts are established along the Gulf and Atlantic coasts.
1566–1568	Pedro Menéndez sends Juan Pardo and soldiers on two expeditions into the interior of La Florida; they leave from Santa Elena and on the second journey reach Tennessee, south of Knoxville.
1572	The Jesuit order withdraws from La Florida.

1573	Franciscan friars arrive at Santa Elena.
1587	The colony at Santa Elena is withdrawn.

References

Alexander, Michael (editor)
  1976 *Discovering the New World, Based on the Works of Theodore de Bry.* Harper & Row, New York.
Aten, Lawrence E.
  1983 *Indians of the Upper Texas Coast.* Academic Press, New York.
Bandelier, Ad. F. (editor)
  1905 *The Journey of Álvar Núñez Cabeza de Vaca and His Companions from Florida to the Pacific, 1528–1536.* Translated by Fanny Bandelier. A. S. Barnes, New York.
Barrientos, Bartolomé
  1965 *Pedro Menéndez de Avilés, Founder of Florida.* Translated by Anthony Kerrigan. University of Florida Press, Gainesville.
Bennett, Charles E.
  1964 *Laudonnière & Fort Caroline, History and Documents.* University of Florida Press, Gainesville.
  1968 *Settlement of Florida.* University of Florida Press, Gainesville.
Blake, Alan
  1987a *A Proposed Route for the Hernando de Soto Expedition from Tampa Bay to Apalachee Based on Physiography and Geology.* De Soto Working Paper No. 2. Alabama De Soto Commission, University of Alabama, State Museum of Natural History.
  1987b *A Proposed Route for the Hernando de Soto Expedition Based on Physiography and Geology. Part II—Apalachee to Chiaha.* De Soto Working Paper No. 4. Alabama De Soto Commission, University of Alabama, State Museum of Natural History.
  1988 *A Proposed Route for the Hernando de Soto Expedition Based on Physiography and Geology. Part III—Chiaha to Mabila. Part IV—Mabila to the Mississippi River.* De Soto Working Paper No. 6. Alabama De Soto Commission, University of Alabama, State Museum of Natural History.
Blakely, Robert L.
  1988 The Life Cycle and Village Organization. In *The King Site, Continuity and Contact in Sixteenth-Century Georgia*, edited by Robert L. Blakely, pp. 17–34. University of Georgia Press, Athens.
Blakely, Robert L., and Bettina Detweiler-Blakely
  1989 The Impact of European Diseases in the Sixteenth-Century Southeast: A Case Study. *Midcontinental Journal of Archaeology* 14:62–89.
Bourne, Edward G. (editor)
  1904 *Narratives of the Career of Hernando de Soto in the Conquest of Florida.* 2 vols. A. S. Barnes, New York.
Brain, Jeffrey P.
  1975 Artifacts of the Adelantado. *Conference on Historic Site Archaeology Papers* 8:129–138.
  1985a Introduction: Update of de Soto Studies since the United States De Soto Expedition Commission Report. In *Final Report of the United States De Soto Expedition Commission*, by John R. Swanton, pp. xi–lxxii. Smithsonian Institution Press, Washington, D.C.
  1985b The Archaeology of the Hernando de Soto Expedition. In *Alabama and Its Borderlands from Prehistory to Statehood*, edited by Reid Badger and Lawrence A. Clayton, pp. 96–107. University of Alabama Press, University.

Brown, Ian W.

1979   Bells. In *Tunica Treasure,* by Jeffrey Brain, pp. 197–205. Papers of the Peabody Museum of Archaeology and Ethnology, vol. 71. Harvard University Press, Cambridge, Massachusetts.

Brown, James A.

1985   The Mississippian Period. In *Ancient Art of the American Woodland Indians,* pp. 93–145. Harry N. Abrams, New York.

Castañeda, Paulino, Mariano Cuesta, and Pilar Hernández

1983   *Transcripcion, Estudio y Notas del "Espejo de Navegantes" de Alonso Chaves.* Instituto de Historia y Cultura Naval, Madrid.

Cordell, Linda

1989   Durango to Durango: An Overview of the Southwest Heartland. In *Columbian Consequences. Vol. 1: Archaeological and Historical Perspectives on the Spanish Borderlands West,* edited by David Hurst Thomas, pp. 17–40. Smithsonian Institution Press, Washington, D.C.

Crosby, Alfred W.

1972   *The Columbian Exchange: Biological and Cultural Consequences of 1492.* Greenwood, Westport, Connecticut.

Cumming, W. P., R. A. Skelton, and D. B. Quinn

1972   *The Discovery of North America.* American Heritage, New York.

Curren, Caleb

1986   *In Search of de Soto's Trail (A Hypothesis of the Alabama Route).* Bulletins of Discovery No. 1. Alabama-Tombigbee Commission, Camden.

1987   *The Route of the de Soto Army through Alabama.* De Soto Working Paper No. 3. Alabama De Soto Commission, University of Alabama, State Museum of Natural History.

Davila Padilla, Augustin

1922   [Narrative, ca. 1560]. In *Early History of the Creek Indians and Their Neighbors,* by John R. Swanton, pp. 231–239. Bureau of American Ethnology Bulletin 73. Smithsonian Institution, Washington, D.C.

Davis, T. Frederick

1935   Juan Ponce de Leon's Voyages to Florida. *Florida Historical Quarterly* 14:5–70.

Deagan, Kathleen A.

1987   *Artifacts of the Spanish Colonies of Florida and the Caribbean, 1500–1800. Vol. 1: Ceramics, Glassware, and Beads.* Smithsonian Institution Press, Washington, D.C.

Delcourt, P. A., and H. R. Delcourt

1981   Vegetation Maps for Eastern North America. In *Geobotany II,* edited by R. Romans, pp. 123–165. Plenum, New York.

DePratter, Chester B., Charles Hudson, and Marvin T. Smith

1983   The Route of Juan Pardo's Explorations in the Interior Southeast. *Florida Historical Quarterly* 62:125–158.

1985   The Hernando de Soto Expedition: From Chiaha to Mabilia. In *Alabama and Its Borderlands from Prehistory to Statehood,* edited by Reid Badger and Lawrence A. Clayton, pp. 108–126. University of Alabama Press, University

DePratter, Chester B., and Marvin T. Smith

1980   Sixteenth Century European Trade in the Southeastern United States: Evidence from the Juan Pardo Expeditions (1566–1568). In *Spanish Colonial Frontier Research,* edited by Henry F. Dobyns, pp. 57–77. Center for Anthropological Research, Albuquerque.

Detweiler-Blakely, Bettina

1988   Stress and the Battle Casualties. In *The King Site, Continuity and Contact in Sixteenth-Century Georgia,* edited by Robert L. Blakely, pp. 87–98. University of Georgia Press, Athens.

Dobyns, Henry F.
1983   *Their Number Become Thinned, Native American Populations Dynamics in Eastern North America.* University of Tennessee Press, Knoxville.

Espenshade, Edward B.
1984   *Goode's World Atlas.* 16th ed. Rand McNally, Chicago.

Ewen, Charles R.
1988   *The Discovery of de Soto's First Winter Encampment in Florida.* De Soto Working Paper No. 7. Alabama De Soto Commission, University of Alabama, State Museum of Natural History.
1989   Anhaica: Discovery of Hernando de Soto's 1539–1540 Winter Camp. In *First Encounters, Spanish Explorations in the Caribbean and the United States, 1492–1570*, edited by Jerald T. Milanich and Susan Milbrath, pp. 110–118. University of Florida Press, Gainesville.

Fairbanks, Charles H.
1968a Early Spanish Colonial Beads. *Conference on Historic Site Archaeology* 2:3–21.
1968b Florida Coin Beads. *Florida Anthropologist* 21:102–105.
1985   From Exploration to Settlement: Spanish Strategies for Colonization. In *Alabama and Its Borderlands from Prehistory to Statehood*, edited by Reid Badger and Lawrence A. Clayton, pp. 128–139. University of Alabama Press, University.

Gagliano, Sherwood H.
1984   Geoarchaeology of the Northern Gulf Coast Shore. In *Perspectives on Gulf Coast Prehistory*, edited by Dave D. Davis, pp. 1–40. University of Florida Press, Gainesville.

Goggin, John M.
1954   Are There de Soto Relics in Florida? *Florida Historical Quarterly* 32:151–162.
1960   *The Spanish Olive Jar, An Introductory Study.* Yale University Publications in Anthropology 62. New Haven.
1968   *Spanish Majolica in the New World.* Yale University Publications in Anthropology 72. New Haven.

Goggin, John M., and William C. Sturtevant
1964   The Calusa: A Stratified Nonagricultural Society (with Notes on Sibling Marriage). In *Explorations in Cultural Anthropology: Essays in Honor of George Peter Murdock*, edited by Ward H. Goodenough, pp. 179–219. McGraw-Hill, New York.

Granberry, Julian
1987   *A Grammar and Dictionary of the Timucuan Language.* Anthropological Notes 1. Horseshoe Beach, Florida.

Hann, John H.
1988   *Apalachee: The Land between the Rivers.* University Presses of Florida, Gainesville.
1989   *Mission to the Calusa.* University of Florida Press, Gainesville, in press.

Haring, C. H.
1963   *The Spanish Empire in America.* Harcourt Brace Jovanovich, New York. Originally published 1947, Oxford University Press, New York.

Harrisse, Henry
1961   *The Discovery of North America: A Critical, Documentary, and Historical Investigation.* Reprinted. N. Israel, Amsterdam. Originally published 1892, London.

Hemming, John
1978   *Red Gold: The Conquest of the Brazilian Indians.* Harvard University Press, Cambridge, Massachusetts.

Henige, David
1986   The Context, Content, and Credibility of *La Florida del Ynca. The Americas* 43:1–24.

Hoffman, Paul E.
1984   The Chicora Legend and Franco-Spanish Rivalry. *Florida Historical Quarterly* 62:419–438.

Hudson, Charles
  1976   *The Southeastern Indians.* University of Tennessee Press, Knoxville.
  1987a An Unknown South: Spanish Explorers and Southeastern Chiefdoms. In *Visions and Revisions, Ethnohistoric Perspectives on Southern Cultures,* edited by George Sabo III and William M. Schneider, pp. 6–24. Southern Anthropological Society Proceedings 20. University of Georgia Press, Athens.
  1987b Juan Pardo's Excursion beyond Chiaha. *Tennessee Anthropologist* 12:74–87.
  1987c *The Uses of Evidence in Reconstructing the Route of the Hernando de Soto Expedition.* De Soto Working Paper No. 1. Alabama De Soto Commission, University of Alabama, State Museum of Natural History.
  1989a *De Soto in Alabama.* De Soto Working Paper No. 10. Alabama De Soto Commission, University of Alabama, State Museum of Natural History.
  1989b *The Juan Pardo Expeditions: Spanish Explorers and the Indians of the Carolinas and Tennessee, 1566–1568.* Smithsonian Institution Press, Washington, D.C., in press.
Hudson, Charles, Chester DePratter, and Marvin T. Smith
  1984   The Hernando de Soto Expedition: From Apalachee to Chiaha. *Southeastern Archaeology* 3:65–77.
  1988   The Victims of the King Site Massacre: A Historical Detectives' Report. In *The King Site, Continuity and Contact in Sixteenth-Century Georgia,* edited by Robert L. Blakely, pp. 101–134. University of Georgia Press, Athens.
  1989   Hernando de Soto's Expedition through the Southern United States. In *First Encounters, Spanish Explorations in the Caribbean and the United States, 1492–1570,* edited by Jerald T. Milanich and Susan Milbrath, pp. 77–98. University of Florida Press, Gainesville.
Hudson, Charles, and Jerald T. Milanich
  1989   *Hernando de Soto and the Florida Indians.* University of Florida Press, Gainesville, in press.
Hudson, Charles, Marvin T. Smith, Chester B. DePratter, and Emilia Kelley
  1989   The Tristan de Luna Expedition, 1559–1561. In *First Encounters, Spanish Explorations in the Caribbean and the United States, 1492–1570,* edited by Jerald T. Milanich and Susan Milbrath, pp. 119–134. University of Florida Press, Gainesville.
Hudson, Charles, Marvin Smith, David Hally, Richard Polhemus, and Chester DePratter
  1985   Coosa: A Chiefdom in the Sixteenth Century Southeastern United States. *American Antiquity* 50:723–737.
Jones, B. Calvin
  1982   Southern Cult Manifestations at the Lake Jackson Site, Leon County, Florida: Salvage Excavation of Mound 3. *Midcontinental Journal of Archaeology* 7:3–44.
Jones, Douglas E. (editor)
  1988   *The Highway Route of the De Soto Trail in Alabama.* De Soto Working Paper No. 8. Alabama De Soto Commission, University of Alabama, State Museum of Natural History.
Ketchem, Herbert E. (editor and translator)
  1954   Three Sixteenth Century Spanish Chronicles Relating to Georgia. *Georgia Historical Quarterly* 28:66–82
Knight, Vernon J., Jr.
  1988   *A Summary of Alabama's de Soto Mapping Project and Project Bibliography.* De Soto Working Paper No. 9. Alabama De Soto Commission, University of Alabama, State Museum of Natural History.
Lankford, George
  1977   A New Look at de Soto's Route through Alabama. *Journal of Alabama Archaeology* 23:11–36.
Larson, Lewis H.
  1980   *Aboriginal Subsistence Technology on the Southeastern Gulf Coastal Plain during the Late Prehistoric Period.* University of Florida Press, Gainesville.

Laudonnière, René
1975 *Three Voyages*. Translated by Charles E. Bennett. University of Florida Press, Gainesville.

Little, Keith, and Caleb B. Curren, Jr.
1981 Site 1Ce308: A Protohistoric Site on the Upper Coosa River, Alabama. *Journal of Alabama Archaeology* 27:117–124.

Lorant, Stefan
1946 *The New World, The First Pictures of America*. Duell, Sloan, & Pearce, New York.

Lyon, Eugene
1976 *The Enterprise of Florida, Pedro Menéndez de Avilés and the Spanish Conquest of 1565–1568*. University of Florida Press, Gainesville.
1982 The Cañete Fragment: Another Narrative of Hernando de Soto. Ms. on file. St. Augustine Foundation. St. Augustine.
1984 *Santa Elena: A Brief History of the Colony, 1566–1587*. Research Manuscript Series 193. South Carolina Institute of Archaeology and Anthropology, University of South Carolina, Columbia.
1988 Pedro Menéndez's Strategic Plan for the Florida Peninsula. *Florida Historical Quarterly* 67:1–14.

Marquardt, William H.
1987 The Calusa Social Formation in Protohistoric South Florida. In *Power Relations and State Formations*, edited by Thomas C. Patterson and Christine W. Gailey, pp. 98–116. Archaeology Section, American Anthropological Association, Washington, D.C.
1988 Politics and Production among the Calusa of South Florida. In *Hunters and Gatherers. Vol. 1: History, Environment, and Social Change among Hunting and Gathering Societies*, edited by David Richies, Tim Ingold, and James Woodburn, pp. 161–188. Berg, London.

Mathews, David S.
1988 The Massacre: The Discovery of de Soto in Georgia. In *The King Site, Continuity and Contact in Sixteenth-Century Georgia*, edited by Robert L. Blakely, pp. 101–117. University of Georgia Press, Athens.

Meyer, William E.
1928 Indian Trails of the Southeast. In *Forty-second Annual Report of the Bureau of American Ethnology*, pp. 727–857. Smithsonian Institution, Washington, D.C.

Milanich, Jerald T.
1988 *Hernando de Soto and the Expedition in Florida*. Miscellaneous Project Report Series No. 32. Department of Anthropology, Florida Museum of Natural History. Gainesville.

Milanich, Jerald T., Ann S. Cordell, Vernon J. Knight, Jr., Timothy A. Kohler, and Brenda J. Sigler-Lavelle
1984 *McKeithen Weeden Island: The Culture of North Florida, A.D. 200–900*. Academic Press, Orlando.

Milner, George R.
1980 Epidemic Disease in the Postcontact Southeast: An Appraisal. *Midcontinental Journal of Anthropology* 5:39–56.

Mitchem, Jeffrey M.
1989a Artifacts of Exploration: Archaeological Evidence from Florida. In *First Encounters, Spanish Explorations in the Caribbean and the United States, 1492–1570*, edited by Jerald T. Milanich and Susan Milbrath, pp. 99–109. University of Florida Press, Gainesville.
1989b *Redefining Safety Harbor: Late Prehistoric/Protohistoric Archaeology in West Peninsular Florida*. Unpublished Ph.D. dissertation, University of Florida. University Microfilms, Ann Arbor.

Mitchem, Jeffrey M., and Dale L. Hutchinson
1987   *Interim Report on Archaeological Research at the Tatham Mound, Citrus County, Florida: Season III.* Miscellaneous Project Report Series No. 30. Department of Anthropology, Florida Museum of Natural History. Gainesville.

Mitchem, Jeffrey M., and Jonathan M. Leader
1988   Early Sixteenth Century Beads from Tatham Mound, Citrus County, Florida: Data and Interpretations. *Florida Anthropologist* 41:42–60.

Mitchem, Jeffrey M., and Bonnie G. McEwan
1988   New Data on Early Bells from Florida. *Southeastern Archaeology* 7:39–48

Mitchem, Jeffrey M., Marvin T. Smith, Albert C. Goodyear, and Robert R. Allen
1985   Early Spanish Contact on the Florida Gulf Coast: The Weeki Wachee and Ruth Smith Mounds. In *Indians, Colonists, and Slaves: Essays in Memory of Charles H. Fairbanks,* edited by Kenneth W. Johnson, Jonathan M. Leader, and Robert C. Wilson, pp. 179–219. Florida Journal of Anthropology Special Publication 4. Gainesville.

Mitchem, Jeffrey M., and Brent R. Weisman
1984   Excavations at the Ruth Smith Mound (8Ci200). *Florida Anthropologist* 37:100–112.

Morison, Samuel Eliot
1971   *The European Discovery of America: The Northern Voyages.* Oxford University Press, New York.

Morse, Phyllis A.
1981   *Parkin: The 1978–1979 Archeological Investigations of a Cross County, Arkansas Site.* Arkansas Archaeological Survey Series 13. Fayetteville.

Newcomb, W. W., Jr.
1961   *The Indians of Texas from Prehistoric to Modern Times.* University of Texas Press, Austin.

Payne, Claudine
1981   A Preliminary Investigation of Fort Walton Settlement Patterns in the Tallahassee Red Hills. *Southeastern Archaeological Conference Bulletin* 24:29–31.

Priestley, Herbert I.
1928   *The Luna Papers, Documents Relating to the Expedition of Don Tristan de Luna y Arellano for the Conquest of La Florida in 1559–1561.* 2 vols. Florida State Historical Society, Publication 8. Deland.

Quinn, David B.
1988   Colonies from the Beginning: Examples from North America. In *Essays on the History of North American Discovery and Exploration,* edited by Stanley H. Palmer and Dennis Reinhartz, pp. 10–34. Texas A&M University Press, College Station.

Quinn, David B. (editor)
1971   *North American Discovery, ca. 1000–1612.* University of South Carolina Press, Columbia.
1977   *North America from Earliest Discovery to First Settlements: The Norse Voyages to 1612.* Harper and Row, New York.
1979   *New American World. A Documentary History of North America to 1612.* 5 vols. Arno Press, New York.

Ramenofsky, Ann F.
1987   *Vectors of Death: The Archaeology of European Contact.* University of New Mexico Press, Albuquerque.

Ribault, Jean
1964   *The Whole & True Discouerye of Terra Florida. A Facsimile Reprint of the London Edition of 1563.* University of Florida Press, Gainesville.

Sauer, Carl O.
1966   *The Early Spanish Main.* University of California Press, Berkeley.
1971   *Sixteenth Century North America: The Land and the Peoples as Seen by Europeans.* University of California Press, Berkeley.

Scarry, John F.

    1984 *Fort Walton Development: Mississippian Chiefdoms in the Lower Southeast.* Unpublished Ph.D. dissertation, Case Western Reserve University. University Microfilms, Ann Arbor.

Shelford, Victor E.

    1963 *The Ecology of North America.* University of Illinois Press, Urbana.

Smith, Bruce D.

    1985 Mississippian Patterns of Subsistence and Settlement. In *Alabama and Its Borderlands from Prehistory to Statehood*, edited by Reid Badger and Lawrence A. Clayton, pp. 64–79. University of Alabama Press, University.

    1986 The Archaeology of the Southeastern United States: From Dalton to de Soto, 10,500–500 B.P. In *Advances in World Archaeology 5*, edited by Fred Wendorf and Angela E. Close, pp. 1–92. Academic Press, Orlando.

Smith, Marvin T.

    1982 "Eye" Beads in the Southeast. *Conference on Historic Site Archaeology Papers 1979* 14:116–127.

    1983 Chronology from Glass Beads: The Spanish Period in the Southeast, 1513–1670. In *Proceedings of the 1982 Glass Trade Bead Conference*, edited by Charles F. Hayes III, pp. 147–158. Research Records No. 16. Research Division, Rochester Museum and Science Center. Rochester, New York.

    1984 A Sixteenth Century Coin from Southeast Alabama. *Journal of Alabama Archaeology* 30:56–59.

    1987 *Archaeology of Aboriginal Culture Change in the Interior Southeast: Depopulation during the Early Historic Period.* University of Florida Press, Gainesville.

    1989 Indian Responses to European Contact: The Coosa Example. In *First Encounters, Spanish Explorations in the Caribbean and the United States, 1492–1570*, edited by Jerald T. Milanich and Susan Milbrath, pp. 135–149. University of Florida Press, Gainesville.

Smith, Marvin T., and Mary Elizabeth Good

    1982 *Early Sixteenth Century Glass Beads in the Spanish Colonial Trade*, Cottonlandia Museum, Greenwood, Mississippi.

Solís de Merás, Gonzalo

    1964 *Pedro Menéndez de Avilés. Adelantado, Governor and Captain-General of Florida.* Translated by Jeannette Thurber Connor. Reprinted. University of Florida Press, Gainesville. Originally published 1923, Florida State Historical Society, Publication 3, Deland.

South, Stanley, Russell K. Skowronek, and Richard E. Johnson

    1988 *Spanish Artifacts from Santa Elena.* Anthropological Studies No. 7. South Carolina Institute of Archaeology and Anthropology, Columbia.

Stahl, Jeremy D.

    1986 *An Ethnohistory of South Florida, 1500–1575.* Unpublished Master's thesis, Department of History, University of Florida, Gainesville.

Sturtevant, William C.

    1962 Spanish-Indian Relations in Southeastern North America. *Ethnohistory* 9:41–94.

    1978 The Last of the South Florida Aborigines. In *Tacachale: Essays on the Indians of Florida and Southeast Georgia during the Historic Period*, edited by Jerald T. Milanich and Samuel Proctor, pp. 141–162. University of Florida Press, Gainesville.

Swanton, John R.

    1946 *The Indians of the Southeastern United States.* Bureau of American Ethnology Bulletin No. 137. Smithsonian Institution, Washington, D.C.

Swanton, John R. (editor)

    1985 *Final Report of the United States De Soto Expedition Commission.* Smithsonian Institution Press, Washington. Originally published 1939. U.S. House of Representatives, 76th Cong., 1st sess, Doc. 71. Washington, D.C.

Tesar, Louis D.

1980 *The Leon County Bicentennial Survey Report: An Archaeological Survey of Selected Portions of Leon County, Florida.* Miscellaneous Project Report Series No. 49. Florida Bureau of Historic Sites and Properties. Tallahassee.

True, David O. (editor)

1945 *Memoir of D. d'Escalante Fontaneda respecting Florida, Written in Spain, about the Year 1575.* Glade House, Coral Gables, Florida.

Varner, John, and Jeanette Varner (translators and editors)

1951 *The Florida of the Inca.* University of Texas Press, Athens.

Weddle, Robert S.

1985 *Spanish Sea, the Gulf of Mexico in North American Discovery, 1500–1685.* Texas A&M University Press, College Station.

Widmer, Randolph

1988 *The Evolution of the Calusa, a Nonagricultural Chiefdom on the Southwest Florida Coast.* University of Alabama Press, Tuscaloosa.

Willey, Gordon R.

1949 *Archeology of the Florida Gulf Coast.* Smithsonian Miscellaneous Collections No. 113. Washington, D.C.

Wood, Peter H.

1974 *Black Majority: Negroes in Colonial South Carolina.* Alfred A. Knopf, New York.

Zubillaga, Felix (editor)

1946 *Monumenta Antiquae Floridae (1566–1572).* Monumenta Historica Societatis Iesu 69; Monumenta Missionum Societatis Iesu 3. Rome.

Chapter 2 ■

Ann F. Ramenofsky

Loss of Innocence: Explanations of Differential Persistence in the Sixteenth-Century Southeast

Despite the plethora of new information on disease introduction and Native American population decline (Baker and Armelagos 1988; Cook 1982; Crosby 1986; Dobyns 1983; Ramenofsky 1987; Smith 1987; Snow and Lamphear 1988; Thornton 1987), there is no theory, or system of knowledge, that unites research efforts and directs inquiry. In the absence of theory, one or another set of implicit or explicit assumptions governs the collection of information and the meaning we infer from the results. Scholars tenaciously hold to their assumptions, accumulating more and more facts in the light of those assumptions, ever hopeful that the scales will tip eventually in their favor.

At various times archaeologists working in the Forested East have supported differing assumptions regarding biological and cultural continuity between history and prehistory. Prior to the late nineteenth century, an assumption of biological and cultural discontinuity prevailed. Following Cyrus Thomas's synthesis of the Mound Builder problem, an assumption of continuity between postcontact and precontact populations was adopted. More recently, as the sixteenth-century disease hypothesis has gained recognition, an assumption of discontinuity and fundamental cultural reorganization has again been adopted.

Unfortunately, we still don't know where, and under what conditions, this discontinuity occurred. As current tribal rosters suggest, not all native populations in the Forested East died in the sixteenth century. Clearly, there were differential responses to disease. Explanatory assumptions come and go, but the problem of persistence or extinction remains.

My intent is to get beyond the polarizing assumptions of continuity or discontinuity during the Columbian period, to evaluate the question of differential persistence or extinction. I do so by building a theoretical model that employs Darwinian evolution to explain differential responses to disease.

The use of Darwinism in the context of disease transmission to North America is a logical and powerful conjunction. Darwinian evolution, or the selectionist model of change (Leonard and Jones 1987), is a robust and elegant theory that explains differential persistence of variability, why some traits survive for very long periods, and other traits become extinct. The central question of this paper from a Darwinian perspective is why there were differential responses to disease: why some areas emptied out and other areas demonstrate persistence into the present.

Answering this question has implications for a number of problems posed by the sixteenth-century disease hypothesis. Determining conditions of decline as opposed to persistence is crucial for building reliable estimates of precontact population size. If decline was ubiquitous and predated initial census counts, uniform adjustment upward to reach precontact maxima is appropriate. If, however, some populations suffered minimal demographic consequences, or if decline postdated documents, then uniform increase in population counts is inappropriate.

Documenting differential persistence of small groups may help explain the form of eighteenth-century miscegenated societies. Records of the eighteenth century contain frequent descriptions of fusion, fission, migration, and relocation. The Creek and Natchez, for instance, were like vacuum cleaners, sucking people into their system. The Bayagoula survived by joining, fighting, and then separating from several groups. Because cultural traits are passengers of individuals, stipulating conditions that promoted or inhibited population loss may, in part, account for the cultural variability of these societies.

I begin with a historical review of the dichotomous assumptions of continuity and discontinuity through the sixteenth century in the Southeast. I then explain how Darwinism relates to the problem of disease contact and population decline. I conclude by presenting a model that will help evaluate assumptions about this important topic against the archaeological record.

Historical Perspective on Population Change

Assumption of Continuity

The archaeological perspective that viewed aboriginal populations of the sixteenth century as being continuous with prehistoric populations can be traced to the resolution of the Mound Builder debate and particularly to the work of Cyrus Thomas (1894). For more than a century preceding Thomas's work, natural historians with an interest in the prehistoric builders of mounds (Atwater 1820; Barton 1787, 1798, 1799; Harris 1835; Haven 1856; Heart 1793; Jefferson 1803 [1784]; Squier and Davis 1848; Stiles 1788; Webster 1787, 1788a, 1788b) had debated the cultural affiliation and fate of the builders. Implicit or explicit in all these discussions was the observation that living native populations in mound-building areas were culturally different from mound-building societies.

With Thomas, however, all questions of mound builders as biologically or culturally distinct from living native populations disappeared. In an effort to give Native Americans back their birthright, Thomas married historical descriptions of native peoples to archaeological manifestations. Although implicit, this marriage was the beginning of the direct historical approach in archaeology (Meltzer 1983; Trigger 1985).

To adopt a direct historical perspective, Thomas had to sidestep certain problems that had plagued all previous investigators. Rather than question whether historical tribes were continuous or discontinuous with the past, Thomas assumed ethnic continuity from present to past. The assumption became possible by pushing forward in time the onset of cultural change.

> One reason why the Indian has been so generally, so persistently, and so unceremoniously refused admission as a possible factor in this problem is because of the opinion, which seems to be almost universally held, that when first encountered on our continent by European explorers, he was the same restless, roving, unsettled, unhoused, and unagricultural savage, wherever found, as we have learned to consider him in more modern times [1894:610–611].

Because change postdated initial descriptions, Thomas used information in historical documents to link historically identified tribes to prehistoric mound types or areas.

Thomas's work has had lasting consequences for American archaeology. Because Thomas pushed forward the beginning of significant demographic or cultural change, native populations of the Forested East were recognized as mound builders, an admission that was long overdue. Researchers in the twentieth century (Bushnell 1986 [1917]; Swanton 1928) would continue to refine the equation between historic tribes and prehistoric mound builders.

The concept of stasis that emerged from Thomas's method had negative consequences. Archaeologists stopped questioning whether or not there were discontinuities between history and prehistory. Ethnic identity from present to past became a constant; archaeologists could discover or document prehistoric ethnicity.

Thomas's intellectual legacy in the Southeast is reflected in two major archaeological trends: the reconstruction of prehistoric identity by means of historic documents and/or the tracing of routes of exploration throughout the Southeast.

The rich sixteenth-century historical record in the Southeast provided an excellent setting for the use of Thomas's approach. Between 1520 and 1570, there were five documented entradas in the Southeast (Parry 1985; Smith 1987; Milanich, this volume). Although the wealth of historical information made the direct historical approach very attractive, evidence of a severe disruption of native populations dates to the same period (Bourne 1904). Archaeologists were aware of the disruptions but assumed, as Thomas had earlier, that the disruptions postdated initial descriptions.

Prior to the development of regional chronologies, historical documents were used to identify the material remains of historic groups (Collins 1927); they anchored developing chronological sequences spatially. In 1936, Ford presented his first chronological sequence of Louisiana, known as the Lower Red River chronology. In building the sequence, Ford relied primarily on the stylistic variation of ceramics. To position this variability spatially, Ford used the direct historical method, defining the Tunica, Natchez, Choctaw, and Caddo complexes. As discussed later in this chapter, once the chronological sequence was built, Ford dropped the direct historical method from his work (Ford and Willey 1941).

By the 1950s, linking historic to prehistoric ethnicity in the Southeast was limited to those areas in which some degree of ethnic or cultural persistence through the sixteenth century could be assumed. In Cole's anniversary volume, Kneberg (1952), Caldwell (1952), and Fairbanks (1952) used the historical material on the Creek, Cherokee, and Muskogee to define, with varying degrees of success, the late prehistory of parts of the interior Southeast.

Swanton's role in the archaeological reliance on history cannot be underestimated. As a historian, he was responsible for translating and publishing numerous documents (e.g., Swanton 1911, 1942, 1946). As an anthropologist, Swanton was concerned with building coherent and integrated descriptions of obviously disrupted societies. Therefore he ignored the temporal dimension and blended traits drawn from prehistory, explorer journals, mythology, language, religion, and archaeology.

Swanton's synthesis of Southeastern Indians (1946) demonstrates the blend. Because of documented historic change, Swanton first summarized post-Columbian abandonment histories of native peoples. A number of areas were targeted, including the Lower Mississippi Valley, trans-Mississippian West, southern Appalachia, and coastal and interior Georgia. Swanton also wanted to account for the origins of historic ethnic units. To accomplish this goal—which was admittedly difficult given the disruptions—he adopted an essentialist ontology that viewed culture as unitary. Continuity of traits implied continuity of ethnic units and systems. In addition, Swanton assumed that change postdated documents.

Within this framework, prehistoric systems were stable; significant, and perhaps terminal, disruptions occurred in the historical period. Fortunately, traits had survived the disruption. Thus, migration myths were employed to describe the march of real discoverable prehistoric units, comparable to historic tribes, down the Mississippi Valley to disrupted historic locations (Smith 1984). Once the reconstructions were in place, archaeologists used them, as if they were real, to resurrect prehistoric ethnicity.

The second major use of documents in the Southeast is to investigate explorer routes. Most attention has focused on de Soto; once again, Swanton's initial synthesis (1939) of the de Soto route was a stimulus. The goals of these types of studies are largely descriptive, as they trace routes and use the archaeological record to flesh out the nature of the earliest postcontact societies. Sixteenth-century European artifacts are index fossils in these investigations, confirming or disconfirming temporal assignments of archaeological sites or the meandering path of the explorer. Unfortunately, there is no consensus regarding how artifacts themselves came to be deposited in particular places.

Brain (Brain et al. 1974; Brain 1985), for instance, assumes that Spanish artifacts were taken out of circulation. Thus, the distribution of Clarksdale bells and halberds indicates de Soto's wanderings.

Researchers reconstructing the interior Southeastern route hold varying opinions (see Boyd and Schroedl 1987 for a similar criticism). Hudson et al. (1984) agree with Brain and suggest that artifacts were removed from circulation. Smith (1987), on the other hand, suggests that artifacts could have been widely traded, with the result that places of acquisition and deposition need not coincide. Because cooperating researchers working on the interior southeastern route do not agree on the aboriginal treatment of the sixteenth-century European artifacts, questions regarding the accuracy and method of de Soto's reconstructed route surface.

Four of the six Coosa towns along de Soto's route (Hudson et al. 1985; Smith 1987) produced index fossils. The question here is whether the artifacts confirm the route. If the artifacts play a confirmatory role, then they could not have been traded into those locations. If artifacts were traded in, they cannot be used to confirm the presence of de Soto. Regardless of the outcome, the presence of Spanish artifacts in Coosa towns must be considered before the route can be accepted.

In summary, the assumption of continuity between prehistoric and sixteenth-century populations stems from Thomas's resolution of the Mound-Builder debate. Because initial explorer descriptions mark the beginning of European contact, evidence of disruption that postdates 1492 but predates documentation is masked. Documents are employed to reconstruct prehistoric ethnicity, or to trace the explorer routes.

Assumption of Discontinuity

Sometime between 1492 and the beginning of European documentation and settlement at regional scales, native peoples had changed. Consequently, assumptions of continuity or ethnic identity from the present to the past are unwarranted. Although observations regarding change in the historic period begin with explorer accounts in the sixteenth century (Bourne 1904; Hariot 1973 [1588]), the assumption of discontinuity, like that of Thomas's continuity, becomes incorporated into the Mound-Builder debate.

Most eighteenth- and nineteenth-century investigators of the mound problem had argued for discontinuity between historic and prehistoric populations. Reasons for the discontinuity varied according to whether native societies were viewed from progressionist or decay perspectives (Ramenofsky 1981). Progressionists believed that social development was directional. Therefore, native populations of the East could never have been mound builders (Atwater 1820; Gallatin 1836, 1845; Harris 1835; Squier and Davis 1848). Building was a characteristic of cultural complexity and, having obtained that stage, it would not be abandoned. Because culture and race were united, racial differences were invoked to explain cultural discontinuity between the present and past. Thus, Tartars (Atwater 1820), Danes (Barton 1787), Toltecs (Morton 1839), or the Spanish (Webster 1787, 1788a, 1788b) had built the mounds.

If, on the other hand, native societies were in a state of decay (Haven 1856; McCulloh 1829; Stiles 1788), then mound builders were autochthonous to the East. Causes for decay had to be suggested; as Haven's work demonstrates, population loss ranked high on the list of causes:

> A mere diminution of numbers, and consequently of power, without any material differences of customs or capacities may perhaps be sufficient to explain the diminution of grandeur in the ceremonies and structures of later inhabitants. The decay of energy and enterprise . . . has led to a discontinuance of works consecrated to religious rites or intended for permanent defense [Haven 1856:18].

Following Thomas's synthesis, discussions of change were quelled for a time, but they resurfaced in the early decades of the twentieth century. When the question of change appeared again, decay was no longer suggested as a reason for discontinuity; disease and warfare were added as causes for population loss. Until very recently, these associations—disease, warfare, population loss, and change—were treated much the way culture historians treated migration or invasion: simple post hoc generalizations to account for obvious discontinuities in the record.

Ford, who in 1936 employed the direct historical method to spatially position ceramic complexes, dropped the use of the method by 1941. In that year, he and Willey argued for discontinuity between prehistory and history. The introduction of disease and population loss were responsible for the discontinuity; the temporally misplaced Southern Cult was the symbol of the disruption. They viewed the Southern Cult as an example of revivalism that occurred in response to the loss of population connected with the arrival of Europeans.

Although the goal of the Phillips, Ford, and Griffin survey (1951) was to build a basement under the Mississippian Tradition, their work became a methodological and substantive watershed for fundamental and far-reaching change. First, Phillips, Ford, and Griffin changed the scale of archaeological investigations from local to regional (Dunnell 1985). The scale of their investigation coupled with sample sizes and temporal control allowed them to use site counts to trace population trends through time. The change in site counts between the Spanish and the French dramatized a substantial decline. Phillips noted the decline, called it "regressive," and linked it to Chickasaw warfare. Regardless of its cause, however, the pattern was unambiguous and required the attention of archaeologists.

It was not until the 1980s that archaeologists began to systematically consider the consequences of disease introduction among native populations. Rather than an empirical generalization about the record, disease and population loss became the focus of hypothesis testing.

Although united on the importance of the problem, researchers hold differing assumptions about the spatial extent of disease diffusion, the magnitude of loss that resulted, or the role of archaeology in the analysis of the problem. Milner (1980, 1988), for instance, argues that geographic or cultural barriers preclude regional-scale diffusion of pathogens. I, on the other hand, think it likely that disease followed trade routes, in which case local outbreaks may have reached regional-scale epidemics. Whereas some researchers accept Dobyns's sixteenth-century hypothesis (Smith 1987) and use it to explain historic discontinuities, I view the disease and population question as empirical matters that must be tested in the context of well-controlled regional investigations. Because some individuals survived in almost all situations, I simply don't know whether the patterns I have documented in some regions of the East (Ramenofsky 1987) occur everywhere.

When viewed from a historical perspective, there is no archaeological agreement regarding the possibility of fundamental population change in the Columbian period. Archaeologists have simply assumed that sixteenth-century populations were either continuous or discontinuous with prehistoric expressions. The result is that we have a patchwork of stable or unstable populations that is more a reflection of archaeological bias than of empirical variability. Although it is certainly possible that there were variable spatial responses to the same pathogen, or that different infections had varying spatial trajectories, the patchwork does not allow for such inferences.

If we want to know why the Tunica, Natchez, or Creek persist, but the Colapissa, Powhatan, or Timucua disappear, we must build theoretical constructs that, in turn, can be translated into measurable variables in the archaeological record.

Darwinian Theory

I restrict my treatment of evolution to that defined by Darwin as "descent with modification." Most models of cultural evolution in anthropology (e.g., Sahlins 1960; Sahlins and Service 1960; White 1949) view cultural development as directional or progressive and adopt a transformational perspective of change. Cultures, viewed as closed systems, transform from bands to tribes by the addition or modification of certain traits. A Darwinian model, on the other hand, adopts a selectionist view of change (Dunnell 1980, 1982; Leonard and Jones 1987). Change in frequencies of traits rather than transformation of systems constitutes descent with modification.

According to Lewontin (1974; Levins and Lewontin 1985), Darwin made two great contributions to natural science. He changed the focus of explanation from idealized types or essences to variation between individuals, and he offered mechanisms that could account for the differential persistence of variation. As long as natural scientists perceived the world from an essentialist ontology, phenomena could only be explained by describing how the particular reflected the ideal. Platonic ideals were real, but not observable; particulars were observable but frequently deviated from the ideal. That deviation was extraneous and often obscured perception.

Within Darwin's materialist ontology, however, ideal types dissolved and were replaced by individual variation. Variation was no longer something extraneous but became the focus of explanation. Why did some variability persist and other variability become extinct?

Second, Darwin offered mechanisms by which differential persistence could be explained. He termed these mechanisms natural selection. One or more of these mechanisms affected the reproductive fitness of individuals. Thus some variability disappeared and other types of variability persisted. The interactions of the mechanisms of natural selection with preexisting variability became the method of analyzing and explaining why phenomena exist.

Variability and selection, then, are the two crucial theoretical concepts within Darwinism. Both are relevant to the question of persistence or decline of aboriginal populations, and both require definition. I take up selection first, and then consider variability.

Not surprisingly, disease is the selective agent. Even when there is some immunity within a population, disease outbreaks can have debilitating effects. When there is no immunity, however, the consequences of disease contact can be devastating. The extinction of the American chestnut, or mortality from the Black Plague are ample evidence of the consequences of disease contact in virgin-soil populations. Despite the effect of such natural catastrophes as earthquakes, I would argue that only since the invention of nuclear warfare have we developed selective agents that have the power of disease.

Mathematical epidemiologists (Bailey 1957; Bartlett 1957) have built descriptive models of the behavior of diseases, such as measles, among populations in which some individuals have immunity from previous exposures. Although helpful for understanding disease as a selective agent, these models differ fundamentally from sixteenth-century America. Because native populations had no immunity to European pathogens, everyone was at risk. The populations of both continents were virgin soil.

When there is some immunity to a disease, a community is divided into three classes: infecteds or sources, susceptibles or recipients (those at risk), and recovereds (those with immunity to the pathogen). As sources contact recipients, the number of individuals who are still at risk decreases and the number of recovereds increases.

Becoming sick, however, does not mean that an individual will die. Mortality rates are typically some proportion of morbidity or infection rates. In a population of 1,000, for example, there are 500 recipients. The expected infection and mortality rates are 10 percent. These figures mean that at time T_1, 50 people will get sick and at T_2, 5 of those 50 will die. These deaths then reduce the total population to 995. This process continues until there are no new recipients.

A loss of 5 individuals from a population of 1,000 does not mean extinction of the population. Expected mortality from the illness is not the only reason people die during a disease event. Other factors can increase or decrease mortality rates and affect the long-term probability of survival or recovery. In sixteenth-century America, factors that elevated mortality are most likely, and some of these have been described in contemporary situations.

First, the distribution of mortality has demographic consequences beyond the disease event. Using population pyramids of virgin-soil populations of Highland New Guinea, Bowers (1971) demonstrated that the greatest mortality was concentrated in the young adult cohort, aged 15–40. Because of the disproportionate loss of reproductively active adults, fewer children were born. The cohort aged 0–4 was depressed accordingly.

Second, the number of sick individuals affects the functioning of the community. Neel (1971) noted that measles morbidity among the Yanomamo was comparable to that among immune populations. Elevated mortality resulted from the disruption of daily life; there was no one to feed the children or care for the sick.

Finally, each incursion of a new pathogen reduces the resistance of individuals, contributing to the probability of secondary infection. In many instances, mortality from these invaders may be higher than that from the primary infection. In the 1918 influenza pandemic, pneumonia caused more deaths than influenza (Jordan 1927; Ramenofsky 1987).

These descriptions suggest that at a local scale, infectious pathogens could have devastated several generations. Other models describe the probability of diffusion between communities. The best fit between spatial diffusion models and empirical situations is obtained when population size or density is added as another parameter to the deterministic model (Haggett 1975, 1976). Probability of contact between sources and recipients is a function of geographic distance. Thus, individuals or communities farther removed from the source are expected to be contacted later in time. As a population drops below the threshold necessary for persistence of the pathogen, the microbe will die out.

In summary, we know that Native Americans were at risk for a suite of diseases (Ramenofsky 1987), some of which were introduced to the Americas in the sixteenth century (Dobyns 1963, 1983). The intersection of these observations can lead to a kind of epidemiological determinism in which pathogenic agents spread like waves across the human landscape. Human populations are passive bystanders who become infected and die.

This scenario is too simplistic from a Darwinian perspective. First, pathogens vary in their reproductive requirements. Some viruses and bacteria reproduce only in humans. Consequently, the interior environment of the individual determines whether or not the microbe will persist. Diseases such as malaria or yellow fever are spread to humans by mosquitos; the environmental constraints of mosquitos, not humans, determine the spatial distribution of the disease. If in the sixteenth century *Anopheles* thrived in the type of ecological conditions that this insect vector prefers today, it is unlikely that malaria reached the Appalachian summit in that century. The current climate and topography of the uplands are inappropriate for its reproduction (Watson and Hewitt 1941).

Disease agents are only one-half of the evolutionary equation; human variability is the other half. Even though the models discussed previously are deterministic, contact between sources and recipients is stochastic. Probabilities will vary according to the infectious period of the microorganism, and according to the location of recipients relative to sources. Although in some cases siblings of an infected individual may miss exposure, cousins or parents may be in the right place at the right time, and become ill. In other cases, the opposite pattern could occur.

The stochastic nature of contact between sources and the susceptible population has evolutionary consequences. The reproductive fitness of some unknown percentage of individuals will be affected, and this will lead to the differential persistence of variability.

Because it is not possible to assess the reproductive fitness of individuals in the archaeological record, investigations of differential persistence are necessarily indirect. Single or multiple archaeological traits must be chosen that can track differential responses to disease selection.

Selecting the appropriate archaeological traits is of some importance. Traditionally, archaeological variables, such as ceramics and projectiles, are tracked until documents appear. Following documentation, archaeological traits are replaced by behavioral traits, such as kinship or religion; the latter are tracked forward. Unfortunately, kinship and religion cannot be tracked backward. If documents postdate catastrophic change, then the traits may be new evolutions. To assume otherwise would mask the variability of interest and place my work squarely within the assumption of continuity. In monitoring differential persistence and decline from disease, archaeological settlement is the appropriate segment of variability to consider.

My focus on settlement stems from several factors. Settlement can be measured archaeologically. In contrast to ceramics or projectiles, settlement occurs at the appropriate scale to monitor the question of differential persistence from disease. I have already shown (Ramenofsky 1987) that settlement relates directly or indirectly to population. As suggested by epidemic models, the spatial distribution of people promotes or retards the spread of pathogens. Consequently, settlement is likely to be a sensitive variable for measuring selection from disease.

Although I am using settlement to monitor disease selection, I am not assuming that certain types of settlement carried greater reproductive advantage than others. Individuals reproduce; settlements do not. I am assuming that settlement is the trait through which selection from disease acted. The distribution of people within settlements either inhibited or promoted disease transmission. The reproductive fitness of individuals living in those places must have been affected.

Because settlement varied across the landscape, the probability that individuals became infected, died, or recovered also varied. To determine what segment of Native American populations persisted or became extinct, we must measure settlement through time.

Model of Differential Persistence

The settlement model is a simple paradigmatic classification (Dunnell 1971) that addresses variability in settlement.

I have restricted settlement variables to those that address the probability of disease transmission. In other words, the classification derives from Darwinian theory of preexisting variability and selection. Those traits of settlement assumed to be most sensitive to disease transmission are the basis of the classification.

The classification has three dimensions and a number of attributes (Table 2-1). Settlement location takes into account whether the settlement is adjacent to or removed from axes of communication. Location of settlement has implications for contact of all sorts, including disease.

Settlement duration describes whether or not a population relocates its place of residence during a year. Its relevance to disease is not simple: I have previously assumed that sedentary settlements should have higher risks of infection than mobile settlements simply because the population remains in one place. Because groups who relocate their settlements may come into contact with more people than those who remain in one place, this assumption may not be correct.

Settlement form focuses on periodic dispersion of part of a community during a year. This dispersion of population may result in higher probabilities of survival than might occur in a nucleated settlement simply becauses the entire population is not clumped together.

Intersecting the attributes of each dimension creates a classification of 12 types of settlement (Figure 2-1). Once single settlements have been investigated, they can be assigned to one of the 12 classes. Because the nature of contact varies according to location and population distribution, each of the 12 classes is likely to have differing probabilities of persistence.

At a general scale, I suspect that classes 1 and 2, nucleated sedentary and nucleated mobile settlements along primary drainages, have the lowest probabilities of persistence simply because settlement location and population distribu-

Table 2-1. Paradigm of Settlement Types

I. SETTLEMENT LOCATION
   A. Near navigable drainage or trail
   B. Near secondary drainage
   C. Removed from axis of communication

II. SETTLEMENT DURATION
   A. Sedentary: population at same location throughout year
   B. Mobile: population relocates throughout year

III. SETTLEMENT FORM
   A. Nucleated: population remains together throughout year
   B. Dispersed: part of population separates during year

		Settlement type			
		Sedentary		Mobile	
		Settlement form			
		Nucleated	Dispersed	Nucleated	Dispersed
Settlement location	Navigable drainage	1	2	3	4
	Secondary drainage	5	6	7	8
	Removed from axis of communication	9	10	11	12

High disease impact   Disease may have less impact   No predictions

Figure 2-1. Classes of settlement types.

tion ensure consistent and frequent contact. Classes 4, 8, and 12, dispersed mobile settlements in all types of locations, have the highest probabilities of persistence. Periodic dispersion of the community makes contact between individuals within the community irregular. The probabilities of persistence of mobile or sedentary settlements located along secondary drainages or in inaccessible places are not known.

This classification can be used at differing analytic scales. At the lowest scale, one can track regional settlement histories through time. It is essential to begin this tracking in late prehistory; variability during this interval promoted or retarded disease transmission. Although it is likely that more than one settlement class is present in a region during the late prehistoric interval, the question is how this variability changes during the Columbian period. Does the variability increase or decrease, and what do these changes mean?

An example will clarify my perspective. The Vacant Quarter hypothesis (Williams 1982) described the abandonment of the Middle Mississippi Valley during the fourteenth century. Morse and Morse (1983) suggested that the region remained uninhabited following abandonment. For some time Lewis (1984, 1988) has been questioning the chronological placement of the Vacant Quarter hypothesis. If his assessment is correct and the purported abandonment occurs in the sixteenth rather than the fourteenth century, then differential persistence from disease is a possible cause of abandonment. Perhaps, the vacant quarter is not vacant. Instead, survivors reorganized settlement following population loss. Perhaps, the large nucleated centers were reduced by disease, but small hamlets evolved and increased in frequency during the sixteenth century.

A change in scale facilitates other types of comparisons. The lower valley could be compared to regions such as the Appalachian summit. The latter may help explain why Swanton (1946) considered the Cherokee one of the largest Southeastern groups and why the lower valley was empty by the seventeenth century.

Conclusions

I began this discussion by arguing that there was no overriding theory in contact period studies of population; in the absence of theory, dichotomous assumptions regarding the relationship between history and prehistory have guided investigations. In conclusion, I want to consider why my model is theoretical and what implications follow from its implementation.

Darwinian evolution, like all theory, is ideational; its purpose is to explain why variability exists. Answering this question depends on particular circumstances. Why the passenger pigeon became extinct in North America is explained by different mechanisms from those responsible for the differential persistence of native populations. Theories are not historically contingent; explanations are particular and necessarily bound in time and space. The passenger pigeon can die out only once.

Although I am sure that my settlement model is theoretically informed, it is not known how well the complexity of the human settlement record will fit the model. Settlement may be the wrong parameter for measuring selection; perhaps my classification is too coarse-grained to measure reproductive success in a disease environment.

The marvelous benefit that accrues when ideas are separated from a messy world is that the latter will refine and adjust ideas. As my ideas become more refined, the fit between differential persistence and ideas will come closer together. This interaction is what I think Popper (1959) was referring to when he defined theory as a net of ideas that is cast on the world. Successive castings draw the net more tightly around the phenomena to be explained.

If the model is at all successful, we will have the beginning of a coherent body of archaeological knowledge that can explain why there was differential persistence from disease, why for instance, the Creek or Choctaw survive in a modified state, but the Quapaw become extinct. Although this classification will not answer all questions related to demographic or cultural change during the Columbian period, it will anchor other, more sophisticated, investigations by building a description of settlement that is comparable across space. Such a description is crucial if we ever hope to go beyond impressionistic statements or archaeological stories about what we think was occurring rather than what was actually occurring.

The implications of such archaeological knowledge are far-reaching. Estimates of precontact population size can be built more reliably. We will have grounded knowledge for evaluating the meanings of historical documents, whether these documents are descriptions of "untouched" populations or those evolving under new selective pressures.

Finally, the evaluation of documents will have important implications for the nature of the twentieth-century ethnographic record. Because ethnologists of the American Historical School assumed, as did Thomas, that change postdated documentation, they defined contact as beginning with face-to-face interactions, and they used initial descriptions to reconstruct what might have been. Whether or not the descriptions accurately capture native societies before the onslaught of change can only be decided by systematic archaeological investigations.

I concur with Julian Steward (1955), who argued that archaeological data are the primary data for determining the nature and magnitude of Native American change in the postcontact period.

Acknowledgments

I would like to thank Bob Leonard, Patrice Teltser, and Robert Dunnell for their insightful comments and critiques of earlier drafts of this paper. They all made helpful suggestions that pushed me to refine my ideas.

References

Atwater, C.
  1820 *Description of the Antiquities Discovered in the State of Ohio and Other Western States.* Transactions and Collections of the American Antiquarian Society, Archaeological Americana, 1. Worcester.
Bailey, N. T. J.
  1957 *The Mathematical Theory of Epidemics.* Charles Griffin, London.
Baker, B. J., and G. J. Armelagos
  1988 The Origin and Antiquity of Syphilis. *Current Anthropology* 29:703–736.
Bartlett, M. S.
  1957 Measles Periodicity and Community Size. *Journal of the Royal Statistical Society, Series A* 120:48–70.
Barton, B. S.
  1787 *Observations on Some Parts of Natural History, Part 1. An Account of Several Remarkable Vestiges of an ancient Date, which have been Discovered in different Parts of North America.* Boston.
  1798 *New View of the Origin of the Tribes and Nations of America.* Philadelphia.
  1799 Observations and Conjectures concerning Certain Articles taken from Ancient Tumulus, or Grave. A Letter from Benjamin Smith Barton to Reverend Joseph Priestly, L. L. D. F. R. S., May 16, 1796. *Transactions of the American Philosophical Society* 4:181–215.
Bourne, E. G.
  1904 *Narratives of the Career of Hernando De Soto.* Vol. 1. A. S. Barnes, New York.
Bowers, N.
  1971 Demographic Problems in Montane New Guinea. In *Culture and Population: A Collection of Current Studies*, edited by S. Polgar, pp. 11–31. Schenkman, Cambridge.
Boyd, C. Clifford, and G. F. Schroedl
  1987 In Search of Coosa. *American Antiquity* 52:840–844.
Brain, J. P.
  1985 The Archaeology of the Hernando de Soto Expedition. In *Alabama and the Borderlands: From Prehistory to Statehood*, edited by R. R. Badger and L. A. Clayton, pp. 96–107. University of Alabama Press, University.

Brain, J. P., A. Toth, and A. Rodriguez-Buckingham

1974   Ethnohistoric Archaeology and the De Soto *Entrada* into the Lower Mississippi Valley. *Conference on Historic Site Archaeology Papers*, 1972, 7:232–289.

Bushnell, D. I.

1986   The Origin and Various Types of Mounds in Eastern United States [1917]. Reprinted in *The Late Prehistoric Southeast: A Source Book*, edited by C. B. DePratter, pp. 43–47. Garland, New York.

Caldwell, J. R.

1952   The Archaeology of Eastern Georgia and South Carolina. In *Archeology of the Eastern United States*, edited by J. B. Griffin, pp. 312–321. University of Chicago Press, Chicago.

Collins, H. B.

1927   Potsherds from Choctaw Villages in Mississippi. *Journal of the Washington Academy of Sciences* 17(10):259–263.

Cook, N. D.

1982   *Demographic Collapse: Indian Peru, 1520–1620*. Cambridge University Press, Cambridge.

Crosby, A.

1986   *Ecological Imperialism: The Biological Expansion of Europe, 900–1900*. Cambridge University Press, Cambridge.

Dobyns, H. F.

1963   An Outline of Andean Epidemic History to 1720. *Bulletin of the History of Medicine* 37:493–515.

1983   *Their Number Become Thinned*. University of Tennessee Press, Knoxville.

Dunnell, R. C.

1971   *Systematics in Prehistory*. Free Press, New York.

1980   Evolutionary Theory and Archaeology. In *Advances in Archaeological Method and Theory*, Vol. 3, edited by M. B. Schiffer, pp. 35–99. Academic Press, New York.

1982   Science, Social Science and Common Sense: The Agonizing Dilemma of Modern Archaeology. *Journal of Anthropological Research* 38:1–25.

1985   Archaeological Survey in the Lower Mississippi Valley, 1940–1947: A Landmark Study in American Archaeology. *American Antiquity* 50:297–300.

Fairbanks, C. H.

1952   Creek and Pre-Creek. In *Archeology of the Eastern United States*, edited by J. B. Griffin, pp. 285–300. University of Chicago Press, Chicago.

Ford, J. A.

1936   *Analysis of Indian Village Site Collections from Louisiana and Mississippi*. State of Louisiana, Department of Conservation, Anthropological Study No. 2. Louisiana Geological Survey, New Orleans.

Ford, J. A., and G. R. Willey

1941   An Interpretation of the Prehistory of Eastern North America. *American Anthropologist* 43:325–363.

Gallatin, A.

1836   *A Synopsis of the Indian Tribes of North America*. Transactions and Collections of the American Antiquarian Society 2:9–422.

1845   *Notes on the Semi-Civilized Nations of Mexico, Yucatan, and Central America*. Transactions of the American Ethnological Society No. 1. New York.

Haggett, P.

1975   Simple Epidemics in Human Populations. Some Geographic Aspects of the Hamer-Soper Diffusion Models. In *Processes in Physical and Human Geography*, edited by R. Peel, M. Chisholm, and P. Haggett, pp. 372–391. Heinemann, London.

1976   Hybridizing Alternative Models of an Epidemic Diffusion Process. *Economic Geography* 52:136–146.

Hariot, T.
1973   A Brief and True Report of the New Found Land of Virginia [1588]. In *Virginia Voyages from Hakluyt [1589]*, edited by D. B. Quinn and A. M. Quinn, pp. 46–76. Oxford University Press, Oxford.

Harris, T.
1835   Researches into the Origin of Indigines of North and South America. Manuscript on file, American Antiquarian Society. Worcester.

Haven, S. F.
1856   *Archaeology of the United States*. Smithsonian Contributions to Knowledge 8:1–168. Washington, D.C.

Heart, J.
1793   A Letter from Major Jonathan Heart to Benjamin Smith Barton, M.D., written in January 1791. *Transactions of the American Philosophical Society* 3:215–222.

Hudson, C., M. T. Smith, and D. B. DePratter
1984   The Hernando De Soto Expedition: From Apalachee to Chiaha. *Southeastern Archaeology* 3:65–77.

Hudson, C., M. Smith, D. Hally, R. Polhemus, and C. DePratter
1985   Coosa: A Chiefdom in the Sixteenth-Century Southeastern United States. *American Antiquity* 50:723–737.

Jefferson, T.
1803   *Notes on Virginia. The Writings of Thomas Jefferson*, II [1784]. Thomas Jefferson Memorial Association, Washington, D.C.

Jordan, E. O.
1927   *Epidemic Influenza*. American Medical Association, Chicago.

Kneberg, M.
1952   The Tennessee Area. In *Archeology of the Eastern United States*, edited by J. B. Griffin, pp. 190–198. University of Chicago Press, Chicago.

Leonard, R. D., and G. T. Jones
1987   Elements of an Inclusive Evolutionary Model for Archaeology. *Journal of Anthropological Archaeology* 6:199–219.

Levins, R., and R. Lewontin
1985   *The Dialectical Biologist*. Harvard University Press, Cambridge, Massachusetts.

Lewis, R. B.
1984   An Examination of the Vacant Quarter Hypothesis in the Northern Mississippi Valley. Paper presented at the 49th annual meeting of the Society for American Archaeology, Portland.
1988   Old World Dice in the Protohistoric Southern United States. *Current Anthropology* 29:759–768.

Lewontin, R.
1974   *The Genetic Basis of Evolutionary Change*. Columbia University Press, New York.

McCulloh, J. H., M.D.
1829   *Researches, Philosophical and Antiquarian concerning the Aboriginal History of America*. Fielding Lucas, Jr., Baltimore.

Meltzer, D.
1983   The Antiquity of Man and the Development of American Archaeology. In *Advances in Archaeological Method and Theory*, Vol. 6, edited by M. B. Schiffer, pp. 1–51. Academic Press, New York.

Milner, G. R.
1980   Epidemic Disease in the Post-Contact Southeast: A Reappraisal. *Midcontinental Journal of Archaeology* 5:3–17.
1988   Population Dynamics and Archaeological Interpretation. Paper presented at the 1988 Midwest Archaeological Conference, Urbana-Champaign.

Morse, D. F., and P. A. Morse
1983   *Archaeology of the Central Mississippi Valley*. Academic Press, New York.

Morton, S. G., M.D.
1839 *Crania Americana; or a Comparative View of the Skulls of Various Aboriginal Nations of North and South America*. J. Dodson, Philadelphia.

Neel, J. V.
1971 Genetic Aspects of the Ecology of Disease in the American Indian. In *The Ongoing Evolution of Latin American Populations*, edited by F. M. Salzano, pp. 561–590. Charles C. Thomas, Springfield.

Parry, J. H.
1985 European Penetration of Eastern North America. In *Alabama and the Borderlands: From Prehistory to Statehood*, edited by R. R. Badger and L. A. Clayton, pp. 83–95. University of Alabama Press, University.

Phillips, P., J. A. Ford, and J. B. Griffin
1951 *Archaeological Survey in the Lower Mississippi Alluvial Valley, 1940–1947*. Papers of the Peabody Museum of Archaeology and Ethnology No. 25. Cambridge.

Popper, K.
1959 *The Logic of Scientific Discovery*. Hutchinson, London.

Ramenofsky, A. F.
1981 Discontinuity and Cultural Decay: A New Perspective on the Mound Builder Debate. Paper presented at the 80th Annual Meeting of the American Anthropological Association, Los Angeles.
1987 *Vectors of Death: The Archaeology of European Contact*. University of New Mexico Press, Albuquerque.

Sahlins, M. D.
1960 Evolution: Specific and General. In *Evolution and Culture*, edited by M. D. Sahlins and E. R. Service, pp. 12–44. University of Michigan Press, Ann Arbor.

Sahlins, M. D., and E. R. Service (editors)
1960 *Culture and Evolution*. University of Michigan Press, Ann Arbor.

Smith, B. D.
1984 Mississippian Expansion: Tracing the Historical Development of an Explanatory Model. *Southeastern Archaeology* 3:13–32.

Smith, M. T.
1987 *Archaeology of Aboriginal Culture Change in the Interior Southeast*. Ripley P. Bullen Monographs in Anthropology and History No. 6. Florida State Museum, Gainesville.

Snow, D. R., and K. M. Lamphear
1988 European Contact and Indian Depopulation in the Northeast. The Timing of the First Epidemics. *Ethnohistory* 35:15–33.

Squier, E. G., and E. H. Davis
1848 *Ancient Monuments of the Mississippi Valley*. Smithsonian Contributions to Knowledge 1. Washington D.C.

Steward, J.
1955 Theory and Application in Social Science. *Ethnohistory* 2:292–302.

Stiles, Ezra
1788 A Letter from the Reverend Ezra Stiles, S.T.D., President of Yale College to the Editor, March 18, 1788. *American Magazine*, April 1788:291–294.

Swanton, J. R.
1911 *Indian Tribes of the Lower Mississippi Valley and Adjacent Coast of the Gulf of Mexico*. Bulletin of the Bureau of American Ethnology No. 43. Washington D.C.
1928 The Interpretation of Aboriginal Mounds by Means of Creek Customs. In *Smithsonian Institution Annual Report of the Board of Regents for 1927*, 495–506. Washington, D.C.
1939 *Final Report of the United States De Soto Commission*. 76th Cong., 1st sess., H.R. 71. Washington, D.C.

1942   *Source Material on the History and Ethnology of the Caddo Indians*. Bulletin of the Bureau of American Ethnology No. 132. Washington, D.C.

1946   *The Indians of the Southeastern United States*. Bulletin of the Bureau of American Ethnology No. 137. Washington, D.C.

Thomas, C.

1894   Report on the Mound Explorations of the Bureau of Ethnology. *Smithsonian Institution Bureau of Ethnology Annual Report* 12:17–742.

Thornton, R.

1987   *American Indian Holocaust and Survival: A Population History since 1492*. University of Oklahoma Press, Norman.

Trigger, B. G.

1985   *Natives and Newcomers*. McGill-Queen's University Press, Kingston.

Watson, R. B., and R. Hewitt

1941   Topographical and Related Factors in the Epidemiology of Malaria in North America, Central America and the West Indies. In *A Symposium on Human Malaria with Special Reference to North America and the Caribbean Region*, edited by F. R. Moulton, pp. 135–147. American Association for the Advancement of Science 15. Washington, D.C.

Webster, N.

1787   Copy of Letter from Mr. Webster to the Reverend Dr. Stiles, President of Yale College, October 22, 1787. *American Magazine*, December 1787:15–19.

1788a   Letter II, from Mr. Noah Webster to the Reverend Dr. Stiles, President of Yale College, containing a particular account of the famous Expedition of Ferdinand de Soto, into Florida, December 15: 1787. *American Magazine*, January 1788:83–87.

1788b   Letter III, from Mr. Noah Webster to the Reverend Dr. Stiles, President of Yale College, on the Remains of the Fortifications in the western country, January 20, 1788. *American Magazine*, February 1788:146–156.

White, L. A.

1949   *The Science of Culture: A Study of Man & Cultivation*. Farrar Straus, New York.

Williams, S.

1982   The Vacant Quarter Hypothesis: A Discussion Symposium. Symposium presented at the 39th Annual Meeting of the Southeastern Archaeological Conference. Memphis.

Chapter 3 ■

Jeffrey M. Mitchem

Initial Spanish–Indian Contact in West Peninsular Florida: The Archaeological Evidence

Research in the western part of the Florida peninsula has yielded a large body of archaeological data pertaining to the late prehistoric and early contact periods (ca. A.D. 900–1550). During this era, the Native American inhabitants of the region, from the Withlacoochee River on the north to at least as far south as Collier County, coalesced into a number of small chiefdoms, with alliances and boundaries that shifted frequently. The Mississippian-influenced artifactual assemblages produced by most of these groups constitute the archaeological culture known as the Safety Harbor culture (Mitchem 1989).

Because of past emphasis on the excavation of mounds, much of our knowledge about the Safety Harbor culture has come from mortuary sites. Mound burial was the norm, often in the form of interments of jumbled bones of many individuals, whose bodies had been stored in a charnel structure. Primary burial of bodies and cremation were also practiced, though less frequently.

Most of the best-known Safety Harbor sites are in the Tampa Bay area, and settlements in this region are generally nucleated villages with middens and associated burial mounds (Mitchem 1989; Willey 1949:476–477). Some settlements include large truncated platform mounds similar to Mississippian mounds elsewhere in the Southeast (Luer and Almy 1981). Away from the Tampa Bay area, however, Safety Harbor sites are usually smaller, more dispersed hamlets or farmsteads. Burial mounds in these areas are typically isolated, not associated with habitation sites (Mitchem 1988).

Ethnohistoric Evidence of Contact

The first recorded entry of Spanish explorers into west peninsular Florida was in the early sixteenth century. The native people they encountered were the producers of Safety Harbor archaeological assemblages. The exploration narratives reveal that separate aboriginal provinces existed, and that each province was ruled by a different cacique (Hernández de Biedma 1973:4–5; Lewis 1984: 153–156).

The expedition of Pánfilo de Narváez landed near Tampa Bay in 1528, and briefly contacted Native Americans in the area before proceeding north. The 300 members of this expedition apparently did not interact with any of the Safety Harbor groups between Tampa Bay and the Withlacoochee River, however, because the narrative indicates that no people, villages, or houses were encountered from the time they left the bay until crossing the Withlacoochee (Núñez Cabeza de Vaca 1983:36).

The Núñez Cabeza de Vaca account (1983) includes evidence that the Tampa Bay residents had been exposed to Europeans before, as a number of Spanish wooden crates were seen by members of the expedition, containing bodies (probably of Europeans) and other European articles. The local inhabitants indicated that the objects and bodies had been retrieved from a vessel that had wrecked in or near Tampa Bay (Núñez Cabeza de Vaca 1983:32–33).

In May of 1539, the expedition of Hernando de Soto arrived near Tampa Bay. In contrast to the Narváez expedition, members of the de Soto entrada interacted repeatedly with Safety Harbor groups over a period of several months in 1539. Although most of the expedition members traveled north, the ships with provisions were left at the landing site for several months. When de Soto reached the main town (Anhaica Apalache) of the Apalachee province, he sent a detachment of soldiers back along the same route with orders for the ship captains to sail north and unload supplies at a port near Anhaica. Some of these soldiers then traveled back overland to Anhaica, apparently again using the same route (Fernández de Oviedo y Valdés 1973:81; Hernández de Biedma 1973: 7–8; Smith 1968:48).

At least one skirmish between members of the de Soto expedition and Native Americans south of the Withlacoochee is recorded (Fernández de Oviedo y Valdés 1973:68). It is safe to assume that a number of undocumented incidents of contact (violent and otherwise) occurred during these travels.

The aims of the Narváez and de Soto expeditions were similar. In both cases, their primary mission for the Crown was to conquer the country of La Florida and to establish Spanish settlements in the region between the Florida peninsula and Mexico (Hodge 1984:3–4; Swanton 1985:76–79).

Prior to his North American entrada, Hernando de Soto had participated in campaigns of conquest in Panama, Nicaragua, and Peru. He had become wealthy from his share of the South American gold and from dealing in Indian slaves (Swanton 1985:68–73). He was granted governorship of the land of North America with explicit instructions from King Charles V to conquer and settle the region (1985:76–79). Naturally, de Soto chose many of his personnel for the expedition from those comrades who had previously served in the South American campaigns.

From the narratives it is apparent that many members of the expedition had not taken the climate and terrain of Florida into account when outfitting themselves, and many items were discarded owing to the summer heat and the difficulty of transporting heavy loads. Iron implements and other objects were buried before part of the expedition left the village of Cale for Anhaica (Smith 1968:40).

The narratives also indicate that many Native Americans (mostly females) were captured and forced to act as bearers of supplies (Hudson et al. 1988:130). More important were those who could act as guides and interpreters. De Soto was fortunate in this regard, because shortly after he landed near Tampa Bay, he rescued a captive Spaniard from Narváez's expedition. This was Juan Ortiz, who was fluent in the local native dialects, but knew little about the surrounding country (Fernández de Oviedo y Valdés 1973:57; Hernández de Biedma 1973:4; Smith 1968:27–33).

From the narratives, it is difficult to discern de Soto's preferred method of dealing with native groups. The Ranjel account indicates that de Soto was cruel and enjoyed killing Native Americans (Fernández de Oviedo y Valdés 1973:59), whereas other narratives suggest that he preferred to obtain information, bearers, and guides by negotiating with caciques and by gift-giving whenever possible (Smith 1968:35). At times, he had caciques taken hostage until they submitted to his wishes. Several instances are also recorded of dogs being used to kill native guides who displeased de Soto (Fernández de Oviedo y Valdés 1973:60; Swanton 1985:92). De Soto also knew from his experiences in South America that the natives feared horses, which were unlike any animals known to them, and he probably used this to his advantage.

From reports of survivors of the Narváez expedition, de Soto knew that food was scarce in many areas (Brain 1985:xx–xxi). Although the expedition carried rations and a herd of pigs, the general strategy was to obtain food from the aboriginal villages and fields. This is clearly noted in the accounts (Fernández de Oviedo y Valdés 1973:64, 68; Smith 1968:37–38). Members of the de Soto expedition also routinely commandeered native dwellings, ransacked temples or charnel structures, and often burned villages from which the inhabitants had fled. These factors resulted in much hostility between the explorers and the native inhabitants, and members of the de Soto force quickly learned not to stray far from the main group of soldiers (Fernández de Oviedo y Valdés 1973:68).

The accounts indicate that from the time the expedition disembarked near Tampa, the Native American groups of west peninsular Florida generally either fled or took up arms upon the arrival of the Spaniards. This response probably resulted from previous experiences with European slavers and members of the Narváez expedition.

In most instances, the cacique of the region was informed of the presence of the Spaniards by eyewitnesses, and messengers were sent to determine the intent of the Spaniards (Smith 1968:33–36). In one case, the cacique Mococo, who released Juan Ortiz from captivity, went to speak with de Soto upon his arrival (1968:33–34). He apparently had cordial relations with de Soto, who presented Mococo with gifts of clothing (1968:34).

As the expedition moved north, instances of conflict increased, probably because the Spaniards appropriated food and took captives (Fernández de Oviedo y Valdés 1973:68). These skirmishes were generally acts of harassment, which consisted of a small group of native bowmen shooting arrows and fleeing (Fernández de Oviedo y Valdés 1973:68–69).

In general, the strategy of the Native Americans in this region was to persuade the Spaniards to move out of the area as quickly as possible. This was accomplished by the aforementioned attacks and by telling the Spaniards that gold was to be found in provinces to the north (Smith 1968:36). Sparse populations and the lack of large amounts of maize in the region probably aided the Native Americans in persuading the Spaniards to proceed north.

Archaeological Evidence of Contact

Archaeological data from west peninsular Florida provide additional evidence for some of the observations gleaned from the narratives, as well as information on other effects of contact (Figure 3-1). The early sixteenth-century data are of two types: (1) private and museum collections, which often have little or no provenience information; and (2) information obtained from scientific archaeological investigations.

In Florida, it is often difficult to determine the period of European contact at aboriginal sites. This is because Spanish contact and occupation of Florida lasted for several centuries, and little is known about the exchange of European artifacts between aboriginal groups. Recent research on specific artifact types, especially glass beads, has revealed that certain types of artifacts are very useful for dating early sixteenth-century sites (Deagan 1987; Smith and Good 1982).

One glass bead type (Nueva Cadiz beads) has proven especially valuable in identifying sites of this time period. Archaeological research has demonstrated that these distinctive tubular beads with a square cross section are found in the New World only on Spanish contact sites predating 1550 (Deagan 1987:162–164; Smith and Good 1982:11).

In west peninsular Florida, Nueva Cadiz beads have been recovered from several archaeological sites (Mitchem 1989; Mitchem and Leader 1988:Table 4; Smith and Good 1982:Table II). Significantly, very few of these beads have been recovered from sites south of Tampa Bay. This supports the contention that both the Narváez and de Soto expeditions probably landed near Tampa Bay, rather than at Charlotte Harbor (the next major bay south of Tampa Bay).

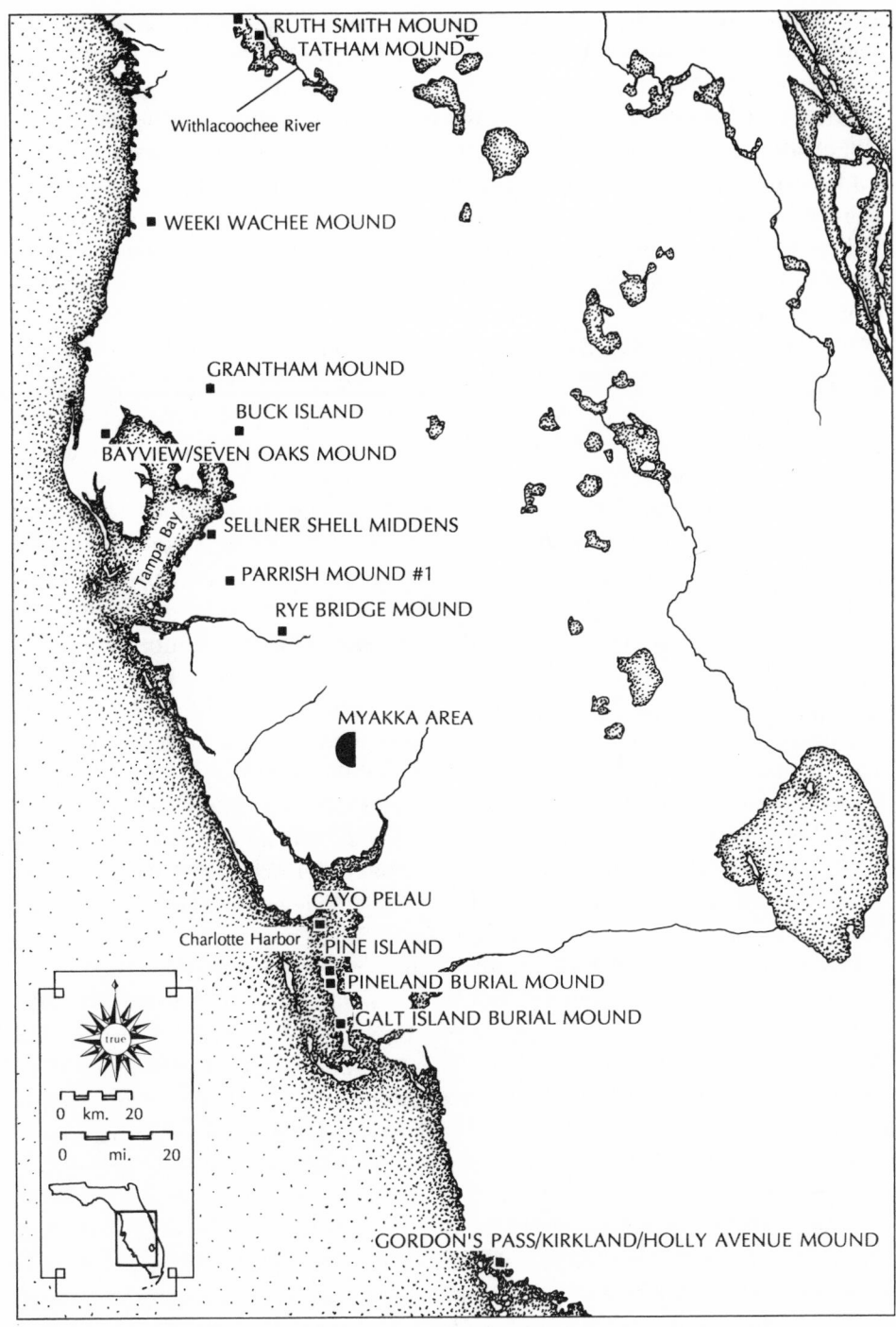

Figure 3-1. Sixteenth-century archaeological sites in west peninsular Florida.

The southernmost known Safety Harbor site is a mound in Collier County known as the Gordon's Pass Sand Mound, the Kirkland Mound, or the Holly Avenue site (8Cr57). It was looted for many years, and a large number of European artifacts were recovered, along with aboriginal ceramics and human burials (Mitchem 1989:291–295). Among the European materials was a single Nueva Cadiz Plain bead and one faceted chevron bead (another type often recovered from early sixteenth-century contexts, although it is also found in later contexts). However, the great majority of European artifacts date from the late sixteenth or seventeenth centuries, so the Nueva Cadiz bead may have been an heirloomed item.

At the Galt Island Burial Mound (8LL81) in Charlotte Harbor (Lee County), a faceted Nueva Cadiz Plain bead was recovered, along with other bead types suggesting a late sixteenth- to eighteenth-century period of contact (Mitchem 1989:284–285). These artifacts are in a private collection, and no provenience information is available.

At the Pineland Burial Mound on Pine Island in Charlotte Harbor, two Nueva Cadiz Plain beads, at least seven faceted chevron beads, and two blue striped olive-shaped beads suggest an early sixteenth-century episode of Spanish contact (Mitchem 1989:274–277). Many late sixteenth- and seventeenth-century artifacts are also present in collections from the site, however. Unfortunately, all of these objects were excavated by looters in the 1960s, and no intrasite provenience information is extant. At another (unrecorded) burial mound on Pine Island, three probable Nueva Cadiz beads were recovered by looters, along with European metal items. No provenience information is available.

On another island in Charlotte Harbor is a burial mound, the Cayo Pelau site (8Ch1), sometimes called Cayo Palu or Carapileu. This mound has been vandalized by looters for decades, and a large number of European artifacts have been removed from the site (Mitchem 1989:232–238; Willey 1949:344–345). A single Nueva Cadiz bead reportedly came from Cayo Pelau, but the other artifacts indicate a late sixteenth- and seventeenth-century period of contact.

These four sites have yielded the only evidence of possible early sixteenth-century contact in the vicinity of Charlotte Harbor. In each case, the lack of contextual information and the presence of later European artifacts suggests that the early beads were anomalous, possibly curated or heirloomed items. Assemblages from this coastal region south of Tampa Bay suggest that the main European contact in the area occurred during the late sixteenth and seventeenth centuries.

At the Parrish Mound #1 (8Ma1) in Manatee County, European artifacts indicate a late sixteenth- or seventeenth-century date for contact, but a single large Nueva Cadiz Plain bead and a red striped olive-shaped bead suggest a possible early sixteenth-century episode of contact (Mitchem 1989:148–150). This site is close to the southern end of Tampa Bay, in the area where de Soto may have disembarked.

Four Nueva Cadiz Plain and two blue striped olive-shaped beads are in a collection of material from the Rye Bridge Mound (8Ma715). This mound was destroyed by looters, and yielded many European artifacts (Mitchem

1989:194–196). The Nueva Cadiz Plain and striped beads indicate an early sixteenth-century date, but many other beads from the site suggest a late sixteenth-century date as well. The different assemblages indicate more than one episode of contact or curation of the earlier bead types.

A large collection of glass beads was recovered from one or more sites in the Myakka area in southeast Manatee County or northeast Sarasota County. The private collection, obtained by uncontrolled digging, includes 37 Nueva Cadiz Plain beads and several other early sixteenth-century types (Mitchem 1989: 199–201). A number of later types, including some typical of Seminole occupations, are also in the collection. This collection contains the largest assemblage of indisputable early sixteenth-century beads from any Safety Harbor site south of Tampa Bay, but the lack of specific provenience information hinders interpretation of their significance.

When the region around Tampa Bay is examined, the archaeological evidence for early European–Native American contact is surprisingly scarce. On the south bank of the Little Manatee River at the southern end of the bay, Works Progress Administration (WPA) excavations in 1937 at an extensive shell midden complex known as the Sellner Shell Middens (8Hi30) uncovered a long glass bead and bones of pigs and horses (or cows) (Bullen 1952:72–73; Mitchem 1989:119). Unfortunately, all of these artifacts have since disappeared, so it is impossible to determine if the bead is a Nueva Cadiz type and to verify the identification of the faunal species. The site could be related to the de Soto expedition, which may have camped in the area (Swanton 1985:138).

Two sites in northern Hillsborough County have yielded early sixteenth-century artifacts. At the Buck Island site (8Hi6), a looter reportedly found a Nueva Cadiz bead with a burial (Mitchem 1989:111). Two faceted chevron beads have also been recovered at the site, along with gold and silver artifacts. A single Nueva Cadiz Twisted bead was recovered from the Grantham Mound near the town of Lutz in 1920 (Mitchem 1989:116). These sites provide the only indisputable evidence of early sixteenth-century contact in the area on the east side of Tampa Bay.

In Pinellas County, along the western shore of Tampa Bay, only one site has yielded definite early sixteenth-century artifacts. This is a burial mound known as the Bayview (8Pi7) or Seven Oaks Mound (8Pi8). Large quantities of European materials were excavated from this mound in the 1880s and 1960s (Mitchem 1989:61–72). Spanish ceramics, along with two Nueva Cadiz Plain, eight faceted chevron, and other early glass bead types suggest some early sixteenth-century contact, but the great majority of the Spanish artifacts from the mound are late sixteenth-century types. Most of these are probably the result of a visit by Pedro Menéndez de Avilés to the area in the 1560s (Solís de Merás 1964:223–229).

North of Tampa Bay, only three early sixteenth-century Safety Harbor sites are known. These are all burial mounds, and have yielded excellent data concerning the nature and results of contact between Spanish explorers and Native Americans.

The Weeki Wachee Mound (8He12) was partly excavated in 1970 (Mitchem 1989:41–42; Mitchem et al. 1985). A total of 63 burials, 127 glass beads, 151 silver beads, and 1 amber bead were recovered (Mitchem 1989:41). All of the glass beads were early sixteenth-century types (including Nueva Cadiz and faceted chevrons), and most were recovered from three burials (Mitchem et al. 1985:Table 7).

The Ruth Smith Mound (8Ci200), near the Withlacoochee River, was vandalized for many years. A total of 32 glass beads, 51 silver beads, 2 gold beads, a large iron chisel, 3 rolled iron beads, interlocking brass rings (possibly chain mail), and a sherd of Green Bacín pottery have been recorded (Mitchem 1989:25–26; Mitchem et al. 1985:202). The glass beads included Nueva Cadiz and faceted chevron varieties, indicating an early sixteenth-century date.

A few kilometers away is the Tatham Mound (8Ci203), which was excavated in 1985 and 1986 (Mitchem 1989:Chapter 3). This undisturbed mound yielded 153 glass beads, 298 metal beads (silver, gold, brass, bronze, and iron), 2 iron chisels, an iron armor plate, and other European artifacts. The beads included Nueva Cadiz, faceted chevron, and other early sixteenth-century types. Most were recovered from primary burials. Excavations at this site also uncovered evidence of a mass burial of at least 77 individuals. The most likely explanation for this large number of primary burials is a disease epidemic, probably introduced by the Spaniards. Violent interaction between Spaniards and Native Americans is demonstrated by two bones (a left humerus and a right scapula) with wounds produced by an edged metal weapon such as a sword. Archaeological evidence indicates that the mound was abandoned shortly after the large group of individuals was buried.

Conclusions

Since no sites in peninsular Florida have been identified as campsites of Spanish expeditions, our interpretations of the archaeological data must be based on evidence from aboriginal sites. The best evidence comes from the Weeki Wachee, Ruth Smith, and Tatham Mounds. The European assemblages from these sites are extremely similar (in terms of specific bead varieties), and they undoubtedly represent contact with the same Spanish expedition, probably that of de Soto. They are the only known postcontact Safety Harbor sites north of the Tampa Bay area, and have yielded the best corpus of archaeological data on the initial period of Spanish–Native American contact in peninsular Florida.

Research north of Tampa Bay has revealed that there are virtually no Safety Harbor sites in the region that date later than the early sixteenth century. It appears that the area was depopulated, probably shortly after contact with the de Soto expedition (Mitchem 1989). The presumed epidemic revealed at the Tatham Mound may have affected all of the populations in the northern Safety Harbor area, not just the Tatham population. The aboriginal survivors apparently moved south to the Tampa Bay area, as nucleated settlements were still present around Tampa Bay in the late sixteenth century.

It is interesting that there is no evidence to suggest that the nucleated settlements around Tampa Bay were severely disrupted by Spanish-introduced diseases, whereas groups in the more sparsely populated northern area were. This may be due to inadequate samples. However, the depopulation of the northern area certainly had profound effects on Safety Harbor populations in terms of the disruption of exchange systems and sociopolitical boundaries. It is possible that adjacent groups, such as the Calusa (Solís de Merás 1964), were able to expand their territories by displacing weakened Safety Harbor caciques.

Archaeology has contributed to our understanding of the interaction of Native Americans and Spanish explorers in peninsular Florida in several ways. First, it has allowed us to observe some of the ethnological information and events described in the narratives. An example is the boundary between the aboriginal province of Cale and the unnamed province south of it mentioned in the de Soto narratives (Fernández de Oviedo y Valdés 1973:67–68). The boundary is clearly revealed by archaeological research in the northern part of the Safety Harbor culture area, where Safety Harbor sites are found south of the Withlacoochee River, but are absent north of the river (replaced by sites with a different material assemblage).

The burial of iron implements at Cale (Smith 1968:40) may be reflected in the recovery of a number of iron artifacts at both the Tatham and Ruth Smith mounds. The populations buried at Tatham and Ruth Smith were probably in contact with the Cale residents north of the Withlacoochee River.

Finally, the Tatham Mound data demonstrate that violent clashes between Spaniards and Native Americans did occur in this region, as mentioned in the narratives. Much greater effects on aboriginal culture were produced by the diseases inadvertently introduced by the Spaniards, however. The area occupied by Safety Harbor groups was drastically reduced, and major changes in sociopolitical structure followed.

Acknowledgments

Much of the information presented in this chapter was gathered while writing my doctoral dissertation at the University of Florida. The number of people who provided information on sites and artifacts is too great to mention them individually, but their contributions are gratefully acknowledged. I would like to thank Bonnie McEwan for reading and commenting on an earlier version of this paper.

References

Brain, Jeffrey P.
    1985   Introduction: Update of De Soto Studies since the United States De Soto Expedition Commission Report. In *Final Report of the United States De Soto Expedition*, by John R. Swanton, pp. xi–lxxii. Reprinted. Smithsonian Institution Press, Washington, D.C. Originally published 1939, U. S. House of Representatives, 76th Cong., 1st sess., Doc. No. 71. Government Printing Office, Washington, D.C.
Bullen, Ripley P.
    1952   *Eleven Archaeological Sites in Hillsborough County, Florida*. Report of Investigations No. 8. Florida Geological Survey, Tallahassee.
Cabeza de Vaca, Álvar Núñez
    1983   *Adventures in the Unknown Interior of America*. Translated by Cyclone Covey. Re-

printed. University of New Mexico Press, Albuquerque. Originally published 1961, Crowell-Collier, New York.

Deagan, Kathleen
  1987 *Artifacts of the Spanish Colonies of Florida and the Caribbean, 1500–1800. Vol. 1: Ceramics, Glassware, and Beads.* Smithsonian Institution Press, Washington, D.C.

Fernández de Oviedo y Valdés, Gonzalo
  1973 A Narrative of de Soto's Expedition Based on the Diary of Rodrigo Rajel, His Private Secretary. Translated by Edward Gaylord Bourne. In *Narratives of the Career of Hernando de Soto in the Conquest of Florida*, vol. 2, edited by Edward Gaylord Bourne, pp. 41–150. Reprinted. AMS Press, New York. Originally published 1922, Allerton, New York.

Hernández de Biedma, Luys
  1973 Relation of the Conquest of Florida. Translated by Buckingham Smith. In *Narratives of the Career of Hernando de Soto in the Conquest of Florida*, vol. 2, edited by Edward Gaylord Bourne, pp. 1–40. Reprinted. AMS Press, New York. Originally published 1922, Allerton, New York.

Hodge, Frederick W.
  1984 Introduction (to the Narrative of Alvar Núñez Cabeza de Vaca). In *Spanish Explorers in the Southern United States, 1528–1543*, edited by Frederick W. Hodge and Theodore H. Lewis, pp. 3–11. Reprinted. Texas State Historical Association, Austin. Originally published 1907, Charles Scribner's Sons, New York.

Hudson, Charles, Chester DePratter, and Marvin Smith
  1988 The Victims of the King Site Massacre: A Historical Detectives' Report. In *The King Site: Continuity and Contact in Sixteenth-Century Georgia*, edited by Robert L. Blakely, pp. 117–134. University of Georgia Press, Athens.

Lewis, Theodore H. (editor)
  1984 The Narrative of the Expedition of Hernando de Soto by the Gentleman of Elvas. In *Spanish Explorers in the Southern United States, 1528–1543*, edited by Frederick W. Hodge and Theodore H. Lewis, pp. 127–272. Reprinted. Texas State Historical Association, Austin. Originally published 1907, Charles Scribner's Sons, New York.

Luer, George M., and Marion M. Almy
  1981 Temple Mounds of the Tampa Bay Area. *Florida Anthropologist* 34:127–155.

Mitchem, Jeffrey M.
  1988 Some Alternative Interpretations of Safety Harbor Burial Mounds. *Florida Scientist* 51:100–107.
  1989 *Redefining Safety Harbor: Late Prehistoric/Protohistoric Archaeology in West Peninsular Florida.* Unpublished Ph.D. dissertation, University of Florida. University Microfilms, Ann Arbor.

Mitchem, Jeffrey M., and Jonathan M. Leader
  1988 Early Sixteenth Century Beads from the Tatham Mound, Citrus County, Florida: Data and Interpretations. *Florida Anthropologist* 41:42–60.

Mitchem, Jeffrey M., Marvin T. Smith, Albert C. Goodyear, and Robert R. Allen
  1985 Early Spanish Contact on the Florida Gulf Coast: The Weeki Wachee and Ruth Smith Mounds. In *Indians, Colonists, and Slaves: Essays in Memory of Charles H. Fairbanks*, edited by K. W. Johnson, J. M. Leader, and R. C. Wilson, pp. 179–219. Florida Journal of Anthropology Special Publication No. 4. Florida Anthropology Student Association, Gainesville.

Smith, Buckingham (translator)
  1968 *Narratives of de Soto in the Conquest of Florida.* Reprinted. Palmetto, Gainesville, Florida. Originally published 1866, The Bradford Club, New York.

Smith, Marvin T., and Mary Elizabeth Good
  1982 *Early Sixteenth Century Glass Beads in the Spanish Colonial Trade.* Cottonlandia Museum Publications, Greenwood, Mississippi.

Solís de Merás, Gonzalo
   1964   *Pedro Menéndez de Avilés, Adelantado, Governor and Captain-General of Florida. Memorial.* Translated by Jeannette Thurber Connor. Reprinted. University of Florida Press, Gainesville. Originally published 1923, Florida State Historical Society, DeLand.
Swanton, John R.
   1985   *Final Report of the United States De Soto Expedition Commission.* Reprinted. Smithsonian Institution Press, Washington, D.C. Originally published 1939, U.S. House of Representatives, 76th Cong., 1st sess., Doc. No. 71. Government Printing Office, Washington, D.C.
Willey, Gordon R.
   1949   *Archeology of the Florida Gulf Coast.* Smithsonian Miscellaneous Collections No. 113. Smithsonian Institution, Washington, D.C.

Chapter 4 ■

Dale L. Hutchinson

Postcontact Biocultural Change: Mortuary Site Evidence

European attempts at exploration and colonization of the New World, which increased after the mid-fifteenth century, brought about changes for populations on both sides of the Atlantic. During this time a variety of previously isolated ecozones, biological populations, and cultures came into contact at an increased tempo (see Crosby 1986; Quinn 1977). These contacts varied in purpose, duration, and effect for all the populations involved.

This discussion focuses on the nature of the contact between Europeans and Indians, and some factors that might have influenced the health of Native American populations. These include epidemiological considerations, and the information mortuary sites supply on changes in the prevalence of infectious disease and other parameters of human health. The populations examined are from the central Gulf coast region of Florida and date to the Safety Harbor period, a protohistoric period in this region (Willey 1982). Included in this geographical locality are the reconstructed routes of two early entradas, those of Pánfilo de Narváez and Hernando de Soto.

Health and Disease: The Old World and the New

Ramenofsky (1987), Dobyns (1983), and others (e.g., Smith 1987), have argued that direct contact with European populations in the New World was preceded in many areas by introduced infectious diseases. Hypotheses about the biological consequences of contact are not limited to the effects on Native American populations, however. Crosby (1972), for instance, hypothesizes that venereal syphilis originated in the New World, citing the epidemic proportions of the disease in Europe following the venture of Columbus in 1492 and the documentary evidence of European physicians at the time who unequivocably stated that it was a new disease.

Unfortunately, the early documentary records present a distorted view of population health prior to contact between the Old and New World. Although there is abundant documentary evidence for infectious diseases in the Old World, such evidence is absent for all but a few New World populations. Epidemics of the plague, for instance, are well-documented in the literature of Europe after A.D. 1346 (McNeil 1976). Does the absence of similar records for the New World suggest that diseases prior to European contact played a relatively minor role in the lives of indigenous populations?

Actually, several metabolic disturbances and infectious diseases were present among prehistoric and protohistoric populations and would likely have predisposed those afflicted to newly introduced infectious diseases. Tuberculosis, for instance, has been demonstrated in Chilean populations dated to A.D. 700 in specimens of soft tissue in which the acid-fast bacilli were isolated (Allison et al. 1973). It is also thought to have been present in several North American populations (see Buikstra 1981). Skeletal responses characteristic of treponemal diseases (e.g., endemic syphilis and yaws) have been noted for precolumbian populations in Illinois (Cook 1976), Alabama (Powell 1988), Georgia (Powell 1987), Florida (Bullen 1972), North Carolina (Bogdan and Weaver 1989), and Louisiana (Robbins 1978).

Ethnohistorical Background for the New World

The earliest *recorded* Spanish and Indian contacts in the Southeast were short attempts at exploration or at capturing Indians as curiosities and slaves. An often-cited reason for the "recruitment" of Native Americans was to replace the already decimated populations that formed the labor force on the Caribbean sugar and tobacco plantations (Gómarra, in Vedia 1852–1853).

Most of the sustained activity by the Spanish, however, was in the form of exploratory entradas, one by Narváez in 1528 (Cabeza de Vaca 1966), and the most intensive beginning in 1539 by de Soto (Oviedo 1945:4:15–71; Smith 1968). Few attempts were made to start settlements in the Southeast during the earliest stages of Spanish involvement; these include Ayllón's ill-fated endeavor at Chicora in 1526 (Oviedo 1945:10:261–290) and one by Tristán de Luna in 1559 (Priestley 1936).

The interactions between the Spanish and Native Americans ranged from amicable to hostile. Ranjel (Oviedo 1945:4:15–71), for instance, reports that during the initial meeting between the Indians and the de Soto expedition two horses were killed and injuries were sustained by both groups.[1] In other interactions, the entrada was well received, as in Cofitachequi. Accounts of the de Soto expedition agree, however, that the Spanish placed demands on Native American food stores, and captured Indians to serve as bearers, translators, and probably concubines.

The ethnohistoric narratives relevant to the Southeast often refer to the Europeans as being sick (Cabeza de Vaca 1966; Smith 1968), but the sickness may have been due to starvation as well as infectious diseases. Elvas (in Smith 1968:68), however, mentions fever for one Spaniard and Cabeza de Vaca (Smith 1966:41–47) reports that the number of Spaniards sick at Aute increased by the day and by the hour. It may have been a disease unknown to them as they did not have a cure. Elvas (Smith 1968) does not mention illness with regard to Native Americans except for the often-cited reference to depopulated towns near Cofitachequi containing European artifacts attributed to the Ayllón colony (see Blakely and Detweiler-Blakely 1989:73; Milner 1980:43–44; Ramenofsky 1987:55; Sauer 1971:302; Smith 1987:55). The account of Cabeza de Vaca (1966), on the other hand, contains numerous references to illness among the Indians.

Epidemiological Considerations

The probable impact of new infectious diseases would vary immensely between those contacts of shorter duration and those that occurred over a lengthy period of time. In addition, the point of origin of the entrada, places of stopover, and length of ocean voyage are important considerations. The Narváez expedition, for instance, was at sea for 54 days, probably too long for diseases with a short infectious period like smallpox to remain infectious. De Soto, on the other hand, sent scouting parties ahead of the main entrada to search for a harbor and to capture Indians for translators; two were brought back to Cuba, exposed to populations there, and then the whole entrada traveled from Cuba to Florida in 7 to 12 days, depending on the ethnohistoric source consulted.

Introduced infectious diseases would have had various effects on the indigenous population, depending on previous exposure, the health and nutrition of the individual, the route of transmission, and population density. The sociopolitical structure of the populations, as well as cultural practices, may have in turn influenced these factors.

Mortuary Sites and Skeletal Remains

Analysis of human skeletal remains and other information derived from the study of mortuary sites has proven particularly useful for testing hypotheses on biocultural issues. For instance, previous research has provided several new and useful insights into changes in health associated with subsistence regime such as agricultural products (Cohen and Armelagos 1984), injury indicative of aggression between sociopolitical groups (Harn et al. 1985; Owsley et al. 1977), and other aspects of human health. Unfortunately, few early contact period skeletal series have been investigated from the Southeast.[2] In one study, however, Blakely and his coworkers (Blakely 1988) reported on remains from the King site in Georgia, where several of the inhabitants had apparently been the victims of a massacre.

Artifacts recovered in mortuary contexts are useful for establishing chronology, as well as trade in exotic items. M. Smith (1987) has provided a four-period chronology for the Southeast based on chronologically sensitive European artifacts. Some items were undoubtedly recovered from shipwrecks, particularly along the south Florida Gulf and Atlantic coasts, where ships from Mexico and South America were sometimes lost in storms. Nonetheless, it is the opinion of several researchers (e.g., Smith 1987; Trigger 1985:153–157) that these prestige items quickly entered the mortuary record, and were removed from circulation.

Consequently, early contact mortuary sites in the Southeast can be dated fairly accurately and the remains may shed some light on skeletal responses to environmental stressors, and thus on human health. It takes time for the skeleton to respond to environmental stressors, however, so that diseases present in epidemic proportions would likely only be apparent in the skeletons of survivors. Moreover, not all diseases affect the skeleton, and studies of disease epidemics in previously unexposed populations demonstrate that often it is secondary infections, such as bronchopneumonia, that are responsible for increased mortality (Neel 1977).

Health and Disease in Central Gulf Coast Florida

Biological adaptation has been a focus of research on Mission period populations (see Larsen et al., this volume), but adaptive responses to new or accentuated environmental stresses are less likely to be detectable during the period of European exploration. Rather, the mortuary record is more likely to preserve indications of the aggressive interactions mentioned in the ethnohistoric narratives, chronic diseases present in the indigenous populations, and increased mortality, possibly due to new epidemic diseases.

These issues have been studied in three mortuary populations from the central Gulf coast of Florida (see Figure 3-1): Safety Harbor (Griffin and Bullen 1950; Stirling 1930, 1931; Willey 1982),[3] Tatham Mound (Mitchem and Hutchinson 1986, 1987; Mitchem, Weisman et al. 1985), and Weeki Wachee (Mitchem, Goodyear et al. 1985). Burials in the upper stratum at Tatham Mound and at Weeki Wachee had associated European trade items, dating them between 1525 and 1560 (see Mitchem, this volume; Smith and Good 1982; Smith 1987), although more securely so at Tatham. One other site, the Ruth Smith Mound, produced artifacts dating to the same time period as Tatham Mound and Weeki Wachee, but previous looting and subsequent bulldozing of the mound preclude the analysis of human skeletal material (Mitchem, Goodyear et al. 1985; Mitchem and Leader 1988). Because analysis is still in progress, only burials that have been studied in depth are included, and interpretations remain tentative.

Three distinct types of burial were delineated during the excavation at Tatham:

individuals articulated at the time of interment, individuals interred as bundle burials, and isolated skeletal elements not attributable to specific individuals. Secondary burials and isolated elements were located above and surrounding the primary interments, and were probably the result of a mortuary program that included curation and later reburial in a ceremonial event (Lorant 1965; Romans 1962; Thwaites 1896–1901:10:279–305). Most burials at Weeki Wachee were secondary interments, many involving more than one individual, although a few primary burials were also delineated (Mitchem, Goodyear et al. 1985). The only record of burial position for Safety Harbor indicates that most interments were secondary (Willey 1982).

Although response to environmental stressors evident in skeletal elements from secondary contexts provides information on the population as a whole, interpretations are usually limited to a description of a general bone response, most often osteomyelitis or periostitis (Ortner and Putschar 1985). Such descriptions provide little insight into specific diseases. Periosteal reactions, for instance, can be the result of several factors, which include treponemal infection, mycotic diseases, anemia, scurvy, trauma, and osteomyelitis (Ortner and Putschar 1985). Disease processes that are generally manifested only in specific skeletal elements or that affect bone in a similar manner to other diseases are most difficult to diagnose differentially when the relatedness of elements is in doubt.

For instance, several skeletal elements from the Gulf coast sites exhibited extreme periosteal reactions with probable endosteal involvement (osteomyelitis).[4] The most common bone response was localized accelerated bone apposition, usually in the process of healing. Radiographs reveal that although some elements did show evidence of endosteal remodeling, others exhibited only superficial endosteal involvement.

Some individuals from Tatham and Weeki Wachee exhibited signs of periosteal elevation in several elements, with nearly the entire diaphysis involved, but endosteal involvement was only superficial. The pattern of the postcranial lesions in three individuals from Tatham, combined with stellate lesions on the frontal and parietals, suggests a treponemal infection. One cranium from Safety Harbor also exhibits stellate lesions, suggesting that the same chronic infection was also present in that population. Postcranial skeletal elements similar in pathology to those in the Tatham Mound and Safety Harbor populations are also present for a few Weeki Wachee individuals. At least some of the elements exhibiting similar pathology in these cases are likely the result of that disease.

Skeletal elements indicative of trauma in the Tatham population included healed fractures, and several elements *suggested* injury by metal weapons. However, only two have been convincingly assigned to this latter category (Mitchem and Hutchinson 1986, 1987). Both of these were secondary elements, not associated with specific burials, and neither shows any signs of healing. One, a right scapula, had the acromian process severed completely, and the other, a left humerus, had been cut almost completely through and then had snapped. This pattern is common in wounds from wedge-shaped weapons, such as knives or swords (Knowles 1983; Ortner and Putschar 1985).

A third wound probably made by a metal weapon matches the configuration and location of wounds in the King site population from Georgia (Mathews 1988). It is located on the proximal lateral portion of the left femur diaphysis of a single-individual secondary burial. No healing had occurred and no other elements were affected. Distal to this wound is a large nodular periosteal reaction. Radiographs revealed that only the periosteum was affected with only very slight endosteal involvement, and that a large cavitation remained that did not penetrate into the medullary cavity.

After consulting with several individuals in the Department of Anthropology and School of Veterinary Sciences at the University of Illinois, I concluded that some foreign body remained in the leg of this individual, irritating the periosteum. The large amount of muscle mass in this area of the femur suggests that the object was a projectile of some type, which broke off and was consequently left to irritate the periosteum. No skeletal elements suggestive of metal weapon wounds were found in either the Safety Harbor or Weeki Wachee series.

Investigations of burial form or associated artifacts have thus far failed to reveal any pattern that might suggest different parts of the mound were used at different times. In fact, the placement of primary burials in the mound as revealed during excavation suggests a well-planned scheme for placing burials in roughly linear rows. Efforts continue to delineate informative patterns and associations. One archaeological feature that merits discussion is a greasy black stain directly underneath the majority of primary burials and areas of the mound associated with European artifacts. Tests for lipids are planned to determine if they are human or vegetable in composition. The former would suggest the decomposition of human remains and the formation of a fatty substance called *adipocere*, the latter a mound surface prepared for use with Palmetto fronds or other vegetation.

The composition of the Tatham Mound population with regard to gender deviates from normal demographic patterns. There are many more females than males,[5] and European artifacts are predominantly associated with females. Mathews (1988) reports that victims of wounds made by metal weapons at the King site were primarily from two age categories: 20–30 and 40–60. Those in the younger age group were all female, except for one male, whereas those of the older age group were distributed evenly. Unfortunately, because of the secondary nature of cut elements at Tatham, the gender of wound victims is unclear.

Discussion

Mortuary sites vary in the length of time utilized, the individuals included (e.g., different lineages, status, age), mortuary program and burial form, spatial organization, and location. Therefore they cannot be treated as homogeneous entities. For example, at the King site (Blakely 1988), burials were predominantly interred as single or multiple-individual primary interments. The population that interred its dead at Tatham Mound and the other Florida sites, on the other hand, utilized a very different approach.

If only secondary burials from these sites were used as the basic unit of interpretation in this analysis, systemic infections would be harder, if not impossible, to detect. However, other pathology would likely be underestimated.

The severed elements attest to rapid death after traumatic injury, probably in direct Spanish and Indian confrontation. Other elements indicate that a form of endemic treponemal infection was present in these populations from the central Gulf coast of Florida.

Changes in lifeway for indigenous New World populations were undoubtedly the result of various types of contact, ranging from the appearance of "new" exotic items of European origin, traded both through European and aboriginal networks, to the direct effects of European explorers who invoked trauma, induced food shortages, and possibly infected native populations with diseases of respiratory and vectored transmission. Data recovered from mortuary sites can be used to test hypotheses regarding these various biocultural changes and serve as a valuable supplement and check to ethnohistoric accounts.

Acknowledgments

Several people have contributed to this study. First, I thank Jerald Milanich, the principal investigator, for including me in this project, and Jeffrey M. Mitchem, coworker in the field. The three field crews and various volunteers who helped excavate Tatham maintained their good spirits in the face of hard labor, hot sun, and annoying insects. They often helped elevate our spirits when the task of excavating this site seemed more than we could accomplish.

Several people have offered their insights and interpretations, although I remain solely responsible for the final interpretations. In particular, I benefited from discussions with Doug Brewer, Leslie Eisenberg, Jo Ann Eurell, Linda Klepinger, Clark Larsen, R. Barry Lewis, William Maples, Jerry Pijanowski, Mary Powell, Jeffrey Mitchem, Deborah Bakken, and Kristin Hedman. Bill Burger called attention to the Safety Harbor materials. I thank Trina Bennett and Denise Goddard for assistance in the laboratory. Finally, I received excellent editorial assistance from Jacqueline McDowell and the staff at the Smithsonian Institution Press.

Funding sources include the Department of Anthropology and the Graduate College of the University of Illinois, the Florida Museum of Natural History, and especially an anonymous private donor.

Notes

1. The Spanish were extremely successful in warfare in other geographical areas (e.g., Peru and Mexico), particularly because of their advantage while on horseback. In the Southeast, however, the Spanish horses encountered swamps, large rivers, and less open space, and the Indians employed a more guerrilla-like approach to warfare (Smith 1968:57). Consequently, ethnohistoric accounts often mention the stealth of the Southeast Indian warrior, who was able to penetrate armor and quickly adapt to chain mail by using cane arrows.

2. The term *early contact* as used in this chapter refers to the period prior to the first successful permanent settlements in the Southeast, in other words, after the establish-

ment of Spanish St. Augustine in 1565. The French established settlements on the Atlantic coast between 1561 and 1565, and although these are beyond the scope of the present discussion, they do have implications concerning introduced diseases.

3. Part of this series is curated at the National Museum of Natural History. All observations reported here refer to a part of the collection currently in the custody of New College, Sarasota, Florida.

4. Pattern of skeletal lesions and specific types of bone response are usually necessary for differential diagnosis of diseases.

5. This is not an artifact of the sample included in this chapter; field observations support the bias toward females.

References

Allison, Marvin J., D. Mendoza, and A. Pezzia
  1973 Documentation of a Case of Tuberculosis in Pre-Columbian America. *American Review of Respiratory Disease* 107:985–991.
Blakley, Robert L. (editor)
  1988 *The King Site: Continuity and Contact in Sixteenth-Century Georgia.* University of Georgia Press, Athens.
Blakely, Robert L., and Bettina Detweiler-Blakely
  1989 The Impact of European Diseases in the Sixteenth-Century Southeast: A Case Study. *Midcontinental Journal of Archaeology* 14:62–89.
Bogdan, G., and David S. Weaver
  1989 Probable Treponemal Skeletal Symptoms in Eight Pre-Columbian Coastal North Carolina Ossuary Samples. *American Journal of Physical Anthropology* 78:194.
Buikstra, Jane E. (editor)
  1981 *Prehistoric Tuberculosis in the Americas.* Scientific Papers No. 5. Northwestern University Archeological Program, Evanston.
Bullen, Adelaide K.
  1972 Paleoepidemiology and Distribution of Prehistoric Treponemamiasis (Syphilis) in Florida. *Florida Anthropologist* 25:133–175.
Cabeza de Vaca, Alvar Nuñez
  1966 *Relation That Alvar Nuñez Cabeça De Vaca Gave of What Befel the Armament in Indias.* Translated by Buckingham Smith. Reprinted. March of America Facsimile Series No. 9. University Microfilms Incorporated, Ann Arbor. Originally Published 1871, Estate of Buckingham Smith, Brooklyn.
Cohen, Mark N., and George J. Armelagos (editors)
  1984 *Paleopathology at the Origins of Agriculture.* Academic Press, Orlando.
Cook, Della C.
  1976 *Pathologic States and Disease Process in Illinois Woodland Populations: An Epidemiological Approach.* Unpublished Ph.D. dissertation, University of Chicago, Department of Anthropology.
Crosby, Alfred W., Jr.
  1972 *The Columbian Exchange: Biological and Cultural Consequences of 1492.* Contributions in American Studies No. 2. Greenwood Press, Westport, Connecticut.
  1986 *Ecological Imperialism.* Cambridge University Press, Oxford.
Dobyns, Henry F.
  1983 *Their Number Become Thinned: Native American Population Dynamics in Eastern North America.* University of Tennessee Press, Knoxville.
Griffin, John W., and Ripley P. Bullen
  1950 *The Safety Harbor Site, Pinellas County, Florida.* Florida Anthropological Society Publication No. 2. Gainesville.

Harn, Alan D., Sharron K. Santure, Nicholas K. Klobuchar, and Duane Esarey
  1985 The Oneota Mortuary Component at Norris Farms #36. Paper presented at the 30th Annual Meeting of the Midwest Archaeological Conference, East Lansing.
Knowles, A. Keith
  1983 Acute Traumatic Lesions. In *Disease in Ancient Man,* edited by Gerald D. Hart, pp. 61–83. Clarke Irwin, Agincourt, Ontario.
Lorant, Stefan (editor)
  1965 *The New World: The First Pictures of America.* Reprinted. Duell, Sloan and Pearce, New York.
McNeil, William H.
  1976 *Plagues and Peoples.* Anchor Press, Garden City.
Mathews, David S.
  1988 The Massacre: The Discovery of De Soto in Georgia. In *The King Site: Continuity and Contact in Sixteenth-Century Georgia,* edited by Robert L. Blakely, pp. 101–116. University of Georgia Press, Athens.
Milner, George R.
  1980 Epidemic Disease in the Postcontact Southeast: An Appraisal. *Midcontinental Journal of Archaeology* 5:39–56.
Mitchem, Jeffrey M., and Dale L. Hutchinson
  1986 *Interim Report on Excavations at the Tatham Mound, Citrus County, Florida: Season II.* Miscellaneous Project Report Series No. 28. Department of Anthropology, Florida State Museum, Gainesville.
  1987 *Interim Report on Excavations at the Tatham Mound, Citrus County, Florida: Season III.* Miscellaneous Project Report Series No. 30. Department of Anthropology, Florida State Museum, Gainesville.
Mitchem, Jeffrey M., Albert C. Goodyear, Marvin T. Smith, and Robert R. Allen
  1985 Early Spanish Contact on the Florida Gulf Coast: The Weeki Wachee and Ruth Smith Mounds. In *Indians, Colonists, and Slaves: Essays in Memory of Charles H. Fairbanks,* edited by Kenneth W. Johnson, Jonathan M. Leader, and Robert C. Wilson. Special Publication No. 4. Florida Journal of Anthropology, Gainesville.
Mitchem, Jeffrey M., and Jonathan M. Leader
  1988 Early Sixteenth Century Beads from the Tatham Mound, Citrus County, Florida: Data and Interpretations. *Florida Anthropologist* 41:42–60.
Mitchem, Jeffrey M., Brent R. Weisman, Donna L. Ruhl, Jennette Savell, Laura Sellers, and Lisa Sharik
  1985 *Preliminary Report on Excavations at the Tatham Mound (8-Ci-203), Citrus County, Florida: Season I.* Miscellaneous Project Report Series No. 23. Department of Anthropology, Florida State Museum, Gainesville.
Neel, James V.
  1977 Health and Disease in Unacculturated Amerindian Populations. In *Health and Disease in Tribal Societies,* Ciba Foundation Symposium 49 (n.s.), pp. 155–168. Elsevier, Amsterdam.
Ortner, Donald J., and Walter G. J. Putschar
  1985 *Identification of Pathological Conditions in Human Skeletal Remains.* Reprinted. Originally Published 1981. Smithsonian Contributions to Anthropology No. 28, Smithsonian Institution Press, Washington, D.C.
Oviedo, Gonzalo Fernando de
  1945 *Historia General y Natural de las Indias: Islas y Tierra-Firme del Mar Oceano.* 16 vols. Editorial Guarania, Asuncion del Paraguay.
Owsley, Douglas W., Hugh E. Berryman, and William M. Bass
  1977 Demographic and Osteological Evidence for Warfare at the Larson Site, South Dakota. *Plains Anthropologist Memoir* 3:119–131.

Powell, Mary L.

1987 On the Eve of Conquest: Life and Death at Irene Mound, Georgia. *American Journal of Physical Anthropology* 72:243.

1988 *Status and Health in Prehistory: A Case Study of the Moundville Chiefdom.* Smithsonian Institution Press, Washington, D.C.

Priestley, Herbert Ingram

1936 *Tristán De Luna, Conquistador of the Old South: A Study of Spanish Imperial Strategy.* Arthur H. Clark, Glendale, California.

Quinn, David B.

1977 *North America from Earliest Discovery to First Settlements: The Norse Voyages to 1612.* Harper & Row, New York.

Ramenofsky, Ann F.

1987 *Vectors of Death: The Archaeology of European Contact.* University of New Mexico Press, Albuquerque.

Robbins, Louise

1978 Yawslike Disease Process in a Louisiana Shell Mound Population. *Medical College of Virginia Quarterly* 14:24–31.

Romans, Bernard

1962 *A Concise Natural History of East and West Florida.* Reprinted. University of Florida Press, Gainesville. Originally published 1775, Printed for the Author, New York.

Sauer, Carl O.

1971 *Sixteenth Century North America.* University of California Press, Berkeley.

Smith, Buckingham (editor)

1968 *Narratives in the Career of Hernando De Soto in the Conquest of Florida.* Translated by Buckingham Smith. Reprinted. Kallman, Gainesville. Originally published 1866, Bradford Club, New York.

Smith, Marvin T.

1987 *Archaeology of Aboriginal Culture Change in the Interior Southeast.* Ripley P. Bullen Monographs in Anthropology and History No. 6, Florida State Museum. University of Florida Press, Gainesville.

Smith, Marvin T., and Mary Elizabeth Good

1982 *Early Sixteenth-century Glass Beads in the Spanish Colonial Trade.* Cottonlandia Museum Publications, Greenwood, Mississippi.

Stirling, Matthew W.

1930 Prehistoric Mounds in the Vicinity of Tampa Bay, Florida. In *Explorations and Field Work of the Smithsonian Institution in 1929*, pp. 183–186. Washington, D.C.

1931 Mounds of the Vanished Calusa Indians of Florida. In *Explorations and Field Work of the Smithsonian Institution in 1930*, pp. 167–172. Washington, D.C.

Thwaites, Ruben Gold (editor)

1896–1901 *The Jesuit Relations and Allied Documents: Travels and Explorations of the Jesuit Missionaries in New France 1610–1791.* 73 vols. Burrows Brothers, Cleveland.

Trigger, Bruce G.

1985 *Natives and Newcomers: Canada's "Heroic Age" Reconsidered.* McGill-Queen's University Press, Kingston and Montreal.

Vedia, Enrique de (editor)

1852–1853 *Historiadores Primitivos de Indias.* 2 vols. Madrid.

Willey, Gordon R.

1982 *Archaeology of the Florida Gulf Coast.* Reprinted. Florida Book Store, Gainesville. Originally Published 1949. Smithsonian Miscellaneous Collections, Vol. 113, Smithsonian Institution Press, Washington, D.C.

Chapter 5 ■

Rochelle A. Marrinan, John F. Scarry, and
Rhonda L. Majors

Prelude to de Soto: The Expedition of Pánfilo de Narváez

"In 1492, Columbus sailed the ocean blue," and the world was never the same. In 1513, Juan Ponce de León discovered La Florida, and the world of the South-eastern Indian was never the same. Within 50 years of Ponce's discovery, Spain had launched seven major expeditions to La Florida (Lyon 1981) and the native polities were in shambles. Each of the expeditions failed in the attempt to find wealth, but like the major successes in New Spain and Peru, these ill-fated un-dertakings provided some of the earliest direct contact between native groups and Europeans and ultimately led to irrevocable changes in the native societies.

Perhaps the greatest failure was the expedition of Pánfilo de Narváez, the man Morison (1974:518) called "the most incompetent of all who sailed for Spain." The company of explorers and would-be colonizers accompanying Narváez ar-rived at the shores of the Florida peninsula 11 years before the expedition of de Soto. In contrast to de Soto, however, Narváez and his expedition are poorly known in the historical record and in the popular imagination, folklore, and tourist trade of the Southeast. Why is this so? Narváez began with the same charge as de Soto: exploration and settlement. Like de Soto he was granted the titles of adelantado and governor of La Florida, an area stretching from the

Florida peninsula north to the Chesapeake Bay and west to Tampico, Mexico.

The surviving chronicles of the Narváez expedition are the *Relaciones* of Álvar Núñez Cabeza de Vaca, stories of men forced to survive in circumstances foreign to their experience, among people often hostile, and in conditions of great deprivation. Perhaps the Narváez expedition in the Southeast is forgotten because Vaca's narrative is usually associated with the legend of the Seven Cities of Cibola and the American Southwest, where the tales of Vaca and his companions served as stimulus for the expedition of Francisco Vásquez de Coronado (Bolton 1949).

We propose to take a closer look at the Narváez entrada and its impact on the native peoples of Florida.

The Expedition

In a very real sense, the path that Narváez followed in La Florida was set long before he landed at Tampa Bay. It was determined by the European worldview in the Age of Exploration and by Narváez's experiences in the New World. Helms (1988:211) has characterized the medieval European cosmography as one that peopled the far frontiers with beings "whose point of contrast with 'normal' society ultimately lay . . . in the realm of the physically and/or morally deformed." For example, Todorov has noted that Columbus's descriptions of the natives of the Caribbean islands always occur among his discussions of nature, "somewhere between birds and trees." He goes on to argue that the Indians were "to Columbus' eyes, deprived of all cultural property . . . characterized, in a sense, by the absence of customs, rites, religion" (1984:34–35). This worldview was particularly well-suited to exploration and conquest of the native societies of the New World.

Narváez was associated with Diego de Velasquez in the conquest and colonization of Cuba beginning in 1511. He served Velasquez as a leader of Spanish forces against the Cubeños, the aboriginal population of the island (Wright 1910). Within a decade, the native population of Cuba was reduced to such small numbers that African slaves were imported to provide a labor force. First seen on Hispaniola, rapid native depopulation was a pattern in the islands of the Caribbean. A young Dominican priest, Bartolome de las Casas, witnessed the cruelties suffered by the Cubeños at the hands of soldiers under the command of a seemingly disinterested Narváez. The brutalities catalogued by Las Casas on Cuba were to become commonplace in further explorations in the Indies giving rise to the leyenda negra.

Narváez also figured in Cortez's conquest of Mexico. Governor Velasquez sent him to arrest the rebellious Cortez and ensure his return to Cuba. Instead, Cortez took Narváez hostage, releasing him two years later. One of Narváez's sailors infected with smallpox introduced this devastating illness to the Central American population. The epidemic that ensued was a major factor in the fall of the Aztec empire (Parkes 1970:56).

Narváez returned to Spain and was rewarded by the Emperor Charles V with the contract for exploration and colonization of the area east of the Rio de las

Palmas (Mexico) or La Florida. At his own expense, he assembled a force of some six hundred men and five vessels. This expedition sailed from Spain for Santo Domingo on June 27, 1527. Although the expedition was led by Narváez, he is probably less well known than his second in command, the treasurer and aguacil mayor, Álvar Núñez Cabeza de Vaca.

Álvar Núñez Cabeza de Vaca was a young nobleman, grandson of Pedro de Vera, a conqueror of the Canary Islands. Vaca was the author of at least three, perhaps four, documents that relate his experiences during the journey from Florida to Mexico. After arriving in Mexico City in 1536, three of the four expedition survivors, the hidalgos Andrés Dorantes, Alonso del Castillo Maldonado, and Vaca prepared a report for Viceroy Antonio de Mendoza. This document was forwarded to the empress by the viceroy, but is not among the extant versions used by scholars today. In addition, the three produced a report for the audiencia of Hispaniola (Santo Domingo). Smith (1866:7–8) suggested that this document was deliberately vague about places and observations because Dorantes and Vaca hoped to return with their own expedition.

In 1542, Vaca published his own account. This document was translated by Fanny Bandelier and is probably the most popular account (Bandelier 1905). A final version, published by Vaca in 1555 is known as the *Naufragios*, or the "shipwrecked ones." This account also includes his further adventures as govenor of the Rio de la Plata area of South America. Recently, John Hann has made translations of Vaca's 1555 version. His work also provides a comparison with previously published translations (Hann 1988b). We use Hann's translation because it is the most literal and because Hann takes into account nuances of the language that can give information useful to an archaeological inquiry.

Vaca was appointed second in command of the expedition, a position that seemed to put him immediately at odds with Narváez. From the narrative, we get the impression that Narváez gave him the dangerous or mundane assignments, but we have little to use in evaluating Vaca's presentation of himself and his position in the narrative. He appears to be loyal to his king, imbued with a strong sense of family honor, resolute, a man of deep faith, and a keen observer of his circumstances. He also seems to have had sounder ideas about the conduct of the expedition than Narváez, but it is difficult to tell how much of this portrayal is an advantage of hindsight.

Narváez's expedition set out from Hispaniola in 1527 for La Florida. The expedition had lost 140 men to desertion on Hispaniola, which necessitated a stop at the port of Santiago, Cuba, to secure more men and provisions. With his fleet of five vessels, Narváez set sail for La Trinidad, Cuba, to pick up additional provisions. He sent Vaca ahead with two vessels to secure promised provisions, but a severe hurricane hit the island. Both vessels with Vaca were lost along with 60 men and 20 horses. So fearful of the Caribbean storms were the members of the expedition that they convinced Narváez to remain on Cuba until spring. In April of 1528, they set sail for Florida, arriving on the 12th. It is believed that they landed on the west cost of Florida, but the specific area is a point of debate. Some argue for the Charlotte Harbor area, others for Tampa Bay (see Figure 1-2).

Within several days, Narváez had disembarked the majority of his force and the 40 horses that survived the voyage. After several days of reconnoitering, Narváez decided to explore the country. On May 2, he set out with 40 horsemen and 260 men on foot. He had contrived the plan of having his ships search for a port from the sea while his force moved in the same direction ashore. Narváez would never again see his ships. Vaca records that he had counseled against this plan, believing it to be folly, but determined to accompany his leader as a matter of family honor rather than remain with the ships as Narváez had ordered.

Interaction with native peoples was initially friendly, but quickly became hostile. Vaca records the use of force against natives in the area of their landing several days after the expedition disembarked. He also records that native people contacted within those first few days assured them that the food and gold they sought could be found in a place to the north called Apalachen.

The march from the landing place to Apalachen required some 56 days. Vaca noted that during the first 15 days, they encountered no Indians and little that was edible. After they forded a swift river, the expedition was approached by some 200 Indians. Following a brief exchange, Narváez judged their intentions to be hostile, and ordered his men to the attack. Several Indians were taken prisoner and used as guides. Narváez secured some foodstuffs from their village to feed his men, but Vaca indicates that the expedition was in desperate need of food. Swanton (1939:113) proposed that the most likely place for this encounter was in the vicinity of the Withlacoochee River.

Always seeking Apalachen, the expedition moved on. Vaca records that they were shunned by native people. Not until June 17 does the *Relación* describe their meeting a chief, ostensibly an enemy of Apalachen. With this chief, Dulchanchellin, as a voluntary guide, the expedition continued to make its way toward Apalachen. The next day, the death of an impatient horsemen who tried to ford a broad and deep river was recorded as the first Spanish fatality. The expedition required a day and rafts to effect a crossing. Swanton (1939:114) has suggested that this occurred in the crossing of the Suwannee River.

Two days later, the expedition arrived at the village of the chief Dulchanchellin. On awakening the next morning, the Spaniards found that all of the natives had fled. The expedition marched on. There were minor hostilities as the group entered a forested region. Vaca records that the terrain was difficult to traverse because of many large, fallen trees. The expedition finally came within sight of Apalachen the day after St. Johns Day.

Narváez and his men entered the territory of Apalachen on June 25. Soon afterward, they encountered the first Apalachee settlement, also called Apalachen by Vaca. Swanton (1939:114) identified this settlement as Ivitachuco (Figure 5-1). The identification seems quite probable given Vaca's description of their subsequent journey. Eleven years later, Ivitachuco was the easternmost Apalachee settlement encountered by de Soto. It was also the name of the easternmost Apalachee mission in the seventeenth century (Hann 1988a:34).

When Narváez entered this village, the only inhabitants were women and children; all of the adult males were absent. The Spaniards assaulted the town and captured its residents. The men returned peacefully several days later and asked to have the women and children freed. Narváez complied, but seized the

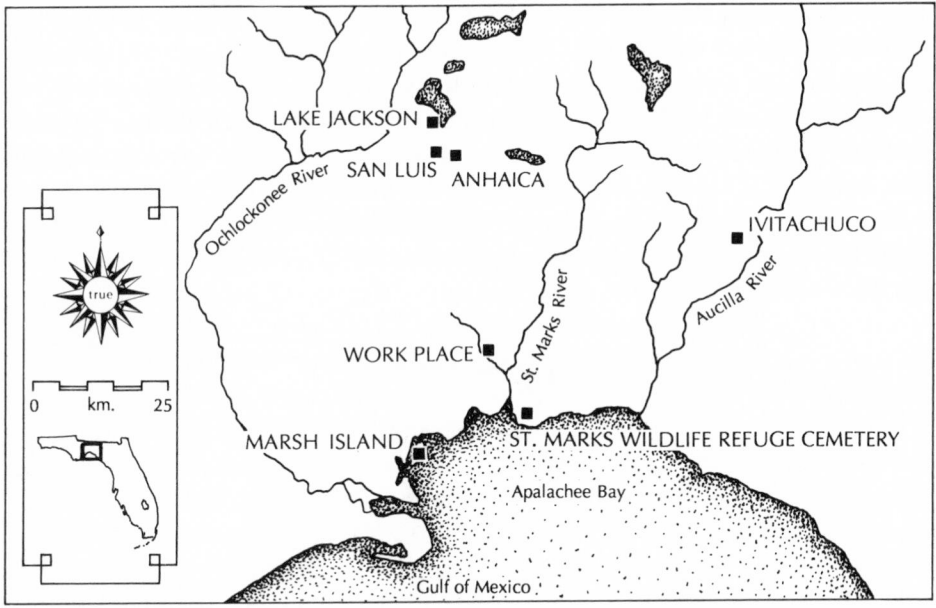

Figure 5-1. Key archaeological and historical sites in Apalachee Province.

Apalachee chief. This action dramatically changed the relationship between the Spaniards and the Apalachee. The following day, 200 Apalachee attacked the Spanish encampment, setting the village aflame. The next day, the Apalachee attacked again. This time their force was augmented by warriors from other villages (Hann 1988b:8).

After 25 or 26 days, Narváez and his company left Ivitachuco for the village of Aute, a settlement said to have much food and to be near the sea. The expedition reached Aute after nine days' journey. Along the way, they were repeatedly attacked by the Apalachee. When they reached Aute, the town and many of the maize fields had been burned.

In Aute, many of the Spaniards, Narváez included, became ill. Dobyns (1983:261; personal communication 1988) believes that their illness may have been typhoid or typhus. Three days after their arrival, Narváez sent Vaca with a contingent to find the sea. Returning, Vaca reported that he found "arms of the sea," presumably the tidal salt marshes of Apalachee Bay. On August 3, the entire force made its way to the coast and began the arduous process of building the boats they hoped would take them to Mexico. Many were ill, some were dying. They were forced to eat their horses. Vaca states that every third day, a horse was killed and the meat distributed among the workers and the sick. The Apalachee continued to harass the Spaniards as they transformed the metal of their weapons and tack, the manes and hides of their horses, into boats and waterskins. Eleven years later, men of the de Soto expedition would identify this site from the forge and horse skulls. Vaca calls this place "the Bay of Horses."

Narváez started inland with over 300 men and 40 horses, but only about 250 men and no horses left Apalachee. The Apalachee had killed some of them, but at least 40 had died of illness. The worst was yet to come. The sea was not close to the point where the boats were constructed. The Spaniards struggled through the marshes for several days before reaching open water. The Apalachee continued their attacks. Once launched, the expedition hugged the Gulf coast. Those who survived as far as the Texas coast were wrecked and others blown out to sea. Eight years after they set out for La Florida, four survivors—the hidalgos Vaca, Andrés Dorantes, and Alonso del Castillo Maldonado, and Esteban, a black slave of Dorantes—reached Mexico.

Archaeological Evidence for Narváez

A group of European cultural materials has become the standard by which chronological affiliation of early Spanish sites in Florida is assessed (see Brain 1975). This group includes items of brass such as the Clarksdale bells, glass beads including faceted chevron beads and Nueva Cadiz beads, and silver or gold of Central or South American origin.

Evidence of a Narváez route is complicated by the presence of materials from the de Soto expedition 11 years later, Spanish activity in the area after the settlement of St. Augustine in 1565, and materials salvaged from shipwrecks. In addition, if we are correct that the first river mentioned by Vaca is the Withlacoochee River, we would expect little cultural material from this expedition on the lower end of the march other than in the vicinity of the landing site. Between the Withlacoochee and the Suwannee Rivers, there are currently no data to support the passage of either the Narváez or de Soto expedition.

Once within Apalachee territory, the evidence becomes more tangible. Researchers in Apalachee province today are basically in agreement with Swanton's identification of Ivitachuco as Apalachen. The expedition entered Apalachen immediately after crossing a river into Apalachee territory. The historic (and archaeological) eastern boundary of Apalachee territory appears to have been the Aucilla River. According to Vaca's account, the expedition made its way through the sandy forests between the Tallahassee Red Hills zone and the coastal marshes. Scout groups may have reconnoitered the Red Hills zone, but it seems clear from Vaca's description of the terrain that the main body of the expedition did not.

The location of Aute is not certain, but several possible sites have been identified. Mitchem (1988) has examined the existing archaeological and ethnohistorical evidence and follows Swanton in arguing for a location in the vicinity of St. Marks, Florida. There are three known sites with early historic components near there (Figure 5-1): Marsh Island (Moore 1902:274–281); the St. Marks Wildlife Refuge Cemetery (Goggin 1947, Griffin 1947, Johnson 1969; Kary 1939, 1940); and the Work Place (Willey 1949:296).

The Marsh Island site (8WA1) was excavated early in this century by C. B. Moore (1902). Moore removed seven intrusive burials of multiple individuals in association with quantities of European materials that included scissors, iron tools, sleigh bells, tubular brass beads, and brass bracelets. European materials appear to have been more common than native artifacts. Mitchem (1988) suggests that the Marsh Island materials may be later than Narváez, given the presence of glass seed beads in the inventory. Two aboriginal vessels illustrated by Moore (1902:Figure 241) also support Mitchem's interpretation; the vessel forms are late, perhaps as late as the seventeenth century (Scarry 1985). One of the vessels is Point Washington Incised, *var. Crowder*, which is found in seventeenth-century contexts in Apalachee province. This collection is held by the Museum of the American Indian, Heye Foundation, and has not recently been studied.

Little is known of the Work Place site (8WA11) that provides an accurate date for it. Willey and Woodbury collected Fort Walton Incised and Lamar Complicated Stamped pottery and a single sherd of a "European-made vessel" (Willey 1949:296). The Lamar sherds suggest that the site dates to late in the Velda phase (ca. 1550) or perhaps even to the Mission Period San Luis phase (ca. 1633–1704; Scarry 1989a).

The best candidate for a Narváez-related site is clearly the St. Marks Wildlife Refuge Cemetery site (8WA15). European artifacts from the site include Clarksdale bells, faceted chevron beads, Nueva Cadiz beads, and purple glass beads. These are good sixteenth-century markers, particularly the Clarksdale bells and Nueva Cadiz beads, which have been found only on sites dating to the first half of the sixteenth century (Deagan 1987:163; Mitchem and McEwan 1988:41). Because it lacks an identified habitation area, this site does not meet the criteria for Aute. The cemetery may have served Aute, however.

Despite not knowing the exact location of Aute, we support Mitchem's and Swanton's overall thesis regarding the general location of the site. Although neither Apalachen nor Aute have been identified, artifacts recovered from the St. Marks–Apalachee Bay locality indicate a strong sixteenth-century interaction between aboriginal inhabitants and Spaniards. Given the possibility that the materials could have originated from other contacts, we would argue that the Narváez expedition is responsible for the concentration of early sixteenth-century material.

Legacy of Narváez

Narváez died a failure, but his attempt to conquer La Florida made a lasting impact on his successors and on the native peoples he encountered. His impact on Hernando de Soto was direct and clear-cut. De Soto, who assumed Narváez's charter from the Crown, learned from Narváez's experiences. He had access to written records and talked with Vaca. As a consequence, de Soto took more men and more horses. To counter the chronic food shortages suffered by Narváez's expedition, he took about 300 swine to provide food for his men. He took a slightly different route that led him to richer native polities with more maize. He also sought Apalachen, both because of the reports that gold was to be found there and because of its known food productivity.

Although de Soto was better prepared because of Narváez's experiences, his way was made more difficult by the natives' experiences. He met more indigenous peoples who had previous interactions with Spaniards. He met more hostility. The difference in native response is particularly noticeable in the Apalachee case. When Narváez entered Apalachen, he was not attacked, even after seizing women and children. It was not until he took a chief as hostage that hostilities ensued. The hostile skirmishes continued for the duration of the expedition's stay in Apalachee territory.

When de Soto entered Apalachee territory, his progress was contested at the border. The first village of Apalachee, Ivitachuco, was ablaze as he approached. De Soto's relations with the Apalachee did not improve. According to Biedma, de Soto had to send horsemen out to scour the area because the Apalachee were constantly attacking (Hann 1988c:23). According to Ranjel, "although the Spaniards pursued them and burned them, they never showed any desire to come to peace" (Hann 1988d:18). It was no doubt with relief that de Soto and his men left Apalachee in the spring of 1540.

Although Narváez's impact on de Soto and subsequent Spanish exploration in La Florida was considerable, it pales against the impact he had on native peoples. The Apalachee held their own militarily against both Narváez and de Soto, but their society could not survive against the biological, cosmological, and social onslaught of European contact.

The biological impact of European contact on Native Americans is widely recognized (Dobyns 1983; Ramenofsky 1982; Smith 1987; Crosby 1972). From the contagion that struck the Spaniards at Aute, Vaca reports the death of 40 members of the expedition (Hann 1988b:15). There is no mention of native deaths, but Dobyns (1983:231) estimates a 50 percent mortality rate. To date, archaeological evidence in support of early sixteenth-century population decline in Apalachee province is limited, although examination of survey data from the Apalachee heartland suggests significant decreases in population during the sixteenth century (Marrinan and Bryne 1985; Smith and Scarry 1988, 1989).

The cosmological impact of European contact was no less significant, if less widely recognized. The increasing frequency of interactions with Europeans and European goods undermined the political and religious systems. Helms has suggested that native worldviews characterized Europeans (or any distant strangers) "as superhuman beings, as wise strangers with exceptional power, much of which was expressed and evidenced by their access to quantities of unusual material goods and by their technical ('magical') skills and capacities" (1988:205).

The first Europeans to enter La Florida were "men" of a different sort, unlike the native himself or his neighbors. Their appearance was different; they had lighter skin, facial hair, and strange clothes. They had strange and powerful weapons and animals that did their bidding. In Helms's view, as the European worldview predisposed the Spaniard to conquest and exploitation, the native worldview predisposed them to be exploited.

In many societies, material goods are used as tangible expressions of political and ideological concepts. This was undoubtedly true in the Southeast, where objects of shell, stone, and metal were crafted into symbols of office, authority, and power. If the Apalachee valued exotic goods of copper made in Mississippian chiefdoms to the north, what would they have thought of artifacts of glass, brass, silver, and gold, materials unlike any they had seen before, brought to their land by Narváez and his men, people unlike any they had seen before?

The social impact of European contact was also dramatic. To a great extent, social cohesion was weakened as the ineffectiveness of native magico-religious practices against the biological invasion became clear. Potentially destabilizing seizures of native leaders were common practice, further stressing the native political system. The consequences of epidemic illness and population loss on native social and political organization are only conjectural since written accounts are not available. However, if many Apalachee died as a result of Narváez's passage through their territory, particularly if they died in anything approaching the numbers estimated by Dobyns, the social consequences would have been far-reaching. Local community and political structure may well have collapsed as a result. Certainly the Apalachee appear less cohesive and much less sure of their power by the beginning of the seventeenth century (Scarry 1988, 1989b).

Apalachee cosmography may have initially characterized the Spaniards as supernatural beings and potential sources of authority and power for the native elite. The Spaniards, however, did not act properly. Instead of legitimizing the power of the elite, they abused the local leaders and tortured many others. These actions represent an unprecedented blow to chiefly authority. At a more concrete level, the Spaniards and the diseases they brought with them would have provided unmistakable evidence of the lack of power of the local leaders. The chiefs could not drive the Spaniards out, nor could they prevent death from European diseases. The connection of the appearance of the diseases and the Spaniards undoubtedly was made by many native groups.

Conclusions

According to his contract with the Spanish Crown, Narváez was to conquer and settle the territories from the Rio de las Palmas to the Cape of Florida. He failed to achieve these goals. Yet, in failure, the impact of the passage of this expedition was felt not only by the native groups contacted, but by other Europeans who would, in the following years, take up the same charter.

In Florida, Narváez's treatment of native peoples set a precedent for the abuses of de Soto. The native peoples of Florida endured four major attempts at exploration and settlement by Spain before 1565. Each was unsuccessful. When a permanent settlement was finally established in 1565, it was on the east coast of Florida. St. Augustine remained relatively isolated for many years, reaching out to incorporate native peoples slowly through missionization. Nearly a century passed before the people of Apalachee province were brought into the mission chain.

In more ways than one, this expedition was a prelude to de Soto. None of the explorers found in Florida the riches they sought. Wealth in gold and silver was not to be found in the land of Apalachen. Those who survived the Narváez expedition remained not as rich landholders served by native retainers, but as struggling, impoverished refugees forced to live by their wits. Perhaps this adventure was forgotten because of the shocking magnitude of the disaster. For the natives of the Southeast, the expedition signaled massive cultural change. Narváez shook the world of the native peoples in Florida. De Soto and those who followed destroyed it.

Acknowledgments

Jennifer Hamilton of the South Florida Museum graciously allowed us to examine artifacts from the St. Marks Cemetery site in the Montagu Tallant collection housed at the museum. Nick Fallier lent us his collection of St. Marks artifacts and provided firsthand information about the excavations at the site during the 1930s. Jeffrey Mitchem provided insights about the archaeology of sixteenth-century Spanish explorations in Florida in several discussions about Narváez and St. Marks. This paper is better for their contributions.

References

Bandelier, Fanny (Translator)
  1905   *The Narrative of Álvar Núñez Cabeza de Vaca. The Trail Makers.* A. S. Barnes, New York.
Bolton, Herbert E.
  1949   *Coronado: Knight of Pueblos and Plains.* University of New Mexico Press, Albuquerque.
Brain, Jeffrey
  1975   Artifacts of the Adelantado. *Conference on Historic Site Archaeology Papers* 8:129–138.
Crosby, Alfred
  1972   *The Columbian Exchange: Biological Consequences of 1492.* Greenwood Press, Westport.
Deagan, Kathleen
  1987   *Artifacts of the Spanish Colonies of Florida and the Caribbean, 1550–1800. Vol. 1: Ceramics, Glassware, and Beads.* Smithsonian Institution Press, Washington, D.C.
Dobyns, Henry F.
  1983   *Their Number Become Thinned: Native American Population Dynamics in Eastern North America.* University of Tennessee Press, Knoxville.
Goggin, John M.
  1947   Manifestations of a Southern Cult in Northwest Florida. *American Antiquity* 12:273–276.
Griffin, John W.
  1947   Some Comments on a Site in the St. Marks Wildlife Refuge, Florida. *American Antiquity* 13:182–183.
Hann, John H.
  1988a *Apalachee: The Land between the Rivers.* Ripley P. Bullen Monographs in Anthropology and History No. 8. University Presses of Florida, Gainesville.
  1988b Translation of the Florida Section of the Álvar Núñez Cabeza de Vaca Accounts of the 1528 Trek from South Florida to Apalachee led by Pánfilo de Narváez. Ms. on file, Florida Bureau of Archaeological Research, Tallahassee.
  1988c Translation of the Florida Section of the Report of the Outcome of the Journey that Hernando de Soto made and of the characteristics of the land through which he traveled written by Luys Hernández de Biedma. Ms. on file, Florida Bureau of Archaeological Research, Tallahassee.

1988d Translation of the Apalachee Section of the Narrative about the de Soto Expedition written by Gonzalo Fernández de Oviedo y Valdéz and based on the Diary of Rodrigo Ranjel, de Soto's Private Secretary. Ms. on file, Florida Bureau of Archaeological Research, Tallahassee.

Helms, Mary W.
1988 *Ulysses' Sail: An Ethnographic Odyssey of Power, Knowledge, and Geographical Distance.* Princeton University Press, Princeton.

Johnson, Jay K.
1969 Two Sites on the St. Marks Wildlife Refuge. Unpublished Bachelor's thesis, Department of Anthropology, Florida State University, Tallahassee.

Kary, William W.
1939 Log of Mound's Tower Archaeological Expedition, August 23–25, 1939. Ms. on file, Florida Bureau of Archaeological Research, Tallahassee.
1940 Report on Mound's Tower. Ms. on file, Florida Bureau of Archaeological Research, Tallahassee.

Lyon, Eugene
1981 Spain's Sixteenth-century North American Settlement Attempts: A Neglected Aspect. *Florida Historical Quarterly* 59:275–291.

Marrinan, Rochelle A., and Stephen C. Bryne
1985 Apalachee-Mission Survey: Final Report. Vol. 1. Ms. on file, Florida Bureau of Historic Preservation, Tallahassee.

Mitchem, Jeffrey M.
1988 Archaeological and Ethnohistorical Evidence for the Location of Narváez's Aute. Paper presented at the 52nd Annual Meeting of the Florida Academy of Science, Tampa.

Mitchem, Jeffrey M., and Bonnie G. McEwan
1988 New Data on Early Bells from Florida. *Southeastern Archaeology* 7:39–49,

Moore, Clarence B.
1902 Certain Aboriginal Remains of the Northwest Florida Coast, Part II. *Journal of the Philadelphia Academy of Natural Sciences* 12:128–358.

Morison, Samuel Eliot
1971 *The European Discovery of America: The Northern Voyages.* A.D. *500–1600.* Oxford University Press, New York.
1974 *The European Discovery of America: The Southern Voyages.* A.D. *1492–1616.* Oxford University Press, New York.

Parkes, Henry B.
1970 *A History of Mexico.* Houghton Mifflin, Boston.

Ramenofsky, Ann F.
1982 *The Archaeology of Population Collapse: Native American Response to the Introduction of Infectious Disease.* Unpublished Ph.D. dissertation, University of Washington. University Microfilms, Ann Arbor.

Scarry, John F.
1985 A Proposed Revision of the Fort Walton Ceramic Typology: A Type-Variety System. *Florida Anthropologist* 38:199–233.
1988 Stability and Change in the Apalachee Chiefdom: Centralization, Decentralization, and Social Reproduction. Ms. on file, Florida Bureau of Archaeological Research, Tallahassee.
1989a A Provisional Chronological Sequence for Apalachee Province. Ms. on file, Florida Bureau of Archaeological Research, Tallahassee.
1989b The Rise, Transformation, and Fall of Apalachee: A Case Study of Political Change in a Chiefly Society. In *Lamar Archaeology: Mississippian Chiefdoms in the Deep South,* edited by M. Williams and G. Shapiro. University of Alabama Press, Tuscaloosa, in press.

Smith, Buckingham (Translator)

1866   *Narratives of the Career of Hernando de Soto in the Conquest of Florida*. Bradford Club, New York.

Smith, Marion F., Jr., and John F. Scarry

1988   Apalachee Settlement Distribution: The View from the Florida Master Site File. *Florida Anthropologist* 41:351–364.

1989   A Disquieting Synthesis of Apalachee Fort Walton: Micro-scales for Mississippian Research. Paper presented at the 54th Annual Meeting of the Society for American Archaeology, Atlanta.

Smith, Marvin T.

1987   *Archaeology of Aboriginal Culture Change in the Interior Southeast: Depopulation during the Early Historic Period*. Ripley P. Bullen Monographs in Anthropology and History No. 6. University Presses of Florida, Gainesville.

Swanton, John R.

1939   *Final Report of the United States De Soto Expedition Commission*. U.S. House of Representatives, 76th Cong., 1st sess., Doc. 71. Government Printing Office, Washington, D.C.

Todorov, Tzvetan

1984   *The Conquest of America: The Question of the Other*. Translated by Richard Howard. Harper Torchbooks, New York.

Willey, Gordon R.

1949   *Archeology of the Florida Gulf Coast*. Smithsonian Miscellaneous Collections 113. Government Printing Office, Washington, D.C.

Wright, Irene A.

1910   *The Early History of Cuba*. Macmillan, New York.

Chapter 6 ■

Charles R. Ewen

Soldier of Fortune: Hernando de Soto in the Territory of the Apalachee, 1539–1540

When Christopher Columbus discovered the New World for Spain he was searching for a quick route to the riches of the East Indies. The enormity of this discovery, although apparently lost on its discoverer, was quickly realized by his more astute colleagues. Columbus discovered and explored much of the Caribbean, but was unable to exploit his discoveries. Others, such as Hernan Cortéz and Francisco Pizarro, realized great fortunes and became known as conquistadors. Within 50 years of Columbus's first voyage of discovery, the circum-Caribbean peoples had succumbed to the process of exploitation by their conquerers. However, the local populations to the north proved to be far more difficult to subdue.

Three Spanish conquistadors tried to subdue La Florida prior to 1539. All three failed, dying in the attempt. In the meantime a more capable conquistador was proving his mettle in the New World.

Imperial Ambitions

Hernando de Soto demonstrated that he possessed a good military sense and leadership ability while serving under Francisco Pizarro. A key figure in the conquest of the Inca empire, his success in Peru brought him great wealth but little satisfaction.

Using the wealth gained from his Peruvian exploits, de Soto assembled one of the youngest, best-equipped, and most disciplined armies to sail to the New World. He landed with a force of over 600 people (including two Spanish women), over 200 horses, a herd of swine, a few mules, and dogs trained for combat.

The asiento, or contract, with the king of Spain was quite explicit as to what was required of de Soto. He was expected to pay for the expedition but would receive big rewards if it was successful. So, if all went well, the Spanish Crown would gain territory and income at no risk while the conquistador gained wealth and titles. However, failure to live up to the terms of the asiento was grounds to be tried for treason.

Such were the motivations of the conquistadors in general, and Hernando de Soto in particular. These were not, as the Black Legend paints them, inhuman monsters driven by an insatiable lust for gold. Rather, they were ambitious men, in difficult circumstances, with a lot at stake. The native inhabitants of the New World presented a challenge to these ambitions to be overcome by negotiation, intimidation, or warfare, whichever was most expedient. The native responses varied with the particular circumstances: alliance, resistance, or flight. However, the biological consequences of European contact eventually rendered the native responses moot.

The Assault on La Florida

Hernando de Soto set sail from Havana on May 18, 1539 and arrived off the coast of Florida seven days later (Figure 1-3). The previous experiences of the expeditions convinced de Soto to adopt an aggressive policy of intimidation with the natives rather than negotiation. Pressing its way northward through the Florida peninsula, the army arrived on the banks of the Aucilla River on October 1 (Swanton 1985:310). This river marked the eastern boundary of the Apalachee Province (see Figure 5-1).

Throughout the peninsula the Spaniards had heard tales of the rich and powerful chiefdom of the Apalachee. The Apalachee hotly contested the entry of de Soto's army into their territory. Failing to halt the Spaniards' advance, they burned the first village that the Spaniards encountered, Ivitachuco, rather than allow it to fall into enemy hands (Hann 1988f:3). By October 6 the expedition had advanced to the principal town of Anhaica, which the Apalachee had hastily abandoned. According to the Gentleman of Elvas, a Portuguese knight on the expedition, "in this settlement, the field master, whose duty it is to assign and provide lodging, lodged everyone round about this settlement" (Hann 1988d:21). He goes on to describe the Apalachee territory.

> At [a distance] half a league and a league [from Anhaica] there were others [settlements] where there was a great deal of maize, squash, and beans and dried plums of the land that are better than those of Spain and that grow through the

fields without their being planted. From these settlements on to Anhaica Apalache the provisions were gathered that appeared would be sufficient to last through the winter [Hann 1988d:21–22].

De Soto seized the opportunity to set up a winter headquarters, as a sixteenth-century chronicler of the expedition relates:

> With these intentions he ordered the collecting of all the provisions that should be possible. He ordered the building of many houses in addition to those that the village had so that it would have suitable lodging for all his soldiers. He had the site fortified, which seemed to him to be appropriate for the security of his people [Hann 1988e:84].

The rest that de Soto's army sought was not to be found at Anhaica that winter. The five-month encampment at Anhaica passed under siege conditions.

> The natives of this province during the entire time that the Spaniards were wintering in their land showed themselves [to be] very warlike and eager and that they showed concern and persistence in attacking the Castillians without losing an opportunity or occasion, no matter how slight it might be in which they might be able to wound or to kill those who strayed from the camp [Hann 1988e: 135].

Despite the fact that the village of 250 structures was fortified and sentries posted, the Apalachee succeeded twice in setting part of the camp on fire (Hann 1988c:11). Neither side lamented when the entrada broke camp on March 3, 1540, and moved north into Georgia.

Three years later the battered army limped into a Spanish outpost in northern Mexico. The campaign had cost the lives of half the army and its leader, Hernando de Soto. The native population, however, were the real victims. The passing of the Spaniards had irrevocable consequences, which doomed the ab-original way of life.

The Quest for Anhaica

The large, heavily equipped Spanish expedition traveled the Southeast for four years and yet few material remains of its passing have been discovered. Jeffrey Brain, in his introduction to the reprinted edition of Swanton's "Final Report of the United States DeSoto Expedition Commission," thought that the site of Anhaica would be one of the best opportunities on the entire route to identify a de Soto campsite:

> The possibilities are fairly well circumscribed and within the scope of a realistic program of archaeological research. Furthermore, the stay was a lengthy one by the entire army, and many buildings and fortifications were constructed that should be manifest in architectural features contrasting with native constructions. Finally, only in its first year, the army was still well accoutered and recently re-supplied from its base camp at the landing [Swanton 1985:xxi].

However, the exact location of de Soto's first winter encampment eluded the searches of historians and archaeologists for over a century. All scholars agreed that the site must be within or very near the present city of Tallahassee, but there agreement ended—until 1987.

The Martin site (named after former Florida governor John Martin, whose mansion dominates the site) was serendipitously discovered in March 1987 by B. Calvin Jones, an archaeologist with the Florida Bureau of Archaeological Research. Jones, who has been responsible for locating the sites of nine seventeenth-century mission sites in north Florida (see Jones and Shapiro, this volume), had suspected for some time that a ridgetop east of the Florida Capitol Building was the site of a Spanish mission. The ridge was occupied by an established residential neighborhood, so there was no urgency to test this hypothesis. However, plans made in early 1987 to develop part of this ridge into an office complex prompted Jones to investigate.

Anhaica Revealed

Initial testing by Jones unearthed aboriginal pottery and pieces of Spanish Olive Jar, which led him to believe that a Spanish mission had, indeed, been located. The developers granted a two-week delay in construction, allowing Jones to hastily assemble a crew of volunteers to conduct salvage excavations. Mobilizing the volunteers, Jones was able to open several units and recover an impressive array of artifacts. These included early-style Olive Jar fragments (A.D. 1492–1570), late Fort Walton period aboriginal ceramics (A.D. 1450–1600), wrought iron nails, blown glass beads (Figure 6-1), and small links of iron (which were correctly interpreted as chain mail armor; Figure 6-2).

The artifacts puzzled Jones and other local archaeologists since they tend to predate the seventeenth century. In addition, the material assemblage lacked the Spanish tin-glazed majolica tablewares and Leon-Jefferson period ceramics that characterize the missions of north Florida. It became apparent that the site represented contact prior to the seventeenth century. In the Tallahassee area, Spanish artifacts dating to the sixteenth century are most reasonably from the

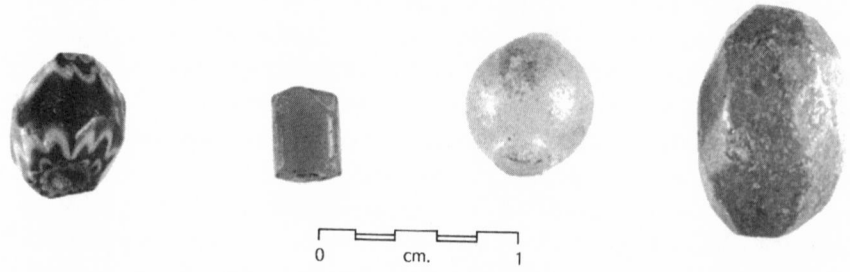

0   cm.   1

Figure 6-1. Sixteenth-century beads from the Martin site. Left to right: faceted chevron, Nueva Cadiz, blown glass, faceted.

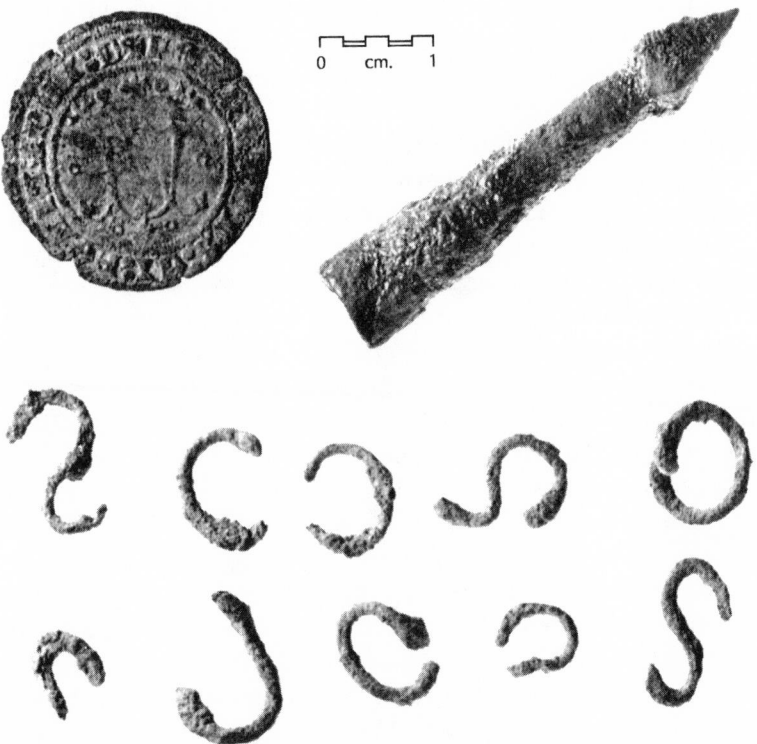

Figure 6-2. Metal artifacts from the Martin site: Spanish four-maravedi coin (top left), crossbow quarrel (top right), iron chain mail links (bottom).

de Soto entrada, although initially the earlier expedition of Pánfilo de Narváez (1528) could not be ruled out.

The suggestive nature of the early finds prompted more formal excavation under the codirection of Jones and myself. Taxing the meager budget and the patience of the developers to the limit, eight months of full-scale excavation were performed. Formal analysis of the material, completed by the end of 1988, described a material assemblage consistent with what would be expected of Hernando de Soto's winter base camp in Florida.

Aboriginal artifacts account for approximately 90 percent of the material assemblage. The encampment was, after all, in an Apalachee village. The majority of the ceramics recovered were late Fort Walton types (A.D. 1450–1600), including Lake Jackson Plain, Lake Jackson Incised, several varieties of Fort Walton Incised, and many specimens of a punctated type that has been tentatively identified as Carrabelle Punctate *var. Meginnis* (Scarry 1985:211). This last type was formerly reported as Lake Jackson Fingernail Impressed (Griffin 1950:106) but later renamed in order to fit the type-variety system devised by Scarry (1985).

Spanish ceramics, as might be expected of a military exploratory expedition, are relatively uncommon at the Martin site. The prevailing Spanish ware is Olive Jar, used by the Spaniards to transport wine, water, olive oil, and a variety of other commodities. Ubiquitous to Spanish sites in the New World, the utilitarian Olive Jar can be distinguished on the basis of rim type and vessel form (Goggin 1960:28). Identifiable rim and handle fragments from the Martin site can be classified as early style (Deagan 1987:28). Other Spanish ceramics recovered were Columbia Plain (A.D. 1492–1650), including a green variant that tends to date before 1550 (Deagan 1987:56); Caparra Blue (A.D. 1492–1600); and an unnamed variety of lead-glazed coarse earthenware with a soft red, sandy paste that dates to the first three-quarters of the sixteenth century (Deagan 1987:53).

European trade beads recovered from the site helped to place it in its chronological context and tied it to other de Soto contact sites in the Southeast. Many of these beads (e.g., small seed beads) could not be assigned to a specific time range. However, some types were good sixteenth-century index artifacts (Figure 6-1). These types included a gooseberry bead, 7 blown glass beads, a faceted amber bead, a small Nueva Cadiz bead, and 12 faceted chevron beads. With the exception of the amber bead, all of these bead types have been found at other sites thought to be associated with the de Soto expedition. Beads similar to the blown glass beads found at the Martin site have been reported from the Poarch Farm site in northern Georgia, located along the expedition's route. However, the uncertain provenience of these blown beads suggests a possible recent date of manufacture (Smith 1989).

Metal artifacts account for a significant portion of the material assemblage from the Martin site. Dozens of wrought iron nails and tacks of various sizes and types were retrieved. One unusual type, with a peaked head, has also been reported from a site in New Mexico, and is possibly associated with the Coronado expedition (Vierra 1987). Coronado's expedition was exploring the Southwestern United States at approximately the same time de Soto was exploring the Southeast.

The military nature of the expedition was evident in a crossbow quarrel recovered from the Martin site (Figure 6-2). The crossbow was, in fact, the principal weapon of de Soto's army. Coats of mail, at least initially, were worn by the Spaniards as protection against personal attack. However, an incident involving a captured Apalachee bowman (Hann 1988e:104–106) convinced them of the ineffectiveness of this armor.

> The Spaniards . . . wanted to see how good the highly polished coats were in which they had such great confidence . . . they placed a basket in the plaza . . . and having chosen the most valued coat of mail among those which they brought, they placed it over the basket . . . and, releasing an Indian from those of Apalachee from the chain in which he was, they gave him a bow and arrow and ordered him to shoot at the coat of mail, which was fifty paces from them. The Indian . . . fired the arrow. The latter passed through the coat of mail and basket so cleanly and with such force that, had it encountered a man on the other side, it would also have passed through him.

Placing a second coat of mail over the first did not effectively mitigate the results. This, then, prompted the Spaniards to throw their iron armor aside in favor of quilted coats.

Although it seems unlikely that the Spaniards would have actually discarded this expensive equipment, many individual iron and brass links have been recovered from the Martin site (Figure 6-2). It may be that the iron armor was showing the effects of long marches through swamps, rivers, and the tropical downpours that characterize summer afternoons in Florida. The scattered nature of the links indicate the loss of individual links rather than the disposal of entire coats of mail.

The public's imagination was captured most by five copper coins that found their way onto the front page of several newspapers, T-shirts, and even Paul Harvey's "News at Noon." Like the mail, the coins were found scattered across the site. This suggests deposition as a result of loss rather than intentional burial. Two of the coins were Spanish maravedis (Figure 6-2), coins of little worth to the Spaniards, and were probably brought along incidentally. They were minted in Spain between 1505 and 1517 specifically for trade in the Indies (Mitchell 1987:10). The other three coins, although badly corroded, appear to be Portuguese ceitils dating to the sixteenth century or even earlier (William Bischoff: personal communication).

All of these artifacts placed the site in an early sixteenth-century context, but could not definitely distinguish between affiliation with either the Narváez or de Soto expeditions. During the final month of the excavation conclusive evidence, in the form of the shattered jawbone of a pig, was unearthed in association with a sixteenth-century structure. The Narváez expedition was reduced to eating their leather and horses by the time they reached the Apalachee territory (Hann 1988a, 1988b). Learning from his predecessor's mistakes, de Soto brought along a heard of swine to serve as "food on the hoof" when the army was unable to live off the land. It was de Soto who, in fact, introduced pigs to north Florida.

The Importance of the Martin Site

The site of Hernando de Soto's first winter camp is one of the most significant sites to be excavated in recent years (see Ewen 1989; Shapiro 1988). Historically, the expedition was Spain's most ambitious exploratory venture into North America. The impact of the Spaniards' passing, particularly in a biological sense, was tremendous. Widespread losses to the aboriginal population due to disease introduced by de Soto's party resulted in demographic shifts and social upheaval (see Smith 1987). Later, during the seventeenth century, Spanish soldiers and missionaries in the Apalachee province described an aboriginal culture that must have been greatly changed from that encountered by the de Soto expedition. It has even been suggested that the process of population loss was already under way as a result of the earlier Narváez visitation (Dobyns 1983:23). The Martin site represents one of the latest protohistoric sites in the Apalachee province and has begun to shed light on the cultural transition from the Fort Walton period to the Mission period in north Florida.

The Martin site is unique in that, at least for one of its components, a precise real-time date can be assigned to it. It is documented that the Spaniards spent from October 1539 to March 1540 at Anhaica. Thus the site will serve as a chronological anchor and can be used to help seriate other Apalachee sites and refine the local ceramic sequence. The Spanish artifacts are already being used for comparative purposes by other researchers to trace the route of de Soto through the Southeast.

There can be no question of the significance of the social, demographic, ecological, and ideological consequences of the de Soto entrada. It quite literally marked the end of the native hegemony in the Southeast and the beginning of European dominance, for better or worse. Yet this momentous event is given little coverage in modern history texts and most schoolchildren only know de Soto as the "discoverer" of the Mississippi River. Archaeological studies such as this one are important educational tools that encourage a greater understanding of the role of Spain in the history of the New World. They also serve to focus popular attention on the native population and the tragic consequences of European contact. It is important that the general public understand why the scholarly community has elected to commemorate rather than celebrate events such as the 450th anniversary of de Soto's landing or the Columbian Quincentenary.

References Cited

Deagan, Kathleen A.
  1987 *Artifacts of the Spanish Colonies of Florida and the Caribbean 1500–1800. Vol. 1: Ceramics, Glassware, and Beads*. Smithsonian Institution Press, Washington, D.C.
Dobyns, Henry F.
  1983 *Their Number Become Thinned: Native American Population Dynamics in Eastern North America*. University of Tennessee Press, Knoxville.
Ewen, Charles R.
  1989 Apalachee Winter. *Archaeology* 42:37–39.
Goggin, John M.
  1960 *The Spanish Olive Jar: An Introductory Study*. Yale University Publications in Anthropology No. 62. Yale University Press, New Haven.
Griffin, John W.
  1950 Test Excavations at the Lake Jackson Site. *American Antiquity* 16(2):99–112.
Hann, John T. (translator)
  1988a Translation of the Florida Section of the Álvar Núñez Cabeza de Vaca Accounts of the 1528 Trek from South Florida to Apalachee Led by Pánfilo de Narváez. Ms. on file, Bureau of Archaeological Research, Tallahassee.
  1988b Translation of the Apalachee Section of the Account Written by Álvar Núñez Cabeza de Vaca about the Expedition Led by Pánfilo de Narváez and about His Own Experiences. Ms. on file, Bureau of Archaeological Research, Tallahassee.
  1988c Translation of the Apalachee Section of the Narrative about the de Soto Expedition Written by Gonzalo Fernandez de Oviedo and Based on the Diary of Rodrigo Ranjel, de Soto's Private Secretary. Ms. on file, Bureau of Archaeological Research, Tallahassee.
  1988d Transcription and Translation of the Apalachee Section of the Hidalgo de Elvas' True Relation of the Labors that the Governor Don Fernando de Souto and Certain Portuguese Gentlemen Experienced in the Exploration of the Province of Florida. Now Newly Made by a Gentleman of Elvas. Ms. on file, Bureau of Archaeological Research, Tallahassee.
  1988e Transcription and Translation of the Apalachee Section of Garcilaso de la Vega's

Florida of the Inca. Ms. on file, Bureau of Archaeological Research, Tallahassee.

1988f Transcription and Translation of the Apalachee Section of Luys Hernandez de Biedma's Report of the Outcome of the Journey that Hernando de Soto Made and of the Characteristics of the Land through Which He Traveled. Ms. on file, Bureau of Archaeological Research, Tallahassee.

Mitchell, Mary

1987 Finding, Significance, and Excavation of the De Soto Site. Ms. in possession of the author.

Scarry, John F.

1985 A Proposed Revision of the Fort Walton Ceramic Typology: A Type-Variety System. *Florida Anthropologist* 38(3):199–233.

Shapiro, Gary

1988 Trailing the Apalachee. *Archaeology* 41(2):58–59.

Smith, Marvin T.

1987 *Archaeology of Aboriginal Culture Change in the Interior Southeast: Depopulation during the Early Historic Period*. University Presses of Florida, Gainesville.

1989 Glass Beads from the Governor Martin Site. Ms. on file, Bureau of Archaeological Research, Tallahassee, Florida.

Swanton, John R.

1985 *Final Report of the United States De Soto Expedition Commission*. Reprinted. Smithsonian Institution Press, Washington, D.C. Originally published U.S. House of Representatives, 76th Cong., 1st sess., Doc. 71. Government Printing Office, Washington, D.C.

Vierra, Bradley J.

1987 A Sixteenth-Century Spanish Campsite in the Tigeux Province: An Archaeologist's Perspective. Paper presented to the 65th Annual Meeting of the Southwestern Social Science Association, Dallas.

Chapter 7 ▮

John F. Scarry

Beyond Apalachee Province: Assessing the Evidence for Early European–Indian Contact in West Florida

The approach of the Columbian Quincentenary has done much to spur interest in the sixteenth-century Southeast. In recent years we have learned a great deal about the native polities, the first European explorers of La Florida, the early settlements at Santa Elena and St. Augustine, and the missions in Timucua, Guale, and Apalachee. But there are still many gaps in our knowledge, gaps that limit our understanding of the social and political organization of the native peoples in particular. It is difficult to trace the routes taken by the early explorers in any save the most general terms, and the sites associated with particular expeditions can be counted on the fingers of one's hands (for example, the National Park Service has identified only one site as being positively associated with the de Soto expedition; National Park Service 1989:Table 1). We are beginning to learn about the responses Europeans made to life in the New World, but we know next to nothing of the responses the Native Americans made. We know the names, histories, and in many instances the locations of missions, but what do we know of the motives of the peoples of the Southeast who converted to Catholicism? We know there were many contacts between European and native, but how adequately have we examined the variety of those contacts? A simple illustration of that variety, and how little is known of it, can be seen in a comparison of Apalachee Province and Choctawhatchee Bay in northwestern Florida.

The Apalachee were one of the first native groups to encounter Spanish explorers and settlers. Alonso de Pineda may have touched land in their territory in 1519, Pánfilo de Narváez spent two months there in 1528, and Hernando de Soto spent five months there in 1539–1540. According to their charters from the Crown, both Narváez and de Soto were to explore and settle La Florida, and they both carried supplies of European goods such as bells and beads to trade with the people they met (Brain 1975). Given all this, Apalachee Province would seem a most likely place to find evidence of early contact.

The available documentary evidence for Apalachee is good, at least compared with the evidence for other groups from the Southeast. The archaeological evidence, however, is neither as abundant nor as clear as one might hope. Despite considerable effort, de Soto's encampment was not found until 1987 (Ewen and Jones 1988; see Ewen, this volume). Only three other sites from the area have yielded European goods, and only one of those can be even tentatively tied to a particular expedition or time (see Marrinan et al., this volume).

The Choctawhatchee Bay area of northwest Florida stands in contrast to Apalachee Province. It was not a focus of early Spanish exploratory or colonial efforts. The major sixteenth-century expeditions bypassed it. There were no missions established there. There were no early colonial settlements there. Nevertheless, sites around Choctawhatchee Bay have yielded evidence of early contact between Europeans and Native Americans. As early as 1901 Clarence B. Moore discovered European artifacts in association with native burials (Moore 1901).

Surprisingly enough, neither Moore's discoveries nor later finds have sparked the interest that the Apalachee sites and artifacts have. There has been little effort to learn more about the archaeology of the Choctawhatchee Bay area. We know far more about Apalachee Province—about the Europeans who might have been there and the natives who lived there, and therefore about the contact between the two peoples—than we do about Choctawhatchee Bay.

In this chapter I examine the little that is known about sixteenth-century Choctawhatchee Bay, beginning with the archaeological evidence of European–Native American contact in the area. I also look at the parties involved and the nature and results of their contact.

The Evidence of Contact

The evidence of European–Native American contact in the Choctawhatchee Bay region is limited but clear. It consists of artifacts of European manufacture found as offerings in native burials. There are no historic accounts that unambiguously describe meetings between Europeans and natives in the area. There is nothing like the de Soto chronicles that describe the contact in Apalachee Province.

The European artifacts from Choctawhatchee Bay sites are varied and include glass beads and finger rings, objects of iron, brass and copper bells, and a single

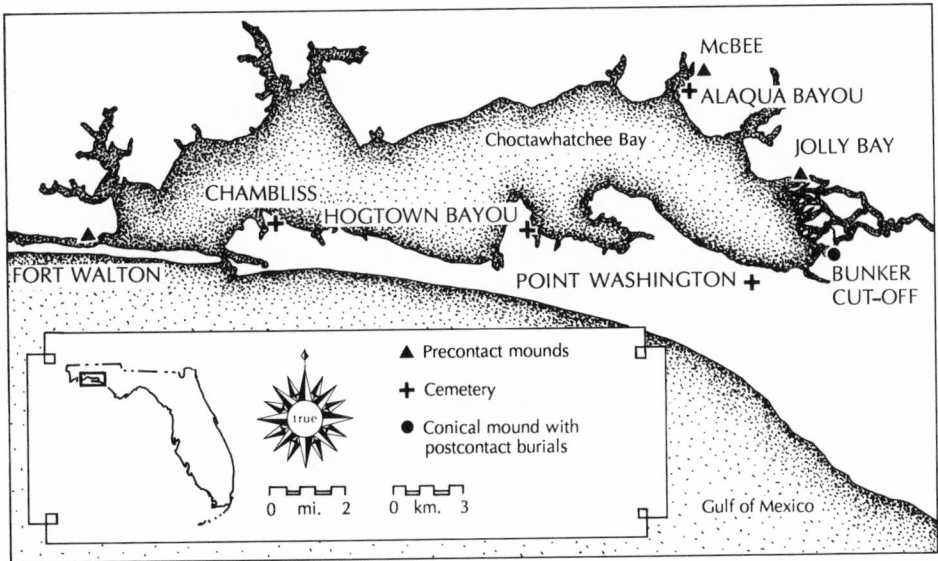

Figure 7-1. Late prehistoric and protohistoric sites of the Choctawhatchee Bay area.

copper coin. For the most part, the artifacts could be from the standard explorer's kit of "goodies" (Brain 1975). Unfortunately, many of the artifacts are poorly described and those discovered by Clarence B. Moore early in this century may not be available for study. For this reason, some of the suggested identifications in this chapter are just that, suggestions.

Four Choctawhatchee Bay sites have yielded European goods: Point Washington, Bunker Cut-off, Hogtown Bayou, and Alaqua Bayou (Figure 7-1). All are mortuary sites. There are no European artifacts from habitation sites. Clarence B. Moore excavated at the Point Washington site in 1901 (1901:472–496) and at Bunker Cut-off (1918:519–520) and Hogtown Bayou (1918:535–541) in 1918. Willey (1949:220, 225–227) was unable to find the sites during his 1940 survey, but William Lazarus relocated Point Washington (1959) and Hogtown (1958) in the late 1950s and conducted minor investigations at both sites. Fairbanks (1965:259) made a cursory examination of the Bunker Cut-off site in the late 1950s. Fairbanks (1965:259) also excavated at Hogtown Bayou in the late 1950s. Most recently, one of the site's owners donated a large collection of aboriginal pottery to the Florida Bureau of Archaeological Research. Alaqua Bayou escaped Moore and was not discovered until the late 1950s. Lazarus conducted limited excavations there in 1957.

The Point Washington cemetery contained both single and multiple burials. There were single skulls, skulls and long bones, bundle burials, and mass deposits of bone. All were secondary interments. Moore excavated over 100 burials during his work at the site. At Point Washington, Moore found some European goods associated with burials and others not associated with skeletal remains. The European items included glass beads, glass finger rings, an iron chisel, and undescribed iron objects. The glass beads were associated with several burials, as was the iron chisel (Moore 1901:478). The glass rings were loose in the sand and not associated with particular burials. During his excavation, Lazarus found several unidentified pieces of iron (1959).

Bunker Cut-off was a small mound (ca. 1 m high and 13 m in diameter) containing aboriginal burials. Moore excavated nine burial pits, only seven of which contained recognizable remains. All the burials were single secondary interments. The European assemblage from Bunker Cut-off was very limited. Moore (1918:519) found a single large iron spike in "the sand thrown back by our men in the demolition of the mound." When Fairbanks revisited the site, he found a small copper harness bell in Moore's backdirt (Fairbanks 1965:259).

The Hogtown Bayou site was another cemetery. Moore described it as a duplicate of the cemetery at Point Washington. It also contained both single burials and multiple secondary burials consisting of single skulls, skulls and long bones, bundle burials, and mass deposits. Moore found glass beads, objects of iron (including a pair of scissors), brass bells, and a disk of tin. The scissors and one of the brass bells were associated with a multiple secondary burial that also contained shell beads. Moore (1918:540) described this bell as resembling a sleigh bell or possibly a hawksbell, although he thought that it was large for the latter possibility. He found a tubular glass bead with a single skull also accompanied by a small celt, three projectile points, and two sheet copper objects that he called lance points (Moore 1918:540). From the description, they may have been headdress ornaments similar to those found at Etowah (Larson 1959) and Lake Jackson (Jones 1982). During his excavations, Fairbanks (1960:150, 1965:259) found one Ichtucknee Blue glass bead.

The Alaqua Bayou site was also a cemetery. Lazarus (1957, 1964, 1965) found a single copper two-maravedi coin in limited excavations there. He also mentions a possible fragment of gold or pyrite in a collection from the site (1957). Fairbanks (1965:259) mentions having seen a "piece of roughly reworked iron" in a collection from the site.

All the European artifacts from the Choctawhatchee Bay area were recovered from mortuary contexts, which are usually excellent sources of information about social and political organization. This is not the case for the Choctawhatchee Bay data. There are no complete reports on any of the sites (if you ignore Moore's reports). The excavators did not report the precise provenience data needed to reconstruct individual grave lots. The major excavations at the sites were conducted by people primarily interested in recovering whole or reconstructible vessels. Screens were only rarely used and individual artifacts were, by and large, poorly provenienced. With one exception, the critical European artifacts have been inadequately described. The situation is further complicated by the fact that at least some of the artifacts were not associated with individual burials. For these reasons, the Choctawhatchee Bay cemeteries must be treated as single units at this time.

Fortunately, rough dates can be calculated for the sites. Both the European artifacts and the aboriginal ceramics found in the sites yield chronological information. The most easily and precisely datable object is the copper coin from Alaqua Bayou. The coin is a two-maravedi piece from the reign of Charles I of Spain. It was minted in Santo Domingo between 1532 and 1557 (Lazarus 1964:136). The one complication in using the coin to date the Alaqua Bayou site is the possibility that it was curated before being placed in the cemetery. It was pierced, probably so that it could be worn.

Glass beads are often used to date early contact sites since they are among the most common European artifacts and many of them can be dated quite precisely (e.g., Smith and Good 1982). Unfortunately, only one of the Choctawhatchee beads has been securely identified. At Hogtown Bayou, Fairbanks (1965:269) found an Ichtucknee Blue bead. This type is common on seventeenth-century sites in La Florida but it has been found on sixteenth-century sites as well. Deagan (1987:171) dates Ichtucknee Blue beads to the period 1575–1720. One other possible clue about the age of the Choctawhatchee Bay sites can be obtained from glass beads. Moore (1918:540) found tubular glass beads at Hogtown Bayou. Tubular Nueva Cadiz beads are markers for early sixteenth-century contact (Smith and Good 1982) and have been found at sites associated with Narváez and de Soto. If the Hogtown Bayou bead was a Nueva Cadiz bead, it should date to the first half of the sixteenth century (Deagan 1987:163). Unfortunately, the Hogtown Bayou bead is not securely identified as a Nueva Cadiz bead, and other tubular glass beads were in use throughout the seventeenth century.

Like glass beads, bells can be good chronological markers for early contact sites (Brain 1975; Brown 1979; Mitchem and McEwan 1988). Two of the Choctawhatchee Bay sites, Hogtown Bayou and Bunker Cut-off, have yielded bells. Unfortunately, like the glass beads from Choctawhatchee Bay, they cannot be identified from the available descriptions. The Choctawhatchee Bay bells might be sixteenth-century Clarksdale bells or they might be seventeenth-century Flushloop bells.

The aboriginal ceramics from the Choctawhatchee Bay sites can also provide chronological information. Although there are no quantified inventories of aboriginal ceramics from any of the contact sites around the Bay, they do contain types and varieties that appear to be chronologically sensitive markers.

All of the sites contain Pensacola series types and varieties including Moundville Incised, *var. Douglas,* Mound Place Incised, *var. Waltons Camp,* and Pensacola Incised, *vars. Pensacola, Perdido Bay, Bear Point,* and *Moore* (Fuller and Stowe 1982). These types are found on protohistoric Bear Point phase sites in Mobile and Perdido bays, although Mound Place Incised, *var. Waltons Camp,* and Pensacola Incised, *var. Pensacola,* are also found on prehistoric sites and Pensacola Incised, *var. Perdido Bay,* may first appear in very late prehistoric contexts. Fuller (1985) estimates that the Bear Point phase dates to A.D. 1500–1700.

The sites also contain chronologically sensitive Fort Walton series types and varieties including Fort Walton Incised, *vars. Choctawhatchee, Englewood, Fort Walton,* and *Safety Harbor,* Point Washington Incised, *vars. Chambliss, Hogtown Bayou,* and *Point Washington,* Lamar Complicated Stamped, *var. Early,* and Leon Check

Stamped (Scarry 1985). Fort Walton Incised, *var. Choctawhatchee*, is largely re-stricted to the Choctawhatchee Bay area and has only limited utitity for dating the contact sites. However, two of Moore's illustrated examples are stylistic equivalents of D'Olive Incised, *vars. D'Olive* and *Arnica*, both of which are found on Bear Point phase sites to the west (Fuller 1985; Fuller and Stowe 1982). The other Fort Walton types are all found on sixteenth-century Velda phase sites in Apalachee Province (e.g., Velda, St. Marks Fire Tower Cemetery, and the de Soto encampment site; Scarry 1989). Some can also be found on seventeenth-century San Luis phase sites, but as a whole they are more common at earlier sites.

On the basis of the available evidence, I would suggest that the early contact period sites around Choctawhatchee Bay date to the sixteenth century, and most of the contact appears to have taken place in the mid- to late 1500s. The sites are undoubtedly contemporaneous with the Bear Point phase sites of the Mobile Bay area.

The Parties to the Contact

The Natives

A fundamental problem in the archaeology of sixteenth-century Chocta-whatchee Bay is that the identity of the people responsible for the archaeolo-gical remains is unknown. So is their name. Even the limits of their territory are unknown. Early documents provide little information about the area or its inhabitants. Indeed, they provide little information on any part of the area be-tween Apalachee and Pensacola Bay. The sixteenth-century record is particu-larly poor, and the seventeenth-century record is not much better.

From the sixteenth century there are the accounts of three major Spanish ex-peditions that passed through northwestern Florida: the Narváez, de Soto, and Luna expeditions. From the Narváez expedition the accounts of Cabeza de Vaca provide some information on the peoples of the area, but they mention no native groups by name and it is difficult to tell where Narváez and his men were. From the de Soto expedition there are the accounts of Maldonado's expedition to Ochuse (which Swanton [1939:164] places at Pensacola Bay). Again there is little information provided about the people, and the location of Ochuse is vaguely described (60 leagues west of Apalachee Bay). From the Luna expedition there are descriptions of Pensacola and Mobile Bay but not of Choctawhatchee Bay. It is clear, however, that Luna thought Maldonado's Ochuse was Pensacola Bay and that Narváez's second major encounter with Native Americans after leaving Apalachee was at Mobile Bay.

If the sixteenth-century documents provide little information about the people of Choctawhatchee Bay, the seventeenth-century documents provide little more. Spanish efforts in the 1600s focused on St. Augustine and the missions of Timucua, Guale, and Apalachee. Spaniards did travel beyond Apalachee but they tended to lump the peoples of that area into a single "pagan Indian" category. The various accounts do mention five or six groups living in the area beyond Apalachee that might include the descendants of the sixteenth-century Choctawhatchee Bay peoples. The trans-Apalachee groups included the Chacato, the Chisca, the Pansacola, the Chine, the Savacola, and the Tawasa (Hann 1988b). Of these groups, the Pansacola and Chine are most likely.

The Chacato, the Chisca, the Savacola, and the Tawasa were probably not the people responsible for the protohistoric archaeological remains around Choctawhatchee Bay. In the seventeenth century, the Chacato lived along the Upper Chipola River. Archaeological data from that area suggest considerable continuity from the protohistoric, back to ca. A.D. 1200 or so (Gardner 1966, 1969; Calvin Jones, personal communication; Scarry 1984). The Chisca are mentioned in sixteenth-century documents and also those of the seventeenth century, but in the 1500s they appear to have been located far to the north of Apalachee (Hann 1988b:75). The Savacola are not mentioned until late in the seventeenth century. At this time they were located on the Apalachicola River and were linked with the Apalachicola communities that lived upstream on the Chattahoochee (Hann 1988b:86–87).

The ancestors of the Pansacola or the Chine might have been the sixteenth-century inhabitants of the Choctawhatchee Bay area. The Pansacola are not mentioned by name until late in the seventeenth century. At that time they lived around Pensacola Bay (Hann 1988b:80–81). Swanton (1946:119) considered the Chine to be a Chacato community, but Hann (1988b:84–85) argues that they have a distinct identity. One important fact about the Chine is their reputed knowledge of the coast west of Apalachee, and Chine served as pilots for voyages from Apalachee to Pensacola (Hann 1988b:85). Unfortunately, the accounts of the Chine all date from the late 1600s, when they were living in mission communities in Apalachee Province.

The archaeological remains from sites in the Choctawhatchee Bay area (and here I mean the ceramic assemblages recovered from sites in the area) suggest that the people living there were a distinct group. The ceramic complex shares types with the Bottle Creek and Bear Point phases of the Mobile Bay area to the west and with the Velda phase of the Apalachee area to the east. The Choctawhatchee Bay complex is not identical to the complexes found in either of these neighboring areas, however. The differences suggest that the people who lived around the bay had a discrete identity. Lazarus (1971) studied ceramic complexes along the northwest Florida coast and noticed that they varied by drainage. Sites within a single bay system had similar assemblages, and those assemblages differed from those of sites in neighboring bays. In particular, Lazarus found that the frequency of shell tempering varied from bay to bay, increasing from east to west.

If the people who lived around Choctawhatchee Bay were an independent group, what were they like? How were they organized and how did they live? Unfortunately, our archaeological and ethnohistorical data provide little evidence on their social and political organization or their subsistence.

We know that there were at least two classes of sites in the late prehistoric period: sites with pyramidal mounds (Fort Walton, Jolly Bay, and McBee [Figure 7-1]) and sites without. What is not clear is whether this constitutes a settlement hierarchy indicative of a hierarchical political organization. It is a possibility.

The burial populations in the Choctawhatchee Bay mortuary sites do not suggest status differentiation. The distribution of items does not cross-cut age and sex differences. There is nothing to suggest that certain individuals received greater expenditures of community labor or wealth. There is no evidence that some burials were spatially segregated. But we do not know how complete the mortuary data are.

The four known cemetery sites from the bay area (Chambliss, Hogtown Bayou, Point Washington, and Alaqua Bayou) are spaced at roughly equal 10-km intervals along the coast (Figure 7-1). This spacing suggests that there might be two additional cemeteries along the north shore of the bay. The spacing may reflect competition between equivalent population and political units or the subordination of several communities under a higher-level political authority at the two large mound centers (Fort Walton and Jolly Bay).

The subsistence base of the native inhabitants of Choctawhatchee Bay is also unclear. Their ceramic assemblage and the pyramidal mounts at Jolly Bay and Fort Walton look like those constructed by Mississippian peoples in the interior Southeast. The Mississippian peoples relied on cleared field agriculture for most of their food, but did the Choctawhatchee Bay people?

Three pieces of evidence suggest that they did not. First, the sandy soils around Choctawhatchee Bay are not conducive to maize agriculture even today. Second, accounts from both the Narváez and Luna expeditions suggest that the coastal area was not occupied by large-scale farming groups. In his first sustained contact with native peoples after leaving Apalachee, Narváez traded maize for fish and water (Hann 1988a:17). Given the state of the Narváez expedition at that time, it is unlikely that they would have traded maize away. When Luna's expedition set off inland from Pensacola Bay, the group found no significant settlements immediately inland from the bay, but only a small population scattered along the banks of the Escambia River (Hann 1988b:61). Third, skeletal remains from the area show a low incidence of caries and appreciable wear (Lazarus 1971).

Although there is little evidence for aboriginal maize production, there is evidence for the use of marine resources—fish and shellfish. The habitation sites around the shores of Choctawhatchee Bay are shell middens. There are no quantified studies of faunal remains from Choctawhatchee Bay sites, but Claassen (1985) has studied shellfish remains from Mississippian-age sites in the Pensacola Bay system just to the west. She found that they were collected in late summer and early fall. In his account of the Narváez expedition, Vaca reports finding dried mullet and roe at settlements along the coast (Hann 1988b:61) and Narváez traded maize for fish. Luna found sites with small maize fields around Pensacola Bay but nothing like the extensive fields of Mississippian groups like the Apalachee.

The Europeans

The Europeans who were the sources of the artifacts from Choctawhatchee Bay are no more securely identified than the natives who received them. Among the possibilities are the sixteenth-century expeditions of Alonso de Pineda, Pánfilo de Narváez, Hernando de Soto, and Tristán de Luna. Other possibilities are slave raiders and shipwreck victims.

Pineda explored the Gulf coast in 1519, landing near Apalachee Bay and discovering Mobile Bay and the Mississippi River (Harrisse 1892:173). He may have encountered the people of Choctawhatchee Bay, but his voyage was too early for him to be a likely source of the known European goods.

Narváez is a better candidate. After leaving Apalachee in 1528 he and his men sailed along the Gulf coast. They had two significant encounters with native peoples before they passed far beyond the Choctawhatchee Bay area. The first encounter took place when the expedition took shelter inside a headland. There they were met by natives in canoes. Since they were in great need of water, they followed the canoes for about a league to a village beside the water. Narváez gave the cacique "beads and hawksbells and maize" in exchange for fish and water (Hann 1988a:17).

The second encounter took place four days after they left the first site. Again the Spaniards were in need of drinking water and met natives in canoes. This time two members of the expedition went in search of water while several native hostages remained with the barges of the expedition. The two Spaniards never returned (Hann 1988a:18–19). Swanton (1946:38–39) suggests that this second encounter took place in Mobile Bay, since the de Soto expedition heard reports that two Spaniards had been killed in Piachi on the Alabama River upstream from Mobile Bay. He also suggests that the natives were Choctaw or were related to the Choctaw, since they wore their hair long. If Swanton is correct about the location of the second encounter, the first encounter may well have been in Choctawhatchee Bay. Narváez and his men could have met the inhabitants of the Choctawhatchee Bay area and given them beads and bells, but they were there too early to account for the maravedi coin at Alaqua Bayou.

De Soto's lieutenant Francisco Maldonado led an expedition west from Apalachee in 1539–1540 in search of a good harbor. Sixty leagues from Apalachee Bay he found a "port sheltered from all winds, capable of handling many ships and with good depth" (Hann 1988c). The harbor was located in a province called Ochuse. After returning to Apalachee Province, Maldonado was sent to Cuba to obtain additional provisions and bring them to Ochuse to meet the expedition. De Soto and his men never made it to Ochuse, of course. Ochuse could have been the Choctawhatchee Bay area. It is close to 60 leagues (using the *lengua legal*, Chardon 1980) from Apalachee Bay to Choctawhatchee Bay. But, again, Maldonado was there too early to account for all the known artifacts.

Tristán de Luna attempted to establish a colony on Pensacola Bay in 1559. He thought that it was the location of Maldonado's Bay of Ochuse. Apparently he did not go to Choctawhatchee Bay. Nevertheless his expedition was in the area at the right time and might have been the source of at least some of the artifacts from Choctawhatchee Bay.

The Nature of the Contact

Some things about the contact between Europeans and the natives of Choctawhatchee Bay are clear. The remains are not from an encampment of one of the major expeditions. They are not from a major Spanish settlement. They are not from Spanish missions.

What they probably represent are the results of several contacts between Europeans and Native Americans, perhaps over the course of several generations during the middle to late sixteenth century. The contact was not sustained. It did not lead to attempts to settle or establish missions in the area. The Spaniards apparently did not pay it much heed. Such intermittent, but continued contact was unlike the interaction between the Spaniards at St. Augustine and the Timucuan peoples of northeastern Florida. It was also unlike the early intense contact between large Spanish expeditions and the Apalachee or the later sustained Mission period contact between the Apalachee and the Spaniards.

Conclusions

There was contact between Europeans and Native Americans in the Choctawhatchee Bay area in the sixteenth century. The evidence is incontrovertible. The available evidence also points to a sixteenth-century date for some if not all the contact. At this point we stop dealing in certainties and start dealing in possibilities.

The current data do not allow secure identification of the actors on either side of the contact indicated by the archaeological remains. We do not know who the native people were and we cannot securely identify the Spaniards who were the ultimate sources of the beads, bells, and other artifacts. Possible sources of the Choctawhatchee Bay artifacts are the expeditions of Narváez, Maldonado, and Luna, but other contacts are also possible if not probable.

The European–native contact in Choctawhatchee Bay was not like that seen around St. Augustine or in Apalachee Province (Deagan 1985; Hann 1988d). It was less sustained, more intermittent and episodic. It should provide a good case study to compare with St. Augustine and Apalachee. Unfortunately, much more work will have to be done before those comparisons can be made. The archaeological data on early contact in the Choctawhatchee Bay are limited and often of questionable quality. The few descriptions of the contact by contemporary Spanish reporters lack the detail seen in descriptions of the contact in Apalachee or around St. Augustine. Since it seems unlikely that new sources of ethnohistoric data will appear, there is a clear need for more and better archaeological data. Both surveys and excavations are needed to provide data on the native inhabitants of the area and on the dating, nature, and intensity of the contact between those natives and the Europeans who came to their land.

If the nature of the contact was different, the final result may not have been.

Who were the people who lived around Choctawhatchee Bay in the sixteenth century? We do not know. We do know that they are no more. The archaeological remains from the bay area point to a flourishing society in the late prehistoric period. That society apparently did not exist by the time Europeans were established in the area. Its demise could have been a result of that poorly understood sixteenth-century contact. The association of European goods and mass burials is certainly suggestive.

References

Brain, Jeffrey P.
    1975 Artifacts of the Adelantado. *Conference on Historic Site Archaeology Papers* 8:129–138.
Brown, Ian W.
    1979 Bells. In *Tunica Treasure*, edited by Jeffrey P. Brain, pp. 197–205. Peabody Museum of Archaeology and Ethnology Papers No. 71. Harvard University Press, Cambridge, Massachusetts.
Chardon, Roland
    1980 The Elusive Spanish League: A Problem of Measurement in Sixteenth-century New Spain. *Hispanic American Historical Review* 60:294–302.
Claassen, Cheryl
    1985 Shellfish Utilization during Deptford and Mississippian Times in Escambia Bay, Florida. *Florida Anthropologist* 38:124–135.
Deagan, Kathleen A.
    1985 Spanish–Indian Interaction in Sixteenth-century Florida and Hispaniola. In *Cultures in Contact*, edited by W. Fitzhugh, pp. 281–318. Smithsonian Institution Press, Washington, D.C.
    1987 *Artifacts of the Spanish Colonies of Florida and the Caribbean, 1500–1800, Vol. 1: Ceramics, Glassware, and Beads.* Smithsonian Institution Press, Washington, D.C.
Ewen, Charles R., and B. Calvin Jones
    1988 Hernando de Soto's First Winter Encampment: Discovery and First Season of Excavation. Paper presented at the 53rd Annual Meeting of the Society for American Archaeology, Phoenix.
Fairbanks, Charles H.
    1960 Notes and News, Southeast. *American Antiquity* 26:149–150.
    1965 Excavations at the Fort Walton Temple Mound, 1960. *Florida Anthropologist* 18:239–264.
Fuller, Richard S.
    1985 The Bear Point Phase of the Pensacola Variant: The Protohistoric Period in Southwest Alabama. *Florida Anthropologist* 38:150–155.
Fuller, Richard S., and Noel R. Stowe
    1982 A Proposed Typology for Late Shell Tempered Ceramics in the Mobile Bay/Mobile-Tensaw Delta Region. In *Archaeology in Southwest Alabama: A Collection of Papers*, edited by C. Curren, pp. 45–94. Alabama Tombigbee Regional Commission, Camden, Alabama.
Gardner, William M.
    1966 The Waddells Mill Pond Site. *Florida Anthropologist* 19:43–64.
    1969 An Example of the Association of Archaeological Complexes with Tribal and Linguistic Grouping: The Fort Walton Complex of Northwest Florida. *Florida Anthropologist* 22:1–11.
Hann, John H.
    1988a Translation of the Florida Section of the Álvar Núñez Cabeza de Vaca Accounts

of the 1528 Trek from South Florida to Apalachee Led by Pánfilo de Narváez. Ms. on file, Florida Bureau of Archaeological Research, Tallahassee.

1988b Florida's Terra Incognita: West Florida's Natives in the Sixteenth and Seventeenth Centuries. *Florida Anthropologist* 41:61–107.

1988c Translation of The Florida of the Inca: History of the Adelantado, Hernando de Soto, Governor and Capitan General of the Kingdom of Florida. Ms. on file, Florida Bureau of Archaeological Research, Tallahassee.

1988d *Apalachee: The Land between the Rivers*. Ripley P. Bullen Monographs in Anthropology and History No. 7. University Presses of Florida, Gainesville, Florida.

Harrisse, Henry

1892 *The Discovery of North America. A Critical, Documentary, and Historic Investigation.* H. Stevens and Son, London.

Jones, B. Calvin

1982 Southern Cult Manifestations at the Lake Jackson Site, Leon County, Florida: Salvage Excavation of Mound 3. *Midcontinental Journal of Archaeology* 7:3–44.

Larson, Lewis H., Jr.

1959 A Mississippian Headdress from Etowah, Georgia. *American Antiquity* 25:109–112.

Lazarus, William C.

1957 Notes on the Alaqua Bayou Site, 8WL30. Ms. on file, Florida Master Site File, Florida Bureau of Archaeological Research, Tallahassee.

1958 Notes on the Hogtown Bayou Site, 8WL9. Ms. on file, Florida Master Site File, Florida Bureau of Archaeological Research, Tallahassee.

1959 Notes on the Point Washington Site, 8WL16. Ms. on file, Florida Master Site File, Florida Bureau of Archaeological Research, Tallahassee.

1964 A Sixteenth Century Spanish Coin from a Fort Walton Burial. *Florida Anthropologist* 17:134–138.

1965 Coin Dating in the Fort Walton Period. *Florida Anthropologist* 18:221–224.

1971 The Fort Walton Culture West of the Apalachicola River. *Southeastern Archaeological Conference Newsletter* 10(2)40–48.

Mitchem, Jeffrey M., and Bonnie G. McEwan

1988 New Data on Early Bells from Florida. *Southeastern Archaeology* 7:39–49.

Moore, Clarence B.

1901 Certain Aboriginal Remains of the Northwest Florida Coast, Part I. *Journal of the Philadelphia Academy of Natural Sciences* 11:419–497.

1918 The Northwestern Florida Coast Revisited. *Journal of the Philadelphia Academy of Natural Sciences* 16:513–581.

National Park Service

1989 *De Soto Trail National Historic Trail Study Draft Report*. National Park Service, Southeast Regional Office, Atlanta.

Scarry, John F.

1984 *Fort Walton Development: Mississippian Chiefdoms in the Lower Southeast*. Unpublished Ph.D. dissertation, Case Western Reserve University. University Microfilms, Ann Arbor.

1985 A Proposed Revision of the Fort Walton Ceramic Typology: A Type-variety System. *Florida Anthropologist* 38:199–233.

1989 A Provisional Chronological Sequence for Apalachee Province. Ms. on file, Florida Bureau of Archaeological Research, Tallahassee.

Smith, Marvin T., and Mary Elizabeth Good

1982 *Early Sixteenth Century Glass Beads in the Spanish Colonial Trade*. Cottonlandia Museum, Greenwood, Mississippi.

Swanton, John R.

1939 *Final Report of the United States De Soto Expedition Commission*. U.S. House of Representatives, 76th Cong., 1st sess., Doc. 71. Government Printing Office, Washington, D.C.

1946 *The Indians of the Southeastern United States*. Bureau of American Ethnology Bulletin No. 137. Government Printing Office, Washington, D.C.

Willey, Gordon R.

1949 *Archeology of the Florida Gulf Coast*. Smithsonian Miscellaneous Collections No. 113. Government Printing Office, Washington, D.C.

Chapter 8 ■

Charles M. Hudson, John E. Worth, and
Chester B. DePratter

Refinements in Hernando de Soto's Route through Georgia and South Carolina

To reconstruct the route of the Hernando de Soto expedition one must first construct a narrative of the long sequence of events that occurred during the expedition, and then fit this narrative to the landscape and to the archaeological record of the late prehistoric Southeast. Such a narrative can be pieced together from the information contained in the several documents that have come down to us from the expedition. The problems in this first step of the research are like those in any historical research. It is in the next two steps that they become so very difficult.

The landscape to which our narrative must be fitted is a relatively stable entity. However, that landscape is not the one that we see today, but the one that existed in the sixteenth century. Hence, it must be reconstructed through scholarship, and as the scholarship advances, the picture of this landscape is accordingly modified. Fortunately, the basic structural features of the Southeastern landscape have not changed since the sixteenth century—that is, the mountains of today are in the same place as they were when de Soto saw them, and rivers and creeks run in much the same channels, although some of them have meandered considerably. But even if one had a full and accurate reconstruction of the sixteenth-century Southeastern landscape, the descriptions of geographical features in the de Soto documents are so sketchy and so haphazardly mentioned that it would still be impossible to fit the narrative to this landscape in an unambiguous way.

The archaeologist's reconstruction of the cultural and social picture of the late prehistoric Southeast is far more incomplete than our reconstruction of the landscape. Large areas of the Southeast are so poorly known archaeologically that even a modest research effort can radically alter the overall picture. Hence the possibilities for error are great when one goes about fitting one's narrative of the de Soto expedition to what is known about the late prehistoric Southeast. Because of these gaps in our knowledge of the archaeological record, no reconstruction of the de Soto route can claim to be the "last word." Reconstructing the route is a matter of achieving a best fit, not infallible exactitude, and it must be assumed that any reconstruction can be improved and made more precise through additional research.

Hudson, Smith, and DePratter (1984) were aware of these difficulties when they published the first segment of their new and comprehensive attempt to reconstruct the route of the de Soto expedition. This was the route from Apalachee to Chiaha (Figure 8-1). Five years have passed since that publication, and new information has come to light that makes it necessary to modify the route in several particulars. This is what we propose to do in this chapter. At the same time, we try to show that our search for a best-fit de Soto route is not simply obsessive scholarship, but that the more precise the reconstructed route the more the gains that may be made in understanding the native people of the sixteenth-century Southeast.

Apalachee to Toa

Since the recent discovery of the Martin site (8Le853), we are much more confident that de Soto and his men departed from present Tallahassee and vicinity on March 3, 1540 (Ewen and Jones 1988; Ewen, this volume). Their route to the north is much as we indicated in our 1984 paper. Events that occurred while de Soto and his men traveled up the Flint River led us to suggest that there were two polities—Capachequi to the south and Toa to the north—with an unpopulated wilderness in between.

In 1984 the archaeology of the Flint River was little better than anecdotal. But through the recent research efforts of John Worth, the late prehistoric picture of the Flint River has been greatly improved. On the basis of an informal survey, Worth (1989) has collected information suggesting that Capachequi was located, as we proposed, in and around Chickasawhatchee Swamp. This swamp constitutes the largest and most well-developed expanse of floodplain bottomland in the entire Lower Flint River drainage. It is composed of extensive wetlands with many flood channels, matching the de Soto accounts very well. The two known multiple-mound sites along with several contemporaneous sites near Chickasawhatchee Creek represent the only recognized Mississippian occupation on the Lower Flint River drainage, and ceramic collections indicate that this

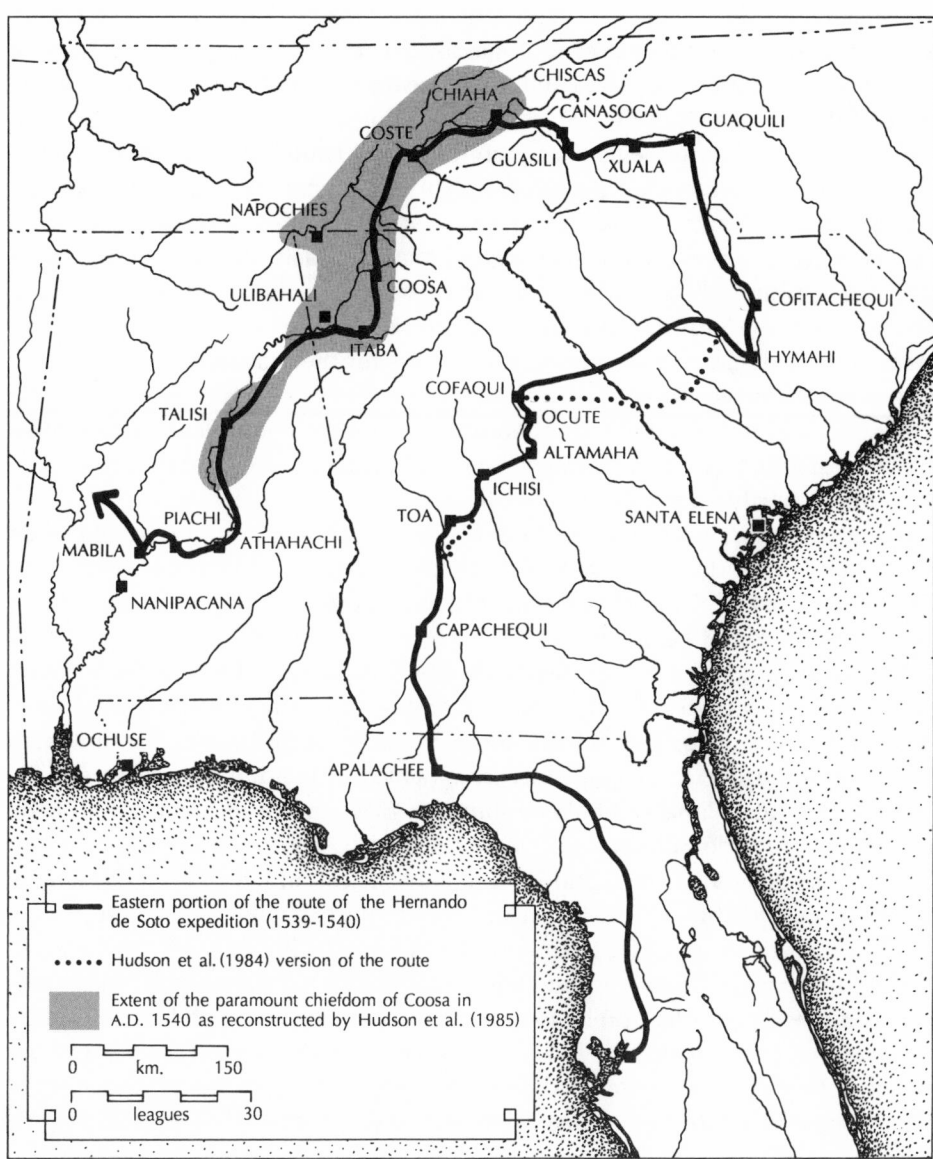

Figure 8-1. Postulated route for the eastern portion of the Hernando de Soto expedition (1539–1540).

area was definitely occupied during the sixteenth century. Closer examination of these ceramics reveals that our characterization of Capachequi as a Lamar chiefdom may be incorrect. Both the ceramics and the pyramidal configuration of at least three and possibly five of the six mounds in this area imply a closer relationship to the Fort Walton culture area, suggesting that Capachequi was affiliated culturally and perhaps politically with Apalachee, its immediate neighbor to the south.

A closer reading of Rodrigo Ranjel's narrative in the original Spanish (Ranjel 1959:163) reveals mention of a unique geographical feature that sustains our reconstruction. On March 11, upon de Soto's arrival at the first town of Capachequi, Ranjel notes that it was among *arcabucos*, perhaps best translated as "densely wooded hills" (Gooch and Paredes 1978:64). As anyone who has seen Chickasawhatchee Swamp will know, this is far from hilly terrain. But there is a ridge line of several pronounced hills, rising to as much as 70 feet, that border the swamp on the south. They are outstanding landmarks on the flat limestone Dougerty Plain, and today appear to be wooded in part with cherry laurel trees, a broadleaf evergreen that contrasts sharply with the pine uplands surrounding the swamp. These little hills are as notable today as they were in 1540. At least one and possibly two sixteenth-century sites are situated next to this ridge, and may thus be candidates for the first town of Capachequi that de Soto visited.

We still feel that the mound site on Magnolia Plantation (9Du1) is the most likely location of the town where de Soto and his men rested for six days before continuing northward. But we wish to correct an error first made by the U.S. De Soto Commission (Swanton 1939:174) and then compounded by us. That is, 9Du1 is not located on Pine Island. Rather, it is on the margin of Chickasawhatchee Swamp and some distance to the northeast of Pine Island, which itself has not been surveyed.

When de Soto and his men departed from Capachequi, they ended their first day of travel at another unusual geographical feature. They came to what Ranjel termed the "White Spring," which had a great flow of good water that contained fish. We would like to propose that this was James Pond, a very large and remarkably isolated lime sinkhole in southern Lee County. It is located directly on the trail that de Soto was probably following, and the modern location of Byne Crossroads at James Pond suggests that it continued to be important to travelers in later times. The pond measures approximately 2,500 feet across, with streams flowing both into and out of it. Certainly the perimeter of this pond should be surveyed to determine whether it might have been habitually used as a camping site for late prehistoric Indians in transit. To reach James Pond de Soto and his army would have had to travel about 17.5 miles, the upper limit of what they ordinarily traveled in a day. But their long rest at Capachequi would have made this task easier than if they had been on the trail for several days.

On March 18 they departed from White Spring and proceeded to the bank of the Flint River and then headed north, marching for three days on a trail paralleling the west bank of the river. On March 21 they came to the crossing of the river where on the day they arrived they began building a bridge to cross to the other side. They built two bridges, one after the other, which failed to hold against the powerful current of the river. The third bridge, which was cleverly cross-braced, held, and on March 22 the entire group crossed to the east bank, where they bivouacked in a pine forest.

John Worth's (1988) intensive survey of the Middle Flint River has given us a much more precise location for the chiefdom of Toa, whose territory appears to coincide with the distribution of the Lockett Phase. It was a small chiefdom with two platform mound centers located near the Fall Line. Lockett Phase sites appear to be associated with the Flint River floodplain for approximately 15 miles below the Fall Line. Although excavations in this area have been limited to stratigraphic testpits in both known mounds, Worth did recover a fragment of a crystalline quartz bead in Hartley-Posey Mound (9Tr12). The method of manufacture suggests that the bead is an early sixteenth-century Spanish artifact.

One of the problems Worth encountered with the archaeological evidence from Lockett Phase sites is that for a long time he was unable to locate a site on the eastern side of the Flint River near the southern edge of the polity. De Soto had clearly first encountered a town of Toa after crossing to the eastern side of the river. Recently Worth has located a possible candidate for this town— the Redneck Hunting Club Site, which does appear to possess a Lockett Phase component, and may be a spatially extensive site. It is the southernmost Lockett Phase site currently known, and it is on the eastern side of the river.

In the light of this new archaeological information on Toa, we now propose to locate de Soto's second crossing of the Flint River approximately 16 miles north of where we placed it in our 1984 route. This crossing was probably at a ford in the Flint River, which is shown on the original 1821 survey of District 15 of Houston County (present Macon County). From Capachequi to this ford it was about 72 miles. De Soto and his men were on the trail for four and a half days, and they could have covered this distance averaging 16 miles per day.

This is the northernmost ford across the Flint below the Fall Line, and as such, this is the narrowest channel of the Flint that de Soto could have crossed short of going all the way to the Fall Line. This crossing would have been located only two leagues to the south of the Redneck Hunting Club site, which de Soto reached early the next day. The trail he followed may have lain on or near a well-documented nineteenth-century stagecoach road along the eastern bluff of the river.

This reconstruction of the de Soto route matches the conditions described in the narratives in another way. Between the Chickasawhatchee Swamp area and the southern end of the Lockett Phase, the Georgia site files show no record of any significant sixteenth-century occupation, despite several surveys in this stretch of the river.[1]

This constellation of geographical features and sixteenth-century archaeological complexes fits the narratives of the de Soto expedition extremely well. We cannot find any other solution north of the Tallahassee area that fits better. Certainly there is nothing to support the route of the U.S. De Soto Expedition Commission, which placed Capachequi on the headwaters of Spring Creek, in eastern Miller County and adjoining parts of Baker and Early counties, and which placed Toa in Chickasawhatchee Swamp.[2]

Toa to Cofaqui

This more precise location of Toa puts the route de Soto and a small party of cavalry followed from Toa to Ichisi at a slightly different place from what we initially proposed. Their travel to the River of Ichisi (the Ocmulgee) would have been on a trail on or near Georgia Highway 127 rather than Highway 224. Beyond present-day Perry, they may have taken the southern fork of a trail shown on the 1847 Bonner map, leading to the Buzzard's Roost landing, which lay on the southern end of the broad expanse of floodplain below the Fall Line of the Ocmulgee River. Here, at the end of an extraordinarily long and strenuous day of travel, de Soto and his cavalry crossed a difficult stretch of water during darkness. This crossing was perhaps in the swamps bordering the Ocmulgee River. De Soto and his men bivouacked not far beyond this point.

The first town of Ichisi they came to was on an island in the Ocmulgee River. After this, they proceeded up the western bank of the river, and while crossing a bad passage of a swamp—possibly Thompson Mill Creek—Benito Fernandez fell into the channel and drowned. After passing some other towns, they met messengers from Ichisi at a town that is at present unlocated, but near Warner Robbins, and here they waited for the remainder of the army to catch up with them.

On March 29, the army was reunited, and resumed its march, crossing a small stream that rose very rapidly—almost certainly Echeconnee Creek. Then de Soto and his men arrived at the town of a chief subject to Ichisi—probably the Cowart's Landing site (9Bi14)—where they spent two nights. A short march northward brought them to the Ocmulgee River, where they were ferried across to the main town of Ichisi, which was located at the Lamar site (9Bi2).

Little more can be said about their march along the western bank of the Ocmulgee River until further archaeological research is done. Further excavation both at the Lamar Mound site and at other sites is needed, as well as a distributional study of known Cowart's phase sites. At present, the geographical limits of the Cowart's phase and the Ichisi chiefdom are not precisely known.

From Ichisi to Cofaqui, a tributary town of the paramount chief of Ocute, their route was as we indicated in our 1984 paper. Williams and Shapiro (1986) have established that the Shoulderbone site is not as imposing as was previously thought and that there may have been only a small sixteenth-century occupation there. This has thrown some doubt on our contention that the Shoulderbone site was the central town of the chiefdom of Ocute (Williams 1989). But until some other candidate for the central town comes to light, the Shoulderbone site is still where we place the center of the paramount chiefdom.

Cofaqui to Cofitachequi

From Cofaqui onward, we propose a change in our 1984 route that will provide a better geographical fit. Since the area de Soto and his men entered beyond Cofaqui was an uninhabited wilderness, archaeological information offers no help until they reached what is today central South Carolina (see Levy et al., this volume). The expedition must have set out from Cofaqui on April 13 or 14 instead of April 15, as proposed by Swanton (1939:315). This April 13 departure date allows for nine days of travel across the wilderness, as attested by Elvas (1866:59).

Although in our 1984 paper we proposed a day-by-day itinerary for the expedition across the wilderness beyond Cofaqui, the evidence cannot sustain such a detailed itinerary, except in a hypothetical way. The army was uncertain about its whereabouts in the forested Piedmont, because it was not following trails and did not have competent guides. Members of the expedition had no clear idea of where they were, so that drawing a single route across the wilderness can only be done using a very broad line.

It is clear from the four existing chronicles that the expedition forded three large rivers between Cofaqui and the place where the expedition halted on April 21, 1540. In our 1984 publication, we argued that these three rivers were the Savannah, the south fork of the Edisto, and the Broad. We were correct in naming the Savannah and the Broad, but the small size of the south fork of the Edisto should have eliminated it from consideration. The Saluda River is a much better candidate for the second river.

Now, if the three rivers were indeed the Savannah, the Saluda, and the Broad, where was each river crossed? The crossing places for these three rivers would be impossible to determine if we did not have evidence that fixes the starting and ending points for this part of the expedition. We have argued that the expedition set out from Cofaqui (vicinity of the Dyar site) on April 13, and that it stopped after crossing the third major river, which we conclude was the Broad, on April 21. On the 21st, the army halted with the future of the expedition in jeopardy. During nine days of travel, the trails had become progressively indistinct, the group saw no signs of Indian occupation, and, what is more important, they found no stores of corn on which the expedition depended for food. By the time de Soto bivouacked on the banks of the Broad River on April 21, the expedition was in desperate straits, and he immediately took decisive action. He ordered pigs slaughtered to provide an emergency ration for his men and he sent out scouts to search for signs of life (Ranjel 1922:95; Biedma 1922:12; Elvas 1866:60).

De Soto himself rode 5 to 6 leagues beyond the camp looking for signs of Indian habitation (Elvas 1866:59–60), but he found none. On April 22, several captains were sent out in various directions, but each returned without success (Ranjel 1922:95). In a final desperate act, de Soto dispatched three captains to search for Indian towns, each with 10 days of rations, in three directions (Ranjel 1922:94–95; Biedma 1922:12). Baltasar de Gallegos was to travel upstream (along the Broad) to the northwest, Juan de Añasco downstream to the southeast, and Juan Ruiz Lobillo inland to the north (Ranjel 1922:94–95). Gallegos and Añasco set out on April 23, and Lobillo departed one day later, on the 24th.

Of the three, only Añasco was successful in his mission. On Sunday, April 25, Añasco returned to the camp, reporting that he had found a town, Aymay (or Hymahi), located downstream from the camp. Elvas (1866:62) says that Aymay was 12–13 leagues downstream from the camp, and Garcilaso (1962:293) places the distance at 12 leagues. This distance would seem to be confirmed by the fact that when de Soto and the army set out for Aymay on the 26th, only de Soto and a few others of "the best mounted, all riding the hardest possible" were able to reach Aymay in a single day; the rest of the army remained scattered 2–4 leagues short of their goal, some not arriving until noon on the second day (Elvas 1866:63; Ranjel 1922:96; Garcilaso 1962:294).

If the distance of 12–13 leagues between the camp and Aymay is correct, and if Aymay was truly located near present-day Wateree, as we have argued elsewhere (DePratter et al. 1983:138; Hudson et al. 1984:72), then we have but to measure 12–13 leagues upstream from Wateree to find the approximate location of the April 21–26 camp site. Such a measurement, done on the U.S. Geological Survey 1:250,000 series maps, places the camp between present-day Montgomery and Wallaceville on the east bank of the Broad River. Along this stretch of river are several sets of islands, including (beginning upstream) Haltiwanger Island, Huffman Island, Bookman Island, and another unnamed island farther downstream. This downstream island, called Boatright's Island in Robert Mills's Lexington District map (Mills 1980), is indicated as the site of a ford. Any of these islands could have served as the crossing point for the "very large river and hard to cross which was divided into two streams," as it was described by Ranjel (1922:94). The April 21–26 camp would then have been located on the east bank of the river approximately 15–20 miles upstream from Columbia.

With their beginning and ending points established, what points did they visit in between? We know that from Cofaqui they were headed east, and there is no reason whatever to think that they traveled in circles while crossing the "wilderness of Ocute." Starting out from Cofaqui, their most likely route would have been to the east, across the northern watershed of the Little River, and this was probably the small stream on whose bank they bivouacked on the night of April 16. The next day they came to the Savannah River, where the stream was divided into two arms. This was probably at Paces Island and Winns Island, where a ferry crossing was located in the early nineteenth century (Mills 1980:Edgefield District). This is a distance of about 65 miles, and in their four and a fraction days of travel time, they could have made this distance averaging less than 16 miles per day. From here their most likely route was to the northeast to cross the Saluda River, possibly near the mouth of Little Saluda River. This was a distance of about 48 miles, which they could have traveled in three days, averaging 16 miles per day.

Chester DePratter's examination of collections at the South Carolina Institute of Archaeology and Anthropology indicates that there are no known mid-sixteenth-century sites on the Saluda and Broad Rivers. This hiatus in the archaeological record is consistent with their having crossed an uninhabited wilderness on this segment of their journey.

We remain convinced that Cofitachequi was in the vicinity of Camden, South Carolina. In our previous publication, we argued that the Mulberry site (38Ke12) was the location of Talimeco, but recent research (DePratter 1989; DePratter and Judge 1986; Judge 1987) indicates that Mulberry is a more likely candidate for the location of the town of Cofitachequi. The Adamson site (38Ke11), also referred to in our 1984 publication, may be the site of Talimeco.

Discussion

To recapitulate, de Soto and his army crossed the Flint River 16 miles further upstream and the Savannah River 26 miles further upstream than we indicated in our 1984 paper, and then crossed the Saluda rather than the south fork of the Edisto. Why do these details matter?

They matter because with a precise reconstruction of the de Soto route in hand, the information and incidents of the expedition can then be linked to archaeological information, and in this way we can build a picture of the social geography of a significant potion of the sixteenth-century southeastern United States. This social geography will in turn make it possible to begin making detailed comparisons of native societies, caught in an instant of historical time, from Tampa Bay to east Texas.

For example, the Gentleman of Elvas states that the Spanish saw a kind of domestic architecture and dress at Toa (he spells it Toalli) that they had not seen before, which suggests that a major difference in cultural adaptation had occurred between Capachequi and Toa. Here is what he says:

> On Wednesday, the 21st of the month, we came to a town called Toalli. Beyond that place, a difference was seen in the houses, for those behind were covered with hay and those of Toalli were covered with canes in the manner of tile. Those houses are very clean and have some of their walls plastered and appear to be made of mud. Throughout the cold lands, each of the Indians has his house for the winter plastered inside and out. They shut the very small door at night and build a fire inside the house so that it gets as hot as an oven, and stays so all night long so that there is no need of clothing. Besides those houses they have others for summer with kitchens nearby where they build their fires and bake their bread. They have barbacoas in which they keep their maize. This is a house raised up on four posts, timbered like a loft and the floor of canes. The difference which the houses of the lords or principal men have from those of the others is that besides being larger they have large balconies in front and below seats resembling benches made of canes; and round about many large barbacoas in which they gather together the tribute paid them by their Indians, which consists of maize and deerskins and native blankets resembling shawls, some being made of the inner bark of trees and some from a plant like daffodils which when pounded remains like flax. The Indian women cover themselves with these blankets, draping one around themselves from the waist down and another over the shoulder with the right arm uncovered in the manner and custom of gypsies. The Indian men wear only one over the shoulders in the same way and have their privies covered with a truss of deerskin resembling the breechclouts formerly worn in Spain. The skins are well tanned and are given the color that is desired; and so perfectly that if the color is vermillion, it seems to be very fine-grained cloth, and that colored black is splendid. And of this same they make shoes. They give the same colors to the blankets.[3]

Now, this is most interesting in light of the fact that what is currently known of the archaeology of the Flint River also suggests that a fundamental cultural difference existed on this stretch of the river. Namely, the archaeological culture for Capachequi southward is Fort Walton, while the Lockett Phase at Toa resembles Lamar phases in northern Georgia, northern Alabama, and South Carolina.[4] Hence the Flint River would seem to offer the opportunity for conducting a most interesting detailed study in cultural ecology.

Such a study might throw light on the observation of the de Soto chroniclers that the villages beyond Toa were larger than they had seen before arriving at Toa. It is notable in this regard that the sixteenth-century Fort Walton settlement pattern may have been one of dispersed farmsteads around a hamlet (Payne 1982:12–13), in contrast to the nucleated villages of Lamar societies immediately to the north.

On a more general level, the distribution of native societies with respect to one another and to the uninhabited wildernesses is interesting, although it may prove difficult to interpret. From the experience of the de Soto expedition else-where, wildernesses frequently indicate that the societies on either side of a va-cant area were hostile toward each other (DePratter 1983). This would seem to be the case with Capachequi and Toa, and also with Toa and Ichisi. But this raises the question, Who were the allies of Capachequi and Toa? Cultural simi-larity would suggest that Capachequi was affiliated with Apalachee. But more compelling evidence will be needed, because cultural similarity does not always coincide with social or political boundaries. One might look for Toa's affiliations to be either with Coosa, to the north, or with the unnamed society that lay on the Chattahoochee River to the west, and it is of course possible that Toa was affiliated with or subject to neither of these.

Whether there are any cultural or social lessons to be derived from placing the crossing of the Savannah River at Pace's Ferry as opposed to Augusta is du-bious, because this entire area was a wilderness. It is possible that this change in our route only makes for a better geographical fit. The Saluda River is a far better candidate for being a big river than is the south fork of the Edisto. And a Pace's Ferry crossing makes for a better fit because it places de Soto's fording of the Savannah at a place where the river carried less water and was therefore easier to cross. Finally, these refinements explain one of the puzzles we had with our 1984 solution. Namely, if the group's destination was eastward to the Savan-nah River at present-day Augusta, why did it first go northward from Ocute to Cofaqui? One reason, as we now see, is that this placed it closer to the point at which it would ford the Savannah River.

In conclusion, we are half tempted to apologize for belaboring such details. But as we have said before, only after a "best-fit" de Soto route has been achieved will it be possible to proceed to the more interesting next step of inter-preting and explaining the social, economic, and political nature of the South-eastern United States at the time of earliest European penetration.

Notes

1. Worth found no evidence of sixteenth-century occupation down to Dooly County, and a reexamination of other survey collections from Macon County (Howry 1979) re-vealed no Lamar ceramics. Frank Schnell (1975) reported similar results from his survey of Lake Blackshear.

2. When one attempts to fit a narrative of the de Soto expedition to the locations proposed by the U.S. De Soto Expedition Commission, a veritable welter of contradictions and inconsistencies present themselves:

a. The Georgia site files contain no evidence for sixteenth-century sites in eastern Miller and adjacent parts of Early and Baker Counties. The floodplain of Spring Creek is very narrow and thin, and did not offer an especially attractive habitat for Mississippian people.

b. If one uses the U.S. De Soto Commission route, Ichawaynochaway Creek has to be the River of Toa. But the distance from this creek to the proposed location for Capachequi would have been only 20 miles—a distance that would not have taken four days to traverse.

c. Little Ichawaynochaway Creek would have presented a difficult crossing for de Soto's army only if it had been flooded, but if it had been flooded, its waters would have been so wide that even a bridge would not have made a crossing possible. Moreover, the current in sluggish Ichawaynochaway Creek would hardly have been strong enough to tear out two bridges before they could be completed and used.

d. This solution to the route would locate the chiefdom of Toa in and around Chickasawhatchee Swamp, but there is no evidence in the documents that Toa was located in a swamp.

e. This solution makes it necessary to identify the Flint River as the River of Ichisi. But this would locate the chiefdom of Ichisi in the unpopulated wilderness mentioned above.

f. More important, this solution to the route puts Ocute on the Ocmulgee River and Cofitachequi on the Savannah River. This leads one into two serious inconsistencies: first, it locates no native people on the Oconee River, which was very densely populated in the sixteenth century; and second, it locates the grand chiefdom of Cofitachequi on the Savannah River, which is known to have been the center of a vast uninhabited wilderness in 1540.

g. The claim is sometimes made that the Flint River at Bainbridge more closely matches the narrative than the river at Newton. But the only conditions that must be met are that the river be deep and swift, and that it be so wide that a Spaniard could not throw a stone across it. The river was deep and swift in both places, and it is wide enough in both places. Although the river was approximately 300 feet wide at Bainbridge before the construction of the reservoir and only 250 feet wide at Newton, the latter is nonetheless a very long throw, unless the Spaniards happened to have a sixteenth-century Joe Montana along with them.

3. Elvas (1866:74–76). Luis Hernandez de Biedma also mentions a change in architecture, but in much less detail, and he recalled (incorrectly) that the change first occurred at Capachequi.

4. The name Chickasawhatchee may derive from the Apalachee word *chicasa*, "abandoned town or area." Hence, in Apalachee, Chickasawhatchee would have meant "old town creek." This, of course, only indicates that this was the Apalachee name for this creek and not necessarily that a dialect of Apalachee was spoken by the people of Capachequi.

References

Biedma, Luis Hernandez de
    1922 Relation. In *Narratives of the Career of Hernando De Soto*, edited by Edward G. Bourne, pp. 3–40. Allerton, New York.

DePratter, Chester B.
1983 *Late Prehistoric and Early Historic Chiefdoms in the Southeastern United States.* Unpublished Ph.D. dissertation, Department of Anthropology, University of Georgia, Athens.
1989 Cofitachequi: Ethnohistoric and Archaeological Evidence. In *Studies in South Carolina Archaeology: Essays In Honor of Robert L. Stephenson,* edited by G. T. Hanson and A. C. Goodyear. South Carolina Institute of Archaeology and Anthropology, Anthropological Study No. 9, in press.

DePratter, Chester, Charles Hudson, and Marvin Smith
1983 The Route of Juan Pardo's Explorations in the Interior Southeast, 1566–1568. *Florida Historical Quarterly* 62:125–158.

DePratter, Chester B., and Chris Judge
1986 A Provisional Late Prehistoric and Early Historic Ceramic Sequence for the Wateree River Valley, South Carolina. Paper presented at the LAMAR Conference, May 9–10, Macon, Georgia.

Elvas, Gentleman of
1866 *True Relation of the Vicissitudes That Attended the Governor Don Hernando De Soto and Some Nobles of Portugal in the Discovery of the Province of Florida,* translated by Buckingham Smith. Bradford Club, New York.

Ewen, Charles R., and B. Calvin Jones
1988 Hernando De Soto's First Winter Encampment: Discovery and First Season of Excavation. Paper presented at the 53rd Annual Meeting of the Society for American Archaeology, Phoenix.

Garcilaso de la Vega
1962 *The Florida of the Inca.* Translated by J. G. Varner and J. J. Varner. University of Texas Press, Austin.

Gooch, Anthony, and Angel Garcia de Paredes (editors)
1978 *Cassell's Spanish-English Dictionary.* Macmillan, New York.

Howry, Jeffrey C.
1979 *Cultural Resources Mitigation Program for the Flint River Pulp Plant.* Environmental Research and Technology, Atlanta.

Hudson, Charles M., Marvin T. Smith, and Chester B. DePratter
1984 The Hernando De Soto Expedition: from Apalachee to Chiaha. *Southeastern Archaeology* 3:65–77.

Judge, Chris
1987 *Aboriginal Pottery Vessel Function in South Appalachian Mississippian Society: A Case Study from the Mulberry Site (38Ke12).* Unpublished Master's thesis, Department of Anthropology, University of South Carolina, Columbia.

Mills, Robert
1980 *Atlas of the State of South Carolina, 1825.* Southern Historical Press, Easley, South Carolina.

Payne, Claudine
1982 Farmsteads and Districts: A Model of Fort Walton Settlement Patterns in the Tallahassee Hills. Paper presented at the 39th Annual Meeting of the Southeastern Archaeological Conference, October 29, Memphis.

Ranjel, Rodrigo
1922 Narrative. In *Narratives of the Career of Hernando De Soto,* edited by Edward G. Bourne, pp. 43–150. Allerton, New York.
1959 Narrative. In *Historia General y Natural de las Indias,* edited by Gonzalo Fernandez de Oviedo. Edicionas Atlas, Madrid.

Schnell, Frank T.
1975 An Archaeological Survey of Lake Blackshear. *Southeastern Archaeological Conference Bulletin* 18:117–122.

Swanton, John R.
1939 *Final Report of the United States De Soto Expedition Commission.* Government Printing Office, Washington.

Williams, Mark
1989 Hernando De Soto in Northeast Georgia. Draft manuscript in possession of the author.

Williams, Mark, and Gary Shapiro
   1986 Shoulderbone was a 14th-Century Frontier Town. Paper presented at the 43rd Annual Meeting of the Southeastern Archaeological Conference, November 7, Nashville.
Worth, John E.
   1988 *Mississippian Occupation on the Middle Flint River.* Unpublished Master's thesis, Department of Anthropology, University of Georgia, Athens.
   1989 Mississippian Mound Centers along Chickasawhatchee Swamp. *LAMAR Briefs* 13:7–9.

Chapter 9 ■

David J. Hally, Marvin T. Smith, and
James B. Langford, Jr.

The Archaeological Reality of de Soto's Coosa

Considerable effort has been devoted in recent years to tracing the routes of sixteenth-century Spanish explorers through the Southeast (Brain 1985; DePratter et al. 1983, 1985; Hudson et al. 1985, 1989; Hudson 1987; Lankford 1977; Smith 1976, 1987). To the extent that such research is successful in determining where different expeditions traveled and who they encountered, it will permit us to bridge the critical gap between archaeologically and historically documented societies in the region. The end result of such research, of course, will be greater understanding of the nature of those societies.

The paramount chiefdom of Coosa, visited by the de Soto, Luna, and Pardo expeditions between 1540 and 1567, has received an especially large amount of scholarly attention. Primarily through the work of Hudson and his colleagues (Hudson et al. 1985) it can now be geographically delineated and identified with a number of archaeological sites and phases.[1] In this chapter, we attempt to add to the growing body of knowledge concerning Coosa by reviewing some of the archaeology relating to it. More specifically, we examine settlement data from the region that Hudson and his colleagues identify as the paramount chiefdom of Coosa and draw several conclusions about the nature of the polity's aboriginal settlement and political systems.

Our research indicates that the paramount chiefdom of Coosa contains at least seven clusters of contemporary archaeological sites, plus several scattered sites that may represent additional clusters. We argue that the clusters represent largely independent chiefdoms that were unified, perhaps only briefly, by Coosa, the chiefdom represented by the largest and geographically most central site cluster.

We begin with brief historical background and methodological statements. These are followed by a review of the archaeological data pertaining to the nature of individual sites, site clusters, and the paramount chiefdom itself. Sites and site clusters are discussed in greater detail as they are the most visible settlement units in the archaeological record; we can find little archaeological evidence for the larger Coosa paramount chiefdom described in the historical literature.

The Historical Record

During the sixteenth century, three major Spanish expeditions entered the province of Coosa. Hernando de Soto visited Coosa in 1540 and spent over three months traveling through the territory subject to it (Ranel 1922; Elvas 1968; Biedma 1968; Vega 1962). In 1560, the Sauz detachment from the Tristán de Luna expedition revisited Coosa and spent several months in the capital (Hudson et al. 1989; Priestly 1928; Swanton 1922). Finally, Juan Pardo explored the northern end of the paramount chiefdom in 1567 (Bandera 1569), and one of his soldiers apparently reached the capital itself. Figure 8-1 illustrates several of the named places visited by these expeditions.

As reconstructed by Hudson and his associates, the paramount chiefdom of Coosa extended approximately 400 km along the Tennessee and Coosa River drainages in the Valley and Ridge physiographic province of Alabama, Georgia, and Tennessee. They place the northernmost province, Chiaha, at Zimmerman's Island in the French Broad River; they locate the southernmost province, Talisi, near present-day Childersburg, Alabama; and they identify the Little Egypt archaeological site in northwest Georgia as the principal town of Coosa.

Although it is impossible to treat the historical documentation for the Coosa paramount chiefdom (see Hudson et al. 1985) in depth here, a number of relevant points can be made. First, the Spanish accounts discuss many "provinces" within the paramount chiefdom, each consisting of several towns. Named provinces or capitals of provinces include Chiaha, Coste, Coosa, Ulibahali, Talisi, and that of the Napochies. Some towns are listed as "subject to" another town, and it is clear that provinces could contain as many as six or eight towns. Ranjel (1922:108) mentions passing through five or six villages the day the de Soto expedition left Chiaha. In 1540 Elvas (1968:76) described Coosa as being "thickly settled in numerous and large towns, with fields between, extending from one to another." An account of Coosa in 1560 notes that "there were seven little hamlets in its district, five of them smaller and two larger than Coza itself" (Swanton 1922:231).

Some towns mentioned by name are not indicated as belonging to any province. These include Tali, Talimachusy, Itaba, Toasi (de Soto accounts), Huchi, Chalahume, Satapo, Cosaque, Tasqui, Tasquiqui, and Oltifar (Pardo accounts). Given the historical references to multitown provinces and the archaeological evidence for spatially delineated site clusters presented in this chapter, it is unlikely that these towns were geographically and politically isolated. Indeed, one such town, Itaba, may be part of an archaeological site cluster that contains at least three large towns.

The accounts indicate that "provinces" are separated by unoccupied areas. For example, de Soto and his men traveled for four days between Tali and Tasqui and three days between Tuasi and an unnamed town as they approached Talisi (Ranjel 1922:111,115), and Pardo traveled through unpopulated territory for three days between Chiaha and Chalahume (Bandera 1569). As de Soto generally traveled about 20–24 km per day (Hudson et al. 1985), these particular uninhabited areas must have been between 60 km and 95 km wide.

In addition, many, if not all, of the towns de Soto encountered were located along rivers. Coste, Tali, Coosa, Itaba, Ulibahali, and Talisi are mentioned in conjunction with rivers. Referring to the province of Coosa, Fray Anunciación reports, "All the towns that there are in this country are on the banks of the rivers, for all the rest is so densely wooded that it can by no means be inhabited" (Priestly 1928:1:239).

There is also some information about the towns. Although there is evidence of depopulation by the time of the Luna expedition, Fray Anunciación says of the towns of Coosa, "so far we have seen none which contains as many as one hundred and fifty houses, and very few which number above forty or fifty" (Priestly 1928:1:239). He goes on to discuss summer houses and winter houses that are earth-covered, with crops growing on them. All the towns have a good-sized plaza on the outskirts, and each has a pole for sports. Some towns are fortified, and some have temples (Priestly 1928:Volume 1). The historian Garcilaso, who we should caution is often inaccurate, mentions three mounds in Coosa, the only mention of earthworks in this part of the expedition (Vega 1962).

The Archaeological Picture

The Data Base

Figure 9-1 shows those sites located within the area controlled by the chief of Coosa that we believe date to the mid-sixteenth century. Sites were identified with this period on the basis of one or more criteria. Sites known to contain sixteenth-century European artifacts were included (see Smith 1987). In Georgia, ceramic chronology has been refined to the point where sites with Barnett and Brewster phase pottery can be dated to the middle decades of the sixteenth century. In Alabama and Tennessee, ceramics have not proven as useful in dating sites. The Kymulga, Dallas, and Mouse Creek phases were in existence during the sixteenth century, but Kymulga continues into the seventeenth century, Dallas covers almost 300 years beginning in the fourteenth century, and Mouse Creek is traditionally identified using nonceramic criteria that are not chronologically sensitive. We have relied on such markers as rattlesnake gorgets, mask gorgets, and the ceramic type DeArmond Incised in an attempt to further refine the chronology for eastern Tennessee. Because of the imprecision involved in some of these criteria, we have included in our analysis some archaeological sites that have "possible" sixteenth-century occupations.

Dating sites is also facilitated by the lack of aboriginal occupation in an area either immediately before or after (or both) the mid-sixteenth century. The upper Coosa, lower Etowah, and Hiwassee drainages appear not to have been occupied immediately before and after the mid-sixteenth century. Most of the Coosawattee and perhaps Little Tennessee drainages appear to have been abandoned shortly after the mid-sixteenth century. The middle Coosa drainage, on the other hand, appears to have had continuous occupation throughout the latter half of the sixteenth century and into the seventeenth century.

The settlement data that we have had to work with are not as complete and reliable as we would like. Systematic site survey has been conducted in three parts of the Coosa region: the Hiwassee River (Lewis and Kneberg 1941; Smith 1988), the Little Tennessee River (Kimball 1985), and the middle Coosa River (Knight 1985; Knight et al. 1984). In each case, however, survey was restricted to river floodplains and adjacent terraces.

Settlement data from the upper Coosa, lower Etowah, and lower Coosawattee rivers are the product of nonsystematic surveys and an active group of amateurs (see Hally and Langford 1988). Upland sites and small sites in the river bottoms are probably underrepresented in site samples from these areas, but all indications are that the latter are rare. Settlement data for the Tennessee River from Chattanooga to the French Broad River above Knoxville are least reliable. Urban growth and reservoir construction have taken a heavy toll of sites. We have information from amateurs and early twentieth-century professional projects on mound sites, but little record of nonmound sites.

In summary, settlement data are better for some areas than others, and are probably biased toward large sites with or without mounds that are located in river bottomlands.

Sites and Site Clusters

Several of the provinces mentioned in the Spanish narratives as being subject to Coosa were themselves made up of multiple towns. This situation is clearly reflected in the archaeological record. Seven clusters of sites can be identified within the geographical area of the paramount chiefdom (Figure 9-1). These are located on the Little Tennessee and Hiwassee rivers, the Tennessee River near Chattanooga, the Coosawattee River below Carters Dam, the lower Etowah River near Cartersville, the upper Coosa River near Rome, and the middle Coosa

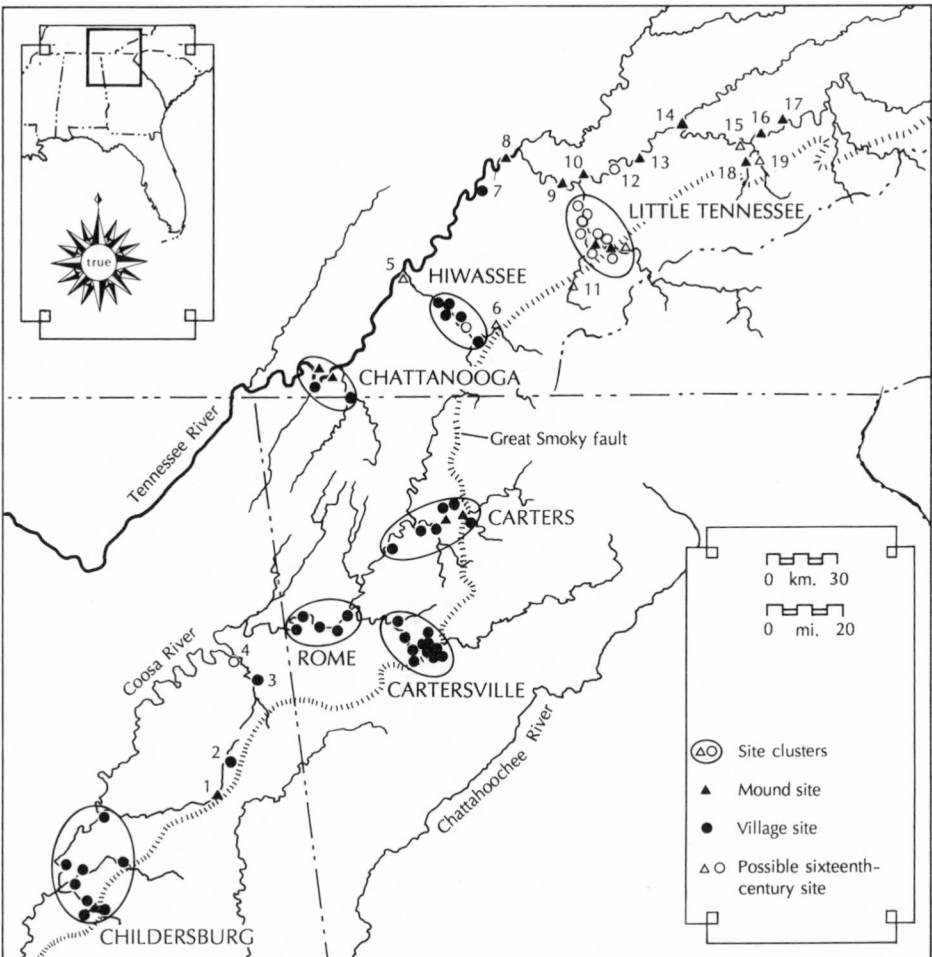

Figure 9-1. Mid-sixteenth-century archaeological sites and site clusters in the region of the paramount chiefdom of Coosa. (1) Davis Farm (1CA196), (2) ICA42, (3) ICE308, (4) Terrapin Creek (1CE309), (5) Hiwassee Island (40MG31), (6) Hiwassee Old Town (40PK3), (7) Upper Hampton (40RE), (8) DeArmond (40RE12), (9) Henry Island (40LD53), (10) Bussel Island (40LD17), (11) Great Tellico (40MR12), (12) Prater (40BT2), (13) Post Oak Island (40KN23), (14) Brakebill (40KN55), (15) Henderson 1 (40SV9), (16) Zimmerman's Island (40JE2), (17) Fains Island (40JE1), (18) McMahan (40SV1), (19) Henderson 2 (40SV4).

River and its tributaries in the vicinity of Childersburg, Alabama. Other clusters of sites probably exist in the vicinity of mound sites dating to the sixteenth century on Choccolocco Creek in eastern Alabama (Holstein and Little 1987), on the Tennessee River near Kingston, Loudon, and Knoxville, and on the French Broad River near Dandridge (Polhemus 1987). There has not been sufficient survey work in these locations, however, to demonstrate the existence of actual site clusters.

The number of known sites in each of the seven identifiable clusters ranges from 5 to 13 (Table 9-1). Most of these are larger than 1 ha and probably represent permanent towns inhabited by several hundred people. Sites smaller than 1 ha may represent farmsteads or locations where specialized activities took place. Although survey coverage is in general too limited to estimate how common small sites are, the number of sites larger than one hectare in each cluster is large enough to identify them as the major settlement type throughout the region. Presumably the great majority of people associated with each site cluster resided in such settlements.

Excavations at several large sites—King (Hally 1988), Little Egypt (Hally 1980), Toqua (Polhemus 1987), Mouse Creek, Ledford Island, and Rymer (Sullivan 1986)—have revealed habitation zones that were tightly packed with substantially built square domestic structures. In most clusters, at least one large site has a platform mound and a plaza. The extensively excavated King and Ledford Island sites do not have mounds but do have plazas and a large structure that is located either in or adjacent to the plaza. These features almost certainly functioned in communitywide political and ceremonial activities. If they are characteristic of all large nonmound sites in the region, and there is no reason to doubt that they are, we can conclude that each town was politically organized and to some extent administered by resident leaders. People residing in farmsteads, if any, probably had political and ceremonial affiliations with a nearby town.

Table 9.1 Estimated Size and Population of Sites

| | | | | Estimated Population | |
| | | | | 5.9 People/ House | 11.0 People/ House |
Site Cluster	Site Number	Site Name	Size of Site (ha)	(Naroll 1962)	(Cook 1972)
Childersbsurg[a]	1TA25		6.6	826	1540
	1TA115	Sylacauga Water Works	—	—	—
	1TA150	Hightower	1.5	189	352
	1TA153	Collins Farm	5.0	625	1166
	1TA171	Rodgers—CETA	8.0	1003	1870
	1TA213	Hudson Branch	7.5	944	1760
	1TA238	Ogletree Island	—	—	—
	1TA285		0.4	53	99
	9FL5	King	2.0	254	473
Rome[b]	9FL49	Johnstone	0.5	—	—
	9FL155	Mohman	2.3	289	539
	9FL161	Coosa Country Club	—	—	—
	9FL175		2.2	277	517
	9BR1	Etowah	5.6	702	1309
Cartersville[c]	9BR2	Leake	1.7	212	396
	9BR54		3.0	378	704
	9PA39		1.0	—	—
	9MU21		3.2	401	748
Carters[d]	9MU102	Little Egypt	4.9	614	1144
	9MU103	Potts Tract	—	—	—
	9GO1	Poarch	3.3	413	770
	9GO4	Thompson	2.4	307	572
	9GO8	Baxter	2.0	254	473
	9GO67	Brown Farm	5.5	690	1287
	9GO70	Swancy	1.7	218	407
	40HA60	Williams Island	—	—	—

Site size can be reliably estimated for King, Little Egypt, and Toqua, which have been extensively excavated. Size can be estimated for an additional 38 sites using measurements of surface artifact distributions (Table 9-1). These latter estimates must be treated with caution, especially since some sites have multiple components. Size estimates are reasonably consistent among the various site clusters, except for the Childersburg and Chattanooga clusters. Estimates for the former average twice the size of sites in other clusters, and at least one researcher familiar with the region (Vernon J. Knight, personal communication) considers them suspect. Estimates for sites in the Chattanooga cluster average less than half as large as sites elsewhere and are suspect for other reasons as well. We have excluded site size estimates for both of these clusters from further analysis.

Large sites in the Rome, Cartersville, Carters, Hiwassee, and Little Tennessee clusters range from 1 ha to 5.6 ha, and average 2.8 ha. We believe we can estimate the number of domestic structures that existed at most of these sites with some accuracy. We divided the area excavated at King (Hally 1988), North Mouse Creek, South Mouse Creek, Rymer, and Ledford Island (Sullivan 1986) sites by the number of contemporaneous domestic structures recorded at each

Table 9.1 cont'd.

Chattanooga[e]	40HA65	Citico	1.3	177	330
	40HA84	Audubon Acres	1.4	177	330
	40HA146	Hampton Place A	1.5	189	352
	40HA146	Hampton Place B	1.0	124	231
	40MN3	Mouse Creek North	—	—	—
Hiwassee[f]	40MN3	Mouse Creek South	—	—	—
	40BY11	Rymer	1.9	242	451
	40PK1	Ocoee	—	—	—
	40BY7		1.1	136	253
	40BY13	Ledford Island	5.0	637	1188
	40BY59		3.1	395	737
	40BT7	Chilhowee	—	—	—
Little Tennessee[g]	40LD42	Negro Hollow	3.2	401	748
	40LD75		1.1	136	253
	40LD107		0.9	112	209
	40MR6	Toqua	1.7	200	385
	40MR7	Citico	2.2	—	—
	40MR28	Mayfield III	0.5	60	110
	40MR67	Peery I	0.5	60	110
	40MR108		0.5	60	110
	40MR134		0.5	60	110
	40MR164		1.4	177	330
	40MR166		0.1	12	22
	40MR168		0.1	12	22

[a] University of Alabama site files. Figures for site size and population are not reliable.
[b] University of Georgia site files.
[c] University of Georgia site files.
[d] University of Georgia site files.
[e] McCullough and Bass 1983, Hatch 1976; Evans and Vicky 1984; Evans, et al. 1981. Figures for site size and population are not reliable.
[f] University of Tennessee site files; Smith 1988.
[g] Kimball 1985.

to arrive at an average amount of site area per house. This figure is 470 m². Divided into the estimates site area for 21 sites larger than 1 ha in the Rome, Cartersville, Carters, Hiwassee, and Little Tennessee clusters, this figure yields a range of 21 to 119 domestic structures per site and an average of 59.

The floor area of 47 domestic structures mapped at the King (Smith 1987), North Mouse Creek, South Mouse Creek, Rymer, and Ledford Island (Sullivan 1986) sites averaged 61m². Depending on whether the formula for estimating household size from dwelling space proposed by Naroll (1962) or by Cook (1972) is used, the average structure at each of these sites would have been occupied by 5.9 or 11.0 people. Applying the smaller figure to all sites with presumably accurate site size estimates, we find that the resident population of towns ranged from 124 to 702 and averaged 350. With the larger figure, population ranged from 253 to 1,309 and averaged 652 (Table 9-1).

Site clusters contain four to seven sites that are larger than 1 ha. The average number of large sites per cluster is 5.3. These figures are almost certainly on the low side, but not by much. Intensive survey would probably turn up additional large sites in the Childersburg, Rome, and Chattanooga areas. Amateur and professional surveying has been fairly thorough in the Coosawattee, Etowah, Hiwassee, and Little Tennessee drainages, however, and it is unlikely that there are more large sites in these areas. Some of the known sites in the Little Tennessee River may actually predate the mid-sixteenth century.

The estimated total population for the Carters cluster, the only one for which we have reasonably accurate size estimates for all known sites, is 2,847 by the Naroll formula and 5,401 by the Cook formula. This cluster contains the greatest number of contemporary, large sites in the paramount chiefdom.

Four clusters—Childersburg, Carters, Chattanooga, and Little Tennessee—contain one or more sites with platform mounds. Mound sites may also have been part of the Cartersville, Rome, and Hiwassee clusters. There is stratigraphic evidence that the Brewster phase inhabitants of the Etowah site, located on the Etowah River where it crosses the Great Smoky Fault, utilized Mound B; a platform mound in downtown Rome, reported to have yielded a silver ornament and gold beads, and to have been destroyed in the late nineteenth century, could have been part of the Rome cluster (Jones 1861:82); and late Mississippian pottery is abundant around the mound at the Hiwassee Old Town site, located on the Hiwassee River where it crosses the Great Smoky Fault (Richard Polhemus, personal communication).

The Carters, Chattanooga, and Little Tennessee clusters may have had more than one mounded site, but only in the Carters cluster is there strong evidence for mound site contemporaneity. Here mound construction episodes are stratigraphically dated to the mid-sixteenth century at the Little Egypt site, while at the Thompson site, there is only one component that can be reasonably identified with mound construction, and it also dates to the mid-sixteenth century.

In the Carters cluster, Little Egypt has two, possibly three, mounds (Hally 1980), while Thompson (Figure 9-2) has one (Langford and Smith 1986). The Chattanooga and Little Tennessee clusters also have one multimound site. The Carters cluster, and possibly the other two, can be characterized as having a

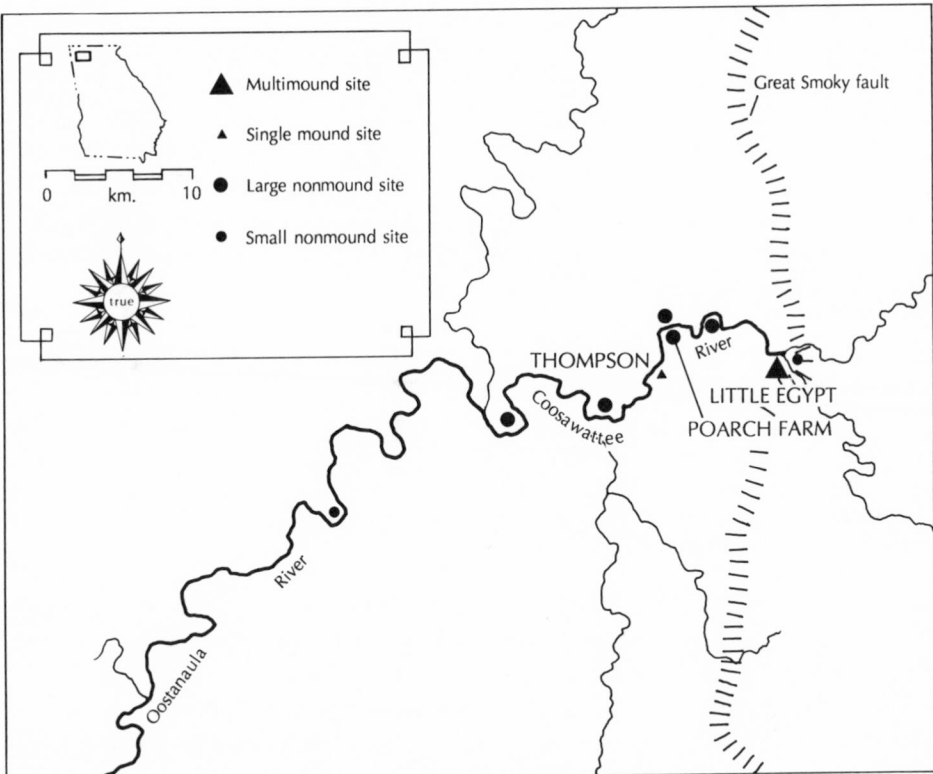

Figure 9-2. The Carters site cluster.

three-level settlement hierarchy (four-level if farmsteads were a common settlement type), and a two-level administrative hierarchy (three-level if towns managed some of their internal affairs).

Large sites tend to be strung out along river courses in most site clusters (Figure 9-1). This linear configuration may reflect the lack of survey in upland areas and along small tributary streams. It is supported, however, by Spanish documents that repeatedly describe large towns as occupying floodplains of major streams. The Childersburg site cluster is the only one that diverges from this pattern.

The geographical size of site clusters, measured as the linear distance between the two most widely separated large sites, ranges from 10.8 km to 23.5 km and averages 19.5 km (Table 9-2). If the site of Hiwassee Old Town does have a sixteenth-century component, the Hiwassee cluster would be the largest, with a maximum dimension of 26 km. Straight-line distances between nearest neighbor large sites within clusters range from 0.1 km to 13.8 km and average 5.5 km. Distances are lowest in the Carters cluster with an average spacing of 3.3 km and highest in the Childersburg cluster with an average of 7.6 km.

All seven site clusters are separated from their nearest neighbors by considerable distances. Mound sites, including those believed to exist in the Rome, Cartersville, and Hiwassee River clusters, are separated from their nearest

Table 9-2. Settlement Characteristics of Site Clusters

	Number				Cluster Size:		Distance between Mound Centers of Nearest Neighbor Site Clusters	Distance between Sites on Edge of Nearest Neighbor Site Clusters[a]
	Mid-Sixteenth Century Sites	Possible Mid-Sixteenth Century Sites	Sites >1 ha	Average Size²	Average Distance between Sites[a]	Maximum Distance between Sites[a]		
Childersburg	8		6	5.4	7.8	23.5	62	42
Rome	5		3	2.1	6.7	20.0	45	20
Cartersville	3	9	4	3.4	4.4	10.8	45	32
Carters	8	1	7	3.3	2.9	18.7	54	42
Chattanooga	5		4	1.3	7.3	18.0	69	50
Hiwassee	5	2	6	2.8	3.4	22.5	48	29
Little Tennessee	3	11	7	1.9	4.4	23.0	29	16

Note: Distances in the last four columns are in kilometers.
[a] Sites refered to are >1 hectare

neighbor in adjacent clusters by distances of between 29 km and 69 km (average 49 km). The shortest distance between large nonmound sites in neighboring clusters ranges from 16 km to 50 km and averages 33 km.

We believe that the site clusters discussed here represent politically integrated societies that have centralized administrative hierarchies and are by and large politically autonomous. The evidence in support of this interpretation can be summarized as follows.

1. Sites with platform mounds, present in most if not all site clusters, can be reasonably identified as the administrative centers for each polity.
2. The number of large sites that constitute each site cluster approximates the optimum number of communities that can be administered by the leader of a single level of an administrative hierarchy (Johnson 1982).
3. Geographical size of clusters (approximately 20 km) is small enough in terms of travel time (Cherry 1987; Johnson 1987; Renfrew 1975; Spencer 1987) to permit leaders to exercise direct control over all communities within their polity.
4. Distances between mound centers in adjacent clusters exceed 30 km and are too great for leaders to efficiently exercise direct control over neighboring polities.
5. The absence of sites from areas between site clusters suggests that the spaces between polities were largely uninhabited. Such space could have served as military buffer zones between competing polities and as procurement territories and population reservoirs for natural food resources such as white-tailed deer (Hickerson 1966).

A similar settlement pattern—where distances separating highest-order central places average 40 km and where distances to settlements furthest removed from the center seldom exceed 20 km—has been noted for prestate complex societies throughout the world (Helms 1979; Johnson 1982, 1987; Kowalewski et al. 1989; Renfrew 1975). According to Renfrew (1975) and Spencer (1987), this pattern reflects the maximum geographical size that politically centralized polities can attain in prestate times.

We choose to refer to the polities represented by site clusters as chiefdoms. The Spanish narratives indicate that they were incorporated into a larger polity, the paramount chiefdom of Coosa. However, we believe that they could, and at various times probably did, exist as autonomous political systems. The province of Toa, located on the Flint River in southwest Georgia (Worth 1988), appears from the de Soto narratives to have been politically autonomous, and it closely resembles in archaeological details the site clusters in the Tennessee and Coosa River drainages.

Central place theory holds that administrative centers should be located near the geographical center of polities so as to minimize the cost, in travel time, of administration (Cherry 1987; Steponaitis 1978) and maximize the accessibility of the center to its supporting population (Johnson 1987). This may be the case for the Chattanooga cluster, where Citico (which has two mounds) is centrally located with respect to the other known sites making up the cluster. It is not the case in the other clusters, most of which have distinctly linear configurations. Five clusters are located on small rivers where they leave the more mountainous Piedmont and Blue Ridge physiographic provinces and enter the Valley and Ridge province. The administrative center in the Kymulga, Carters, and Little Tennessee clusters, represented by a mound site or the site with the largest number of mounds, is located immediately adjacent to the Great Smoky Fault, which separates the Valley and Ridge province from the Piedmont and Blue Ridge provinces. This places the center at one end of the site cluster. If Etowah and Hiwassee Old Town had mid-sixteenth-century mound construction episodes, then the Cartersville and Hiwassee clusters conform to this pattern as well.

Several explanations may account for this seemingly anomalous location of centers.

1. It would have enhanced the ability of the chief to control two important subsistence resources, food crops and fish, since the richest alluvial soils and largest shoals are located at the fault and immediately downstream from it (Earle 1987; Hally and Langford 1988; Larson 1971a).
2. It would have enabled the chief to better control the flow of Piedmont and Blue Ridge subsistence resources and people into the polity (Larson 1971a).
3. It would have enabled the chief to better control long-distance trade in prestige goods originating from polities located in the Piedmont and farther east.
4. Finally, topography and the location of shoals on east-west flowing rivers such as the Etowah and Coosawattee combine to form a natural artery for overland travel along the fault line itself. Aboriginal trails followed this artery for much of its length in Tennessee and Georgia in the historic period (Goff 1953; Meyer 1928). The junctions of these trails with east-west flowing rivers suitable for canoe travel form a series of "crossroads" that could have served as important nodes for trade and communication.

The Paramount Chiefdom of Coosa

Spanish sources refer to at least five provinces that were under some form of control by the chief of Coosa. These were spread out over a distance of almost 400 km with the province of Coosa and its head town, Coosa, located in the approximate center. Each province had a capital town where its chief resided. Provinces were separated from one another in some cases by as much as 90 km of uninhabited territory.

Chiefs of subordinate provinces acknowledged "being subject to" the chief of Coosa, but the narratives say very little else about the nature of the relationship between the two types of leader. Military alliance and coordination is suggested by a plot to ambush Juan Pardo's expedition in 1567 that was apparently organized by the chief of Coosa and involved warriors from several towns or provinces (Bandera 1569). At least some provinces paid tribute to the paramount chief, as is indicated by the Napochie pledge "to pay as tribute, thrice a year, game, or fruits, chestnuts, and nuts in confirmation of their (Coosa's) superiority" (Swanton 1922:239).

From an archaeological perspective, the paramount chiefdom of Coosa appears to have consisted of at least 7 and possibly as many as 10 chiefdoms (Figure 9-1). Each was separated from its neighbors by a distance of 20–50 km. Each consisted of 4 to 7 towns, one of which may have had a platform mound and served as the administrative center for the polity. Most towns were 2–4 ha in size and had between 200 and 1,000 inhabitants. Each town may have had a plaza and one or more large structures that probably functioned in the ceremonial and political life of the community. In most cases, towns comprising a chiefdom were strung out along a single river at intervals of 3–5 km for a total straight-line distance of approximately 20 km.

The chiefdom of Coosa (represented by the Carters site cluster) consisted of at least seven large towns, including the capital, and may have had a population in excess of 5,000 people (Figure 9-2). The capital of this chiefdom and of the paramount chiefdom, represented by the Little Egypt site, covered approximately 5 ha and had two or three platform mounds. It was located at the eastern edge of the chiefdom where the Coosawattee River enters the Great Valley. A lower-level administrative center existed at the single mound Thompson site, which was located 8.5 km downstream from the capital at the geographic midpoint of the chiefdom.

There is little archaeolgical evidence for the preeminent position that Little Egypt and the Carters polity held in the paramount chiefdom of Coosa. Little Egypt is large and has more mounds than most other mound sites. But it is not the only multimound site, nor even the only one with three mounds, since Chilhowee on the Little Tennessee River is reported to have had three mounds (Thomas 1894). The mounds at Little Egypt, standing only 3–4 m high, are rather small in comparison with those at Citico (8 m) in the Chattanooga polity (Hatch 1976) and Toqua (7 m) in the Little Tennessee polity (Polhemus 1987). No burials with mortuary characteristics suggestive of exalted status are known from the site, although they may exist (Hally 1980).

The Carters chiefdom contains more large sites than most other chiefdoms, and these are larger on the average than towns in most other chiefdoms. It is not, however, exceptional in these respects. Future research, furthermore, may result in upward revision in the size of other polities. The Carters chiefdom is somewhat unusual in having a two-tiered administrative hierarchy. It is not, however, necessarily the only polity with this characteristic, since the Chattanooga and Little Tennessee chiefdoms may also have had two levels.

Little Egypt and the Carters site cluster may have been the politically most important town and chiefdom in the region in A.D. 1540, but it is difficult to tell this from the available archaeological evidence. Their architectural and settlement features are certainly not comparable in magnitude to those of Etowah (Larson 1971b) and Moundville (Peebles 1987) in the fourteenth and fifteenth centuries.

There is also little archaeological evidence outside the Carters area for the larger political system of which the chief of Coosa was acknowledged head. The uninhabited areas separating site clusters suggest that the chiefdoms were not integrated into a larger politically centralized system. There is, as we have already noted, little evidence for the kind of settlement hierarchy that we might expect to accompany Coosa's regional hegemony.

To the extent that the chief of Coosa exercised any control over subordinate chiefdoms and was able to maintain peaceful relations among them, we might expect a certain amount of stylistic uniformity to develop in the region as a result of increased contact between chiefdoms. This does not appear to be the case, at least with respect to pottery. Ceramics of the Dallas culture chiefdoms in the Tennessee River drainage and the Lamar culture chiefdoms in the Coosa River drainage are quite distinct. Furthermore, the pottery complex of every chiefdom for which ceramic counts are available can be distinguished at the phase level (Hally and Langford 1988; Polhemus 1987; Sullivan 1986).

The distribution of the Citico-style gorget (Muller 1966) conforms closely to the area of the Coosa paramount chiefdom (compare Figure 9-3 with Figure 8-1). As such, it is a part of the archaeological record that may be attributable to the existence of that political system. Citico-style gorgets are found exclusively with adult female and subadult burials (Seckinger 1977; Hatch 1975). Other grave associations indicate that these individuals had relatively high status within their community. We may never know the ideological significance of the Citico-style gorget or why it was associated with females in mortuary contexts. It is not beyond reason, though, to suggest that it may have been a symbolic representation of the paramount chief and an identity marker for those people under his political control.

Conclusion

Other types of evidence and analyses may someday help us identify the paramount chiefdom of Coosa in the archaeological record. For the present, however, it is essentially invisible. We feel this situation says something about the nature of the political control that the chief of Coosa had over those provinces described as subject to him. If paramount chiefdoms such as Coosa involved primarily personal relationships between chiefs and subordinate chiefs and

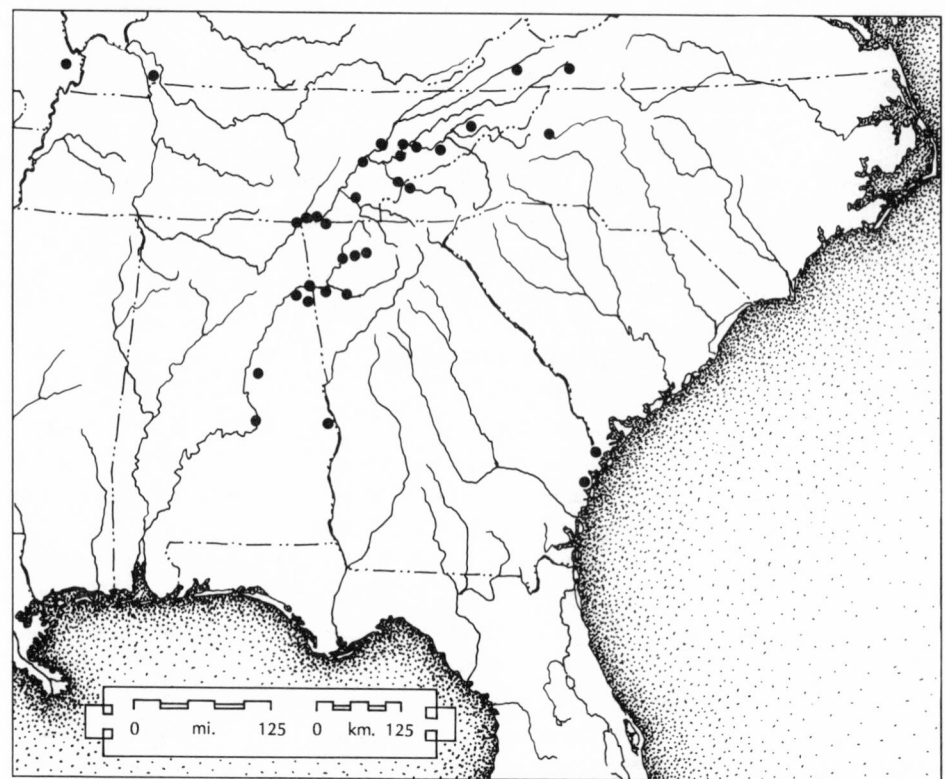

Figure 9-3. Distribution of Citico-style rattlesnake gorgets.

these were largely of a symbolic nature, if paramount chiefs made few demands (Wright 1977; Earle 1987) of subordinate chiefs and their provinces, and if paramount chiefdoms were rather unstable and short-lived (Earle 1987), archaeological evidence of them may be virtually nonexistent.

Acknowledgments

Vernon J. Knight provided us with site data for eastern Alabama. Dick Polhemus, Jefferson Chapman, and Nick Fielder each contributed useful information on the archaeology of eastern Tennessee. We are grateful to the Tennessee Valley Authority, especially J. Bennett Graham and Jill Elmendorf, for permission to use unpublished information from M. Smith's survey in the Chickamauga reservoir. Charles Hudson and Steve Kowalewski read early drafts of this paper and provided useful comments. To each of these people we offer our sincere thanks.

Notes

1. Although Little and Curren (this volume) dispute the findings of Hudson and his associates as to the location of sixteenth-century Coosa, we accept the Hudson recon-

struction as being the most consistent with historical and archaeological evidence. For the Hudson reconstruction, see Hudson et al. (1985, 1987). For the reconstruction of Coosa by Little and Curren, see this volume. Hudson (1989) and Smith (1989) have recently critiqued various aspects of the de Soto route reconstruction of Little and Curren.

References

Bandera, Juan de la
  1569 *Proceeding of the Account Which Captain Juan Pardo Gave of the Entrance Which He Made into the Land of the Floridas*. Archivo General de Indias 54-5-9. Copy in the North Carolina State Archives, Raleigh.
Biedma, Luys Hernandez de
  1968 Relation. In *Narratives of Hernando de Soto in the Conquest of Florida*, translated by Buckingham Smith, pp. 229–261. Palmetto Books, Gainesville, Florida.
Brain, Jeffrey P.
  1985 Update of de Soto Studies since the United States de Soto Expedition Commission Report. In *Final Report of the United States De Soto Commission*, written by John R. Swanton, pp. xi–lxxii. Smithsonian Institution Press, Washington, D.C.
Cherry, J. F.
  1987 Power in Space: Archaeological and Geographical Studies. In *Landscape and Culture: Geographical and Archaeological Perspectives*, edited by J. M. Wagstaff, pp. 146–172. Basil Blackwell, Oxford.
Cook, Sherburne F.
  1972 *Prehistoric Demography*. Addison-Wesley Module in Anthropology 16. Addison-Wesley, Reading, Massachusetts.
DePratter, Chester, Charles Hudson, and Marvin T. Smith
  1983 The Route of Juan Pardo's Explorations in the Interior Southeast, 1566–1568. *Florida Historical Quarterly* 62:125–58.
  1985 The de Soto expedition: From Chiaha to Mabila. In *Alabama and the Borderlands, From Prehistory to Statheood*, edited by Reid Badger and Lawrence Clayton, pp. 108–127. University of Alabama Press, Tuscaloosa.
Earle, Timothy
  1987 Chiefdoms in Archaeological and Ethnohistorical Perspective. *Annual Review of Anthropology* 16:279–308.
Elvas, Gentleman of
  1968 Relation. In *Narratives of Hernando de Soto in the Conquest of Florida*, translated by Buckingham Smith, pp. 5–203. Palmetto Books, Gainesville, Florida.
Goff, John H.
  1953 Some Major Indian Trading Paths across the Georgia Piedmont. *Georgia Mineral Newsletter* 6(4): 122–131.
Hally, David J.
  1980 *Archaeological Investigation of the Little Egypt Site (9Mu102), Murray County, Georgia, 1970–72 Seasons*. Submitted to the Heritage Conservation and Recreation Service, U.S. Department of the Interior, Contract Nos. 14-10-9-900-390, 1910P21041, 9911T000411, C5546.
  1988 Archaeology and Settlement Plan of the King Site. In *The King Site: Continuity and Contact in Sixteenth-Century Georgia*, edited by Robert L. Blakely, pp. 3–16. University of Georgia Press, Athens.
Hally, David J., and James B. Langford, Jr.
  1988 Mississippi Period Archaeology of the Georgia Valley and Ridge Province. University of Georgia Laboratory of Archaeology Series Report No. 25.
Hatch, James W.
  1974 *Social Dimensions of Dallas Mortuary Patterns*. Unpublished Master's thesis,

Department of Anthropology, Pennsylvania State University, University Park.

1975 Social Dimensions of Dallas Burials. *Southeastern Archaeological Conference Bulletin* 18:132–138.

1976 The Citico Site (40Ha65): A Synthesis. *Tennessee Anthropologist* 1:75–103.

Helms, Mary W.

1979 *Ancient Panama: Chiefs in Search of Power.* University of Texas Press, Austin.

Hickerson, Harold

1966 The Virginia Deer and Intertribal Buffer Zones in the Upper Mississippi Valley. In *Man, Culture, and Animals,* edited by A. Leeds and A. P. Vayda, pp. 43–65. American Association for the Advancement of Science Monograph.

Holstein, Harry O., and Keith Little

1987 *A Short-term Archaeological Investigation of the Davis Farm Archaeological Complex, A Multicomponent Prehistoric Site in Calhoun Co., Alabama.* Archaeological Resource Lab Research Series No. 1. Jacksonville State University, Jacksonville, Alabama.

Hudson, Charles

1987 Juan Pardo's Excursion Beyond Chiaha. *Tennessee Anthropologist* 12:74–87.

1989 Critique of Little and Curren's Reconstruction of De Soto's Route through Alabama. Manuscript circulated to the Alabama De Soto Commission.

Hudson, Charles, Marvin Smith, David Hally, Richard Polhemus, and Chester DePratter

1985 Coosa: A Chiefdom in the Sixteenth Century Southeastern United States. *American Antiquity* 50:723–737.

1987 Reply to Boyd and Schroedl. *American Antiquity* 52:845–856.

Hudson, Charles, Marvin Smith, Chester DePratter, and Emilia Kelly

1989 The Tristan de Luna Expedition, 1559–1561. *Southeastern Archaeology,* 8:31–45

Johnson, Gregory A.

1982 Organizational Structure and Scalar Stress. In *Theory and Explanation in Archaeology,* edited by C. Renfrew, M. J. Rowlands, and B. A. Segraves, pp. 389–421. Academic Press, New York.

1987 The Changing Organization of Uruk Administration on the Susiana Plain. In *The Archaeology of Western Iran,* edited by Frank Hole, pp. 107–140. Smithsonian Institution Press, Washington, D.C.

Jones, Charles C., Jr.

1861 *Monumental Remains of Georgia.* John M. Cooper, Savannah.

Kimball, Larry R.

1985 *The 1977 Archaeological Survey: An Overall Assessment of the Archaeological Resources of Tellico Reservoir.* Report of Investigation No. 40. Department of Anthropology, University of Tennessee, Knoxville.

Knight, Vernon James, Jr.

1985 East Alabama Archaeological Survey 1985 Season. Report of Investigations No. 47. University of Alabama, Office of Archaeological Research, Moundville, Alabama.

Knight, Vernon James, Jr., Gloria Cole, and Richard Walling

1984 An Archaeological Reconnaissance of the Coosa and Tallapoosa River Valleys, East Alabama: 1983. Report of Investigations No. 43. University of Alabama Office of Archaeological Research, Moundville, Alabama.

Kowalewski, Stephen A., Gary M. Feinman, Laura Finsten, Richard E. Blanton, and Linda M. Nicholas

1989 *Prehistoric Settlement Patterns in Tlacolula, Etla and Ocotlán, the Valley of Oaxaca, Mexico.* University of Michigan Museum of Anthropology Memoirs, No. 23. Ann Arbor.

Langford, James B., and Marvin T. Smith

1986 Recent Investigations in the Core of the Coosa Province. Paper presented at the LAMAR Institute Conference of South Appalachian Mississippi, Macon, Georgia.

Lankford, George E.
 1977 A New Look at De Soto's Route through Alabama. *Journal of Alabama Archaeology* 23(1): 11–360

Larson, Lewis H., Jr.
 1971a Settlement Distribution during the Mississippi Period. *SEAC Bulletin* 13(1970):19–25.
 1971b Archaeological Implications of Social Stratification at the Etowah Site, Georgia. In *Approaches to the Social Dimension of Mortuary Practices*, edited by James A. Brown, pp. 58–67. Memoirs of the Society for American Archaeology No. 25, Washington, D.C.

Lewis, T.M.N., and Madeline Kneberg
 1941 The Prehistory of the Chickamauga Basin in Tennessee, a Preview. Tennessee Anthropology Papers No. 1. Division of Anthropology, University of Tennessee, Knoxville.

Meyer, William E.
 1928 Indian Trails of the Southeast. *Annual Report of the Bureau of American Ethnology* 42:727–857.

Muller, Jon D.
 1966 Archaeological Analysis of Art Style. *Tennessee Archaeologist* 22:25–39.

Naroll, Raoul
 1962 Floor Area and Settlement Population. *American Antiquity* 27:587–589.

Peebles, Christopher S.
 1987 Moundville from 1000 to 1500 A.D. as Seen from 1840 to 1985 A.D. In *Chiefdoms in the Americas*, edited by Robert D. Drennan and Carlos A. Uribe, pp. 21–42. University Press of America, New York.

Polhemus, Richard R. (editor)
 1987 *The Toqua Site: A Late Mississippian Dallas Phase Town*. Report of Investigations No. 41. Department of Anthropology, University of Tennessee, Knoxville.

Priestly, Herbert I.
 1928 *The Luna Papers*, 2 vols. Florida State Historical Society, Deland, Florida.

Ranjel, Rodrigo
 1922 Narrative. In *Narratives of the Career of Hernando de Soto*, edited by Edward G. Bourne, pp. 43–150. Allerton, New York.

Renfrew, Colin
 1975 Trade as Action at a Distance: Questions of Integration and Communication. In *Ancient Civilization and Trade*, edited by Jeremy A. Sabloff and C. L. Lambert-Karlowsky, pp. 3–59. University of New Mexico, Albuquerque.

Seckinger, Ernest W., Jr.
 1977 Social Complexity during the Mississippian Period in Northwest Georgia. Unpublished Master's thesis, Department of Anthropology, University of Georgia, Athens.

Smith, Marvin T.
 1976 The Route of de Soto through Tennessee, Georgia, and Alabama: The Evidence from Material Culture. *Early Georgia* 4(1 & 2):27–47.
 1987 *Archaeology of Aboriginal Culture Change in the Interior Southeast: Depopulation during the Early Historic Period*. University Presses of Florida, Gainesville.
 1988 Mississippian Settlement in Eastern Tennessee: The View from the Chickamauga Reservoir. Paper presented at the Southeastern Archaeological Conference, New Orleans.
 1989 Review of "A Spatulate Axe from the Demopolis, Alabama Area" by Keith Little, Caleb Curren, Curtis Hill, and Harry Holstein. Manuscript circulated to the Alabama De Soto Commission.

Spencer, Charles S.
 1987 Rethinking the Chiefdom. In *Chiefdoms in the Americas*, edited by Robert

Drennan and Carlos Uribe, pp. 369–389. University Press of America, New York.

Steponaitis, Vincas P.
  1978 Location Theory and Complex Chiefdoms: A Mississippian Example. In *Mississippian Settlement Patterns*, edited by Bruce D. Smith, pp. 417–453. Academic Press, New York.

Sullivan, Lynne Anne Peters
  1986 *The Late Mississippian Village: Community and Society of the Mouse Creek Phase in Southeastern Tennessee*. Unpublished Ph.D. dissertation, Department of Anthropology, University of Wisconsin-Milwaukee.

Swanton, John R.
  1922 *Early History of the Creek Indians and Their Neighbors*. Bureau of American Ethnology Bulletin No. 3. Government Printing Office, Washington, D.C.

Thomas, Cyrus W.
  1894 *Report on the Mound Explorations of the Bureau of Ethnology*. Smithsonian Institution, Bureau of Ethnology, Twelfth Annual Report. Washington, D.C.

Vega, Garcilaso de la
  1962 *The Florida of the Inca*. Translated by J. G. Varner and J. J. Varner. University of Texas Press, Austin.

Worth, John E.
  1988 Mississippian Occupation of the Middle Flint River. Unpublished Master's thesis, Department of Anthropology and Linguistics, University of Georgia, Athens.

Wright, Henry T.
  1977 Recent Research on the Origin of the State. *Annual Review of Anthropology* 6:379–397.

Chapter 10 ■

James B. Langford, Jr.

The Coosawattee Plate: A Sixteenth-Century Catholic/Aztec Artifact from Northwest Georgia

Recent efforts to delineate the routes of the sixteenth-century Spanish notables Hernando de Soto and Tristán de Luna have determined that the core of the indigenous province of Coosa was located along a 20-km stretch of the Coosawattee River in Northwest Georgia (Hudson et al. 1985; Langford and Smith 1986). The villages in this corridor share striking similarities with respect to ceramic assemblages and other cultural remains within the Barnett phase designation (A.D. 1450–1600) (Hally 1979:202).

Artifact collectors working on these Barnett phase sites have found a number of sixteenth-century European-type artifacts in direct association with indigenous materials within burials (Langford and Smith 1986). Most of these artifacts are assumed to be of Spanish origin since the area was abandoned by the seventeenth century (Smith 1987:76) and not reoccupied until the early eighteenth century. So far, these materials yield little additional information as to the specific expedition with which they may be associated.

Recently, however, an unusual copper "plate" or modified gorget found by an artifact collector at the Poarch Farm site (9Go1) is beginning to yield new and valuable information about these early expeditions. An incised picture on the plate suggests that it was manufactured in Mexico in the middle sixteenth century by an Aztec Indian. Such manufacture, if accurately identified, would place the artifact with the Luna colonizing expedition of 1559–1561. The plate was brought to Northwest Georgia by a member of the expedition (perhaps as a book cover or other ornament), traded or given to a native inhabitant, modified into a gorget, and buried with presumably its last owner, a child of 10–11 years of age.

The Poarch Farm Site

The Poarch Farm site is one of seven known Barnett phase sites located on the Coosawattee River below the main Carter's Dam (see Figure 9-2). The principal village of Coosa is thought to be located at the Little Egypt site (9Mu102) now covered by the reregulation lake immediately below Carter's Dam (Hudson et al. 1985). The Poarch Farm site is located approximately 7.6 km from the Little Egypt site.

Collectors worked extensively at the site during the late 1970s and early 1980s and excavated 300–400 burials in the Barnett phase occupation area. The property has changed hands in the past few years and the new landowner has stopped all digging on the site.

Collectors recovered several European artifacts including glass beads (faceted chevron, Nueva Cadiz plain, and blown), iron spikes and wedges, Clarksdale brass bells, and pieces of swords and knives. All of the European items were found in seemingly aboriginal burials and almost always accompanied by other grave goods of indigenous manufacture. Most of the burials containing European artifacts occurred in a limited part of the site that was possibly a plaza.

In the fall of 1984, two collectors probing and excavating in the western end of the site uncovered a thin copper plate in a flexed burial. The skeletal remains were in a very poor state of preservation. No other grave goods were present in the burial pit. Examination of the teeth from the burial indicate that the individual was a subadult of 10–11 years of age beginning to experience changes in dentition from deciduous to permanent teeth (Robert Blakely, Bettina Detweiler, personal communication 1987).

Cleaning and Laboratory Analysis

The general condition of the plate is relatively poor; various states of corrosion, chemical stabilization, and bronze disease exist on the face of the artifact. The plate measures approximately 18 cm × 8.5 cm × .098 cm. Owing to the brittle nature of the metal and the relatively unfavorable environmental condition of interment, the plate is broken into 23 contiguous pieces and numerous other discontiguous fragments. At least two holes measuring 0.4 cm in diameter were drilled in the center of the plate as it was adapted by Indians in the Southeast for use as a gorget. Two additional holes were punched or drilled approximately 1.0 cm from the edge of both left and right sides of the plate. Other features of the plate are the 26 raised "punch" marks around the intact portions of the perimeter of the plate. Originally, these probably extended around the entire perimeter. Examination of these punch marks has not revealed whether the marks were a decorative feature or served the functional purpose of securing the plate to leather or fabric.

During extensive laboratory analysis and conservation, soils and some sulfides were carefully removed from the artifact. However, no attempt was made to remove most of the corrosive deposits from the plate surface because preliminary examination of these deposits revealed many kinds of organic material preserved by the copper sulfides. Also, the incised lines are very shallow and almost obliterated in some areas where corrosive activity has been most destructive. Removal of the sulfide deposits would destroy the remaining traces of incised lines in these areas.

Examination of the incised lines revealed that the lines were made via a "step-cut" method utilizing a stone tool (John Leader, personal communication 1987). This repoussé technique involves the careful retracing of lines or pictorial representations. Because these lines were repeatedly retraced, no "stray" lines have been found on the artifact. Each line was carefully and purposefully cut into the face of the plate.

Metallic composition of the plate is presumed to be predominantly copper. Because of the corroded nature of the discontiguous fragments, meaningful neutron activation analysis was not possible. Uncorroded metal is present in some of the contiguous pieces, but the removal of metal for testing would necessitate defacement, albeit minor, of artistically significant areas. Such a trade-off at this time seems unnecessary, at least with regard to determining the origin of manufacture. Incising techniques and stylistic treatment provide sufficient information to ascertain where and by whom the plate was made.

Figure 10-1. The Coosawattee plate.

Analysis of the Elements of the Incising

Understanding the meaning of the incised design requires an analysis of (1) the individual elements, (2) the style of aggregation of the elements, and (3) the historical and cultural context of the artifact. This analysis demonstrated a blend of Christian and Aztec religious ideas representative of the ethnohistorical context of mid-sixteenth-century Mexico. The plate has three incised characters that we call Characters A, B, and C. Character A is in the center of the plate and Characters B and C appear on the left and right sides of the plate, respectively (see Figure 10-1).

We can begin the analysis of the individual elements with the most dominant figure, Character A. The hand of this figure is relatively oversized in relation to the rest of the figure and the index finger extends prominently, while the thumb holds down the other fingers. The left hand clasps the end of a flowering or leafed branch that rests on the left shoulder.

The raised hand and open mouth indicate that the character is speaking. Some Aztec postconquest codices contain "speech scrolls" emanating from the mouths of those who are speaking. Other illustrations of the same period lack such speech designations even when speech is obviously intended. Lack of consistency in this regard can probably be attributed to differences in artistic style and expression. The almost vertical position of the hand and arm indicates that Character A is agreeing to or accepting a command or request, and the horizontal position of the extended arm and hand of Character B confirms this relationship between the two characters (Troike 1975).

The clothing of Character A features the stamped rectangular neck design of the traditional *huipilli* worn by Aztec Indian women of early colonial period and preconquest Mexico (Anawalt 1981:52–53). The hair of Character A appears to flow over the shoulders and down the back, which probably denotes a young woman. In sixteenth-century drawings young women usually have longer hair (Lienzo de Tlaxcala 1979:Lamina 7). Drawings of Marina, Cortez's interpreter and wife of a lieutenant of Cortez, depict her with both long and short hair styles (Lienzo de Tlaxcala 1979:Lamina 2–4; Sahagún 1950–1969:12:Illustrations 1, 22, 44).

The flowers or flowering branch could be one of several types of flowers described in the Florentine Codex. The blossoms most closely resemble the *azcalxochitl* or the *iopixochitl* (Sahagún 1950–1969:11:Illustrations 707, 708). Cross-referencing these flower types with the Sahagún texts regarding Aztec deities or even everyday life has thus far not produced any correlations. The fact that the sixteenth-century documents lack any pictorial representations of females carrying flowers in such a manner is probably significant. Occasionally, women and deities are shown carrying plants and even flowers, but such depictions of flowers are quite different from the Coosawattee Plate and the manner of carrying or presenting them is always with the items held away from the body (Sahagún 1950–1969:2:Illustrations 5–12).

Another notable incised feature of the female character on the plate is the slightly diagonal line (with hash marks across it) that appears on the lower section of the skirt. This design was cut carefully and repeatedly in the same manner as the rest of the incising and therefore carries some significance as a decoration or symbol. One reference in the text of the Florentine Codex may provide a valuable clue to the meaning of the design. The reference is to "torn and mended skirts" that Aztec women wore at certain times as a means of appearing more modest and less attractive (Sahagún 1950–1969:12:118).

Some pictorial precedents do exist for the display of stitching on the seams of skirts of Aztec women, but not stitching that is perpendicular to the natural seams of the skirts in the manner of the Coosawattee Plate. Representations that display the stitched seams are usually associated with women of lower status, even drunken and downtrodden (Anawalt 1981:54). The practice of wearing old skirts continues into present-day Mexico among Indian and mixed-race rural women when they come to trade in the marketplace. Presumably, these women strive to look more modest in order to enhance their bargaining positions (John Aguilar, personal communication 1987).

Because of the care taken to depict other rather delicate details (eyes, ears, and even shading of some areas), we can infer that the diagonal design on the skirt is exactly what it appears to be—a jagged and straight tear that has been mended. The reason for showing this woman to be modest in appearance will become clearer as we analyze the other elements of the design, the intentions of the artist, and the blended Aztec and Christian influences.

Character B is wearing the traditional *tilmatli*, or cloak, worn by Aztec men of sixteenth-century and preconquest Mexico (Anawalt 1981:30). The cloak is knotted at the neck. The figure is also wearing what appears to be a closed-sleeve shirt or camisa (Patricia Anawalt, personal communication 1989). Shirts of this kind were not common in preconquest Mexico but appear to be somewhat more prevalent in the postconquest sixteenth century. The Florentine Codex shows several examples of Aztec males wearing the cloak and the camisa together (Sahagún 1950–1969:9:Illustrations 58, 59; 10:Illustrations 53, 51).

Representation of the hair, including very light striations depicting the "grain" of the hair styling, is almost identical to examples in the sixteenth-century sources (Sahagún 1950–1969:9:Illustration 58; 12:Illustrations 22, 71, 101; Wauchope 1975:14:3:Figure 70). In preconquest Mexico, head adornments and clothing styles reflected important delineations of social status. Usually the cloak was knotted at the right shoulder. However, certain nobles and priests apparently were allowed to knot the cloak in the front. High-status individuals would also wear various types of colored feathers in the hair as a corresponding badge of rank (Anawalt 1981:30). Character B wears no such head adornments, a fact somewhat inconsistent with the cloak knotted at the neck. However, examples do exist that clearly show messengers from Montezuma to Cortéz who have cloaks knotted in the front but who also do not have head adornments of any kind (Sahagún 1950–1969:12:Illustrations 22, 25, 26).

The right hand of Character B is relatively oversized and extends toward Character A with the palm up and the index finger extended. As previously mentioned, the horizontal position of the arm and hand indicates that Character B is making a request or command (Troike 1975).

Character B is carrying either a torch or a flower, possibly a rose, in the left hand. The identification of the torch was made after reviewing the sixteenth-century Mexican codices and comparing the item to representations of fire, smoke, torches, and plumed (feathered) staffs. Although a duplicate example of the item has not been found in the sixteenth-century references or in any later codex, the smoke may be inferred by comparison with the Florentine Codex (Sahagún 1950–1959:12:Illustrations 5, 25, 49). Several examples of plumed staffs exist in the sixteenth-century codices, and these are distinctly different from the item represented on the copper plate (Sahagún 1950–1969:12:Illustrations 5, 25, 49). The item could also represent an oversized flower such as a rose. The historical and artistic context, discussed later in this chapter, lend credence to this possibility.

Character C appears on the right side of the face of the copper plate and on Character A's left side. Character C is an animal-type figure with a pronounced snout and multiclawed or cloven foot. These features appear inconsistent with easily recognizable animals. A review of the various sixteenth-century sources reveals a limited number of creatures that resemble Character C. The representation is not consistent with sixteenth-century Aztec examples of indigenous dogs or catlike creatures. Both animals are always drawn with the teeth displayed and the ears usually pointed (Sahagún 1950–1969:11:Illustrations 1–14).

Besides horses, sixteenth-century drawings of domesticated animals introduced by the Spanish are very rare. However, we could speculate that the figure is a horned animal such as a goat, sheep, or bull. Among European domesticated animals, the closest possible matches would probably be an ox or a pig. The "clawed" foot could be a cloven hoof and the earlike flap could represent a downturned horn or an oversized and rounded ear (Sahagún 1950–1969:12:Illustration 1).

Another kind of animal, the *axolotl*, might also fit the features of the animal depicted on the plate. The *axolotl* was an amphibious creature that occupied a special place in Aztec mythology as a feared man-eating anomaly. The *axolotl*, as drawn and described in the Sahagún documents, had strong short limbs with powerful claws. The nose was blunted and the mouth had no teeth. Alongside the head grew fanlike gills that were quite distinctive and the neck had skin folds similar to the horizontal bands on the neck of the incised animal (Sahagún 1950–1969:11:Illustration 218). These features fit a variety of actual salamander-like animals and one in particular carries the name *axolotl* today. It is probably the same *axolotl* of the preconquest Aztec.

Interpretation of the Incising

Detailed study of the aggregation of the incised elements represented on the Coosawattee Plate begins to reveal more about the message intended by the artist and presents us with two potential interpretations: (1) the scene depicts an event important in the life of some individual Aztec, or a historical or religious event important to a somewhat wider number of Aztecs, or (2) the incising graphically represents the blending of a European-style Virgin Mary with Aztec metaphors in order to depict a specific event of Christian or Aztec religious nature. The aggregations of elements is consistent with sixteenth-century depictions of the Annunciation and also with the sixteenth-century syncretic origins of the Marian cult of the Lady of Guadalupe de Tepeyac.

The first scenario would imply that the incising substantially carries the style and elemental arrangement of sixteenth-century Aztec artistry. While the individual elements of the scene depicted on the plate are undoubtedly sixteenth-century Aztec in nature (Charles Dibble, Jesse Jennings, personal communication 1987), the evidence is compelling that the style of the aggregation or use of elements contained in the scene is very different from any known Aztec or Mexican contexts of any time period (Patricia Anawalt, Hasso von Winning, personal communication 1989).

The second potential interpretation of the aggregated images incised on the plate is that the plate displays an attempt by an Aztec artist to incorporate Aztec characters into a Christian-influenced religious scene. The arrangement of the elements in the incising corresponds substantially with religious scenes on various European book covers, especially Bibles, and other ornaments from the period A.D. 1200–1700.

Two of the most common types of scenes and motifs feature a female as the cental character. These females are the Virgin Mary at the moment of the Annunciation of the coming of Christ (the visitation by the angel Gabriel) or as part of the Nativity at the birth of Christ, and the Woman of Revelation, as described in Chapter 12 of the Book of Revelations. Religious leaders in Europe debated the distinction between the two female characters and finally declared at the Council of Trent in 1556, perhaps as an admission of the evolution of common belief, that the Woman of Revelation was, in fact, the Virgin Mary (Henkel 1973:18).

Depictions of the Virgin Mary in both the Annunciation and the Nativity usually included some representation of a Tree of Life, also called a Tree of Jesse, in close proximity to the female character. Sometimes the Virgin is shown actually holding a budded branch or blossoming flowers (usually lilies, called Annunciation lilies, and occasionally roses). This foliage represents multiple meanings: the lineage of Jesse out of which the prophet Isaiah predicted that Christ would come, and the fertility of the Virgin. In some artistic renderings of the Virgin, the foliage is shown as a prominent motif and sometimes as merely a decorative border (Child and Colles 1971:88–89, 159, 243). Scenes of the Annunciation often include foliage or flowers even held and presented to the Virgin by the angel Gabriel. The angel usually appears on the left side of Annunciation scenes and the Virgin appears on the right (Rothenstein 1951:19, 21, 29; Emily Umberger, personal communication 1987).

The Coosawattee Plate has a combination of elements consistent with European scenes of the Annunciation. The male figure could represent the angel Gabriel delivering a message of instruction, indicated by the extended hand and arm, to the female figure. The female responds in agreement as indicated by the raised and almost vertical arm. She carries the flowers or branch consistent with other Annunciation scenes, and the artist portrays her as a woman of modest background by use of the symbolic torn and mended skirt. This portrayal of modesty would be consistent with the teachings of the Franciscans in postconquest Mexico who often represented the Virgin as a modest housewife, easily approached (Taylor 1987).

The angel carries a torch to offer illumination in the same way that rays of the sun penetrate the room of the Virgin in some European examples of the Annunciation. Ellen Baird (personal communication, 1989) suggests that the "torch" might instead be an oversized representation of a rose, which would also be consistent with some artistic versions of the Annunciation. The animal is not consistent with European representations of the Annunciation, but animals do appear quite frequently in other scenes involving the Virgin, especially the Nativity scenes where oxen and donkeys are most common (Child and Colles 1971:89).

An alternative scenario would argue that the scene represents the appearance of the Woman of Revelation as described in the Book of Revelations. This part of the Bible provided an extremely rich source for graphic representations of all kinds of miraculous events, creatures, and superhuman characters. These representations became quite prevalent in architecture, art, and ornaments as the official church became more obsessed with keeping a vigilant watch for the coming of the Apocalypse and the subsequent arrival of the Kingdom of God.

One of the most commonly reproduced scenes from Chapter 12 of Revelations describes a woman who appeared in the sky "clothed with the sun and the moon under her feet, and upon her head a crown with twelve stars: And her being with child cried out" (Henkel 1973:88).

Artistic renderings of this woman in the sky are surprisingly similar from the eighth through the sixteenth century. The modest demeanor, the cloak (or sometimes crown) with stars, the crescent moon at the feet, the rays of the sun, and the child are elements present in most artistic representations during that period. The artistic representation of the Lady of Guadalupe de Tepeyac, supposedly painted by miraculous means, is almost an exact duplicate of European representations of the Woman of Revelation from the fifteenth and sixteenth centuries. Some historians believe that the painting was made in 1556, more than 20 years after the miraculous event supposedly responsible for its creation (LaFaye 1976:241).

The central female character of the Coosawattee Plate does not have any of the characteristics normally associated with the Woman of Revelation, although some might argue that the animal figure is an *axolotl* and therefore represents the Beast of the Apocalypse that threatens the Woman of Revelation, as it does in some other European pictorial representations of the sixteenth century. The incising does, however, have elements consistent with the legendary origin of the Lady of Guadalupe de Tepeyac.

According to the popular legend, this painting miraculously appeared on the cloak of an Aztec convert, Juan Diego, in 1531 after a woman mysteriously appeared to him three times on or near the hill of Tepeyac, the site of traditional Aztec rituals in celebration of the goddess Tonantzin. The woman instructed Diego to go and pick flowers from the hill and bring them to her. When he returned, she took them from him and then gave them back. She instructed him to take them to the archbishop, Zumárraga. Upon unfolding his cloak before the archbishop, he noticed the beautiful color painting that had miraculously appeared on his cloak.

The story was actually created in 1648 by Miguel Sanchez and closely parallels the appearance of the Lady of Guadalupe de Estremadura in Spain in the thirteenth century (LaFaye 1976:217–224), but the story may also have roots in pictorial representations of other religious events such as the Annunciation. While the copper plate may represent a specific Christian religious event, it does so with Aztec characters and features a Virgin Mary in Aztec clothing. Some researchers believe that the Aztecs related the Virgin to a female in their own belief system, probably Cihuacoatl, also called Tonantzin, or "Our Mother" (LaFaye 1976:215). This created a syncretic female that became a bridge between the traditional beliefs of the Aztecs and the new Christian ideas being so pervasively and urgently presented to them by the new rulers of Mexico.

Conclusions

The Coosawattee Plate was found buried with an Indian child at the Poarch Farm site in Northwest Georgia where investigations reveal a Barnett phase occupation that was abandoned before the seventeenth century. Research also indicates that the Poarch Farm site was one of the larger villages of the capital of Coosa, which was visited by de Soto in 1540 and a small contingent of the Luna expedition in 1560. The Luna group left Mexico City in 1559 to found a colony in the southeastern United States (see Milanich, this volume).

The method of manufacture of the Coosawattee Plate and the stylistic treatment of the incised characters indicate that the plate was made by an Aztec Indian in central Mexico during the middle sixteenth century and no later than 1559, the date of departure of the Luna party from Mexico City. While the artifact could have been manufactured en route to Northwest Georgia, it is proposed here that a more likely setting for the manufacture of the plate would have been a metal workshop in Mexico City. Such a workshop could have been a church-sponsored or sanctioned activity where native artisans were encouraged to use their talents for the benefit of the church and its ongoing educational efforts among the native populations.

The possibility does exist that the artifact was made in the Southeast by some member of the Luna expedition. However, the uniformity of thinness of the plate, its brittleness, and lack of annealing exfoliation suggest that it was manufactured by someone who had the right tools and conditions to produce a metal object of relatively high quality.

The purpose of the plate was to serve as an adornment for a book (probably a Bible) or some other religious item. Oval-shaped copper plates that were engraved and also enameled or pigmented were used as Bible cover ornaments in Europe during and after the sixteenth century. Such plates were also used as decorative additions to Bible boxes, wooden boxes used for the storage of Bibles and other objects. These boxes were also used as writing desks and for the storage of documents (Day 1907:167–180). Until now, no copper ornaments with pictorial incising such as the Coosawattee Plate are known to have been manufactured in Mexico during the sixteenth century (Hasso von Winning, personal communication 1989). The artist or metalworker may have seen a similar ornament of European origin and copied the style of manufacture and incising.

We can speculate that this book or box ornament was given (and perhaps created) as a gift to one of the Dominican priests who accompanied the Luna expedition from Mexico City to the coast of La Florida and eventually to Northwest Georgia. While trying to associate the artifact with a particular person may be stretching the imagination, we do know that one of only about 200 people (the size of the smaller contingent of the Luna expedition) brought the artifact to Northwest Georgia and only two of the group, the priests Domingo de la Anunciación and Domingo de Salazar, were likely to be in possession of books or boxes that might be decorated in such a way. Biographical information about Anunciación reveals that he possessed a Bible box in which he stored personal documents (Dávila Padilla 1955:622). The coincidence of the ordained name, Anunciación, and the potential interpretation of the incising regarding the Annunciation at least merits mention. His biography also details his extensive work with the native population in Mexico during which he could have encountered a student who made the plate as part of a personal gift, or he could have acquired it in any number of other ways.

After being made in Mexico and brought to Northwest Georgia, the plate or perhaps an entire book or box was given or traded to some aboriginal individual at Coosa. The plate was then adapted for use as a gorget and buried with a child.

Regarding the incising, the native artisan chose to either copy a scene depicted in the same or in another medium or to extract images from various sources in order to visually convey a religious idea. Whether the incised scene was a copied or original design, European iconographic and artistic style influences are unmistakably present. The incised design probably depicts the Annunciation of the birth of Christ to the Virgin Mary, but does so by using distinctively Aztec characters and artistic elements.

The plate, therefore, reflects in style and message the blending of Aztec and Catholic religious ideas that ethnohistorical sources relate when discussing the early days of the Marian cult of the Lady of Guadalupe. The artifact also helps delineate a trend in the development of the cult: the gradual change from a decidedly Aztec deity origin to a Europeanized Woman of Revelation/Virgin Mary. Changes in the visual representation of the Tonantzin/Guadalupe character during the sixteenth century reflected the conscious influence of the official church as it endorsed images and ideas that did not deviate significantly from accepted European Catholic ideology. The well-known painting of the Lady of Guadalupe demonstrates the influence of the church on this trend as the church embraced the painting and gave it special status in the new basilica established in 1555.

Jacques LaFaye (1976:242) explains how Miguel Sanchez in 1648 crystallized and embellished the oral tradition of the origin of the Lady of Guadalupe and left behind a well-defined story complete with apparitions, miracles, and quaint characters. Thus armed with a visual representation and a story, the official church in New Spain moved forward in its task of spreading the gospel through-out the hemisphere under the protecting and nurturing image of the patroness. But as William Taylor (1987) has recently pointed out, the Indian population from the seventeenth century to the nineteenth century may not have been as devoted to the patroness as the Spanish and mixed populations. One reason proposed here is that the Europeanized version of the Lady of Guadalupe and its embracement by the church may have moved the cult away from its Indian roots too far and too fast as the church searched for a way to endorse this popular "pagan" devotion.

With regard to archaeological and ethnohistorical significance, the plate is an additional piece of evidence to support the research of Charles Hudson and his colleagues regarding the routes of de Soto, Luna, and Pardo through the Southeast. Their research and the supporting evidence demonstrate that the capital of the sixteenth-century paramount chiefdom of Coosa was located on the Coosawattee River in Northwest Georgia. This capital comprised at least six villages, the main political center being the Little Egypt site.

However, the Luna accounts also relate that two other villages in this capital core or polity were larger than the capitol village (Hudson 1988). The Poarch Farm site was probably one of these two villages, and the copper plate and the other trade items found at the site indicate that significant interaction occurred there between the Indian population and the Luna expedition. It is surprising that medallions and cruciforms of various kinds have not been found at this site or other sites visited by Luna. Of course, most of the expedition's supplies were lost in Pensacola Bay and among the lost items may have been the religious trade items. Further investigations at the Poarch Farm site and other Luna contexts may yet yield other European or Mexican religious items.

The Coosawattee Plate provides a tangible and remarkable example of the crosscurrents of change sweeping through the Western Hemisphere in the sixteenth century. The history of the artifact parallels the history of the era: manufactured by a native of Mexico, influenced by the Christian religion of Europe, carried hundreds of miles to an unsettled frontier, traded for food or given as a gift, adapted for use by another culture, and finally buried with a child in a village soon thereafter abandoned.

Our scientific methods generally require that we remain cautious and even detached from discussions of simple and particular human motivations associated with the history of a single artifact. Occasionally, however, an artifact and its context compel the researcher to try to understand those individuals who created and possessed the item in order to extract something more personal from the artifact than mere data. The Coosawattee Plate richly deserves such an indulgence.

Acknowledgments

The story of this intriguing artifact could be called one chronicle of the early history of the Americas, or perhaps some might call it a mere footnote. But it is also a detective story that winds its way from a bait shop in Calhoun, Georgia, to museums and universities and laboratories in a dozen states and Mexico. I found it necessary to draw upon the advice and experience of many people from several different disciplines in order to begin the process of unraveling the mystery of the artifact—a process that may continue for years to come. For their professional and personal opinions and the time they gave me, I extend many thanks to John Aguilar, Patricia Anawalt, Ellen Baird, Robert Blakeley, Bettina Detweiler, Charles Dibble, Mike Gannon, Kathryn Jakes, Jesse Jennings, Steve Kowaleski, John Leader, Jerry Milanich, Susan Power, Barbara Stark, Emily Umberger, and Hasso von Winning. David Hally and Charles Hudson provided invaluable reference and logistical advice. Richard Bryant lent his significant photographic skills to the project, as did Jack Shrum who provided the photomacroscope expertise. Neil Shulman arranged the X-ray studies, and Julie Barnes-Smith and Jodie Lewis spent many hours working on drawings. Kerry McBrayer processed and organized many of the notes and reference material. I am thankful for the time they donated so eagerly. Wayne Long, John Long, Jon Wear, Quentin Haynes, and Mike Holland provided critical information to the effort. I am also quite grateful to Jon Griffin who was particularly generous in his contribution to the research. Also, I extend special thanks to Marvin Smith for his considerable encouragement and support.

References

Anawalt, Patricia R.
  1981 *Indian Clothing before Cortéz.* University of Oklahoma Press, Norman, Oklahoma.
Child, Heather, and Dorothy Colles
  1971 *Christian Symbols, Ancient and Modern.* Charles Scribner's Sons, New York.
Dávila Padilla, Fray Augustín
  1955 *Historia de la Fundación y Discursos de la Provincia de Santiago de Mexico, de la Orden de Predicadores.* 3rd ed. Editorial Academia Literaria, Mexico.
Day, Lewis F.
  1907 *Enamelling: A Comparative Account of the Development and Practice of the Art.* B. T. Batsford, London.
Hally, David J.
  1979 *Archaeological Investigation of the Little Egypt Site (9Mu102) Murray County, Georgia, 1969 Season.* University of Georgia Laboratory of Archaeology Series Report No. 18. Athens.
Henkel, Kathryn
  1973 *The Apocalypse.* Museum Press, Washington, D.C.
Hudson, Charles M.
  1988 A Spanish-Coosa Alliance in Sixteenth-century North Georgia. *Georgia Historical Quarterly* 72:599–626.
Hudson, Charles M., Marvin T. Smith, David J. Hally, Richard Polhemus, and Chester DePratter
  1985 Coosa: A Chiefdom in the Sixteenth-century Southeastern United States. *American Antiquity* 50:723–737.
LaFaye, Jacques
  1976 *Quetzalcóatl and Guadalupe: The Formation of National Consciousness 1531–1813.* University of Chicago Press, Chicago.

Langford, James B., Jr., and Marvin T. Smith
  1986 Recent Investigations in the Core of the Coosa Province. *Lamar Archaeology: Mississippian Chiefdoms in the Deep South.* University of Alabama Press, Tuscaloosa.
Lienzo de Tlaxcala
  1979 *Lienzo de Tlaxcala.* Edited by Alfred Chavero. Reprinted. Litoimpresores, S.A., Mexico. Originally published 1892, *Antigüedades Mexicanas.* Junta Colombina de Mexico. Mexico City: Secretaría de Fomento.
Rothenstein, Elizabeth (editor)
  1951 *The Virgin and the Child.* William Collins Sons, London.
Sahagún, Fray Bernardino de
  1950–1969 *Florentine Codex: General History of the Things of New Spain.* Translated and edited by Arthur J. O. Anderson and Charles E. Dibble. Monographs of the School of American Research No. 14, pts. 2–13. University of Utah and the School of American Research, Santa Fe, New Mexico.
Smith, Marvin T.
  1987 *Archaeology of Aboriginal Culture Change in the Interior Southeast—Depopulation during the Early Historic Period.* University of Florida Press/Florida State Museum, Gainesville.
Taylor, William B.
  1987 The Virgin of Guadalupe in New Spain: An Inquiry into the Social History of Marian Devotion. *American Ethnologist* 14:9–33.
Troike, Nancy P.
  1975 The Meanings of Postures and Gestures in the Mixtec Codices. Paper presented at the 40th Annual Meeting of the Society for American Archaeology, Dallas.
Wauchope, Robert (general editor)
  1975 *Handbook of Middle American Indians.* University of Texas Press, Austin.

Chapter 11 ■

Janet E. Levy, J. Alan May, and David G. Moore

From Ysa to Joara: Cultural Diversity in the Catawba Valley from the Fourteenth to the Sixteenth Century

Within the Spanish Borderlands, some regions were more distant and peripheral than others. De Soto in 1540 and Pardo in 1566–1568 entered one of these distant reaches of the borderlands when they passed through the center of the province of Cofitachequi and moved northward. Here, they were further from their original bases in the Caribbean than at any other time. After Pardo's second expedition in 1567–1568 and the abandonment of his short-lived forts, the Spanish never returned to this distant part of the borderlands.

In this chapter we discuss the Spanish experience, who they met, and what impact they had on the native peoples. We review some of the early historic evidence and consider archaeological evidence from the Catawba River Valley of the western piedmont of North Carolina (Figure 11-1). In particular, we are concerned with the relationship of this area to the polity of Cofitachequi and with the nature of the interaction between the Spanish and the native populations.

There are four well-known accounts of de Soto's explorations (see Bourne 1904; Varner and Varner 1980) and three short accounts of Pardo's expeditions (see Ketcham 1954). In addition, a fourth, much longer, account of Pardo's expeditions has recently been analyzed (DePratter et al. 1983). It is clear from all these

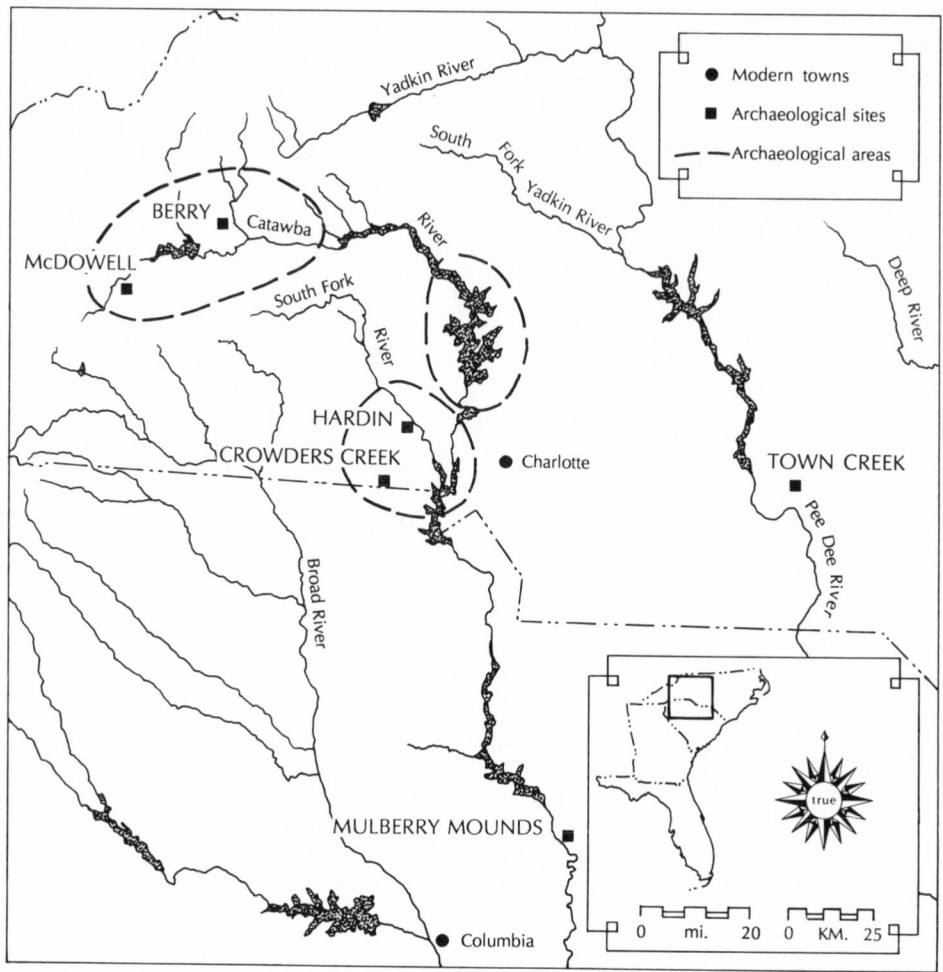

Figure 11-1. Catawba River Valley showing excavated sites. Dotted lines indicate approximate boundaries of upper, middle, and lower valley.

accounts that the Spanish visited communities of various sizes after leaving the main town of Cofitachequi and that the next large town they visited was a place that de Soto called Xualla and Pardo called Joara, some seven or eight days' march north or northwest of Cofitachequi. This town was affiliated in some way, perhaps quite intimately, with Cofitachequi. The accounts of Pardo's journeys give more names and a little information about the communities between Cofitachequi and Joara (including the important town of Ysa—hence our title) than do the de Soto accounts. Although it is unlikely that de Soto passed through all of the same towns as Pardo, it is likely that both explorers followed similar routes.

The De Soto Commission (Swanton 1985 [1939]) placed Cofitachequi somewhere on the Savannah River, probably near Augusta, and Xualla somewhere in northwestern South Carolina. More recently, however, Baker (1974) and Hudson and his colleagues (DePratter et al. 1983; Hudson et al. 1984) have persuasively argued that the central town of Cofitachequi is represented by the Mulberry Mounds site (38Ke12) near Camden, South Carolina, on the Wateree River (see Figures 1-3 and 11-1). Hudson and his colleagues argue that both explorers traveled up the Catawba-Wateree River Valley, reaching Xualla or Joara somewhere on the upper Catawba River near present-day Marion, North Carolina. We have accepted this general reconstruction of the routes of exploration north of Cofitachequi. In addition to locational information, the Spanish documents provide some linguistic and social information about the peoples that the explorers met, although these accounts must be interpreted with the usual care required by ethnohistoric documents. We return to this information later.

There was no firmly documented Spanish exploration of the area after Pardo, and no missions were established; thus, there are no other written accounts of the Catawba River Valley until after 1650, when English explorers and settlers began visiting the area either from Virginia settlements to the north or from Charleston to the south. At this point, much of the Catawba Valley was apparently uninhabited as most of the native population was clustered just south of the present-day North Carolina–South Carolina border in a society that was soon to become known as the Catawba nation (Merrell 1982; see also Wilson 1983). Contact with the Spanish in the sixteenth century may well have contributed to these settlement and social changes visible in the seventeenth century.

The Chiefdom of Cofitachequi

Hudson interprets the accounts of the de Soto and Pardo expeditions to suggest that the polity of Cofitachequi encompassed a very large area from the coastal plain of South Carolina to the edge of the Blue Ridge in western North Carolina (Hudson 1986:Figure 1; see also DePratter et al. 1983). More recently, DePratter (1987) suggested that Cofitachequi was smaller and possibly reached only to the vicinity of the current North Carolina–South Carolina border. This suggestion is congruent with our understanding of the region.

A notable characteristic of Cofitachequi in de Soto's time was that it was ruled by a woman. The Spanish documents do not record that either the native people or the Spanish found this unusual, although politically powerful women are not noted elsewhere in the Southeast. In Pardo's day, the central town of Cofitachequi was apparently ruled by a man, but women chiefs existed at Quatariaatiqui (Ketcham 1954:72) and Guatary (Ketcham 1954:79). The Pardo documents imply that Guatary is northeast of the main route from Cofitachequi to Joara and it may have been on what is now the Yadkin River. In any case, the Lady of Cofitachequi was not unique in this region of the borderlands. Elvas (Bourne 1904:72) and Garcilaso (Varner and Varner 1980:330) both say that the power of the Lady of Cofitachequi extended at least as far as Xualla. But Garcilaso also refers to Xualla as a different province than Cofitachequi. The Pardo documents are silent about the geographic extent of the power of the chief at the main town of Cofitachequi, although Pardo met chiefs from towns subsidiary to the main chief.

The Spanish documents also suggest that the polity of Cofitachequi had more than one level of elite hierarchy. The de Soto documents provide only hints about the hierarchy; for example, Garcilaso (Varner and Varner 1980:298) speaks of six men who are principal men but who are also vassals of the Lady of Cofitachequi. The Pardo documents are more detailed, speaking of many chiefs at several communities between Cofitachequi and Joara. At some towns, there are multiple chiefs (e.g., Tagaya) and at others only one chief (e.g., Tagaya the Lesser). At a town called Ysa, Pardo notes the presence of a "great chief" and a large number of other chiefs. Although this variability could be due to different observers, the differences between the de Soto and Pardo documents are sufficiently striking that it is possible that the organization of authority in the larger area of Cofitachequi changed between 1541 and 1566.

To supplement the specific information about Cofitachequi, there is evidence that these several levels of authority were apparently characteristic of other southeastern polities encountered by the Spanish both before and after they reached Cofitachequi. According to Elvas (Bourne 1904:68), the chief of Chiaha was a subject of Coosa; and according to Ranjel (Bourne 1904:90), Camumo, chief of Altamaha, was subject to the greater chief of Ocute. These data, incomplete as they are, are congruent with extensive ethnographic and ethnohistoric evidence about chiefdoms in general (Earle 1987; Steponaitis 1986:391). These midlevel, ranked societies tend to have more than one level of elite, and relations among elite leaders are fluid. Typically, chiefdoms fluctuate in size and stability, expanding and contracting over time as individual chiefs compete with varying success for status and power in the arenas of warfare and of ritual. A leader's authority varies with the situation; as Fried (1967:133) so aptly put it, "leaders can lead, but followers may not follow." A community may owe nominal allegiance to a distant, quite powerful chief, participating in important but infrequent religious rituals at that chief's center, while running the rest of their affairs without reference to the chief's wishes. At the same time, local leaders may attempt to manipulate those local affairs and various religious rituals to gain prestige and expand their sphere of influence.

This model of chiefly politics is relevant to understanding both the Spaniards' and the natives' experiences in this area of the Spanish Borderlands. Among other things, it might explain Garcilaso's otherwise confusing statement that Xualla was another province than Cofitachequi, but also owed allegiance to the Lady. The large size alone of the proposed province of Cofitachequi (Hudson 1986:140), taken with the general model of chiefly politics described above, suggests that it was not a unified polity fully controlled by the chief at the central town. In addition, linguistic evidence suggests at least three language families (Muskoghean, Catawban, and one unidentified) existed in the region from Cofitachequi to Joara, at least during Pardo's expedition (Rankin et al. 1984); this linguistic diversity could be related to political diversity. Furthermore, although de Soto's chroniclers do not provide much specific information about political jockeying in this area, information from nearby areas gives hints about the situation in Cofitachequi. For example, Ranjel reports that the Camumo, the chief of Altamaha who was subject to Ocute, asked de Soto, known as "The Governor," "to whom should he give tribute in the future, whether to the governor or to Ocute; and the Governor suspected that this question was put with cunning" (Bourne 1904:90). This episode suggests that secondary chiefs attempted to manipulate events for their own benefit. There is also archaeological evidence, discussed below, that is relevant to this model. Overall, even in de Soto's time, when the Lady of Cofitachequi was perhaps experiencing a period of successful expansion of her influence, it is likely that her "authority" over the further reaches of Cofitachequi was limited, a matter of ritual respect rather than firm political control.

In summary, our reading of the Spanish documents suggests that the land from Cofitachequi to Joara was not a single, unified polity even in de Soto's day. Although the elite from the center of Cofitachequi had influence throughout the region at the time de Soto arrived, this was possibly a short-lived situation within a more complex history of competing elites and fluctuating polities. Even at this point, local leaders probably maintained some independence from the main chief of Cofitachequi. At Joara, which was after all at least a week away from the center, this independence may have been considerable. This proposed political arrangement is similar to the situation in Coosa described by Hally et al. (this volume). We now turn to the archaeological evidence for this region. Although incomplete, our analysis of these data provides preliminary support for this proposed reconstruction of regional politics.

Archaeological Evidence

Introduction

Because the historical records are limited for the sixteenth century and nonexistent for the century between Spanish and English contact, the contact experience in this area must be investigated through archaeological data. Until recently, however, there was little systematically recovered archaeological evidence from the region. Cyrus Thomas (1891, 1985 [1894]) reported the presence of both the Mulberry Mounds (then known as the McDowell Mounds) along the Wateree and several mound sites along the upper Catawba. In addition, Thomas found mounds in the upper Yadkin River drainage just to the north of the upper Catawba (Figure 11-1). Some survey work was conducted in the upper Catawba Valley in the 1960s (Keeler 1971) and in the middle valley in conjunction with the creation of Lake Norman. Some small-scale cultural resource management, investigations have been conducted in the 1970s and 1980s. Analysis of these materials has so far been limited. Even with the recent excavations reported here, archaeological research is much less advanced in this area than in the Georgia piedmont, for example.

A review of existing site location data suggests that no mounds exist along the Catawba-Wateree system between the cluster of sites near Camden, South Carolina (Mulberry, Adamson, etc.) and the cluster of sites in the upper Catawba Valley between Marion and Morganton, North Carolina, including the Berry and McDowell sites (although Thomas [1891] makes brief mention of a possible mound in Catawba County between these two areas; this was not visited by Thomas's investigators and cannot be identified today).

Since 1985, test excavations have been conducted at four sites in the Catawba Valley: Crowders Creek (31Gs55) and Hardin (31Gs30) in Gaston County, Berry (31Bk22) in Burke County, and McDowell (31Mc41) in McDowell County (Figure 11-1).

The Crowders Creek site and the Hardin site are nonmound sites. The Berry site is the only mound site discussed by Thomas that can be identified today. The recent excavations suggest that a remnant mound also exists at the McDowell site, although Thomas apparently did not identify this mound (this mound should not be confused with the nineteenth-century name for the Mulberry Mounds site in South Carolina). DePratter and his colleagues (1983) suggested that the McDowell site is Joara; although Joara was probably in the area, this specific identification cannot yet be confirmed or disproved.

Excavation Evidence

The four excavated sites are located in alluvial bottoms or terraces. All have been disturbed by modern plowing; artifacts and ecofacts were recovered from one or more plowzones and from subsurface features. Post-molds are the most frequent subsurface features discovered at all four sites; in addition, shallow, cob-filled basins, refuse-filled pits of various shapes and sizes, hearths or roasting pits, and burial pits have been discovered. Maize is common at all four sites; however, floral analyses are not complete for Crowders Creek and Hardin. The chipped stone tool assemblages are dominated by small triangular points, often made on flakes and predominantly manufactured from locally available quartz, rhyolites, and other metavolcanics. Lamar-style ceramics predominate at these sites (see below).

Crowders Creek Site (31Gs55): This site is located on a small tributary of the South Fork Catawba River, itself the largest tributary of the Catawba (May 1987). The plowzone of this site yielded the broadest chronological range of artifacts of any of the four, with a significant Archaic component; however, most of the features seem to date to the late prehistoric period. Structure patterns are not well defined, but at least one circular to oval structure seems to be present. No daub was recovered. The most distinctive artifact recovered was a finely made, zoomorphic, ceramic pipe. Three radiocarbon dates from feature contexts (including the feature yielding the pipe) suggest a fourteenth- to sixteenth-century occupation.

Hardin Site (31Gs30): This site is located on the South Fork Catawba River and has been partly eroded by the river, which changed its channel (with human encouragement) in the twentieth century (Levy 1987). Incomplete patterns of two circular structures were uncovered. Burned daub, with plant impressions, was recovered from three pits but not from the plowzone. The most distinctive artifact recovered was a finely polished, biconcave discoidal, or chunkey stone.

Numerous ceramic discs and pipestem or tube fragments were recovered. A small, rolled copper tube, recovered from plowzone, is the only possible Spanish artifact; it resembles an "aglet" or lacing tip, but could be a native bead. Three radiocarbon dates suggest a fifteenth- and sixteenth-century occupation, but two other radiocarbon dates fall within the eleventh-twelfth century. However, the ceramics are more congruent with the fifteenth- to sixteenth-century date (DePratter and Judge 1986).

Berry Site (31Bk22): This site is located on Upper Creek, a tributary of the Catawba River (Moore 1987, 1990). The mound that Thomas identified was partly bulldozed in the 1960s, but the recent excavation revealed remaining undisturbed, basket-loaded mound fill. Part of a circular structure pattern was delineated adjacent to the mound, along with two large features interpreted as holes for large game posts. Uncontrolled excavations in the mound in the 1960s yielded ceramics, pipe fragments, shell beads, and animal bones. One oval, shaft and chamber burial pit and one atypical, rectangular, shaft and chamber burial pit were excavated. The adult male buried in the latter was accompanied by copper disks (possibly ear spools) and an artifact bundle containing a turtle carapace, a pipe, a stoneworking tool kit, and an Early Archaic point. An iron knife was found on his chest; this knife may date from the sixteenth to the eighteenth century. The lack of other historic artifacts at the site suggests the earlier date, as does the association with the soapstone-tempered ceramic pipe (see "Ceramics" below); however, the rectangular pit and the extended position are more typical of eighteenth-century native burials. The question remains open.

Two radiocarbon dates suggest a fifteenth-century occupation. Recent analysis of the floral remains (Gremillion 1989) shows that small amounts of gourd and beans are present as well as corn. Knotweed, chenoped, little barley, and various nuts and fruits are also present.

McDowell Site (31Mc41): This site is located on the floodplain of the Catawba River (Moore 1987, 1990). The remnant of a subsurface mound is present. One Pisgah house pattern, square with rounded corners and entryway trenches (Dickens 1976), was uncovered; this style of structure is common in the mountains to the west of the site. Parts of a probable palisade were uncovered. A large (about 12 m in diameter) burned feature was uncovered but not further excavated; this feature, next to the mound, may be a burned and collapsed public structure and is possibly an earth lodge. Deep plowing has significantly disturbed features at this site. Small amounts of daub were discovered in the plowzone. The most distinctive artifact discovered was a stone pipe incised with a stylized *uktena* (i.e., the mythical Cherokee winged serpent). Some very small iron fragments recovered from the plowzone have been tentatively identified as bits of chain mail.

Two available radiocarbon dates are not congruent; one is late fifteenth century and one is eleventh century. The ceramics, including the presence of Pisgah ceramics and later Burke-like ceramics (see below), are more congruent with the fifteenth-century date. The eleventh-century date comes from a timber from the large burned structure. Recovered botanical remains are similar to those from Berry (Gremillion 1989).

Discussion

The radiocarbon dates for these four sites, especially in conjunction with the ceramics (see "Ceramics" below), suggest major occupation in the fourteenth to sixteenth centuries; eleventh- to thirteenth-century occupations are also suggested. At present, we cannot propose finer chronological divisions, although we recognize that finer chronological controls are needed. We find the radiocarbon dates sufficiently homogeneous to consider the four excavated sites as contemporaneous in a general sense, although, clearly, we cannot be sure they were all occupied at exactly the same time. Among the sites identified through surface collections in the upper valley (Keeler 1971) and in the Lake Norman area of the middle valley (Moore 1990) are many with ceramic assemblages similar to those of the excavated sites. These surface collections thus provide limited, but useful, information about other contemporaneous sites. Our discussion should therefore be considered a preliminary interpretation of the fourteenth- to sixteenth-century cultures in the Catawba Valley. We emphasize the term "preliminary"; this interpretation will, no doubt, be modified as more detailed chronological information becomes available.

Artifactual evidence of Spanish contact is limited. The possible copper lacing tip and fragments of chain mail are both plowzone finds, while the iron knife remains insecurely dated. Thomas (1985 [1894]:335) illustrates iron artifacts recovered from the Nelson Triangle in the upper Yadkin River Valley immediately north of our study area. These resemble iron objects known to date to the sixteenth century (Smith 1987:34–36). No Spanish artifacts have been reported from Mulberry Mounds, the putative center of Cofitachequi (Ferguson 1974). Smith (1987:37) suggests that sixteenth-century Spanish artifacts were frequently used as grave goods in elite native burials. Future excavation of burials in the Catawba Valley may yield securely identified Spanish artifacts.

The excavation data suggest regional variability in structure patterns in the Catawba-Wateree Valley. The only excavated structure from the Mulberry Mounds site is rectangular, apparently a combined domestic and craft-production locale (Grimes 1986). This contrasts with the round or oval structures from Crowders Creek, Hardin, and Berry, and the Pisgah-style house from the McDowell site. The burned structure at McDowell differs from the others in its large size, but very likely is not a domestic structure like the others. Only the McDowell site has evidence of a palisade. These data suggest the possibility of contemporaneous variability in domestic structures and village enclosures within the region.

Ceramics

The ceramics from Catawba Valley sites are the major source of information about the cultural affiliations of the prehistoric communities. Variability within and between ceramic assemblages is due to both chronological and cultural differences between communities. At present we are able to discuss spatial variability in more detail than chronological variability, and additional chronological information may well modify our interpretation. The spatial variability is relevant to the model of chiefly politics developed above. However, the results discussed here are preliminary as the ceramic analysis is still under way (see Moore 1990).

The analyzed ceramics include excavated assemblages of 1,498 sherds from the McDowell site, 3,691 sherds from the Berry site, 915 sherds from the Hardin site, and 1,065 sherds from the Crowders Creek site. Surface collections analyzed include 3,461 sherds from 47 sites in the upper valley (McDowell, Burke, and Catawba counties) and 3,188 sherds from 116 sites from the Lake Norman reservoir in the middle and lower valley (Catawba, Lincoln, and Mecklenburg counties). There appear to be at least two geographic areas of ceramic variability in the Catawba Valley: Burke series ceramics found in the upper valley, and an unnamed series in the lower valley resembling ceramics from the Mulberry Mounds and other sites in the Wateree Valley (DePratter and Judge 1986).

In the lower valley, dominant surface treatments are plain, burnished plain, and complicated stamped, both rectilinear and curvilinear (Figure 11-2). At Crowders Creek, plain and burnished plain sherds make up about two-thirds of the assemblage, and complicated stamped sherds are about 10 percent of the collection; in contrast, at Hardin, the assemblage is dominated by about 50 percent complicated stamped sherds and about 25 percent plain and burnished

Figure 11-2. Ceramics from Catawba Valley sites. Provenience: Hardin site (left, top two rows; right, top row), Berry site (left, bottom row; right, bottom row), Crowders Creek site (right, middle row).

plain. At both sites, cob-impressed sherds make up 5 to 10 percent of the assemblage and small numbers of brushed and check-stamped sherds are present. Burnished interiors are frequent. Temper is predominantly sand and grit (mostly crushed quartz) in varying amounts.

There are no complete vessels among the collections studied from the lower valley, but rim sherds indicate the presence of constricted neck jars, straight-sided bowls and jars, and small globular bowls. Rims are predominantly notched or finger-impressed, punctated or notched applique strips, and plain. Ticks on the shoulder are occasionally observed, notably at Crowders Creek, and a small number of simply incised rims are present.

No systematic investigations have taken place in the middle valley, with the exception of the 1962 Lake Norman survey. From these limited data, it appears that the general characteristics of the lower valley ceramics extend into the middle valley.

The upper valley is marked by the presence of the distinctive soapstone-tempered Burke series pottery (Keeler 1971; Boyd 1986). Exterior surface finishes are predominantly curvilinear complicated stamped (50 percent) along with burnished plain (20 percent; often incised, resembling Lamar Incised) and plain (20 percent). Minority finishes include cob impressed, simple stamped, rectilinear complicated stamped, check stamped, roughened, and brushed. Interiors are smoothed or burnished. Vessel forms include straight-sided and carinated bowls and straight-sided and constricted neck jars. Jars often feature notched rims or finger-pinched or punctated folded rims. Carinated bowls are usually plain or burnished plain and often feature complicated incised shoulders and rims (Figure 11-2). The Berry site assemblage exemplifies this series.

Further ceramic variability occurs at the head of the Catawba Valley, immediately west of the Burke series core area. Most of the sites in this area feature Pisgah ceramics (Dickens 1976). Five sites feature both Pisgah and Burke ceramics, as well as vessels exhibiting attributes of both series. The McDowell site assemblage is the largest in the area and consists of soapstone-, sand-, and grit-tempered wares. As elsewhere, complicated, stamped-surface finishes predominate (47 percent); however, the McDowell assemblage features a much larger proportion of rectilinear complicated stamped to curvilinear complicated stamped than do sites in other parts of the valley. Plain (30 percent) and burnished (12 percent) surfaces also occur, as do minority finishes, including simple stamped, cord marked, cob impressed, roughened, and brushed.

Whole vessels are not represented but appear to include straight-sided bowls and jars, carinated bowls, and constricted neck jars. Bowl rims are often notched or punctated and the constricted neck jars often exhibit the typical punctated Pisgah collared rim (50 percent) or a folded rim (16 percent).

The late prehistoric and protohistoric Catawba Valley ceramics fall within the general Lamar style (Jennings and Fairbanks 1939; Hally 1986). The ceramics from the lower Catawba Valley show strongest similarities in temper, surface treatment, and rim decoration to the McDowell and Mulberry phase assemblages of the central Wateree Valley defined by DePratter and Judge (1986). They date these phases to A.D. 1350–1550, which is congruent with most of the radio-carbon dates from Crowders Creek and Hardin sites. In the upper valley, the Pisgah pottery from the McDowell site is believed to be slightly earlier than the Burke material at the same site. Pisgah ceramics, with predominantly rectilinear complicated stamping, date to A.D. 1000–1450 (Dickens 1976), while the curvilinear, Lamar-style designs typical of the Burke series resemble Qualla phase and Tugalo phase ceramics (Anderson et al. 1986:42), both of which date to circa A.D. 1450–1600.

Overall, comparisons of these Catawba Valley assemblages with assemblages from central and northwestern South Carolina, northern Georgia, and western North Carolina support fourteenth- to sixteenth-century dates for the excavated sites reported here. However, the Catawba Valley ceramics are different from contemporary assemblages in piedmont North Carolina to the east, where the major surface decorations are plain, simple stamped, check stamped, net, and brushed (Davis 1987).

In the most general sense, these stylistic patterns suggest that the cultural affiliations and social interactions of the late prehistoric Catawba Valley population were focused to the west and south rather than to the east. This area, along with the southern Appalachian summit region, was the most northerly extent of the Lamar tradition. It was a Lamar borderland as well as a Spanish one.

To summarize, considerable regional variation can be discerned within this larger, Lamar-affiliated tradition. Variation exists in temper, proportions of common surface treatments, and types of rim decoration. At least two ceramic sub-regions can be distinguished within the Catawba Valley: the lower (and, possibly, the middle) valley, including the Crowders Creek and Hardin sites, and the upper valley, including the Berry site and others with distinctive, soapstone-tempered ceramics. The head of the valley, including the McDowell site, exhibits Burke ceramics influenced by Pisgah and Qualla traditions to the west.

Conclusions

We are now in a position to draw together several lines of evidence about the chiefdom of Cofitachequi. We suggest that the Catawba-Wateree Valley was not a unified polity in the late prehistoric and protohistoric period, but a region with fluctuating interrelations among political and social units of different sizes and, possibly, different cultural identities.

Our interpretation of the archaeological evidence suggests significant cultural variability within this region. This is most striking in the ceramics, but is hinted at as well in the evidence of site features, including the contrast between shaft and chamber burials in the upper valley and simple oval pits in the lower valley. Furthermore, if the mound sites were political centers of various sizes in the late prehistoric Southeast, the distribution pattern of mounds within the Catawba-Wateree Valley suggests at least two centers or groups of centers, one on the central Wateree and one on the upper Catawba. The archaeological evidence also suggests that the Catawba Valley could be distinguished culturally from much of the central North Carolina piedmont. The archaeological evidence of stylistic diversity complements evidence of linguistic diversity in the region, as well as the ethnohistoric evidence reviewed above. (However, it is possible that the linguistic diversity recorded in the Pardo documents reflects population movement due to the impacts of contact with the de Soto expedition.) General ethnographic data about chiefdoms provide additional support for our interpretation.

We see several small polities, which are probably affiliated periodically with the main center of Cofitachequi but maintain a high degree of autonomy. These polities were not egalitarian; at least two kinds of stratification were present. First, the chief of Cofitachequi, in times of expanding influence, probably could require tribute, labor, and allegiance from much of the region. The de Soto documents hint that the early 1540s were such a period. Second, within the smaller polities, elite individuals probably had authority over a general population, both in the chief's town and in surrounding subsidiary communities, even when the influence of the elite at Cofitachequi was minimal. In fact, the influence of local chiefs may have expanded as the influence of the chief at Cofitachequi waned. This seems to have been the case at the time of the Pardo expeditions. We cannot, at this point, be more specific about the degree or organization of stratification within the region. In any case, the political situation in the Catawba-Wateree Valley in the fourteenth to sixteenth centuries was probably a shifting one.

This model of chiefly politics helps us to understand the contact experience of both the Spaniards and the natives. First, the Spaniards could not confidently rely on a single ruler easing their way forward, even within a putative unified polity. Every major town could have presented a new political situation for the Spanish to cope with. The side trip to Guatary made by Pardo's expedition may have exposed the Spanish to yet another new cultural system; if Guatary was located along the Yadkin to the east, as DePratter and his colleagues (1983) suggest, this would have brought the Spanish to what the archaeological evidence suggests is a different cultural area.

Second, the natives did not experience the Spanish passively, overwhelmed by their horses and weapons. Not only was physical attack a possible response, as attempted at Mabila, but familiar political maneuvering was probably the first strategy for dealing with these unfamiliar intruders. Because the people of Ocute and Cofitachequi and other contemporary chiefdoms lived in stratified societies where public ritual, sumptuary display, and jockeying for power were familiar, the Spanish were not as strange as we might think. They could be treated as a new kind of chief, possibly rather dangerous but not completely unfamiliar.

Although the fluctuating political system probably existed in de Soto's time, we suggest that by the time of Pardo's trips, the fluidity of chiefly politics in the region had increased. The chief of the main town, Cofitachequi, was apparently experiencing a period of contracting influence although still remaining a significant figure. Leaders of numerous towns were jockeying for prestige and influence in the region.

The increased fluidity of the political system was probably due, in part, to the first impact of disease on the area. Ramenofsky (1987) has demonstrated that European diseases, especially smallpox, may have preceded face-to-face contact; by the 1560s, the people of Cofitachequi could have been exposed to disease indirectly from the Ayllón visit to the coast in 1526 as well as directly from de Soto's men. The high death rates from these introduced diseases would have disrupted kinship and political systems, leading to uncertainty about the inheritance of elite positions and thus to increased political jockeying. This may explain, at least in part, the strikingly large number of chiefs that Pardo met, although some of them may also have been nonchiefly elders or members of town councils. Even if future archaeological evidence modifies our understanding of the route of Spanish explorers, this interpretation of the impact of disease on the Catawba Valley will not be weakened because smallpox and other European diseases could reach communities that never had direct contact with the Spanish.

It is likely that introduced diseases continued to have a significant impact into the seventeenth and eighteenth centuries, leading to population movements. Although the data are imperfect, no native sites with post-1600 artifacts are known from the upper valley (except the knife of uncertain date from the Berry site). Given that historical documentation indicates active European trade efforts in the Virginia and Carolina piedmont from at least 1670 (Merrell 1982:62–67), this lack of seventeenth- and eighteenth-century trade goods in the upper valley suggests that there were few people in the area to receive them.

However, there is extensive historic (Merrell 1982, especially Chap. 2) and, at present limited, archaeological evidence (Wilson 1983:455) of post-sixteenth-century Native American occupation of the lower valley. These are the communities that come to be known around 1700 as the Catawba. Merrell (1982:248) describes the formation of the historic Catawba: "Out of the congeries of independent peoples scattered through river valleys of the Carolina interior emerged the historic Catawba Nation. From the profusion and confusion of names emerged a single name which, while disguising complex ethnic realities, also came to define and to identify a people from that day to this." This process is very possibly the result of population disruptions, movements, and reorganizations following devastation by introduced disease, as described by Ramenofsky (1987) and Smith (1987; see also Merrell 1982:190, 251, 158).

Merrell presents a persuasive picture of the late seventeenth- and eighteenth-century Catawba actively pursuing control over their own fate through trade, alliances, and military action. This is parallel to what we think happened in the sixteenth century at the time of the Spanish entrada. The native peoples were active participants in the contact experience. Their earlier experience with existing political relationships provided them a strategy by which they tempered and manipulated the potential impact of these new "chiefs." Ultimately, it was disease, rather than political or military failure, that led to the final disruption of sixteenth-century native cultures.

Acknowledgments

We wish to thank the large number of colleagues, volunteers, and students who have worked on our excavations and contributed to processing and analyzing the materials discovered. These archaeological projects are truly community efforts. The projects have been supported financially by the state of North Carolina; the Schiele Museum of Natural History, Gastonia, North Carolina; the National Park Service through a Survey and Planning grant administered by the Office of State Archaeology, North Carolina Division of Archives and History; the Historic Burke Foundation; the University of North Carolina at Chapel Hill; and the University of North Carolina at Charlotte. We are also grateful for the interest and support of our archaeological colleagues in the Carolinas and elsewhere in the Southeast.

References

Anderson, David G., David J. Hally, and James L. Rudolph
  1986 The Mississippian Occupation of the Savannah River Valley. *Southeastern Archaeology* 5:32–51.
Baker, Steven G.
  1974 *Cofitachique: Fair Province of Carolina*. Unpublished Master's thesis, Department of History, University of South Carolina, Columbia.
Bourne, Edward Gaylord (editor)
  1904 *Narratives of the Career of Hernando De Soto*. A. S. Barnes, New York.
Boyd, Clifford
  1986 *An Evolutionary Perspective on the Prehistory of Upper East Tennessee*. Unpublished Ph.D. dissertation, Department of Anthropology, University of Tennessee, Knoxville.
Davis, R. P. Stephen
  1987 Pottery from the Fredericks, Wall, and Mitchum Sites. In *The Siouan Project: Seasons I and II*, edited by Roy S. Dickens, H. Trawick Ward, and R. P. Stephen Davis, pp. 185–216. Research Laboratories of Anthropology, University of North Carolina, Monograph Series No. 1. Chapel Hill.
DePratter, Chester
  1987 Cofitachequi: Ethnohistorical Sources and Current Archaeological Knowledge. Paper presented at the 44th Southeastern Archaeological Conference, Charleston.
DePratter, Chester, Charles M. Hudson, and Marvin T. Smith
  1983 The Route of Juan Pardo's Explorations in the Interior Southeast, 1566–1568. *Florida Historical Quarterly* 62:125–158.
DePratter, Chester, and Chris Judge
  1986 A Provisional Late Prehistoric and Early Historic Ceramic Sequence for the Wateree River Valley, South Carolina. Paper presented at the LAMAR Institute Conference on the South Appalachian Mississippian, Macon, Georgia.
Dickens, Roy S.
  1976 *Cherokee Prehistory: The Pisgah Phase in the Appalachian Summit Region*. University of Tennessee Press, Knoxville.
Earle, Timothy K.
  1987 Chiefdoms in Archaeological and Ethnohistorical Perspective. *Annual Reviews of Anthropology* 16:279–308.

Ferguson, Leland (editor)
  1974 Archaeological Investigations at the Mulberry Site. *Notebook* 6:57–122. University of South Carolina, Institute of Archaeology and Anthropology, Columbia.
Fried, Morton
  1967 *The Evolution of Political Society*. Random House, New York.
Gremillion, Kristen
  1989 Report on Plant Remains from Berry and McDowell Sites. Ms. on file. Research Laboratories of Anthropology, University of North Carolina, Chapel Hill.
Grimes, Kimberly M.
  1986 Dietary Choices at the Mulberry Mound Site. Paper presented at the 43rd Southeastern Archaeological Conference, Nashville.
Hally, David J.
  1986 An Overview of Lamar Culture. Paper presented at the Ocmulgee National Monument 50th Anniversary Conference, December 13.
Hudson, Charles M.
  1986 Some Thoughts on the Early Social History of the Cherokees. In *The Conference on Cherokee Prehistory*, compiled by David G. Moore, pp. 139–153. Warren Wilson College, Swannanoa, North Carolina.
Hudson, Charles M., Chester DePratter, and Marvin T. Smith
  1984 The Hernando De Soto Expedition: From Apalachee to Chiaha. *Southeastern Archaeology* 3:65–77.
Jennings, J. D., and C. H. Fairbanks
  1939 Type Descriptions of Pottery. *Newsletter, Southeastern Archaeological Conference*, Vol. 1, No. 2. Lexington, Kentucky.
Keeler, Robert W.
  1971 *An Archaeological Survey of the Upper Catawba River Valley*. Unpublished Bachelor's Honors thesis, Department of Anthropology, University of North Carolina, Chapel Hill.
Ketcham, Herbert E. (editor and translator)
  1954 Three Sixteenth Century Spanish Chronicles Relating to Georgia. *Georgia Historical Quarterly* 38:66–82.
Levy, Janet E.
  1987 Archaeological Investigations at 31Gs30, Gaston County, North Carolina. Paper presented at the 44th Southeastern Archaeological Conference, Charleston.
May, J. Alan
  1987 Archaeological Investigations at 31Gs55, Gaston County, North Carolina. Paper presented at the 44th Southeastern Archaeological Conference, Charleston.
Merrell, James
  1982 *Natives in a New World: The Catawba Indians of Carolina, 1650–1800*. Unpublished Ph.D. dissertation, Department of History, Johns Hopkins University, Baltimore.
Moore, David G.
  1987 Archaeological Investigations in the Upper Catawba River Valley, North Carolina. Paper presented at the 44th Southeastern Archaeological Conference, Charleston.
  1990 *Late Prehistoric and Protohistoric Aboriginal Settlements in the Upper Catawba Valley*. Unpublished Ph.D. dissertation, Department of Anthropology, University of North Carolina, Chapel Hill.
Ramenofsky, Ann F.
  1987 *Vectors of Death: The Archaeology of European Contact*. University of New Mexico Press, Albuquerque.
Rankin, Robert L., Charles M. Hudson, and Karen Booker
  1984 Linguistic Affiliation of the Juan Pardo Expedition Place Names. Paper presented at the 83rd Annual Meeting of the American Anthropological Association, Denver.

Smith, Marvin
> 1987 *Archaeology of Aboriginal Culture Change in the Interior Southeast: Depopulation during the Early Historic Period*. Ripley P. Bullen Monographs in Anthropology and History No. 6. University Presses of Florida, Gainesville.

Steponaitis, Vincas P.
> 1986 Prehistoric Archaeology in the Southeastern United States, 1970–1985. *Annual Reviews of Anthropology* 15:363–404.

Swanton, John R.
> 1985 *Final Report of the United States De Soto Expedition Commission*. Reprinted. Smithsonian Institution Press, Washington, D.C. Originally published 1939, Government Printing Office, Washington, D.C.

Thomas, Cyrus
> 1891 *Catalogue of Prehistoric Works East of the Rocky Mountains*. Smithsonian Institution, Bureau of Ethnology Bulletin No. 12. Washington, D.C.
> 1985 *Report on the Mound Explorations of the Bureau of Ethnology*. Reprinted. Smithsonian Institution Press, Washington, D.C. Originally published 1894, Government Printing Office, Washington, D.C.

Varner, John Grier, and Jeannette Johnson Varner (translators and editors)
> 1980 *The Florida of the Inca*. University of Texas Press, Austin.

Wilson, Jack H.
> 1983 *A Study of the Late Prehistoric, Protohistoric, and Historic Indians of the Carolina and Virginia Piedmont: Structure, Process, and Ecology*. Unpublished Ph.D. dissertation, Department of Anthropology, University of North Carolina, Chapel Hill.

Chapter 12 ■

Keith J. Little and Caleb Curren

Conquest Archaeology of Alabama

Conquest archaeology is a specialized field of study dealing with subjects pertinent to the Spanish conquest of the New World. This research covers both the European groups involved in the conquest and the native groups affected by the initial European actions. During the past two decades, there has been a great deal of activity in this field in the southeastern United States (Brain 1975; Brain et al. 1972; Curren 1989; Curren et al. 1981; DePratter et al. 1985; Ewen 1988; Lankford 1977; Little 1989; Smith 1976). Much of the investigative effort in the Southeast has centered on correlating archaeological and geographical data with documentary evidence derived from sixteenth-century accounts of the de Soto and de Luna expeditions. This chapter integrates these various data into a reasonable model of sixteenth-century aboriginal political spheres for the present state of Alabama.

In order to make full use of the potential resources available in the early Spanish documents, it is first necessary to establish the geographic localities of the native polities described in the early accounts and to correlate specific archaeological manifestations with these polities. The geographic localities of the aboriginal populations encountered by the de Soto and de Luna expeditions must also be identified before these data can be applied to anthropologically oriented research.

We use several lines of evidence to interpret the geographic locations and political alignments of the native groups encountered by sixteenth-century Spanish expeditions through present-day Alabama: documentary evidence of the Spanish activities, later historic data concerning the locations of historic aboriginal populations, linguistic data, the archaeological record, and physiographic data. To deal with such diverse data, we found it necessary to use a multidisciplinary methodology, and therefore turned to ethnohistoric archaeology (see Brain et al. 1972:232), which draws its data from the disciplines of ethnography, history, and archaeology.

We obtained our primary documentary evidence from four chronicles of the 1540 de Soto expedition and documentation of the 1560 de Luna expedition (Bourne 1904a, 1904b; Priestly 1928; Varner and Varner 1951). These records supply ethnographic, linguistic, and physiographic data, as well as distance statistics. The problems associated with the de Soto chronicles have been discussed by several researchers (Brain et al. 1972; Curren 1989; Little 1989). However, the distance statistics derived from the de Soto chronicles deserve special attention.

Researchers have repeatedly attempted to solve the mystery of the de Soto route through interpretations of the distance data derived from the de Soto chronicles (Hudson 1987; Swanton 1939). This has usually involved establishing a key location and estimating the number of miles that equal a day of travel in the de Soto narratives. Given this base, it would appear to be a simple matter to plot distance on a map from the key location and determine all other localities along the map. This methodology has, however, failed to accurately predict the localities of the towns encountered by the early Spanish explorers. Archaeological evidence has refuted some of Swanton's postulated locations that were based on distance statistics (DeJarnette 1958), as well as locations recently proposed by Charles Hudson and his colleagues (see the appendix to this chapter). We suggest that one of the major problems with this approach is its untenable assumptions concerning the accuracy of the Spanish estimates of distance and days of travel as well as the emphasis on this single data source (Little 1988b, 1989).

This is not to say that this type of evidence should not be used. It can help rule out distances between postulated localities that are too incongruent with chronicle estimates for us to consider at all. We would rule as unacceptable any distance requiring travel of 20 or more miles per day. Although distance data are not entered into our model, elsewhere we have examined the distance estimates between these localities and at no point were 18 or more miles of travel per day required (Curren 1989).

The archaeological record provides data for inferences and can be used to evaluate the accuracy, validity, and utility of the various hypotheses incorporated into our model. The value of the archaeological record in studies of the Spanish conquest goes beyond that of simply establishing the presence of European objects and dating the aboriginal sites to the sixteenth century. Through pottery-distribution studies, we have correlated specific archaeological phases with chiefdoms encountered by the Spanish. In some cases, archaeological settlement pattern studies have also been correlated with early descriptions of native settlements. In addition, we have used linguistic correlations with pottery types to establish certain political boundaries described in the Spanish accounts, and through archaeological investigations in several areas we have linked sixteenth-century Mississippian populations to their historic descendants.

Late Mississippian Archaeology

We are now able to identify specific late Mississippian archaeological phases of Alabama as sixteenth-century aboriginal manifestations. These phases incorporate several lines of archaeological evidence into a single analytical unit that has proven to be particularly useful in this study. The following summaries describe the geographic extent, settlement patterns, pottery, and documentation of European artifacts associated with each phase.

Barnett Phase

Barnett phase pottery types (Hally 1970, 1979) include Lamar Plain, Lamar Bold Incised, and Lamar Complicated Stamped in association with shell-tempered plain and incised wares. The Terrapin Creek, Ohatchee Creek, and Choccolocco Creek basins of the Upper Coosa River drainage in northeast Alabama exhibit pottery assemblages very similar to the Barnett phase of northwest Georgia (Harry O. Holstein, personal communication 1989; Holstein and Little 1985; 1986; Little 1989; Little and Curren 1981). In northeast Alabama and northwest Georgia, Barnett phase sites consistently yield associations of sixteenth-century European manufactured artifacts (Langford and Smith n.d.; Little 1985; Little and Curren 1981; Moorehead 1932; Morrell 1964; Smith 1975, 1976, 1977, 1979). Barnett phase sites in the upper Coosa region of Alabama exhibit a regional settlement pattern oriented toward occupations along the eastern tributaries of the Coosa River. Known settlements along the main river in this area tend to be confined to locations at the sites of major eastern stream confluences with the Coosa River (Little 1989).

Kymulga Phase

Kymulga phase pottery types (Knight 1985b, 1986; Knight et al. 1984; Nance 1986) are very similar to those of the closely related Barnett phase. Again, Lamar Plain, Lamar Bold Incised, Lamar Complicated Stamped, and shell-tempered types are important assemblage constituents. The sites appear to occur only in the Talladega County area of Alabama. Several sixteenth-century European artifacts have been recovered from Kymulga phase sites (Harry O. Holstein, personal communications, 1989; Knight 1985b; Knight et al. 1984; Wilson 1987). Like the closely related Barnett phase sites of Alabama, the settlement pattern is oriented away from the main river and toward occupations along the eastern tributaries of the Coosa River (Knight 1988; Knight et al. 1984).

Avery Phase

Avery phase pottery types include Lamar Plain, Lamar Bold Incised, and Lamar Complicated Stamped (Knight 1980). Avery phase sites are found in the upper Tallapoosa River drainage (Hubbert and Wright 1983). Although no European artifacts have been recovered from Avery phase sites, the relationship of the associated Lamar pottery types with those of the neighboring Barnett and Kymulga phases certainly suggests contemporaneity.

Shine II Phase

Shine II phase pottery types include Lamar Plain, Lamar Bold Incised, and Lamar Complicated Stamped co-occurring with shell-tempered types (Knight 1985a). Shine II phase sites are situated in the lower Tallapoosa River region. Although the exact provenience is unknown, sixteenth-century European artifacts have been recovered from the lower Tallapoosa River area (Smith 1976). Moreover, similarities with Kymulga and Barnett phase assemblages suggest a sixteenth-century date for the Shine II phase. The Shine II phase settlement pattern is oriented toward occupations along the Tallapoosa River (Curren 1989; Knight 1988).

Moundville III–Related Phase

An undefined Moundville III–related phase has been identified on the upper Alabama River. Pottery illustrated in Moore (1899) and survey collections indicate the presence of Moundville III phase occupations in the upper Alabama River region (Ned Jenkins, personal communication). We documented a large collection of sixteenth-century European artifacts recovered by C. B. Moore from a mound at the Charlotte Thompson Site, a major Moundville III–related phase site of the region (Curren et al. 1981).

Furman Phase

Furman phase decorated pottery types include a predominance of Pensacola Incised varieties and a consistent presence of Moundville Incised. The Furman phase is differentiated from the closely related Bear Point phase primarily by a marked reduction in D'Olive varieties. Although European objects have not been recovered from a Furman phase context, similarities with the closely related Bear Point phase pottery assemblages confirm a probable sixteenth-century date within the phase. Geographically, the Furman phase extends from Monroe County or southern Wilcox County to the Selma area of the Alabama River drainage (Curren 1989).

Bear Point Phase

Diagnostic decorated pottery of the Bear Point phase includes a predominance of Pensacola Incised varieties and a consistent presence of Moundville Incised and D'Olive types (Fuller 1985). Numerous sixteenth-century European artifacts have been recovered from Bear Point phase contexts (Curren 1989; Stowe 1982). Geographically, the phase extends from the lower Alabama and Tombigbee rivers to the coast, and along the coast from Choctawhatchee Bay to Biloxi Bay.

Moundville III Phase

Diagnostic decorated pottery of the Moundville III phase includes Carthage Incised types (Steponaitis 1980) as well as small amounts of Moundville Incised (Solis and Walling 1982). Sixteenth-century European artifacts have been recovered with related assemblages at the Charlotte Thompson Site (Curren et al. 1981). Geographically, the Moundville III phase appears to extend from the fall line near Tuscaloosa, Alabama, to the mouth of the Black Warrior River in the Demopolis, Alabama, region.

Other Archaeological Evidence

Currently, archaeologists studying the southeastern United States tend to avoid the controversial use of historic aboriginal place names in correlations with earlier sixteenth-century native societies. Although historic place names should certainly be applied with caution, they can still be an important source of evidence as long as they meet archaeological requisites.

Historic place names are eschewed in Southeastern contact period studies primarily because they revealed inconsistencies in Swanton's monumental de Soto route. Swanton associated the eighteenth-century location of the Abihka town of Coosa, situated near present-day Childersburg, Alabama, with the de Soto expedition's Coosa (Swanton 1939). Subsequently, David DeJarnette (1958) conducted archaeological excavations on the site. Although the site yielded evidence of an eighteenth-century occupation, it failed to demonstrate the presence of an earlier sixteenth-century component.

Consequently, archaeologists began to reevaluate the route of the de Soto expedition through Alabama (Curren 1989; Curren et al. 1981; DePratter et al. 1985; Lankford 1977; Little 1989; Smith 1976). Researchers realized that Swanton had failed to consider the possibility of historic aboriginal population relocations. Many researchers were therefore reluctant to base interpretations on associations with historic place names. However, Ewen's (1988, this volume) recent archaeological discovery of the de Soto expedition's winter encampment at Apalachee in present-day Tallahassee, Florida, indicates that this attitude toward place names may represent an overreaction to a problem that has viable alternatives.

Documentation of the geographic stability of the Apalachee situated in northern Florida from the period of early sixteenth-century Spanish contact into the later historic period demonstrates that the location of at least one historic native society can be projected back to the period of initial European contact. Given this example, it would be presumptuous of researchers to totally disregard, or to relegate to secondary importance, the historic localities of aboriginal groups in contact period studies of other Southeastern regions. Nevertheless, historic accounts do document many dislocations of native populations that could lead researchers to erroneous conclusions regarding the locations of early contact period groups. The problem, then, is to find objective criteria for determining when the use of historic place names is appropriate in sixteenth-century contact period studies.

The first, and most obvious, would be a careful scrutiny of protohistoric and historic documentary evidence for indications of recorded relocations and movements. Because more groups were dislocated during the post-1750 historic settlement period, pre-1750 protohistoric records should provide more appropriate locations for projecting back into the sixteenth century. There is little doubt, however, that some early historic group movements were simply not observed or recorded. Therefore, an indication of geographic stability derived from historic documents is not in itself sufficient grounds for making a correlation with an earlier sixteenth century population.

The archaeological record can, however, provide an objective criterion for making such correlations. It is suggested here that, if an indigenous development from the sixteenth century to the succeeding historic period can be demonstrated through studies of archaeological data (e.g., pottery), and the manifestations of the latter period can be associated with a historic place name, then correlations of the historic place names with the earlier contact period manifestations may be appropriate. In turn, the dubious use of a historic place name without first considering the existence of a demonstrable indigenous development in the archaeological record as described above would certainly be questionable. Hence, the use of an archaeological continuum is viewed as a primary requisite for correlating historic place names with earlier archaeological manifestations.

In Alabama there are at least three known areas in which archaeological evidence indicates historic continuity between local late Mississippian manifestations and those of later documented historic populations: Kymulga phase (Talladega County, Alabama), Shine II phase (lower Tallapoosa River), and Bear Point phase (lower Alabama River). Place names from the Spanish accounts and later historic records suggest that these were the regions of Apica, Talisi, and Mauvila, respectively. This archaeological documentation of historic continuity is incorporated in the following model of the locations of sixteenth-century aboriginal polities encountered by sixteenth-century Spanish explorers in the present state of Alabama (see Figure 12-1).

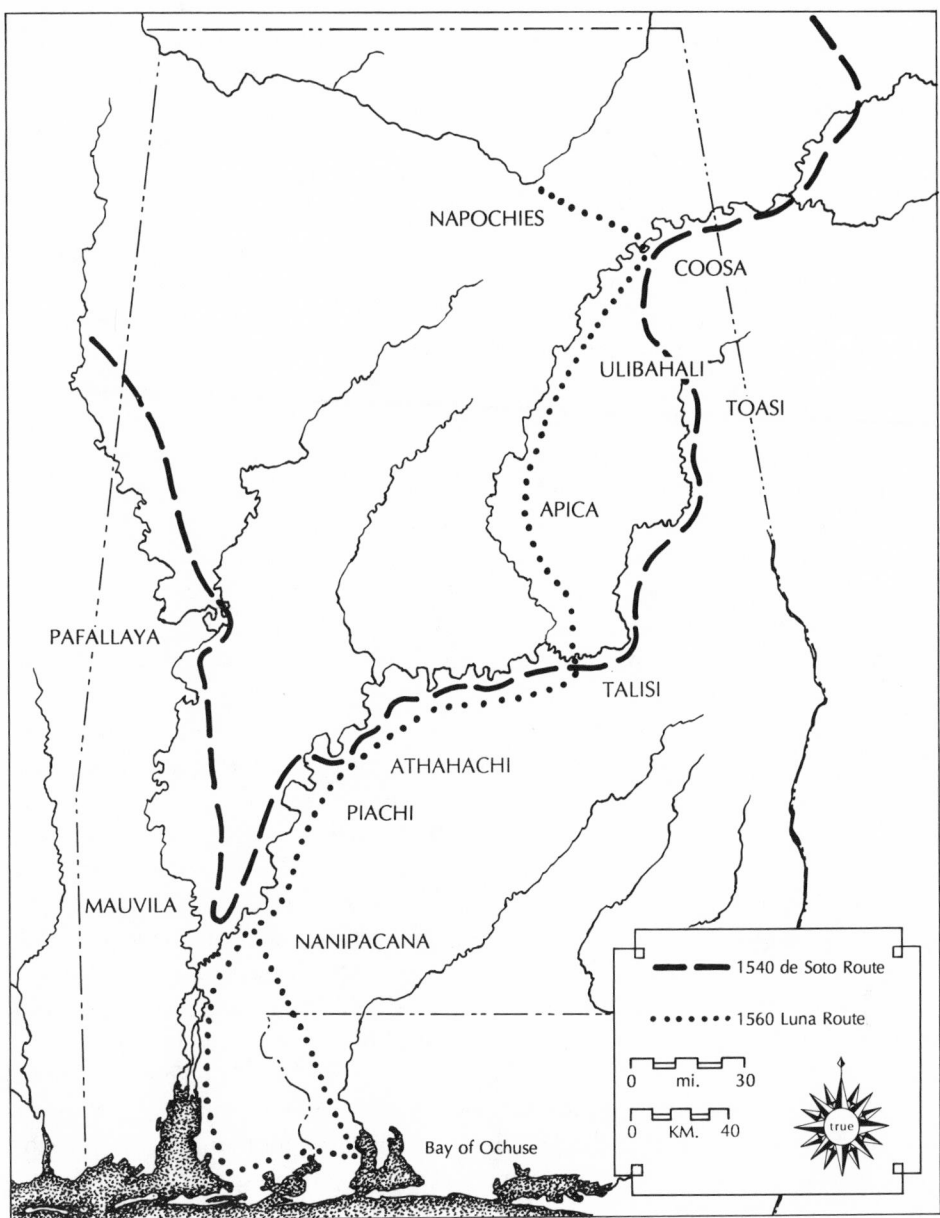

Figure 12-1. Postulated routes of the Hernando de Soto expedition through Alabama.

Sixteenth-Century Aboriginal Polities in Northern Alabama

Coosa

The chiefdom of Coosa was regarded as one of the most powerful polities en-countered by the de Soto expedition on its journey through the southeastern

United States. According to Elvas, Chiaha was the first subject of Coosa encountered by de Soto (Bourne 1904a:68). Elvas also describes the town as situated on a large river island (Bourne 1904a:74). Although the precise location of Chiaha remains to be determined, many researchers agree that the town was located at a Dallas or Mouse Creek phase site, situated on an island, in the Tennessee River drainage of east Tennessee (Brain 1985; DePratter et al. 1985; McCollough and Alexander 1988).

Traveling down the Tennessee River, the expedition came to another island chiefdom, Coste. In 1981, we postulated that the Chattanooga, Tennessee, area was the locality of Coste/Tali (Curren et al. 1981). Independent archaeological investigations concur that Coste and Tali were likely located at a Mouse Creek phase site in the vicinity of Chattanooga (McCollough and Alexander 1988).

Leaving the Coste/Tali area, the de Soto expedition traveled five to six days, passing through several towns subject to Coosa before coming to the principal town of Coosa (Bourne 1904a:81, 1904b:111–112; Varner and Varner 1951:342–343). The Garcilaso de la Vega account gives an often-cited passage indicating the presence of a mound or mounds at the town of Coosa (Varner and Varner 1951:343). The subsequent de Luna expedition accounts give geographic descriptions, including a major stream confluence situated south of an east-west-trending mountain range. These documents also indicate that Coosa was situated in a well-populated valley (Priestley 1928:241).

The geographic descriptions of the de Luna documents restrict the number of localities that could have been the town of Coosa. The possibilities are even further limited by certain items of the archaeological record: (1) if the site is in the Coosa River basin, then it should yield aboriginal artifacts indicative of a sixteenth-century occupation (i.e., Barnett phase); (2) there should be a mound associated with the site; (3) there should be settlements on at least two sides of a stream confluence; (4) there should be other contemporaneous sites in the same stream valley. Only one location being considered by researchers at present fits the geographic descriptions of Coosa derived from Luna documents and cannot be ruled out by the limitations imposed by the other documentary evidence and the archaeological record—the Terrapin Creek site, 1Ce309 (Little 1989).

The Terrapin Creek site is at the confluence of Terrapin Creek, approximately 11 km south of the edge of the Cumberland Plateau mountains. This physiographic setting is congruent with the restrictive de Luna account descriptions. The site is also included in the sixteenth-century Barnett phase. Although professional excavations have not been conducted on the site, Marvin Smith (1976, 1977) has recorded numerous finds of European and aboriginal artifacts recovered during extensive looting activities by collectors during the early 1970s. Included in Smith's inventory of sixteenth-century European objects are faceted chevrons and a Nueva Cadiz bead (Smith 1977). Possible mounds have also been recorded at the site (Smith 1976).

A current survey by the Jacksonville State University Archaeological Resource Laboratory is addressing the remaining two archaeological requisites concerning the presence of other contemporaneous sites in the vicinity and in the area around the junction of Terrapin Creek and the Coosa River. So far, the survey has documented several contemporaneous sites in the lower Terrapin Creek basin that may be correlated with the de Luna passages describing a well-peopled valley (Harry Holstein, personal communication, 1989).

Given that the Terrapin Creek Site was Coosa, then other Barnett phase sites in northwest Georgia, many of which have yielded sixteenth-century European artifacts, probably represent some of the numerous towns encountered by the de Soto expedition while traveling from Coste/Tali to Coosa.

The de Luna party also assisted Coosa in a campaign to realign rebellious Napochie subjects (Priestley 1928:xlii–xliii, 231–233). We have postulated that the Crow Creek phase of the Tennessee River Guntersville basin represents Napochie manifestations (Little 1989). The post-sixteenth-century aboriginal ceramics of the Guntersville basin and the upper Coosa River region are very similar and reflect close ties. Given that Coosa's joint venture with the de Luna soldiers was successful, then post–de Luna links between the Coosa and Napochie populations may be expected; and thus offer a reasonable explanation for so many similarities in post-sixteenth-century pottery assemblages between the upper Coosa River of Alabama and the Guntersville basin.

Apica

Although the de Soto chronicles do not mention the Apica, who were subject to the chiefdom of Coosa, they were encountered by the Luna expedition (Priestley 1928: 225–229). Knight et al. (1984) have pointed out that the Apica referred to in the de Luna correspondence were probably the ancestors of the eighteenth-century Abihka of the Talladega County, Alabama, area. In an earlier locational model, we further postulated that some of the sixteenth-century Kymulga phase sites in Talladega County were the Apica discussed in the Luna documents. An archaeological test was suggested to further evaluate the accuracy and validity of this hypothesis:

> The designation of the Kymulga phase as an Apica manifestation has certain implications for archaeological research. If Kymulga phase sites represent Luna's Apica and the later Upper Creek Abihka are descendents of Luna's Apica, then future pottery analyses should directly link later local Creek Indian ceramics to those of the Kymulga phase [Little 1989].

Since the initial draft of that model was prepared, Vernon Knight, Jr., completed a study of the ceramic developments in the Talladega County area and concluded: "Kymulga phase Lamar of the middle Coosa region is Muskogee, specifically ancestral to the Abihka group of Creek towns" (Knight 1986). Here we have established through archaeological investigations very probable historic continuity between the eighteenth-century Abihka and the sixteenth-century Kymulga phase. Given such a historic relationship and the likelihood that the Abihka were descendants of the Apica, then the Kymulga phase manifestations are surely those of the sixteenth-century Apica. Essentially, Vernon Knight's research documented the validity of the earlier archaeological prediction concerning historic continuity between the Kymulga phase and later historic Creek manifestations of the Talladega County area. We view the fact that Knight's study came after the original hypothesis as very strong supporting evidence for the association of the sixteenth-century Apica with Kymulga phase manifestations of the Talladega County, Alabama, area.

Ulibahali

The Luna Papers (Priestley 1928:225) indicated that Ulibahali was situated between Apica and Coosa. The de Soto expedition traveled to Ulibahali after visiting Coosa (Bourne 1904a:84, 1904b:113). The hypotheses that the town of Coosa was at the Terrapin Creek site and that the Apica were in the Talladega County area compelled us to postulate the location of Ulibahali at a position between these two points—the Davis Farm Site complex near Oxford, Alabama. Archaeological field investigations at the Davis Farm Site complex have recorded the presence of a large mound and verified a later Mississippian component through the recovery of an assemblage of Barnett phase pottery (Hatcher 1979; Luttrell 1882; Holstein and Little 1986; Waselkov 1980). The presence of the mound indicates that the site was an important civic-ceremonial center for the smaller local Mississippian settlements. Hence, the site was postulated as a likely candidate for the principal town of Ulibahali (Little 1989).

Since the hypothesis was first put forth, additional archaeological investigations have provided more supporting evidence that the Davis Farm Site complex represents the town of Ulibahali. Specifically, the Elvas account describes Ulibahali as being situated on a stream with "a town on the opposite shore" (Bourne 1904a:85). Harry Holstein (1986) conducted field investigations at another site, 1Ca190, directly across Choccolocco Creek from the Davis Farm Site complex. The presence of a Barnett phase component documented at 1Ca190 indicates contemporaneity with the Davis Farm Site complex. The locations of the Davis Farm Site complex and 1Ca190, which are situated on opposite banks of Choccolocco Creek, certainly coincide with the Elvas passage describing a town across the stream from Ulibahali. Once again, supporting archaeological evidence acquired after the initial formulation of the hypothesis indicates the accuracy and validity of our association of the Davis Farm Site complex with the town of Ulibahali.

Talisi

In the Garcilaso narrative, Talisi was recorded as the last constituent of Coosa encountered by the expedition (Varner and Varner 1951:346). The de Luna documents only briefly mention Talisi, but concur with the Garcilaso account that it was part of Coosa (Priestley 1928:291). The de Soto chronicles offer descriptions of the settlement system, or at least a part of it, that have direct implications for the archaeological record. Three accounts all indicate that the towns of Talisi were situated along a large river (Bourne 1904a:86, 1904b:115; Varner and Varner 1951:346).

The fact that the Kymulga phase and Barnett phase sites of the Coosa River basin in Alabama exhibit a settlement pattern oriented along major tributaries and away from the main river rules out these areas as logical candidates for the location of Talisi (Little 1988c, 1989; Knight 1988). However, several lines of evidence, including a riverine settlement pattern, support our hypothesis that Shine II phase sites along the lower Tallapoosa River represent towns of the chiefdom of Talisi. As we (Curren 1989) first pointed out and as independent studies by the Alabama De Soto Commission later confirmed (Knight 1988), the Shine II settlements are primarily situated along the Tallapoosa River. This settlement pattern certainly matches the chronicle descriptions of a riverine settlement at Talisi.

Moreover, pottery studies document an indigenous development of later Creek ceramics from the earlier Mississippian traditions of the region. According to Vernon Knight and his colleagues, the ceramics characteristic of historic Big Tallassee were directly derived from earlier Shine II phase pottery types of the lower Tallapoosa River (Knight 1986; Knight et al. 1984). Thus our hypothesis that sixteenth-century Talisi was located in the lower Tallapoosa River basin is well supported in the archaeological record.

Toasi

The de Soto chronicles placed Toasi between Ulibahali and Talisi (Bourne 1904a:84–86, 1904b:113–115). According to the Elvas account, the de Soto expedition encountered another settlement of the Ulibahali chiefdom between the principal town of Ulibahali and Toasi (Bourne 1904a:85). The Elvas narrative also discusses passing through towns subject to the Talisi chiefdom between the towns of Toasi and Talisi (Bourne 1904a:86).

We have postulated that Toasi was situated at an Avery phase site on the upper Tallapoosa River (Curren 1989). This hypothesis is primarily based on the following interpretations: (1) the association of Ulibahali with the Davis Farm Site complex; (2) the fact that Choccolocco Creek closely coincides with a major historic Indian route over the divide to the vicinity of the Tallapoosa River (Royce Map); and (3) the hypothesis that Talisi was located in the lower Tallapoosa River Valley.

Ultimately, these interpretations are linked to the premise that aboriginal sociopolitical boundaries of the Southeast were often tied to specific drainage basins. Given this premise and the association of the Davis Farm Site complex with Ulibahali, a good argument can be made for correlating the other late Mississippian sites of the Choccolocco Creek basin with the chiefdom of Ulibahali. The Elvas account distinguishes the town situated between Ulibahali and Toasi as a subject of Ulibahali. Hence, one of several Barnett phase sites in the upper Choccolocco Creek drainage could represent the other Ulibahali town encountered by the de Soto army between the principal town of Ulibahali and Toasi (Holstein and Little 1985).

Although still within the chiefdom of Coosa, Toasi appears to be of a different local political affinity than Ulibahali. The suggestion of a change in political alignments gives good reason to suspect that Toasi may be situated in a different drainage, if it is assumed that sociopolitical boundaries correlate with specific drainage basins.

A final point concerns the placement of both Toasi and Talisi in the Tallapoosa River basin. The de Soto expedition's line of travel between Toasi and Talisi would probably have closely followed the course of the Tallapoosa River. The towns subject to Talisi described by Elvas between Toasi and Talisi would necessarily have been in the same drainage as Talisi, a location that is consistent with our premise correlating sociopolitical boundaries with drainage basins.

Discussion

Notably, this model of the locations of Ulibahali, Apica, Toasi, and Talisi offers explanations of several discrepancies between the de Soto and de Luna documents that have puzzled researchers for years. For example, the de Soto chronicles did not mention Apica, whereas the de Luna expedition referred to it as an important subject of Coosa. Furthermore, the de Luna documents only briefly referred to Talisi and did not mention Toasi at all. These puzzles are resolved if one considers that the Luna expedition took a different route from the de Soto army through this part of Alabama.

If the Davis Farm Site complex represents the principal town of Ulibahali, then it is reasonable to postulate that the de Soto expedition changed drainages through the mountain passes of the upper Choccolocco Creek drainage while traveling to Toasi in the adjacent Tallapoosa River basin. Thus, the de Soto expedition entirely missed an encounter with the Apica who were located to the south of Ulibahali in the next major eastern tributary, the Talladega Creek drainage. In turn, if the de Luna expedition traveled up the Coosa River instead of the Tallapoosa River, then it would have encountered the Apica populations in the Talladega area that were missed by the earlier de Soto expedition. This would also explain why the de Luna documents did not mention Toasi and only briefly referred to Talisi, both of which were located in the Tallapoosa River drainage. The ability of this ethnohistoric archaeological model to explain these kinds of puzzles with support from several lines of evidence certainly adds even more credibility to the model's accuracy, validity, and utility.

Sixteenth-Century Aboriginal Polities in Southern Alabama

Caxa

The de Soto army left Talisi and traveled the first day to the town of Casiste. The next day the expedition entered the domain of Tascalusa at the town of Caxa (Bourne 1904a:87, 1904b:116). Swanton pointed out that a change from Creek to Choctaw place names corresponds perfectly with these chronicle passages concerning the army's travel from Talisi, the last subject of Coosa, to Caxa, the first subject of Tascalusa.

> In the designations of the towns given us . . . we also recognize the Creek tongue. Talimachusy . . . Itaba . . . [and] Ulibahali . . . are all Creek and . . . names of towns such as Talisi and Casiste [Caxiti in the Luna narratives] reappear in recognizable forms. Not only so but the point where the Creek territory comes to an end and that of the Choctaw-speaking Mobile Indians begins is clearly defined. Casiste is the last town in the Creek country. . . . The next town beyond is called Caxa, a name with the tell-tale Choctaw locative *asha*. . . . Moreover, we do not have to depend merely on names because Elvas says that the day after leaving Casiste the explorers passed through a village and slept in one belonging to the province of Tascaluça, and Tascaluça ("Black Warrior") is a pure Choctaw word [Swanton 1939:51].

The archaeological record reflects this change of polity in the major change in distribution of pottery types in the area of the lower Tallapoosa and upper Alabama rivers. These pottery types can in turn be specifically linked to either Creek or Choctaw. The Shine II phase pottery of the lower Tallapoosa River represents a southern extension of Lamar ceramics. Vernon Knight, Jr. (1986), has documented that the Lamar pottery assemblages of the Barnett, Kymulga, Avery, and Shine II phases all are ancestral to Creek assemblages. Pottery of the Moundville III–related phase of the adjacent upper Alabama River represents the northeastern extent of the closely related Moundville and Pensacola pottery complexes of the Alabama Coastal Plain. Fuller et al. (1984), by tracing the probable pottery development of Pensacola types into related types associated with later historic Choctaw-speaking Mobile and Tomeh Indians, has established a very probable Choctaw connection with Pensacola and related Moundville ceramics.

Given the correlations of Swanton's linguistic data with pottery types, we are compelled to place Caxa at the Charlotte Thompson Mound site or another Moundville III–related site in the upper Alabama River region, the northernmost area of Choctaw pottery distributions. Although the specific site of Caxa is not confirmed, the fact that it is located at one of the Moundville III–related sites of the upper Alabama River is almost certain, particularly in the light of the Creek and Choctaw pottery associations. This kind of confirmation from the archaeological record makes our hypotheses concerning the general locations of Talisi and Caxa some of the best-supported points along the entire de Soto route through the southeastern United States.

Athahachi

The de Soto chronicles described a sparsely occupied area between Caxa and the principal town of Tascalusa. Archaeologically, the region of the Alabama River between the Montgomery cluster of Moundville III–related sites and the contemporaneous Furman phase sites in the Selma area corresponds with the narrative descriptions of a sparsely occupied zone (Jenkins and Paglione 1980; Knight 1988; Little 1988a; Nance 1976).

Athahachi, the principal town of Tascalusa, was encountered after the de Soto expedition traveled through the sparsely populated area lying beyond Caxa. The

Elvas, Ranjel, and Garcilaso accounts all have passages indicating the presence of a mound at the town (Bourne 1904a:87, 1904b:120; Varner and Varner 1951:349). However, *The Luna Papers* (Priestley 1928) did not record a visit to Athahachi during de Luna's trip up the Alabama River, and this difference between the de Soto and de Luna accounts in inventories of native towns presented a real puzzle to earlier researchers. Our hypothesis concerning the location of Athahachi resolves these puzzling issues.

The Furman phase is postulated as a manifestation of the core chiefdom of Tascalusa's political sphere. The Cedar Creek site (1Ds172), on a tributary of the Alabama River, is the most logical candidate for the location of Athahachi (Curren 1989; Curren et al. 1981). Archaeological investigations have recorded the presence of a large Mississippian domiciliary mound on the site, an important feature for correlating the site with the chronicle descriptions (Curren and Little 1982; Jenkins and Paglione 1980). Although pottery recovered from the site demonstrates a Mississippian occupation on the Cedar Creek Site, the sample was not adequate for confirming or refuting the presence of a Furman phase component (Curren 1989). However, this is one point that can easily be addressed through additional excavations on the site.

Further evidence to indicate Athahachi may be associated with the Cedar Creek site is that the de Soto chroniclers do not mention a river at the town. The Cedar Creek site is on the banks of Cedar Creek east of the Alabama River. This location off the main river not only offers a viable explanation of why the de Soto chronicles did not mention a river, but also why the de Luna expedition traveling up the Alabama River did not encounter the town.

Piachi

The chronicles described another major town, Piachi, located in the core chiefdom of Tascalusa. All the de Soto chronicles indicate that Piachi was situated along a river that was crossed by the expedition (Bourne 1904a:89, 1904b:17, 123; Varner and Varner 1951:351). The de Luna expedition also encountered Piachi while traveling up the Alabama River from Nanipacana, thus, confirming that the river was the Alabama (Priestley 1928). One of the late Mississippian, Furman phase sites located in Wilcox County, Alabama, is thought to be the locality of Piachi (Curren 1989).

Mauvila

The de Soto expedition crossed the Alabama River at Piachi and proceeded to Mauvila, also subject to Tascalusa (Varner and Varner 1951:354; Bourne 1904a: 90, 1904b:17, 122). Mauvila was the site of a violent resistance by the natives to the intrusion of the de Soto army. After the battle, the victorious Spaniards remained in the area for almost a month recuperating from wounds received during the battle. Consequently, there are several pertinent passages in the chronicles concerning Mauvila that are amenable to associations with other lines of evidence.

The chronicles described the town of Mauvila as being on a plain (Bourne 1904b:17; Varner and Varner 1951:353). Elvas mentioned the presence of a pond at the site (Bourne 1904a:96). Elvas and Ranjel referred to several native settlements in the Mauvila region (Bourne 1904a:98, 1904b:123).

The location of Mauvila is postulated to be in the region of the lower Alabama River in present-day Clark County, Alabama (Curren 1989). Physiographically, the region is characterized by mature alluvial landforms coinciding with the chronicle descriptions of a plain. Mississippian settlements of the Clark County region are typically situated on high ground adjacent to oxbow lakes, one of which could represent the pond described by Elvas. In addition, archaeological survey and testing has recorded numerous late Mississippian sites in the area, which corresponds with the chronicle description of several settlements in the area (Curren and McKenzie 1988; Curren and Majors 1984; Fuller et al. 1984).

European artifacts recovered from the area also support the hypothesis that Mauvila was located in that vicinity. Collectors recovered several sixteenth-century European objects from a Mississippian burial mound at the Pine Log Creek site (Stowe 1982). These artifacts include a brass candlestick, brass Holy Water container, iron gun barrel, fragments of a sword, a pike head, a "standard" knife, an iron bridle and cheek plate, a horseshoe, an iron kettle fragment, an iron axe, an iron chisel, an iron chisel or wedge fragment, an iron sickle fragment, iron spikes, faceted chevron beads, blue glass beads, and an ear spool made of a Columbia Plain sherd. The artifacts that can be dated with some confidence all support a sixteenth-century date. These artifacts include the glass beads, the Columbia Plain sherd, the candlestick, the Holy Water container, the horseshoe, the pike head, the iron spikes, the iron wedge, and the iron chisels. Two of these items described as a part of a sixteenth-century altar set are particularly significant: the Holy Water container and the candlestick.

The Elvas, Ranjel, and Garcilaso accounts all describe the loss of religious paraphernalia at the battle of Mauvila (Bourne 1904a:97, 1904b:127; Varner and Varner 1951:382). The fact that the Pine Log Creek site artifacts identified as part of an altar set mirror some of those lost in the Mauvila battle is viewed as an important correlation. This is particularly true when consideration is given to alternative ways that these religious artifacts could have come into the possession of the Indians. Surely it would have been considered a blasphemy for a devout Catholic to have traded these items to non-Christian aboriginals. Moreover, these items were considered essential for core rituals required by the Spaniards' religion for their own well-being, a point well documented by the chroniclers. Therefore, the proposition that these items were obtained through trade with other sixteenth-century Spanish expeditions is not viable.

The relatively large and varied assortment of European weapons recovered from the Pine Log Creek site is also unusual. Although the gun barrel and sword fragments have not been dated, the ridged pike point closely resembles fifteenth- to seventeenth-century Spanish examples illustrated in Calvert's *Spanish Arms and Armour* (Calvert 1907:Plates 201 and 202). Notably, these are kinds of artifacts that could be expected from the battlefield of Mauvila.

When the Pine Log Creek inventory of European objects is compared to inventories of sixteenth-century European artifacts recovered from other aboriginal sites in the Southeast, the Pine Log Creek Site stands out. Although the Pine Log Creek site inventory includes the glass beads, iron spikes, iron wedges, and iron chisels more typical of many other sixteenth-century sites in the Southeast, the addition of the weapon assemblage and the altar set makes this site an archaeological anomaly. A reasonable explanation for this anomaly is offered by the hypothesis that the site of sixteenth-century Mauvila is in the region of the lower Alabama and Tombigbee rivers and that these artifacts were recovered from the Mauvila battle site by local natives.

Another important line of evidence supporting the placement of Mauvila in the lower Alabama River and Tombigbee River region is found in later documents describing eighteenth-century French activities conducted in the area. These documents indicate that Mobilians and Tomeh were present in this region (Higginbotham 1966). The archaeological record indicates historic continuity between the sixteenth-century Mississippian populations of the lower Alabama River region and the eighteenth-century Mobilians. Vernon Knight, Jr. (1981), has fervently argued that there is historic continuity between the eighteenth-century Mobile/Tomeh Indians and late Mississippian populations in the lower Alabama River and Tombigbee River area. Knight connected the eighteenth-century Mobile Indians to the Mississippian Bottle Creek site through early French documents. He further argued that economic strategies of the eighteenth-century Mobile have a direct "relationship to those of their immediate prehistoric predecessors in that environment." Fuller et al. (1984:215–217) also noted pottery similarities that indicate continuity between late Mississippian and seventeenth- to early eighteenth-century native populations of the region. If these archaeological indications are accurate, then there can be little doubt that sixteenth-century Mauvila populations were located in the same general area as their historic descendants.

Pafallaya

The de Soto army left Mauvila traveling northward through unoccupied country for five days before arriving at the town of Talicpacana in the chiefdom of Pafallaya (Bourne 1904a:99, 1904b:21, 128–129). An archaeological survey in the upland regions between the Alabama and Tombigbee rivers, north to the confluence of the Black Warrior River, indicates that this area was essentially unoccupied during the sixteenth century (Brose et al. 1983; Curren and Majors 1984; Wimberly 1960). The lack of archaeological evidence of Mississippian occupations in this region coincides with the chronicle descriptions of the route north of Mauvila to Pafallaya (Curren 1989). A cluster of Mississippian sites in the lower Black Warrior River basin region is postulated as the likely locality of Pafallaya (Curren 1989).

In general, researchers concur that these lower Black Warrior River sites are included in the Moundville phase (Peebles 1978:387; Steponaitis 1978:437). Sheldon et al. (1982) specifically documented the presence of late Mississippian

(Moundville III phase) components at 1Ha54 and 1Ha55, and hence support the postulate that the area was probably occupied during the sixteenth century.

Since we first postulated the lower Black Warrior River Mississippian sites as the locale of Pafallaya, additional archaeological evidence has been recorded that further documents the presence of late Mississippian occupations in the area. Collectors recovered a ground stone, perforated spatulate axe from the lower Black Warrior River near Demopolis, Alabama (Little et al. 1989). Not only is this type of axe indicative of late Mississippian occupations, but perforated spatulate axes have consistently been recovered from sites yielding sixteenth-century European artifacts.

Conclusions

We have viewed our research for the past 12 years as a means of getting to a point where we can begin addressing more anthropologically oriented questions. In order to benefit fully from the documentary evidence of the early Spanish explorers as well as the archaeological record, it was first necessary to establish the localities of aboriginal chiefdoms encountered by the sixteenth-century conquistadors in Alabama through the use of archaeological documentation. We believe that this model largely fulfills that requisite and has opened new avenues of anthropological research. The model offers a unique opportunity to understand the geographic extent of some complex Mississippian political spheres.

In summary, this locational model provides a logical basis for postulating the geopolitical extent of a complex network of interacting chiefdoms operating in Alabama during the Spanish conquest. The chiefdom of Coosa covered a vast area from East Tennessee down the Tennessee River drainage as far as the Guntersville basin in Alabama, and from northwest Georgia in the Oostanaula River drainage down the Coosa River to the fall-line hills of Alabama, and from the upper Tallapoosa drainage to an area near its confluence with the Coosa River. Included here are the chiefdoms subject to Coosa and their postulated archaeological correlates: Chiaha (Dallas phase) in the Great Valley physiographic region of east Tennessee; Coste/Tali (Mouse Creek phase) in the Chattanooga, Tennessee, area; the Napochies (Crow Creek phase) in the Guntersville basin of north Alabama; Coosa (Barnett phase) of the Coosa River drainage in northeast Alabama and northwest Georgia; Ulibahali (Barnett phase) of the Choccolocco Creek basin; Apica (Kymulga phase) of the Talladega County, Alabama, area; Toasi (Avery phase) of the upper Tallapoosa River; and Talisi (Shine II phase) of the lower Tallapoosa River.

The chiefdom of Tascalusa also covered a large geographic region. The chiefdom included an area from the upper Alabama River near Montgomery, Alabama, to the Gulf coast and possibly extended into the Black Warrior River basin. Polities and associated archaeological phases include Caxa (Moundville III–related phase), upper Alabama River; Tascalusa (Furman phase), Wilcox County to the Selma area; and Mauvila (Bear Point phase), lower Alabama River region. Although the chronicles did not include Pafallaya as a subject of Tascalusa, there are reasons to suspect a possible connection. If the Moundville III–related sites in the Alabama River area represent a frontier settlement of the Moundville chiefdom, then the fact that these sites were subject to Tascalusa may be extended to associate the rest of the Moundville manifestations with Tascalusa. The attractiveness of this proposition is enhanced by the fact that researchers believe that Moundville had lost much of its influence shortly before the initial European contact.

In conclusion, we are beginning to understand through these conquest archaeology studies the vast geographic extent of several Mississippian chiefdoms. This work clearly discredits the postulate that the complexity of Mississippian organization was declining throughout the Southeast before the first European contact. A more feasible interpretation would be that the locations of major centers (such as Etowah and Moundville) changed as new polities (such as Coosa and Tascalusa) gained control of vast territories. Our hypotheses, through correlations of chronicle accounts with the archaeological record, also open new avenues for studies concerning the effects of the initial European contact with native societies in the Southeast.

Acknowledgments

This project was funded through the generous contributions of numerous supporters throughout the region. The funds are administered through the Mobile Historic Development Commission and the Alabama-Tombigbee Regional Commission. Stalwart support has come from Palmer Bedsole, Senator Ann Bedsole, Kenneth Hannon, and Nicholas Holmes, Jr. Dennis Golladay, dean of humanities at Pensacola Junior College, has been instrumental in providing support facilities. George Alford, executive director of the Alabama-Tombigbee Regional Commission, is commended for years of support with office space, laboratory space, and funding concerning conquest archaeological studies in southwest Alabama. We also are grateful to several archaeologists for sharing data, ideas, and opinions; notably, Harry Holstein, Ned Jenkins, Lawrence Alexander, Craig Sheldon, Roger Nance, McDonald Brooms, and Jeffrey Brain.

Appendix

Charles Hudson and his colleagues (DePratter et al. 1985; Hudson et al. 1985; Hudson, Smith, and DePratter 1987) have presented a reconstruction of the de Soto route through the present state of Alabama that is significantly different from our model of the locations of sixteenth-century polities. Our research indicates that the route proposed by Charles Hudson and his colleagues is invalid, at least throughout the state of Alabama. In this appendix, we document several archaeological inconsistences that refute their reconstruction. Several objective examinations of their reconstructions (Curren 1988; Little 1988a, 1988b, 1988c, 1988d, 1989) have further convinced us that many of the propositions of Charles Hudson and his colleagues are incongruent with both the archaeological data and the sixteenth-century documentary evidence. We have included here some examples of these incongruities.

1. Both the de Soto (1540) and de Luna (1560) expeditions visited the town of Coosa. According to *The Luna Papers* (Priestley 1928:xxi), former members of the de Soto expedition as well as native captives from Coosa accompanied the de Luna party to Coosa. The fact that these individuals traveled with the de Luna group to Coosa offers some assurance that both the de Soto and de Luna expeditions visited the same Coosa (Hudson et al. 1985:725–726; Little 1989).

The de Luna documents described the town of Coosa as being situated south of an east-west-trending mountain range: "There is a mountain range to the north of town, which runs east and west. It is fairly high and well-wooded, but up to this time we do not know where it begins or ends" (Priestley 1928:214). The fact that the passage describes the mountain as "well-wooded" indicates that the observers were actually near enough to the mountain to note its vegetation. Also, the description of not knowing where the mountain range "begins or ends" indicates that they were unable to observe either the western or eastern extremes of the mountains.

Hudson and his associates place Coosa at the Little Egypt site in northwest Georgia (DePratter et al. 1985; Hudson et al. 1985). According to their reconstruction, Cohutta Mountain is the mountain described in the de Luna passages (Hudson et al. 1985:726). Yet, Cohutta Mountain is a ridge within the north-south-running Blue Ridge Mountains. Furthermore, the north-south trending Blue Ridge Mountains are situated east of Little Egypt. Given the fact that the de Luna expedition would have necessarily approached Little Egypt from the southwest via the Coosa River drainage, a western limit is also readily discernible for the Blue Ridge range. Thus, the Little Egypt site is irreconcilable with the description of Coosa's physiographic setting in the de Luna documents.

2. Hudson and his colleagues placed Apica in northwest Georgia at the Johnstone Farm Site (DePratter et al. 1985:119). By reason of their reconstruction, the Apica relocated sometime after the de Soto and de Luna expeditions into the area of Talladega, Alabama, where the historic Abihka are known to have resided (Hudson et al. 1985:729). However, as we have shown in our model, there is ample evidence linking the pottery types of the historic Abihka with the earlier Kymulga phase ceramics in the Talladega area. This evidence of historic continuity strongly implies an indigenous development in the Talladega region rather than a major population movement from northwest Georgia into the Talladega area, as Hudson and associates concluded in their reconstruction.

3. Hudson and his associates placed Talisi at a Kymulga phase site in the Talladega area (DePratter et al. 1985:120; Hudson et al. 1985:731). Archaeologically, the settlement pattern of the Kymulga phase typically consists of sites situated away from the Coosa River along eastern tributaries (Knight et al. 1984; Knight 1988). Yet, three of the de Soto chronicles describe the towns of Talisi as being situated along a large river (Bourne 1904a:86, 1904b:115; Varner and Varner 1951:346). The Kymulga phase, with settlements typically situated away from the river, is certainly incongruent with the chronicle descriptions of riverine set-

tlements at Talisi. Despite the chronicle descriptions and archaeological data concerning the settlement pattern, Hudson and his colleagues still insist that Talisi is situated at a Kymulga phase site in the Talladega County area.

4. Hudson and his colleagues placed Piachi on the Alabama River at Durant Bend (DePratter et al. 1985). This area of the Alabama River is known for its paucity of late Mississippian sites (Curren 1989; Jenkins and Paglione 1980; Knight 1988; Nance 1976). Furthermore, archaeological field investigations have been conducted at Durant Bend and it is now fairly certain that there was no major late Mississippian component present in the vicinity of Durant Bend (Curren 1989; Nance 1976; Craig Sheldon, personal communication). In this case, Hudson and his associates have placed a major aboriginal town, Piachi, in a locality where archaeological investigations have consistently failed to produce evidence of a major sixteenth-century occupation.

5. Charles Hudson and his colleagues placed Mauvila at the Old Cahawba site, at the mouth of the Cahaba River near Selma, Alabama (Hudson et al. 1987). Although the chronicles described many settlements in the vicinity of Mauvila (Bourne 1904a:98, 1904b:123), an archaeological survey conducted by the University of Alabama State Museum of Natural History failed to find evidence of a substantial Mississippian occupation near the vicinity of the Old Cahawba Site (Atchison 1987). Moreover, excavations conducted by the University of Alabama on the Old Cahawba site specifically designed to evaluate the postulate that the site was the locality of Mauvila also failed to produce substantiating evidence outside the presence of daub and fortifications, neither of which is uncommon on Mississippian sites (Knight 1987). Also, as we pointed out in our model, there is ample ethnohistoric archaeological evidence that the later historic Mobilians descended from local Mississippian populations of the lower Alabama River drainage. Conversely, there is absolutely no evidence supporting a major population movement from the north such as would have been necessary for Mauvila to have been in the region of Selma, as suggested by Hudson and his associates. Clearly, to associate the Old Cahawba site with the sixteenth-century battlefield of Mauvila is inconsistent with the archaeological record.

So far, we have shown that at least five sixteenth-century localities presented by Hudson and his associates are incongruent with the archaeological record. Moreover, Charles Hudson himself pointed out that a hazard of methods such as his, which rely heavily on distance estimates, "is that if one town is inaccurately located, the chances are the next one will also be inaccurately located" (Hudson 1987:2). Given Hudson's own reasoning, if any one site is inaccurately placed, then chances are good that this will have a domino effect over the entire route reconstruction. We have identified five such cases, any one of which provides evidence for refuting the reconstructions of Hudson and his colleagues.

There are just too many archaeological inconsistencies with their reconstruction through Alabama to seriously consider it valid. Hence, one is led to ask why this group of researchers reached such conclusions? The following discussion looks at some of the problems with their analysis.

1. The Elvas account described a pond at the sixteenth-century town of Mauvila (Bourne 1904a:96). Charles Hudson and his colleagues suggested that

an artesian well located on the Old Cahawba site was the pond described by Elvas: "Near the site there is an artesian well which could be the 'pond' mentioned by the Gentleman Elvas" (Hudson et al. 1987). The artesian wells at the Old Cahawba site, however, are nineteenth-century features (Linda Derry, personal communication). Moreover, artesian wells reflect a fairly sophisticated technology typically requiring deep drilling through solid rock (Davis and DeWiest 1966), definitely not a capability of sixteenth-century aboriginal societies in the Southeast.

2. The decision by Hudson and his associates to use the *lequa comun* instead of the *legua legal* to approximate distances traveled by Spanish expeditions is founded in questionable conclusions drawn from their own study of the Pardo expedition Vandera documents They said: "Working with the Vandera document, we came to the conclusion that Pardo and his men ordinarily calculated distances in terms of the *legua comun* of 5.57 kilometers or 3.45 miles, not the *legua legal* of 4.19 kilometers or 2.63 miles that was favored by the United States De Soto Commission" (DePratter et al. 1985:109–110). Although the connection is unclear, they appear to have used their *legua comun* conclusions from the Pardo study to justify the use of the same measurement in the de Soto route reconstruction. However, an evaluation of their Pardo studies indicates that their conclusions regarding the league measurement were unwarranted and that their logic was faulty. According to Hudson and his colleagues,

> Vandera noted down a series of puzzlingly inaccurate distances and directions between the string of forts they were building. According to Vandera, Chiaha (i.e., Olamico) was fifty leagues to the west of Joara, whereas in fact the trail distances from Zimmerman's Island to Marion, North Carolina, is only a little over thirty-one leagues, and Zimmerman's Island is slightly to the northwest of Marion. He indicates that Cauchi was twenty-eight leagues to the northwest of Joara, whereas the trail distance from Salisbury to Marion is only thirty leagues or less, and it is very slightly to the northeast. Vandera writes that from Cofitachequi to Santa Elena was fifty-five leagues to the south, whereas in fact Santa Elena is only fifty leagues to the south of Camden. Finally, he notes that from Guatari to Cofitachequi it was forty-five leagues to the southeast, whereas there trail distance from Salisbury, North Carolina to Camden, South Carolina, was only about thirty-four leagues, and Camden is slightly southwest of Salisbury [DePratter et al. 1983:151–152].

These statements reject Vandera's distances and directions with the suggestion that his approximated measurements and directions do not fit the preconceived localities in the route reconstructed by Hudson and his associates. These inconsistencies should have, instead, suggested to the researchers that either their reconstruction was in error or that the Spanish records of distances were ambiguous. In either case, their reconstruction can be criticized for relying too heavily on distance statistics. Furthermore, these ambiguities definitely do not support the conclusion that the Pardo expedition was using the *legua comun* rather than the *legua legal* in references to distances between localities. Hudson and his associates actually demonstrate this point in another dubious statement they made while trying to explain the Vandera discrepancies: "[A] possible explanation for these discrepancies is that in this official summation of the line of forts he had built, Vandera may have been attempting to convert his *legua comun* measurements (3.45 miles to a league), used in everyday affairs, to *legua legal* measurements (2.63 miles to a league), used in juridical matters" (DePratter et al. 1983:152).

In summary, we believe that Hudson and his associates rejected Vandera's distances and directions because these data conflicted with their own reconstruction. Moreover, the rationale of Hudson and his colleagues that Vandera may have been translating from one type of league to another appears to be little more than an attempt to support their unfounded conclusions concerning the accuracy of Vandera's statements.

3. Although distance estimates provide the primary line of evidence used in the Hudson and associates de Soto route reconstructions, there is little consistency in their application of their own ideal upper limit of travel that could be accomplished by the de Soto expedition in a day's march. For instance, Hudson and his associates wrote, "One problem with locating Piachi at Durant Bend is that this would place it 16 leagues or more from where we have located Athahachi. To have reached this place in two days would have required more than 8 leagues of travel each day—well within the army's capability" (DePratter et al. 1985:122). Eight leagues per day is equivalent to 27.6 miles per day using the *legua comun* conversion that Hudson and his colleagues applied to other distances in that paper. Yet, Charles Hudson has argued elsewhere that "seventeen miles should be the upper limit of a day's travel" (Hudson 1988). First, Hudson and his colleagues argue that travel in excess of 27 miles per day is "well within the army's capabilities" and then Charles Hudson contradicts that statement by placing a 17-mile upper limit on a day's travel.

4. Hudson and his colleagues also misquoted a passage from the Elvas account concerning the number of leagues traveled per day by the de Soto expedition. The Elvas account stated: "The amount of travel usually performed was five or six leagues a day, passing through settled country; and when through desert, all haste was made to avoid the want of maize" (Bourne 1904a:85–86). Hudson and his associates erroneously took this to mean that the "five or six leagues a day" referred to travel through unpopulated areas: "When it traveled through unpopulated areas, Elvas says, the expedition covered 5 to 6 leagues per day, or 17.25 to 20.7 miles" (DePratter et al. 1985:110). This is a contradiction of Elvas's statement, which indicates instead that 5 or 6 leagues was an average and that a greater distance was covered in deserted or unoccupied areas. A misquotation of the chronicle accounts such as this provides sufficient grounds for questioning the adequacy and the logical basis of *all* the route reconstructions presented by Hudson and his colleagues.

We have shown through specific examples that the reconstruction of the de Soto route through Alabama presented by Hudson and his associates is incongruent with the archaeological record and that their logical framework is seriously undermined by inadequate research and unsound reasoning. Although this does not necessarily preclude the possibility that they may have accurately predicted one or more locations along the de Soto route in other areas of the Southeast, we view their overall propositions with skepticism.

References

Atchinson, Robert B., Jr.
  1987 *Archaeological Survey in the Lower Cahaba Drainage.* Report of Investigations No. 53. University of Alabama Office of Archaeological Research, Moundville.
Bourne, Edward Gaylord
  1904a *Narratives of the Career of Hernando de Soto*, Vol. 1. A. S. Barnes, New York.
  1904b *Narratives of the Career of Hernando de Soto*, Vol. 2. A. S. Barnes, New York.
Brain, Jeffery P.
  1985 Introduction: Update of de Soto Studies since the United States De Soto Expedition Commission Report. In *Final Report of the United States De Soto Expedition Commission*, by John R. Swanton, pp. xi–lxxii. Reprinted. Smithsonian Institution Press, Washington, D.C. Originally published 1939, U.S. House of Representatives, 76th Cong., 1st sess., Doc. 71. Government Printing Office, Washington, D.C.
Brain, Jeffrey P., Alan Toth, and Antonio Rodriquez-Buckingham
  1972 Ethnohistoric Archaeology and the de Soto Entrada into the Lower Mississippi Valley. *Conference on Historic Site Archaeology Papers*, Vol. 1, 232–289.
Brose, David S., Ned J. Jenkins, and Russell Weisman
  1983 *Cultural Resources Reconnaissance Study of the Black Warrior–Tombigbee System Corridor, Alabama, Vol. 1, Archaeology.* Report submitted to the U.S. Army Corps of Engineers Mobile District.
Calvert, Albert Fredreik
  1907 *Spanish Arms and Armour.* J. Lane, New York.
Curren, Caleb
  1988 A Rebuttal of the "Georgia Reconstruction" of the Soto Route through Alabama. Submitted to the Alabama De Soto Commission.
  1989 The Route of the Soto Army through Alabama. In Spanish Colonial Exploration and Colonization in the Southeast, *American Archaeology* 7(2), in press.
Curren, Caleb, and Keith J. Little
  1982 Archaeological Research concerning Sixteenth Century Spanish and Indians in Alabama. Report on file, Alabama-Tombigbee Regional Commission. Camden, Alabama.
Curren, Caleb, Keith J. Little, and George E. Lankford, III
  1981 The Route of the Expedition of Hernando De Soto through Alabama. Paper presented at the 38th Annual Meeting of the Southeastern Archaeological Conference, November , Asheville, North Carolina.
Curren, Caleb, and Lee McKenzie
  1988 Archaeological Investigations at Three Sites in the "Mauvila Province." Report submitted to the Alabama De Soto Commission.
Curren, Caleb, and Rhonda Majors
  1984 An Archaeological Reconnaissance of Monroe and Clarke Counties in Southwest Alabama. Report submitted to the Alabama Historical Commission.
Davis, Stanley N., and Roger J. M. DeWiest
  1966 *Hydrogeology.* John Wiley and Sons, New York.
DeJarnette, David L.
  1958 An Archaeological Study of a Site Suggested as the Location of the Upper Creek Indian Community of Coosa Visited by Hernando de Soto in 1540. Unpublished Master's thesis, University of Alabama.

DePratter, Chester, Charles Hudson, and Marvin Smith
  1983 The Route of the Juan Pardo Explorations in the Interior Southeast, 1566–1568. *Florida Historical Quarterly*, October. Florida Historical Society.
  1985 The Hernando de Soto Expedition: From Chiaha to Mabila. In *Alabama and Its Borderlands, from Prehistory to Statehood*, edited by R. Badger and L.A. Clayton. University of Alabama Press, University.

Ewen, Charles R.
  1988 *The Discovery of de Soto's First Winter Encampment in Florida*. Alabama de Soto Commission Working Paper Series No. 7. University, Alabama.

Fuller, Richard S.
  1985 The Bear Point Phase of the Pensacola Variant: The Protohistoric Period in Southwest Alabama. *Florida Anthropologist* 38:1–2.

Fuller, Richard S., Diane E. Silvia, and N. R. Stowe
  1984 The Forks Project: An Investigation of the Late Prehistoric–Early Historic Transition in the Alabama-Tombigbee Confluence Basin. Submitted to the Alabama Historical Commission.

Hally, David J.
  1970 *Archaeological Investigation of the Potts' Tract Site (9Mu103), Carters Dam Murray County, Georgia*. University of Georgia Laboratory of Archaeology Series, Report No. 6. Athens.
  1979 *Archaeological Investigation of the Little Egypt Site (9Mu102). Murray County, Georgia, 1969 Season*. University of Georgia Laboratory of Archaeology Series, Report No. 18. Athens.

Hatcher, Eddie M.
  1979 A Preliminary Classification and Cataloging of the Dan W. Josselyn Archaeological Collections. Ms. on file at the Laboratory of Anthropology, University of Alabama, Birmingham.

Higginbotham, Jay
  1966 *The Mobile Indians*. Mobile, Alabama.

Holstein, Harry O.
  1986 Davis Farm I-20 Off-Ramp Site, 1Ca190. Report submitted to the Alabama State Highway Department.

Holstein, Harry O., and Keith J. Little
  1985 An Archaeological Pedestrian Survey of Portions of Northeast Alabama. Report submitted to the Alabama Historical Commission.
  1986 *A Short-Term Archaeological Investigation of the Davis Farm Archaeological Complex, A Multicomponent Prehistoric Site in Calhoun County, Alabama*. Jacksonville State University Archaeological Research Laboratory Research Series No. 1.

Hubbert, Charles, and Richard Wright
  1983 *Archaeological Investigations in the Rother L. Harris Reservoir Area: 1977*. Report of Investigation No. 34. Office of Archaeological Research, University of Alabama, Moundville.

Hudson, Charles
  1987 *The Uses of Evidence in Reconstructing the Route of the Hernando de Soto Expedition*. Alabama De Soto Commission Working Paper Series 1. University.
  1988 Critique of Caleb Curren's De Soto Route. Submitted to the Alabama De Soto Commission.

Hudson, Charles, Marvin Smith, David Hally, Richard Polhemus, and Chester DePratter
  1985 Coosa: A Chiefdom in the Sixteenth Century Southeastern United States. *American Antiquity* 50(4):723–737.

Hudson, Charles, Marvin T. Smith, and Chester B. DePratter
  1987 The Hernando De Soto Expedition: From Mabila to the Mississippi River. Updated paper presented at the symposium "Towns and Temples along the Mississippi," Memphis State University, October 18, 1985.

Jenkins, Ned J., and Teresa Paglione
  1980   An Archaeological Reconnaissance of the Lower Alabama River. Report submitted to the Alabama Historical Commission.
Knight, Vernon James, Jr.
  1980   Cultural Complexes of the Alabama Piedmont: An Initial Statement. *Journal of Alabama Archaeology* 26(1):1–27.
  1981   Late Prehistoric Adaptation in the Mobile Bay Region. Paper presented at the Tulane University Conference on Gulf Coast Archaeology, Avery Island, Louisiana.
  1985a *Tukabatchee, Archaeological Investigations at an Historic Creek Town, Elmore County, Alabama 1984*. Report of Investigation No. 45. Office of Archaeological Research, University of Alabama, Moundville.
  1985b *East Alabama Archaeological Survey, 1985 Season*. Report of Investigation No. 47, Office of Archaeological Research, University of Alabama, Moundville.
  1986   Ocmulgee Fields Culture and the Historical Development of Creek Ceramics. Paper presented at the Ocmulgee National Monument 50th Anniversary Conference. Macon, Georgia.
  1987   A Report of Alabama De Soto Commission/Alabama State Museum of National History Archaeological Test Excavations at the Site of Old Cahawaba Dallas County, Alabama. Submitted to the Alabama Historical Commission.
  1988   A Summary of Alabama's De Soto Mapping Project. Report and map submitted to the Alabama De Soto Commission.
Knight, Vernon James, Jr., Gloria C. Cole, and Richard Walling
  1984   *An Archaeological Reconnaissance of the Coosa and Tallapoosa River Valleys, East Alabama: 1983*. Report of Investigation No. 43. Office of Archaeological Research, University of Alabama, Moundville.
Langford, James B., and Marvin T. Smith
  n.d.   Recent Investigations in the Core of the Coosa Province. Unpublished manuscript.
Lankford, George E., III
  1977   A New Look at De Soto's Route through Alabama. *Journal of Alabama Archaeology* 23(1):10–36
Little, Keith J.
  1985   A Sixteenth Century European Sword from a Protohistoric Aboriginal Site in Northwest Georgia. *Early Georgia* 13:1–2.
  1988a A Critical Evaluation of the Proposed Locality of Mauvila in the Selma, Alabama Vicinity. Submitted to the Alabama De Soto Commission, July.
  1988b A Critical Evaluation of the Hudson and Associates Use of Distance Statistics. Submitted to the Alabama De Soto Commission, August, 1988.
  1988c *The De Soto Route Debates: A Presentation for the General Public*. Bulletins of Discovery No. 2. Alabama-Tombigbee Regional Commission. Camden, Alabama.
  1988d A Critical Evaluation of the Placement of Casiste in the Talladega Springs Area. Submitted to the Alabama De Soto Commission, August, 1988.
  1989   A Segment of the Sixteenth Century Soto Route through Alabama. In Spanish Colonial Explorations and Colonization in the Southeast. *American Archaeology* 7(2), in press.
Little, Keith J., and Caleb Curren
  1981   Site 1Ce308: A Protohistoric Site on the Upper Coosa River in Alabama. *Journal of Alabama Archaeology* 27(2):117–140.
Little, Keith J., Caleb Curren, Curtis E. Hill, and Harry O. Holstein
  1989   A Spatulate Axe from the Demopolis, Alabama Area. Submitted to the *Journal of Alabama Archaeology*.
Luttrell, Elston
  1982   Abstracts from Archaeological Correspondence. In *Annual Report of the Board of Regents of the Smithsonian Institute*. Washington, D.C.

McCollough, Major C.R., and Lawrence S. Alexander
1988 Dating Results for Two Sixteenth Century Spanish Contact Towns in Tennessee. *Southeastern Archaeological Conference Newsletter* 30(2):19.

Moore, Clarence B.
1899 Certain Aboriginal Remains of the Alabama River. *Journal of the Academy of Natural Sciences of Philadelphia* 11. Philadelphia.

Moorehead, Warren K.
1932 *Etowah Papers.* Yale University Press, New Haven, Connecticut.

Morrell, L. Ross
1964 Two Historic Sites in the Coosa River. *Florida Anthropoligist* 17(2):75–76.

Nance, Roger C.
1976 *The Archaeological Sequence at Durant Bend, Dallas County, Alabama.* Alabama Archaeological Society, Special Publication No. 2. Moundville.
1986 Archaeology of the Rodgers-CETA Site A Lamar Village on Talladega Creek, Central Alabama. Unpublished manuscript.

Peebles, Christopher S.
1978 Determinants of Settlement Size and Location in the Moundville Phase. In *Mississippian Settlement Patterns*, edited by Bruce D. Smith. Academic Press, New York.

Priestley, Herbert Ingram
1928 *The Luna Papers.* Florida State Historical Society, DeLand, Florida.

Sheldon, Craig T., Jr., David W. Chase, Teresa L. Paglione, Gregory A. Waselkov, and Elisabeth S. Sheldon
1982 *Cultural Resources Survey of Demopolis Lake, Alabama Fee Owned Lands.* Auburn University Archaeological Monograph No. 6. Auburn.

Smith, Marvin T.
1975 European Materials from the King Site. *Southeastern Archaeological Conference, Bulletin* 18:63–66.
1976 The Route of de Soto through Tennessee, Georgia, and Alabama: The Evidence from Material Culture. *Early Georgia* 4:1–2.
1977 *The Early Historic Period (1540–1670) on the Upper Coosa River Drainage of Alabama and Georgia.* Conference on Historic Site Archaeology Papers No. 11.
1979 European Artifacts from the Little Egypt Site. In Archaeological Investigations of the Little Egypt Site (9Mu102), Murray County, Georgia, 1970–1972 Seasons, by David J. Hally. Report submitted to the National Park Service.

Solis, Carlos, and Richard Walling
1982 *Archaeological Investigation at the Yarborough Site (22Cl814), Clay County, Mississippi.* Report of Investigations No. 30. Office of Archaeological Research, University of Alabama, Moundville.

Steponaitis, Vincas P.
1978 Location Theory and Complex Chiefdoms: A Mississippian Example. In *Mississippian Settlement Patterns*, edited by Bruce D. Smith. Academic Press, New York.
1980 Ceramics, Chronology, and Community Patterns at Moundville, a Late Prehistoric Site in Alabama. Unpublished Ph.D dissertation, University of Michigan, Ann Arbor.

Stowe, Noel R.
1982 *A Preliminary Report on the Pine Log Creek Site 1Ba462.* University of South Alabama Archaeological Research Laboratory, Mobile.

Swanton, John R.
1939 *Final Report of the United States De Soto Expedition Commission.* U. S. House of Representatives, 76th Cong., 1st sess. Doc. 71. Government Printing Office, Washington, D.C.

Varner, John Grier, and Jeannette Johnson Varner
1951 *The Florida of the Inca.* University of Texas Press, Austin.

Walthall, John A.
  1980   *Prehistoric Indians of the Southeast: Archaeology of Alabama and the Middle South.* University of Alabama Press. University.
Waselkov, Gregory A.
  1980   *Coosa River Valley Archaeology,* Vols. 1 and 2. Auburn University Archaeological Monograph 2. Auburn.
Wilson, Robert C.
  1987   A Preliminary Report on the Archaeological Investigations at the Hightower Village Site (1Ta150), Talladega County, Alabama. Unpublished manuscript.
Wimberly, Stephen B.
  1960   *Indian Pottery from Clarke County and Mobile County, Southern Alabama.* Alabama Museum of Natural History Museum Paper No. 36. University.

Chapter 13 ■

Dan F. Morse and Phyllis A. Morse

The Spanish Exploration of Arkansas

Arkansas occupied the northwesternmost extent of La Florida. The discovery and conquest of this region is just now beginning to be understood. However, one might well ask whether Arkansas was conquered by or in fact conquered de Soto during his quest for gold and fame in 1539–1543. The Spanish spent two years exploring almost two-thirds of the future state of Arkansas. At least three-fourths of the Indian polities present in 1541–1543 were directly visited by the expedition. The impact of this contact, and of new diseases and Spanish cruelty, took their toll on the Indians. Yet de Soto died here. The expedition "escaped" to Mexico. The conquest of La Florida was immediately judged a failure by the civilized world.

Arkansas

Arkansas is an area of extreme contrasts. It can be divided into lowland and mountainous regions. The northwest is composed of the Ozark and the Ouachita mountains, which are separated by the Arkansas River. The southwest is part of the Gulf Coastal Plain. The eastern alluvial plain is divided into two unequal

197

parts by the Arkansas River. Within the largest region to the north are major north-south drainages, a central upland with major gravel deposits known as Crowley's Ridge, and an ancient deciduous forest. Southward the alluvial plain narrows considerably and there are no major uplands comparable to the Ozarks or Crowley's Ridge. The vegetation also differs considerably from that of the alluvial plain north of the Arkansas River (Phillips et al. 1951:26–27).

The social differences in the Arkansas of 1541 were also striking. There were two major settlement systems, both based on agriculture and featuring corn, beans, and squash. One system, most characteristic south of the Arkansas River and west of the eastern Lowlands, consisted of a dispersed population with one or a few mound centers for each polity.

This dispersed settlement pattern was also characteristic of northeastern Arkansas societies until about A.D. 1400, when populations nucleated into palisaded villages or towns and people farmed fields near the towns of affiliation. Population nucleation was so dramatic that almost all of southeast Missouri and all but a very small part of the lowlands west of Crowley's Ridge were abandoned to permanent habitation. The large population of southeast Missouri con-

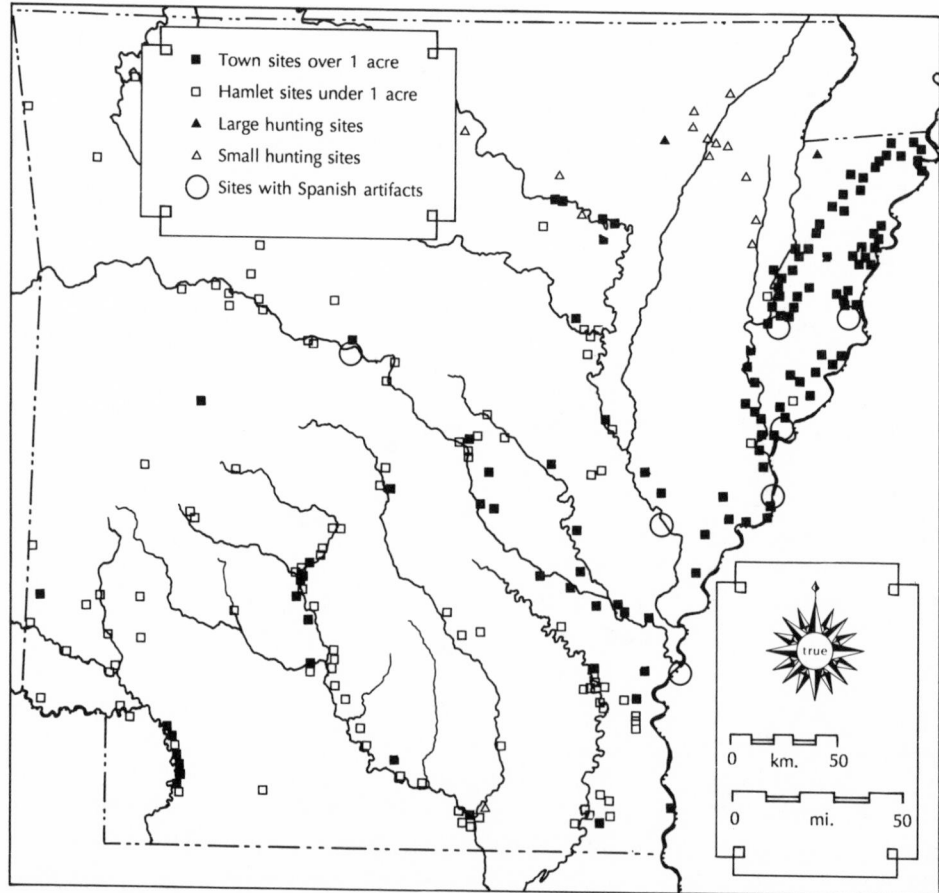

Figure 13-1. Protohistoric sites in Arkansas.

centrated into over 70 sites in northeast Arkansas, while the former population of northeast Arkansas filled the sites along the lower St. Francis and possibly down to the lower Arkansas River, where overcrowding of societies became a critical problem (Morse and Morse 1983). Warfare was characteristic over most of Arkansas in 1541. The Spanish were quick to take advantage of this fragmentation, just as many of the native societies involved were quick to take advantage of de Soto's army for their own goals.

More than 350 archaeological sites have been recorded for the Arkansas of 1541 (Figure 13-1). Over 150 are considered large or major sites with populations probably ranging up to 2,000 for some of the northeastern towns. If one accepts an average population of 500 for major sites (and each polity associated with major Caddo sites), then the total population of Arkansas in 1541 was around 75,000. Since some polities do not have any major sites recorded for them, we probably have not recorded or recognized *all* of the major sites. Indeed, many have been destroyed by erosion, as in the case of sites excavated by C. B. Moore, which no longer exist. However, probably not all of the major sites were contemporaneous, and in 1541 perhaps only half existed. A more precise estimate of total site acreage is needed for 1541 before a firmer maximum figure can be developed. For now, we can assume a maximum population of about 75,000.

By 1673, the next recorded European contact with Arkansas, the Indians were actively trading for European artifacts with several nations. The Michigamea trade probably began in the mid-seventeenth century. However, Spanish trade was active as early as 1600 in the southwestern and southeastern United States. Blue glass beads indicative of trade no earlier than about 1570–1580 are common on Arkansas Indian sites, including those assigned to the Nodena phase, which became extinct or transformed by 1650.

The 1673 population figures for Native Americans in Arkansas, based on Mooney's (1928) and Swanton's (1946) figures for the Tunica, Quapaw, and Caddo (13,000), plus the other five groups shown on the 1673 Marquette map, total a conservative 15,000. The year 1673 marks the beginning of the full Colonial period and the virtual end of the protohistoric Spanish influence and trade in Arkansas, which began in 1541. The Spanish protohistoric period lasted 132 years. French and possibly English trade and influence coexisted for no more than the last 39 years of that period, so the Spanish monopoly in Arkansas lasted approximately one century, from 1541 to about 1640.

"Discovery" of Arkansas

The de Soto expedition did not "discover" the Mississippi River or the Rio Espiritu Santo or Rio Grande. The Spanish already had some knowledge of the Atlantic and Gulf coasts and the northern border marked by the Rio Espiritu Santo (our Tennessee and lower Ohio rivers). The expedition had an astrolabe and an individual capable of using it. With the aid of this individual, Captain Juan de Anasco, and intelligence gained from the Indians, de Soto and Moscoso were able to determine where they were with reference to the known geographical perimeters.

When finally confronted with the Mississippi River a short distance south of present-day Memphis (Hudson 1985), they gazed across at Arkansas with the knowledge of Cabeza de Vaca's experiences in the deserts separating Arkansas from Mexico (see Milanich, and Marrinan et al., this volume). Chapter 2 in the Gentleman of Elvas's account (Bourne 1904:1:5–9) details "How Cabeza de Vaca arrived at court, and gave account of the Country of Florida; and of the persons who assembled at Sevilla to accompany Don Hernando de Soto." The Gentleman of Elvas also states that "they considered the country farther on, beyond the River Daycao, on which they were, to be that which Cabeza de Vaca had said in his narrative should have to be traversed [to get to New Spain], where the Indians wandered like Arabs, having no settled place of residence, living on prickly pears, the roots of plants, and game" (Bourne 1904:1:180). In other words, Moscoso and de Soto knew that the region between New Spain and La Florida was a place in which a large expedition could not survive.

One member of the Narváez expedition, Juan Ortiz, was rescued from the Indians by de Soto. Ortiz had lived among the Indians for 12 years before joining de Soto as his interpreter. He was an extremely valuable person to de Soto. After Ortiz died in Arkansas during the winter of 1541–1542, the expedition was not able to gather intelligence as readily as before. The Gentleman of Elvas relates that "the death was so great a hindrance to our going, whether on discovery or out of the country, that to learn of the Indians what would have been rendered in four words, it became necessary now to have the whole day: and oftener than otherwise the very opposite was understood of what was asked" (Bourne 1904:1:147).

Juan Ortiz was the interpreter when de Soto reached the Mississippi River. He was able to gather important intelligence about the Indians of eastern Arkansas to help de Soto plan his approach. Both Ranjel and Biedma related in their accounts that they learned of Pacaha while in Quizquiz, on the east bank of the Mississippi River (Bourne 1904:125, 138). "They told us that it [Quizquiz] was, with many towns about there, tributary to a lord of Pacaha, famed throughout all the land" (Bourne 1904:2:25).

Later, as Biedma recorded, "on the way to that Province of Pacaha, we came first to the province of another land, called Icasqui [Casqui], against whom he waged severe war" (Bourne 1904:2:26). In Muskhogean "Casqui" means *place where there are many warriors* (Swanton 1939:61). The Casqui capital is probably the Parkin site (3CS29), located inland to the northwest of the Mississippi River crossing point next to the St. Francis River, while the Pacaha capital is probably the Bradley site (3CT7), located to the north, next to the Mississippi River. Evidently the reason de Soto went northwest, then northeast to Pacaha, was to raise an Indian army (Varner and Varner 1951:435).

Exploration of Arkansas

The de Soto expedition crossed the Mississippi River on Saturday, June 18, 1541 (pre-Gregorian calendar). He was successful because, noticing the 200–250 canoes that appeared daily at 3:00 p.m., he crossed early in the morning. De Soto understood bureaucracy very well.

After crossing the Mississippi River, "In Aquixo, Casqui, and Pacaha, they saw the best villages seen up to that time, better stockaded and fortified" (Bourne 1904:2:140). This is an extremely important statement. Later Ranjel comments on "Quiguate, which is the largest village which they saw in that country" (Bourne 1904:2:146). At Coligua, there was a town with "vast provisions" (Bourne 1904:2:147). Autiamque was "suited for our purpose, for there was a town nigh in which was much food" (Bourne 1904:2:34). It contrasted strikingly with the settlements farther west. From Autiamque downriver to Anilco were "other provinces well peopled" (Bourne 1904:2:34). At Anilco "were many other large towns in which was a good quantity of maize, beans, walnuts and dried *ameinas* [persimmons]" (Bourne 1904:1:149).

In the Province of Palisema, "the houses were few and scattered: only a little maize was found" (Bourne 1904:1:134). At Cayas they did *not* see "a large stockaded town" (Bourne 1904:2:147). Southward from Guachoya, according to the chief and information obtained during a reconnaissance trip by Juan Anasco, there were no large towns (Bourne 1904:1:150–154).

Large towns with stored food were important to the expedition, and the accounts clearly indicate that such sites existed to the northeast of the territory explored west of the Mississippi River. Large mapped sites reveal that the primary population of Arkansas was concentrated mostly along the lower Arkansas River and in the northeastern lowlands. "This river passing by Anilco, is the same that flows by Cayas and Autiamque and falls into the River Grande, which flows by Pacaha and Aquixo, near the Province of Guachoya" (Bourne 1904:1:150). "This river" can only be the Arkansas River.

Casqui and Quiguate were on the River of Casqui, which could only be the St. Francis River. A statement by Ranjel suggests that the expedition later returned toward the mouth of the St. Francis River: "It was later known that the banks of this river were thickly populated further down (although they did not find it out there; Bourne 1904:2:146). Coligua, also characterized as having a large town, was on a third large river, which could only be the White River.

By comparing the accounts with the intensive site plotting that has taken place during the past 21 years in Arkansas, it has been possible to determine the basic route. What is particularly significant is that individual Survey archeologists have been concentrating their research in 7 to 17 counties of Arkansas for up to 21 years. In addition, some major contract surveys such as the Cache River survey have been conducted by archeologists familiar with the research potential of de Soto-oriented investigations.

Casqui

The expedition crossed the Mississippi River a few miles south of the Tennessee-Mississippi state line to the province of Aquixo (Belle Meade phase), which was vassal to Pacaha upriver (Nodena phase). The Spanish occupied a town that had been abandoned because of their approach. It was near the river where the four barges were dismantled to preserve the iron. All the towns, including the capital, were similarly abandoned. The Spanish were able to capture some Indians for questioning. On a Wednesday, "they passed through the worst tract for swamps and water that they had found in all Florida" (Bourne 1904:2:138).[1]

Thursday, they entered the province of Casqui (Parkin phase) and on Friday they were at its principal town (Parkin, 3CS29).[2] According to the accounts, the province of Casqui extended about two days' march along the St. Francis River and one day's march along the Tyronza River, a maximum distance of about 50 to 70 km (30 to 45 miles), depending on how one measures a "league" and the rate (probably slow) of march.[3] The actual minimum linear distance of the Parkin phase is 50 km (30 miles) (P. Morse 1981:Figure 19).

The behavior of the Casqui chief provides insight into native Arkansas chiefdoms. This older paramount chief with a large entourage walked "half a league" from the town to greet de Soto. He welcomed de Soto with an elegant speech, forgiving de Soto's killing of his "vassals" downstream and not mentioning the numerous gifts he had sent to de Soto the previous two days. The chief invited de Soto to stay in his house, but de Soto declined. The Casqui chief returned with an entourage of singers, including two blind men he wished cured, and made another eloquent speech. De Soto answered with a speech on the "true God" and soon was invited to erect a large cross on the major mound in the town. Rain at the appropriate time in a period of drought evidently convinced the chief of the power of the new religion and he had himself and others baptized as Christians. Our impression is that Casqui very badly needed an ally of de Soto's power to defeat Pacaha and used all his diplomatic wiles to gain one. He may or may not have known that de Soto needed him just as much. According to Biedma, de Soto was careful to instruct his men "to avoid doing mischief" while they were guests at Casqui (Bourne 1904:2:27).

Pacaha

The provinces of Casqui and Pacaha were at war, and the armies of Casqui and de Soto invaded Pacaha successfully.[4] The Pacaha capital (3CT7) was situated on the southern frontier of the province (the Nodena phase, consisting of about 70 large sites). We learn several things about Pacaha after the peace alliance was made. After the conquest, Casqui had to use extreme diplomacy to preserve the favor of de Soto, who no longer needed Casqui's help. The expedition spent 29 days in the Pacaha capital, using it as a base from which to explore the countryside. The younger paramount chief of Pacaha was able to make a peace treaty and was recognized by de Soto as "a greater lord and more ancient in rank [than the Casqui chief], and he showed in his good customs more of the manners of the courtier after their fashion" (Bourne 1904:2:144). Casqui gave de Soto a daughter and Pacaha gave him a wife, a sister, and "another Indian woman of rank" (Bourne 1904:2:144) or two sisters (Bourne 1904:1:127). This sort of behavior, particularly as it involved daughters and wives, indicates a patrilineal orientation, which is different from the norm in the Southeast, as was the nucleated town and warfare.

Two of probably several exploratory excursions were recorded originating from Pacaha. One was led by Biedma (Bourne 1904:2:29–30) to the northwest for either seven or eight days. "Thirty horsemen and fifty footmen" were in the party (Bourne 1904:1:128). The area was uninhabited except at the furthest point explored. The province of "Caluç" ("Blackwater" in Chickasaw and Choctaw [Swanton 1939:60]) seems to have been located some 120 km (75 miles) directly northwest of 3CT7, the Bradley site, according to archaeological evidence. We characterize sites near the Black River and in the Western Lowlands to the east as "hunting sites" since all but one of those sites are known to have produced a single Nodena point. That site (3LW509) has produced several Nodena points and end scrapers, but no late prehistoric ceramics (Morse 1986). It evidently was a hunting base camp. Biedma described huts that could be taken down and moved readily as the sparse population moved to "wherever many deer were accustomed to range, and a swamp where were many fish" (Bourne 1904: 2:30). We do not know the origin of the name Black River, but it existed in 1815 on a town plat of Davidsonville and probably is Indian in origin. The Arkansas River was called the Red River by the Indians in 1673, and there are also a White River and a Little Red River between these two. The direction and distance from 3CT7 to 3LW509, the hunting nature of the sites in Lawrence County, the lack of anything dating to 1541 in between, and the coincidence of the name "Black" seem to fit with the Biedma account in an almost uncanny way.

A second known excursion is described by Garcilaso. This account almost seems to have been written down as told to Garcilaso (Varner and Varner 1951:449–450) with little of the usual Garcilaso embellishment. Two men, Pedro Moreno and Hernando de Silvera, who was on an identical expedition earlier in Tennessee (Varner and Varner 1951:337, 340), took items to trade and proceeded toward some mountains to check on "yellow metal." After 11 days (probably exaggerated, as was typical of Garcilaso), they returned with salt and copper. "They reported however that the lands they had seen were not good, but sterile and poorly populated" (Varner and Varner 1951:450). Site 23PM5 (Campbell) is located about 95 km (60 miles) up modern Interstate 55, which is located within a relict braided stream terrace that was uninhabited in the sixteenth century. They probably went no farther than this site. It would have taken a total of five Indian days or so for the whole trip. The St. François Mountains where the salt and copper originated are located another 160 km (100 miles) or more further north. The region in between was uninhabited north of Carruthersville, Missouri. That trip would have taken a full 11 Indian days. However, brass bells and at least 24 chevron beads, which are probably sixteenth-century de Soto trade items, have been found at 23PM5. In fact, site 23PM5 contains more sixteenth-century Spanish artifacts than any other known site in Arkansas or immediately beyond.

To the Mountains

The expedition returned to Casqui and then proceeded downriver to Quiguate (Kent phase) trying to gather intelligence to guide them in their quest for gold and food.[5] The Quiguate paramount chief reluctantly made peace after being captured. He told de Soto of Coligua, located to the northwest near some mountains where interpreters and guides could be obtained for western Arkansas. De Soto was also obviously checking mountainous areas systematically for gold and silver. The expedition traveled through an uninhabited region for five days before reaching the White River, which the Spaniards crossed twice since it flows out of the west to meet the Black River, then turns sharply south. The principal village (3IN8) of Coligua (Greenbrier phase) was "a pretty village, between some ridges along the gorge of a great river" (Bourne 1904:2:147). They were told that bison could be hunted nearby. Site 3ST70, located upstream in the next county, is a rock shelter with a bison and arrow motif depicted on its wall. The expedition was then told that Cayas was a province "better provisioned . . . than any other, and more populous" (Bourne 1904:1:133). It was reported to be west-southwest of Coligua (Bourne 1904:2:31–32). This certainly was one way to get rid of an unwelcome guest, especially over 400 of them!

"Wednesday they passed some mountains and came to Calpista [a village of Palisema?], where there was an excellent salt springs" (Bourne 1904:2:147). The only salt known to be available anywhere in the lowlands of northeast Arkansas is located exactly where our interpretation of the accounts indicates (Akridge 1986). This locality was predicted by Hudson and then discovered by Akridge. In the province of Palisema "the houses were few and scattered." The Little Red River phase consists of a dispersed population characterized—with one possible larger exception located upstream and beyond the Spanish area of exploration—by sites of one or very few house mounds.

Between Coligua and Autiamque, the expedition accounts describe (1) populations that were dispersed and (2) mountainous terrain. Again both the geographical and social evidence fits the accounts perfectly. At Tanico (village) in the province of Cayas there were "scattered houses" rather than "a large stockaded town." All the accounts emphasize this because of the contrast with the eastern towns. "Here we found a copious river, which we afterwards discovered empties into the Rio Grande. . . . It is a very rough country of hills" (Bourne 1904:2:32). Tanico (and Cayas) is the Carden Bottoms phase, located on the Arkansas River.[6] Salt was obtained here and the accounts provide a description of typical Indian salt recovery (Bourne 1904:1:136, 1904:2:148).

The Caddo

Disappointed, de Soto decided to go one and a half Indian days southward and upriver (Fourche La Fave) to Tula where "the tongue of that country was different . . . and . . . he and his ancestors [Cayas] had ever been at war with its chiefs" (Bourne 1904:1:137). Site 3YE15 is some 35–40 miles southwest of Carden Bottoms. De Soto advanced with a cavalry unit and 50 infantry and returned with the captured chief of Cayas and his whole army to be met by some of the most well-organized and ferocious fighting he experienced in Arkansas. They were Caddo Indians and site 3YE15 was a Caddo mound center. After considerable carnage and cutting off the noses and right hands of 54 Indian captives, who he sent off to their chief as examples of what he would do to everyone if the chief did not surrender, de Soto was met by weeping and surrender and presents of quantities of bison hides. Bison were available in quantity to the west, near the Arkansas-Oklahoma border.

On the Arkansas River

"The cold of winter had begun to threaten us sharply" (Bourne 1904:2:33). De Soto learned that "toward the west was a thin population, and to the southeast were great towns, principally in a province, abundant of maize, called Autiamque" (Bourne 1904:1:141). He left for there on Wednesday, October 19, and arrived at Autiamque (3JE56?) on November 2. At Quipana (3SA11), located next to a river within a very short distance (less than a day's march) of the edge of the mountains, they learned from captured Indians of the province of Chaguate located to the south. But Autiamque was closer, was known to contain towns with stored corn, and was located on the River of Cayas, which was tributary to the Mississippi River, and via which de Soto hoped to reinforce his army and stock from Cuba (Bourne 1904:1:142). The chief of Chaguate visited de Soto at Autiamque with presents of salt.

The winter of 1541–1542 was particularly harsh and cold, with much snow. In addition, the paramount chief did not want de Soto there and attempted to dislodge him. A local lame chief vassal to Autiamque finally was captured but was released because he had given de Soto presents. Indians were "allowed to go at large in their shackles" (Bourne 1904:1:146). Juan Ortiz died at Autiamque and one of the accounts (Ranjel) inexplicably ended at this time. Even though the expedition left Autiamque on March 6, its members were surprised by a late severe snow. The main interpreter was dead, they kept getting lost, and some of the horses were lame, so it took most of the month of March just to travel to Anilco (3AR4), an extraordinarily large settlement with lots of corn within an area of large settlements (Menard complex). De Soto was opposed by the province of Anilco and was invited by the chief of Guachoya (possibly the Hog Lake phase located south near the Mississippi River) to reside with him since he was at war with Anilco. Nearby to the west was Catalte, possibly the Tillar phase.

The Final Escape

De Soto died and Moscoso became the leader of the expedition. At that point, the remnants of the expedition only wished to return to their Spanish world. They had two choices of routes to New Spain: to build boats and go downstream or to go overland via Chaguate west and south. They chose first to go overland and spent six months on a round-trip that took them into east Texas and back again (Schambach 1988).

We need to mention the ill-fated round-trip through south-central Arkansas (see Schambach 1989 for a full report). Dispersed populations were the order. They were distributed geographically precisely where archaeologists have reconstructed Protohistoric complexes (Chaguate [Middle Ouachita], Aquacay [Little Missouri], Pato [Little River], Amoye [Texarkana], and Naguatex [Belcher]). The salt springs at Chaguate were located near Arkadelphia (3CL27). Those salt springs were extremely important in early Colonial Arkansas.

The expedition continued to capture Indians for service and intelligence. After getting more salt and rest at Aquacay, the expedition headed southwest toward a reported large population concentrated along the Great Bend of the Red River. They may have first gone to 3SU69, located along an old trail, for salt. Pato may be 3LR12. However, specific sites are difficult to pinpoint because most sites look alike, are not very large, and mound centers did not keep the stored corn. The general geography and distances all match well with reconstructed regions, but specific sites may never be identified.

The paramount chief of the Naguatex, after initial defeat, met Moscoso with an entourage, weeping in the Caddo fashion of greeting. An Indian guide who led the expedition astray was literally thrown to the dogs to be torn apart. The expedition "made so many turns, it might be in some of them they had observed our passing [and thought] there were other Christians like us" (Bourne 1904:2:37). At Chaguate, a member of the expedition remained behind with an Indian girl because he was "in fear of being made to pay for gaming debts" (Bourne 1904:1:168). Moscoso continued to have noses and right hands cut off of those he wished to carry messages back to a chief. The expedition found turquoise and cotton traded from the Southwest in the westernmost extent of Arkansas.

On their return trip, despite their scorched-earth policy, Naguatex had been "rebuilt, and the houses full of maize" (Bourne 1904:1:182). The expedition returned to Chaguate, then proceeded to Anilco, discovering a town "they had not seen before" on the route.

Returning to the Mississippi River, "they came to Anilco, where the Governor found so little maize, that there was not enough to last while they made the vessels; for during seedtime, while the Christians were in Guachoya, the Indians in fear of them, had not dared to come and plant the grounds" (Bourne 1904:1:183–184). Fortunately, Moscoso was directed to two towns (3PH20 and 3PH21) two Indian days upriver in the province of Aminoya (Old Town phase).[7] These two regions are about 65 km (40 miles) apart but the presence of numerous swamps could stretch this distance sufficiently to match two Indian days (normally about 95 km, or 60 miles).

At the town of Aminoya, a blacksmithy was established to make nails out of chains and presumably a saw pit was constructed to make lumber. Caulking was manufactured and a cooper made large water casks. They built seven barges ("brigantines"). All but 22 of the remaining horses were jerked, in addition to the hogs. Indians supplied rope, canoes (which were tied together in pairs), labor, and most of the available food.

Moscoso tortured one Indian to learn of a planned surprise attack, then cut off the right hands of another 30 who had planned to spearhead the attack. The chief of Guachoya changed sides and helped Moscoso defeat the others, who included Anilco and Toguanate, located upriver and presumably on the eastern side. It is evident from the accounts that there were other Indian polities nearby ("other neighboring people"; Bourne 1904:1:188). Across the river from the Old Town phase are numerous sites known to be late prehistoric and protohistoric; in fact, they form the basis for Brain et al.'s attempt to have the expedition originally cross the river at this point (literally "Friar's Point"). Evidently this particular region contained several polities that were capable of quickly establishing and breaking alliances. Natchez names predominate but undoubtedly a primary interpreter being used was Natchez. The major (if not all) words recorded in Arkansas are Muskogean, Choctaw/Chickasaw, Natchez, Tunica, and Caddo. Of 35 names identified by Swanton, 21 are considered Natchez. Obviously the Natchez-speaking interpreter played an important role for the expedition.

They spent the winter of 1542–1543, a period of about seven months, in Aminoya. It then took about a month for their barges to reach the mouth of the Mississippi, and they took almost another two months to make Panuco, Mexico.

Remarks

We have presented a "new" reconstruction of the de Soto expedition in Arkansas, that subregion of La Florida located west of the Mississippi River. This reconstruction follows that developed by Charles Hudson with help from a number of individuals. The reconstruction is vital to us because it represents the initial European history of this region as well as the first description of Native American societies. Except in a few cases, we still do not know the names of the polities and their leaders.[8] We have only hints of the elegance of chiefdomship in the region. Refreshingly, the accounts match what we see archaeologically. The archaeology helps us interpret the Spanish (and Portuguese) observations. The cruelty of the Spanish and the various attempts of the Indians to react to their intrusion represents a human drama in which both sides lost. The Spanish defeat was immediate, the Indian defeat had only just begun.

Interaction on the Arkansas borderland was varied. The first Catholic baptisms in Arkansas took place at Casqui and included the paramount chief. The first cross constructed and raised in Arkansas was also at Casqui, where an alliance was engineered between the Spanish and the Native Americans in order to attack Pacaha. The Spanish and Portuguese admiration of the courtly manners at Pacaha and the descriptions of the Native American processions provide insight into both Spanish and Native American character.

The Spanish experience was an incredible feat of exploration. However, the Spanish were extremely cruel to the Indians, possibly because de Soto had developed cruelty as a weapon to use against a foe that greatly outnumbered the Spanish. The Native American reaction to the presence of the Spanish differed in Arkansas. The less-developed Caddo fought back and quickly readjusted to the scorched earth policy of Moscoso. The eastern chiefdoms with all their bureaucracy did not fight well, if at all, and did not readjust well to the depletion of stores.

Disease introduced by the conquistadors was undoubtedly responsible for the population decline in Arkansas, from nearly 75,000 to about 15,000. A quick comparison of the Marquette 1673 map with the Arkansas Archeological Survey map of protohistoric sites clearly demonstrates the demographic collapse in northeastern Arkansas. Native reaction in Arkansas to the beginnings of the Colonial period and decreasing population was manifested in some apparently unusual population nucleation. The end of Bradley Ridge may have supported 25 ha of people in four stockaded towns by the first quarter of the seventeenth century. This Bradley Ridge population may well have become the four villages of the Quapaw near and on the Arkansas River observed by the French explorers of the last quarter of the seventeenth century.[9] French trade may have been initiated by the frontier Illini in the early seventeenth century, while the population still existed on Bradley Ridge. By 1673 the summer village of the Michigamea was located in Arkansas specifically to trade French artifacts including knives, axes, and brass, to the Quapaw for deerskins and bear oil. In 1686 the French established Arkansas Post, probably at the same site of Anilco visited by de Soto in 1542. But when the Quapaw first met the French, they were already growing watermelon and peaches, raising chickens, wearing glass beads, and using steel knives and axes, and evidently they knew more about the French than the French knew about the Quapaw.

Acknowledgments

Our thanks go to Ann Early, Jerry Hilliard, John House, Marvin Jeter, Jamie Lockhart, Martha Rolingson, George Sabo, and Frank Schambach for helping upgrade the Arkansas Archeological Survey files on protohistoric sties to produce a map of sites. We are also grateful to Charles Hudson for helpful comments and for being the main stimulus for our overview of de Soto in Arkansas, and to Marvin Jeter for very helpful editorial comments.

Notes

1. Swanton (1939) and Brain have the expedition crossing the Yazoo Basin in Mississippi. If true, the wetlands between Casqui and Aquixo were hardly "the worst swamps and water" Ranjel experienced in La Florida. One must also note that Biedma (Bourne 1904:2:24) stated the expedition went *northwest* after leaving the vicinity of Tupelo, thus skirting the Yazoo Basin and all its swamps.

2. One Clarksdale bell and one chevron bead have been found at Parkin (Morse 1981) and a group of bells from Parkin were observed in a local collection 35 years ago (Gregory Perino, personal communication).

3. The *legua legal* abolished in 1568 was 2.5943 miles (4.1750 km), the geographical league made mandatory in 1718 was 3.9461 miles (6.3505 km), and the marine league was 3.459 miles (5.5667 km) (Doursther 1840:210). League estimates are and probably were primarily based on time (hourly and daily) of march, which must have varied considerably, depending on factors such as terrain, intelligence and the need of it from Indians, food, and the weather. Indian distance was expressed as days of travel; one Indian

day was equivalent to about 10–12 French leagues, or probably about 48 km (30 miles) (Stubbs 1982:43).

4. A musket ball, possibly from either a sixteenth-century military arquebus or a small cannon, was found at 3CT43, an 11-ha site located 800 m west of 3CT7, which probably measured about 9½ hectares in 1883 before being partly destroyed by a levee. Other major sites near 3CT43 and 3CT7 are 3CT40 (1.6 ha) and 3CT245 (2.8 ha). From the recovery of blue glass and iron beads and cut brass, it appears that all four sites were contemporaneous and lasted into the seventeenth century. The identification of 3CT7 as the town of Pacaha is based on the huge borrow pit adjacent to the once-stockaded site, which was drained by Wapanocca Bayou into the Mississippi River. This unique feature was described by both Elvas and Garcilasco.

5. A Clarksdale bell and a possible arquebus support have been found at 3LE11.

6. A Clarksdale bell from Carden Bottoms near Russellville is in the University of Arkansas Museum collections.

7. Clarksdale bells and halberds have been found in the general vicinity of the Old Town phase sites pinpointed here (Dickinson 1987; Morse 1988). The pattern fits a long-term residency of Spanish trade with surrounding Indian polities for food and supplies.

8. Names such as "Pacaha" and "Casqui" were evidently supplied by the large group of interpreters held by de Soto, and very often are not even in the language of the inhabitants of those towns.

9. There is another village site in the Nodena phase, Campbell in southeast Missouri, that also was inhabited into the seventeenth century and may or may not have become part of the late seventeenth-century Quapaw.

References

Akridge, Scott
  1986 *De Soto's Route in North Central Arkansas. Field Notes* 211:3–7. Newsletter of the Arkansas Archeological Society. Fayetteville, Arkansas.
Bourne, Edward G.
  1904 *Narratives of the Career of Hernando De Soto.* A. S. Barnes, New York.
Dickinson, S. D.
  1987 Arkansas's Spanish Halberds. *Arkansas Archeologist* 24/25:53–62. Arkansas Archeological Society, Fayetteville.
Doursther, Horace
  1840 *Dictionnaire Universel des Poids et Mesures.* Paris.
Hudson, Charles
  1985 De Soto in Arkansas: A Brief Synopsis. *Field Notes* 205:3–12. Newsletter of the Arkansas Archeological Society, Fayetteville.
Mooney, J.
  1928 *The Aboriginal Population of America North of Mexico.* Smithsonian Miscellaneous Collection, Vol. 80, No. 7. Washington, D.C.
Morse, Dan F.
  1986 Prehistoric Hunting Sites in Northeastern Arkansas. In *The Protohistoric Period in the Mid-South: 1500–1700,* edited by David H. Dye and Ronald C. Brister, pp. 89–94. Archaeological Report No. 18, Mississippi Department of Archives and History, Jackson.
  1988 Comments on "Arkansas's Spanish Halberds" by Sam Dickinson. *Field Notes* 222:7–10. Newsletter of the Arkansas Archeological Society, Fayetteville.
Morse, Dan F., and Phyllis A. Morse
  1983 *Archaeology of the Central Mississippi Valley.* Academic Press, New York.
Morse, Phyllis, A.
  1981 *Parkin.* Arkansas Archeological Survey Research Series No. 13, Fayetteville.

Phillips, Philip, James A. Ford, and James B. Griffin
   1951   *Archaeology of the Lower Mississippi Alluvial Valley, 1940–43.* Papers of the Peabody Museum of Archaeology and Ethnology, Vol. 25.
Schambach, Frank
   1989   The End of the Trail: The Route of Hernando De Soto's Army through Southwest Arkansas and East Texas. *Arkansas Archeologist*, vol. 27 and 28, pp. 9–33. Fayetteville.
Stubbs, John
   1982   The Chickasaw Contact with the La Salle Expedition in 1682. In *La Salle and His Legacy: Frenchmen and Indians in the Lower Mississippi Valley*, edited by Patricia Galloway. University Press of Mississippi, Jackson.
Swanton, John R.
   1939   *Final Report of the United States De Soto Expedition Commission.* U. S. House of Representatives, 76th Cong., 1st sess., Doc. 71. Government Printing Office, Washington, D.C.
   1946   *Indians of the Southeastern United States.* Bulletin of the Bureau of American Ethnology No. 137, pp. 1–943. Washington, D.C.
Varner, John, and Jeannette Varner
   1951   *The Florida of the Incas.* University of Texas Press, Austin.

Chapter 14 ■

David H. Dye

Warfare in the Sixteenth-Century Southeast: The de Soto Expedition in the Interior

Members of the Hernando de Soto entrada encountered two related aspects of Indian warfare in their travels through southeastern North America between 1539 and 1543: small-scale guerillalike raids and massive planned and coordinated warfare (Anderson 1987; DePratter 1983:45). In addition, the Spaniards encountered military shows of force aimed at demonstration of power. In this chapter emphasis is placed on conquest warfare because the various strategies and tactics associated with hegemonic control may have been the basis on which ruling elites coped with the de Soto entrada.

In the late prehistoric and early historic period, Southeastern Indian warfare was motivated by political, economic, military, and ideological realities. Technological and organizational constraints set limits on the extent to which Southeastern chiefdoms could dominate their neighbors. Large forces could not be deployed over great distances, nor could chiefs maintain effective political control over distant polities.

The dynamics of sixteenth-century Southeastern warfare can best be understood through archaeological studies and the accounts of members of the Hernando de Soto entrada after they reached Spain (Biedma 1922; Elvas 1922; Ranjel

1922; Varner and Varner 1962). These ethnohistorical sources vary in their treatment of native polities, and provide useful data for positing hypotheses concerning the nature of power struggles in relation to internal political pressures and external military threats.

Social power is expressed in distinct cultural patterns, as is evident in native contact with de Soto's retinue. Indian reaction to Spanish aggression, as portrayed in the early documents, is consistent with Southeastern cultural traditions in the archaeological and ethnohistoric record. Social behaviors established over the centuries evolved from complex political interactions among neighboring polities.

Over 50 autonomous political domains are described, from Florida north to North Carolina and east to Texas. They vary in political complexity and include nine paramount chiefdoms (see Figure 1-3). The de Soto accounts detail chiefdoms engaged in power struggles and political conflicts with neighboring polities. Each varied considerably in population and the area it covered.

Elites, constituting a small percentage of the population, governed by virtue of their power and membership in local ruling lineages and supported chiefs in the administration of political, economic, military, and ideological activities. Commoners produced food and other staples, and served as part-time craftsmen and warriors. They supported governing elites, but the extent to which they did so is uncertain.

Southeastern Chiefdoms

Three types of Southeastern chiefdoms existed during the sixteenth century: independent, paramount, and tributary. Independent chiefdoms are autonomous, multicommunity political domains controlled by a paramount chief. Paramount chiefdoms expand through the forceful incorporation of neighboring polities that yield their sovereignty under the threat or use of force and by so doing become tributary chiefdoms.

Each political domain possessed an administrative structure consisting of two decision-making levels: a paramount chief and town chiefs. The paramount chief and supporting elites reached decisions concerning political, economic, military, and ideological matters, perhaps in conjunction with councils (Elvas 1922:75). Town chiefs enforced decisions made by the paramount chief and his or her supporters. Tributary chiefs were responsible for their commoners and provided tribute to paramount chiefs.

Southeastern chiefdoms have been characterized as existing in a state of chronic warfare (Peebles and Kus 1977:444). During the de Soto expedition polities exercised powerful and forceful threats. But few reports of ongoing warfare or violent conflicts between polities are noted. Elites discussed warfare a great deal, perhaps as was customary. Chiefs may have tried in these discussions to elicit de Soto's aid or to demonstrate their power and authority to the threatening Spanish force.

Warfare

Warfare is a cultural process integrated with the various aspects of social power and is based on "organized, purposeful group action, directed against another group that may or may not be organized for similar action, involving the actual or potential application of lethal force" (Ferguson 1984:5). The occurrence and form of warfare is intimately related to processes of material production and other exigencies of survival (Hassig 1988). The study of war requires attention to human interaction with the natural environment and to economic, political, ideological, and military sources of power.

Warfare can be one result of political relationships among polities. Ruling elites often rely on force and power to further political goals within and among polities. *Force* is direct physical action, exercised only in proportion to its availability and consumed in its application. *Power*, on the other hand, operates indirectly and is not consumed in use. Power is primarily psychological, but must rely on force as one of its primary components. The more a political system relies on power, the more efficient it is. That is, paramount chiefs who utilize power relationships require subordinate or tributary chiefdoms to police themselves. The paramount polity thereby conserves its own force (Hassig 1988; Luttwak 1976). Hegemonic systems use force and power to dominate and control political domains, but emphasize power, particularly in attempts to control tributary polities. Southeastern ruling elites organized and controlled people, materials, and territories through their access to social power. Success in these endeavors depended upon their skill in manipulating the requisite techniques associated with organization, control, logistics, and communication. The relationships between these spheres of power overlap and intersect to some extent (Mann 1986:1). Multiple networks of social power exist among elites that compete for leadership positions. These sources of power provide the institutional means for elites to achieve and maintain their individual agendas and goals. Chiefly polities require hierarchical integration to dominate the sources of power. The interrelatedness of power sources in Southeastern warfare is evidenced in the archaeological and ethnohistorical record. Chiefs may have sought de Soto's aid as an external source of power to subdue neighboring polities, to wage war against traditional enemies, and to reorient local power structures. Casqui entreated aid in his war with Pacaha, Guachoya asked for help in fighting Taguanate and Quiqualtam, and Chicaça sought de Soto's friendship in defeating the Chachiuma.

Chiefly hegemonic systems conquer and indirectly control other polities, usually neighboring chiefdoms. Overwhelming force and extraordinary measures, including terror tactics, may be used in initial conquests to intimidate local ruling elites into continued compliance after the conquerors leave. Hegemonic systems achieve political expansion without direct territorial control. Hegemonic wars are wars of conquest geared to capturing new populations as sources of labor; the limiting factor to production in chiefdoms is control over labor, not access to land (Earle 1987:293).

Past discussions of Southeastern warfare in the late prehistoric and early historic periods have focused on resource scarcity (Larson 1972), social mobility

(Gibson 1974), dietary scarcity (Weisman and Milanich 1976), boundary mainte-nance (Peebles and Kus 1977), materialist and idealist approaches (Dickson 1981), resource scarcity and competition (DePratter 1983), and political evolution (Anderson 1987).

Buffer Zone Warfare

Conflicts among chiefdoms, acting as boundary maintenance mechanisms to se-cure political stability, often were conducted in buffer zones. In the Central Mis-sissippi Valley, for example, buffer zones arose from population consolidation between A.D. 1000 and A.D. 1350 (Morse and Morse 1983:237). In the late four-teenth century subsequent depopulation of large areas of the Mid-South, charac-terized by low carrying capacity, gave rise to "vacant quarters" (Morse and Morse 1983:271). Floodplain habitats with large amounts of arable soils acted to concentrate populations. According to the chiefs Ocute and Cofaqui, organized raids were "carried out through obscure and intricate parts, out of which no one would be expected to issue" (Biedma 1922:11). Boundary maintenance across buffer zones is based on feuding.

Aggression directed across buffer zones may have been confined to elites or those seeking elite status. Knowledge concerning directions to chiefdoms across extensive buffer zones generally was limited to elites. The Apalachee guide, Perico, who may have been a shaman, knew the route from Apalachee to Ocute, a distance of some 360 km (225 miles). As an elite, he may have traveled to dis-tant places to acquire esoteric knowledge (Helms 1979). Guatutima, a man of rank from Aguacaleyquen, "professed to know much of the country beyond [his chiefdom] and gave abundant information" to the Spanish (Ranjel 1922:72). Most commoners, when captured, would not, but often could not, take the en-trada beyond their respective polity boundaries.

Paramount Chiefdoms

The warfare of paramount chiefdoms was based on organized squadrons that sacked civic ceremonial centers and captured ruling elites to subjugate neighbor-ing polities or reconquer unruly vassals in hegemonic wars. Conquest of neigh-boring polities allowed chiefly elites to incorporate conquered groups into their political domains. The result was an increase in the number of tribute-paying commoners, the amount of the chief's finances, and the ruling elite's ability to engage in patronage and conspicuous display without provoking commoner re-volt or desertion (Brumfiel 1983:269).

Chiefdom size, and hence access to large amounts of arable soils, may have been an important factor in subjugating neighboring polities. The chiefdoms of Quizquiz and Aquixo occupied relatively small land bases compared with their paramount chiefdom Pacaha (Morse and Morse 1983). Casqui and Quigate, larger polities and more distant from Pacaha, maintained their independent sta-tus.

Large polities tended to have military and organizational advantages that allowed them to conquer smaller chiefdoms. Political domains of considerable size resulted from the consolidation of polities with access to large tracts of arable soil. Large and powerful independent or paramount chiefdoms tend to be associated with large floodplains, while neighboring hinterland chiefdoms with access to smaller amounts of arable soils would eventually become vassals to larger polities. As larger chiefdoms became unstable and fissioned, smaller polities would again emerge from the overarching political structure.

Critical variables in conquering neighboring chiefdoms may include physical distance, ease or difficulty of travel over intervening terrain, population size of the target chiefdom relative to the paramount chiefdom, relative political complexity of the competing chiefdoms, and settlement type (nucleated vs. dispersed). Chiefs attempting to intensify production through access to social labor pools and to increase their financial base would tend to be more successful in conquering chiefdoms requiring the least investment of time, energy, and resources. In the Central Mississippi Valley chiefs fought their neighbors. For example, the chiefdom of Guachoya was "at war" with Quilquatam to the southeast, Taguanate to the northeast, Aminoya to the north, and Autiamque to the northwest. Those areas to the south and southwest were thinly populated.

Chiefly elites ruled tributary polities from within the structure of the paramount chiefdom. Direct supervision of a tributary polity by a paramount's subordinates would place potential rival elites in positions of power equipped with a labor base and the capacity to become a serious threat. Loyalties would then be divided among kin groups within the paramount chiefdom. Paramounts could apply coercion to vassal rulers in tributary chiefdoms, but they would not be successful in threatening lineage kin who ruled tributary polities, because the political position of ruling elites in chiefdoms generally is insecure. Competition among political rivals exists where leadership is instituted in permanent offices and those offices are unique, where social statuses are filled from a pool of socially qualified individuals (Goody 1966:2), and where the chiefly elite's right to use coercion is limited. Instead, incumbent chiefs may enhance their authority by claims of legitimacy of office through access to supernatural forces, demonstrated effectiveness in warfare, the ability to wield political power, lineage affiliation, and domination over some aspects of the economy.

Paramount chiefs, according to the de Soto accounts, experienced difficulty controlling their tributary chiefdoms. Chicaça requested de Soto's aid in returning the rebellious Chakchiuma to tributary status. Although de Soto suspected Chicaça of setting a trap, the Chakchiuma chief, Miculasa, did return as a vassal to Chicaça after being threatened by a combined Chicaça and Spanish force.

However, other tributary chiefdoms—Aquixo and Quizquiz under Pacaha; Ocita and Moscoso under Paracoxi; Chiaha, Tali, and Ulibahali under Coosa; Mabila under Tascaluza; Hymahi, Guaquili, Chalaque, and Ilapi under Cofitachequi; and Altamaha, Cofaqui, and Patofa under Ocute—did not rebel in de Soto's presence. They may have enjoyed the protection of the paramount chiefdom or may have been willing to accept the tributary status to which they had grown accustomed. Çamumo, vassal of Ocute, expresses Southeastern political and economic reality when he inquires of de Soto, "To whom should I now give tribute in the future?" (Ranjel 1922:90).

Tributary chiefdoms may have been required to produce and transport goods without recompense. The area from which goods could be drawn would have been limited by the ability to transport them efficiently. The economic benefits of incorporating vast areas would be reduced as transportation became less efficient. By leaving the government of conquered areas in local hands, administrative costs would be kept relatively low. The economic benefits of pervasive and dominating political influence depended on exercising political control and extracting goods and services at local expense (Hassig 1988:17–18).

Tribute derived from within the chiefdom appears to have been extracted through authority and kin affiliation, while tribute from vassal or tributary chiefdoms could be obtained through exercise or show of initial force followed by subsequent threats. Internally derived tribute was based on consensus; chiefly coercion is limited because chiefs use mechanisms to reduce internal conflict and tensions within the polity. Paramounts coerced externally derived tribute from tributary chiefdoms.

Southeastern chiefs controlled the labor and tribute of commoners, as is seen in the ability of ruling elites to deliver social labor (carriers) upon request to the Spaniards. Had this not been the case, de Soto would not have captured and held ruling elites hostage while in their polities. De Soto requisitioned social labor for Spanish use without expending Spanish force beyond the ruling elite. The political use of force in any primitive society, and chiefdoms in general, has no formal, legal apparatus of forceful repression (Service 1975:15–16) within the chiefdom, but the relationship between Southeastern paramount chiefs and their tributaries was based on coercive power in order to extract goods and services as tribute.

In some instances social labor was given to de Soto without the use of force. The independent chiefdoms of Ichisi and Talisi and the paramount chiefdom of Ocute and its tributary chiefdom Patofa, Cofitachequi's tributary chiefdom of Chalaque, and Coosa's tributary chiefdom Tali, all gave bearers freely to de Soto. Where such labor is given without force by ruling elites, it is generally given by tributary chiefdoms that perhaps already have been conditioned to deliver social labor to ruling elites, as exemplified by the above case of Çamumo's dilemma.

Slaves, differentiated from social labor, were given by Chiaha to de Soto as gifts. The extent to which slaves were used by elites as labor sources to intensify production is not well understood.

Chiefly political power and authority also may be seen in the treatment of chiefs by their subjects. In particular, chiefs of paramount chiefdoms, such as Cofitachequi, Coosa, Tascaluza, and Chicaça were treated with great respect and deference and indicate the extent to which sixteenth-century chiefs ruled by authority rather than force. Coosa possessed the power to order his people to give up their houses, and they did so willingly (Elvas 1922:82). The niece of the chieftainess Cofitachequi, came "to that town [Cofitachequi] [by the chief's] command to punish capitally some principal Indians who had seized upon the tribute" (Elvas 1922:65). The other end of the political spectrum is Quiguate, who, under de Soto's orders, asked his people to return to their town and serve the Spanish, but they refused (Elvas 1922:131–132). Quiguate's subjects may have been unwilling to serve the Spanish rather than disobey Quiguate, but it still points to his limited control.

The power of various chiefs was known throughout the Southeast. Apalachee "had great fame wheresoever we went" (Beidma 1922:5), Tascaluza was "a powerful lord and one much feared in that land" (Ranjel 1922:115), Pacaha was "famed throughout all the land," and Quigualtam was the "greatest lord of that country" (Elvas 1922:153). The territories they commanded likewise demonstrate their political power: Quiguate was "a large province and country of great abundance (Elvas 1922:129), Caluça, was "a place of much repute," and Nondacao was very populous with plenty of maize.

Customary loyalty oaths acted to acknowledge chiefly power and authority; the majority of chiefs, or their emissaries, with whom de Soto came in contact declared oaths of allegiance. Elvas in particular records numerous pledges. Tributay chiefdoms apparently delivered oaths of fealty to ruling paramounts. The Southeastern Indians met by de Soto may have presented themselves to the Spanish force as allies or vassals by stating required oaths of obedience to their perceived new paramount in order to avoid destruction through de Soto's protection. The powerful chiefs of Coosa, Tascaluza, Casqui, and Cofitacheque opened their stores and aided de Soto in the initial encounters. Paramount chiefdoms may have acted to safeguard their vassals because ruling elites would have vested interests in the well-being of tributary chiefdoms.

Southeastern chiefs dominated and manipulated the economies of their vassals in order to derive a surplus through internal and external tribute that could be invested through the distribution of wealth and staple items to lower-ranking elites. Chiefly elites expropriated a variety of economic goods from their subjects to mollify Spanish demands: maize, dogs, tanned skins, blankets, venison, salt, corncakes, turkeys, persimmon bread, fish, woven mantles, and nut oil. Tribute goods varied in quantity and composition from one area to another. For instance, west of the Mississippi, woven mantles, tanned deer and bison skins, and fish were delivered by virtually all chiefs, while east of the Mississippi maize, small game, turkeys, dogs, tanned deerskins, and venison predominated as gifts to the Spanish.

These items mirror tribute goods obtained by native elites from commoners. For instance, the chieftainess Cofitachequi received a tribute of "gold" (copper) (Elvas 1922:51) and clothing (possibly woven mantles and deerskins). Maize, deerskins, and woven blankets were given as tribute in the chiefdom of Toa to masters or principal men by commoners (Elvas 1922:53). Tanned hides may have been an important tribute item because of their relative scarcity (Gramly 1977). Clothing in general may have been in great demand as a result of the scarcity of leather and the labor-intensive production of textiles and skins. When Moscoso and his allies, the Guachoyans, looted Nilco, the Guachoyans "went to the houses for plunder, filling the canoes with clothing" (Elvas 1922:158). In some instances tribute items were valued as trade goods; the Cayas exchanged salt for skins (tanned hides) and woven mantles.

Through economic domination by political means, elites manipulated two systems of finance to support chiefly institutions (Johnson and Earle 1987:208). Staple finance, generated from the collection of foods and crafts, was received from commoner households as tribute and distributed to "principal people" or those working for the polity. Staple finances in the form of food and clothing were critically important to de Soto and he obtained them primarily by coercing ruling elites. The de Soto expedition sought densely populated areas to seize the large stores of staple finances. The Spanish conquerors had a long history in the New World of subsisting from native storehouses.

Wealth finance (Johnson and Earle 1987:208) involves elite control of the production and distribution of primitive valuables. Wealth is important in establishing and recognizing a person's social position and in attaining and maintaining prestige and associated political office and acts as an indicator of social status that defines an individual's political and economic rights, obligations, and responsibilities in a society. By controlling the distribution of the valuables, ranking chiefs manipulated them as a political currency. Members of the de Soto entrada did not comment upon wealth finance, with the exception of copper used as tribute in the Cofitachequi chiefdom. De Soto hoped to find liquid wealth such as gold, silver, and precious gems. He and his colleagues took advantage of the Central American chiefly tribute system in order to acquire slaves and gold. De Soto hoped to continue this pattern in the Southeast.

Hegemonic Warfare

Chiefly conquest warfare involves three potential types of regional conflict. First, an elite rival might rebel against his paramount either as the ruler of a subordinate town of an independent chiefdom or as the ruling elite of a tributary chiefdom. The former is exemplified by the capital punishment of Cofitachequi's principal elites who attempted to seize tribute, presumably for their own use. The latter is found in Chicaça's attempt to gain de Soto's aid in returning the recalcitrant Miculasa, ruling elite of the Chakchiuma chiefdom, to a state of vassalage.

Second, a chief could extend his chiefdom regionally by annexing adjacent towns that might be either independent or located on the adjacent chiefdom's border. There are no examples of this type of warfare in the de Soto narratives, but the independent towns may have been incorporated in areas lacking buffer zones or sharp territorial boundaries. Frontier towns may have shifted as political boundaries changed. By the sixteenth century, few towns could have survived as independent political domains.

Third, a paramount chief might incorporate adjacent polities through direct coercive action. The actions of the entrada may have been perceived by the Southeastern Indians as an aggressive acquisition of populations.

Southeastern chiefdoms, depending upon their particular political formation (independent chiefdom, paramount chiefdom, or tributary chiefdom) reacted to Spanish presence in a number of ways. First, a polity could disperse its population so that a concentrated force organized into squadrons could not effectively cage or circumscribe them. Town abandonment was an effective means of avoiding vassalage, but it allowed political, economic, military, and ideological structures and associated paraphernalia to be desecrated, looted, or destroyed. In some instances the Indians set fire to their own towns, rather than have them fall into enemy hands. At Nilco they set fire to the chief's house after an unsuccessful show of force and escaped to a nearby lake to avoid being captured by the cavalry. Such drastic measures may have been a reaction to the de Soto expedition as a scorched earth policy is rarely mentioned in the accounts.

Town abandonment was a commonplace strategy in frontier villages as well as major civic/ceremonial towns throughout the Southeast. In some cases Spanish occupation of towns took place for such an extended period that the inhabitants were forced to return and beg for food.

The element of surprise was an important tactic in capturing a resident population, particularly the elite. Native squadrons attacked from four directions in the predawn hours in an effort to successfully cage a targeted population. For example, Chicaça and Tula attacked the Spanish in the early morning hours from cardinal directions.

The third option was to enter into diplomatic relations to seek a mutual settlement or alliance between each party or to send messengers to assess an enemy's strengths and weaknesses. A number of polities, particularly those in the east, sought de Soto's allegiance. In several instances, Indian elites tried to secure alliances through kinship with de Soto. Casqui gave a daughter and Pacaha gave one of his wives, a sister, and a woman of rank. The latter strategy existed throughout the Southeast. "Messengers" with their elite retinue conveyed gifts of labor (carriers), staple finance (food, consisting of venison, fish, dogs, corn; and clothing, comprising skins and mantles), and wealth finance (pearls, a marten-skin mantle) on behalf of chiefly elites. Gifts were offered prior to the host's arrival into the chiefdom.

Messengers, generally regarded by the Spanish as spies (Elvas 1922:149), held the rank of town chief or were members of the elite. Individuals of lesser rank often accompanied chiefly messengers. Helms (1979:134) suggests that sixteenth-century Panamanian elites, rather than commoners, traveled to geographically distant lands.

Chiefs employed spies in nonambassadorial roles. Spies captured by the Spaniards, such as the one sent by Quiguate, were used to ferret out chiefs in hiding. Captured spies from Naguatex informed Moscoso that their chief sent them to discover Spanish numbers and their condition. Uritina, Pacaha, Quiguate, and Anilco sent imposters to spy on de Soto.

A fourth reaction was to threaten the enemy, by displaying one's perceived supernatural, military, and political power and authority. In most instances this show of force was sufficient to threaten one's enemies. The Mississippi River chiefdoms of Quizquiz, Aquixo, Pacaha, and Nilco employed this tactic. In hegemonic systems the first line of defense against enemy aggression is perceived power. The Spanish believed themselves to be morally, spiritually, and militarily superior to the Indians, and the native show of force had an unprecedented negligible effect.

A fifth strategy was to engage the enemy in armed combat as was done by Chicaça, Tascaluza, Alimamu, Tula, Naguatex, Aays, and an aborted attack by Nilco, Taguanate, Guachoya, and Quigualtam. On two occasions several independent polities cooperated in joint attacks against de Soto's entrada.

The Chicaça attack (Biedma 1922:22–23; Carmona 1922:153; Elvas 1922:103; Ranjel 1922:134–135) evidenced much planning to take advantage of the enemy's weaknesses. Harassment through the winter softened expectations of an attack and the steady diet of rabbit provided by the Chicaça may have been followed as sympathetic magic to ensure timidity and cowardice in the Spanish soul and spirit (Hudson et al. 1989). The attacks began at dawn with four squadrons descending upon the Spanish from four directions.

The Tula attack (Biedma 1922:33; Elvas 1922:138; Ranjel 1922:148) also started at daybreak with two to three large squadrons moving in from different directions. The Tula were noted for being the best fighting men the Spanish met.

Quiqualtam (Elvas 1922:155) came across the Mississippi at night to give de Soto battle, but turned back for an unknown reason. Nilco, Taguanate, and Guachoya planned an attack, but the assault was aborted when Moscoso learned of it in time to defeat them singly (Elvas 1922:190). Naguatex (Elvas 1922:170) and two other polities, Maye and Hacanac, cooperated in an attack by sending two squadrons in a ploy to lead the cavalry away from the body of the expedition, so that two other squadrons might attack the remainder of the force in the camp.

Squadron warfare is but one facet of aggression based on hegemonic relationships among neighboring chiefdoms. Alliances through marriage, gift exchange, subterfuge, spies, threats of force, and open hostility characterize the use of political power in gaining access to social labor in the sixteenth-century Southeast.

Summary

Sixteenth-century accounts of the de Soto expedition indicate that two interrelated types of Southeastern Indian aggression existed, and that native coping strategies with Spanish intrusion took place according to traditional rules of political strategies. Spanish presence was militarily devastating, but initial encounters may have been perceived by native chiefs within the context of regional power struggles centered upon differential access to and use of ideology, military, economic, and political bases.

Southeastern chiefdoms attempted to interact with, if not dominate, the Spanish entrada within the context of conquest warfare based upon hegemonic relationships. The variety of aggressive and nonaggressive tactics employed by ruling elites may be subsumed, to some extent, within Southeastern conceptions of political dominance and vassalage among neighboring polities. Southeastern Indian behavior with regard to their reaction to the de Soto entrada may be understood by examining the nature of regional and local political power interrelationships among independent, paramount, and tributary chiefdoms.

Acknowledgments

I wish to thank David Anderson, Janet Levy, and Charles Hudson for their useful comments on this paper. The responsibility for any errors contained in this paper rests solely with the author.

References

Anderson, David
    1987 Warfare and Mississippian Political Evolution in the Southeastern United States. Paper presented at the 20th Annual Meeting of the Chacmool Conference, Calgary.
Biedma, Luis Hernandez de
    1922 Relation of the Conquest of Florida. In *Narratives of the Career of Hernando de Soto*, edited by Edward G. Bourne, Vol. 2, pp. 1–40. Allerton, New York.
Brumfiel, Elizabeth M.
    1983 Aztec State Making: Ecology, Structure, and the Origin of the State. *American Anthropologist* 85:261–284.
Carmona, Alonso de
    1922 Fragments from Alonso de Carmona and Juan Coles. In *Narratives of the Career of Hernando de Soto*, edited by Edward G. Bourne, Vol. 2, pp. 151–157. Atherton, New York.
DePratter, Chester B.
    1983 *Late Prehistoric and Early Historic Chiefdoms in the Southeastern United States.* Unpublished Ph.D. dissertation, University of Georgia, Athens.
Dickson, D. Bruce
    1981 The Yanomamö of the Mississippi Valley? Some Reflections on Larson (1972), Gibson (1974), and Mississippian Period Warfare in the Southeastern United States. *American Antiquity* 46(4):909–916.
Earle, Timothy K.
    1987 Chiefdoms in Archaeological and Ethnohistorical Perspective. *Annual Reviews in Anthropology* 16:279–308.
Elvas, Fidalgo of
    1922 True Relation. In *Narratives of the Career of Hernando de Soto*, edited by Edward G. Bourne, Vol. I, pp. 1–223. Allerton, New York.
Ferguson, R. Brian
    1984 Introduction: Studying War. In *Warfare, Culture, and Environment*, edited by R. Brian Ferguson, pp. 1–81. Academic Press, New York.
Gibson, Jon L.
    1974 Aboriginal Warfare in the Protohistoric Southeast: An Alternative Perspective. *American Antiquity* 39(1):130–133.
Goody, Jack
    1966 Introduction. In *Succession to High Office*, edited by Jack Goody, pp. 1–56. Cambridge University Press, Cambridge.
Gramly, Michael
    1977 Deerskins and Hunting Territories: Competition for a Scarce Resource of the Northeastern Woodlands. *American Antiquity* 42:601–605.
Hassig, Ross
    1988 *Aztec Warfare: Imperial Expansion and Political Control.* University of Oklahoma Press, Norman.
Helms, Mary W.
    1979 *Ancient Panama: Chiefs in Search of Power.* University of Texas Press, Austin.
Hudson, Charles, Marvin T. Smith, and Chester B. DePratter

1989 The Hernando de Soto Expedition: From Mabila to the Mississippi River. In *Towns and Temples along the Mississippi*, edited by David H. Dye and Cheryl A. Cox. University of Alabama Press, University.

Johnson, Allen W., and Timothy Earle
1987 *The Evolution of Human Societies: From Foraging Group to Agrarian State*. Stanford University Press, Stanford.

Larson, Lewis H., Jr.
1972 Functional Considerations of Warfare in the Southeast during the Mississippi Period. *American Antiquity* 37(3):383–392.

Luttwak, Edward N.
1976 *The Grand Strategy of the Roman Empire: From the First Century A.D. to the Third*. Johns Hopkins University Press, Baltimore.

Mann, Michael
1986 *The Sources of Social Power. Vol. 1: A History of Power from the Beginning to A.D. 1760*. Cambridge University Press, Cambridge.

Morse, Dan F., and Phyllis A. Morse
1983 *Archaeology of the Central Mississippi Valley*. Academic Press, New York.

Peebles, Christopher S., and Susan M. Kus
1977 Some Archaeological Correlates of Ranked Societies. *American Antiquity* 42:421–448.

Ranjel, Rodrigo
1922 A Narrative of De Soto's Expedition. In *Narratives of the Career of Hernando de Soto*, edited by Edward G. Bourne, Vol. II, pp. 41–150. Allerton, New York.

Service, Elman R.
1975 *Origins of the State and Civilization: The Process of Cultural Evolution*. W. W. Norton, New York.

Varner, John G., and Jeannette J. Varner
1962 *The Florida of the Inca*. University of Texas Press, Austin.

Weisman, Brent, and Jerald T. Milanich
1976 Dietary Scarcity: A Stimulus for Warfare among Southeastern United States Horticulturalists during the Historic Period. *Florida Journal of Anthropology* 1(1):31–37.

Part 2 ■

The Impact of Hispanic Colonization in the Southeast and Caribbean

Chapter 15 ■

Kathleen A. Deagan

Sixteenth-Century Spanish–American Colonization in the Southeastern United States and the Caribbean

The term "New World" has traditionally been used to refer to the geographic entity of the Americas—an entity that was new only to the Europeans who came there after 1492. We might more appropriately refer to the New World as a new global, social, economic, and political configuration that resulted from interaction and exchange among peoples of the Americas, Europe, Africa, and Asia.

These processes were set in motion by the invasion of the Americas by Europeans following the Columbian voyages of exploration. These earliest ventures of exploration, contact, and conquest had an immediate dramatic impact on the peoples and landscapes of the Americas, and led to a popular image emphasizing conquistadors as a symbol of encounter between the Old World and the Americas. It was, however, the later and less dramatic colonization efforts of the Spaniards (and later of other European powers) that were to define and shape the true New World.

Such colonization efforts required sustained adaptive measures on the part of all people involved, and the resulting modes of interaction and behavior were apparently those that had the greatest long-term effect on Europe and the Americas. They resulted not only in the virtual disappearance of traditional American

Indian society, but also in the emergence of what we refer to today as "Hispanic-American," "African-American," and "Anglo-American" cultural traditions.

Because of the special circumstances of the encounter between the Old World and the Americas, historical archaeology has been a central and irreplaceable resource in our attempts to understand the nature and impact of early colonial centuries. The New World emerged as a result of confrontation and interaction between literate and nonliterate societies, so that it is impossible to rely upon written or material evidence alone in reconstructing its origins. After 1492, American society became part of a global world, and its study thus requires a global and multicultural perspective. Only historical archaeology can bring this special perspective to bear on such problems (see Deagan 1988; Leone 1977; Schuyler 1976); the study of issues addressed in this volume, for example, has depended to a considerable extent on historical archaeology.

Historical archaeologists have enjoyed some notable successes in tracing the emergence and development of life in the New World, as the essays in this volume illustrate for the Southeast. One of the central topics has been the impact of colonialism on indigenous peoples throughout the region, as well as their varied, flexible, and often creative responses to encounters with European intruders (see the chapters in the section; Dyson 1982; Fitzhugh 1985; Proctor and Milanich 1978).

Historical archaeology has also played a central role in our understanding of Euro-Afro-American culture formation, which was a direct consequence of the European colonizing ventures in the Americas, and gave rise to modern American life.

This chapter provides an overview of Spanish colonization strategies and organization, Spanish attempts at colonization in the fifteenth and sixteenth centuries, and the consequences of this colonization from the perspectives of Native Americans, Euro-Americans, and African-Americans.

Spanish Presence in North America

The sixteenth-century colonization of North America and the Caribbean was essentially a Spanish venture. By 1617, when the first permanent English colony was founded at Jamestown, 124 years had already passed since the establishment of the first Spanish colony in the Caribbean and 104 years since Ponce de León delcared Florida a colony of Spain. For more than 300 years—a century longer than this country has been an independent nation—the southern fringe of what is now the United States was occupied by a string of Spanish towns, missions, ranches, trails, and presidios—all the result of the intentional New World colonization strategies of the Spaniards.

The Spanish roots of European colonization in North America are not generally emphasized in traditional treatments of American colonial history, such as those found in textbooks or general historical studies. A now-acknowledged, anti-Hispanic and pro-Anglo bias has permeated the historiography of colonial North America, manifest in *La Leyenda Negra*, or the Black Legend. This term refers to a set of extremely negative beliefs about the Spaniards that developed during the sixteenth century in the English attempt to promote Protestantism. The Black Legend held that Spaniards were by nature bloodthirsty, cruel, proud, lustful, and perfidious. It also implied that the Spanish did not come to America to colonize, but rather to search for gold and exploit the Indians. The English, in contrast, had come to America to establish family and community life, and to build a nation. This sixteenth-century, politically motivated depiction has had a profound influence, as can be seen in the rejection and neglect of Spanish contributions to North America's cultural heritage over the last few centuries.

This perspective has been balanced somewhat in recent decades, owing both to a growing interest in the social history of the North American and Caribbean Spanish colonies (e.g., Jones 1979; Landers, this volume; McAlister 1984; Scardaville 1985), and to the growing body of archaeological research on Spanish colonial sites (for a summary and synthetic treatments, see Deagan 1983, 1985a, 1985b, 1988; Dobyns 1982; Farnsworth 1986; Hoover and Costello 1985; Marrinan 1985; Schuyler 1976). A consideration of the religious, legal, economic, and biological contexts of initial Spanish–American colonization provides us with a more comprehensive and realistic understanding of Spanish colonization in the Americas, and its consequences.

Spanish Colonial Strategies

During the first 25 years of Spanish presence in the New World—an exclusively Caribbean occupation—certain interrelated institutions developed from the Iberian *Reconquista* tradition, and these later radiated with the Spaniards in their subsequent colonizing ventures. Such institutions as religious organization and interaction, new forms of labor organization, political administration, town and settlement patterns, and an exclusively mercantile Spanish economy acquired the forms they were to assume throughout the Spanish New World in the first years of contact (see Elliott 1987; Lockhart and Schwartz 1983; McAlister 1984).

The source of inspiration for initial exploration and settlement throughout Spanish America was often described as "God, Gold, and Glory." Neither historical nor archaeological research has produced information to dispute this suggestion, although it should be noted that those terms also generally describe the motives behind most European colonial ventures.

Old World Precedents

The early Spanish presence in the New World was in many ways a continuation of the well-established medieval tradition in Spain of territorial expansion, conquest, occupation, incorporation of local populations, and permanent feudal rule. This tradition had developed over the 700 years of the reconquista of Spain from the Moors (see Elliott 1987:1–10; Lockhart and Schwartz 1983:61–63; McAlister 1984; Wolf 1959:55–59). The emphasis on God and glory has its roots in the Reconquista, as does the emphasis on gold, which could be obtained through the bounty of war and the acquisition of land. The motives and values that evolved over those seven centuries of holy war emphasized the *hidalgo* status, which built a livelihood on service to God and king, and the acquisition of property and wealth through rewards for honor, valor, and military success.

This pattern of colonization of conquered lands was first translated from the reconquista to the Spanish conquest and colonization of the Canary Islands, which took place under Queen Isabela between about 1477 and 1497. After sustained resistance and dramatic loss of population, the Guanche natives were given the privilege of becoming free Castilian subjects as long as they adopted Christianity and accepted the sovereignty of Spain. The status and privileges of their chiefs were recognized, and intermarriage between Spanish men and Guanche women was not uncommon. Those Guanches who continued resistance, however, were considered appropriate candidates for enslavement and despoliation (for more details on this colonization, see Crosby 1986:73–99; McAlister 1984:63–65).

Antillean Experiments

The arrival of Columbus in the Americas only a few months after the fall of Grenada, the last Iberian Moorish stronghold, had a profound effect on the subsequent development of the Spanish colonies. The first decades of Spanish presence in nearly all parts of the New World were characterized by conquest-oriented expeditions, for which successful conquistadors were rewarded with allocations of land and the servitude of the people who occupied it.

Ideally, that land would contain natural resources with a high and profitable yield, preferably of gold or silver, and a sizable stable population that could be subjected to peonage. The locations and organization of the first Spanish settlements in the Caribbean were based on this principle; however, excesses in extraction and the exploitation of human resources led within 30 years to a nearly complete depletion of both precious metals and the human labor necessary to extract them (Deagan 1988; Sauer 1966:200–204).

Earliest Encounters: A Question of Humanity

Europe's encounter with the Americas in the fifteenth century clearly extended the realm of both the known and the possible and provoked a burst of intellectual inquiry. Such inquiry assuredly also occurred in American Indian thought and intellectual life, but we unfortunately have no written records of this response. One of the earliest and most powerful new questions to arise was where American Indians fit into the prevailing cosmology (see Lockhart and Schwartz 1983:64–72; Pagden 1982:1–56). The question of Indian humanity was essentially one of whether Indians had souls, and for fifteenth-century Catholicism, this would have a critical bearing on the direction of Spain's policies in the New World treatment of the Indians. It was determined in 1500 that Indians did, in fact, have souls, and after this time the Spanish Crown was careful to legally ensure that Indians could not be enslaved (see Simpson 1960 and the sources cited above).

Encomienda: Reducción and the Demise of Indian Workers

Of all the changes provoked by the Spaniards in the Caribbean, the organization and exploitation of native labor had perhaps the most dramatic impact as it resulted in the nearly complete extinction of Caribbean Indians by ca. 1520 (see discussions by Deagan 1985b; Sauer 1966). Southeastern Indian groups in areas under Spanish dominion fared somewhat better than those in the Caribbean, although the Florida Indians were extinct after 1763 (see Deagan 1985b).

Introduced disease was certainly the primary cause of this population decline; in the Caribbean, however, the early Spanish labor practices were also a contributing factor, and the lessons learned by the Spaniards in the Antilles shaped their subsequent Indian policy in other parts of the Americas (see Elliot 1987; Fairbanks 1985:137–8).

Much of the institutional development after the passage of the laws of Burgos was designed to ensure that the "free" Indians would nevertheless be a ready and reliable source of labor. The labor problem was intially resolved by a uniquely American institution, that of the *encomienda.* established in Hispaniola in 1503 (see Deagan 1985b; Elliott 1987; Gibson 1987; Kieth 1971; McAlister 1984:157–166).

Under the encomienda system, those Indians associated with a particular allocation of land were obliged to exchange their labor for instruction in Christianity and civilization. In order to make the system more efficient, the Indians were regularly relocated and consolidated at locations convenient for Spanish labor exploitation and conversion. This process, known as *reducción*, figured centrally in the social disintegration and breakdown of traditional cultural patterns among both Caribbean and North American Indian groups after contact.

The institution of encomienda did not extend widely into North America, ostensibly because the law of 1549 eliminated the obligation of the Indians to provide labor, although special permission was sometimes given to the borderlands conquistadors to establish encomienda. This policy was at least in part a recognition of the devastating losses to the Indian population in the Caribbean (Elliot 1987:47–48); however, one must also consider both the absence in the Southeast of large-scale extractive ventures requiring the consolidation of Indian labor pools, and the organized resistance of native peoples of that region as factors in the relative insignificance of the encomienda institution in North America.

Political Accommodation and Intermarriage

The practice of dealing with the American Indians through their chiefs was developed in the Canary Islands and subsequently extended to the Caribbean. This was to become a cornerstone of Spanish–Indian interaction in those areas of the Americas with strongly differentiated chiefs and stratified societies.

In their relations with the Indians, the Spanish initially stressed respect for and recognition of the political importance of the hereditary leaders of the Indians, their *caciques*. Caciques among the groups in both Florida and the Caribbean held considerable power over their people, came from elite lineages, and had a wide variety of special privileges (see, e.g., Deagan 1978; Feinman and Neitzel 1984; Gibson 1987:377; Hanke 1964:27; Hann 1988:104-108; Hussey 1932; McAlister 1984:180; Milanich 1987; Rouse 1948a; Wilson 1989). By securing the cooperation and alliance of the caciques, the Spanish expected to impose conversion and civilization on the rest of the Indians (Gibson 1987:377; Hanke 1964). This hierarchical approach was appealing to the already hierarchically organized Spaniards, and the recognition of Indian political organization and chiefly privilege was formalized in 1512 by the Law of Burgos (Simpson 1960).

From the fifteenth century onward, this included intermarriage between Spanish conquistadors or soldiers and Indian chieftainesses (Deagan 1985b:304–305; Floyd 1973:59–61; Lyon 1976:148; Morner 1967:37). Intermarriage between conquistadors and caciques was later to be important in subduing and converting Florida, and Spanish–Indian intermarriage in general was to be an important characteristic in Spanish Borderland towns, and of the development of Spanish-American culture (see Deagan 1983:304–306).

The Role of the Church

The Catholic Church played a major role in all aspects of colonial life, including the structure of Spanish–Indian interaction in the Americas (see Gibson 1987:15; Hanke 1964). It served simultaneously as a philosophical base for paternalistic treatment of the Indians, and as a force for the mitigation of abuse. These are illustrated by church-inspired protective legislation—best seen through the writings of Bartolomé de las Casas (1951).

The church also served—particularly in the frontier regions— as a primary agent of hispanicization, acculturation, and labor organization of the native inhabitants. It was in these inseparable areas of conversion and organization for labor that the Catholic Church had the most profound impact on native peoples in the areas of Spanish colonization, primarily through missions.

The mission as it was known in the northern borderlands areas was not an Antillean phenomenon. Friars in the Caribbean traveled to the Indian settlements or worked with caciques (see Hanke 1964). The mission was rather an accommodation to the need to secure and control a vast and isolated territory inhabited by a large but dispersed Indian population (see Bolton 1917 for the original statement of this position). Missions evolved along the frontiers of Spanish America as centers not only of Christianity, but also of Spanish political presence, labor organization, economic production, and defense. The roles and consequences of the missions in the Southeast are treated elsewhere in this volume and are referred to as appropriate in this discussion.

Resistance to Spanish Presence

In neither the Caribbean nor the southeastern United States do we see the pattern of successful extended native resistance to the Spanish invaders that occurred in many parts of the Americas. Such successful resistance was most characteristic of those regions inhabited by semisedentary or nomadic people who were not centrally organized, or who could not be centrally controlled (see Dozier 1970; Hudson 1987; Lockhart and Schwartz 1983:52–53; Simmons 1979; Spicer 1962; Williams 1986). American Indian resistance in the Caribbean, like that of the Guanche peooples in the Canary Islands, was immediate and sustained; however, the population fell to unrecoverable levels so quickly that such resistance was soon ineffective.

Indians in La Florida, although initially organized for strong resistance to the intruders, were subdued in large measure by the end of the sixteenth century (see Canzo 1598, 1600). This appears to have resulted from the combined effects of population loss, mission efforts, and the collaboration of the caciques with the Spaniards.

It is perhaps noteworthy that the chiefdoms of the interior Southeast, which were neither in sustained contact with the Spaniards nor under their direct dominion, had collapsed by the end of the sixteenth century (see Smith 1987:86–89). Those in the region of northern Florida and southeastern Georgia appear to have sustained their political organization under the protection of the Spaniards.

It should also be noted that the Spanish conquistadors in La Florida failed to locate such resources as precious metals or valuable cash crops, and thus did not need to practice extensive reducción for intensive labor. The reducción practices that were so devastating to the Caribbean Indians were not implemented to as considerable an extent in the Southeast.

African Resistance

Another important aspect of both labor organization and resistance is the role of Africans in the earliest Spanish colonies (addressed in this volume by Landers). The loss of the American Indian population was disastrous also for Africans, who came to be enslaved by the thousands for labor on American enterprises. Resistance to enslavement took place almost immediately by the relatively powerless African peoples in the Americas, more often than not in cooperation with American Indians (see Landers, this volume; 1988). The Black (and Indian) *cimarron* communities that were found in colonial times throughout the Spanish Caribbean (see Arrom and García-Arevalo 1986; Chapeaux 1983; Deive 1980; Price 1973; Schelle 1906:volume 1). Legislation was issued in the Caribbean as early as 1518 to prevent interaction between the two groups (Hanke 1964:31).

Social and material exchange between African, Amerindian, and European populations also occurred quite early and quite extensively in the contact period. Although the resulting Afro-Caribbean tradition has been studied in detail (e.g., Armstrong 1989; Crahan and Knight 1979; Deive 1978; Mintz 1974; Price 1973, among others) its origins in the Spanish contact period have been given little archaeological attention. Exceptions include Arrom and García-Arevalo (1986), Smith (1986), and Veloz Maggiolo (1974).

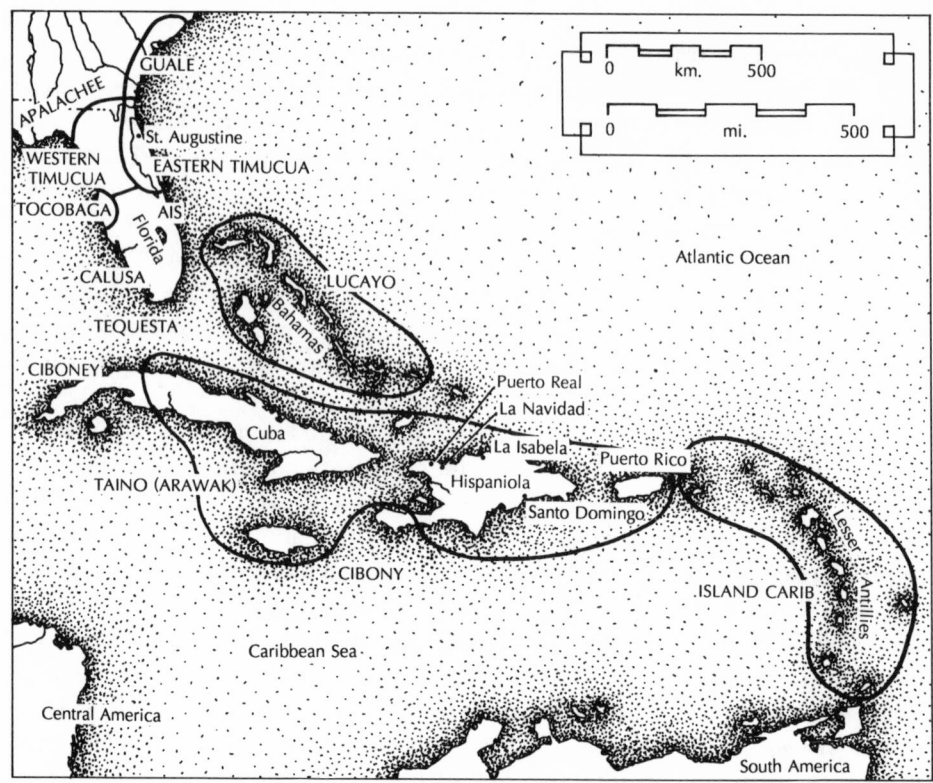

Figure 15-1. Locations of major Native American groups and early Spanish settlements in the Caribbean and La Florida.

Permanent Settlement: Organized Life in Towns

Spain maintained control of early colonies through a complex system of settlement consisting of towns, missions, ranches, *presidos* (fortified places), and roads (Dobyns 1980; Spicer 1962:285–305). Examples of all of these components are found in the southeastern United States borderlands, although they were by no means as numerous or as large as those in other parts of Spanish America (Figure 15-1).

The basic instrument for the establishment of permanent settlement was the Castilian *municipio* concept, which mandated the presence of towns for organized life (McAlister 1984:133–136). Efforts were made from the earliest days to establish permanent towns. The first intentional colony was established by Christopher Columbus in 1493, at La Isabela on the north coast of Hispaniola (see Cruxent, this volume), and efforts to settle towns in the southeastern United States occurred as early as the 1526 Allyón attempt, perhaps located near Sapelo Sound, Georgia (see Hoffman 1984).

The establishment of Spanish towns in the Americas was a closely regulated undertaking, both in the physical and the administrative organization of these settlements, and contradicts the notion that Spaniards did not come to colonize (see Jones 1979). The regulations governing the physical and organizational aspects of towns were codified in 1573 (Crouch et al. 1982), although they were implemented at least in part as early as the establishment of Santo Domingo in 1498, and were developed as a code by the early sixteenth century (McAlister 1984:134–139).

Archaeological evidence has confirmed that even in the remote borderland frontiers these regulations were observed in such towns as Santa Fe and St. Augustine, with occasional modifications to meet local environmental conditions and defensive needs (Crouch et al. 1982; Deagan 1982; Jones 1979:5–11). It was primarily within these towns that the Hispanic-American cultural tradition crystallized (Foster 1960), through processes that can be documented archaeologically. Issues related to town-based interaction and adaptation in Florida and the Caribbean can be found in Chapters 16, 17, 20, and 22.

American Antecedents: The Native Peoples

It was with such established patterns and precedents of conquest and colonization that the Spanish colonizers arrived in the Caribbean in the late fifteenth century, and came to Florida in the mid-sixteenth century. Obviously the precedents developed in Europe and Africa were modified in the Americas in response to the peoples of the Americas and their unique social, ecological, and geographical circumstances. These are briefly considered here to provide a context in which to consider the consequences of colonization in these regions.

It is believed that in 1492 the Caribbean islands were occupied by at least three cultural and linguistic groups: the Taino, the Guanahatabey (also known as Ciboney), and the Island Carib (Figure 15-1). The Taino occupied the Greater Antilles, which were the site of the earliest, most intense, and most sustained interaction between Spaniards and American Indians in the region. For that reason the Greater Antilles and the Taino serve as the focus for this discussion. However, the reader may pursue information about other groups at the time of contact in the sources cited for the Guanahatabey-Ciboney (Keegan 1989; Rouse 1948b, 1986a; Tabio and Rey 1979) and for the Island Carib (Allaire 1977; Boomert 1984; Davis and Goodwin 1988; Haviser 1987; Rouse 1948c).

The Taino were the first Caribbean people to encounter Europeans, and they sustained the most direct and most intense interaction with them during the contact period. Ethnographic data relevant to the Taino can be found in a number of primary accounts (Benzoni 1857; Casas 1951; Bourne 1907; F. Columbus in Keen 1959; Gil and Varela 1984; Martyr D'Anghiera 1970; Oviedo y Valdés 1950, 1959; Varela 1982), as well as in a number of synthetic and secondary sources (Alegria 1978; Deagan 1988; Cassa 1975; Gerbi 1985; Loven 1935; Rouse 1948a; Sturtevant 1961; Wilson 1989). The discussion of Taino ethnography below is derived from these and other cited sources, and because it is necessarily brief owing to space restraints, the reader is encouraged to consult these sources for more complete coverage. An overview of the archaeological research pertinent to the Taino and Caribbean at the time of contact can be found in Deagan (1988).

Taino cultural traits included large village sites (up to 200,000 m^2 in a wide variety of environmental settings), village spatial organization around plazas or ballcourts, manioc-based farming (Sturtevant 1961), hereditary chiefdoms (Alcina Franch 1983; Cassa 1975; Dreyfus 1981; Wilson 1989), Ostionoid ceramic traditions (Rouse 1986b:297), and the development of an elaborate artistic-ritual tradition (Deive 1983; García-Arevalo 1979; Rouse 1986a:114–115). This last tradition was centered around the worship of *zemis* or images representing spirits.

Taino horticulture was based on manioc cultivation. Maize, beans, peanuts, and other minor crops were also grown (Sturtevant 1961). Farming was balanced with a very diversified pattern of marine species exploitation (Wing 1983; Wing and Reitz 1982; Wing and Scudder 1983) that provided an appropriate protein balance for the starch-based horticultural yield. Cotton was also cultivated and was a significant trade item (Rose 1986). The Taino appear from ethnohistorical sources to have been an example of a complex chiefdom society, such as those discussed by Wright (1984:68–69).

Such groups are characterized by strongly differentiated chiefs with centralized powers, ranked social groups, interregional trade, some specialization in economic activities, high population densities, and intensive food production resulting in surplus. The Taino may also have had an incipient system of social class stratification (Wilson 1989). They were among the most densely settled prestate, sedentary societies in the New World, and apparently sustained one of the most strongly differentiated chiefly positions in the Americas, both symbolically and socially (Rouse 1948a; Wilson 1989).

Population estimates for the Taino have varied considerably, ranging from the 100,000 suggested by Rosenblatt (1954), to the higher estimates of 3 million by las Casas (1951:v.2:ch.1) and 6 to 8 million proposed by Cook and Borah (1971) (see also Henige 1978; Moya-Pons 1982). Archaeological data suggest that on Hispaniola, at least, one of the higher figures may have been more accurate, given the site densities encountered in the very few areas of the island that have been surveyed (Rainey 1941:5; Rouse and Moore 1984; Veloz-Maggiolo and Ortega 1980).

The Indians of peninsular Florida, like those of the Caribbean, included several diverse identifiable cultural groups ranging from complex subtropical chiefdoms such as the Timucua (Deagan 1978, 1985a; Milanich 1978) to band-level foragers such as the Ais, Jororo, and Tequesta (Fairbanks 1974; Milanich and Fairbanks 1980).

The Calusa, a powerful chiefdom based largely on foraging and the extraction of tribute, lived in southwest Florida, and apparently interacted with Caribbean groups during the early historic period (see Goggin and Sturtevant 1964; Marquardt 1988; Widmer 1987). Archaeological efforts to document interaction and exchange between the Indians of Florida and the Caribbean have been provocative but, to date, unsuccessful (Bullen 1964; Keegan 1987; Marquardt 1988; Sturtevant 1970).

The native peoples of La Florida who sustained the earliest and most regular interactions with Spanish colonists were the Timucua tribes of northeast Florida and southeast Georgia. The Guale peoples of the Georgia and South Carolina coastal areas were also brought into the sphere of Spanish colonial dominion through the impact of the short-lived colony of Santa Elena (discussed below).

The Timucua and Guale Indians in the areas of initial Spanish colonization in Georgia are known primarily through the casual ethnographic accounts of the early French and Spanish explorers, colonists, and priests, as well as through the excavation of burial mounds (see Deagan 1978; Milanich 1978; Vernon 1983). As is the case among the Taino, very few village sites of the contact period have been systematically excavated. Ethnographic information relevant to the Timucuan and Guale peoples can be found in the overview prepared by Thomas (this volume).

Fitzhugh (1985:271) has characterized the Indians of La Florida as existing in a fragile and unstable interaction environment. This environment, for the former groups, was not only poor in terms of agricultural potential, but also subject to border vulnerability through the absence of significant environmental barriers. Furthermore, there were no regionally integrating political or military institutions, and the resulting fragmented region and delicate environmental balance probably left the inhabitants vulnerable to demographic instability and therefore to external pressures.

A similar environmental vulnerability was characteristic of the Taino as well. Their adaptation to an island environment, although richer in agricultural potential than coastal La Florida, provided limited possibilities for expansion (see Keegan 1985; Keegan and Diamond 1987). The dense population, the political fragmentation of the islands, and the absence of environmental barriers to European technology may have created a similarly unstable situation for the Taino. That the Taino, the Timucua, and the Guale succumbed so rapidly to the rigors of Spanish contact is perhaps a consequence of this instability.

European Arrival and Exploration

Most of the traits described for both the Taino and the Indians of La Florida seem to have disappeared quite rapidly after the arrival of Europeans. Within one year of initial contact in the Caribbean, the Spaniards implemented measures to subdue the land and its inhabitants while extracting profits from both. This enterprise began in 1493 when Columbus established the settlement of La Isabela in Hispaniola. Spanish presence was concentrated in the Caribbean until about 1517, when the focus of colonial attention shifted to mainland Central and South America (see Floyd 1973). This also corresponded to the point in time at which the human and mineral resources of the Caribbean islands were by and large depleted (Sauer 1966:198–204).

Even before Spanish radiation to Mexico and Central America, however, forays were regularly made to Florida in search of slaves and other resources. The initial Spanish presence in Florida was a direct result of circumstances in the Columbus-era Caribbean, in that the first 50 years of Spanish activity in Florida were dominated by exploratory expeditions originating in the Caribbean. The best-known of these ventures were those of Juan Ponce de León, who in 1513 claimed La Florida as a Spanish territory (see Milanich, this volume; Morison

1974; Murga Sanz 1959; Weddle 1985:38–54). Although these visits did not result in immediate colonization, they undoubtedly introduced European pathogens, and encouraged attitudes of distrust and hostility among the people of Florida. Such attitudes were also no doubt reinforced by the exploratory expeditions in 1528 of Pánfilo de Narváez, and Hernando de Soto in 1540 (see Milanich, this volume).

Africans participated—either willingly or unwillingly—in the exploratory and colonizing ventures from the first days of contact (see Landers, this volume). They came as sailors, soldiers, slaves, and settlers, and seem in all parts of the Americas to have quickly established cooperative relationships and alliances with Indians. Africans also intermarried with Spanish and mixed-blood (Indian-African-European) inhabitants of the colonies, and undoubtedly influenced Hispanic-American cultural patterns in ways that we cannot yet recognize.

Spanish Florida in the early contact period included not only present-day Florida, but also the territory north to Virginia and west to the Mississippi. Other than the early exploratory expeditions and sporadic slave raids along the coast, Spanish colonization activity in La Florida was concentrated primarily in the northern, subtropical regions of the peninsula, where agricultural productivity and population densities were greatest (see Milanich, this volume). A short-lived, but nevertheless important colonization effort also took place between 1566 and 1587 at Santa Elena, South Carolina.

The following discussion concentrates on the events and consequences of colonization in those areas where Spanish colonies were successfully established, and does not consider either the initial explorations or the subsequent missions, which, although properly considered as part of the entire spectrum of colonization strategy, are treated elsewhere (see Milanich, Thomas, this volume).

The First Colonies

The earliest site of intentional Spanish settlement in the Americas was at La Isabela, located near present-day Puerto Plata on the north coast of the Dominican Republic (Figure 15-1; Cruxent, this volume; Palm 1945; Varela 1982, 1987). Columbus established La Isabela on his second voyage. He had with him 17 ships and 1,200 men of a variety of social classes and occupations, as well as the range of items and accessories believed necessary to establish a colony (Taviani 1984:2:158–160; Varela 1982, 1987).

It was at La Isabela that European plants, animals, diseases, and cultural institutions were introduced to the New World on a large scale and in a regular manner, and because of this, Isabela has received considerable, if sporadic, archaeological attention. It is currently being studied by Jose F. M. Cruxent with the Office of National Parks of the Dominican Republic (this volume), and the University of Florida under the direction of Kathleen Deagan.

In 1496 a fortress and settlement were established inland from La Isabela to subdue the island's interior, and was named Concepción de la Vega. Archaeological work has been under way at the site intermittently since the 1950s (Goggin 1968:24; Gonzales 1980; Ortega and Fondeur 1978a; Poladura 1980).

Shortly after the founding of Concepción de la Vega and the failure of La Isabela, the first permanent European capital in the New World was established at Santo Domingo in 1497 (Moya-Pons 1971; Varela 1987). Santo Domingo is today a densely populated major urban center, which still contains significant remains of the initial period of occupation. A major research, restoration, and exhibition program has been under way in Santo Domingo for several decades (Council 1975; García-Arevalo 1978; Ortega 1971, 1982; Ortega and Cruxent 1976; Ortega and Fondeur 1978b). Taken as a whole, this research provides an important descriptive resource for the study of the roots of Hispanic-American cultural development in the Caribbean.

By 1503, Santo Domingo was firmly established as the administrative seat of Spanish presence in the Caribbean, and in that year a series of 13 outlying communities was founded throughout Hispaniola in order to subdue the island and its resources (Floyd 1973:62–4; Moya-Pons 1971; Figure 15-1). One of these was the town of Puerto Real, which was occupied between 1503 and 1578 (Hodges 1980; Lyon 1981), and is among the most extensively excavated sites of early European occupation in the Caribbean. The discussion of Puerto Real by Charles Ewen (this volume) illustrates some of the issues addressed by the 10-year-long archaeological program carried out there by the Universtiy of Florida, such as the processes of Euro-American social formation.

Shortly after Puerto Real and the other Hispaniola towns were established, the second wave of Spanish colonization began to occur. The Spaniards radiated from Hispaniola to take over and occupy other parts of the Caribbean. The settlement of Puerto Rico was begun in 1508 and Jamaica in 1509, and in 1511 the conquest of Cuba was begun. Archaeological research of varying intensity has taken place at all of these locations (see Deagan 1988).

Colonial Expansion to Florida

These first sites of Spanish Caribbean occupation were all initially intended to be not only bases from which to control and exploit the Antilles, but also permanent colonies, and most have persisted to the present day. After early expectations were disappointed or modified, however, the mainlands of North, Central, and South America became the focus of colonization efforts. As the Spaniards expanded their areas of colonization, they carried with them a modified version of the attitudes and organization of their first colonial venture, shaped by failures and successes in the Caribbean.

Ponce de León reached and claimed La Florida in 1513, although it was not permanently settled until St. Augustine was founded in 1565 (Deagan 1985b; Lyon 1976). Between the arrival of Ponce de León and the founding of St. Augustine, a number of unsuccessful attempts were made to explore and colonize Florida (summarized by Milanich, this volume; Sauer 1971:32–46, 157–195; Weddle 1985:183–284). Three of these were formal colonization efforts—by Vásquez de Allyón in 1526 near Sapelo Sound (Hoffman 1984), Tristán de Luna at Pensacola in 1559–1561 (Weddle 1985:265–281), and René de Laudonnière at Ft. Caroline near Jacksonville, Florida, in 1562 (Ribault 1964). The French attempts to colonize Florida were the direct cause of the first successful colonial effort in the southeastern United States, by Pedro Menéndez de Avilés at St. Augustine.

The first two colonies were established in St. Augustine (1565) and Santa Elena (1566), which was located near present-day Parris Island, South Carolina. Eugene Lyon's discussion of the organization and precedents of these ventures (this volume) provides a context and framework for the archaeological work in the colonies reported by Deagan (this volume, 1985b), Scarry and Reitz (this volume, Reitz and Scarry 1985), and South (this volume, 1988).

An overriding feature of the Spanish colonies in the Southeastern United States was the failure of the colonists to locate, identify, or exploit valuable resources. This discouraged growth or self-sufficiency in the colonies and kept them poor, isolated, and essentially military outposts. St. Augustine also served as a headquarters and anchor for the Spanish mission system in La Florida, and the conversion of souls figured prominently in the rationale for the colony.

The inability to subdue the Guale Indians and their allies in South Carolina led the Spanish to abandon Santa Elena in 1587, so that St. Augustine remained the only Spanish town in the region until the establishment of Santa Rosa Pensacola in 1720 (see Smith 1965).

St. Augustine was therefore the primary locus of Hispanic-American culture in the southeastern United States for more than two centuries, as well as the site of the most intensive Spanish–Indian–African interaction. It is here, as at Puerto Real, that the consequences of the encounter between the Old World and the Americans can be best seen, beginning with the European adjustments and adaptation that led to the Euro-American cultural tradition. Questions and insights related to these issues in St. Augustine are discussed by Lyon, Scarry and Reitz, and Landers and Deagan (this volume).

American Consequences

Caribbean colonization had been a period of initial encounter, adaptation, and modification of precedent patterns by Spaniards, American Indians, and Africans alike. It had frequently had tragic consequences, particularly from a demographic perspective (Crosby 1986:196; Dobyns 1983; Sauer 1966). These consequences were related in large part to the transmission of alien pathogens into a densely populated and relatively disease-free region that lacked empty hinterland (for a summary and references, see Deagan 1988, 1985a; Dobyns 1983; Henige 1978). The ecological consequences of new plant and animal introductions to unstable and delicate island ecological systems had equally dramatic effects within several decades of contact (Crosby 1986; Sauer 1966).

The consequences were also tragic from certain social perspectives. Uninformed decisions about the structure of contact and interaction with Caribbean Indians exacerbated the rate of disease-induced depopulation. Although this experience influenced Spanish policy in the decades following initial colonization, it did not prevent severe depletion of both human and natural resources in either the Caribbean or other parts of the Spanish Americas.

Archaeological research in the Caribbean has provided concrete illustration of this depletion process, at such sites as the pearl-fishing center of Nueva Cadiz on Cubagua Island off the coast of Venezuela. This site represents quite a different type of early Spanish settlement from those noted above, in that the pearl harvesting carried on there was a single-resource, extractive venture. This was also one of the earliest Spanish contact sites in the Caribbean to be archaeologically investigated (Boulton 1952; Cruxent and Rouse 1958; Goggin 1968:24; Rouse and Cruxent 1963; Willis 1976, 1982).

The town of Nueva Cadiz was established in 1515, and its desert location forced the Spaniards to depend entirely upon imports for everything from food and water to labor. At its peak the colony was occupied by about 300 Spaniards and 1,200 Indian and African slaves. A relatively European way of life was sustained by the Spaniards at Nueva Cadiz, with few apparent adjustments made to the local environment. This was achieved almost completely through the overexploitation of natural and human resources. This pattern persisted until about 1540, when the pearl beds were depleted, the Indian labor force annihilated, and the settlement abandoned.

Archaeology of Resource Depletion: Colono-ware Ceramics

The depletion of human resources has also been documented in the archaeological record. Results of chronological analysis of ceramic remains from sixteenth-century Puerto Real in Haiti apparently reflect the decline and replacement of native Amerindian potters and laborers by what are probably African potters and laborers. Through time at the Spanish town, it can be seen that the indigenous Taino ceramic wares disappear and are replaced by a new, simplified, and comparatively crude locally made pottery that was probably produced by the African laborers who are known to have replaced the American laborers at the site after about 1520 (Smith 1986).

Similar responses can be detected in the ceramic record of other Spanish sites where the forced consolidation of diverse, non-European peoples took place—either for labor or conversion purposes. The process of consolidating native peoples of many different origins into Spanish centers is reflected widely in Caribbean contact period sites of slavery by the presence of a new, crude, and very simplified ceramic tradition, similar to that identified by Smith at Puerto Real as possibly African in influence. These ceramic wares are locally made, and distinct from known pre-Hispanic wares. They sometimes exhibit European formal influence, and suggest both the breakdown of traditional craft and cultural transmission traditions, and the recombination of traits from distinct African and Amerindian ceramic traditions (see Deagan 1988b; Dominguez 1984; García-Arevalo 1978; Ortega and Fondeur 1978b; Smith 1986; Willis 1976).

These wares have a certain functional similarity to those known as "Mission wares," or "colono-wares," that are found throughout the North American Spanish Borderlands (see Boyd et al. 1951; Costello 1985:31–32; Deagan 1983; Otto and Lewis 1974; Smith 1948; Snow 1984). These colono-wares characteristically exhibit European formal elements in tableware forms; however, they are usually found in mission sites rather than town sites. For the most part, native peoples in such frontier and mission sites interacted regularly only with male members of religious orders, who were overtly involved in "civilizing" and directed change activities.

Intermarriage, Integration, and the Emergence of Euro-American Society

The non-European "contact period ceramics" found at Spanish sites throughout the Caribbean and in two sites in Florida are different from the colono-wares in that they occur in sites where native and African peoples were forcibly consolidated, they only occasionally incorporate aboriginal forms, and they are found in Spanish household contexts. The significance of this to our understanding of colonization is twofold: First, it shows that in Spanish town contexts, and in the daily life of Spanish households, non-European wares were regularly incorporated on a large scale. This has implications for the hybridization of Spanish and American elements into a Hispanic-American tradition through consistent incorporation of native traits by Spaniards. This facet of colonization is almost completely undocumented in the Anglo-American colonies.

It has been postulated that this pattern of integration was largely a consequence of the widespread practice of intermarriage among Spaniards, Indians, and Africans in the Spanish colonies, and of the influential role of women in cultural transmission in the home (see Deagan 1973, 1983; Morner 1967). This theme is treated also in Ewen (this volume) and Deagan (this volume).

The second significant aspect of this pattern lies in its insights into native responses to contact: Depopulation, reconsolidation, and movement are clearly reflected in the ceramic traditions of Amerindians. For whatever reason, and there are many to be postulated, new ceramic patterns appear throughout the Caribbean and the region of La Florida shortly after contact (e.g., see Smith 1948). Interestingly, these patterns do not include the incorporation of European traits as a frequent and consistent element (although some does, of course, occur).

Rather, one can see in the "slave wares" of the Caribbean—and in the early historic period Amerindian ceramic traditions of the Southeastern United States—a recombination of non-European traits, be they Indian or African, to produce a distinctly new and non-European tradition. This occurs primarily in Spanish town sites, or in Indian sites associated with Spanish towns. This suggested pattern adds another perspective to the process of Native American acculturation during the contact period, in that a certain amount of observed change may well have been a consequence of acculturation to other non-European Indian and American peoples rather than primarily to the Spaniards (see Deagan, this volume).

Certain other kinds of native accommodation to Spanish culture can be seen clearly in the archaeological record, such as the accommodation of Catholic religious precepts by Indians (and Spaniards) in the mission burial grounds. However, even here Spanish accommodation occurred as well (Marrinan 1985; Milanich and Saunders 1987; Thomas 1988, this volume).

Instead of showing the response of American Indians to contact with Spaniards, archaeological research in the Spanish colonies of both the Caribbean and of Florida has shown a consistent incorporation of Native American elements in the lives of the Spanish colonists, most often in nonsocially visible areas, accompanied by a careful preservation of Spanish identification in visible areas (Deagan 1985a, 1983; Dominguez 1984; Ewen 1987, this volume; Ezell and Ezell 1982; South 1985, 1988). This is at least partly a function of the widespread incorporation of Indian and African women into Spanish households throughout the Americas through intermarriage, concubinage, and servitude. The archaeological record of the earliest Spanish colonies—perhaps even more than the documentary record—has revealed an adaptation to difficult circumstances by both Spaniards and Native Americans based on adherence to a highly structured set of preexisting precepts, but implemented simultaneously with a considerable degree of flexibility and accommodation to local, indigenous conditions.

Initial Spanish colonization in the Americas borderlands represents both an extension of Spanish imperial patterns dating to the Spanish reconquista and alterations to these patterns in response to regional social and environmental differences. Historical archaeology has made indispensable contributions to the investigation of the origins and evolution of Spanish settlement strategies in North America, as well as to the understanding of the formation of Native American responses to these strategies. Ultimately, these contributions should lead us to a clearer understanding of the formation of the Euro-Afro-American tradition that created the New World.

Chronology: Important Dates and Events in the Colonization of Florida and the Caribbean

1492	The fall of Granada and the Moorish empire to Ferdinand and Isabella. Spain is reconquered from the Moors.
October 1492	Columbus completes his first voyage; encounters the Americas.
December 1492	La Navidad, first European settlement in the Americas, is established on the north coast of Haiti by the crew of the sunken *Santa Maria*.
January 1494	Columbus establishes the colony of La Isabela on the north coast of Hispaniola during his second voyage.
1496	Santo Domingo established as capital and headquarters of the Spanish Caribbean. The colony of Isabela declines.
1498	Encomienda first implemented in Hispaniola.
1502–1504	Spanish settlements established throughout Hispaniola, including Puerto Real.
1508	Puerto Rico colonized.
1509	Jamaica colonized, then Panama.
1511	Colonization of Cuba begun.
1513	Florida claimed for Spain by Juan Ponce de León.
ca. 1520	Native Caribbean population greatly depleted; large-scale importation of African labor begins.
1521	Conquest of Mexico by Cortez; emigration of Spaniards from the Caribbean to the mainland begins.

1526	Vásquez de Allyón's unsuccessful attempt to establish San Miguel de Gualdape near Sapelo Sound, Georgia.
1527–1536	Pánfilo de Narváez expedition through Florida and the Gulf coast.
1539–1540	Hernando de Soto expedition through Florida and the Southeast.
1559–1561	Tristán de Luna's unsuccessful attempt to establish a colony at Pensacola.
1565	French colony and inhabitants eliminated by Pedro Menéndez de Avilés.
1565	St. Augustine established.
1566	Santa Elena established near present-day Parris Island, South Carolina.
1566	Jesuit missions in La Florida.
1570–1571	Santa Elena abandoned.
1573	Royal ordinances for town planning formally adopted.
1571	Santa Elena reestablished.
1574	Franciscan missions established in La Florida.
1578	Santa Elena permanently abandoned.
1675	Construction of present Castillo de San Marcos.
1698	Establishment of Pensacola.
1702–1704	Raids of James Moore in Florida; end of the mission chain.
1739	War of Jenkins Ear.
1763	Florida ceded to England by the Treaty of Paris; Spanish, African, and Indian residents leave.

References

Alcina-Franch, J.
   1983   El chamanisimo taìno. In *La cultura Taína: Seminario sobre la situacion de investigacion de la cultura*, pp. 69–80. Biblioteca del v Centenario, Madrid.
Alegria, Ricardo
   1963   *Descubrimiento, conquista, y colonización de Puerto Rico, 1493–1599*. Colección de Estudios Puertorriquenos. San Juan de Puerto Rico, Barcelona.
   1978   *Las primeras representaciones graficas del Indio Americano 1492–1523*. Centro de Estudios Aronzodos, San Juan.
Allaire, Louis
   1977   *Later Prehistory in Martinique and the Island Caribs*. Ph.D. dissertation, Yale University, New Haven.
Armstrong, Douglas
   1989   *The Old Village at Drax Hall Plantation: An Archaeological Study of Afro-Jamaican Settlement*. University of Illinois Press, Urbana.
Arrom, Juan J., and Manuel García-Arevalo
   1986   *Cimarron*. Ediciones Fundación García-Arevalo. Santo Domingo.
Bennett, Charles (editor)
   1975   *Settlements of Florida*. University Press of Florida, Gainesville.
Benzoni, G.
   1857   History of the New World (1725). In The Hacklyut Society Publication No. 21, edited by W. H. Smythe, London.
Bolton, Herbert E.
   1917   The Mission as a Frontier Institution in the Spanish-American Colonies. *American Historical Review* 23:42–61.

Boomert, Arie
   1984   The Arawak Indians of Trinidad and Coastal Guiana, 1500–1680. *Journal of Caribbean History* 19(2):123–88.
Boulton, Alfredo
   1952   *La Margarita*. Caracas.
Bourne, E.
   1907   Columbus, Ramon Pané and the Beginning of American Anthropology. *Proceedings of the American Antiquarian Society* 17:310–348.
Boyd, Mark F., Hale G. Smith, and John W. Griffin
   1951   *Here They Once Stood: The Tragic End of the Apalachee Missions*. University of Florida Presses, Gainesville.
Bullen, Ripley
   1964   *The Archaeology of Grenada, West Indies*. Contributions in Anthropology and History No. 11. Florida State Museum, Gainesville.
Canzo, Gonzalo Mendez de (Governor of Florida)
   1598   Manuscript, AGI 54-5-9 [Letter to the Spanish Crown, February 24, 1598.] Microfilm copy, Lowery Collection, University of Florida.
   1600   Manuscript, AGI 54-5-9 [Letter to the Spanish Crown, January 12, 1600.] Microfilm copy, Lowery Collection, University of Florida.
Casas, Bartolome de las
   1951   *Historia de las Indias*. Edición de Agustín Millares Carlo. 3 vols. Fondo de Cultura Economica, Mexico City.
Cassa, Roberto
   1975   *Los Taínos de la Española*. Universidad Autonoma de Santo Domingo, Santo Domingo.
Chapeaux, Pedro Deschamps
   1983   *Los Cimarrones Urbanos*. Editorial de Ciencias Sociales, Havana.
Cook, S., and W. Borah
   1971   *Essays in Population History. Vol. 1. Mexico and The Caribbean*. University of California Press, Berkeley.
Costello, Julia
   1985   Ceramics. In *Excavations at Mission San Antonio, 1976–1978*, edited by Robert Hoover and Julia Costello. Monographs of the Institute of Archaeology No. 26. University of California, Los Angeles.
Council, R. Bruce
   1975   *Archeology of the Convento de San Francisco*. Unpublished Master's thesis, Department of Anthropology, University of Florida, Gainesville.
Crahan, Margaret, and Franklin Knight (editors)
   1979   *African and the Caribbean: The Legacies of a Link*. John Hopkins University, Baltimore, Maryland.
Crosby, Alfred
   1986   *Ecological Imperialism. The Biological Expansion of Europe, 900–1900*. Cambridge University Press, Cambridge.
Crouch, Dora P., Daniel J. Garr, and Axel I. Mundigo
   1982   *Spanish City Planning in North America*. MIT Press, Cambridge, Massachusetts.
Cruxent, J. M., and Irving Rouse
   1958   *An Archeological Chronology of Venezuela*. 2 vols. Pan American Union Social Science Monographs No. 6. Washington, D.C.
Davis, Dave, and Christopher Goodwin
   1988   Island Carib Origins: Evidence and Non-evidence. *American Antiquity* 54.
Deagan, Kathleen
   1973   Mestizaje in Colonial St. Augustine. *Ethnohistory* 20:55–65.
   1978   Cultures in Transition: Fusion and Assimilation among the Eastern Timucua. In *Tacachale: Essays on the Indians of Florida and Southeastern Georgia during the Historic Pe-*

riod, edited by Jerald Milanich and Samuel Proctor, pp. 89–119. University Presses of Florida, Gainesville.

1983 *Spanish St. Augustine: The Archaeology of a Colonial Creole Community.* Academic Press, New York.

1985a The Archeology of 16th century St. Augustine. *Florida Anthropologist* 38 (1-2):6–33.

1985b Spanish-Indian Interaction in Sixteenth Century Florida and the Caribbean. In *Cultures in Contact*, edited by W. Fitzhugh, pp. 281–318. Smithsonian Institution Press, Washington, D.C.

1988 The Archaeology of the Spanish Contact Period in the Caribbean. *Journal of World Prehistory* 2(2):187–233.

Deive, Carlos Esteban

1978 *El Indio, el Negro y la vida tradicionál Dominicana.* Ediciones del Museo del Hombre, Santo Domingo.

1980 *La esclavitud del Negro en Santo Domingo, 1492–1844.* Ediciones del Museo del Hombre Dominicano, Santo Domingo.

Dobyns, Henry

1983 *Their Number Become Thinned: Native American Population Dynamics in Eastern North America.* University of Tennessee Press, Knoxville.

Dobyns, Henry (editor)

1982 *Spanish Colonial Frontier Research.* Spanish Borderlands Research Series No. 1. Center for Anthropological Studies, Albuquerque.

Dominguez, Lourdes

1984 *Arqueologia colonial cubana. Dos estudios.* Editorial de ciencias sociales, Havana.

Dozier, Edward P.

1970 *The Pueblo Indians of North America.* Case studies in Anthropology, edited by G. and L. Spindler. Holt, Rinehart, and Winston, New York.

Dreyfus, Simone

1981 Notes sur la chefferie Taino D'Aiti: Capaces productrices, ressources alimentaires, pouvoir dans une societe procolombienne de foret tropicale. *Journal de la Société des Americanistes* 67:229–248.

Dyson, Stephen

1982 *Comparative Studies in the Archaeology of Colonialism.* B.A.R. International Series No. 233. Oxford, England.

Elliott, John H.

1987 The Spanish Conquest. In *Colonial Spanish America*, edited by L. Bethell, pp. 1–58. Cambridge University Press, Cambridge.

Ewen, Charles

1987 From Spaniard to Creole: the Archaeology of Hispanic American Cultural Formation at Puerto Real, Haiti. Unpublished Ph. D. dissertation, Department of Anthropology, University of Florida.

Ezell, Paul, and Greta Ezell

1982 Bread and Barbeques at San Diego Presidio. In *Spanish Colonial Frontier Research*, edited by H. Dobyns. Spanish Borderlands Research Series No. 1. Center for Anthropological Studies, Albuquerque.

Fairbanks, Charles H.

1974 *Ethnohistorical Report on the Florida Indians.* Commission Findings, Indians Claims Commission. Garland, New York.

1985 From Exploration to Settlement: Spanish Strategies for Colonization. In *Alabama and the Borderlands: From Prehistory to Statehood*, edited by R. Reid Badger and Lawrence A. Clayton, pp. 128–139. University of Alabama Press, University.

Farnsworth, Paul

1986 Spanish California: The Final Frontier. *Journal of New World Archaeology* 6(4):34–46.

Feinman, Gary, and Jill Neitzel
1984 Too Many Types: An Overview of Sedentary Pre-state Societies in the Americas. In *Advances in Archeological Method and Theory*, Vol. 7, edited by M. Schiffer, pp. 39–42. Academic Press, New York.

Fitzhugh, William
1985 *Cultures in Contact. The European Impact on Native Cultural Institutions in Eastern North America*. Anthropological Society of Washington Special Publication. Smithsonian Institution Press, Washington D.C.

Floyd, Troy
1973 *The Columbus Dynasty in the Caribbean 1492–1526*. University of New Mexico Press, Albuquerque.

Foster, George
1960 *Culture and Conquest*. Viking Fund Publications in Anthropology No. 27. Wenner-Gren Foundation, New York.

García-Arevalo, Manuel
1978 La arqueologia Indo-Hispano en Santo Domingo. In *Unidades y variedads: ensayos en homenaje al Jose M. Cruxent*, pp. 77–127. Centro de Estudios Avanzados, Caracas.

Gerbi, A.
1985 *Nature in The New World*. University of Pittsburgh Press, Pittsburgh.

Gibson, Charles
1987 Indian Society under Spanish Rule. In *Colonial Spanish America*, edited by L. Bethell, pp. 361–399. Cambridge University Press, Cambridge.

Gil, Juan, and Consuela Varela
1984 *Cartas de particulares a Colón y relaciones coetaneas*. Alainza editorial, Madrid.

Goggin, John
1968 *Spanish Majolica in the New World*. Yale University Publications in Anthropology No. 72. Yale University Press, New Haven.

Goggin, John M., and William C. Sturtevant
1964 The Calusa: A Stratified Non-agricultural Society (with Notes on Sibling Marriage). In *Explorations in Cultural Anthropology: Essays in Honor of George Peter Murdock*, edited by W. Goodenough, pp. 179–219. McGraw-Hill, New York.

Gonzales, Jose
1980 Conferencia del Arq. José Gonzales. In *Objectos y ambientes de la Concepción de la Vega*, A. Poladora, coordinador, pp. 34–50. Catálogo de la exposición. Museo Casas Reales, Santo Domingo.

Hanke, Lewis
1964 *The First Social Experiments in America*. Peter Smith, Gloucester, Mass.

Hann, John
1988 *Apalachee: Land between Two Rivers*. Ripley P. Bullen Monographs in Anthropology. University Presses of Florida, Gainesville.

Haviser, Jay
1987 *Amerindian Cultural Geography on Curaçao*. Unpublished Ph.D. dissertation, Rijksuniversiteit Leiden, Holland. Privately printed, Emmastad, Curaçao.

Henige, David
1978 On the Contact Population of Hispaniola: History as Higher Mathematics. *Hispanic America Historical Review* 58(2):219–237.

Hodges, William
1980 Puerto Real Sources. Typescript. Musée de Guahaba, Limbé, Haiti.

Hoffman, Paul
1984 *The Spanish Crown and the Defense of the Caribbean 1535–1585*. Louisiana State University Press, Baton Rouge.

Hoover, Robert L., and Julia Costello (editors)
1985 *Excavations at Mission San Antonio, 1976–1978*. Monographs of the Institute of Archaeology No. 26. University of California, Los Angeles.

Hudson, Charles
   1987   An Unknown South: Spanish Explorers and Southeastern Chiefdoms. In *Visions and Revisions, Ethnohistoric Perspectives on Southern Cultures*, edited by George Sabo III and William M. Schneider, pp. 6–24. Southern Anthropological Proceedings No. 20. University of Georgia Press, Athens.
Hussey, Raymond
   1932   Text of the Laws of Burgos Concerning the Treatment of the Indians. *Hispanic American Historical Review* 12:301–326.
Jones, Oakah
   1979   *Los Paisanos; Spanish Settlers on the Northern Frontier of New Spain*. University of Oklahoma Press, Norman.
Keegan, William
   1985   *Dynamic Horticulturalists: Population Expansion in the Prehistoric Bahamas*. Unpublished Ph.D. dissertation, University of California, Los Angeles. University Microfilms, Ann Arbor.
   1987   Diffusion of Maize from South America: The Antillean Connection Reconstructed. *Emergent horticultural*
   1989   Creating the Guanahatabey (Ciboney): The Modern Genesis of an Extinct Culture. *Antiquity* 63(239):373–380.
Keegan, William, and Jared Diamond
   1987   Colonization of Islands by Humans: A Biogeographical Perspective. In *Advances in Archaeological Method and Theory*, edited by M. Schiffer, Vol. 10:49–91. Academic Press, New York.
Keen, Benjamin (translator)
   1959   *The Life of The Admiral Christopher Columbus by his Son, Ferdinand*. Rutgers, New Brunswick, New Jersey.
Kieth, Robert
   1971   Encomienda, Hacienda and Corregimiento in Spanish America. *Hispanic-American Historical Review.* 51:431–466.
Landers, Jane
   1988   *Black Society in Spanish St. Augustine, 1784–1821*. Unpublished Ph.D. dissertation, Department of History, University of Florida, Gainesville.
Leone, Mark P.
   1977   Foreword to *Research Strategies in Historical Archaeology*, edited by S. South. Academic Press, New York.
Lockhart, James, and Stuart B. Schwartz
   1983   *Early Latin America*. Cambridge Latin American Studies No. 46. Cambridge University Press, Cambridge.
Loven, Sven
   1935   *The Origins of Tainan Culture, West Indies*. Flanders, Göteburg.
Lyon, Eugene
   1976   *The Enterprise of Florida*. University Presses of Florida, Gainesville.
   1981   Puerto Real: Research on a Spanish Town on Hispaniola's North Coast. Project historian report on file. Florida State Museum, University of Florida, Gainesville.
Marquardt, William H. (editor)
   1988   *Culture and Environment in the Domain of the Calusa. Report of Interdisciplinary Investigations in Southwest Florida, 1984–1987*. University of Florida, Institute of Archaeology and Paleoenvironmental Studies, Monograph No. 1. Gainesville.
Marrinan, Rochelle
   1985   The Archaeology of the Spanish Missions of Florida: 1565–1704. In *Indians, Colonists, and Slaves*, edited by K. Johnson, J. Leader, and R. Wilson, pp. 241–252. Florida Journal of Anthropology Special Publication No. 4. Gainesville.
Martyr D'Anghiera, Peter
   1970   *De Orbe Novo*, translated by F. A. MacNutt. 2 vols. Burt Franklin, New York.

McAlister, Lyle N.
 1984   *Spain and Portugal in the New World, 1492–1700.* University of Minnesota Press, Minneapolis.
Milanich, Jerald T.
 1978   The Western Timucua: Patterns of Acculturation and Change. In *Tacachale: Essays on the Indians of Florida and Southeastern Georgia during the Historic Period*, edited by Jerald Milanich and Samuel Proctor, pp. 59–88. University Presses of Florida, Gainesville.
 1987   Corn and Calusa, De Soto and Demography. In *Coasts, Plain, and Deserts: Essays in Honor of Reynold J. Ruppe*, edited by S. W. Gaines, pp. 173–184. Anthropological Research Papers No. 38. Arizona State University, Tempe.
Milanich, Jerald T., and Charles H. Fairbanks
 1980   *Florida Archaeology.* Academic Press, New York.
Milanich, Jerald T., and Rebecca Saunders
 1987   Investigation of the 1686–1702 Mission/Castillo of Santa Maria on Amelia Island. Paper presented at the Society for Historical Archaeology, Savannah, Georgia.
Mintz, Sidney
 1974   *Caribbean Transformations*, Aldine, Chicago.
Morison, Samuel E.
 1974   *The European Discovery of America: The Southern Voyages. 1492–1616.* Oxford University Press, New York.
Morner, Magnus
 1967   *Race Mixture in the History of Latin America.* Little, Brown, Boston
Moya-Pons, Frank
 1971   *La Española en el Siglo XVI.* Universidad Católica Madre y Maestra. Santiago, R.D.
 1982   Los trabajadores indígenas y la estructura social de la Española en 1514. *Museo del Hombre Dominicano Boletín* 17:119–133. Santo Domingo.
Murga Sanz, Vincente
 1959   *Juan Ponce de León.* Ediciones de la Universidad de Puerto Rico, San Juan.
Ortega, Elpidio
 1971   Informe de las excavaciones arqueológicas realizadas en la plazoleta y en la Calle Juan Baron. *Revista Dominicana de Arqueología y Antropología* 1(1):25–37.
 1982   *Arqueología colonial en Santo Domingo.* Fundación Ortego-Alvarez, Santo Domingo.
Ortega, E., and J. M. Cruxent
 1976   Informe preliminar sobre las excavaciones en las ruinas del Convento de San Francisco. *Actas del XLI Congreso Internacional de Americanistas* 3:674–689.
Ortega, Elpidio, and Carmen Fondeur
 1978a *Arqueología de los monumentos históricos de Santo Domingo.* San Pedro de Macoris, Universidad Central del Este, Dominican Republic.
 1978b *Estudio de la ceramica del periodo Indo-Hispano de la Antigua Concepción de la Vega.* Fundación Ortega Alvarez. Serie Cientifica 1. Santo Domingo.
Otto, John, and Russell Lewis
 1975   A Formal and Functional Analysis of San Marcos Pottery from Site SA-16-23, St. Augustine. Florida Department of State, Bureau of Historic Sites and Properties Bulletin No. 4. Tallahassee.
Oviedo, y Valdes, Gonzalo Fernando de
 1950   *Sumario: Historia general y natural de las Indias.* Fondo de la Cultura Economica. Mexico.
 1959   *Historia generál y naturál de las Indias.* Biblioteca de Autores Españoles, Madrid.
Pagden, Anthony
 1982   *The Fall of Natural Man: The American Indian and the Origins of Comparative Ethnology.* Cambridge University Press, Cambridge.

Palm, Erwin
   1945   Excavations at La Isabela, White Man's First Town in the Americas. *Acta Ameri-cana* 3:298–303.
Poladura, Atala de (coordinator)
   1980   *Objetos y ambientes de la Concepción de la Vega.* Exposición catálogo. Museo Casas Reales, Santo Domingo.
Price, Richard
   1973   *Maroon Societies—Rebel Slave Communities in the Americas.* John Hopkins University Press, Baltimore, Maryland.
Proctor Samuel, and Jerald Milanich (editors)
   1978   *Tacachale: Essays on the Indians of Florida and Southeastern Georgia during the Historic Period.* University Presses of Florida, Gainesville.
Rainey, Froelich
   1941   *Excavations in the Ft. Liberté Region, Haiti.* Yale University Publications in Anthropology No. 23. New Haven.
Reitz, Elizabeth, and Margaret Scarry
   1985   *The Reconstruction of Historic Foodways.* Special publication of the Society for Historical Archaeology, No. 3.
Ribault, Jean
   1964   *The Whole and True Discouerie of Terra Florida.* Facsimile reprint of the 1563 London edition. University Presses of Florida, Gainesville.
Rose, Richard
   1986   Lucayan Lifeways at the Time of Columbus. *Proceedings of the First Annual San Salvador Conference: Columbus and His World*, edited by D. Gerace, pp. 321–340. San Salvador, Bahamas.
Rosenblatt, Angel
   1954   *La población de America en 1492. Viejos y nuevos calculos.* Mexico City.
Rouse, Irving
   1948a The Arawak. In *Handbook of South American Indians*, vol. 4. The Circum-Caribbean Tribes, edited by J. Steward. Bureau of American Ethnology Bulletin 143(4):507–546.
   1948b The Carib. In *Handbook of South American Indians*, vol. 4. The Circum-Caribbean Tribes, edited by J. Steward. *Bureau of American Ethnology Bulletin* 143(4):547–566.
   1948c The Ciboney. In *Handbook of South American Indians*, vol. 4. The Circum-Caribbean Tribes, edited by J. Steward. *Bureau of American Ethnology Bulletin* 143(4):497–506.
   1986a *Migrations in Prehistory.* Yale University Press, New Haven.
   1986b Origin and Development of the Indians Discovered by Columbus. In *Proceedings of the First San Salvador Conference: Columbus and His World*, edited by D. Gerace, pp. 293–312. San Salvador, Bahamas.
Rouse, Irving, and José Cruxent
   1963   *Venezuelan Archaeology.* Yale University Press, New Haven.
Rouse, Irving, and Clark Moore
   1984   Cultural Sequence in Southwestern Haiti. *Bureau National D'Ethnologie Bulletin* 1:25–38. Port-au-Prince.
Sauer, Carl O.
   1966   *The Early Spanish Main.* University of California Press, Berkeley.
   1971   *Sixteenth Century North America.* University of California Press, Berkeley.
Scardaville, Michael C.
   1985   Approaches to the Study of the Southeastern Borderlands. In *Alabama and the Borderlands: From Prehistory to Statehood*, edited by R. Reid Badger and Lawrence Clayton, pp. 184–196. University of Alabama Press, University.
Schelle, G.
   1906   *La traite negriére aux Indes de Castile.* Contratset Traites d'Assiento, Paris.

Schuyler, Robert L.
  1976   Images of America: The Contribution of Historical Archaeology to the National Identity. *Southwestern Lore* 42(4):27–39.
Simmons, Marc
  1979   History of Pueblo-Spanish Relations to 1821. In *Southwest*, edited by Alfonso Ortiz, pp. 206–223. Handbook of North American Indians, vol. 9, William C. Sturtevant, general editor. Smithsonian Institution, Washington, D.C.
Simpson, Leslie (translator and editor)
  1960   *The Laws of Burgos 1512–1513: Royal Ordinances for the Good Governance and Treatment of the Indians.* John Howell, San Francisco.
Smith, Hale G.
  1948   Two Historical Archeological Periods in Florida. *American Antiquity* 13(4):313–319.
  1965   *Santa Rosa Pensacola.* Florida State University Notes in Anthropology No. 10. Tallahassee.
Smith, Marvin
  1987   *Archaeology of Aboriginal Culture Change in the Interior Southeast.* Ripley P. Bullen Monographs in Anthropology and History No. 6. Florida State Museum, Gainesville.
Smith, Greg
  1986   A Study of Colono-ware and Non-European Ceramics from Sixteenth-century Puerto Real, Haiti. Unpublished Master's thesis, University of Florida, Gainesville.
Snow, David H.
  1984   Spanish American Pottery Manufacture in New Mexico: A Critical Review. *Ethnohistory* 31(2):93–113.
South, Stanley
  1985   Excavation of the Casa Fuerte and Wells at Ft. San Felipe 1983. Research Manuscript Series No. 190. Institute of Archeology and Anthropology, University of South Carolina, Columbia.
  1988   Santa Elena: Threshold of Conquest. In *The Recovery of Meaning*, edited by M. Leone and P. Potter, pp. 27–72. Smithsonian Institution Press, Washington, D.C.
Spicer, Edward
  1962   *Cycles of Conquest.* University of Arizona Press, Tucson.
Sturtevant, William
  1961   Taino Agriculture. In *The Evolution of Horticultural Systems in South America: Causes and Consequences—A Symposium.* Anthropological Supplement No. 2. Caracas.
  1970   The Significance of Ethnological Similarities between Southeastern North America and the Antilles. In *Papers in Caribbean Anthropology*, compiled by S.W. Mintz. Yale University, Publications in Anthropology, pp. 57–64.
Tabio, Ernesto, and Estrella Rey
  1979   *La prehistoria de Cuba.* Editorial de Ciencias Sociales, Havana.
Taviani, Emilio Paolo
  1984   *I viaggio di Colombo*, 2 vols. Instituto Geografico de Agostini Novaro, Rome.
Thomas, David Hurst
  1988   Saints and Savages at Santa Catalina: An Alternative Hispanic Design for Colonial America. In *The Recovery of Meaning in Historical Archeaology*, edited by Mark Leone and Parkson Potter, pp. 73–140. Smithsonian Institution Press, Washington D.C.
Varela, Consuela
  1982   *Cristobal Colón. Textos y docmentos completos.* Editorial Alianza, Madrid.
  1987   La Isabela: vida y ocaso de una ciudad efemera. *Revista de Indias* XVLII (181):733–744. Madrid

Veloz-Maggiolo, Marcio
  1974 Remanentes Culturales Indigenas y Africana en Santo Domingo. *Revista Dominicana de Antropología e História* 7–8:19–26. Santo Domingo.
Veloz-Maggiolo, Marcio, and Elipidio Ortega
  1980 Nuevos hallazgos arqueológicos en la costa norte de Santo Domingo. *Boletin del Museo del Hombre Dominicano* 9(13):11–48. Santo Domingo.
Vernon, Richard
  1983 Northeast Florida Prehistory: Synthesis and Regional Research Design. Unpublished Master's thesis, Florida State University, Tallahassee.
Weddle, Robert
  1985 *Spanish Sea*. Texas A&M University Press, College Station.
Widmer, Randolph J.
  1987 *The Evolution of the Calusa, a Non-agricultural Chiefdom of the Southwest Florida Coast*. University of Alabama Press, Tuscaloosa.
Williams, Maurice
  1986 Sub-surface Patterning at 16th Century Spanish Puerto Real, Haiti. *Journal of Field Archaeology* 13(3):283–296.
Willis, Raymond
  1976 *The Archeology of 16th century Nueva Cadiz*. Unpublished Master's thesis, Department of Anthropology, University of Florida.
  1982 Nueva Cadiz. In *Spanish Colonial Frontier Research*, edited by H. Dobyns, pp. 27–40. Center for Anthropological Studies, Albuquerque.
Wilson, Sam
  1989 *The Conquest of the Caribbean Chiefdoms*. University of Alabama Press, Tuscaloosa, in press.
Wing, Elizabeth
  1983 La adaptación humana a las medioambientes de las Antillas. In *La cultura Taina: Las culturas de America en la época del descubrimiento*, pp. 87–105. Biblioteca del V centenario, Madrid.
Wing, Elizabeth, and Elizabeth Reitz
  1982 Prehistoric Fishing Economies of the Caribbean. *Journal of New World Archaeology* 5(2):13–32. Los Angeles.
Wing, Elizabeth, and Sylvia Scudder
  1983 Animal Exploitation by Prehistoric Peoples Living on a Tropical Marine Edge. In *Animals and Archeology: 2. Shell Middens, Fishes and Birds*, edited by C. Grigson and J. Clutton-Brock, pp. 197–210. B.A.R. International Series No. 183. Oxford, England.
Wright, Henry
  1984 Prestate Political Formation. In *The Evolution of Complex Societies: Essays in Honor of Harry Hoijer*, edited by T. Earle, pp. 41–78. Anthropology Department, University of California, Los Angeles.
Wolf, Eric
  1959 *Sons of the Shaking Earth*. Columbia University Press, New York.
  1982 *Europe and the People without History*. University of California Press, Berkeley.

Chapter 16 ■

José Maria Cruxent

The Origin of La Isabela: First Spanish Colony in the New World

Cristopher Columbus set out on his second voyage to the New World in 1493 with the intention of establishing a permanent settlement at La Navidad (at the site known today as En Bas Saline, Haiti; see Deagan 1986). This proved to be an unfortunate decision. He found La Navidad burned and most of its 39 Spanish occupants gone, except for a few multilated corpses. Columbus had left these men there during his first voyage (see Morison 1940).

As he sailed eastward in search of another place for what would be America's first (European) settlement, Columbus bypassed several locations that looked promising. He wanted to get as far away as possible from La Navidad and to find a good harbor as close as possible to the allegedly gold-rich region of Cibao (the central plain of the Dominican Republic still known by that name today).

The coast of Hispaniola was already known to Columbus, for he had examined it closely during his first voyage. In fact, he had spent the night near the bay of Isabela, under the protection of Punta Roja (Punta Isabela) (Jane 1960:156). He navigated due east from La Navidad until he reached a bay that he at once christened La Isabela.

The expedition disembarked and gave thanks to the Almighty. As his men unloaded the ships, Columbus "ordered everything to be put on a plain" (las Casas 1987:1:363). The afflicted and tired passengers (about 1,400 persons) were undoubtedly grateful to touch land after a difficult three-month voyage.

Although there has been a great deal of speculation on the exact location of this first disembarkation, it has not yet been precisely identified. This information is essential if researchers hope to discover, identify, and interpret the first colony in America.

According to Chanca, the settlement is referred to in documents both as La Isabela and as La Ciudad Marta (Navarrete 1945:1:346). This has created some confusion concerning its identity and location. These documents indicate that 200 dwellings were constructed at La Isabela. Thus it can be regarded as the first regular town in the New World. The question is, were these dwellings built at the site commemorated as La Isabela today (known locally as Isabela el Castillo), where stone foundations dating to the fifteenth century have been identified? Or was the first settlement at a separate place altogether, known as Ciudad Marta?

Much of the confusion and apparent contradiction in the original narrative sources pertaining to the establishment of La Isabela may have been due to insufficient topographic knowledge on the part of the narrators, or perhaps simply to forgetfulness in some instances. The former seems to have been the case in the area of Rio Isabela (the Isabela River) or the Bay of Isabela. Another problem is that the chronicles were not always written in La Isabela, but were often composed in faraway lands by someone who had not even been present at the site. Furthermore, the narrators concentrated on details that they thought might have political, military, ecclesiastic, or economic value and thus overlooked some aspects of the colony that we now consider important.

When our archaeological study of La Isabela began in 1987, we were fully aware of the poor condition of the site at Isabela–El Castillo. The ruins had been neglected for many years and reached a low point at the time of the famous "cleaning" of the fields with a tractor.[1] The tractor destroyed the stratigraphy and pushed almost all the remains of the structures and their contents (potsherds, metals, etc.) into the sea. The entire area that is today encompassed by the National Park at Isabela–El Castillo (El Solar de las Americas) was cleared in this way.

This type of situation constitutes a real challenge for the archaeologist. The present condition of the site of Isabela–El Castillo has forced archaeologists to adopt a salvage approach to their research there, the primary objective of which is to reconstruct the settlement as far as the present circumstances will allow. This undertaking and the methods required to carry it out have created problems of all kinds.

Early Investigations

The preliminary results of studies currently under way suggest that La Isabela consisted of two settlement nuclei located about 1,700 m apart. This discovery may help clarify the confusion that possibly started with Chanca, the chief chronicler of La Isabela, and that subsequent works have perpetuated.

In the 1950s, I and my colleagues Emile Boyrie Moya and Louis Chanlatte realized that bricks, roof-tiles, and perhaps pottery were produced locally at La Isabela. We reasoned that it should therefore be possible to find the remains of the kilns, a search that we postponed as we were not equipped to explore the area at that time.

The primary goal of the study I began in 1987 has been to locate the remains of these kilns. We suspected that they would have been associated with the 200 dwellings constructed when Columbus and his men disembarked.

We found the site of the kilns after becoming acquainted with the local oral tradition of the villagers in what is today the pueblo of Isabela–El Castillo. A local guide to the ruins at La Isabela, Celestino Torres, revealed that his mother, who had been dead for many years, had told him that across the bay in a place known as Las Coles there had formerly been a very old bakery.

I immediately associated a "bakery" with ovens or kilns, and without wasting time began to explore Las Coles. There I found large quantities of earthenware pottery in situ that appeared to date to the fifteenth century. The site was designated El Tamarindo. Soon afterward, a local resident of Las Coles, Negro Dulce, took us to a site that we named La Breña, where we surface-collected earthenware and Spanish majolica. These specimens dated from the fifteenth century and were similar to those we had found at El Tamarindo. The area known as Las Coles is therefore a likely candidate for the location of Columbus's initial disembarkation and settlement in the New World.

Some maps of the area refer to Le Cole (an irremissible gallicism) instead of the usual Las Coles. It should also be pointed out that there is another place known as Las Coles in Cotui, in the Dominican Republic's municipality of Villa Riva, Duarte.

After many years of searching, I believe that we have found the exact place of the first landing. By examining topographic maps, we also located the "first sector of La Isabela, the Ciudad Marta," pointed out by Chanca.

Documentary Sources and Geographical Correlations

The following discussion presents some of the comments on La Isabela in the primary sources along with my interpretations and firsthand observations.

Las Casas stated that when Columbus was first looking for a place to start a settlement, he turned shoreward "around three leagues from where a big river flows out to the sea" (las Casas 1987:1:362). This "big river" was none other than the Isabela, or Bajabonico River, located in the Isabela Bay between Punta Devora and Estero Hondo.

The strip of coast between these two features faces west; to the south of it, we find the bay that Chanca described as being about "ten leagues from Monte Cristi" (Navarrete 1945:1:346). This is the Bay of Isabela. Just to the northeast of the Isabela (Bajabonico) River we find the famous *peña bien acomodada* (well-situated rock) that Columbus described as offering good protection. This is the location of the present-day National Park of La Isabela (El Solar de las Americas). The area of Las Coles lies to the south of the Bajabonico River.

The fact that Columbus was looking for a place "where a big river flows to the sea" suggests that he would not have installed a settlement in a place where freshwater was not abundant. Freshwater is available in Las Coles, but there is no freshwater near "the well- situated rock" of Isabela–El Castillo.

Las Casas (1987:1:62) also noted that "there is a port, which although open to the northwest wind the rest is good, where he decided to come to ground at an Indian town that was there." If las Casas was referring to the area between the mouth of the Isabela River and the "well-situated rock," his idea of "a good port" would be questioned today. When the wind blows from the north, northwest, and west, this area cannot be used as a port, and fishermen have to move their boats farther north where they will find better protection. Such a point can be found at the Isabela River itself, rather than adjacent to Isabela–El Castillo, and appears to have been the "port" used by Columbus.

Although las Casas refers to "an Indian town that was there," we have found no evidence of an Indian town at the place we believe to be the landing port. We have known for many years that an important Indian settlement existed at El Perenal, although unfortunately it has been somewhat disturbed. It was studied by archaeologist Elpidio Ortega:

> We located the settlement of Perenal close to the hill of Candelon in front of the dry bed of the Bajabonico River. It was investigated a few years back by Veloz Maggiolo, Guerrero, Luna Calderon y Ortega, and has the characteristics of a large settlement of Mellacoide and Chicoide [peoples], who for us were contemporary with the conquest of the island by Christopher Columbus and his people [Ortega 1988:13].

Evidence suggests that these Indians had a port for canoes at the foot of the hill of El Perenal, at a place where a large meander of the Bajabonico River touches the foot of the hill. Columbus had navigated to this point during his first voyage, before he established the settlement, and thus probably knew of the Indian town that was there. The distance, as the crow flies, from the mouth of the Isabela River where we believe Columbus disembarked to the Indian port is about 2,900 m.

Chanca (in Navarrete 1945:1:346) recorded: "We were to land in the best place and disposition that we could select, where there is a good port and a great fishery." It is difficult to imagine a "good" landing on a beach. As mentioned earlier, we believe the port was probably northwest of the mouth of the Isabela (Bajabonico) River. Las Casas (1987:1:362) clearly states the landing took place "where a big river flows out to the sea"; this can only be the Isabela River. This thesis is supported archaeologically by the presence of fifteenth-century ceramics in Las Coles in an area only 250 m from the left bank of the river.

This interpretation also fits in with the narrative, according to which Columbus ordered that everything be unloaded "on a plain." Consider the difficulty of unloading 1,400 people, a good number of domestic animals, and the cargo of 17 ships. The ideal site is not a beach. The best candidate is found on the left bank of the Isabela River, at the western edge of the "plain" of Las Coles, where we believe the 200 dwellings were constructed.

Chanca's Confusion

Navarrete (1945:1:346) notes that "The land is very propitious for everything; it has nearby a major river, and another reasonably abundant of singular water nearby . . . [we] built on the bank of the river in Ciudad Marta." The two rivers are the Isabela River, which ran north of Las Coles, and the Unijica River to the south. The Unijica's original course has deviated since the fifteenth century, passing to the north of what is today the settlement of Dieguito, and eventually becoming a tributary of the Isabela River. In the fifteenth century, it probably disgorged on the north side of the Lake of Las Coles.[2]

Chanca's narrative becomes confusing after he identifies the Ciudad Marta, for he seems to treat the "ciudad" (which we believe to have been at Las Coles) and the "well-situated rock" as if they were one entity. He then continues: "At Ciudad Marta, the place borders with the sea, so that half of the city is surrounded by water with a sheer cliff or rock that serves as a barrier so that there is no need for any kind of defense; the other half is surrounded by thick forest."

Having scrupulously examined the topography of Las Coles, we concluded that the most practical and intelligent choice would have been to establish a port on the left bank of the Isabela River. The agricultural lands started to the east of this area. Chanca tells us: "We had to take land in the best place and disposition that we could select where there is a good port and great fishery" (Navarrete 1945:1:346). Close to the mouth of the river, there is an anchoring place, and fish are abundant in the ocean as well as in the river.

The Disembarkation Site

As already noted, it is difficult to imagine that a beach could be used for a large unloading operation. The more tranquil and accessible bank of the river, where one could also quickly establish a community of 200 dwellings, seems a better choice.

The left bank of the Isabela River would have served perfectly for the landing, loading, and unloading. It offered still waters, provided the ships protection against running aground, and meant that the crew would not have to drag heavy loads across the sand. Strong waves are never absent on the beach during windy days and would have impeded the unloading. Furthermore, there is only a short distance between the probable river landing place and the area of Las Coles where we have found fragments of earthenware with a strong Moorish style dating to the fifteenth century.

Settlement at Las Coles

Las Casas (1987:1:362) also reported that "going up-river [we saw] there is an open and fruitful plain and that the river could be diverted with the help of trenches [canals] that would go inside the town; and also to build water mills and to build other commodities." This apparently refers to the ample and fertile lands to the east of the Isabela River (today known as Dieguito). The canals were to be used for irrigation by the farmers of Las Coles. When he says "the river could be taken out with the help of trenches [canals] that would go inside the town," there can be no doubt that we are dealing with La Isabela, as the river could not have run through the middle of La Isabela–El Castillo ("the well-situated rock" where the National Park is located today). This would have required a major diversion of more than a kilometer. Agricultural irrigation canals and diverting an arm of the river are quite different things.

Referring to the decision to settle at La Isabela, las Casas (1987:1:362) noted: "which seen, in the name of the second trinity, he determined to settle there." Upon disembarking, the expedition settled and blessed the future site of Spain's colony. Las Casas (1987:1:363) says that the settlement was "on a plain . . . beside a rock well suited to build on it its fortress." Nowhere does he say *on* the *Peña bien aparejada* (the well-situated rock), which, at the time of arrival, Columbus had commented on because it afforded good protection.

The memory of La Navidad and the fear of other dangers no doubt led the settlers to believe that one of their first priorities was to construct a fortress. Before this could be done, they had to put up dwellings for the expedition and organize a strategy for developing the colony. All of this leads us to conclude that La Isabela comprised two distinct settlements with different patterns (La Isabela–Las Coles and La Isabela–El Castillo). Both settlements, however, were part of a single community, La Isabela.

When Columbus stated that "on this site I begin to settle a town that is the first of all these Indies" (las Casas 1987:1:363), he was no doubt referring to Isabela–Las Coles. This suggestion is supported by the presence of fifteenth-century ceramics at Las Coles.

Settlement Priorities

Another important statement to look at is las Casas's (1987:1:363) comment that "there were good rocks for quarrying and to make lime, and good soil to make bricks and roof tiles, and all good materials and . . . very fertile and benevolent and blessed land." The limestone quarry referred to by las Casas has been located and identified at a spot between the Isabela River and the present National Park. Archaeological and soil studies have also demonstrated that "good soil to make bricks and roof-tiles" is found at Las Coles in the site known as El Tamarindo. Not only are clay soils located there, but we have found evidence of a ceramic kiln and its by-products (see also Deagan 1989).

The report that the settlement of La Isabela had "close by a major river, and another reasonably close of very regular water" (Navarrete 1945:1:346) suggests that it *was located between two rivers*, probably the Isabela (Bajabonico) River to the south and the Unijica River to the north. Although most historians agree that Isabela was situated between two rivers, they are referring to La Isabela–El Castillo, which until now was the only location considered to have been La Isabela. This site is not "between two rivers," at least not today.

The strategic location between two rivers was one of the reasons Columbus chose Las Coles. It allowed the Spanish to settle and build houses immediately, and to avoid the problem of supplying water for the people and animals.

The "well-situated rock" that was the site of Isabela–El Castillo has no water, and people could not have settled there immediately. Moreover, to bring water to the site would have taken considerable engineering, and it seems unlikely that the exhausted expedition could have waited that long to disembark and settle.

Another comment that suggests the Unijica River was the northern boundary is the one referring to "another [river] reasonably abundant and of very regular water." Apparently the other river was thought to have better water than the Isabela. According to people living in the area today, this is still the case.

Shortly after their arrival, the Spanish began planning to develop irrigation and water canals from the river "by bringing an arm of the river, which, the masters say, should be brought through the middle of the place" (Navarrete 1945:1:347). This declaration by Chanca confirms that the Spanish saw the need to develop this "arm of the river," implying that there were two sectors, and one of them had no water. That can only be "the well-situated rock" of Isabela–El Castillo.

We know that the settlement of La Isabela (at Las Coles) consisted of 200 cabins, and from the accounts of Michel de Cuneo, that it was a functioning community by September of 1494: "The last day of September, with God's help, we arrived to the safety of our cabins in La Isabela." We believe that Cuneo was referring to Isabela–Las Coles in this instance. There were probably some huts and cabins on the site of Isabela–El Castillo, but we suspect they would have been occupied by the workers and service personnel associated with the fort, and that the soldiers would have had separate cabins in the area for the troops. We do not believe, however, that Cuneo or anyone else could call the area of La Isabela–Fortaleza a *village*.

Cuneo states: "When our small village was constructed, the inhabitants of the island from one to two leagues around came to see us in a brotherly manner, saying that we were men of God that came from the sky," and Las Casas (Navarrete 1945:1:347) adds, "They trade the gold and supplies and everything they bring for lacetips for beads, and pins for pieces of escudillas and plates." Again Cuneo is referring to the community at Las Coles that was baptized La Isabela when they landed, in honor of the Queen of Spain. His comments suggest that the Spanish community was not on the site of an Indian town, but rather some leagues distant.

Trade and exchange were part of the Spaniards' early contacts with the inhabitants of the New World. Las Casas's comments concerning the Indians' eagerness for even the most worthless of Spanish items reflects the Indians' belief that the Spaniards were godlike beings that had come from the sky. At no point can it be said that the Indians were cheated or deceived in this trade.

This helps account in part for the absence of large quantitites of archaeological remains at Isabela–Las Coles, as well as at other sites of the first contact. In these places the archaeological remains were taken by the Indians. At Las Coles, the spot we consider to be the first one that the Spaniards settled, the material is very sparse for this reason, in addition to natural causes.

Archaeological Remains from Las Coles

Ceramic pieces were recovered from the surface and from test excavations at Las Coles, but they have not yet been analyzed fully. Nonetheless, there can be no doubt about their fifteenth-century origin. There are a few remains of items brought from Spain (*Melado* glazed ware, for example) but most of the ceramics were made locally at Las Coles, and two pieces exhibit characteristics of the Spanish-Moorish style.

At present, a team of researchers from the Florida Museum of Natural History, University of Florida, is carrying out a survey of the lands of the community of Castillo de La Isabela and at Las Coles, under the direction of Kathleen Deagan, in conjunction with the Office of National Parks and J. M. Cruxent of the Universidad Nacional Francisco de Miranda de Coro, Venezuela. The team is attempting to locate evidence of the extent of fifteenth-century occupation at both Isabela–El Castillo and at Las Coles.[3]

The present work should be considered only a preliminary investigation into the origins of La Isabela. It offers the first fruits of our documentary, archaeological, and geographic research, which suggests that La Isabela consisted of two nuclei, one of which was Las Coles. As our studies continue, we hope to gain further insight into the reasons why the Spanish selected and established the first regular settlement in the New World at the places we suggest.

Notes

This essay was translated and edited by Kathleen Deagan and Gianna Brown. Dr. José F. Maria Cruxent has been living at Isabela el Castillo for two and a half years, conducting archaeological excavations at La Isabela, the site designated as Columbus's first intentional New World settlement. His work there has led him to question the traditional assumption that all colonial defensive, domestic, religious, and administrative activities were located at the same central place. This essay argues that the very first European New World colony did *not* follow that template; rather, it was composed of multiple nonadjacent nuclei.

1. Local tradition at La Isabela holds that in preparation for a visit of Trujillo to the site during the 1950s, the present road was constructed and much of the site was "cleaned" with heavy equipment. It is said that in the process many of the standing ruins and much of the surface of the site were pushed into the sea.

2. The previous bed of the Unijica can be clearly seen in air photo no. DR-b 57/V 15-14/11 December 1967/No. 232 and 9948, Instituto de Cartrografia Nacional, Santo Domingo.

3. This study was completed in May 1989 (see Deagan 1989). The subsurface transect

tests indicated extremely sparse remains in both areas, but particularly so at Las Coles, where artifacts were recovered from 50-cm square holes. At Isabela–El Castillo, artifacts were recovered from holes covering an area of abouat 200 m².

References

Casas, Bartolomé de las
   1987   *Historia De Las Indias*. Sociedad Domicana de Bibliofilos, Santo Domingo.
Colon, Cristobal
   1972   *Diario de Colon*. 2nd ed. Prólogo Gregorio Marañón, Madrid.
   1985   *Historia Del almirante*. Luiz Arranz, Madrid. Historia 16.
Cruxent, J. M. and Irving Rouse
   1982   *Arqueologia Cronologica de Venezuela*. Unidad Prehispánica de las Asociación "Juan Llovera," Ernesto Armitano, Caracas.
Deagan, Kathleen
   1986   First Colony, Lost Colony. *National Geographic* 172(5):672–676.
   1989   *Report on the 1989 Sub-surface Test Program at La Isabela, Dominican Republic*. Florida Museum of Natural History, Gainesville.
Jane, Cecil (translator and editor)
   1960   *The Journal of Christopher Columbus*. Clarkson Potter, New York.
Morison, S. E.
   1940   The Route of Columbus along the North Coast of Haiti and the Site of La Navidad. *Transactions of the American Philosophical Society* 31(4):239–285.
Navarrete, Martín Fernandez de
   1945   *Coleccion de Los Viajes y Descubrimientos Que Hicieron Por Mar Los Espanoles*. Editorial Guarania, Buenos Aires.
Ortega, Elpidio José
   1988   *La Isabela y La Arqueologia en La Ruta de Colon*. Universidad central del Este, vol. 68, ser. 5. Ediciones de la Fundación Ortega Alvarez, San Pedro de Macoris, R.D.
Varela, Consuelo
   1982   *Cristobal Colon*. Textos y Documentos completos. Relaciones de viajes, cartas y memoriales. Prologo y Notas de Consuelo Varela. Editorial Alianza, Madrid.

Chapter 17 ▪

Charles R. Ewen

The Rise and Fall of Puerto Real

Few events in history have had the impact of the meeting between the New World and the Old. Whether it be the stirring exploits of the conquistadors or the tragic demise of the native populations, the discovery and exploration of the New World is usually portrayed in dramatic fashion. Popular and scholarly interests have focused on the spectacular successes and failures of this period. However, most of the history of this era, though not spectacular, is no less important to understanding the Spanish colonial experience in the New World. Hispaniola, the first Caribbean island to be colonized, is a case in point.

The Caribbean, during the sixteenth century, was wholly subservient to Spain. Exploitation, more than development, characterized Spanish colonial policy. According to McAlister (1984:81) Spain and its colonists had similar, but conflicting interests.

> The Crown wished to convert and patronize the indigenous population, establish exclusive sovereignty in its American possessions and, at the same time gain a profit from the enterprise. Conquerors and settlers wanted to exploit the natives, acquire *señorios* and become wealthy.

The result was that the Indies were developed only to the point of being profitable to the investor.

The Enterprise of the Indies

Hispaniola was the first island to receive the dubious benefits of Spanish attention. Precious metals, particularly gold, attracted the Spaniards to the island. Columbus, during his first voyage, mentions that the native Arawaks possessed gold and that he intended to obtain it (Dunn and Kelly 1989:71). Reports of gold in the Cibao region, in the eastern part of Hispaniola, prompted a serious effort to colonize the island. Columbus, however, was not equal to the task. A consummate sailor and explorer, he lacked the administrative skills to establish a viable colony.

The complete subjugation of Hispaniola occurred during the governorship of Nicolas de Ovando (1502-1509). With brutal efficiency, Ovando extended Spanish administrative sway throughout the entire island. He established 15 new towns (Sauer 1966:151) to secure Spanish authority over the native inhabitants. Puerto Real was one of these communities.

Boomtown

Founded in 1504, Puerto Real was originally envisioned as a mining colony. However, prospecting in the mountainous hinterland produced no gold and what copper deposits there were proved too meager to make exploitation worthwhile (Sauer 1966:154). The area around Puerto Real did, however, serve as a source of labor for other, more profitable, districts. If Puerto Real had no need of slave labor itself, then it could serve as middleman, supplying labor to those areas that required it.

The decline of the native population, coupled with the rise in demand for labor, prompted Spanish slaving raids on the nearby Bahamas. Puerto Plata and Puerto Real were the ports that serviced these slaving operations (Sauer 1966:159). A bone from a species of muskrat native to south Florida was recovered from excavations at Puerto Real. This suggests that the slave raids were not confined to the Bahamas (Ewen 1989). A total of 40,000 Indians debarked at these two ports (Hodges 1980:3). As these imported Indians succumbed to disease and mistreatment, African slaves were brought in in increasing numbers to replace them. Analysis of the locally manufactured ceramics from Puerto Real has disclosed a corresponding change in ceramic attributes with demographic shifts at Puerto Real. The recognized Arawak ceramic traditions quickly give way to a thick, undecorated ware. Smith (1986:101) claims that the distribution of locally produced ceramics "offers strong support for the replacement of Indian tradition ceramics through time, a replacement which was primarily accomplished through African ceramic manufacture."

The decline in the Arawak slave trade compelled the inhabitants of Puerto Real to explore other economic options. Leather was much in demand in Europe and the Indies possessed an abundance of cattle. Hides from the Indies revived the leather-working industry in Spain that had been initiated by the Moors. Ornamental leather goods, jackets, and the famous gloves of Ocaña and Ciudad Real were made from West Indian hides and sold throughout Europe (Lynch 1984:125). Evidence of this industry came to light during excavations of an activity area at Puerto Real. The large amount of cattle bone recovered here implies that this location represented an area where refuse from skinning and meat preservation was processed into tallow and other cattle industry by-products. The combination of household artifacts and faunal remains suggests that it was used for possibly both residential and commercial purposes (Reitz 1986:327).

The settlement's early years were its most lucrative. In the first decade of the sixteenth century, Puerto Real boasted a thriving community of 100 households (Haring 1947:207n). Archaeological investigations have revealed that the town followed the classic grid pattern, with its masonry houses grouped around a central plaza. Large public buildings, such as the church, faced on the plaza. There are also indications that the plaza served as a marketplace (Willis 1984:303).

An analysis of artifacts recovered during a preliminary survey of the town indicates the presence of economically differentiated neighborhoods (Williams 1986). It was also possible to identify areas associated with specialized crafts or specific commercial activities. By using the data collected from a systematic subsurface survey of the site and comparing it with patterns defined by archaeological work at St. Augustine (cf. Deagan 1983), three basic patterns of occupation could be defined. The first type represented the dwelling of a Spanish colonist; the second, the household of a lower-status individual, possibly an African or Arawak slave; and the third, a nonresidential structure, probably associated with commercial activity.

After the Gold Rush

After the initial gold deposits on the island were exhausted, Hispaniola became a base for further exploration of the New World. After the real mineral wealth of the New World was discovered on the mainland, the population drain of Hispaniola began in earnest (Andrews 1978:54). The mainland gold rush did more than just draw off manpower; it diverted shipping away from the less profitable island ports.

The convoy system of shipping, first implemented in 1542, was designed to ensure that precious metals from Mexico and Peru arrived safely in Spain. For the most part, ships were required to sail in convoy and visit only those ports on the convoy's route. Very few ships received licenses to sail to ports not on the route. One need only glance at the routes of the treasure fleets (Figure 17-1) to see that Puerto Real is located well away from the *Carrera de las Indias*. The mercantile policies of Spain decreed all colonial commerce would be conducted exclusively with the mother country. By this time the economy of Puerto Real depended upon the hide trade. Unfortunately, the bulky, relatively low-value hides could not compete with silver and gold for the limited cargo space of the fleets.

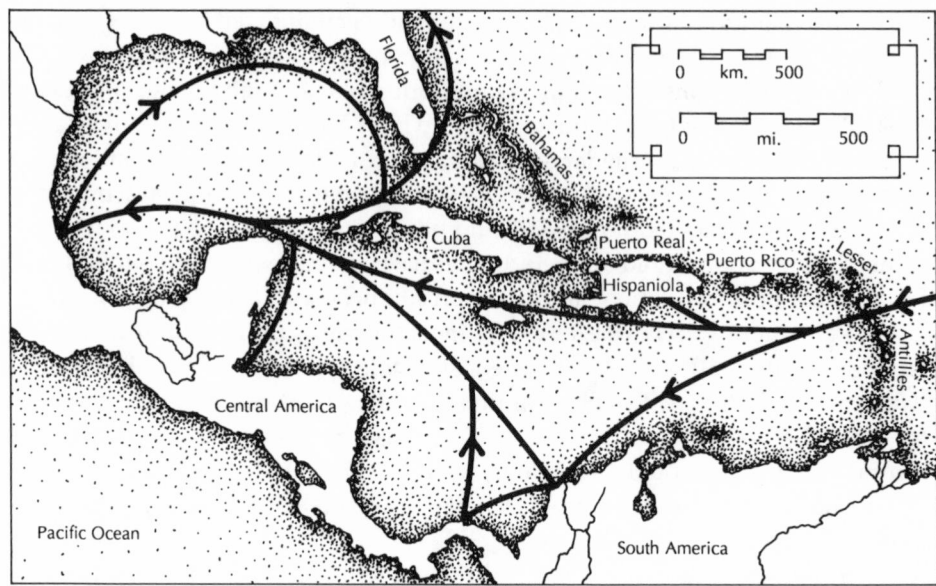

Figure 17-1. Mid-sixteenth-century routes of the Spanish treasure fleets.

Living on the Edge

The consequences of the convoy system were crippling to the economic well-being of Puerto Real. Denied access to regular shipping, the colonists were forced to seek alternative means of satisfying their material requirements. The colonists resorted to substituting indigenous commodities for imported goods. This is abundantly evident in the material assemblage recovered from Puerto Real. Locally manufactured wares account for nearly half of the ceramics from an upper-class household excavated at Puerto Real (Ewen 1989). Also, the faunal assemblage shows that many regionally available species such as marine fishes, turtles, and shellfish were incorporated into the colonial diet. Fragments of manioc griddles recovered from another part of the site suggest that cassava bread became a substitute for imported wheat bread (McEwan 1983:64).

Eventually, the colonists turned to the *rescate* or illegal trade. Smuggling became the only source for European goods. There is little tangible evidence of this illegal activity at Puerto Real. Skowronek (1989:10) points out, with some effect, that there is little archaeological evidence for smuggling at Spanish colonial sites. However, Andrews (1978:182) states that textiles were the leading contraband item of the French smugglers. Perhaps much of the other contraband was perishable and, so, left little trace in the archaeological record. Ming porcelain, reported from Puerto Real, provides some evidence, however, of the illegal trade (Ewen 1989; McEwan 1983; Willis 1984). Ming porcelain was not available in the Caribbean until at least 1550 and then only through Portuguese corsairs. Not until 1573, with the beginning of the Manila Galleon trade, did Spain begin supplying its colonies with Chinese porcelain (Deagan 1987:96). Since Puerto Real was abandoned a scant five years after the commencement of the legitimate trade in porcelain, it seems likely that Portuguese smugglers were responsible for the presence of porcelain at Puerto Real.

Such was the paradox that confronted the citizens of Puerto Real. They could obey the law and rely on local industries to exclusively satisfy their material needs, or they could trade illegally with smugglers and enjoy European goods unavailable to them by other means. Another consideration of the colonists involved the trading practices of the smugglers, who were not above transacting business at gunpoint. Often, the colonists faced the choice of trading with the corsairs or becoming their victims by resisting their advances. The latter occurred when the French corsair Jean Bontemps entered the ports of Monte Christi, Puerto Real, and La Yaguana. He seized 12 vessels and burned the port facilities of Puerto Real in 1566 (Andrews 1978:96). It is therefore not surprising that most of the hides produced at Puerto Real found their way into the illegal trade system.

The Empire Strikes Back

After 1560, the situation went from bad to worse for the dwindling citizenry of Puerto Real as both natural and human elements worked against the port city. An earthquake, which shook the city in 1562, was followed by the depredations of pirates in 1566. That same year, ironically enough, saw the revocation of Puerto Real's registry because of its association with smugglers. Puerto Real was able to regain its license after filing suit, but it was only a couple of years before it was lost again, this time for good.

It was the presence of these smugglers, not the loss of revenue, that brought down the wrath of the Spanish Crown. The financial importance of the hide trade did not particularly concern Phillip II. As Andrews (1978:195) points out, "Hides were the virtual offal of the Indies, left for Lutherans and mulattos to haggle over by Spaniards occupied with transactions of a higher order—in sugar, dyes and precious metals." No, the fear of losing its exclusive monopoly in the Caribbean was the motivating force behind Spanish reprisals against its own colonists.

And Spain had good reason to fear the foreign presence in the Caribbean as nearly everyone, at least in the ports of northern and western Hispaniola, was somehow involved with the rescate (Andrews 1978:208). All attempts to curb these smuggling activities by Spain were in vain. Unable to adequately supply its more remote colonies, Spain was helpless against the opportunistic corsairs who operated with the cooperation of the Crown's own officials. A drastic solution taken in 1578 involved the establishment of a new settlement, Bayaha, midway between Puerto Real and Monte Christi. The population of these two towns was forced, at gunpoint, to relocate to Bayaha. The Spanish Crown reasoned that it would be easier to stop the smuggling at a single point than all along the coast. However, this was not the case. Smuggling continued with the collusion of the town officials. Spain's ultimate response was to abandon the western third of the island in 1605. This ended the Spanish chapter of Puerto Real and allowed the French to occupy what was to become Haiti.

The material record corroborates the historical record. No seventeenth-century Spanish artifacts have been recovered from any of the excavations that have been conducted at Puerto Real. Willis (1984:351) found evidence of some squatter activity around the plaza area that postdated the Spanish occupation of the town. For all practical purposes, Puerto Real ceased to be a viable community in 1578.

The Spanish Borderlands Reexamined

The unifying theme of the diverse essays in this volume is the concept of the Spanish Borderlands. How do we define the Spanish Borderlands? Does Puerto Real fit the criteria for inclusion? If we adhere to Bolton's original concept, it does not.

Bolton (1921:vii) defined the Spanish Borderlands as

> the regions between Florida and California, now belonging to the United States, over which Spain held sway for centuries. These were the northern outposts of New Spain, maintained chiefly to hold the country against foreign intruders and against the inroads of savage tribes. They were far from the centers of Spanish colonial civilization, in the West Indies, Central America, Mexico, and Peru.

Although the geographic criteria may be dismissed as Bolton's attempt to fit the Spanish Borderlands into the "Chronicles of America" series, Puerto Real is still not described by any of these conditions. It was not on the northern border of the Spanish empire; it was not under Spanish sway for centuries; and, although it was initially settled to establish control over the northwestern part of Hispaniola, it never really served as a defensive buffer. Furthermore, in a strict geographic sense, Puerto Real was not far from the centers of Spanish colonial civilization.

Yet, Puerto Real *was* on the fringe of the Spanish empire, if not in the Boltonian apprehension, then by an economic definition. After the collapse of the Arawak slave trade, Puerto Real turned to the export of leather. However, bulky hides could not compete with precious metals for the limited cargo space of the fleets and, so, the town ceased to be an asset to the empire. Proof of its low regard can be seen in the fact that it was omitted from the route of the trade convoys. To make matters worse, Puerto Real was isolated geographically from the rest of Hispaniola so that even overland access to the viable port of Santo Domingo was difficult. The town became an economic backwater and probably would have died with a whimper had it not started trafficking with smugglers. Participation in the rescate demoted Puerto Real from nonasset to liability.

Puerto Real represents a different kind of Spanish Borderland: a forgotten frontier. Settlements such as St. Augustine and Santa Elena were defensive outposts on the geographic fringes of the Spanish empire. Settlements such as Puerto Real and Monte Christi were commercial outposts on the economic fringes of the Spanish empire. The former settlements were maintained out of strategic necessity, while the latter, lacking even strategic importance, were abandoned. The fact that Spain so readily and completely abandoned Puerto Real corroborates this assertion.

Puerto Real is an example of a failed Spanish colonial experiment. Present-day Haiti, unlike other former Spanish possessions, bears very little trace of its Hispanic heritage. Too often modern researchers fall prey to an emotional reaction to Spanish colonial activity in the New World, be it *la leyenda negra* or *blanca*. The history of Puerto Real serves to shake us from the idealistic notions of Spain's imperial ambitions and compels a more sober and pragmatic examination of the Spanish enterprise in the New World.

References

Andrews, Kenneth
    1978   *The Spanish Caribbean Trade and Plunder, 1530–1630.* Yale University Press, New Haven.

Bolton, Herbert E.
    1921   *The Spanish Borderlands: A Chronicle of Old Florida and the Southwest.* Chronicles of America Series Vol. 23. Yale University Press, New Haven.

Deagan, Kathleen A.
    1983   *Spanish St. Augustine: The Archaeology of a Colonial Creole Community.* Academic Press, New York.
    1987   *Artifacts of the Spanish Colonies of Florida and the Caribbean 1500-1800. Vol. 1: Ceramics, Glassware, and Beads.* Smithsonian Institution Press, Washington D.C.

Dunn, Oliver, and James E. Kelley, Jr. (translators)
    1989   *The Diario of Christopher Columbus's First Voyage to America 1492-1493.* University of Oklahoma Press, Norman.

Ewen, Charles R.
    1991   *From Spaniard to Creole: The Archaeology of Hispanic American Cultural Formation at Puerto Real, Haiti.* University of Alabama Press, University.

Haring, C. H.
    1947   *The Spanish Empire in America.* Harcourt, Brace, and Jovanovich, New York.

Hodges, William
    1980   Puerto Real Sources. Ms. on file, Musée de Guahaba, Limbe, Haiti.

Lynch, John
    1984   *Spain under the Habsburgs.* Vol. 1. New York University Press, New York.

McAlister, Lyle
    1984   *Spain and Portugal in the New World, 1492–1700.* University of Minnesota Press, Minneapolis.

McEwan, Bonnie
    1983   *Spanish Colonial Adaptation on Hispaniola: The Archaeology of Area 35 Puerto Real, Haiti.* Unpublished Master's thesis, Department of Anthropology, University of Florida, Gainesville.

Reitz, Elizabeth
    1986   Vertebrate Fauna from Locus 39, Puerto Real, Haiti. *Journal of Field Archaeology* 13:317-328.

Sauer, Carl O.
    1966   *The Early Spanish Main.* University of California Press, Berkeley.

Skowronek, Russell K.
    1989   Empire and Ceramics: The Changing Role of Illicit Trade in Spanish America. Paper presented at the Annual Meeting of the Society for Historical Archaeology, Baltimore.

Smith, Greg C.

    1986 *Non-European Pottery at the Sixteenth Century Spanish Site of Puerto Real, Haiti*. Unpublished Master's thesis, Department of Anthropology, University of Florida, Gainesville.

Williams, Maurice

    1986 Sub-surface Pattering at Puerto Real: A Sixteenth Century Spanish Town on Haiti's North Coast. *Journal of Field Archaeology* 13:283-296.

Willis, Raymond

    1984 *Empire and Architecture at 16th century Puerto Real. Hispaniola: An Archaeological Perspective*. Unpublished Ph.D. dissertation, Department of Anthropology, University of Florida, Gainesville.

Chapter 18 ■

Manuel García-Arevalo

Transculturation in Contact Period and Contemporary Hispaniola

Cultural interaction between Spaniards and American Indians took place on the island of Santo Domingo (Hispaniola) most intensely during the early contact period (A.D. 1492–1550). This period is also known in Hispaniola as the "Indo-Hispanic period" (García-Arevalo 1977). During this period, which occurred before the demise of the Taino, Spanish–Indian transculturation and native religious syncretism took place intensely throughout the Antilles. The most pronounced archaeological manifestations of these processes are the postcontact changes in traditional Taino-Arawak pottery. A premise of this paper is that the cultural alterations manifest in these ceramic changes also had an important influence on the patterns of *criollo* Hispanic-American culture as it exists today in the Dominican Republic.

Taino Ceramic Traditions in Hispaniola

The Taino peoples who inhabited most of the Greater Antilles at the time of discovery had already undergone a long process of indigenous cultural evolution in an island environment by the time Columbus arrived. Their cultural and linguistic origins were most likely related to those of the South American Arahuacan peoples (Rouse and Cruxent 1963).

The Taino at contact had developed an extensive and elaborate ceramic industry, characterized by well-defined styles and decoration emphasizing symbolic expression. This pottery is distinguished by elaborate anthropomorphic and zoomorphic figural representations, which serve both as adorno decoration and decorative appliqued handles. These applied figural elements occur in combination with diverse incised and punctuated geometric motifs, which appear either as abstract designs or in enclosed banded zones that generally surround the superior part of the vessel close to the rim (see García-Arevalo 1977; Veloz 1972:127–150).

This distinctive Taino pottery is known as the Chicoide Style in Caribbean archaeological literature, after the nomenclature developed by Irving Rouse (1964) from the site of Boca Chica near Santo Domingo, capitol of the Dominican Republic. The style was developed between the thirteenth and fifteenth centuries A.D.

"Culture and Conquest"

The Spanish conquest of the Greater Antilles stimulated changes in the forms, decorative motifs, and circumstances of use for Taino pottery. In analyzing these changes and their variations it is useful to refer to the model of Spanish-American culture change proposed by George Foster (1960) to explain Indo-Hispanic interaction in Mexico. That model was subsequently employed by Kathleen Deagan in her study of Spanish criollo society in colonial St. Augustine, Florida (Deagan 1983).

In Foster's model of encounter between the nations of the New and Old Worlds, the Spanish newcomers are referred to as bearers of the "donor culture," while the Mexican Indians are characterized as the "recipient culture." Furthermore the donor culture is depicted as having two aspects: One can be called "conquest," which refers to the exercise of some form of political and military control over the recipient culture; and the other can be referred to as "contact," in which control is informal in nature and less restrictive to the recipient group. The conquest aspect implies the use of formal measures to control a group and bring about directed change, while the contact aspect implies that culture change occurs without formal sanctions of a political or military nature (Foster 1960; Deagan 1983:66).

These distinctions in Foster's model of postcontact culture change in Mexico are useful for the analysis and interpretation of stylistic change in the Taino ceramics of the postcontact period in the Antilles, as detailed in the following discussion.

The Contact Phase: Informal Influence

During the first stage of the Indo-Hispanic period in the Antilles, it is evident that some Taino pottery was produced in a contact situation and was influenced by Hispanic ceramic styles and forms. From the chroniclers of the era, we know that Spanish majolica and other ceramics brought to the Americas by the first colonists were received by the Taino with admiration and pleasure. This new ceramic ware, in contrast to the Taino wares, was of brilliant colors, and had a resplendent glazed enamel. This was extremely appealing to the Indians, to the extent that ceramic sherds were among the most common articles used by the Spaniards in their barter and commerce with the Caribbean Indians.

Christopher Columbus wrote in 1492 in his diary that "they would save even the pieces of *escudillas* [carinated bowls] and the fragments of broken glass" (1968:29).

Later the Admiral added in his navigation diary,

> [They] would barter with some pieces of gold hanging from the nose, that which they would willingly give for a *cascabel* for the feet of sparrow hawks, (hawksbell), and for glass beads, that are so little that they are nothing. This is true for any little thing you would give them: they also held a great wonder at our coming, and they thought that we had come from the sky [1968:129].

Similarly, Fray Bartolome de las Casas, in his *History of the Indies* (1965:1:206), comments: "The estimation that the Indians have for the Christians, truly thinking that they had descended from the sky, and for this reason, anything that belonged to them [the Christians], even if it was a piece of an escudilla or dish, they held for relics, and so they would give [for it] whatever they had."

Columbus and las Casas were not in error when they interpreted Taino reaction as a belief that Spanish objects had a divine character. Sherds of majolica have been found in archaeological excavations at Taino sites believed to have been in contact with Spanish conquistadors. These sherds were associated with a number of Taino burials, and were probably used as funeral offerings. This association reveals the importance that the Indians gave to Hispanic ceramics, particularly since it was recorded that the Taino believed in supernatural life, and buried their dead with their most prized personal possessions.

From this, we can suggest that the European materials that reached the Taino during the earliest stage of Spanish domination were acquired through a process of trade or exchange. In the Taino context, these items were those that denoted status, and were used as substitutes for traditional objects. Metal bells and glass beads, for example, were used in place of the "cibas," or stone beads, traditionally found in Taino burials (Deagan 1987:162–71; García-Arevalo 1978a:84–87).

It should also be noted, and has been argued elsewhere (García-Arevalo 1978a) that Spanish majolica introduced by the conquistadors influenced the forms of native Taino vessels. At several aboriginal sites of the contact period examples of Taino pottery appear to have departed from traditional designs and have adopted new forms of Spanish vessels. This can be seen in Cuba, as well as in the Dominican Republic, at such sites as Yayal in Holguien (Dominguez 1978), Bani, and other indigenous settlements.

These sites contain locally made pottery that imitates Spanish jars and dishes, and suggests a widely dispersed pattern of aboriginal stylistic change throughout the Antilles after contact. Such change reflects the process of aboriginal transculturation during the contact period (Dominguez 1978; García Castañeda 1938, 1949; Morales and Perez 1946; Rouse 1942).

It can also be suggested that this Indo-Hispanic pottery produced during the contact period manifests a process of postcontact religious syncretism among the Taino. As they borrowed and reproduced European forms, they combined them with traditional symbolic decorative elements and motifs, thereby possibly attempting to appropriate the supposed magical attributes that the Taino conferred upon the conquistadors.

The Conquest Phase

The second aspect of Indo-Hispanic interaction was the conquest phase. The interactions manifest in this phase, in contrast to the contact phase, indicate a more profound acculturative impact on the Old World newcomers than can be seen in the noncoercive contact phase. In their efforts to conquer and colonize the Antilles, the Spanish conquistadors and the African laborers who accompanied them assimilated a number of Taino cultural and linguistic elements. This assimilation took place as a consequence of cohabitation with the native peoples, and the Spaniards' necessary adaptations to a new and unfamiliar environmental setting. Many indigenous Taino traits were adopted as an appropriate response to the challenges posed by the American landscape.

Taino Cultural Legacies

Dietary patterns and foodways were among the most important of the Taino contributions to be integrated into colonial culture. The preparation of cassava bread from manioc (*Manihot esculenta*) was a Taino staple, and came to be known as the "bread of the conquest." It is still a staple today in the Dominican diet, as are other Taino foods such as corn (*Zea mays*) and sweet potato (*Ipomea batatas*). The botanical repertoire of the Taino also contributed a great deal of knowledge about the nutritional and medicinal qualities of numerous other indigenous plants.

One of the most important of the Taino legacies to be integrated into colonial culture was vernacular architecture; the wattle and daub or wood and thatch *buhío*. This type of primitive structure is still in use today throughout Hispaniola. Other indigenous traits adopted during the period of conquest included navigation in canoes and *cayucos*; the use of the *hamaca* (hammock); the use of *higueros* (gourds) as receptacles and musical instruments; the production of *bateas* (dugout canoes); the use of palm thatching for house roofs and basketry; the fabrication of many kinds of woven mats, baskets, cordage, and fabrics from endemic plants such as cotton (*Goddypium* sp.), *guano* palm (*Coccothrinax argentea*), the *cabuya* (*Frucraea hexapetala*), and hemp (*Agave sisalana*); and the smoking of tobacco (*Nicotiana tabacum*), which was an important element of Taino rituals. Most of these traits were adopted by Spaniards and Africans during the interaction and transculturation that occurred in the early stages of colonization.

Indigenous languages—particularly that of the Taino—also enriched Spanish and other European languages with a number of words that are today commonly used to designate plants, animals, people, and objects. The names of countless locations and geographical features of the New World also have native origins (see Henriquez-Urena 1947; Tejera 1977). A few examples that suffice to illustrate the wide diffusion of these Taino words include *hurucan* (hurricane), *canoa* (canoe), *hamaca* (hammock), *macana* (club or cudgel), *sabana* (savannah), *barbacoa* (barbeque), and *cacique* (cassique).

There is no doubt that despite the elapsed centuries, the Antillean toponymy has sustained the marked presence of indigenous terms. This phenomenon suggests that the assimilation of the Taino language by the Spaniards and Africans must have been intense.

The Dominican humanist Pedro Henriquez-Urena recognized Hispaniola's native legacy more than three decades ago in his essay, *History of Culture in Hispanic America*:

> Thirty years ago it would have been believed unnecessary to speak of indigenous culture when dealing with civilization in Hispanic America. Today, with the advance and dissemination of sociological and historical studies in general, and of ethnography and archaeology in particular, it is considered differently: if indeed the structure of our civilization, and its essential orientations come from Europe, not a few of the materials used for its construction are indigenous [1947:10].

Even earlier, in his note to Mariano Picon-Salas's book, *From Conquest to Independence*, Henriquez-Urena comments on native survivals in the Americas: "The fusion reaches not only the arts, it is ubiquitous. On the important and ostensible, we see the European model imposed; in domestic and daily traditions we see many indigenous traits preserved."

In his analysis of the true dimensions of the Taino legacy in Dominican culture, Bernardo Vega states:

> The indigenous must not be exaggerated in our culture; genetic factors by themselves explain the greater weight of European and African culture in the origin and development of our own. What is fair to point out, however, is the surprising persistence of certain indigenous cultural legacies, given the very brief period of contact [1981:12].

Taino Genetic Legacies

It should also be pointed out, however, that racial mixing is a poorly studied and understood phenomenon in the Antilles, despite the fact that it played a fundamental role in the development of colonial societies, particularly in the dispersed rural areas. Isolated, but nevertheless revealing documentary testimony from that era indicates the magnitude of unions between the Spaniards and the Indians—a union that gave rise to the first American mestizos.

Fray Bartolomé de las Casas, writing about the abundant Indo-Hispanic mixing that occurred in Hispaniola, comments:

> I came to know the life of a town, some years after we arrived in this island, that
> was established on the same spot where the King Behecio had his royal house; of
> 60 or 70 *vecinos* (Spanish citizens with rights to own land), all of them married to
> the daughters and kinswomen of the nobles, that were so beautiful that they
> would be considered the most beautiful women in our Castile [Las Casas 1967:2:310].

Las Casas also informs us of a number of other Indian–Spanish unions that
occurred in other parts of the island: "In La Vega I came to know women married
to Spaniards and to nobles, (who lived as) 'ladies of the town.' Others from the
town of Santiago married with them, their beauty is admirable and almost white
like the women of Castile" (1967:1:178).

Another account of the results of such racial amalgam was provided by Captain Francisco de Barrionuevo in 1533, on his return from the Sierra del Bahoruco
after settling a peace treaty with the Cassique Enriquillo: "There are a lot of mestizos here, sons of Spanish and Indians, that generally are born in uninhabited
places, and outside this city [Santo Domingo] everything else can be said to be
uninhabited" (Muñoz 1981:368).

Racial mixing was one of the most strikingly characteristic traits of Iberian conquest in the New World. The number of Spanish women who came to the Indies
during the early stages of the colony was very low and, as Rosenblatt (1954:18)
points out, "Spanish women were scarce during all of colonial history. Even during the most stable period of colonization more men than women came to the
Indies; a phenomenon general to all migration."

From the beginning of colonization the authorities encouraged marriage between Spaniards and chieftainesses (*cassiquas*) for strategic reasons. This is illustrated in the instructions given by Cardinal Cisneros (Regent of Spain) in 1516
to the friars in charge of the civil government of the Indies. These pointed out
that such unions were "very helpful and can save many expenses" (Morner
1969:46).

To this effect, mixed marriages were permitted by the royal decree of January
14, 1514:

> It is our own will that the Indians have—as it should be—the liberty to marry
> who they wish, with Indians who are the natives of these kingdoms or with
> Spaniards born in the Indies, and that with this they shall be given no impedi-
> ment, and we mandate that no order we have given shall impede or prohibit mar-
> riage between Indians and Spaniards, and that they all enjoy complete freedom to
> marry whom they wish, and that our officials ensure that it is obeyed and en-
> forced [Perez de Bamadas 1948:64].

We know from the list that appears in the 1514 *repartimiento* census made by
Rodrigo de Albuquerque that there were 70 land-owning citizens (*encomenderos*)
who were married to "chieftainesses" in Hispaniola (Rosenblatt 1954:2:19;
Demorizi 1971:16). But even more typical and numerous than these marriages
were the many unions outside of wedlock that comprised the widespread institution of concubinage. Not all of these were voluntary; in addition to those entered into by choice, many of the Indian servants (known as "naborias") were

forced to engage in relations with their masters. All of these factors led to the genetic importance of *mestizaje* during the colonial period.

Miscegenation between black and Indians was also quite common, both among black slaves who lived and worked with Indians on plantations and in the mining zones, and in the fugitive slave ("cimmaron") communities (*manieles*). The inhabitants of these illicit cimmaron communities were generally fugitive runaway slaves, and would frequently assault small villages and capture Indian women, retaining them in their manieles (Cassa 1974; Deive 1980:429–63).

According to a report from Archbishop Alonso de Fuenmayor concerning the economic, ecclesiastical, and political state of Hispaniola in 1545, there were, in 29 sugar mills belonging to prominent people on the island, 5,778 Indians laboring side by side with 3,300 blacks. This observation provides an indication of the intensity of interracial cohabitation in Santo Domingo during the first half of the sixteenth century (Mañón 1978; Peguero 1978).

(It should be clarified that the majority of the Indians represented in these figures would not have been of Taino origin, but rather Indian slaves brought from other areas. Their presence is nevertheless important in order to evaluate the Amerindian presence in the demographic composition of Hispaniola during the first half of the sixteenth century.)

Mestizaje in the Antilles did not reach the magnitude experienced in other parts of Latin America, owing to the rapid disintegration of aboriginal society through disease. Interracial relationships are nevertheless recognized today as one of the critical elements upon which Dominican society is founded. Such authors as Hugo Tolentino, for example, do not hesitate to state, "It is much to our sorrow that the persistence of mestizo presence in Santo Domingo has not been emphasized. It cannot be denied that it contributed to the racial and ethnic conformation of the Dominican people" (1974:101–102). This point has also been stressed by Alvarez (1973):

> The biological presence of the indigenous peoples of the Antilles in contemporary Dominican Society also cannot be denied, and this presence is very accentuated in some areas, and practically nonexistent in others. With the passing of the years, the indigenous elements were diluted in both the dynamics of miscegenation and the social structure of the colonial period, giving rise to the blending of these components with those of Spanish or African origin. It is still possible today, however, in remote and isolated mountain areas, to find the genetic remnants of the indigenous Dominican race.

(For a discussion of Amerindian community survival in Cuba, see Manuel Rivera de la Calle's "Antropologia Fisica de los Tainos," in *Las Culturas de America en La Epoca del Descubrimiento: Seminario sobre la Situacion de la Investigacion de la Cultura Taina*.)

The persistence of a Taino genetic component in contemporary Dominican life, along with the survival of certain undeniably indigenous beliefs and traditions (kept alive in rural areas and passed along through oral tradition) requires the recognition of a native substratum in our midst today. This proposition corroborates that of Jose Arrom (1975:18), who affirms,

Figure 18-1. Vessels made by Taino natives, reproducing Spanish models. These pitchers were found at the site of Juandolio, on the southeastern coast of Santo Domingo.

In the case of the Taino population, the creations and beliefs of these people had a greater influence than we suspect on the present actual culture of the Antilles. There exists ample documented evidence to demonstrate that the natives were decimated but not exterminated. In the initial processes of cohabitation and transculturation, not only material and visible traits, but also something of their latent vision and ways of feeling were transmitted. By knowing how they perceived the world and represented natural forces, we can approach the hidden roots of many religious beliefs and artistic creations found among today's *Antillanos*.

Taino and Indo-Hispanic Contact Period Ceramics

The adoption of Spanish ceramic traits by the Taino has been discussed above in the context of Indo-Hispanic contact. The following paragraphs document some of the changes manifested in Taino pottery as a consequence of this contact (see Figure 18-1).

The earthenware vessels made by the Tainos were praised by Christopher Columbus himself, when he entered in the diary of his first voyage: "They would bring water to us in gourds and in earthenware jars of Castilian quality" (1967:121). Las Casas also noted and appreciated Taino pottery, writing that the Indians would offer the admiral "water in earthenware jars, very well done and painted on the outside like red ochre" (1965:273).

Archaeological excavations carried out in the first Spanish settlements of Hispaniola have shown that the Spaniards used objects produced by the Taino in their culinary activities from the beginning of the conquest period. Aboriginal

Figure 18-2. Handmade plates imitating Spanish wheel-turned examples of the period. These vessels exhibit a degree of transculturation in which indigenous potters used traditional techniques to imitate ceramic types introduced by the conquistadors.

methods of pottery manufacture also continued to be used through the Colonial period to fill some of the everyday kitchen needs (Figure 18-2).

Between about 1515 and 1530, however, a gradual loss of the traditional Taino ceramic decorative elements can be seen. This undoubtedly occurred as a consequence of the exclusively culinary role that Taino ceramics had when used in the Spanish contexts, and the dominance of the Spaniards over the Indians. As part of this dominance we can suggest that decorative motifs and the symbolic content of Taino ritual design were suppressed or eliminated, for they were thought to be related to "Zemi" (small idols) worship and other pagan beliefs contrary to the evangelical interests of the conquistadors (see García-Arevalo 1978b; Smith 1986:13; Cusick 1989:5).

New European dietary elements, as well as food-preparation techniques, also influenced the changes occuring in Taino ceramics during the Indo-Hispanic period. New vessel forms were required to suit Spanish tastes, and vessel walls had to be thicker in order to make them more impervious to heat (García-Arevalo 1978b; Smith 1986; Cusick 1989). A general postcontact tendency toward simpler forms requiring less ceramic specialization has also been noted (Deagan 1987:725).

Postcontact Taino pottery shows dramatic technical changes in response to these factors, which tended to suppress ritual and artistic aspects and emphasize utilitarian aspects. These changes—which include thicker vessel walls, simpler surface finishes, and the absence of molded decoration (zemis)—ultimately gave rise to a new style known as Creole Pottery (a study and illustration of Creole Pottery is currently under way, to be published by the Fundación García-Arevalo, Santo Domingo).

The Creole Pottery tradition of the Dominican Republic incorporated Taino elements during the Indo-Hispanic period and retained them over the span of centuries, filling the domestic needs of many of the populations. It has persisted to the present day in various rural areas of the country and remains as one of the most evocative examples of Dominican craftsmanship found today in the Dominican Republic.

Conclusions

The arrival of the Spanish and their cultural dominance in Hispaniola dramatically altered the way of life of the island's native inhabitants, particularly that of the Taino. These alterations are reflected in the postcontact Taino ceramic traditions, which materially embodied important ideological, social, technical, symbolic, and dietary aspects of Taino life. These altered traditions give testimony to the interaction and cohabitation that characterized the Indo-Hispanic period in the Antilles.

During the initial contact phase, the native peoples had great esteem for European objects, attributing divine qualities to them. They were used in Taino burial ritual while it still existed in its traditional forms, thus illustrating religious syncretism and symbolic substitution.

Archaeological evidence also demonstrates that Spanish ceramic forms—such as jars, dishes, and escudillas—influenced Taino ceramics. Taino potters attempted to imitate these new shapes during the early contact period, often creating aberrant forms that diverged from both Spanish and Taino traditional models.

These new types were stimulated in the early contact phase by an influx of Spanish elements to Taino communities through trade and exchange. The emerging syncretic ceramic tradition was abruptly interrupted, however, by the effects of Spanish conquest and subjugation of the native inhabitants, and the imposition of new socioeconomic and cultural patterns. These effects suppressed freedom of expression for Taino craftsmen.

Thus during the conquest phase the Taino ceramic industry—often located in Spanish establishments—again changed dramatically, marked by artistic impoverishment, and the disappearance of the richly symbolic iconographic traits that characterized Antillean pottery in precontact times. This loss can be explained by Spanish hostility toward elements that were inspired by Taino magico-religious belief and mythology, and that were contrary to the goals of Spanish Catholic evangelization.

Spanish dietary practices, as well as preferences in ceramic use, were imposed on the Taino, and also contributed to the simplification and loss of artistic and ritual elements. This process was accelerated by the postcontact breakdown of Taino social organization, including the loss of specialized craftsmen. The conquistadors were interested primarily in extracting manual labor from the Indians and did not nurture or take advantage of the class of skilled potters existing at the time of contact.

Despite these adverse factors, the techniques of Taino ceramic production, as with various other discrete Taino production methods, did not disappear completely under Spanish domination. Instead they evolved, developing new forms and finding different uses, and giving rise to a new style known as Creole Pottery. This creole ceramic style is an index and reflection of Indo-Hispanic transculturation in Hispaniola, and is part of the aboriginal legacy assimilated by the Spaniards and later by the African blacks.

Thus the Indians of Hispaniola contributed in a singular way to the criollo cultural and social patterns that crystallized during the process of conquest. These contributions, which were incorporated in the earliest stages of colonial life, have been preserved as tradition, passed on from generation to generation, and now constitute an important part of the language, craftsmanship, and national folklore of the Dominican Republic.

Notes

This chapter was translated by Kathleen Deagan, Gianna Brown, and Ricardo Fernandez-Sardina.

References

Arrom, José Juan
    1975 *Mitologías y artes prehispánic de las Antillas*. Siglo XIX Editores, S. A. Fundación García Arévalo, Mexico.
Casas, Fray Bartolomé de las
    1965 *Historia de las Indias*. 3 vols. Edición de Agustin Millares Carlo y Prólogo de Lewis Hanke. Fondo de Cultura Económica, Mexico.
    1967 *Apologética Historia Sumaria*. 2 vols., Edición, notas y prólogo de Edmundo O'Gorman. U.N.A.M., Mexico.
Cassá, Roberto
    1974 *Los taínos de la Española*. U.A.S.D., Santo Domingo.
Columbus, Christopher
    1968 *Diario*. Prólogo de Gregorio Marañón Instituto de Cultura Hispánica, Madrid.
Cusick, James
    1989 *A Study of Postcontact Stylistic Change in Taino Ceramics at En Bos Saline, Haiti*. Unpublished Master's thesis, University of Florida, Gainesville.
Deagan, Kathleen
    1983 *Spanish St. Augustine. The Archaeology of a Colonial Creole Community*. Academic Press, New York.
    1987 *Artifacts of the Spanish Colonies of Florida and the Caribbean, 1500–1800. Vol. 1: Ceramics, Glassware and Beads*. Smithsonian Institution Press, Washington, D.C.
Deive, Carlos Esteban
    1980 *La esclavitud del negro en Santo Domingo (1492-1844)*. Museo del Hombre Dominicano, Santo Domingo.
Demorizi, Rodriguez
    1971 Los Dominicos y las Encomiendas de Indios de la Isla Española. Santo Domingo.
Domínguez, Lourdes
    1978 *La transculturación en Cuba (S. XVI–XVII)*. Cuba Arqueológica, pp. 33–50, Santiago de Cuba.
Foster, George M.
    1960 *Culture and Conquest: America's Spanish Heritage*. Viking Fund Publications in Anthropology No. 27. New York.

García-Arevalo, Manuel A.
  1977   *El arte taíno de la República Dominicana*. Publicación de la Fundación García Arévalo, Barcelona.
  1978a   *Influencia de la dieta indo-hispánica en la cerámica taína*. Boletín del Museo del Hombre Dominicano 9, Santo Domingo.
  1978b   *La arqueología indophispana en Santo Domingo*. Publicado en "Unidad y variedades, ensayo en homenaje a J. M. Cruxent". Centro de Estudios Avanzados. Ivic, Caracas.
García Castañeda, José A.
  1938   *Asiento Yayal*. Revista de Arqueología1(1) 44–58. La Habana.
Henriquez-Urena, Pedro
  1947   *La Historia de la Cultura en Hispanoamerica*. Santo Domingo.
Mañón Arredondo, Manuel
  1978   *Importancia arqueológica de los ingenios indo-hispánicos de las Antillas*. Boletín del Museo del Hombre Dominicano 10:139–172. Santo Domingo.
Morales Patiño, Oswaldo and Roberto Pérez de Acevedo
  1946   *El período de transculturación indo-hispánico*. La Habana. Revista de Arqueología y Etnología. 1(1):5–135.
Morner, Magnus
  1969   *Race Mixture in the History of Latin America*. Little Brown, Boston.
Muñoz, Juan Bautista
  1981   *Santo Domingo en los manuscritos de Juan Bautista Muñoz*. Transcripción y glosas de Roberto Marte. Fundación García Arévalo, Barcelona.
Peguero, Luis Joseph
  1975   *Historia de la conquista de la isla española de Santo Domingo. Transumptada el año de 1762*. Vol. 1. Edición, Estudio Preliminar y Notas de Pedro J. Santiago. Publicaciones del Museo de las Casas Reales, Santo Domingo.
Picón-Salas, Mariano
  1947   *De la conquista a la indepéndencia*. Fondo de la Cultura Económica, Mexico.
Rosenblatt, Angel
  1954   *La Población de América en 1492*. Nuevos y Viejos Calculos, Mexico City.
Rouse, Irving
  1942   *Archeology of the Maniabon Hills, Cuba*. Yale University Publications in Anthropology No. 26. New Haven.
  1964   Prehistoric in the West Indies. *Science* 144(3618):499–513.
Rouse, Irving, and J.M. Cruxent
  1963   *Arqueología venezolana*. Instituto venezolano de Investigaciones Científicas, Caracas.
Smith, Greg Charles
  1986   *Non-European Pottery at the Sixteenth Century Spanish Site of Puerto Real, Haiti*. Unpublished thesis, University of Florida,
Tejera, Emilio
  1977   *Indigenismos*. 2 vols. Sociedad Dominicana de Bibliófilos, Barcelona.
Tolentino, Hugo
  1974   *Raza e historia en Santo Domingo*. U.A.S.D., Santo Domingo.
Vega, Bernardo
  1981   *La heréncia indígena en la cultura dominicana de hoy*. Ensayos sobre la cultura dominicana, pp. 11–59. Museo del Hombre Dominicano, Santo Domingo.
Veloz-Maggiolo, Marcio
  1972   *La arqueología prehistórica de Santo Domingo*. McGraw-Hill, Singapore.

Chapter 19 ■

Eugene Lyon

The Enterprise of Florida

Among the remarks that have been made on the nature of history is the popular dictum: "History is about things we don't know, written by people who weren't there." More to the point are two remarks of Eugen Weber, a modern historian: first, "there are only partial histories"; but also "the future inevitably enriches the past and colors it" (Weber 1984).

As a partial hedge against the distortion of the past, historians have formed a concept analogous to the "ethnographic present," which might be termed "the historical present." In reaching for this historical present, we seek context through valid and sufficient primary sources, much as archaeologists do in assigning proper provenience to artifacts recovered in the field. We strive to detect intrusive elements, using our own time-tested canons about the authenticity of documents.

How, then, can historians and their sources best be utilized in the pursuit of ethnohistorical reality, that merging of the ethnographic and historical presents? Reviewing that question, a thoughtful essayist has said "the historian becomes more important when the archaeologist moves beyond simple chronology and secondary studies into discussions of social status, population size and composition, sources and forms of the supply of material (culture) items and similar complex . . . questions" (Hoffman 1983). In such an ethnohistoric collaboration, need one discipline be the other's handmaiden? Can we not seek objective interchange? Can we avoid the contamination of the historic present by clearly intrusive elements?

The following may be one such intrusion; succeeding the original "Black Legend" about sixteenth-century Spain is another that might be termed "The New Black Legend." As demographers continue to develop their findings about population decline among Native Americans, it appears that important European and African disease may have decimated the southeastern Indians to a degree not unlike that in Hispaniola, the Bahamas, and Mexico. A parallel and progressive destruction of native cultures also occurred in the colonial period (Cook and Borah 1963; Crosby 1972; Dobyns 1983; Lyon 1988b; Zambardino 1980–1981).

It is not this undeniable body of fact, but rather its possible effect upon scholarly inquiry, that is in question. In its extremes, reaction against these facts has taken the form of a total rejection of the Spanish expansion into the Americas, as if it had never occurred. Last fall, for instance, a Mexico City newspaper headline proposed: "¡Colón al paredón!" (Columbus to the wall!). In our country, some historians have expressed these sentiments: Either we should not glorify the "oppressors" by studying the period of initial European expansion at all, or we should strongly deemphasize it by concentrating upon what followed. The New Black Legend.

How does this sort of ideological emphasis affect us? Does it make of some of us Hispanophiles, carrying water for Pedro Menéndez, apologists for Pizarro, laborers in the vineyard of the modern North American Hispanics? Are other scholars then by definition compelled through concern over the decimation and degradation of native peoples to become their passionate advocates?

Perhaps that is where our studies and inclinations may leave us. Regardless of that, it is suggested here that all peoples in the historical present of the sixteenth century are valid subjects for scholarly inquiry; let us neglect none of them. How else can we attempt to comprehend the determinants of the cosmic fusion that has produced us? Which is one historian's way of expressing solidarity with David Thomas's cubist statement (1989).

In the interests, then, of Columbian Cubism, in this chapter I discuss the origins and events of the entrepreneurial Spanish conquest of Florida of 1565 to 1577. I attempt to describe some of the impact of their complex cultures upon Native Americans. I endeavor to reproduce, at least in part, the rich societal mosaic that once was present here, and that has left material culture remains for the patient fieldworkers who now uncover the Spanish past at Santa Elena, on St. Catherine's Island, in St. Augustine, or elsewhere in the Southeast.

Foundations of Outreach: The Origins of the Private Side of Conquest

The impulse for Spanish colonization that led Pedro Menéndez de Avilés to Florida began long before the Columbus voyages, with its roots in the reconquest of Spain and overseas experience in the Canary Islands (Bishko 1956; Zavala 1948). Once Spaniards reached the Indies, two fundamentally different models of settlement entered into opposition.

The first model, that of Mediterranean mercantilism, was embodied in Christopher Columbus's vision of a Crown monopoly to exploit the riches, as he thought, of Asia. This New World vision openly conflicted with Castile's long tradition of expansion through the assimilation of new lands by Castilians who shared in the enterprise. This conflict makes more understandable Columbus's eventual relegation to the status of a residual estateholder in the New World enterprise. The subsequent history of Spanish expansion in the Americas featured continual tension between the Crown's wish to control the process and its own scarce resources, which forced it to rely upon "private conquerors." These were royal surrogates called adelantados, whose precursors had been developed during the conquest of Andalusia from the thirteenth through the fifteenth centuries. This relationship was incorporated into the royal contracts with all the sixteenth-century adelantados (González 1951; Hill 1913; Lyon 1976:1–7, 1985).

Thus a traditional process of land assimilation, originated during the Reconquest, was transmitted intact to the Americas (Council of the Indies 1671). It was widely used for diplomatic and economic reasons in the sixteenth century, despite the increasing strength of the absolutist Hapsburg monarchy and the parallel development of fiscal, juridical, and vice-regal institutions in the New World.

The private side of the Florida enterprise, which developed into a joint venture between the Spanish Crown and its adelantado, Pedro Menéndez de Avilés, was an essential underpinning of the conquest effort. This private interest was embodied in a coterie of followers, a whole conquest-group interrelated by blood, place of origin, marriage, or economic interest (Lyon 1976:71–77, 1979).

Florida Expectations

What were the expectations of Pedro Menéndez and his followers in Florida? Since most of the control group that they constituted were Asturians, they hoped to reproduce their *país*, their homeland. Asturias—a fair, green, but mountainous land—received adequate rainfall and had flourishing pastures, vineyards, and nut groves. However, its growing population put heavy pressure upon the limited arable land. Many ambitious youths, like Menéndez, were forced out upon the adjacent sea to seek their livelihood.

Still the exiles from the remembered country preserved their individual dreams of the ownership of land. Land, measured in *días de bueyes*, the days it took a team of oxen to plow a tract, was the currency of wealth in Asturias. It was bought and sold, leased, share-cropped, and mortgaged readily among a number of small or large proprietors.[1]

Spaniards transferred their land hunger to the Indies, where it underlay Spain's impulse for New World settlement. The king promised Florida contractholder Lucas Vázquez de Ayllón "your own land . . . to farm, with all its pastures, woods, meadows, waters and rivers" (Ayllón 1523). This hunger for land is overlooked by those who would characterize the motivations of Spanish expansion by the words "God, Gold and Glory" (Lyon 1981).

Although kings might award large tracts to important nobles like Menéndez, an efficient mechanism enabled ordinary Spaniards to obtain land in the Indies. Municipal councils possessed the power to divide royal lands (*tierras de realengo*) among their citizens (Morse 1962).

In addition to his dream of replicating Asturias, Pedro Menéndez de Avilés had another model: the Oaxaca empire founded by Hernán Cortéz and his successors in the Valley of Mexico. Menéndez's promised Florida land grant of 25 leagues squared would support the title of marquis, which had been given Cortez.

Other benefits for emigrants, perfected during the Antillean, New Spain, and South American conquests, were defined as the "rights of conquerors." These included tax exemptions and rights in Native American labor and tribute. The structured use of native labor and the payment of tribute also were planned for Spanish Florida.

In addition to planning his estate in Florida, Pedro Menéndez was a visionary on a continental scale. He sought to find the Northwest Passage through North America and thus open Spain's route to China. In a Florida writ large, Menéndez planned to fortify the east coast up to 50 degrees North Latitude and patrol the Newfoundland codfishing banks. Turning westward, he proposed to erect a line of mission forts across the Mississippi, and master the Gulf of Mexico. Later in his conquest, he applied for another royal contract, this time for Pánuco, on New Spain's border. Thus, he could link Spain commercially with the mines of Guanajuato and Zacatecas by way of Florida (Lyon 1985; Menéndez 1566, 1568; Vigneras 1969).

The Spaniards in Florida: Cultural Baggage

Apart from their desire to recreate their Spanish homeland, and to be individual shareholders in the profits of that re-creation, what other cultural baggage did Spaniards bring to the enterprise of Florida? It was as diverse as the persons engaged, incorporating a variety of selected cultural imports. Among these were the presence of and adherence to a number of institutions, belief systems, and other cultural entities present in early modern Spain (Foster 1960).

This was to be what has been termed "a deferential society," strongly influenced by the class structure and corporatism of Iberian life. Most of the ranks of society except the very highest, those of grandee and royal family, would be represented in Florida. The deference among these orders would, however, be tempered by the presence of the ever-sturdy and individualistic Spaniard. Moreover, a degree of mobility did exist in Spanish society, often involving advancement through commercial ties (Pike 1966:37–39).

Although he was no high nobleman, and did not use the honorific "Don," Pedro Menéndez aspired to grandee status, and planned to "ennoble" Florida, populating it with hidalgos (Menéndez 1565b). Guiding the Florida enterprise through its patron Adelantado Menéndez would be what Asturians call a *comuño*—a grouping of families joined for social advancement and common profit through blood, marriage, or other association (Lyon 1976:71–77, 1979). The lesser relationships of client and patron were also evident among those who gathered to undertake the conquest of Florida.

For good or ill, the new colony would be strongly influenced by the seafaring or military past of its people. Menéndez and many of his chief followers were sailors whose experiences colored their continental strategies and settlement tactics (Lyon 1987a:40–42). Many of Menéndez's captains and soldiers were veterans of the French or Italian wars, and, as he charged, were used to "banquets, booty and wine" (Menéndez 1566), and accustomed to the semi-independent life of the Spanish infantry company.

Spanish Florida, a branch of the sacramental, Tridentine Mother Church, was destined to be a community suffused with religiosity. It would, in microcosm, partake of the bewildering variety of devotions, orders, and lay organizations of Counter-Reformation Spain. Its cities and missions would number their hours by the church bells, while their soldiers and settlers would count their days by the feasts and Holy Days of the Christian calendar.

Initial Contact in Spanish Florida

Native American Cultures and Spanish-Indian Law

The Native Americans in Florida at the time of contact with the Spaniards in 1565 consisted primarily of the Calusa, Ais, Timucua, Apalachee, Guale, and some lesser groups (Deagan 1978b; Hann 1988; Lewis 1978; Lyon 1967, 1980; Thomas et al. 1978; Widmer 1988). Although there were substantial cultural differences among them, it appears that these peoples all exhibited evidence of coherent social and political integration and were part of ordered, ritualized societies. Their organizations usually featured hereditary chieftainships and strong clan systems. In sum, they held their cultures as a powerful shield against the "Other" described by Todorov (1984). Unless and until those shields could be broken or voluntarily laid aside, no attempted Spanish domination of these peoples could succeed.

By 1565, long-continued disputes over the treatment of the native Americans had culminated in successive Spanish codifications establishing regulations for Indian protection and for their religious conversion. Pedro Menéndez's royal contract for Florida required him, as a primary obligation, to convert the Indians to the Catholic religion and bring them to obedience to the King (Philip II 1565). Where the Florida contract of the second Vázquez de Ayllón forbade him to establish encomiendas of Indians, Menéndez's agreement made no such prohibition. In fact, despite the rhetoric of the rights of Native Americans, two-life repartimiento and three-life encomienda with tribute payments were allowed by the royal ordinances for new discovery and settlement (Philip II 1573:58, 61, 145, 146, 149). Moreover, the "Just War" doctrine, which permitted Spaniards to war upon rebelling Indians under certain circumstances, was still very much alive in 1565.

Possession Taking and First Contact

Pedro Menéndez's first act upon landing in St. Augustine in September 1565 was to formally take possession of the whole of Florida and its peoples, in the name of the Crown of Castile. The event was properly certified and recorded, and followed the certified possession acts of previous explorers. These actions validated the Spanish king's continental title, which was granted through the donation of Pope Alexander VI and had previously been debated in the Council of the Indies (1565).

The possession taking also constituted the lands of North America as *tierras de realengo*. Thus it gave the Spanish Crown or its legally designated representatives the power to retain lands or alienate them to third parties. It was the semifeudal basis for the power of treaty making with the native peoples, in the name of a king who now suddenly owned, and could dispose of, the continent that they inhabited.

But before the Spaniards could deal with the Indians whom they met in Florida, they had to overcome obstacles to mutual communication created by the barrier of language. It was perforce necessary to utilize or develop intermediaries who could make each party intelligible to the other. Interpreters, many of whom were Frenchmen or Spaniards released from Indian captivity, were put on Menéndez's regular payroll (Lyon 1987a).

But simple translation of spoken or written words did not bring immediate understanding. As they did in colonial New England, examples of mutual misapprehension abound in Spanish Florida documentation (Cronon 1983; Lyon 1967).

These misapprehensions were exacerbated by Spanish preconceptions. For instance, Pedro Menéndez was preoccupied with French influence over the Indians; there were, of course, actual instances of Florida native cooperation with the French (Bushnell 1983). But Pedro Menéndez also believed that the French Calvinist "heretics" held Satanic beliefs that were strangely compatible with Native American religious rites. Thus his relations with the eastern Timucua were darkened by suspicion (Lyon 1987b:49).

Alfred Thomas describes two Spanish strategies in dealing with the Native Americans, "one preventive and the other punitive. First they tried to make peace with the Indians; . . . the second technique was to make campaigns in Indian territory" (Thomas 1968). Certainly the Spaniards practiced the making of peace with the Florida Indians through written treaties. Texts of some of these compacts and descriptions of others have survived (Gutiérrez de Palomar 1571; Quirós 1580). The agreements fixed the Indians as vassals to the suzerain Philip II, to whom they swore fealty and promised to pay tribute, all of this being recorded by a notary. Since the violation of sworn fealty was, in America, grounds for waging "just war," the treaties were taken seriously by the Spaniards. This "just war" was graphically described as the logical outcome of Indian disobedience in the Requerimiento, since 1514 a standard harangue to the Indians (Todorov 1984:147). It puzzled and frustrated the Spaniards that agreements often had to be signed more than once with the same Indian groups.

Another factor that confused the mutual contact relationship was the private aspect of the Florida enterprise. This was especially evident in matters of trade with native peoples, which was called *rescate*. Florida governors often had to instruct expedition captains to restrain the cupidity of their soldiers, as they sought to trade privately for ambergris or precious metals and coins the Indians had recovered from shipwrecks (Lyon 1987a:2). In fact, the officials themselves were at times accused of complicity in such illegal trade (Lyon 1976:176).

Tribute payments were also regularly "privatized," and it was sometimes difficult to determine if the gifts given to Native American leaders by the Spaniards represented official presents or consideration for goods or services furnished to the Spanish leaders for their own account. These presents to the Indians were made up of a great variety of items (Gayón 1568).

The Development of Spanish Culture in Florida

The Religious Influence

Pedro Menéndez noted that the Florida colony celebrated the days of Sts. Augustine and Matthew, commemorating his sighting of Florida in 1565 and his capture of Fort Caroline. September eighth, the Day of Our Lady, when the Spaniards celebrated the first Mass in St. Augustine, and All Saint's Day, the day of Menéndez's defeat of the French at Cape Canaveral, were also observed. Further demonstrating the linkage between Menéndez's feats of arms and the militant Counter-Reformation Church, the adelantado asked for papal indulgences for the commemorative feast days, and for all of his colonists and soldiers, if they were to die without confession during the conquest (Menéndez 1571a).

In the Florida cities or at its most remote outposts, the religious influence was manifest. City life featured the processions of the Easter cycle, and of the True Cross in Santa Elena, where the confraternity of the same name paraded (Confraternity of the True Cross 1576; Olmos 1576). In the fort mission of Tequesta on Biscayne Bay, Jesuit Francisco Villareal staged two morality comedies on "the war between vices and virtues" at the mission for the entertainment and enlightenment of the soldiers (Villareal 1568).

Social Structure

Pedro Menéndez's Florida adelantamiento was directly accountable to King Philip II through his Council of the Indies in the person of Menéndez, who filled the top military and civil commands as governor and captain-general. He was at the top of the Florida legal appeals channel, an onerous position, for he ruled a litigious tribe. But dominating any formal legal structure in Florida was the shallow government of the *comuño*; examination of the major Florida offices during this time discloses that the majority of them, including fiscal posts supposedly answerable only to the Crown, were in reality manipulated by *comuño* figures (Lyon 1979; List of Governors ca. 1576).

The Florida legal cases disclose much about the society of sixteenth-century Spanish Florida. They depict, for instance, the arrogance of Governor Don Diego de Velasco, the legitimized grandson of the constable of Castile, who had married Menéndez's illegitimate daughter María. Velasco struck the tailor Alonso de Olmos for refusing to work on the rebuilding of the Santa Elena fort. Later, Olmos—also a farmer, moneylender, and tavernkeeper—filed suit against the same governor for insulting his daughter during a religious procession. He also alleged that Velasco villified him by crying out, "See the Lutheran going to the synagogue!" During the trial, the tailor averred that, as against Don Diego de Velasco, he held himself "to be as honorable as he" (Lyon 1984b; Olmos 1576).

Another distinct social order was that of the *criados*, or servants. One of these, Juan Rodríguez, slept on the floor outside his mistress's chambers in St. Augustine. One Captain Miguel Enriquez had a gardener at his house. The adelantado, who kept court like any high Indies official, had as retainers another type of *criado*, noble aides like Juan and Hernán de Quirós (Enriquez 1567; Rodríguez 1576; Quirós 1572).

The settlers themselves, especially at Santa Elena, constituted a strong interest group quite distinct from the soldiers or *comuño* members (Enriquez 1567). After an unsuccessful attempt to bring colonists from the Azores, Pedro Menéndez took his first settler group from the *meseta* of central Spain. Menéndez had originally promised his own soldiers land for farming and stock raising, and the settlers who came in 1568 and later were *labradores*, small farmers with large families (Menéndez 1565a; Settlers of Florida 1568). Once established at Santa Elena, the settlers built houses, worked at their lands and livestock, and engaged in trade, but also involved themselves in the city government (Settlers of Florida 1569).

The continuing role of military tradition in Spanish Florida was shown in the nearly disastrous mutinies that swept the colony from north to south in 1566, and virtually destroyed Pedro Menéndez's enterprise before it could fairly begin. The semi-independent company commanders and their brawling infantrymen often had to be subdued by force before peace could be restored (Lyon 1984a).

The Florida Material Culture

Several archaeologists have described the colonial Florida material culture (Deagan 1978a; Griffin et al. 1982; Milanich and Fairbanks 1980; Thomas 1987). Other studies have been made of status as revealed in archaeological investigations (Deagan 1974; Thomas et al. 1977).

A basic list of material culture items from Spanish Florida between 1565 and 1569 has been extracted from the Florida accounts by Paul Hoffman (1976). These included tools of agriculture and other crafts and many different types of cloth. Containers, nails, and other fasteners were imported or made in Florida (Lyon 1988c).

In addition, simple personal goods were listed in the property inventories of deceased soldiers: hats, swords, a guitar or vihuela, a jacket. Their issue clothing and equipment had included a jacket, breeches, hat, sword-belt, shirts, sandals or shoes, stockings, and a blanket. A typical Florida-bound soldier named Diego Flores de Robles also received an arquebus with powder flasks, and a bullet mold. Archaeologist Stanley South has found a bullet mold in the Santa Elena fort moat (Soldiers' Inventories 1576; Flores 1575; South et al. 1988:80, 89).

In contrast, the property of nobles, officials, and others of higher status was of a different order of magnitude. It included more expensive items of clothing and many other personal possessions. When the adelantado moved to Santa Elena with his wife Doña María de Solís, he brought valuable personal household and stable furnishings—costly canopy beds and carpets, linens and table settings in silver and pewter, saddles and tack (Menéndez 1571b). After his death at the hands of the Indians at Sapelo in Guale, the adelantado's nephew Pedro Menéndez the Younger left expensive possessions. The assets of Don Diego de Velasco, the elder Menéndez's son-in-law, seized at his arrest in Santa Elena, constitute another list of costly items. Interestingly, they also included a large number of promissory notes and other papers relating to his private business affairs in Florida (Menéndez the Younger 1576; Velasco 1576).

In addition to basic foodstuffs, articles of clothing, and standard military and household equipment, many luxury goods were imported for resale by the adelantado's factors. His agent Diego Ruiz sold swords, clothes, and majolica for Menéndez in Santa Elena. Other items sold to settlers and soldiers included waistbands, ribbons, ornamental braid (*bordado*), Toledo bonnets, hourglasses, combs, *vihuela* strings, and marzipan. Imported delicacies included dates, almonds, figs, capers, raisins, sugar fritters, hazelnuts, quince paste, and anise seed (Menéndez 1571b; Ruiz 1574).

Religious materials entering Florida included a painted retable for the parish church, with a gilded cross and an image of Santa Clara, the patron saint of Avilés, which had been donated by the adelantado's wife (Confraternity of the True Cross 1576; Lyon 1984b:20, n. 25).

Economic Activity in Spanish Florida

The adelantado's vision for the economic future of his colony was closely linked with his own personal design. In 1569 he told the Council of the Indies that he wished to attract merchants to join the enterprise so that Crown, adelantado, and commercial interests would all profit. He looked to develop naval stores, sugar cultivation, silk production, and lumbering in Florida (Menéndez 1569).

Documents for this period in Spanish Florida reflect the trades, crafts, or activities of whaling; viniculture; the raising of wheat, barley, corn, fruit, and vegetable crops; fishing; hunting; fur trading; carpentry; shoemaking; tailoring; charcoal burning; prostitution; moneylending; lumbering; the gathering of root crops; smithing; lime burning; the production of pitch and other naval stores; cattle raising and the raising of chickens, goats, sheep, and horses; the import and sale of goods; the operation of boardinghouses, taverns, and gambling establishments; the making of matchcord from the cabbage palm; and the fabrication of suits of padded cotton armor.

The use and cultivation of maize became important in Spanish Florida. At Santa Elena after 1570, and in St. Augustine later, it became a large-scale activity. Both sassafras and lumber were exported from Florida during the Menéndez years (Lyon 1984b; Reitz and Scarry 1985).

Because of the wealth of timber resources, shipbuilding took place in Florida during this time. On the Fort Caroline ways and at Santa Elena, Pedro Menéndez had two *fregatas* constructed (Astudillo 1571).

In sum, one might surmise where Spanish Florida was heading: toward an economic base of hides, tallow, and local meat consumption, like that of the later Rio de la Plata or Spanish California, plus some production of lumber and naval stores. In later years, this is what had begun to develop (Bushnell 1981).

Later Events and Results of the Conquest

Spanish Indian Policies in Practice

From 1565 to 1573, Pedro Menéndez and his lieutenants followed the two-track path with the Native Americans. They executed treaties with many groups. Nonetheless, Indian troubles began immediately. Open warfare broke out with the Ais between Cape Canaveral and the Spanish fort at Santa Lucía. Father Pedro Martínez, one of the first Jesuit missionaries to arrive in Florida, was killed by Indians in the Mocamo area in 1566. Now, as disturbances and ambushes multiplied in Timucua, the Spaniards sent out armed punitive expeditions. In 1567, Captain Andrada and his whole troop were killed on such an entrada in Potano. Then, in 1568, not long after the entire Spanish garrison at Tocobaga on Tampa Bay had been massacred, Timucuan allies guided Dominique de Gourges to the mouth of the St. Johns River. There the Frenchman took the Spanish blockhouses and captured Fort San Mateo. Indian war tactics forced Menéndez to change his own methods; he employed crossbows and padded cotton armor to return the Indians' rapid arrow fire and protect his soldiery (Lyon 1976:150, 170, 198–201, 203; Menéndez 1566).

Alternately offering the sword and the olive branch, the Spaniards used another strategem with the Indians: They took, and sometimes gave, hostages in an attempt to guarantee peace (Gutiérrez de Palomar 1571; Lyon 1987a:5). But Spanish claims to political and religious sovereignty posed a danger, as perceived by the Native Americans, to the inherent values of their cultures. When Spaniards exercised their supposed right to interfere with Indian leadership by appointment or deposition, the basic structure of the native group was affected. The zealous Jesuit missionaries, using a technique of working with elites that had been successful in Europe and utilizing experience with other peoples illiterate in Spanish, still made little headway in their conversion efforts. The missionaries' claim for exclusivity of the Christian God negated the Indians' offer of placement in a pantheon of other deities. While apprehension and misapprehension continued to build, individual acts of agression on both sides exacerbated the disturbances.

In this state of chronic sporadic warfare, treaty making, hostage taking, trade, and Indian gift giving continued. In 1572, after the attempt to establish a mission at the Chesapeake ended in the death of all the missionaries, the Jesuits withdrew from Florida.

So great was Menéndez's frustration at his failures with the Native Americans that he proposed to the king in 1573 that he be permitted to enslave them and send them to the islands of the Antilles. The king refused the request (Menéndez 1573b). Still, the request had been in the tradition of the "just war," which had recently been reaffirmed in New Spain (Lyon 1984b:21, n.32).

It certainly appears that institutionalized forms of Indian labor, such as the encomienda and repartimiento, were planned for, and did exist in, Spanish Florida. After the death of Menéndez, a lengthy request by a succeeding adelantado petitioned for the family and associates "the encomiendas and rights of conquerors" (Adelantado of Florida n.d.). Although no grants of encomienda have been found in the documents on Spanish Florida, there exists evidence of a number of forced Native American labor arrangements. These appeared along the Guale coast and in Apalachee. This labor supply system appeared to be governed much like the Peruvian *mita*. It resembled, in fact, what Lyle McAlister has termed the "new repartimiento," in which native caciques sent labor drafts, ostensibly paid, to serve on Spanish works and to toil in the private fields of Spaniards (McAlister 1984:211). The labor repartimientos were still operating in Guale by the mid-seventeenth century (Argüelles 1663).

The Final Stage of the Conquest

With the failure of the South Florida forts and missions, Spanish Florida shifted northward after 1568 (Lyon 1988a). In 1569 there occurred a general crisis in Menéndez's finances. After four royal councils met to consider Florida, a royal subsidy was approved in 1570. Then Menéndez brought more settlers and his own family to Santa Elena, the new colonial capital, near his planned estate at Guatari. He entrusted its government to his sons-in-law (Menéndez 1573a, 1574; Valdés 1565). In 1574, on a naval assignment in Spain, Pedro Menéndez died.

After the removal of its chief figure, the Florida colony showed signs of internal disorder, as disputes arose among the Menéndez heirs. Although a new Franciscan mission experienced some degree of success in Guale, the friars had to work with all the contradictions of the Indian relationships. They condemned but could not prevent the cruelties of Menéndez's governors at Santa Elena and in Guale. Menéndez's successor, Hernando de Miranda, was forced to abandon Santa Elena in the face of a hostile confederation of the Guale and Orista. When the next governor, Pedro Menéndez Marqués, took office, he instituted a series of severe punitive raids. Nothing had changed for the better.

In the end, the sixteenth-century Florida enterprise failed to achieve its aims of settlement and prosperity for Spaniards, and obedience and Christianity for Native Americans. The resources of the adelantado and the Crown were insufficient to carry out their multiple purposes. The soldiery was therefore spread too thin to defend the colony or its settlers adequately, and the threat of Indian warfare kept the Spaniards confined to a coastal perimeter. In their turn, the Spanish settlers' inability to reach the better Piedmont soils of the interior limited severely their possibilities for success (Lyon 1984b).

Conclusions

Spanish Florida was, in its elements, consistent with Spain's outreach in other parts of the Indies. Its entrepreneurial conquest, or *adelantamiento*, was much like others in the Spanish Indies. This vigorous thrust of sixteenth-century Spain was a major cultural transfer, for Spanish Florida in the sixteenth century represented direct if selective transplants from Asturias and other regions. The Menéndez years exhibited all the rhetoric and reality of the contacts with Native Americans that occurred in other parts of the Spanish Indies.

By 1577 the interaction of cultures had led to a degree of mutual acculturation between Spaniards and Native Americans. It was, however, already evident that those Indians who most fully maintained their isolation and independence from the European invaders—those who kept their shield raised against the Other—had the best chance for continued cultural survival.

Notes

The fifteenth- and sixteenth-century records of innumerable land transactions are found in profusion in the private archives relating to the north of Spain, including those for the Menéndez, Valdés, and other affiliated families, in the Archivo de los Condes de Revillagigedo. A microfilm copy of the entire archives is held at the P. K. Yonge Library of Florida History, University of Florida, and at the St. Augustine Foundation at Flagler College. Following is a key to the abbreviations used in the references:

ACR Archivo de los condes de Revillagigedo
AGI Archivo General de Indias
AIDVJ Archivo del Instituto de Valencia de Don Juan (Madrid)
CAN *Canalejas*. From ACR.
EC *Escribanía de Cámara* ⎤
IG Indiferente General ⎬ In the AGI
JU *Justicia* ⎦
PAT *Patronato Real*
SAFD St. Augustine Foundation Database
SD *Santo Domingo*. In the AGI

References

Adelantado of Florida
  n.d. Some points in the contract which the Adelantado of Florida must propose

and grants which must be requested about the conquest and discovery of the said provinces. From ACR CAN 50, No. 3.

Argüelles, Captain Antonio de
1663 Services. From AGI SD 23.

Astudillo, Gaspar de
1571 Registry of supplies to build *fregatas*, two in Florida. From AGI JU 817, No. 5, piece 6.

Ayllón, Lucas Vázquez de
1523 Contract with Emperor Charles V for the conquest and settlement of Florida. From AGI IG 415.

Bishko, Charles Julian
1956 The Iberian Background of Latin-American History: Recent Progress and Continuing Problems. *Hispanic American Historical Review* 36(1):50–80.

Bushnell, Amy
1981 *The King's Coffer: Proprietors of the Spanish Florida Treasury 1565–1702.* University Presses of Florida, Gainesville.
1983 The French in Florida from 1565 to 1609. Unpublished Ms. on file, St. Augustine Foundation.

Confraternity of the True Cross
1576 Visit and Inventory of Possessions. From AGI EC 154A, fol. 370–377vo.

Cook, Sherburne F., and Woodrow Borah
1963 *The Aboriginal Population of Central Mexico on the Eve of the Spanish Conquest.* Ibero-Americana No. 45. University of California Press, Berkeley.

Council of the Indies
1565 Proofs of Royal Title to Florida. From AGI IG 738, ramo 7, no. 73-A.
1671 Affirmation that Indies Adelantados held powers equal to those of Castile. From AGI SD 23.

Cronon, William
1983 *Changes in the Land.* Hill and Wang, New York.

Crosby, Alfred W., Jr.
1972 *The Columbian Exchange: Biological and Cultural Consequences of 1492.* Greenwood Press, Westport, Connecticut.

Deagan, Kathleen
1974 *Sex, Status and Role in the Mestizaje of Spanish Colonial Florida.* Unpublished Ph.D. dissertation, Department of Anthropology, University of Florida, Gainesville.
1978a The Material Assemblage of Sixteenth Century Spanish Florida. *Historical Archaeology* 12:25–50.
1978b Cultures in Transition: Fusion and Assimilation among the Eastern Timucua. In *Tacachale*, edited by Jerald T. Milanich and Samuel Proctor, pp. 88–119, University Presses of Florida, Gainesville.

Denevan, William M. (editor)
1976 *The Native Population of the Americas in 1492.* Madison.

Dobyns, Henry F.
1983 *Their Number Become Thinned.* University of Tennessee Press, Knoxville.

Enriquez, Miguel
1567 Crown Prosecuting Attorney against Captain Miguel Enriquez, AGI JU 999.

Flores, Diego
1575 Merits and Services. From AGI JU 927, No. 5.

Foster, George M.
1960 *Culture and Conquest: America's Spanish Heritage.* Chicago.

Gayón, Gonzalo
1568 List of Indian trade goods sent to Florida. From AGI *Contaduría* 299, No. 2, pliego 107. In microfilm, St. Augustine Foundation.

González, Julio
    1951   *Repartimiento de Sevilla*. 2 vols. Consejo Superior de Investigaciones
        Científicas, Madrid.
Griffin, John W. et al.
    1982   *Excavations at the Granada Site*. Archaeology and History of the Granada Site
        No. 1. Florida Division of Archives, History and Records Management, Tallahassee.
Gutiérrez de Palomar, Juan
    1571   Merits and Services. From AGI JU 908, No. 6.
Hann, John H.
    1988   *Apalachee: The Land between the Rivers*. University Presses of Florida, Gainesville.
Hill, Roscoe R.
    1913   The Office of Adelantado. *Political Science Quarterly* 28(4):648–668.
Hoffman, Paul Everett
    1976   Objects of Material Culture in Florida, 1565–1569. SAFD, Item 1399.
    1983   The Historian in Historic Sites Archaeology. In *Forgotten Places and Things*,
        compiled by Albert E. Ward. Center for Anthropological Studies, Contribution
        No. 3, pp. 37–47. Albuquerque.
Lewis, Clifford M.
    1978   The Calusa. In *Tacachale*, edited by Jerald T. Milanich and Samuel Proctor, pp.
        19–49. University Presses of Florida, Gainesville.
List of Governors
    ca. 1576   From AGI EC 154-A, fol. 122 vo.-123.
Lyon, Eugene
    1967   More Light on the Indians of the Ays Coast. Ms. on file, P. K. Yonge Library
        of Florida History, University of Florida, Gainesville.
    1976   *The Enterprise of Florida*. University of Florida Press, Gainesville.
    1979   The Control Structure of Spanish Florida. Ms. on file, St. Augustine Foundation.
    1980   Utilization of Marine Resources by the Keys and Coastal Indians of the Pre-
        contact and Contact Periods. In *Florida's Maritime Heritage*, edited by Barbara A.
        Purdy, pp. 10–12. Florida State Museum, Gainesville.
    1981   Spain's 16th Century North American Settlement Attempts: A Neglected As-
        pect. *Florida Historical Quarterly* 59(3):275–291.
    1984a The Spanish Mutineers. *Tequesta* 44:44–61.
    1984b *Santa Elena: A Brief History of the Colony*. Institute of Archaeology and Anthro-
        pology, University of South Carolina, Columbia.
    1985   Continuity in the Age of Conquest. In *Alabama and the Borderlands*, edited by
        R. Reid Badger and Lawrence A. Clayton, pp. 154–161. University of Alabama
        Press, University.
    1987a Cultural Brokers in Sixteenth-Century Spanish Florida. Paper presented at the
        conference on the Provinces of Florida, Johns Hopkins University, Baltimore.
    1987b Aspects of Pedro Menéndez the Man. *El Escribano* 24:39–52.
    1988a Pedro Menéndez' Strategic Plan for the Florida Peninsula. *Florida Historical
        Quarterly* 67(1):1–14
    1988b Demographic Trends: Florida and the Gulf. Paper presented at the conference
        on Florida and the Gulf Territories in the Age of Charles III, Miami.
    1988c Towards a Typology of Spanish Nails. In Stanley South et al., *Spanish Artifacts
        from Santa Elena*, 327–330.
McAlister, Lyle N.
    1984   *Spain and Portugal in the New World, 1492–1700*. University of Minnesota Press,
        Minneapolis.
Menéndez, Pedro
    1565a Agreements with his private soldiers about service, rations, and land-grants.
        From AGI JU 879, No. 3, piece 1.

1565b Letter to the Crown, December 2, from Matanzas. From AGI SD 71.

1566 Letter to the Crown, October 20. From AGI SD 115.

1568 Letter to Francesco Borgia. From Felix Zubillaga, *Monumenta Antiquae Floridae*, pp. 228–234.

1569 Declaration to the Council of the Indies. From AIDVJ *Envío* 25-H, No. 162. On color slides, St. Augustine Foundation.

1571a Letter to Francesco Borgia, Seville. In Felix Zubillaga, *Monumenta Antiquae Floridae*. Monumenta Historica Societatis Iesu, Rome, 1946.

1571b Goods imported into Florida from the account of Pedro Menéndez. From PAT 19, ramo 15; fol. 133-140. Also from AGI JU 817, No. 5, piece 6, and AGI CD 548, No. 8, piece 5.

1573a Dower Agreement with Don Diego de Velasco. From AGI 153-A, fol. 72vo.

1573b Damages done by the Indians of Florida. From AGI PAT 259, No. 3, ramo 20.

1574 Dower agreement with Hernando de Miranda. From AGI EC 1024-A, piece 4.

Menéndez the Younger, Pedro

1576 Inventory of goods made after his death. From ACR CAN 47, No. 10. On microfilm at St. Augustine Foundation, reel 106, images 670–671.

Milanich, Jerald T., and Charles H. Fairbanks

1980 *Florida Archaeology*. Academic Press, New York.

Morse, Richard M.

1962 Some Characteristics of Latin American Urban History. *American Historical Review* 67:317–338.

Olmos, Alonso de

1576 Lawsuit against Governor Don Diego de Velasco. From AGI EC 154-A, fol. 467-505.

Philip II

1565 Contract with Pedro Menéndez de Avilés for the conquest of Florida. From AGI *Contratación* 3309, Piece 1.

1573 Ordinances concerning new discovery and settlement. From *Colección de documentos in-éditos . . . de Indias*, Vol. 8. Real Academia de la Historia, Madrid, 1842–1985.

Pike, Ruth

1966 *Enterprise and Adventure: The Genoese in Seville and the Opening of the New World*. Cornell University Press, Ithaca.

Quirós, Juan and Hernán

1572 Debts owed to the Adelantado by Juan and Hernán Quirós, his *criados*, for money loaned them to outfit themselves. From AGI JU 817, No. 5, piece 6.

Quirós, Tomás Bernaldo de

1580 Services. From AGI SD 125, No. 150-D.

Reitz, Elizabeth J., and C. Margeret Scarry

1985 *Reconstructing Historic Subsistence with an Example from Sixteenth-Century Spanish Florida*. Special Publication Series No. 3. Society for Historical Archaeology, Ann Arbor.

Rodríguez, Review of the Case of Juan

1576 From AGI EC 154-A, fol. 570–599.

Ruiz, Diego

1574 Testament. From AGI EC 154-A, fol. 765–780vo.

Settlers of Florida

1568 List of settlers at Cádiz, ready to embark for Florida. From AGI PAT 19, No. 1, ramo 15.

1569 Memorial of the settlers in . . . Santa Elena. From AGI CD 941.

Soldiers Inventories

1576 Soldiers' inventories. From AGI EC 154-A, fol. 782–797vo.

South, Stanley, Russell K. Skowronek, and Richard E. Johnson
  1988   *Spanish Artifacts from Santa Elena.* Anthropological Studies No. 7. Institute of Archaeology and Anthropology, University of South Carolina, Columbia.
Thomas, Alfred Barnaby
  1968   *Teodoro de Croix.* University of Oklahoma Press, Norman.
Thomas, David Hurst
  1987   *The Archaeology of Mission Santa Catalina de Guale.* American Museum of Natural History Anthropological Papers 63(2):47–161.
  1989   Columbian Consequences: The Spanish Borderlands in Cubist Perspective. In *Columbian Consequences. Vol. 1: Archaeological and Historical Perspectives on the Spanish Borderlands West,* edited by David Hurst Thomas. Smithsonian Institution Press, Washington, D.C.
Thomas, David Hurst, Stanley South, and C. S. Larson
  1977   *Rich Man, Poor Men: Observations on Three Antebellum Burials from the Georgia Coast.* American Museum of Natural History Anthropological Papers 54:(3):395–420. New York.
Thomas, David Hurst, Grant D. Jones, Roger S. Durham and Clark Spencer Larsen
  1978   *The Anthropology of St. Catherine's Island.* American Museum of Natural History Anthropological Papers 55(2).
Todorov, Tzvetan
  1984   *The Conquest of America: The Question of the Other.* Translated from French by Richard Howard. Harper and Row, New York.
Valdés, Pedro de
  1565   Marriage to Ana Menéndez and dower agreement with Pedro Menéndez de Avilés. From ACR *Valdés* 14, no. 1.
Velasco, Don Diego de
  1576   Inventory of his possessions. From AGI EC 154-A, fol. 641-646vo.
Villareal, Francisco
  1568   Letter to Father Juan Rogel, Tequesta. From Zubillaga, *Monumenta Floridae Antiquae,* 234–240.
Vigneras, Louis-André
  1969   A Spanish Discovery of North Carolina in 1566. *North Carolina Historical Review* 46(4):398–414.
Weber, Eugen
  1984   Book Review. *New York Times Book Review,* July 22, pp. 13–14.
Widmer, Randolph J.
  1988   *The Evolution of the Calusa: A Nonagricultural Chiefdom on the Southwest Florida Coast.* University of Alabama Press, Tuscaloosa.
Zambardino, Rudolph A.
  1980–1981 Mexico's Population in the Sixteenth Century: Demographic Anomaly or Mathematical Illusion? *Journal of Interdisciplinary History* 11:1–27.
Zavala, Silvio
  1948   La conquista de Canarias y América. In *Estudios indianos,* Mexico, esp. p. 13.

Chapter 20 ■

Kathleen A. Deagan

Accommodation and Resistance: The Process and Impact of Spanish Colonization in the Southeast

The observance of the Columbian Quincentenary has focused attention on the consequences of an encounter between two worlds—the Old World and the Americas. The most visible and enduring of these consequences was the emergence of a "new world," that is, the constellation of new, worldwide social, economic, ecological, and ideological relationships that emerged after 1500. This "new world" was shaped by the interactions among America, Africa, and Europe, which certainly affected all of those continents. It was in the Americas, however, that the consequences of this new world were most dramatically manifested.

Some of the consequences of the encounter were tragic. The depopulation, disruption, and disenfranchisement of Native American society was catastrophic, as was the rise of economic systems based on large-scale slave labor, which exploited the African people in the Americas. Much has been written and discussed in recent years about these negative aspects of the encounter, and they are undeniable.

Without diminishing the disastrous effects of the encounter, social scientists also recognize another kind of dramatic consequence in the Americas: the formation and development of a vital, hybrid Euro-Afro-American culture. Within a century of Columbus's first voyage, a flourishing and distinctly new form of society was emerging in the Americas, one based on global colonial interactions. The roots of modern life, including our contemporary global economic and political organization, lie in this development.

The emergence of the "new world" is therefore both interesting and important for a wide range of social scientists, and historical archaeology has a critical role to play in understanding it (see Deagan 1988; Leone 1977; Wallerstein 1974; Wolf 1982). It evolved from the confrontation between literate and nonliterate societies. Because this interaction was not fully recorded, both archaeological and historical perspectives are essential in studying the roots of the new world.

This chapter is specifically concerned with the Hispanic-American segment of the new world, although it was but one of many multicultural expressions after 1500 in the Americas. It was, however, the earliest, and patterns and precedents established by the Spaniards in their first century of occupation in the Americas shaped the experiences of subsequent Euro-African-American expressions.

For a variety of reasons discussed at length elsewhere (Gibson 1971; Scardaville 1985; Thomas 1988), North Americans have only a vague appreciation, if any at all, of the Spanish presence and impact in our post-Columbian past. A great deal of the effort related to the Quincentenary has been devoted to helping correct that situation, and this discussion—along with its companion papers on Columbian Consequences—is intended to contribute to the effort from the perspective of historical archaeology in the North American Hispanic colonies.

The emphasis here is on multi-ethnic colonial encounter and response, as manifested in North America's earliest European colony, St. Augustine, Florida. St. Augustine was first settled in 1565, and has been occupied ever since. It was a site of early encounter among Europeans, American Indians, and Africans, and subsequent coexistence of all groups for more than two centuries.

The consequences of these early encounters—particularly from the perspective of Amerindian, African, and nonelite European participants—are among the most elusive and least understood aspects of colonization in the Americas. Virtually no written documentation other than that relevant to demographic change expresses the responses of these largely illiterate groups to contact with one another, or their ways of coping with the resulting changes. Even in those cases of simultaneous historical-archaeological focus on colonial adaptations, the research and its conclusions have been devoted largely to European adaptations. This is now changing to some extent with the current emphasis on research in mission Indian villages (see Thomas, this volume).

Apart from the relative absence of documentation, there are other inherent difficulties in studying colonial Amerindians and Africans. One of these is the very rapid decline and disappearance of the native peoples of Florida and the Caribbean after contact. Few sites of colonial Amerindian occupation outside of missions have been identified, and those that have are often greatly damaged by development (see, for example, Smith and Bond 1981). It is also extremely difficult to isolate African occupation and culture in the Spanish colonies of North America. Slavery precluded most direct movement of African materials themselves, and we have not yet learned as scholars to recognize the patterns in which African-Hispanic people recombined European and Amerindian elements in ways that were meaningful to African cultural expression. Although this, too, is slowly changing through the work of such scholars as Jane Landers (this volume) and others, African-Hispanic responses and adjustments are for the moment extremely difficult to study in the archaeological record.

Although also difficult, the recovery of information for American Indians and nonelite Europeans in the colonies has been more successful than the effort to study African-Hispanic adaptations. Using a combination of archaeological and historical investigation, researchers have gained some insights into the colonial adaptations of these people under certain circumstances such as those found at St. Augustine.

An ongoing program of historical, archaeological, and ethnobiological research has been under way in St. Augustine since 1972 through the University of Florida, and before that through Florida State University (for summary works, see Deagan 1983, 1985; King 1981; Reitz and Scarry 1985; Zierden 1981). The program has addressed a variety of anthropological, methodological, historical, educational, and archaeological issues, all of which have been related in general to the overarching issue of the adaptive strategies and mechanisms that resulted in the emergence and development of new world Euro-American society. In every instance, however, the central task has been to define and predict the patterns of interaction, accommodation, resistance, and invention that shaped the post-1500 societies of Spanish Florida. As a consequence, there exists an extremely large systematic data base, appropriate to the issues at hand, covering the 200 years of Spanish occupation of the town.

St. Augustine is also both fortunate and unusual in the historical documentation available to scholars of the colonial period. Detailed records were maintained by government bureaucrats, bookkeepers and priests, and these records permit the reconstruction of demographic patterns and vital statistics for a large portion of St. Augustine's colonial population. Church parish registers and mission censuses have been particularly useful in this, providing such information for nearly all individual Spanish colonists, and many of the Indian and African colonists.

Friars also made periodic censuses of the mission towns located in the vicinity of St. Augustine from about 1600 onward. It is therefore in fact possible to develop a reasonable estimation of the size and composition of St. Augustine's population through the colonial period. When combined with the archaeological data pertinent to their occupations, we can begin to better define patterns of adaptive responses among various groups in the colony.

This essay considers the responses of American Indians and Spaniards to the unique circumstances of colonial St. Augustine. It constitutes a rather crude attempt to assess the archaeological data base in terms of a single and familiar category of data: Amerindian ceramics as they occur in European-American contexts. Observable patterns in this data category are compared with documented demographic information for the Indian population of the colonial town, and suggestions made concerning the meaning of the archaeological patterns in terms of encounter and response.

Certain aspects of St. Augustine's history and occupation, central to the arguments offered here, are discussed in the following section. Detailed background information about St. Augustine's history and development, and about the excavation of the sites themselves, can be found elsewhere (for a summary, see Deagan 1985, 1983 and the references cited in Tables 20-1 and 20-2).

St. Augustine

St. Augustine was settled initially by Pedro Menéndez de Avilés in partnership with Philip II, the king of Spain. The Crown was eager to eliminate the French Huguenot colony of Fort Caroline, which had been established near present-day Jacksonville, Florida, in 1562 (Ribault 1964 [1563]). The French settlement posed a serious threat to the burgeoning Spanish empire in the Caribbean, as well as in South America and Central America. Menéndez was willing to try to eliminate the French presence in exchange for support from the Crown in his colonizing venture (for a detailed discussion of the founding of Florida and Menéndez's role, see Lyon 1976, this volume). Menéndez's rewards were to be such riches and titles as would accrue from the founding and governorship of the Florida colony.

Menéndez was successful in eliminating the French presence, and established the town of St. Augustine in its present vicinity (Figure 20-1). The initial fort and settlement were slightly apart from the contemporary location of downtown

Table 20-1. Distribution of Aboriginal Ceramics in Colonial St. Augustine

Period	Timucua, St. John No.	Percent[a]	Guale San Marcos No.	Percent[a]	All Other No.	Percent[a]	Total Aboriginal No.	Total Percentage of All Ceramics	Ceramics
1700–1730	383	.136	2,294	.801	186	.065	2,863	.677	4,230
1650–1700	919	.226	2,933	.722	212	.052	4,064	.711	5,716
1600–1650	1,294	.502	1,008	.391	275	.107	2,577	.526	4,900
1580–1600	2,833	.530	1,897	.355	612	.114	5,342	.593	9,007
1565–1580	733	.856	40	.047	83	.097	856	.504	1,699
Total	6,162		8,172		1,368		15,702		25,552

Note: Based on closed undisturbed contexts from the following sites: SA-34-2 (Ewen 1984; King 1982); SA-26-1 (Deagan 1983; King 1981; Singleton 1976; Zierden and Caballero 1979); SA-34-1 (Deagan 1983; Piatek 1985; Vernon 1980); SA-36-4 (Deagan 1983; King 1981; Poe 1978); Fountain of Youth (Chaney 1987).
[a] Percentage of all aboriginal ceramics.

Table 20-2. Christian Indian Population in St. Augustine (Documentary Accounts: 1565–1783)

Year	Number Listed				Source
	Total	Timucua	Guale/Yamassee	Other	
1602	200	200			Bermejo (1602)
1606	216	216			Altamirano (1606 [1606])
1655					Geiger (1940:125)
1675	90				Calderón, in Wenhold (1936)
1689	225	100	125		Compostela (1689)
1711	358	88	107	163[b]	Corcoles y Martinez (1711)
1714	401				Phillipe V, King of Spain (1714)
1717	952	256[a]	619	77[c]	Escobar (1717)
1726	1,011	177	354	480[d]	Valdes (1729)
1728	1,350				Benavides (1738)
1736	477				Arredondo (1736)
1737	276	108	114	54[e]	Arredondo (1737) (map key)
1752	152				Gelabert (1752)
1759	100				Grinan, in Scardaville and Belmonte (1979)
1760	79				Solana (1760)
1763	86				Puente, cited in Deagan (1978)

[a] Includes Eastern and Western Timucuans after this date. [b] Costa, Apalachee. [c] Jororo, Apalachee. [d] South Florida, Apalachee, "mixed." [e] Costa, "mixed."

St. Augustine, in the vicinity of the important chiefly town of Seloy (Chaney 1988; Lyon 1976). The first North American Indian mission, Nombre de Dios, was established there in 1565 about 0.8 km north of the present Castillo de San Marcos (Gannon 1965:27). Today the site is occupied by the Fountain of Youth Park tourist attraction, and has been the subject of intermittent test excavations over the past 30 years (Chaney 1986, 1988; Goggin 1952, 1968; Merritt 1977; Seaberg 1951). This original settlement was, however, moved after less than a year to a site about a mile away, where the present town of St. Augustine has remained to the present day.

La Florida was considerably larger in the sixteenth century than the state is today—it encompassed much of what is now the Southeastern United States. A second settlement was established in 1565, several months after the establishment of St. Augustine, at what is today Parris Island, South Carolina. This community, called Santa Elena, was the capital of La Florida between 1566 and 1587 (South 1988, this volume). The colony at Santa Elena provided a channel for interaction between peninsular Florida and the more northern parts of the southeastern coastal plain.

Menéndez's hopes for riches in La Florida were never realized, owing to the absence in the region of such commodities as the precious metals or minerals that had made the fortunes of conquistadors in other parts of the Spanish empire. Furthermore, the native populations in the Atlantic coastal area of La Florida were low in density, were dispersed, and did not have an intensive agricultural tradition that could be turned to the Spaniards' advantage.

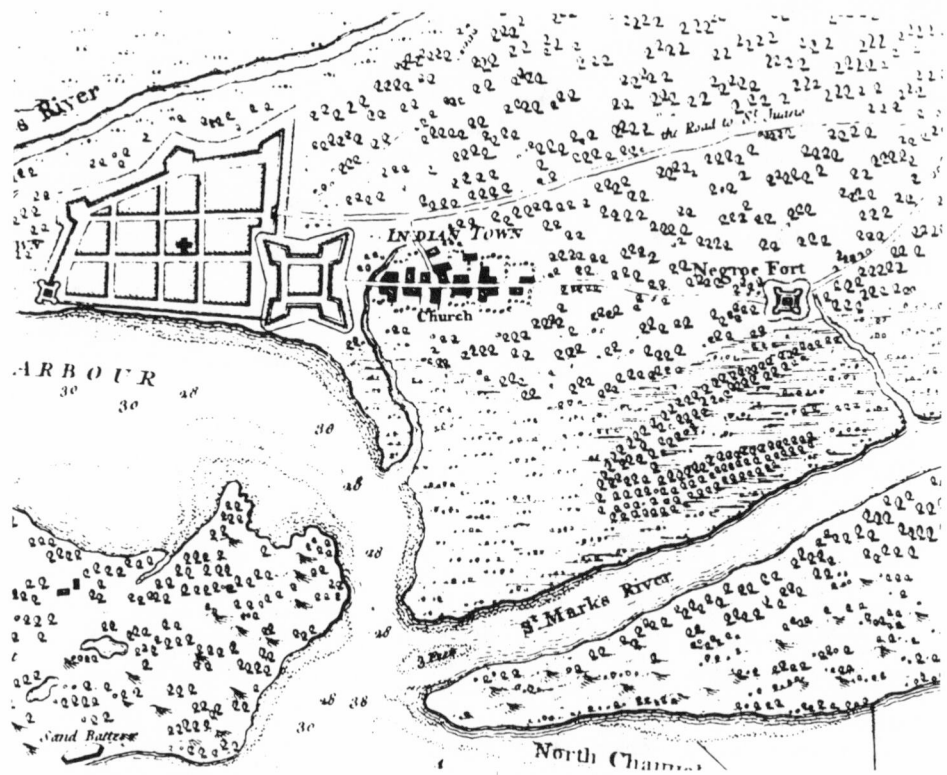

Figure 20-1. The Thomas Jeffries map (1762) depicting the multiracial and ethnic composition of eighteenth-century St. Augustine. It was drawn from information gathered during James Oglethorpe's 1740 raid. "Indian towns" are shown on the original map outside the town walls to the north and south (courtesy of the St. Augustine Historical Society, map 11).

The Menéndez family's control of the colony ended in 1570, when La Florida become a Crown colony, subsidized by an annual government allocation of funds and supplies referred to as the *situado*. Despite the poverty of exploitable resources in La Florida, St. Augustine was supported because of its strategic value in maintaining the defenses and economic functions of the Caribbean and New Spain colonies (see Hoffman 1980). From St. Augustine, the Straits of Florida and the Bahama Channel could be protected from foreign powers. These waters afforded routes that were critical in the safe transport of the treasure fleets from New Spain to Spain (Haring 1964). As a northern outpost, St. Augustine was also a buffer between the Spanish empire and the English colonies established in the Southeastern United States during the first decades of the seventeenth century. Another important purpose of the St. Augustine colony was to convert the Indians and establish missions, and this shaped much of the interaction between Europeans and American Indians in Florida (for detailed histories of this endeavor see Gannon 1965; Hann 1988; Lanning 1936).

Original Inhabitants

The native inhabitants of the St. Augustine area were the Eastern Timucua Indians (Deagan 1978), well known through the engravings by Theodore DeBry of Jacque LeMoyne's paintings (Lorant 1946). They included a number of warring groups of allied tribes, with centralized chiefly authority.

The Timucua's neighbors to the north were the Guale chiefdoms of coastal Georgia and South Carolina. The Jesuit mission effort was implemented among the Guale in about 1570, but it ended in revolt in 1597 (see Gannon 1965; Jones 1978; Larson 1978). A more enduring and successful Franciscan system was reestablished after 1604. Mission activity was extended to the interior (Western) Timucua groups after 1607 (Milanich 1978:71); and in 1633 to the Apalachee chiefdoms, descendants of Florida's only Mississippian group (Hann 1988; Scarry 1985).

Much of the interaction between the town of St. Augustine and these outlying areas occurred through the mission system, which also functioned to organize trade, tribute, and labor on the Spanish frontier. Menéndez had originally established an obligatory tribute from the Indians in Florida, and this was continued until some unknown date in the early eighteenth century. This payment was generally in the form of corn, animal skins, and labor (Bushnell 1983, 1982; Deagan 1985; Lyon 1976:118–119), and resulted in the intermittent presence in St. Augustine of nonlocal Indians and Indian materials.

The friars worked through the Indian caciques to implement the tribute system, control trade, organize labor, and convert the Indians to Christianity (see

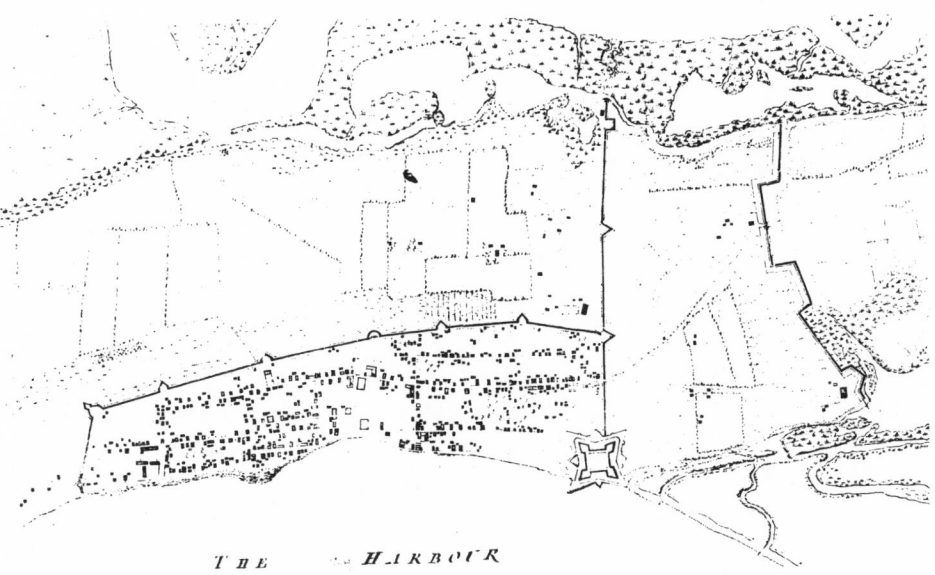

Figure 20-2. This anonymous map of St. Augustine was published ca. 1765, at the end of the first Spanish period. The small structures depicted outside the town walls are Indian settlements, including the towns of Nombre de Dios, Tolomato, Costas, Pocotalaca, and La Punta (courtesy of the St. Augustine Historical Society, map 133).

Deagan 1985b). The Christian Indian towns were not exclusively on the frontier, however. Many of the Eastern Timucua peoples who had originally inhabited what is today St. John's County, Florida, continued to live in the vicinity of St. Augustine, where they were often joined by Indians from outside the region. These people, who chose to live in proximity of the town, remained in small, primarily Christian villages, just outside the town walls (Figure 20-2). Over the centuries there were always between 2 and 10 of these villages within 2 miles of the town (see the references in Table 20-2).

In precontact time, Timucua sites in the vicinity of St. Augustine contained the Timucua-associated St. Johns series ceramics almost exclusively, along with very small quantities of nonlocal trade wares. With the arrival of Europeans, and the accompanying shifts in interaction patterns in the aboriginal Southeast, a wider variety of Southeastern Indian ceramics found their way into the St. Augustine area. Their numbers and varieties fluctuated with perturbations in the tribute and mission systems (Piatek 1985), and appear to have been influenced significantly by the mission system. Supporting data come from preliminary analysis of the materials from the site of the Convento de San Francisco in St. Augustine, which was the mission system anchor and headquarters. There, a wide variety of nonlocal native Southeastern Indian pottery has been identified, surpassing that of other sites so far excavated in St. Augustine (Hoffman 1989).

The groups who interacted with the Spanish town were characterized by distinct and recognizable ceramic traditions, in both precontact and postcontact times. The native Eastern Timucua made and used St. Johns series wares almost exclusively. This was a distinctive chalky pottery tempered with sponge spicules and was either plain or check-stamped (Goggin 1952; Thanz and Shaak 1977).

The Guale are known to have made a sand and grit-tempered, rectilinear stamped series of ceramics known variously as San Marcos (Otto and Lewis 1974; Smith 1948), Altamaha, and sometimes Chicora ware (South 1983). At contact, Irene incised ceramics were also associated with the Guale. The Apalachee were associated in postcontact times with the Leon-Jefferson ceramics series (Boyd et al. 1951; Smith 1948), and the Western Timucua with a variety of wares including Leon-Jefferson ceramics, St. Johns ceramics, and Potano ceramics (Milanich 1978).

Florida Indian Demography in Eighteenth-century St. Augustine

The Timucua population of St. Augustine declined steadily after contact; however, by the mid-seventeenth century, their numbers were supplemented by refugee Guale mission Indians who were relocated to St. Augustine for protection from the British and their Indian allies. A major increase in the Indian population of the town took place after 1704, when James Moore's devastating raids brought an end to the Spanish mission system outside of St. Augustine (see Boyd et al. 1951; Arnade 1959), and refugee Indians from many areas were relocated to the town.

The Spanish inhabitants of St. Augustine interacted with the Indians in these towns, through labor arrangements, trade, intermarriage, and concubinage.

Spanish–Indian intermarriage began immediately and continued consistently through the two centuries of Spanish occupation (Deagan 1973).

A major consequence of such interaction, and particularly of intermarriage, was the incorporation of native pottery into Spanish households as a primary cooking ware. Such Amerindian pottery (some of which may actually have been African in inspiration) constitutes more than 50 percent of the pottery at all Spanish sites excavated to date (Table 20-1).

One of the great assets of historical archaeology is the ability to establish narrowly defined date ranges for deposits, on the basis of the Terminus Post Quem of well-documented material categories, and other tools such as stratigraphy, documented event dates, the mean ceramic date, and pipestem formulas (see South 1979). In St. Augustine it has been possible to define the ranges seen in Table 20-1, in some cases down to as little as 20 years.

This capability, along with the historically documented demographic figures and the well-established association of Indian groups with material types, has made it possible to suggest that the archaeological remains from the Spanish town provide a reasonably reliable reflection of demographic circumstances for the poorly known Native American component of the colony. The data upon which this assertion is based can be seen in Figures 20-3 and 20-4, which show, respectively, the proportions through time of the various group-affiliated aboriginal ceramics, and the fluctuations in Indian population as revealed in the mission censuses.

Numerical population figures are not present for the Eastern Timucua in the vicinity of St. Augustine prior to 1600, but we can be confident that they were

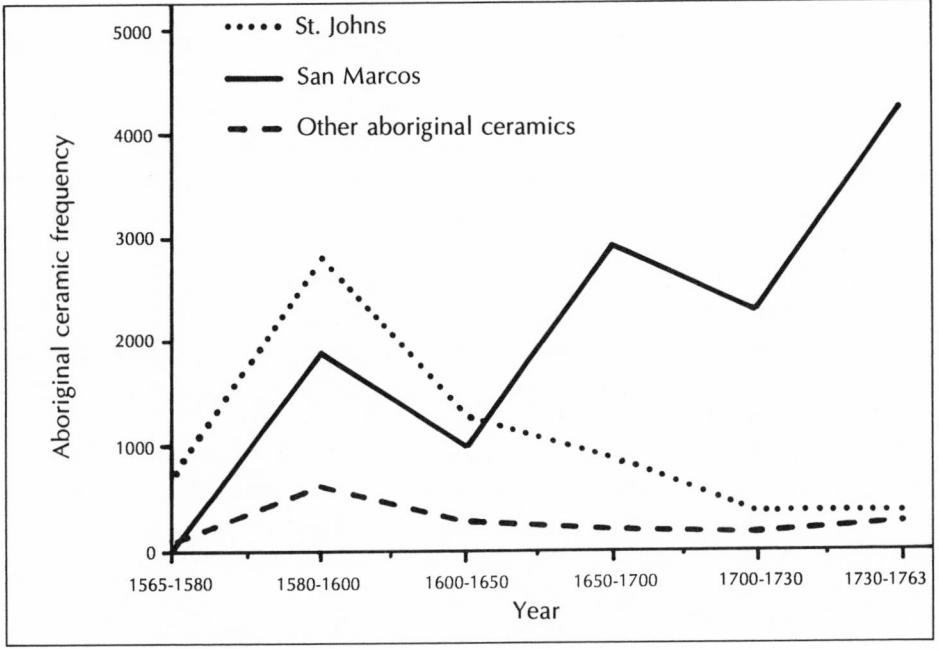

Figure 20-3. Distribution of aboriginal ceramics in colonial St. Augustine.

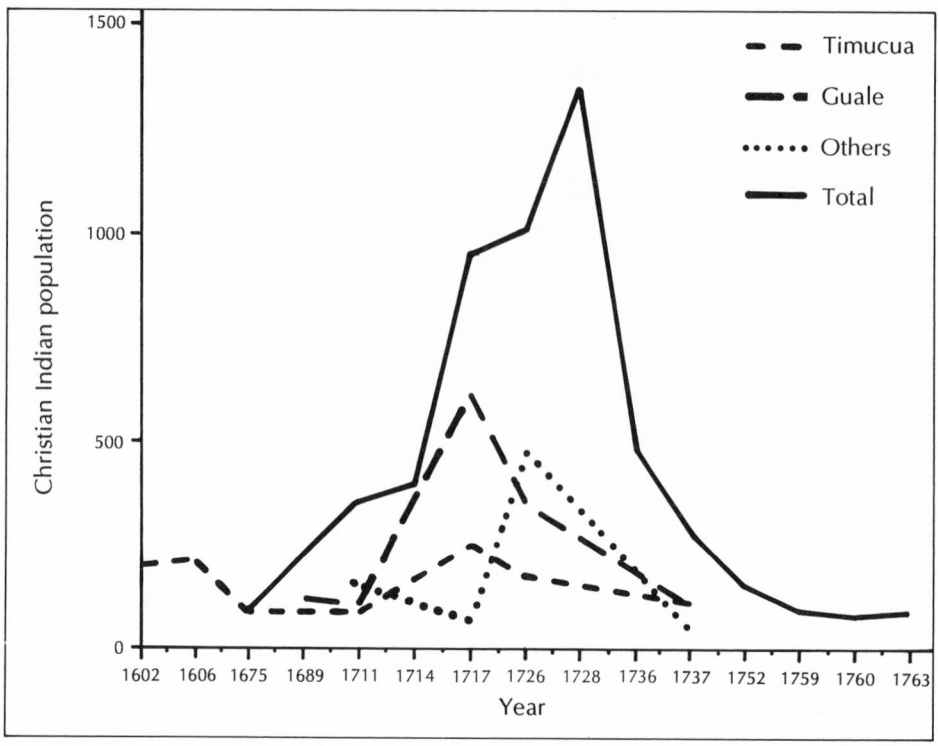

Figure 20-4. Christian Indian population in St. Augustine (based on documentary accounts, 1565–1783).

considerably higher than those of the post-1600 period, by which time several epidemics had taken their toll (see, e.g., Dobyns 1983). A replacement of Timucua by the Guale and, to a lesser extent, other Indian groups, is reflected both in the census figures and in the archaeological record. This occurs markedly after 1650, and corresponds to two demographically important events. One was the relocation of many of the Georgia coastal Guale mission Indians after this date to St. Augustine (Lanning 1936:221; Phillipe V 1660; Swanton 1946:135–36), and the other was one of the most severe epidemic periods recorded in colonial Florida. Three epidemics took place between 1649 and 1659, from which both the Timucua and the Spaniards suffered terribly. (Bushnell 1982:13; Dobyns 1983:285). This decline and replacement are reflected in the archaeological data (Table 20-1) by the considerable increase in Guale ceramics in the Spanish households of the town, at the expense of Timucua wares.

The Indian population of St. Augustine grew most markedly in both numbers and diversity after the collapse of the mission system in 1704. As Table 20-2 indicates, the non-Timucua and non-Guale Indian population of St. Augustine increased steadily after 1711, including Apalachee, Jororo, Costa, Western Timucuans, and South Florida Indians. This diversity is not, however, reflected as clearly in the archaeological record. Neither an increase in the proportion of "other" ceramics, nor the appearance of ceramic wares traditionally associated with these groups, is found in the record of the Spanish town. During the eighteenth century, the "other" ceramic category remains very small in size, and comprises previously undefined or unreported grog and grit-tempered plain ceramics.

Incorporation and Resistance in the Hispanic-Indian Material World

It is known that the catastrophic events of the early eighteenth century resulted in the relocation and consolidation of a large number of different—and decimated—remnant tribal groups. The corresponding patterns in the archaeological record suggest either (1) that the ceramic traditions associated with these peoples did not persist in the face of cultural disruption, and that the already established Guale ceramic tradition dominated the Indian material world; or (2) that the Spanish preferred Guale ceramics and the remnant groups continued to make their traditional wares in their own domestic contexts. The latter hypothesis is suggested on the basis of the documentary marriage records, which show Guale women making up an overwhelming number of Spaniards' brides. The former hypothesis is suggested on the basis of the archaeological record, which shows that such traditional Florida Indian ceramics as the Leon-Jefferson wares, or the Potano wares, from Spanish contexts, did not disappear until after the collapse of the mission system. Such wares were incorporated in the town before the relocation of their respective groups (Hoffman 1989; Piatek 1985).

Obviously these assertions require testing through the excavation of eighteenth-century Indian town sites in St. Augustine. This has not been possible yet for a variety of reasons, including site destruction as a result of residential and commercial development, the lack of funds, and established program priorities. Nevertheless, even in the absence of such work, it can be seen that the sample of Amerindian materials from the Spanish town can be used to examine certain aspects of cultural change, adaptation, and demography in colonial Native American society.

Even more important from the perspective of this essay, however, is that these data reflect the extent to which the Spaniards consistently and regularly incorporated non-European elements into their daily lives. This practice increased steadily through time (Table 20-1).

One of the most interesting features of the Indian pottery found in the Spanish sites is that the great majority of it is unmodified from its traditional forms—neither shape nor decoration show European influence in most cases. This is an important observation, because it demonstrates, first, that traditional Amerindian crafts persisted in a largely unaltered form through the entire colonial period, and, second, that there did not appear to be any serious directed effort on the part of the Spaniards to influence change in favor of Spanish tastes.

It has been shown in one case that during the sixteenth century the Spanish inhabitants of St. Augustine had a preference for check-stamped over plain St. Johns pottery, but this was interpreted to have been a function of the better handling and heat-holding properties of the stamped ware during cooking, which was its primary use. No evidence for change in vessel forms or the introduction of new design elements was noted (Herron 1978).

Even in the face of disruption, depopulation, relocation, forced contact with other Indian groups, as well as new social, religious and economic structures, cultural information about the making of Guale and Timucua pots continued to be transmitted largely unaltered for over 200 years. If this was the case for craft traditions, what other elements may have successfully resisted alteration and continued as traditional Indian cultural elements? This finding suggests not only a resiliency in Southeastern Indian culture, but also a resistance to or disinterest in the alteration of at least some traditional ways in favor of European influence.

These circumstances stand in contrast to two other contemporary Spanish colonial situations—those of the Spanish missions outside of St. Augustine, and of the sixteenth-century Spanish Caribbean colonies. In most of the missions, a considerable proportion of the Indian ceramic assemblage exhibits European formal elements (see Boyd et al. 1951), while in the Caribbean sites an entirely new, simplified, technically unsophisticated local ware appears (Deagan 1988; Dominguez 1978, 1984; Smith 1986). Several potential hypotheses can be offered to explain these differences, all of which would require additional archaeological work. One of the simplest explanations at the mission sites is the poverty and isolation, coupled with the expense and difficulty of transporting ceramics overland. Indian pottery substitutes for Spanish tablewares may have been requested by the friars for their own use.

In the Caribbean it has been variously suggested that the appearance of a crude new ceramic ware is associated with the devastating population declines and the breakdown of cultural transmission systems, as well as with the replacement of the initial Amerindian labor pool by African slaves, who may have replaced not only the Indians but also their pots. This suggestion has been explored elsewhere (Deagan 1988; Smith 1986).

The patterns of unmodified aboriginal pottery use documented in St. Augustine are undoubtedly related to the incorporation of Indian women into households as either wives, concubines, or servants, and to their role in food preparation. Indian cooks may have preferred unmodified Indian pots to cook in. European tableware forms, available in the capital, were used as needed on European tables. This pattern of incorporation of native traits in non–socially visible areas, particularly women's activities, coupled with the maintenance of Spanish social identification in socially visible areas, has been documented as highly characteristic of the Spaniards' early colonial adaptive strategy (Deagan 1983; Ewen 1987).

The same pattern of aboriginal trait incorporation in the Spanish town suggests different things about Amerindian responses to coexistence with Spaniards. In contrast, we see a maintenance of and continuity in native craft traditions and foodways throughout the colonial period in Florida. The direct impact of Spanish culture, beyond population loss and relocation, on the daily lives of colonial Amerindians may have been considerably less than we have traditionally assumed; or perhaps native resistance to European influence was stronger than archaeologists have often considered.

There are other factors that must ultimately be considered in assessing these suggestions. We cannot yet gauge, for example, the impact of interaction and exchange among the various Indian and African peoples of St. Augustine. It is possible that interaction with other Amerindian groups may have had as pronounced an impact on colonial Indian life as did interaction with Europeans. These hypotheses are archaeologically testable.

Conclusions

The results of the preceding exercise underscore certain aspects of Spanish colonial adaptation, and suggest others:

1. Spanish domestic adaptive strategy was consistently based on the incorporation of unmodified Indian cultural elements in kitchen activities, probably through Indian mates. This resulted in a genuinely new, multicultural expression that ultimately crystallized as New World criollo culture and stands in sharp contrast to Anglo-American culture.

2. Several southeastern ceramic traditions of people in daily contact with Europeans persisted unmodified for nearly 200 years of Spanish–Indian interaction. This suggests a resistance to, or disinterest in, the alteration of traditional crafts in favor of European elements, and is reminiscent of the same kind of resistance seen in early Chinese-American sites in California (Greenwood 1982). It also suggests that systems for the transmission of crafts and symbolic information through generations were not fully disrupted by the depopulation, relocation, and other severe traumas of the contact period, at least for these groups. This itself implies a remarkable cultural resiliency.

3. The disappearance of traditional Amerindian ceramic wares in situations of extreme population decline can be seen clearly in the archaeological record of the colonies, particularly for the Caribbean Indians and the non-Timucuan, non-Guale populations of St. Augustine. This may reflect the disintegration of cultural transmission systems at a certain point of population loss, or it may reflect bias in the archaeological record.

4. On a methodological level, the results of this exercise suggest that, in the predictable absence of direct information about historic-period native peoples, it is possible to draw upon data from the better-studied European contexts to gain some insight into postcontact Indian demography and cultural responses.

Notes

The following abbreviations are used in the references: AGI, Archivo General de las Indias; HSAPB and SCUF, Stetson Collection, P. K. Yonge Library of Florida History, University of Florida, Gainesville.

References

Altamirano, Juan de las Cabezas de
    1606   Bishop Altamirano to the King of Spain, June 27, 1606. Manuscript, AGI 54-5-20. SCUF Photostat.

Arnade, Charles
    1959   *The Siege of St. Augustine in 1702*. University of Florida Press, Gainesville.

Arrendondo, Antonio de
    1736   Arrendondo to the Crown of Spain, November 27, 1736. Manuscript letter. AGI 87-1-1/60. SCUF Photostat.
    1737   Plano de la ciudad de Sn. Agustin de la Florida y sus contornos situada en al altura. May 15, 1737. Map photostat, Historic St. Augustine Preservation Board.

Benavides, Antonio de
    1738   Governor Benavides to the Crown, April 24, 1738. Manuscript letter, AGI 58-2-16/45. SCUF Photostat.

Bermejo, Frey
    1602   Letter of Frey Bermejo to the Crown of Spain, Sept. 2, 1602. Manuscript, AGI 54-5-20/5. SCUF Photostat.

Boyd, Mark F., Hale G. Smith, and John W. Griffin
    1951   *Here They Once Stood: The Tragic End of the Apalachee Missions*. University of Florida Presses, Gainesville.

Bushnell, Amy
    1983   Cross, Pole and Banner: The Balance of Power in the Province of Seventeenth Century Florida. Paper presented at the Southern Historical Association meetings, Memphis, Tennessee.
    1982   *The King's Coffer*. University of Florida Presses, Gainesville.

Caballero, Olga, and Martha Zierden
    1979   Excavations at SA–28–1 (Spanish Hospital Site), St. Augustine, 1979. Ms. project report on file, HSAPB.

Chaney, Edward
    1988   Survey and Evaluation of Archaeological Resources in the Abbott Tract and North City, St. Augustine, Florida. Project report on file, Florida Museum of Natural History, Gainesville.

Compostela, Diego Euclino
    1689   Bishop of Cuba to the Crown of Spain. Manuscript letter, September 28, 1689. AGI 54-3-2/9. SCUF Photostat.

Corcoles y Martines, Francisco de
    1711   Governor of Florida to the Crown of Spain, April 9, 1711. Manuscript letter, AGI 58-1-3/20. SCUF Photostat.

Deagan, Kathleen
    1973   Mestizaje in Colonial St. Augustine. *Ethnohistory* 20:55–65.
    1978   Cultures in Transition: Assimilation and Fusion among the Eastern Timucua. In *Tacachale: Essays on the Indians of Florida and Southeastern Georgia During the Historic Period*, edited by Jerald Milanich and Samuel Proctor, pp. 89–119. University Presses of Florida, Gainesville.
    1983   *Spanish St. Augustine: The Archaeology of a Colonial Creole Community*. Academic Press, New York.
    1985a The Archaeology of 16th Century St. Augustine. *Florida Anthropologist* 38(1–2):6–33.
    1985b Spanish–Indian Interaction in Sixteenth Century Florida and the Caribbean. In *Cultures in Conflict*, edited by W. Fitzhugh. Anthropological Society of Washington Special Publication, pp. 281–318. Smithsonian Institution Press, Washington, D.C.

1988   The Archaeology of the Spanish Contact Period in the Caribbean. *Journal of World Prehistory* 2(2):187–233.

Dobyns, Henry
   1983   *Their Number Become Thinned: Native American Population Dynamics in Eastern North America*. University of Tennessee Press, Knoxville.

Dominguez, Lourdes
   1978   La transculturación en Cuba (s. XVI–XVII). *Cuba Arqueológica* I, pp. 33–50. Editorial Oriente, Santiago de Cuba.
   1984   *Arqueología colonial cubana: Dos estudios*. Editorial de ciencias sociales, Havana.

Escobar, Juan de Ayala
   1717   Governor of Florida to the Crown of Spain, April 18, 1717. Manuscript letter, AGI 58-1-1-30/64-65. SCUF Photostat.

Ewen, Charles
   1984   Final Report on Excavations at the Ximenez-Fatio House (SA-34-2), St. Augustine. Project report on file, Florida Museum of Natural History, Gainesville.
   1987   *From Spaniard to Creole: The Archaeology of Hispanic American Cultural Formation at Puerto Real, Haiti*. Unpublished Ph.D. dissertation, Department of Anthropology, University of Florida, Gainesville.

Gannon, Micheal V.
   1965   *The Cross in the Sand*. University of Florida Press, Gainesville.

Geiger, Maynard
   1940   *The Franciscan Conquest of Florida*. Washington, D.C.

Gelabert, Jose
   1752   Jose Gelabert to the Crown of Spain, January 10, 1752. AGI 87-1-14/2. Manuscript letter. SCUF Photostat.

Gibson, Charles
   1971   *The Black Legend: Anti-Spanish Attitudes in the Old World and the New*. Knopf, New York.

Goggin, John M.
   1952   *Space and Time Perspective in Northern St. Johns Archaeology*. Yale University Publications in Anthropology No. 47. New Haven.
   1968   *Spanish Majolica in the New World*. Yale University Publications in Anthropology No. 72. Yale University Press, New Haven.

Greenwood, Roberta S.
   1982   The Chinese on Main Street. In *Archaeological Perspectives on Ethnicity in America*, edited by Robert Schuyler. Baywood Press, Farmingdale.

Hann, John
   1988   *Apalachee*. University Presses of Florida, Gainesville.

Haring, Clarence H.
   1964   *Trade and Navigation between Spain and the Indies in the Time of the Hapsburgs*. Reprinted. Peter Smith, Gloucester, Massachusets. Originally published 1918.

Herron, Mary
   1978   *A Formal and Functional Analysis of St. Johns Ceramics from Two Sites in St. Augustine*. Unpublished senior honors thesis, Department of Anthropology, Florida State University, Tallahassee.

Hoffman, Katherine
   1989   Interim report on excavations at the National Guard Armory (Convento de San Francisco), St. Augustine. Project report on file, Florida Museum of Natural History, Gainesville.

Hoffman, Paul
   1980   *The Spanish Crown and the Defense of the Caribbean 1535–1585*. Louisiana State University Press, Baton Rouge.

Jones, Grant
   1978   The Ethnohistory of the Guale Coast through 1684. In *The Anthropology of St.*

Catherine's Island. 1. Natural and Cultural History, by D. H. Thomas et. al., pp. 178–210. American Museum of Natural History Anthropological Papers 55(2). New York.

King, Julia
1981 *An Archaeological Investigation of 17th Century St. Augustine*. Unpublished Master's thesis, Florida State University, Tallahassee.

Lanning, John T.
1936 *The Spanish Missions of Georgia*. University of North Carolina Press, Chapel Hill.

Larson, Lewis H., Jr.
1978 Historic Guale Indians of the Georgia Coast and the Impact of the Spanish Mission Effort. In *Tacachale: Essays on the Indians of Florida and Southeastern Georgia during the Historic Period*, edited by Jerald Milanich and S. Proctor, pp. 120–140. University Presses of Florida, Gainesville.

Leone, Mark
1977 Foreword. *Research Strategies in Historical Archaeology*, edited by S. South. Academic Press, New York.

Lorant, Stefan (editor)
1946 *The New World: The First Pictures of America*. Duell, Sloane & Pierce, New York.

Lyon, Eugene
1976 *The Enterprise of Florida*. University Presses of Florida, Gainesville.

Merritt, James D.
1977 *Excavations at a Coastal Eastern Timucua Village in Northeast Florida*. Unpublished Master's thesis, Department of Anthropology, Florida State University, Tallahassee.

Milanich, Jerald T.
1978 The Western Timucua: Patterns of Acculturation and Change. In *Tacachale: Essays on the Indians of Florida and Southeastern Georgia during the Historic Period*, edited by Jerald Milanich and Samuel Proctor, pp. 59–88. University Presses of Florida, Gainesville.

Otto, John, and Russell Lewis
1974 *A Formal and Functional Analysis of San Marcos Pottery from Site SA-16-23, St. Augustine*. Florida Department of State, Bureau of Historic Sites and Properties Bulletin 4. Tallahassee.

Phillipe V, King of Spain
1660 Cedula to the Governor of Florida. Feb. 26, 1660, AGI 54-5-10/87. SCUF, Gainesville.
1714 Royal Cedula of Phillipe V of Spain to Governor Corcoles y Martinez of Florida, Sept. 26, 1714. Manuscript, AGI 58-1-23/494. SCUF Photostat.

Piatek, Bruce
1985 Non-local Aboriginal Ceramics from Early Historic Contexts in St. Augustine. *Florida Anthropologist* 38(1–2):81–89.

Poe, Charles B.
1978 Status Variability in *Criollo* Culture in St. Augustine. Paper presented at the Society for Historical Archaeology Annual Meeting, Nashville, Tennessee.

Reitz, Elizabeth, and Margaret Scarry
1985 *The Reconstruction of Historic Foodways*. Special Publication of the Society for Historical Archaeology No. 3.

Ribault, Jean
1964 *The Whole and True Discouery of Terra Florida*. Facsimile reprint of the London edition of 1563. University of Florida Press, Gainesville.

Seaberg, Lillian
1951 Archaeological Report on Excavation of the Indian Cemetery at the Fountain of Youth Park, Florida. Unpublished manuscript, Florida Museum of Natural History, Gainesville.

Scardaville, Michael C.
 1985   Approaches to the Study of the Southeastern Borderlands. In *Alabama and the Borderlands: From Prehistory to Statehood*, edited by R. Reid Badger and Lawrence Clayton, pp. 184–196. University of Alabama Press, University.

Scardaville, Michael, and Jesus Marie Belmonte
 1979   Florida in the Late Spanish Period: The 1756 Grinan Report. *El Escribano* 16:1–24. St. Augustine Historical Society.

Scarry, Margaret M.
 1985   The Use of Plant Foods in Sixteenth Century St. Augustine. *Florida Anthropologist* 38(1–2):70–80.

Singleton, Teresa
 1976   *The Archaeology of a Pre-eighteenth Century Household in St. Augustine*. Unpublished *Master's thesis, University of Florida, Gainesville.*

Smith, Greg
 1986   *A Study of Colono-Ware and Non-European Ceramics from Sixteenth Century Puerto Real, Haiti.* Unpublished Master's thesis, Department of Anthropology, University of Florida, Gainesville.

Smith, Hale G.
 1948   Two Historical Archaeological Periods in Florida. *American Antiquity* 13(4): 313–319.

Smith, James, and Stanley Bond
 1981   Phase III Archaeological Survey of St. Augustine. Report on file, Historic St. Augustine Preservation Board.

Solana, Juan Joseph
 1760   Report of J. Solana to the Crown of Spain, April 9, 1760. Manuscript AGI 86-7-21/41. SCUF Photostat. Transcription, HSAPB.

South, Stanley
 1979   *Method and Theory in Historical Archaeology*. New York: Academic Press.
 1983   *Revealing Santa Elena*. Manuscript Series 188. Research Institute of Archaeology and Anthropology, University of South Carolina, Columbia.
 1988   Santa Elena: Threshold of Conquest. In *The Recovery of Meaning*, edited by M. Leone and P. Potter, pp. 27–72. Anthropological Society of Washington. Smithsonian Institution Press, Washington, D.C.

Swanton, John
 1946   *The Indians of the Southeastern United States*. Bureau of American Ethnology Publication No. 137.

Thanz, Nina, and Graig Shaak
 1977   A Correlation of Environmental and Cultural Changes in Northeast Florida during the Late Archaic Period. *Florida Journal of Anthropology* 2(1):3–22.

Thomas, David Hurst
 1988   Saints and Savages at Santa Catalina: An Alternative Hispanic Design for Colonial America. In *The Recovery of Meaning in Historical Archaeology*, edited by Mark Leone and Parkson Potter. Smithsonian Institution Press, Washington D.C.

Valdes, Bishop of Cuba
 1729   Report of the Bishop of Cuba to the Crown of Spain, Jan. 14, 1729. Manuscript, AGI 58-2-15/25. SCUF Photostat.

Vernon, Richard
 1980   Field Report on Excavations at the Trinity Site (SA-34-1) St. Augustine. Project report, Florida Museum of Natural History, Gainesville.
 1984   *Northeast Florida Prehistory: A Synthesis and Research Design*. Unpublished Master's thesis, Department of Anthropology, Florida State University, Tallahassee.

Wallerstein, Immanuel
 1974   *The Modern World System I: Capitalist Agriculture and the Origins of the European World-Economy in the Sixteenth Century*. Academic Press, New York.

Wenhold, Lucy
    1936   A Seventeenth Century Letter of Gabriel Diaz Vara de Calderon, Bishop of Cuba Describing the Indians and Missions of Florida (1675). *Smithsonian Miscellaneous Collections* 95(1–b):1–14.

Wolf, Eric
    1982   *Europe and the People without History*. University of California Press, Berkeley.

Zierden, Martha
    1981   *The Archaeology of the Nineteenth Century Second Spanish Period in St. Augustine, Florida*. Unpublished Master's thesis, Department of Anthropology, Florida State University, Tallahassee.

Zierden, Martha, and Olga Caballero
    1979   Field Report on Excavations at the Josef de Leon site (SA-26-1), St. Augustine. Unpublished M.S., Florida Museum of Natural History, Gainesville.

Chapter 21 ■

Jane Landers

African Presence in Early Spanish Colonization of the Caribbean and the Southeastern Borderlands

The upcoming commemoration of the Columbian Quincentenary has stimulated a wide range of international scholarship on the many consequences of Columbus's voyages of discovery. The popular image of encounters between Europeans and peoples of the so-called New World is one of whites meeting aborigines. The Spaniards, the first Europeans who undertook to build an empire in the western hemisphere, designed a colonization model based upon two republics—that of the Spaniards and that of the Indians, as they mistakenly called the native peoples. In fact, African-Americans played significant roles in Spain's exploration and settlement of the Americas, and one of the important consequences of the linkage of Old and New worlds was the enslavement of 10 to 12 million Africans who were brought to the Americas to labor for Europeans (Curtin 1969; Mintz 1984; Mintz and Price 1976).

The African presence in the New World is coterminous with that of the Europeans, yet Africans remain largely "invisible" in the literature. This lacuna is due, in part, to the difficulty of the sources, and in part to the lack of interest among earlier scholars. But the Spaniards were meticulous bureaucrats and the sources for Afro-Caribbean history are rich and varied. These records are available in the Archive of the Indies in Seville, in regional and national archives in the Caribbean, and in microfilm collections in the United States. The records range from the accounts of wages paid to day laborers to the deliberations of the king and the Council of the Indies, and African-Americans appear in all of these. Although it requires some effort, it is possible to reconstruct, from the documentary record, the structures and some of the details of the African experience in the Spanish colonization of the circum-Caribbean. Historical archaeology of Afro-Caribbean sites is also offering important new insights into the material life of Africans in the Hispanic colonies.

The basic range and limitations of economic, political, and social opportunities for African-Americans evolved during the first Antillean phase of Spanish exploration and settlement. As the Spaniards spread out from their base in Hispaniola, European pathogens, warfare, and overwork took a catastrophic toll on the native populations they encountered. Although estimates of the original populations and their decline after contact vary greatly, researchers agree that some islands were rapidly depopulated and white manpower was limited. This demographic imperative made Africans important players in the geopolitical contests for control of the circum-Caribbean, and their labor and military skills helped sustain Spanish colonization. The role of Africans in this process cannot be understood without some idea of their legal and social status in the Spanish world.

Africans in Spain

The presence of Sub-Saharan Africans in Spain dates back at least to the Moslem presence in the peninsula (711–1492). Although some were enslaved, others served as soldiers and couriers in Moslem armies and intermarried with the natives of Andalusia. As the Christian armies of Spain advanced the Reconquest, they too began to acquire African slaves. Like the Portuguese merchants who dominated the Sub-Saharan trade, the Spaniards justified their activities by claiming the slaves were captured in a "just war." By this they meant that the Africans had rejected Spain's attempts to convert them to the "True Faith," and as an impediment to the extension of Christianity, were subject to legal enslavement. During this period, however, slavery was not equated with a particular race. Moors, Jews, white Christians, and Canary Islanders were also enslaved (Rout 1976).

King Alfonso X (Alfonso the Wise) incorporated provisions regarding slaves into Castilian law in the thirteenth century. His *Siete Partidas* and its later adaptations formed a body of law that was based on the belief that slavery was against the laws of nature, for man was a noble and free creation of God. Slavery was considered an accident of fate, and an aberration in nature, rather than a preordained or perpetual condition. These codes recognized that slaves had a moral and juridical personality, and Castilian legislation specifically granted slaves rights and protections not found in other slave systems. They had the right to personal security and legal mechanisms by which they might escape a cruel master. Moreover, Spanish slaves were incorporated into the church where they enjoyed all its sacraments, including marriage. The sanctity of the family was protected as the law prohibited the separation of family members, and owners could even become extended members of their slaves' families when they entered into fictive kinships as sponsors at slave marriages and baptisms. Social and religious values in Spanish society promoted honor, charity, and paternalism, which often ameliorated the hardships of bondage, and sometimes led to manumission. Further, slaves had the right to hold and transfer property and to initiate legal suits. Thus, they had the extremely important right of self-purchase and the mechanisms to pursue it. In theory, slaves of all races were accorded equal legal consideration. Although some Africans acquired freedom in fifteenth-century Spain, their social mobility and status were severely circumscribed by Spanish notions of their racial inferiority (Klein 1969; Mörner 1967; Rout 1976; Pike 1976; Tannenbaum 1946).

Africans in the New World

The Europeans who "discovered" and conquered the Americas transplanted their racial stereotypes, as well as Africans, to the New World. It is believed that a free African sailed on Columbus's first voyage of discovery, and there were certainly slaves among the earliest expeditions to Puerto Rico (1508), Jamaica (1509), Cuba (1511), and Florida (1513) (Deagan 1988; Deive 1980; Díaz Soler 1970; Kopytoff 1978; Larrazábal Blanco 1967). By the time Nicolás de Ovando arrived in Hispaniola in 1503, some of the first African slaves had already run away and found refuge among the Indians in the mountains. The problem of social control was critical and Ovando recommended no more slaves be sent from Spain. He charged that the runaways, known as *cimarrones*, were teaching the Indians "bad customs," a theme that would be reiterated many times in other areas of Hispanic conquest. Although Isabella enacted Ovando's suggested ban, Ferdinand was more concerned about his revenues than the moral endangerment of the Indians, and in 1505 he reauthorized the introduction of African slaves to extract Hispaniola's gold and copper ores (Deive 1980; Larrazábal Blanco 1967).

Within a brief time the indigenous populations of the Caribbean islands had declined dramatically, and in 1517 Father Bartolomé de las Casas warned they would soon disappear. Although not the first, he was perhaps the best-known advocate of importing African slaves to relieve labor demands on the native populations (Díaz Soler 1970; Larrazábal Blanco 1967). Hispanic colonists contended that blacks were more hardy and that one African could do the work of four Indians. They also claimed the Crown could not hope to populate and develop the islands unless African laborers were introduced in large numbers. In 1518 Charles V granted an *asiento*, or contract, to import 4,000 slaves into Hispaniola, Cuba, Jamaica, and Puerto Rico and the floodgates were opened (Díaz Soler 1970). Most of the newly imported and unacculturated Africans or *bozales* were first employed in mining, as in Hispaniola, or in animal husbandry, as in Jamaica and Puerto Rico (Kopytoff 1978).

By the mid-sixteenth century, however, plantation agriculture absorbed most of the Caribbean labor force and a more regimented and demanding slave regime was established (Deagan 1988; Mintz 1974). Las Casas came to regret his earlier pro-slavery stance, and reported that when Africans were forced to work in sugar mills, the excessive labor demands and access to alcohol led to disease, high mortality, and violent rebellion against oppression (Larrazábal Blanco 1967)

African Resistance

One scholar described the Spanish–African relationship as a cold war that periodically escalated into fierce fighting (Guillot 1961). The first recorded slave uprising broke out on the sugar estate of Diego Colon in Hispaniola and was led by Wolof slaves from the Senegambia region of West Africa. During Christmas of 1522 the Wolofs rebelled and, gathering slave recruits along the way, sacked sugar estates and killed approximately 20 Spaniards. In five days of fierce fighting the Spaniards employed Indians and superior arms to overcome the Africans, and then placed their heads on spikes to horrify the rest of the enslaved. The Crown reviewed the incident, concluded the Wolofs were influenced by Moslem teachings and therefore could not be trusted, and thereafter attempted to prohibit their introduction into the New World (Larrazábal Blanco 1967; Rout 1976).

Nevertheless, violent racial conflict continued. In 1533 and 1538 slave revolts wracked Cuba, and this time Cuban and Yucatecan Indians fought on the side of the slaves (Instituto de Ciencias Históricas 1986). It soon became apparent that rebelliousness was not the exclusive nature of the Wolofs, for in the 1540s slaves rose against Spanish masters in Mexico, Central America, and the northern coast of South America. Hardly a decade passed without some significant insurrection by the slaves, and despite repeated defeats, Africans continued their armed struggle against slavery until it was eventually abolished (Guillot 1961; Rout 1976).

As we have already seen, other Africans resisted slavery by flight. Communities of runaway slaves were common to all slaveholding societies, but they challenged the Spanish concept of civilized living as well as the hierarchical racial and social order that colonial administrators sought to impose. The Crown sought to promote public order and righteous living by establishing towns and Indian missions. The Spaniards thought urban living would facilitate evangelization, but beyond that, they attached a special value to living a *vida politica*. They believed "people of reason" distinguished themselves from nomadic "barbarians" by living in stable urban situations (Hardoy 1975). Royal legislation reflected an ongoing interest in reforming and settling the so-called vagabonds of all races within the empire (Konetzke 1953–1962).

The primary focus of efforts to reduce non-Spaniards to village life was, of course, the Indians, but as black and mixed populations grew, so did Spanish concerns about how these elements would be accommodated into civilized society. The "two republics" of Spaniards and Indians gave way to a society of castes, which increasingly viewed the unforeseen and unregulated groups with hostility.

Some maroon communities or *palenques* posed a serious economic threat, for they survived by raiding Spanish settlements and enticing or stealing away slaves. They were a plague to Spanish authorities, yet repeated military efforts to eradicate these communities were, more often than not, unsuccessful (Acosta Saignes 1967; Arrom and García-Arevalo 1986; Guillot 1961; Palmer 1976; Price 1973). Recent archaeological excavations of an early eighteenth-century *palenque*, the Maniel de José Leta, in southeastern Hispaniola have begun to enrich the limited evidence for the lifeways of the maroons. There the inhabitants subsisted primarily on wild pigs, although it is presumed they also grew garden crops and gathered wild honey. Although the site was only briefly occupied, investigators found slag piles and metallurgical tools as well as metal-tipped arrows, knives, nails, metal bracelets, and a metal dagger. Archaeologists also uncovered other evidence of craft production such as incised clay pipes and water jugs. It appears the site was evacuated quickly, perhaps as Spanish slavecatchers approached (Arrom and García-Arevalo 1986).

African Accommodation

Although conditions for Africans living among the Spanish were less harsh, people of color were nonetheless assigned to the bottom of the social hierarchy. Blacks and mulattos, even if free, suffered penalties for having descended from slaves. As conquered people, they were subject to tribute payments, although these were rarely collected anywhere in Latin America. African-Americans were also subject to elaborate social controls and a great body of discriminatory legislation evolved throughout the Indies. Nevertheless, the emphasis on a slave's humanity and rights, and the lenient attitude toward manumission embodied in Spanish slave codes and social practice, made it possible for a significant free black class to exist in the Spanish world where its members filled various important economic and military functions (McAlister 1984; Mörner 1967; Tannenbaum 1947). These free persons of African descent had some access to education and could own and sell property. As they had in Seville, free Africans associated along ethnic-linguistic lines in *cofradías* or lay brotherhoods chartered by the Catholic Church in the sixteenth and seventeenth centuries. Members participated in religious ceremonies and supported a variety of charitable activities that benefited their members as well as the less fortunate (Deive 1980; Larrazábal Blanco 1967; Ortiz 1920).

Africans in Spanish Florida

The African experience was as varied in Spanish Florida as it was in other areas of the Hispanic world. Spanish explorers found no precious metals or major Indian civilizations to exploit there and the land did not support intensive agricultural production. Florida's significance resided almost solely in its strategic location, and it became a military outpost of the Spanish empire when Pedro Menéndez de Avilés established St. Augustine in 1565 (Lyon 1976). A royal charter granted Menéndez permission to import 500 African slaves to help settle

Florida, but Menéndez never filled that contract and evidence suggests that fewer than 50 may have accompanied the first settlers (Lyon 1976). Life in St. Augustine was not easy for any of the colonists, but disease and hard work took an especially harsh toll on the hard-working slaves. In 1581 the Crown ordered Havana to send royal slaves to supplement the dwindling slave force, and by 1583 officials in St. Augustine were able to report that the king's slaves had built several structures, including a church, a blacksmith shop, and a platform for artillery (Chatelain 1941; Connor 1924–1930). The slaves also made repairs on the fort, sawed timber, and cleared land for planting. They were soon harvesting enough to feed themselves "with no other expense but their oil and salt." When the work at St. Augustine was completed, 10 of the most skilled slaves were sent to help with the construction of the fort at Santa Elena, Spain's northern-most settlement in America (Chatelain 1941).

The Crown considered black labor indispensable to the maintenance of Florida, noting that the work of cutting and sawing wood for fortifications and ships was unceasing and that the entire *situado*, or government subsidy, would not suffice if wages had to be paid for these tasks (the king to Captain General Sancho de Alquía 9 April 1618, SD 225, AGI). Africans also provided military reserves for the understaffed Spanish garrison and were formed into a militia unit by at least 1683 (Roster of the Free *Pardo* and *Moreno* Militia of St. Augustine, 20 September 1683, SD 226, AGI).

Some slaves in St. Augustine led lives of unceasing toil and misery, while others lived fairly comfortably in the homes of their Spanish owners. The royal government was the main employer in Spanish Florida and found many uses for its slaves. Slaves served as auctioneers, town criers, and messengers. They worked in the royal hospital and barracks and served the military by cutting firewood, maintaining weapons, tending mounts, and providing their music. More strenuous labor was required of slaves working on public construction projects, or in the stone quarries or lime kilns. Slaves were the cowboys, field hands, and lumberjacks in the countryside. St. Augustine's coastal location and its network of interior rivers and creeks meant that the lives of other slaves revolved around the water and Florida's important shipping trade. Slaves hunted, trapped, fished, and grew food for themselves and the larger community, and they were its artisans, domestics, musicians, sailors, and soldiers. They were included in dowries, bequeathed in wills, traded and exchanged in contract and property transactions, and even posted as bonds. In short, slaves were a critical component in the economic structure of Spanish Florida (Landers 1988).

Over time, freedmen, like slaves, came to play important roles in Spanish Florida. A few were manumitted by owners, or were already free when they came to the province from Cuba or other areas of the Spanish empire. Another group of slaves became free by astutely manipulating the Anglo-Spanish contest for empire in North America. In 1670 England challenged Spain's claim to exclusive sovereignty in the Southeast by establishing the colony of Carolina. Although the small force at St. Augustine could make no major response, a campaign of harassment was initiated against the colony, which included slave raids by the Spanish and their African and Indian allies. These contacts may have pointed the way to St. Augustine and suggested the possibility of a refuge among the enemy, for by 1687 slaves from the English plantations were beginning to escape to St. Augustine (TePaske 1975; Wood 1974; Wright 1924). Despite an early ambiguity about the legal status of the runaways, the Spanish welcomed the labor and military services they offered. Rather than return them as the English owners demanded, Spanish officials sheltered them, instructed them in Catholic doctrine, and employed them, ostensibly for wages. The fugitives claimed to seek conversion to the "True Faith," and in 1693, on this basis, the Spanish king decided to free them, "granting liberty to all . . . the men as well as the women . . . so that by their example and by my liberality . . . others will do the same" (Royal Edict, 7 November 1693, SD 58-1-2/74 in ST, PKY).

In the next decades more slaves sought asylum in Florida, and they were frequently aided in their escapes by Indians. The Carolinians complained bitterly of the provocation inherent in the sanctuary policy, for not only did each runaway represent an economic loss, but by the beginning of the eighteenth century blacks outnumbered whites in the English colony, which increased the settlers' chronic fears of slave uprisings. Carolina experienced slave revolts in 1711 and 1714 and the following year many slaves joined the Yamassees in their war against the English (Wood 1974). Moreover, the Spaniards continued to send parties of escaped slaves and Indians back to raid Carolina plantations. In 1728 the frustrated planters launched an unsuccessful retaliatory raid against St. Augustine, and Africans fought bravely in the town's defense (TePaske 1964). Still, not all were immediately freed.

The leader of the slave militia that fought to maintain Spanish sovereignty in Florida was Francisco Menéndez. Menéndez was of the Mandingo "nation," whose West African homelands stretched between the Senegal and Niger rivers. Like the Wolofs, the Mandingos were said to be fierce warriors, influenced by the Moslems, but they were also noted for their superior culture and literacy (Acosta Saignes 1967). Menéndez was first a slave of the English in Carolina, but he escaped and joined the Yamassee uprising. After three years of warfare against his former captors Menéndez made his way to St. Augustine in the company of the Yamassee chieftain, Jorge. There he hoped to claim the freedom promised by the Spanish Crown, but he was betrayed by a non-Christian Indian named Mad Dog and sold back into slavery. Menéndez repeatedly petitioned the Spanish governors and the Bishop of Cuba for his liberty and that of other escaped slaves who had not been freed. Chief Jorge of the Yamassee also petitioned on behalf of his old allies.

The Free Black Town of Gracia Real de Santa Teresa de Mose

Finally, in 1738, Governor Manuel de Montiano investigated the matter, belatedly freed the petitioners, and established the first free black town in the present-day United States, Gracia Real de Santa Teresa de Mose, about 2 miles north of St. Augustine. Menéndez, his wife María, and some 37 other families became homesteaders at the site, and the grateful freedmen vowed to "shed their last drop of blood in defense of the Great Crown of Spain and the Holy

Faith, and to be the most cruel enemies of the English" (Manuel de Montiano to the King, 3 March 1738, Memorial of Chief Jorge, 3 March 1738, and Memorial of the Fugitive Slaves from the Carolina Plantations to the King, 10 June 1738, SD 844, on microfilm reel 15, PKY).

Although the governors and the Crown stressed the religious and humanitarian grounds for establishing Mose, the primary function of the town was to serve as a buffer against foreign encroachment. Mose was strategically located across land and water routes to St. Augustine so that the freed slaves could defend against invasions by their former masters. A white military officer supervised the construction at Mose and a student priest saw to the spiritual guidance of the new converts. Although the Franciscan lived at Mose, there is no evidence the white officer ever did. It seems rather that Francisco Menéndez was responsible for ruling the settlement, for in one document Governor Montiano referred to the others at Mose as the "subjects" of Menéndez. His leadership and military skills were recognized by the Spaniards, who may have regarded him as a sort of natural lord, akin to an Indian *cacique*, through whom they could communicate and enact their objectives. Francisco Menéndez was captain of the Mose militia, continuing the military role he had filled since 1726. Spanish titles and support may have reinforced Menéndez's status and authority in the community.

The case of Menéndez raises interesting questions about the cultural identifications of the inhabitants of Mose. Among the West African "nations" represented at Mose were the Mandingo, Carabalí, and Congo. Most of the townspeople had spent at least some time in an English slave society from which they risked great harm to escape. Some had intimate contact for several years with the Yamassee Indians and hostile contacts with non-Christian native peoples before reaching the Spanish colony. Some became slaves of the Spanish prior to achieving a free status, and once free they associated closely with the remnants of seven different nations aggregated into outlying Indian towns. Meanwhile, new infusions of Africans were incorporated into the original Mose community as runaways continued to filter into St. Augustine from Carolina and Georgia (Landers 1988).

The first settlement at Mose was short-lived, for in 1740 James Oglethorpe led a land and naval attack on St. Augustine and his forces occupied Mose. Captain Francisco Menéndez led the free black militia on dangerous reconnaissance missions into enemy-controlled areas. His unit also participated in the surprise attack that recaptured Mose at great cost to the enemy. The governor commended Menéndez's bravery in two letters to the king, and Menéndez petitioned to receive regular military pay for his services, but there is no evidence of any royal response (Manuel de Montiano to the King, 27 December 1740, and Memorial of Francisco Menéndez, 21 November 1740, SD 2658, AGI).

Mose's original structures were destroyed during Oglethorpe's raid and the displaced settlers lived in St. Augustine until a second Mose was rebuilt by the freedmen in 1752. At the new settlement a walled fort enclosed a large church, the priest's house, a lookout, a well and guardhouses, and a moat topped with Spanish bayonet surrounded the fort. The villagers lived in 22 thatched huts described as resembling those of the Indians (Father Juan de Solana to Don Pedro Agustin Morel de Santa Cruz, 22 April 1759, SD 516 on microfilm reel 28K, PKY). A house-by-house census of the village identifies 37 men, 15 women, 7 boys, and 8 girls by name and age and details the relationships of the people in the household (Census of Fray Ginés Sánchez, 11 February 1759, SD 2604, AGI). Several of the households were composed solely of men, but parish registers reveal that some of them had slave wives and children living in St. Augustine. The same records reveal that several of the men were married to women from nearby Indian towns (Black Marriages and Baptisms on microfilm reels 284 C, 284 L, 284 F, 284 J, PKY).

Kathleen Deagan, of the Florida Museum of Natural History, heads an inter-disciplinary team currently conducting an archaeological investigation of Mose that will add to the documentary record material evidence about daily life at this unique site. Although the village site still eludes them, in two seasons of excava-tions the team has uncovered the foundations and earthen walls of the fort, parts of the palisade, sections of the moat, and several of the interior structures. They have also recovered military artifacts such as bullets, gunflints, and but-tons, and domestic items such as bone buttons, pins and thimbles, clay pipe bowls, beads, and a variety of eighteenth-century ceramics and bottles. One unique find is a handmade St. Christopher's medal of pewter. Preliminary anal-yses of floral and faunal remains from the site indicate the inhabitants subsisted largely on estuarine fish and shellfish and other wild, locally available foods. In future investigations archaeologists hope to learn more about subsistence and environmental use practices at the site and better determine patterns of cultural adaptation. It is clear that the Africans living at Mose were remarkably adapta-ble. Not only did they escape to freedom and survive, they also learned to use Spanish legal institutions and by persevering were ultimately successful in ap-peals to Spanish justice and *honor*. In return for liberty, they vowed fealty and armed service, and established themselves as vassals of the Spanish King, de-serving of royal protection. They also formed ties of reciprocal obligation with important members of both the white and black communities through the mech-anism of *compadrazgo*, or ritual brotherhood. Governor Montiano commended their industry as they worked to establish and cultivate Mose, and the adaptive behavior of Menéndez and his "subjects" seems to have earned them at least a limited autonomy.

Such autonomy is evident in the operations of both the black and Indian mili-tias who operated on St. Augustine's frontiers, and whose role in the defense of the Spanish colony has not yet been fully appreciated. These cavalry units served in frontier reconnaissance and guerrilla operations. They had their own officers and often operated independently, although Spanish infantry officers also commanded mixed groups of Spaniards, blacks, and Indians on scouting missions (Manuel de Montiano to the King, 27 December 1740, SD 2658, AGI, and Manuel de Montiano to Captain General Güemes y Horcasitas, 13 March 1742, SD 2593, AGI).

The Mose settlers may have spoken several European and Indian languages in addition to their own, and were exposed to a great variety of subsistence techniques, craft and artistic traditions, labor patterns, and foodways. Several of the men were skilled carpenters, soldiers, and trackers, but the full range of their occupations is not clear in the historical record. Historical records are similarly deficient in informing us about women's work, but archaeology may provide the missing data.

More is known about the way the people at Mose adapted to religious expectations in Spanish Florida. Since their sanctuary was based upon religious conversion, it was incumbent upon them to exhibit their Catholicism. Their baptisms, marriages, and deaths were faithfully recorded in the parish registers. But a rich syncretic tradition has been noted in other Spanish Caribbean and Southeastern colonies and it is possible the people of Mose also observed some of their former religious practices (Ortiz 1920, 1973; Savannah Unit, Georgia Writers' Project 1940; Thompson 1984). Archaeologists hope to determine what mixture of customs the Africans may have adopted in many other areas of daily life, and what of their traditions may have influenced the culture of their hosts. Mose is the only colonial black settlement in the Americas to be examined in such depth and its history will shed new light on the nature of multiethnic New World societies (Mintz and Price 1976).

Mose was occupied until the Spanish were forced by treaty to evacuate Florida in 1763. At that time the population of Mose joined the general exodus to Cuba (Gold 1969; Evacuation report of Juan Jorge Eligio de la Puente, 22 January 1764, SD 2595, AGI). This last diaspora scattered the African-American community of first-period Spanish Florida, but Spanish functionaries continued to record bits of their lives in Cuba.

It has accurately been noted that those who write history, shape it. Florida became a part of the American South, where most persons of color remained anonymous. Even had they been interested, historians of earlier years may have assumed the lives of its African-Americans were impossible to recover. But, if one approaches Florida history from a Caribbean perspective, assumptions are dramatically altered, and inquiry can proceed. One has only to look at the histories of Cuba, the Dominican Republic, Jamaica, coastal Mexico, Venezuela, and Colombia, for example, to know that the African-American experience must be incorporated into any history of a Spanish colony in the "Negroid littoral" (Acosta Saignes 1967; Campbell 1975; Deive 1980; Klein 1969; Kopytoff 1976; Ortiz 1973; Palmer 1976).

The Africans of the Spanish "borderlands," like those at Mose, often lived on the periphery of Spanish society—sometimes between the Spanish and their enemies. The interstitial location of settlements such as Mose parallels the social position of their inhabitants—persons who straddled cultures, astutely pursued their own advantage, and in the process helped shape the colonial history of the circum-Caribbean as well as an Afro-Hispanic culture.

Acknowledgments

Research for this paper at the Archive of the Indies and in the P.K. Yonge Library of Florida History was supported by the Florida Legislature, the Program for Cultural Cooperation between Spain's Ministry of Culture and U.S. Universities, the Spain-Florida Alliance, and the Department of History, University of Florida. I would like to thank Lyle McAlister, Kathy Deagan, James Amelang, Cheryll Cody, Peter Wood, and Bertram Wyatt-Brown for their thoughtful comments on various drafts of this work and their encouragement, while acknowledging personal responsibility for its shortcomings.

References

Manuscript Collections

Archivo General de Indias, Seville, Spain, Section Five, Audiencia de Santo Domingo, La Florida, cited as SD.
Legajos 844, 2583, 2595, 2604, 2658.
P. K. Yonge Library of Florida History, University of Florida, Gainesville, Florida, cited as PKY.
Audiencia of Santo Domingo, on microfilm, Legajo 844. Cathedral Records, Saint Augustine Parish, on microfilm.
Black Baptisms, reels 284 F, 284 J.
Black Marriages, reels 284 C, 284 L.
Black Burials, reels 284 D, 284 L.
John B. Stetson Collection, photostatic copies, cited as ST. SD 58-1-2/74.

Books, Articles, Dissertations, and Papers

Acosta Saignes, Miguel
1967 *Vida de los esclavos negros en Venezuela*. Ediciones Hespérides, Caracas.
Arrom, Juan José, and Manuel A. García-Arevalo
1986 *Cimarron*. Fundación García-Arevalo, Dominican Republic.
Bolton, Herbert E., and Mary Ross
1968 *The Debatable Land: A Sketch of the Anglo-Spanish Contest for the Georgia Country*. Reprinted. Russell and Russell, New York.
Campbell, Leon.
1975 The Changing Racial and Administrative Structure of the Peruvian Military under the Late Bourbons. *Americas* 32:117–133.
Chatelain, Verne E.
1941 *The Defenses of Spanish Florida, 1565 to 1763*. Carnegie Institute, Washington, D.C.
Coll y Toste, Cayetano
1971 *Historia de la esclavitud en Puerto Rico*. Jorge Casa, Barcelona.
Connor, Jeanette Thurber (editor)
1924–1930 *The Colonial Records of Spanish Florida: Letters and Reports of Governors and Secular Persons*. 2 vols. Florida State Historical Society, Deland.
Curtin , Philip
1969 *The Atlantic Slave Trade: A Census*. University of Wisconsin Press, Madison.
Deagan, Kathleen
1988 The Archaeology of the Spanish Contact Period in the Caribbean. *Journal of World Prehistory* 2:187–233.
1982 *Spanish St. Augustine: The Archaeology of a Colonial Creole Community*. Academic Press, New York.

Deive, Carlos Esteban
 1980 *La esclavitud del negro en Santo Domingo*. Museo del Hombre Dominicano, Santo Domingo.
Díaz Soler, Luis M.
 1970 *Historia de la esclavitud negra en Puerto Rico*. Editorial Universitaria, San Juan.
Foster, George M.
 1953 Cofradía and Compadrazgo in Spain and Spanish America. *Southwestern Journal of Anthropology* 9:1–28.
Gold, Robert L.
 1969 *Borderland Empires in Transition: The Triple-Nation Transfer of Florida*. Southern Illinois University Press, Carbondale and Edwardsville.
Guillot, Carlos Federico
 1961 *Negros rebeldes y negros cimarrones*. Fariña editorial, Montevideo.
Hardoy, Jorge (editor)
 1975 *Urbanization in Latin America: Approaches and Issues*. Anchor Press, Garden City, New York.
Instituto de Ciencias Históricas
 1986 *Esclavitud en Cuba*. Editora de la Academia de Ciencias de Cuba, Havana.
Klein, Herbert S.
 1969 Anglicanism, Catholicism and the Negro Slave. In *Slavery in the New World, A Reader in Comparative History*, edited by Laura Foner and Eugene D. Genovese, pp. 138–165. Prentice-Hall, Englewood Cliffs, New Jersey.
 1961 The Colored Militia of Cuba: 1568–1868. *Caribbean Studies* 6:17–27.
Konetzke, Richard (editor)
 1953–1962 *Colección de documentos para la historia de la formación social de Hispanoamérica, 1493–1810*. 3 vols. Madrid.
Kopytoff, Barbara Klamon
 1978 The Early Political Development of Jamaican Maroon Societies. *William and Mary Quarterly* 35:287–307.
Landers, Jane
 1987 *Historical Report on Gracia Real de Santa Teresa de Mose*. Ms. submitted to the Florida Museum of Natural History, Gainesville, Florida.
 1988 *Black Society in Spanish St. Augustine, 1784–1821*. Unpublished Ph.D. dissertation, Department of History, University of Florida, Gainesville.
Larrazábal Blanco, Carlos
 1967 *Los negros y la esclavitud en Santo Domingo*. Julio D. Postigo y hijos Editores, Santo Domingo.
Lyon, Eugene
 1976 *The Enterprise of Florida: Pedro Menéndez de Avilés and the Spanish Conquest of 1565–1568*. University Presses of Florida, Gainesville.
 1985 Continuity in the Age of Conquest: The Establishment of Spanish Sovereignty in the Sixteenth Century. In *Alabama and the Borderlands, From Prehistory to Statehood*, edited by R. Reid Badger and Lawrence A. Clayton, pp. 154–161. University of Alabama Press, University.
McAlister, Lyle
 1984 *Spain and Portugal in the New World, 1492–1700*. University of Minnesota Press, Minneapolis.
Mintz, Sidney W.
 1984 *Caribbean Transformations*. Johns Hopkins University Press, Baltimore.
Mintz, Sidney M., and Richard Price
 1976 *An Anthropological Approach to the Afro-American Past: A Caribbean Perspective*. Occasional Papers in Social Change. Institute for the Study of Human Issues, Philadelphia.

Mörner, Magnus
  1967 *Race Mixture in the History of the Americas.* Little Brown, Boston.
Morse, Richard
  1975 A Framework for Latin American Urban History. In *Urbanization in Latin America: Approaches and Issues*, edited by Jorge Hardoy, pp. 57–107. Anchor Press, Garden City, New York.
Ortiz Fernández, Fernando
  1920 La fiesta Afro-Cubana del Día de Reyes. *Revista Bimestre Cubana* 15:5–16.
  1973 Los cabildos afrocubanos. In *Orbita de Fernando Ortiz*, edited by Julio le Riverand, pp. 121–134. Unión de Escritores y Artistas, Havana.
Palmer, Colin
  1976 *Slaves of the White God—Blacks in Mexico, 1570–1650.* Cambridge University Press, Cambridge.
Pike, Ruth
  1976 *Aristocrats and Traders: Sevillian Society in the Sixteenth Century.* Cornell University Press, Ithaca, New York.
Price, Richard (editor)
  1973 *Maroon Societies—Rebel Slave Communities in the Americas.* Anchor Press, Garden City, New York.
Rout, Leslie B. Jr.
  1976 *The African Experience in Spanish America, 1502 to the Present Day.* Cambridge University Press, Cambridge.
Savannah Unit, Georgia Writers' Project
  1940 *Drums and Shadows: Survival Studies among the Georgia Coastal Negroes.* University of Georgia Press, Athens.
Tannenbaum, Frank
  1946 *Slave and Citizen: The Negro in the Americas.* Alfred A. Knopf, New York.
TePaske, John J.
  1964 *The Governorship of Spanish Florida, 1700–1763.* Duke University Press, Durham.
  1975 The Fugitive Slave: Intercolonial Rivalry and Spanish Slave Policy, 1687–1764. In *Eighteenth-Century Florida and Its Borderlands*, edited by Samuel Proctor, pp. 1–12. University of Florida Press, Gainesville.
Thompson, Robert Farris
  1984 *Flash of the Spirit: African and Afro-American Art and Philosophy.* Vintage Books, New York.
Wood, Peter H.
  1974 *Black Majority: Negroes in Colonial South Carolina, from 1670 through the Stono Rebellion.* W.W. Norton, New York.
Wright, Irene.
  1924 Dispatches of Spanish Officials Bearing on the Free Negro Settlement of Gracia Real de Santa Teresa de Mose. *Journal of Negro History* 9:144–193.

Chapter 22 ■

Stanley South

From Thermodynamics to a Status Artifact Model: Spanish Santa Elena

Colonization at the city of Santa Elena in Port Royal Sound, South Carolina, from 1566 to 1587 was a major effort by Spain to gain a foothold in the New World. The significance of this capital city of Spanish Florida has been outlined by historians (Conner 1925; Hoffman 1978; Lyon 1976; Ross 1925; Salley 1925), and archaeological research has been carried out on the site under my direction since 1979 (South 1979, 1980, 1982, 1983, 1984, 1985, 1988; South and Hunt 1986; South et al. 1988).

Santa Elena was the city from which Juan Pardo led his expedition into the interior of the Carolinas and from which a mission in the Chesapeake Bay area was established. In the 1560s the population at Santa Elena numbered more than 400. The settlement represented a major effort by Spain to curb the French exploration and settlement begun in the Port Royal area in 1562 (Bennett 1975; Connor 1925, 1927, 1930; Judge 1988; Lorant 1946; Lyon 1984).

Three forts were erected to guard the city of Santa Elena, which had over 60 houses in 1580 (Conner 1930:283). One of these, Fort San Felipe, was attacked by Indians in 1576, and the settlement had to be abandoned for a year. It was reoccupied the following year, but was abandoned again in 1587 after Sir Francis

Drake burned St. Augustine. This exodus brought to a close the 21-year period of Spanish presence at Santa Elena (Hoffman 1978; Conner 1925; Lyon 1976; Ross 1925; Salley 1925).

Archaeological Background

Many projects have been undertaken on the Parris Island site of Santa Elena from 1979 to 1985. These have resulted in the partial excavation of the forts of San Felipe and San Marcos and the ruins of Santa Elena. The interior of Fort San Felipe and the northwest bastion have been excavated. A 50-by-70-foot fortified house ruin was found inside the fort as well as three wells. A 30-by-100-foot section was excavated in Santa Elena, and several 20-by-30-foot archaeological windows revealed details of the buried city. In one area a small round hut, built in the Indian manner, and thought to be the residence of a servant or a soldier, was found. Rectangular buildings were positioned around what appears to be a courtyard.

Spanish and Indian artifacts were recovered in abundance and a volume on these has recently been published (South et al. 1988). An additional project, in which Eugene Lyon is translating Spanish documents relating to Santa Elena, is currently under way. Reports on all projects have been published (South 1979, 1980, 1982, 1983, 1984, 1988; South et al. 1988).

Method and Theory

Exploring world cultural systems and the process of their operation as they utilize the available energy resources through class distinctions is a major concern of my research (Adams 1975, 1982, 1988; Finley 1954:397; Green 1986a; Harris 1980; Lewis 1984; Marx 1906; Odum and Odum 1981; Wallerstein 1974; White 1949, 1959, 1975; Wolf 1982). All life, as well as cultural systems, is based on the control of energy flowing from storage in plant, animal, mineral, and human cultural resources (Green 1986a; Odum and Odum 1981; White 1949:364–365). Models for expressing the energy flow from processes represented by the artifacts historical archaeologists recover, in relation to the cost of obtaining the energy, are needed if we are to express the archaeological record in terms of energy theory (Odum and Odum 1981). This chapter presents such a model based on my research at Santa Elena.

The primary role of the Spanish cultural system was *economic exploitation, fortification for protection of the settlement population,* and *control of the native people,* through the mechanism of *evangelization* into the Catholic faith (Lyon 1976, 1984). The primary function of culture is to harness energy for man's use. Because the control of energy resources from the environment leads to the concentration of power in the hands of individuals and families, and because this power tends to become fixed as socioeconomic status levels within a society, it behooves archaeologists to focus on such status levels in their studies of world cultural systems (Adams 1975, 1982, 1988; Finley 1954; Green 1986a; Harris

1980:111, 228; Lewis 1984; Nash 1981; Odum and Odum 1981:3; Wallerstein 1974, 1980; White 1949, 1959, 1975). Fortunately, the archaeological record lends itself to such analysis since this socioeconomic status-related social process leaves its indelible mark upon the archaeological record.

In our research at Santa Elena we have illustrated the importance of arguments of relevance as links bonding evolutionary energy theory to the appropriate artifact types, classes, and groups as seen in the archaeological record. The power of the use of evolutionary theory to address the energy exploitative processes of cultural systems lies in the compatibility between theoretical concepts and material remains within the archaeological record. Evolutionary theory equips the historical archaeologist with the necessary power to address the cultural processes at the scale of the world cultural systems with which we deal (South 1988).

The exploration of status differences at Santa Elena has been used as a theoretical approach since the project began. Because the founder of the settlement, Pedro Menéndez, and his family were obviously from the upper class, and controlled the laboring class and others in their exploitation of energy resources available through the colonization effort, the study of socioeconomic status is an important archaeological strategy. The archaeological study of the ruins of a city such as Santa Elena can be organized within the framework of the utilization of energy.

Thus, *status, ethnicity, fortification, social structure of the Indians, social structure of the Spanish colonial system, trade, settlement,* and *evangelization* can be seen to vary with the net capture ratio of energy resources by those controlling classes involved. Analyses of the remains of the Spanish colonial system at Santa Elena over the past years have focused on the *elite vs. the soldiers, the domestic Spaniards vs. the Indians, the local Indians vs. those represented by St. Johns Indian pottery imported to Santa Elena from the area of St. Augustine,* and so on (South 1979, 1980, 1982, 1983, 1984, 1985).

Given the theoretical framework outlined above, the methods we have used at Santa Elena to demonstrate that status differences reflect differential access to energy resources will continue to be used in our research. We now know, for instance, that larger structures reflect greater access to energy resources such as access to Ming porcelain, decorated majolica, bordado, glassware, and chickens associated with them. We know that this can be monitored by examining refuse thrown into daub-processing pits in the courtyard area of the structures. When these were full of refuse, the area above such pits continued to be used for refuse disposal.

This refuse is still located in a relatively undisturbed context in the lower "B zone," as well as in the plowed soil zone overlying it. Variability in the distribution of such refuse has been successfully monitored in totally excavated areas by the use of SYMAP (South 1979, 1980, 1984, 1985). Status/energy-related artifacts have been examined by means of the Status Artifact Model, a measure of socioeconomic status level I have developed for use with sixteenth-century Spanish colonial artifacts. This model is presented in the following section.

From Thermodynamics to a Status Artifact Model

In developing the Status Artifact Model, we have drawn on three data sets from Santa Elena:

1. a humble hut, only 12 feet across, built in the Indian manner with a central hearth and thought to be the residence of a worker or slave or possibly a soldier, all individuals of lower socioeconomic level in Santa Elena (South 1980);
2. the entire collection of artifacts in the moat and inside Fort San Felipe, the place where soldiers were carrying out their role of protecting Santa Elena, and who were known to be "suffering need for everything" (Conner 1925:307, 313); and
3. finally, the collection of all artifacts from the 30-by-100-foot excavated area in which three rectangular Spanish houses of the more affluent citizens of Santa Elena were found (South 1982), one structure measuring 42 feet in length.

From these three contexts we might expect the small hut and the area occupied by the soldiers to contain a higher ratio of lower socioeconomic artifacts than the Santa Elena residential area where the three houses were located. Indeed, a comparative study of chicken bones (an upper-class indicator), Ming porcelain, and decorated majolica, has revealed the greater presence of these upper status–related artifacts in association with the three Spanish houses (South 1982). An outline of the model follows.

Archaeological fragments of teacups, porcelain, earthenware, glassware, bowls, buttons, buckles, armor, shot, and other by-products of a cultural system form a close parallel to the pieces of a jigsaw puzzle in a box. The natural and cultural formation processes of the archaeological record make their impact felt, as they form increasing disorder through time similar to the disarrangement inside the puzzle box as it is shaken. Stephen W. Hawking (1988:144–146) has used this image to illustrate the second law of thermodynamics, which states that in a closed system disorder or entropy increases through time. Leslie White (1959:38) and Richard Adams (1975:122, 1988:31) have emphasized that this law is applicable to cultural systems as well as to other material systems.

All life depends on a flow of energy from the sun, which passes through the life system and is dissipated into space as heat. Human history is the story of how we have learned to tap ever greater amounts of that energy flow. Archaeological remains are the physical evidence of this story. The archaeological challenge is not only to trace the pathway of fragments of past cultural systems back in time to their more whole, less disordered state within the cultural system, but also to attempt to determine something of the cultural processes of which the artifacts were once a functioning part. These cultural processes function to tap the available energy resources to serve the needs of man. Energy is the ability to do work or labor. White (1959:40) has expressed this as E (energy) times T (the technological means of using the energy) which results in P (product), serving the needs of man.

How can we monitor energy in cultural systems through historical archaeology and fulfill the challenge with which I have goaded the field (South 1988:25–28)? Richard Adams has examined energy and social structure in developing a theory of social power in the evolution of cultural systems based on nineteenth- and twentieth-century data from British history (Adams 1975, 1982, 1988), expanding on the foundation laid by Leslie White (1959). Halcott Green (1986a) has examined evolution and power and has developed a disequilibrium hypothesis relevant to many fields, which allows predictions at the level of the collectivist (USSR) vs. noncollectivist (individualistic, USA) societies (Green 1986b).

Implementing these energy-based theories using site-specific historical archaeology data sets is no easy task because there is a quantum leap in scale from theory designed to deal with the evolution of state systems to the level of artifact fragment analysis. The challenge offered by energy-based evolutionary theory has been virtually ignored in historical archaeology with the notable exception of the dissertation of Jack Marvin Jackson, which deals with a theory of social evolution for historical archaeology (1988).

The "Status Artifact Model" was built on the data base provided by almost a decade of archaeological excavation at the Santa Elena site using an energy theory framework useful in examining class structure and other culture processes reflected in the archaeological record. The following sequence outlines the argument-of-relevance steps from theory to method to technique, in a decreasing order of generality.

Theory

1. Human processes can be best understood by thinking of them in energy terms (Adams 1982:122, 1988).

2. Energy-based evolutionary theory is best understood through the dissipative structure concept of the laws of thermodynamics (Adams 1982:123, 1988:31–36, 129–136; Hawking 1988:102–105).

3. Marx emphasized that traditional societies are divided into two strata or "classes," and Fried has emphasized that such stratified societies evolve into states (Adams 1975:243–247; 1988:164–165).

4. In traditional societies the minority ruling class dominates a majority subordinate class held in some form of bondage (White 1959:313).

5. In those societies the dominant class controls the labor of the subordinate class, and labor is used as a measure of the value of production, along with the net capture ratio of energy from technology and the degree of scarcity of the raw materials and the finished product (White 1959:338).

6. In White's view, "On the average the magnitude of value of a product will be proportional to the amount of human labor, or energy, expended in its production" (1959:336).

7. The control of energy resources (the ability to do work), such as labor, tools, technology and transportation, by the dominant class leads to the concentration of power in the hands of dominant families and individuals (Finley 1954; Green 1986a; Harris 1980:111, 228; White 1959:329–353).

8. An important mechanism of coordination and integration in the economic system of a society is the merchant, who is a vital fulcrum between production and consumption (White 1959:346).

9. Throughout history the merchant has also been a pirate, which prompted Nietzsche to observe that "even today mercantile morality is really nothing but a refinement on piratical morality" (White 1959:346). This stems from the fact that the merchant performs a public function with the private gain going to the merchant (White 1959: 348).

10. The merchandizing process leads to the concentration of wealth and power into the hands of fewer and fewer individuals and families (White 1959: 351).

Santa Elena

11. Spanish Florida with its two sister cities, St. Augustine and Santa Elena (1566–1587), was a colonial state-church controlled by Pedro Menéndez and the Menéndez Associated Families in America (MAFIA) (Hoffman 1977) through a contract with the king (Lyon 1976:42, 118, 147, 185), a classic example of the concentration of power in the hands of a family through an individual.

12. Menéndez was the epitome of the merchant benefiting from trade, commerce, tribute and Royal bounty, while at the same time enjoying the booty from privateering in the model of the merchant-pirate, taking many French prizes in his forays in the Indies (Lyon 1976:7, 208, 1977, 1984a:7; Manucy 1985:44).

13. Two socioeconomic levels or "classes" characterized Santa Elena: the controlling Menéndez family, along with attorneys, justices of the peace, and other officials on the one hand, with the settlers consisting of slaves, soldiers, artisans, craftsmen, and farmers and their wives and children, on the other (Lyon 1976, 1977, 1984:6; Manucy 1985:45).

14. Often the plight of the soldiers and settlers was so bad that they were close to starving, suffering "extreme need of everything" (Connor 1925:307, 313).

Problem

No model exists in historical archaeology for effectively measuring, through artifacts, the two dramatically contrasting, dominant and subordinate, socioeconomic-status levels documented to have been present in Santa Elena. Such a model is needed to express in energy terms the *labor, tools, technology, scarcity, production, and transportation costs* of artifacts reflecting the two known socioeconomic levels at Santa Elena. If these two status levels cannot be accurately measured from artifacts from Spanish colonial sites, we will have failed to take the first basic step toward a meaningful expression of the archaeological record in energy theory terms.

The Status Artifact Index Model

15. A socioeconomic-status index or scale of measurement can be constructed using a selected group of artifacts known to have higher or lower value *on the basis of the amount of labor and nonhuman energy resources involved in their production.*

Thus, porcelain, requiring far higher temperatures (more heat energy) than lead-glazed earthenware and a special kiln construction, has a higher energy expenditure and economic value than glazed earthenware, which requires a simple kiln and far less fuel consumption.

16. *Porcelain*, being made of special products—kaolin clay and steatite— cannot be made without these specialized ingredients. Earthenware, being made of many types of locally obtainable clays, can be made in many places from a variety of common clays. Thus, porcelain, due to the *scarcity of raw materials* in the productive process, requiring transport of raw materials to the production site, has a greater economic value than glazed earthenware.

17. Porcelain, because it was manufactured only in China during the sixteenth century, had to be transported by ship to the opposite side of the world at Acapulco, Mexico, then across Mexico by expenditure of human and nonhuman energy, loaded again onto ships to be carried to Spanish Florida. This represents a *high expenditure of labor and transportation costs*, which put a value on porcelain at the time of Santa Elena that was equal to its weight in silver (Cervantes 1976, 1977; Kamer 1956; South 1988:58). This is a far *higher expenditure of energy* than that reflected by more readily made *glazed earthenware*.

18. White (1959:335) has pointed out that "the labor that goes into the manufacture of a glazed and painted pottery bowl is more significant, as a rule, than the natural abundance of clay." In turn, the labor that went into the decoration of a piece of Spanish *polychrome majolica* in Seville in the mid-sixteenth century is more significant, as a rule, than that involved in the manufacture of a piece of *Columbia Plain majolica* (Goggin 1968:117), which has no decoration.

19. *Decorative braid* made of fine silver, gold, and copper wire was used to form decorative borders (*bordado*) on upper-socioeconomic-level Spanish clothing in the mid-sixteenth century (South et al. 1988:140–142). This *bordado* could not be afforded by the lower classes and was not worn by them (South et al. 1988:140–142; South 1988:58). Therefore, its presence in a refuse dump of that period is a clear indication of the presence of upper socioeconomic-status individuals.

20. *Personal items* of apparel such as jewelry and other ornaments, coins, keys, book hinges, crucifixes, and the like are reflective of upper socioeconomic status in sixteenth-century Spanish colonial contexts (South et al. 1988:157–171). *The amount of labor and specialized tools and technology* involved in the production of small figas, scallop shells, crosses of jet, to be sewn onto clothing as amulets or charms to help in preventing the effects of the evil eye, places these items far above the purchasing power of those in lower socioeconomic levels.

21. *Glassware* is rare in sixteenth-century Spanish colonial contexts (South et al. 1988:25–29). The glass that is present on such sites is very thin and fragile in the extreme. Paintings of the period reveal the use of such ware in upper socioeconomic-level households. The *transportation* of such fragile items required careful and special packing to allow them to arrive unbroken, and labor and expertise beyond that required by more mundane and easily transported items.

22. *Furniture* hardware is also rare in sixteenth-century Spanish colonial

households (South et al. 1988:69–74). From descriptions of soldiers' possessions, it is clear that they did not own furniture items, as reflected by the tacks, balusters, and latches found at Santa Elena. Furniture such as chests, tables, and other large items took up considerable space on board ship and thus the *transportation costs* were prohibitive for those not in the upper socioeconomic level. Those in the lower socioeconomic level could not afford to own such pieces owing to the labor and tools and technology involved in producing them in Spain and then shipping them to the New World. The houses of those in the lower socioeconomic levels were more likely to have been furnished by *items that took less energy to produce, were locally made, cost less to produce and used less expensive tools and technology, and had low labor costs.*

23. By using the *fragment count* of the above upper and lower socioeconomic level items, we can compare the value of artifacts from contexts representing the two socioeconomic levels and thus identify the status level represented by artifact assemblages and, by association, those structural remains associated with the artifacts.

24. To construct such a Status Artifact Index Model I have divided the low-cost artifacts mentioned above (coarse earthenware and Columbia Plain majolica) by the high-cost artifacts (Ming porcelain, decorated majolica, bordado, personal items, glassware, and furniture hardware). Thus, equal numbers of fragments of low-cost artifacts and high-cost artifacts would produce a Status Artifact Index number of 1. Twice the number of low-status artifact fragments to upper-status artifact fragments would produce an index number of 2, while triple the number of lower socioeconomic-status items in relation to upper-status

Table 22-1. Sixteenth-Century Spanish Colonial Status Artifact Model

Status Artifact Index Model

Low-Cost Item Fragments	100	200	300	400	500	600	700	800	900	1000
Divided by High-Cost Item Fragments	100	100	100	100	100	100	100	100	100	100
Equal Status Index No.	**1**	**2**	**3**	**4**	**5**	**6**	**7**	**8**	**9**	**10**

Application of Data to Model

Hypothesized Menéndez Family Data	1.00				
Actual Town of Santa Elena Data		3.60			
Hypothesized Midstatus Household			5.00		
Actual Fort San Felipe Data				9.80	
Hypothesized Servant or Slave Data					10.00
Actual Hut Dwelling Data					10.70
	Upper-Status Index No. Range			Lower-Status Index No. Range	

artifacts would produce a Status Artifact Index number of 3. Ten times the number of low-status items divided by one of the upper-status artifacts would reveal a Status Artifact Index number of 10, which would reflect a lower socioeconomic-level artifact assemblage. Thus we have a model based on a scale of 1 to 10, expressed as the ratio of lower socioeconomic-level artifact fragments to upper-status items. An assemblage with a Status Artifact Index of 1 to 5 would indicate a high socioeconomic level is represented by the assemblage. A Status Artifact Index of 6 through 10 would reveal a low socioeconomic level is represented (Table 22-1).

25. I predict that applying this model to the Spanish refuse associated with the upper socioeconomic-level Spanish colonial households in Santa Elena will reveal a low Status Artifact Index. I also predict that the refuse from the soldiers living inside Fort San Felipe will have a high Status Artifact Index, reflecting their low socioeconomic-status level. I also predict that the artifacts associated with the small hut dwelling will have a high Status Artifact Index, reflect-

Table 22-2. Deriving Status Index Numbers from Santa Elena Assemblages

	Upper Socioeconomic Status **Town of Santa Elena** Domestic Occupation	Lower Socioeconomic Status **Fort San Felipe** Military Occupation	Lower Socioeconomic Status **Hut Dwelling** Servant or Soldier Hut
High-Cost Fragments			
Ming Porcelain	67	18	1
Decorated Majolica	235	678	11
Bordado (gold braid)	9	3	—
Personal Items	9	56	—
Glassware	34	48	3
Furniture Hardware	9	6	—
Total Costly Items	**363**	**809**	**15**
Low-Cost Fragments			
Coarse Earthenware	412	3857	93
Columbia Plain Maj.	894	4081	68
Total Cheap Items	**1306**	**7938**	**161**
Low-cost/High-cost Equals	1306/363 - 3.6	7938/809 - 9.8	161/15 - 10.7
Low- to High-Cost Ratio	**3.6 to 1**	**9.8 to 1**	**10.7 to 1**
Status Index Number			

Low-Status Ratio - 6–10 Times the Number of Low- to High-Cost Items
High-Status Ratio - 1–5 Times the Number of Low- to High-Cost Items

Provenience Data	*Levels and Features 38Bu162C(South1982: 64–65, 70–71)*	*Levels and Features 38BU162E,G.H (South 1983:65,67; 1984:116,125,146, 156; 1985:107,123, 125, 126)*	*Levels 38Bu162A (South: 1980: 22–23)*

ing their low socioeconomic-status level within the Spanish colonial system.

26. When we tabulate the artifacts from these three assemblages using the Status Artifact Index Model, we find that the Index number for the town of Santa Elena is 3.6, reflecting a fairly *high socioeconomic status level* for the assemblage (see Table 22-2). When we do the same for Fort San Felipe, a Status Artifact Index number of 9.8 is derived, with the hut dwelling having an Index number of 10.7, both revealing a *low socioeconomic status level* for the assemblages. This is in keeping with expectations independent of data related to artifact frequency (architectural and historical documentation).

27. I intend to further test the Status Artifact Index with new data from Santa Elena and to comb the literature of sixteenth-century Spanish colonial sites to derive other assemblages to test this Status Artifact Index Model. I feel this method of classifying and analyzing artifacts in relation to socioeconomic status on the basis of the *energy cost of labor, tools, technology, scarcity, and transportation* will prove to be a valuable analytical tool in historical archaeology for studying socioeconomic status through artifacts from sixteenth-century Spanish colonial sites. The model is of value in demonstrating how energy-related theory can help us understand social processes from historic site artifacts from sixteenth-century Spanish colonial assemblages.

28. A broader application of this energy-based research is expected to be in addressing questions such as the following. In the late sixteenth century and the early seventeenth century, two attempts were made to establish European settlements in southeastern America: Spanish Santa Elena in 1566 and the English settlement at Jamestown in 1607. The James River estuary English attempt was successful, whereas the Port Royal Sound Spanish effort as Santa Elena failed. Why? The answer lies in the difference between the energy input/outflow of the two colonization efforts expressed in terms of social bifurcation, support from Europe, enterprise scale, commodity exports, and so on. A first step toward addressing such questions is the application and testing of the Status Artifact Model presented here as a tool for exploring, through the archaeological record, the cultural process of controlling energy through social bifurcation.

Acknowledgments

Funding for the above projects has been provided by the National Geographic Society, the *National Geographic* Magazine, the National Science Foundation, the National Endowment for the Humanities, the Explorers Club of New York, the University of South Carolina, the United States Marine Corps, and the government of Spain. Total funding thus far is almost a half million dollars, as research continues on this important Spanish colonial city.

References

Adams, Richard N.
  1975 *Energy and Structure: A Theory of Social Power*. University of Texas Press. Austin.

1982   *Paradoxical Harvest: Energy and Explanation in British History, 1870–1914.* Cambridge University Press. Cambridge.

1988   *The Eighth Day: Social Evolution as the Self-organization of Energy.* University of Texas Press. Austin.

Bennett, Charles E. (editor)

1975   *Three Voyages, Rene Laudonnière.* University Presses of Florida, Gainesville.

Cervantes, Gonzalo Lopez

1976   *Cerramic Colonial en La Ciudad de Mexico.* Instituto Nacional de Anthropologia Arqueologia No. 38. Mexico.

1977   *Porcelana Oriental en la Nueva España. Anales de Antropología e Historia.* Epoca 8a. Tomo I, INAH, Mexico.

Connor, Jeannette T. (editor)

1925   *Colonial Records of Spanish Florida: Letters and Reports of Governors and Secular Persons.* Translated and edited by J.T.C. Vol. 1. Florida State Historical Society Publication No. 5. Deland.

1927   *Jean Ribault, The Whole and True Discovery of Terra Florida.* Florida State Historical Society. Deland.

1930   *Colonial Records of Spanish Florida: Letters and Reports of Governors and Secular Persons.* Translated and edited by J.T.C. Vol. 2. Florida State Historical Society Publication No. 5. Deland.

De Bry, Theodore

1591   *America.* ii. Frankfurt.

Finley, M. I.

1954   *The World of Odysseus.* Viking Press, New York.

Goggin, John M.

1968   *Spanish Majolica in the New World.* Yale University Publications in Anthropology No. 72. New Haven.

Green, Halcott P.

1986a *Power and Evolution: The Disequilibrium Hypothesis.* (Occasional Papers No. 1. Institute of International Studies, University of South Carolina. Columbia.

1986b Original Sin and the Social Order: The Social Prediction of the Disequilibrium Hypothesis. Ms. on file, Institute of International Studies, University of South Carolina. Columbia.

Harris, Marvin

1980   *Cultural Materialism: The Struggle for a Science of Culture.* Vintage Books, New York.

Hawking, Stephen W.

1988   *A Brief History of Time from the Big Bang to Black Holes.* Bantam Books, New York.

Hoffman, Paul E.

1977   Sixteenth Century Fortifications on Parris Island, South Carolina. Manuscript on file, National Geographic Society. Washington, D.C.

Jackson, Jack Marvin

1988   The Self-organization of the American Frontier: A Theory of Social Evolution for Historical Archaeology. Ph.D. dissertation on file at the University of Texas. Austin.

Judge, Joseph

1988   Between Columbus and Jamestown: Exploring our Forgotten Century. *National Geographic* 173 (3):330–363.

Kamer, Aga Oglu

1956   Late Ming and Early Ching Porcelain Fragments from Archaeological Sites in Florida. *Florida Anthropologist* 8(4):1-51.

Lewis, Kenneth E.

1984   *The American Frontier: An Archaeological Study of Settlement Pattern and Process.* Academic Press, New York.

Lorant, Stephan

1946   *The New World.* Duell, Sloan, and Pearce, New York.

Lyon, Eugene
1976　*The Enterprise of Florida*. University Presses of Florida, Gainesville.
1977　St. Augustine 1580: The Living Community. *El Escribano*.
1984　*Santa Elena: A Brief History of the Colony, 1566–1587*. Research Manuscript Series 193. University of South Carolina, Institute of Archaeology and Anthropology, Columbia.
Manucy, Albert
1985　The Physical Setting of Sixteenth Century St. Augustine. *Florida Anthropologist* 38(1–2), Part 1:34–53.
Marx, Karl
1906　*Capital*. Modern Library, New York.
Nash, June
1981　*Ethnographic Aspects of the World Capitalist System*. Annual Review of Anthropology.
Odum, Howard T., and Elizabeth C. Odum
1981　*Energy Basis for Man and Nature*. McGraw-Hill, New York.
Ross, Mary
1925　The Spanish Settlement of Santa Elena (Port Royal) in 1578. *Georgia Historical Quarterly* 9:352–379. (Essentially a translation of the inspection of Fort San Marcos by Alvaro Flores de Valdes.)
Salley, Alexander S., Jr.
1925　The Spanish Settlement at Port Royal, 1565–1586. *South Carolina History Magazine* 26:31–40.
South, Stanley A.
1979　*The Search for Santa Elena on Parris Island, South Carolina*. Research Manuscript Series 150. University of South Carolina, Institute of Archaeology and Anthropology, Columbia.
1980　*The Discovery of Santa Elena*. Research Manuscript Series 165. University of South Carolina, Institute of Archaeology and Anthropology, Columbia.
1982　*Exploring Santa Elena*. Research Manuscript Series 184. University of South Carolina, Institute of Archaeology and Anthropology, Columbia.
1983　*Revealing Santa Elena 1982*. Research Manuscript Series 188. University of South Carolina, Institute of Archaeology and Anthropology, Columbia.
1984　*Testing Archaeological Sampling Methods at Fort San Felipe 1983*. Research Manuscript Series 190. University of South Carolina, Institute of Archaeology and Anthropology, Columbia.
1985　*Excavation of the Casa Fuerte and Wells at Ft. San Felipe 1984*. Research Manuscript Series 196. University of South Carolina, Institute of Archaeology and Anthropology, Columbia.
1988　Santa Elena: Threshold of Conquest. In *The Recovery of Meaning*, edited by Mark Leone and Parker B. Potter, Jr. Anthropological Society of Washington. Smithsonian Institution Press, Washington, D.C.
South, Stanley, and William B. Hunt
1986　*Discovering Santa Elena West of Fort San Felipe*. Research Manuscript Series 200. University of South Carolina, Institute of Archaeology and Anthropology, Columbia.
South, Stanley, Russell K. Skowronek, and Richard E. Johnson
1988　*Spanish Artifacts from Santa Elena*. Anthropological Studies No. 7. University of South Carolina, Institute of Archaeology and Anthropology, Columbia.
Wallerstein, Immanuel
1974　*The Modern World-system*. Academic Press, New York.
1980　*The Modern World-System II: Mercantilism and the Consolidation of the European World-Economy, 1600–1750*. Academic Press, New York.
White, Leslie
1949　*The Science of Culture*. Grove Press, New York.

1959   *The Evolution of Culture: The Development of Civilization to the Fall of Rome*. McGraw-Hill, New York.

1975   *The Concept of Cultural Systems: A Key to Understanding Tribes and Nations*. Columbia University Press, New York.

Wolf, Eric R.

1982   *Europe and the People without History*. University of California Press, Los Angeles.

Chapter 23 ■

C. Margaret Scarry and Elizabeth J. Reitz

Herbs, Fish, Scum, and Vermin: Subsistence Strategies in Sixteenth-Century Spanish Florida

Over the past ten years, we have collaborated on research designed to increase our understanding of the impact of colonization on Spanish and Native American foodways. To this end, we have combined documentary evidence with analyses of plant and animal remains to examine subsistence strategies in sixteenth-century Spanish Florida. Our investigations have provided information about the modifications the Spaniards made to their diet in order to survive (Reitz and Scarry 1985). Unfortunately, our attempts to balance the picture and examine the effects of contact on native diets have been hampered by limited data. Thus the material presented here emphasizes the effects of colonization on Spanish foodways.

Historical Background

Spanish colonies were organized ventures subject to contracts and ordinances designed to establish Iberian social, political, religious, and economic structures in the New World (Lyon 1976:115–116, 1981:280). The goal of recreating Iberian order in novel settings was an impossible dream that was nowhere fully realized. In frontier colonies with few immediately exploitable resources, replicating Old World structures was akin to tilting at windmills.

From the Spanish perspective, La Florida was a backwater region with few attractions. Thus, concerted efforts at colonization were not begun until the activities of French settlers on the Atlantic coast threatened Spanish domain. In response to these activities, Pedro Menéndez de Avilés, accompanied by 600 to 800 soldiers and settlers, arrived in Florida in September of 1565. The Spaniards set up their first camp in the village of the Timucuan chief Seloy. Early in 1566, Menéndez established a second colony at Santa Elena. In the summer of that year, tensions between the Spaniards and the Timucuans led Menéndez to relocate his initial camp (Paul Hoffman, personal communication 1982). The Spaniards moved a short distance south of Seloy's village and founded St. Augustine (see Figure 20-2).

Although established as garrisons, the settlements were expected to be economically self-sufficient (Lyon 1977:23). The colonists who accompanied Menéndez were lured to Florida by dreams of earning fame and fortune by creating Iberian-style estates (Lyon 1981:277–278). These were not idle fantasies. Menéndez's contract with the Crown stipulated that he should allot land for each settler and provide the basic supplies required to make the dreams come true. Thus, the expedition set out for Florida supplied with seedstock for planting wheat and other cereal grains and cuttings for starting vineyards. Also on board were 200 calves, 400 pigs, 400 sheep, and unspecified numbers of goats and chickens intended to serve as breeding stock for the venture (Solís de Merás 1923:262).

Unfortunately for the colonists' aspirations, the locations of the settlements were chosen for reasons of political and military strategy. The towns, built on low rises near good harbors, were surrounded by salt marshes and tidal creeks. The climate was permanently humid with warm winters and hot wet summers (Mehta and Jones 1977:10; Schwartz 1977:52, 199). Moreover, the poorly drained, sandy soils were infertile and had limited agricultural potential. These conditions were unsuitable for replicating the traditional Iberian subsistence economy. Cereal grains rotted or withered on the stalk and wine grapes and olives would not grow (Connor 1925:146–149). Pigs, chickens, and to a lesser extent cattle adjusted to the climate (Connor 1925:88–89), but sheep—the preferred meat source—did not thrive (Defourneaux 1966:64; Williamson and Payne 1978:19).

Unable to pursue traditional economic strategies, the settlers had to forgo their dreams of wheat fields and sheep flocks and modify their subsistence practices. Documentary evidence concerning the colonists' efforts to adapt to the new environment is skimpy. There are reports that list some of the crops and livestock the settlers attempted to raise (Arnade 1959:9, 37; Connor 1930:227; Cumbaa 1975:115). Unfortunately, such records lack detail and disagree on the success of these efforts. Accounts range from rave reviews to cries of privation (Arnade 1959:33; Connor 1925:99, 147–149, 1930:227). At a hearing held in 1573 to decide the fate of the colony, one soldier testified that rations were often short and that "when there was nothing they ate herbs, fish and other scum and vermin" (Connor 1925:98–99). Only six years later, however, Pedro Menéndez Marqués, then governor of the colony, wrote in glowing terms about the abundance and variety of fruit and vegetables the colonists were producing in their gardens (Connor 1930:226–227).

Whatever the accuracy of these reports, we do know that the goal of economic self-sufficiency was never fully achieved. The colonists depended on supply ships and trade with the Native Americans for some provisions. In 1570, the situado, an annual subsidy and payroll provided by the Spanish Crown, was instituted. The arrival of a situado ship undoubtedly brought a temporary abundance of desired foodstuffs, but the ships did not come at regular intervals (Lyon 1977:22). The unpredictable timing of the subsidy prevented the settlers from depending on situado supplies for their daily bread. Instead, the Spaniards relied more on food acquired from the Native Americans to make up for shortfalls in their own production efforts (Bushnell 1981:11–12).

Archaeological Background

Documentary evidence about foodways in sixteenth-century Florida is fragmentary and contradictory. Fortunately, analyses of archaeologically recovered animal bones and plant remains provide data that help fill the gaps and resolve the discrepancies in the contemporary accounts. By combining information gleaned from the historical and archaeological records we can gain new insights about the development of Spanish colonial subsistence strategies.

To round out the picture drawn from historical accounts, we use biological data recovered from three sixteenth-century settlements. The earliest settlement was at the Fountain of Youth Park site (8SJ31). Despite its name, this site was not the location of Ponce de León's fabled fountain. It was, however, the location of a precontact and contact period Timucuan village, a pre-1571 Spanish occupation that was probably Menéndez's first camp, and a later sixteenth-century mission that was probably Nombre de Dios (Chaney 1987; Merritt 1983). In 1985 and 1987, the site was excavated by University of Florida field school students directed by Kathleen Deagan and supervised by Edward Chaney (Chaney 1987). The field school excavations produced abundant faunal remains but very limited plant remains from precontact Timucuan deposits at the Fountain of Youth site. Large quantities of both plant and animal remains were recovered from Spanish features, including a well, associated with Menéndez's camp (Chaney 1987). Like the precontact deposits, the mission deposits at Fountain of Youth produced faunal remains but few plant remains. Only the precontact and pre-1571 data are described below (see Reitz, this volume, for a discussion of the Mission period fauna).

Besides the precontact and early contact data from the Fountain of Youth site, we have data from later sixteenth-century contexts at both Santa Elena and St. Augustine. Santa Elena served as the capital of La Florida from its founding in 1566 to 1587, when it was abandoned owing to hostilities between the Spaniards and the local Guale populations. Our data from Santa Elena come from Stanley South's excavations in the town and in San Felipe, one of a series of three forts built to protect the settlement (South 1980, 1982, 1983, 1984, 1985). Thus, we have data from civilian and military contexts for Santa Elena.

St. Augustine was founded in 1566 when Menéndez moved his followers out of Seloy's village. Beginning in 1976, Kathleen Deagan directed excavations focused on the sixteenth-century community at St. Augustine (Deagan 1978a, 1978c, 1980, 1981, 1985; Deagan et al. 1976). This work resulted in the recovery of faunal remains from seven households and plant remains from five households. Artifact inventories indicate that these households form a socioeconomic cross section of the sixteenth-century community.

Biological Data

Bone preservation at the three sixteenth-century settlements was generally excellent. As a result, we have faunal data from a range of contexts including sheet midden, trash pits, and wells. The Fountain of Youth faunal remains were recovered from 6.2-mm (1/4″) and 1.7-mm (1/16″) screens, those from Santa Elena from 3.1-mm (1/8″) screens and flotation samples, and those from St. Augustine from 6.2-mm (1/4″) screens and flotation samples (for detailed descriptions of sampling and analytical procedures see Reitz 1988b; Reitz and Scarry 1985). Elizabeth Reitz analyzed the faunal remains. She used minimum number of individuals (MNI) to quantify the data for this paper. The MNI were estimated by considering the evidence for symmetry, age, and sex for each species and calculating the number of individuals necessary to account for the identified elements. Comparisons between assemblages are made using percentages of MNI for selected groups of animals. Invertebrates are not included in our discussions. Undoubtedly they were important sources of food at these coastal settlements, but the Spaniards used tabby made from crushed shell as a building material, and this makes it difficult to measure the dietary contribution of shellfish. Because we were interested in examining the use of animals for food, commensal animals such as frogs, toads, mice, and rats were excluded when percentages of MNI were calculated.

The preservation of plant food remains ranged from poor to extraordinary. In contexts where plants would have to be carbonized to be preserved, plant remains were sparse. Thus we have limited plant data from precontact features at the Fountain of Youth and from sheet middens and trash pits at Santa Elena and St. Augustine. Fortunately, wells have been excavated from Menéndez's camp at the Fountain of Youth, from the town and fort at Santa Elena, and from the sixteenth-century households at St. Augustine. Abandoned wells were often used for refuse disposal. Fine-screen and flotation samples taken from the waterlogged fill of the wells have yielded abundant plant remains (for detailed descriptions of sampling and analytical procedures see Reitz and Scarry 1985; Scarry 1989). The data from the wells form the basis for our discussions of plant food use. Margaret Scarry analyzed most plant material included in our discussions; however, the remains from one well at Santa Elena were analyzed by Paul Gardner (1982). Plant foods are quantified by count with each seed and nutshell fragment counted as one. Comparisons between the plant assemblages are based on percentages calculated from the seed counts. As with the faunal data, commensals such as grasses, weeds, and other plants with no known economic value are omitted from the analyses presented below.

Subsistence Strategies

Because the colonists were unable to depend on Old World crops and animals for food they had to modify their traditional diet. They did not do so in a vacuum, however. By the time Santa Elena and St. Augustine were founded, Europeans had been exploring and colonizing parts of the New World for over 70 years. Thus, the Spaniards arrived in La Florida armed with information acquired from the experiences of settlers in other New World colonies. More important, Menéndez and his followers initially lived in a Timucuan village and once the towns were established the Spaniards and Native Americans continued to interact. Throughout the early years, the Spaniards not only obtained foodstuffs from the Native Americans, but many of the settlers formed liaisons, legal and otherwise, with local women (Deagan 1973).

Undoubtedly, the Native Americans through example and exchange influenced the development of Spanish colonial foodways. Thus, it is logical to begin our investigation of the colonists' subsistence strategies by examining the strategies of their Native American neighbors. By comparing the Native American patterns of food use with those of the Spaniards at Menéndez's camp and with those of Spaniards in Santa Elena and St. Augustine, we can begin to trace and understand the development of Spanish Colonial foodways.

Native American Subsistence

Native American populations living on the South Atlantic coast pursued subsistence strategies that combined reliance on estuarine resources with farming and foraging. Studies of faunal collections from several coastal sites indicate intense use of fish and shellfish (Reitz 1988a, 1988b; Smith et al. 1981). For example, in the assemblage from the precontact Timucuan component at the Fountain of Youth site, sharks, rays, and bony fishes constitute 96 percent of the MNI (Table 23-1). The most common remains are from small to medium-sized sea catfishes and drums. The size range and species composition of the assemblage suggest capture in near-shore waters of fishes that were available year round. Other animals such as deer, small mammals, birds, and turtles were occasionally eaten. Their contribution to the diet, however, was small compared with the estuarine resources.

There are no systematic studies of plant assemblages from precontact coastal sites. Fortunately, ethnohistoric accounts and incidental reports of plant remains give some indications of plant use (Deagan 1978b; Larson 1978; Laudonnière 1975; Swanton 1946). The Timucuans and other coastal groups raised maize, beans, squash, and sunflowers. They were, however, apparently less dependent on agriculture than their contemporaries in the more fertile interior regions of the Southeast. The coastal groups reportedly did not produce sufficient crops

Table 23-1. Summary of Selected Faunal Categories from Sixteenth-Century Contexts in La Florida

Category	Fountain of Youth Precontact (MNI)		Fountain of Youth Spanish Contact (MNI)		Santa Elena and St. Augustine Sixteenth Century (MNI)	
	No.	Percent	No.	Percent	No.	Percent
Domestic mammals					86	5.3
Domestic birds					86	5.3
Wild terrestrial mammals	4	1.9	6	4.3	110	6.7
Wild birds	1	0.5	2	1.4	110	6.7
Turtles/alligators	2	0.9	11	7.8	96	5.9
Sharks/rays/fishes	204	96.7	122	86.5	1,142	70.1
Total	211		141		1,630	

Source: Data taken from Reitz and Scarry (1985) and Reitz (1988b).

to last from one harvest to the next. To supplement their harvests, the Native Americans gathered a varied assortment of nuts and wild fruits. The precontact deposits at the Fountain of Youth yielded too few plant remains to quantify, but the samples do indicate the use of maize, hickory nuts, acorns, persimmons, grapes, and cabbage palm berries.

Contact Period Spanish Subsistence

The biological data from Menéndez's camp at the Fountain of Youth site provide information about food use during the initial period of contact between the Spaniards and the Timucuans. The features from which these data were recovered were clearly the result of Spanish activities (Chaney 1987). The majority of the data are from a well and its construction pit. According to artifact inventories, these features date to Menéndez's occupation, not to the later sixteenth-century mission at the site.

The origin of the food debris in the well is less certain, however. It is clearly not precontact. The samples contain some remains from Old World plants and animals. The well samples also contain fragile, uncarbonized seeds. Unless these seeds were deposited in the well soon after they were discarded, they would have decayed or been eaten by scavengers such as gulls or rodents. It seems most likely that the debris in the well is Spanish, either deposited by the Spaniards themselves, or thrown in by the Timucuans when they cleared the site after the Spaniards relocated their camp. It is possible, however, the refuse is from contact period Timucuan activities.

The faunal assemblage from the Fountain of Youth contact period deposits is similar to that from precontact Timucuan deposits (Table 23-1). There are no bones from domestic animals, although the mandible of a European house mouse attests to the early introduction of this pest. Sharks, rays, and bony fishes account for 86 percent of the MNI. Exploitation of inshore waters is indicated by the abundance of small to medium sea catfishes and drums. While fish clearly dominate the assemblage, the proportions of deer, wild birds, and turtles are slightly higher than in the precontact deposits.

Like the faunal assemblage, the plant assemblage from the Fountain of Youth contact period deposits, with a couple of notable exceptions, is similar to what one would expect to find at a precontact Timucuan site (Table 23-2). Maize remains are abundant and squash, beans, and sunflower are also present. Together these indigenous crops account for 21 percent of the food assemblage. Nutshells from acorns and hickory nuts constitute 51 percent. Acorn shell is considerably more abundant than hickory shell. Wild fruits are also well represented. There are almost 500 seeds from nine different wild fruits, including persimmon, maypop, prickly pear, and creeping cucumber.

Besides the locally available crops and wild plants, remains from three nonlocal crops were recovered from the Fountain of Youth well. Old World crops are represented by a single wheat grain and 54 melon seeds. There are also 167 seeds from *Cucurbita moschata*. Prehistorically this squash species was grown on the Caribbean islands and in Mesoamerica, but not in southeastern North America. The wheat, melons, and moschata squashes must have been introduced to La Florida by the Spanish colonists. It is worth noting, however, that both melons and moschata squashes could have been grown locally from imported seedstock.

The biological data from the contact period Fountain of Youth deposits can be interpreted in two ways. If the refuse was discarded by the Spaniards, then the assemblage suggests that in the initial settlement period the colonists' diet was very similar to that of their Timucuan hosts. This is quite plausible. When the Spaniards arrived in Florida, Menéndez dispatched his largest ship before many of the supplies on board were unloaded (Lyon 1976:120). As a result, after defeating the French, Menéndez spent much of the first year attempting to arrange for supplies to be shipped from the Caribbean to his fledgling settlements. Shipments were erratic at best. To survive, the colonists must have relied heavily on foodstuffs acquired locally. Some they may have procured or produced on

Table 23-2. Summary of Selected Plant Categories from Sixteenth-Century Contexts in La Florida

Category	Fountain of Youth Spanish Contact		Santa Elena and St. Augustine Sixteenth Century	
	No.	Percent	No.	Percent
Old World crops	55	1.90	226	13.66
Indigenous crops	597	20.60	849	51.30
Exotic New World crops	167	5.76	55	3.32
Wild nuts	1,481	51.10	447	27.01
Wild fruits	487	16.80	78	4.71
Wild tubers	111	3.83		
Total	2,898		1,655	

Source: Data taken from Gardner (1982), Reitz and Scarry (1985), and Scarry (1989).

their own. The presence of melon seeds suggests they may have planted gardens; melons spoil rapidly and would be unlikely to survive the rigors and delays of shipping. Much of the food consumed by the settlers, however, was probably supplied willingly or unwillingly by the Timucuans.

On the other hand, if the refuse in the Fountain of Youth contact period deposits was discarded by Timucuans, then the data suggest that the Spanish presence initially had limited impact on the Native Americans' subsistence practices. A few new crops were raised, but overall the economic strategy remained largely the same. Such a conclusion is in line with Elizabeth Reitz's (this volume) findings for later sixteenth-century mission contexts at the Fountain of Youth site.

Late Sixteenth-Century Spanish Colonial Subsistence

The biological assemblages from sixteenth-century Santa Elena and St. Augustine indicate that as the colonists settled in, they developed subsistence strategies that were not strictly Iberian or Timucuan. The faunal assemblage from the two towns is more diverse than those from the precontact and contact period deposits at the Fountain of Youth site (Table 23-1). Estuarine resources remained very important; sharks, rays, and bony fishes constitute 70 percent of the MNI. The fish assemblage, however, contains larger individuals and more mullets than the collections from the precontact and contact collections at the Fountain of Youth. This suggests the townsfolk were fishing in deeper water and using capture techniques, such as cast nets, that were different from those used by the Timucuans. The populations in Santa Elena and St. Augustine also consumed more deer, wild birds, and turtles than did the various occupants of the Fountain of Youth. This may reflect a Spanish preference for game rather than fish. The increase in wild birds is probably due to the Spanish use of fowling pieces. Pork, chicken, and beef were consumed by the townspeople but may not have been widely or regularly available. Domesticated animals account for only 10 percent of the MNI.

The plant assemblage from Santa Elena and St. Augustine indicates an emphasis on cultivated plants (Table 23-2). Indigenous crops, especially maize, served as staple foods. A variety of Old World crops were also consumed. The most abundant Old World plants were peaches, melons, and watermelons. These fruits were probably raised in the colonies from introduced seedstock. Remains from wheat, olives, and other traditional Iberian staples that could not be raised locally are extremely rare. Moschata squashes, chili peppers, and lima beans also have been recovered from the two towns. These exotic New World crops could have been part of food shipments sent from other colonies or they could have been grown locally from imported seedstock. Wild resources appear to be considerably less important than in the contact period deposits. Nutshell drops from 51 to 27 percent of the food remains and the relative importance of acorns and hickory nuts is reversed. The townspeople used hickory nuts, which are primarily sources of oils and fats, more than they used acorns, which are sources of carbohydrates. Besides the change in nut use, there is also a sharp decrease in the use of wild fruits. Not only are seeds from wild fruits proportionately less abundant but fewer types of wild fruit were used. It seems that the colonists' success in producing traditional Iberian fruits, such as peaches and melons, led to a decreased use of the smaller wild fruits.

Spanish Colonial Foodways: Deprivation or Dissatisfaction?

The historical and archaeological evidence suggests that the Spanish colonists incorporated food resources from both hemispheres into a viable subsistence strategy. Initially, the settlers' diet was much like that of the Timucuans with whom they were bivouacked. Within a short time, however, the colonists developed new foodways that wove together the various elements available to them.

To adjust their subsistence strategy to their new situation the colonists took the following steps. They curtailed production of traditional Iberian resources such as sheep, wheat, wine grapes, and olives that were unsuited to the coastal environment. In place of familiar Old World crops, the colonists focused their agricultural efforts on indigenous crops—maize, beans, and squash—that could be grown locally. To supplement these staple foods, the settlers grew a few Old World cultigens, primarily fruits, which could tolerate the local conditions. They also introduced and raised some exotic New World cultigens. For meat, the Spaniards husbanded those Old World domesticated animals that could survive with limited attention in humid, forested conditions. Most of their protein, however, they obtained from fish and shellfish harvested in nearby estuaries and game hunted in the fields and forests around their settlements. Finally, the colonists used imported foodstuffs when they could get them. Unreliable shipments, however, prohibited the settlers from depending on such supplies for their daily sustenance.

The local production of some Old World livestock, fruits, and vegetables gave the colonists' foodways a superficially Iberian character. Like the Native American coastal strategy, however, the Spaniards' strategy emphasized reliance on estuarine resources and indigenous crops. Indeed, the Native Americans should be considered part of the Spaniards' strategy, since the colonists obtained significant quantities of food through trade and tribute. Although never fully self-sufficient nor satisfied, the settlers adopted a system that allowed St. Augustine, at least, to survive.

The results of our investigations provide a perspective from which to judge the "feast or famine" portrayals in the contemporary documents. Clearly, the more glowing reports of the colonies' promoters were exaggerated, but so were the cries of chronic starvation. Undoubtedly there were periods of extreme hardship, but the abundant estuarine resources, the "herbs, fish, scum, and vermin" literally at the colonists' doorsteps would have made starvation unlikely.

What then do we make of the reports of extreme privation? First we should recognize that most of these reports are contained in official correspondence or in testimony about conditions in the colonies. The situation may have been intentionally misrepresented in an effort to elicit increased support for the backwater towns (Bushnell 1981:11–12).

Privation is also partly a state of mind. Spaniards felt deprived if they did not have wheat bread, olive oil, and wine (Bushnell 1981:12; Crosby 1972:65). Because these commodities could not be produced locally and supply ships arrived irregularly, there were chronic shortages of familiar Iberian foodstuffs. The colonists often found themselves eating corn bread and fish rather than wheat bread and mutton.

There may have been another factor that contributed to the Spaniards' dissatisfaction with the available foods. In Spain, as elsewhere in sixteenth-century Europe, only the wealthy could afford to eat meat regularly (Defourneaux 1966:152; Goody 1982:135–140). Peasants and the urban poor ate bread, dairy products, and fish (Defourneaux 1966:64–65, 103). In other words, the Spanish colonists' diet was closer to that of a peasant than an hidalgo. For those who came to the New World with dreams of improving their social standing, this must have been a grave disappointment.

Acknowledgments

We would like to thank Kathleen A. Deagan and Stanley A. South for making us part of their sixteenth-century research teams, and thereby giving us the opportunity to work on the biological remains from the Fountain of Youth, St. Augustine, and Santa Elena. Over the years, historians Amy Bushnell, Paul Hoffman, and Eugene Lyon have read our reports and discussed our ideas with us. Although we have not always taken their advice, our work has benefited from their criticism. A number of students and lab assistants have helped with the analyses of the biological materials. We would like to thank H. Catherine Brown, Marc Franc, Jim Greenway, Tom Gresham, Yvonne Narganes, Lisa O'Steen, Kay Wood, Timothy Young, Carter Vest, and University of Georgia Instructor Barbara Ruff for their work on the faunal remains. Likewise we want to thank Bridget Beers, Frank Keel, Marilyn Masson, Scott Perry, and Dana Stetson for their work on the plant remains. Funds for the various St. Augustine projects were provided by grants from the Florida Board of Regents Star Grant No. 77–081, the National Endowment for the Humanities Grants RO-32537-78-1425 and RS-20293-82, the St. Augustine Foundation, Inc., the Florida Chapter of the Colonial Dames of America, the Dupont Foundation, the University of Florida Division of Sponsored Research, the Florida State Museum, the Wentworth Foundation, and the Florida Bureau of Historic Preservation Historic Grant-in-Aid Program. Funds for the Santa Elena analyses were provided by the National Geographic Society, the National Endowment for the Humanities, the National Science Foundation, and the Explorers Club of New York.

References

Arnade, Charles W.
  1959 *Florida on Trial: 1593–1602*. University of Miami Hispanic American Studies No. 16. University of Miami Press, Coral Gables.

Bushnell, Amy Turner
 1981   *The King's Coffer: Proprietors of the Spanish Florida Treasury, 1565–1702.* University Presses of Florida, Gainesville.
Chaney, Edward E.
 1987   Report on the 1985 Excavations at the Fountain of Youth Park Site (8–SJ–31), St. Augustine, Florida. Ms. on file, Department of Anthropology, Florida Museum of Natural History, Gainesville.
Connor, Jeannette Thurber
 1925   *Colonial Records of Spanish Florida 1.* Florida State Historical Society, Deland.
 1930   *Colonial Records of Spanish Florida 2.* Florida State Historical Society, Deland.
Crosby, Alfred W., Jr.
 1972   *The Columbian Exchange: Biological and Cultural Consequences of 1492.* Greenwood Press, Westport, Connecticut.
Cumbaa, Stephen L.
 1975   *Patterns of Resource Use and Cross-Cultural Dietary Change in the Spanish Colonial Period.* Unpublished Ph.D. dissertation, University of Florida. University Microfilms, Ann Arbor.
Deagan, Kathleen A.
 1973   Mestizaje in Colonial St. Augustine. *Ethnohistory* 20:5565.
 1978a The Archaeology of First Spanish Period St. Augustine, 1972–1978. *El Escribano* 15:1–22.
 1978b Cultures in Transition: Fusion and Assimilation among the Eastern Timucua. In *Tacachale,* edited by J. Milanich and S. Proctor, pp. 89–119. Ripley P. Bullen Monographs No. 1. University Presses of Florida, Gainesville.
 1978c The Material Assemblage of 16th Century Spanish Florida. *Historical Archaeology* 12:25–50.
 1980   Spanish St. Augustine: America's First "Melting Pot." *Archaeology* 33(5):22–30.
 1981   Downtown Survey: The Discovery of Sixteenth-Century St. Augustine in an Urban Area. *American Antiquity* 46:626–634.
 1985   The Archaeology of Sixteenth Century St. Augustine. *Florida Anthropologist* 38:6–33.
Deagan, Kathleen A., John Bostwick, and Dale Benton
 1976   A Sub-surface Survey of the St. Augustine City Environs. Ms. on file, St. Augustine Restoration Foundation, St. Augustine.
Defourneaux, Marcelin
 1966   *Daily Life in Spain in the Golden Age.* Translated by Newton Branch. Praeger, New York.
Gardner, Paul S.
 1982   Appendix IV: Plant Remains from Features 117 and 141, Santa Elena, South Carolina. In *Exploring Santa Elena, 1981,* by S. South, pp. 165–170. Institute of Archaeology and Anthropology, Research Manuscript Series 184. University of South Carolina, Columbia.
Goody, Jack
 1982   *Cooking, Cuisine and Class: A Study in Comparative Sociology.* Cambridge University Press, Cambridge.
Larson, Lewis H.
 1978   Historic Guale Indians of the Georgia Coast and the Impact of the Spanish Mission Efforts. In *Tacachale,* edited by J. Milanich and S. Proctor, pp. 120–140. Ripley P. Bullen Monographs No. 1. University Presses of Florida, Gainesville.
Laudonnière, René
 1975   *Three Voyages.* Translated by Charles E. Bennett. University Presses of Florida, Gainesville.

Lyon, Eugene
  1976 *The Enterprise of Florida: Pedro Menéndez de Avilés and the Spanish Conquest of 1565–1568.* University Presses of Florida, Gainesville.
  1977 St. Augustine 1580: The Living Community. *El Escribano* 14:20–34.
  1981 Spain's Sixteenth-century North American Settlement Attempts: A Neglected Aspect. *Florida Historical Quarterly* 59:275–291.
Mehta, A. J., and C. P. Jones
  1977 *Matanzas Inlet, Glossary of Inlets.* Report No. 5. Florida Sea Grant Program, Report 21. Gainesville.
Merritt, James D.
  1983 Beyond the Town Walls: The Indian Element in Colonial St. Augustine. In *Spanish St. Augustine: The Archaeology of a Colonial Creole Community*, edited by K. Deagan, pp. 125–147. Academic Press, New York.
Reitz, Elizabeth J.
  1988a Evidence for Coastal Adaptations in Georgia and South Carolina. *Archaeology of Eastern North America* 16:137–159.
  1988b Faunal Remains from the Fountain of Youth Park Site (8-SJ-31). Ms. on file, Department of Anthropology, Florida Museum of Natural History, Gainesville.
Reitz, Elizabeth J., and C. Margaret Scarry
  1985 *Reconstructing Historic Subsistence with an Example from Sixteenth-century Spanish Florida.* Society for Historical Archaeology Special Publication Series No. 3.
Scarry, C. Margaret
  1989 Plant Remains from the Fountain of Youth Park Site (8SJ31). Ms. on file, Department of Anthropology, Florida Museum of Natural History, Gainesville.
Schwartz, Gilbert
  1977 *The Climate Advisor.* Climatic Guide, Flushing, New York.
Smith, Robin L., C. O. Braley, N. T. Borremans, and E. J. Reitz
  1981 *Coastal Adaptations in Southeastern Georgia: Ten Archaeological Sites at Kings Bay.* University of Florida Final Report on Secondary Testing at Kings Bay, Camden County, Georgia. Ms. on file, U.S. Department of Defense, Washington, D.C.
Solís de Merás, Gonzalo
  1923 *Pedro Menéndez de Avilés.* Translated by Jeannette T. Connor. Florida State Historical Society, Deland.
South, Stanley A.
  1980 *The Discovery of Santa Elena.* Research Manuscript Series No. 165. University of South Carolina Institute of Archaeology and Anthropology, Columbia.
  1982 *Exploring Santa Elena 1981.* Research Manuscript Series No. 184. University of South Carolina Institute of Archaeology and Anthropology, Columbia.
  1983 *Revealing Santa Elena 1982.* Research Manuscript Series No. 188. University of South Carolina Institute of Archaeology and Anthropology, Columbia.
  1984 *Testing Archaeological Sampling Methods at Fort San Felipe 1983.* Research Manuscript Series No. 190. University of South Carolina Institute of Archaeology and Anthropology, Columbia.
  1985 *Excavation of the Casa Fuerte and Wells at Ft. San Felipe 1984.* Research Manuscript Series No. 196. University of South Carolina Institute of Archaeology and Anthropology, Columbia.
Swanton, John R.
  1946 *The Indians of the Southeastern United States.* Bureau of American Ethnology Bulletin No. 137. Government Printing Office, Washington, D.C.
Williamson, G., and W. F. A. Payne
  1978 *An Introduction to Animal Husbandry in the Tropics.* Longman, London.

Part 3 ■

The Missions of La Florida

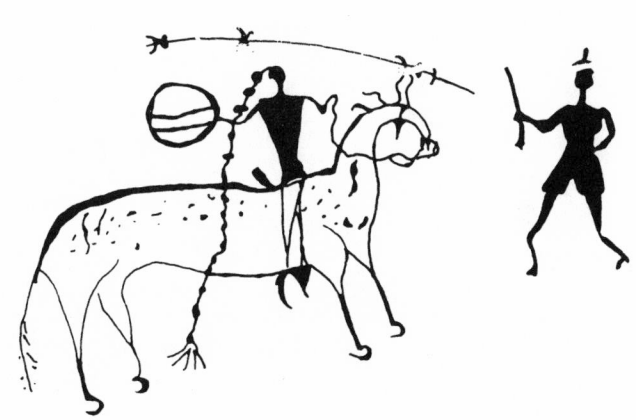

Chapter 24 ■

David Hurst Thomas

The Spanish Missions of La Florida: An Overview

This overview recapitulates what is currently known about the once-extensive mission system of La Florida. My own effort is significantly enhanced by John Griffin's firsthand narrative (this volume) describing the changing fashions in scholarly thinking about this mission system (see also Marrinan 1985), and also the chapters by Elizabeth Reitz, Donna Ruhl, and Rebecca Saunders summarizing the present status of archaeological investigations at these missions.

The Native American Context

The Spanish Crown initially employed the term *La Florida* to denote an extensive, if ill-defined territory covering practically all of the eastern half of the present United States. But by the Mission period, La Florida had contracted to about 70,000 square miles—roughly the size of New England—embracing the state of Florida, the Georgia coast, and the southeastern coast of South Carolina (up to Port Royal Sound).

Despite its dramatic gains elsewhere in the Indies, Spain found the conquest of La Florida to be a demanding hurdle. Several of the earlier chapters in this volume have chronicled this pioneering phase of exploration and colonization (see especially the overviews by Milanich and Deagan). At first, part of the difficulty was geographic, as the terrain of La Florida tenaciously resisted Spanish efforts at subsistence agriculture and contributed to the perceived deprivation and destitution that characterized the so-called First Spanish Period.[1] The scarcity of significant east-west rivers also hampered Spanish movement from the capital at St. Augustine, restricting early expansion to the coastal zone.

But viewed from the sixteenth-century Spanish perspective, the most significant environmental shortcoming of La Florida was the lack of metallic mineral resources. Although the Spanish conquered more formidable environments elsewhere in the New World, these places generally boasted rich deposits of gold and silver, and thus provided the necessary incentives to persist and conquer. The early conquistadors in Middle and South America also encountered more sedentary Native Americans, groups that could be profitably exploited after their subjugation.

Such was not the case in La Florida, where the Spanish found, according to one mid-nineteenth-century historian, a "land sparsely peopled by a barbarous

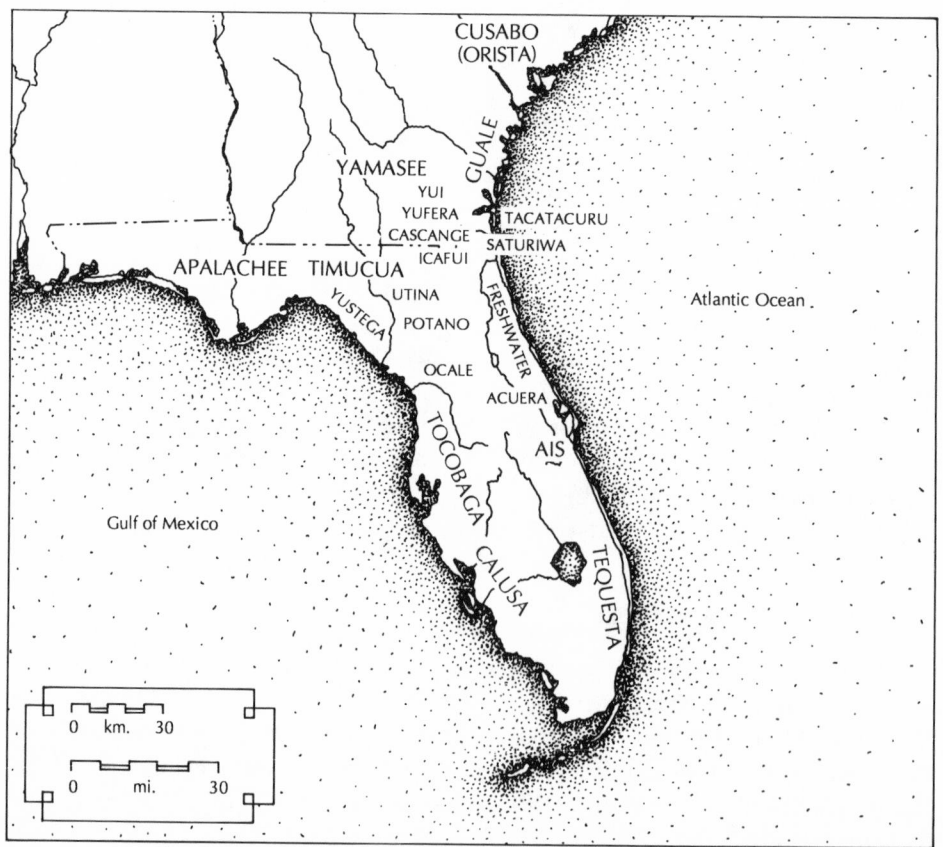

Figure 24-1. Native American groups in La Florida at the time of European contact.

and quarrelsome race of savages, rent asunder into manifold petty clans, with little peaceful leisure wherein to better their condition, wasting their lives in aimless and unending internecine war" (Brinton 1969 [1859]:111). Yet even the untrained Spanish eye of the conquistadors and early missionaries penetrating La Florida quickly determined that the Native American populations divided into roughly seven major tribal groups (Figure 24–1):

The Apalachee: Warlike and prosperous, the Apalachee were considered by the Spaniards to be the most sophisticated, unified, and powerful group living in La Florida.

The Timucua: An agricultural people controlling the northern one-third of peninsular Florida, they were perceived to be as progressive and numerous as the Apalachee, but unable to consolidate under a single chief.

The Guale: A coastal confederation of numerically small, but apparently well-integrated people, the Guale were capable of perpetuating long-distance trade, extended political networks, and social contacts.

The Cusabo: Also called the Orista, this northernmost group remained closely aligned with their Guale neighbors.

The Calusa: To the south, the numerous and commanding Calusa lived not by tilling, but by maintaining elaborate exchange networks through which they redistributed the surpluses of the coastal waters, savannahs, and wetlands. Much of the complex political organization observed in south Florida arose in alliance with, or in response to Calusa society, which consisted of a higher class (chief and nobles), an underclass (vassals and commoners), and slaves (see Goggin and Sturtevant 1964; Marquardt 1986, 1987; Milanich and Fairbanks 1980:241–250).

The Ais: A hunting and gathering society, the Ais subsisted along the Atlantic coastal lagoons and inlets. When Quaker Jonathan Dickinson visited the Ais in 1696, he was astounded at their impassioned, at times even torrid, dances and celebrations (Andrews and Andrews 1975:37–39).

The Tequesta: A nonagricultural group around the Miami area, these people were united under a single headman. Living in large coastal villages for part of the year, the Tequesta also dispersed into satellite camps to exploit animal and plant resources in the adjacent swamps and wetlands (Milanich and Fairbanks 1980:236; Sturtevant 1978).

Because three of these native groups—the Guale, the Timucua, and the Apalachee—eventually attracted the brunt of Spanish evangelical attention, we examine their precontact lifeways in more detail (see also Smith 1956; Smith and Gottlob 1978).

The Guale

The Guale were among the first indigenous peoples met by Europeans exploring north of present Mexico. After brief contact with the Spanish in 1526, this Muskhogean-speaking group later encountered the French in 1562–1563 and then, beginning in 1566, they were exposed to a long and intensive period of Spanish colonization. By 1684, the gradual withdrawal of the Spanish to the south and the correlative expansion of the Carolina colony southward fostered relocation and reorganization of the vastly reduced Guale population. The most important sources on the precontact and Mission period Guale people include

Jones (1978), Larson (1969, 1978, 1980), Sturtevant (1962), and Swanton (1922, 1946); see also Crawford (1975), Crook (1986), C. C. Jones (1873), G. Jones (1980), Larsen (1982), and Thomas (1987).

Patterns of Guale Subsistence. According to Larson's (1969, 1980) interpretation, precontact Guale people congregated almost exclusively along the lagoons and marshes of the Georgia coast. This area is characterized by a broad variety of floral and faunal resources, the most important of which, for aboriginal subsistence, included the hardwood forest (on high ground), molluscs and fish in the aquatic range, a variety of birds, and, of course, the white-tailed deer; Larson believes that the strands and deltas contained insufficient resources to attract a large or stable aboriginal population. The interior pine barrens were likewise thought to offer little of value to aboriginal populations beyond seasonal fishing or perhaps limited horticulture along the floodplain. Unfortunately, the details of Guale subsistence and social organization remain in some dispute. "The 'ethnohistoriographic' problems inherent in a study of the Guale are immense" (Jones 1978:242).

We can be certain that the Guale planted maize, beans, and varieties of squash and melons (for a review of the primary evidence, see Ruhl, this volume); but little is known about the specific agricultural technology. Investigators have long assumed that the Guale practiced a form of swidden agriculture based on a series of fallow cycles. Clearly, the production of maize was sufficient to last in storage from the late summer harvest through at least April, when planting began anew. One seventeenth-century English account suggested that more than one crop could be harvested each year (Hilton 1911).

Much of our knowledge of Guale subsistence and ecology derives from a 1570 account by Jesuit Father Rogel:

> The Indians were so reluctant to receive the Catholic religion that no admonitions would curb their barbarity—a barbarity based on liberty unrestrained by the yoke of reason, and made worse because they had not been taught to live in the villages. They were scattered about the country for nine of the twelve months of the year, so that to influence them at all, one missionary was needed for each Indian [Barcía 1951:152].

Rogel's letter, written after he returned from 11 months in Guale, goes on to rationalize the failure of the Jesuit efforts. He blamed two problems in particular: First, the missionaries were unable to concentrate the Indians in permanent settlements because the soil of the region would not allow intensive agriculture, and, second, the Spanish garrisons depended on the Indians for food and many disturbances ensued as a result.

Another Jesuit, Father Sedeño, wrote a similar letter from Guale on March 6, 1570:

> It is full of huge pines and barren forests; and . . . the few Indians that are there are so scattered; because as they do not have that with which to clear the trees for their fields they go where they find a small amount of land without forest in

order to plant their maize; and as the land is so miserable they move with their households from time to time to seek other lands that they can bring to productivity [cited in Larson 1980:208].

In his pioneering analysis of environment and subsistence technology on the Georgia coast, Lewis Larson took the Jesuit letters at face value, then reinforced and extended the Jesuit position by arguing that because suitable agricultural soils along the Georgia coast are isolated and rare—most of the land is poorly drained, highly permeable, and characterized by acidity and poor moisture retention—the Guale diet was heavily supplemented with nonagricultural sources (Larson 1969, 1980; see also Thomas 1987:60). Whereas swidden agriculture was indeed practiced in late prehistoric times, "its importance seems to have been slight. . . . The Guale were a coastal people whose economy was centered on the tidal waters where they derived a subsistence from fishing. Agriculture and hunting were of relatively minor importance" (Larson 1978:122, 137). The poor land resources were thought to have had such limited horticultural productivity that only a highly dispersed, seasonally mobile population could have survived there.

Grant Jones has proposed an alternative model for precontact Guale ecology, and his position is reinforced by the rather controversial demographic evidence assembled by Henry Dobyns (1983; see also Fairbanks 1985): "On the empirical level I believe that it [the conventional wisdom] has led to an overstatement of the isolation of Guale from the interior, the unproductivity of Guale horticulture, and the scattered quality of Guale settlements" (Jones 1978:189). Reinterpreting the Jesuit accounts cited above, Jones argues instead,

> Guale horticulture, I suggest, was sufficiently productive, in combination with other subsistence and productive activities, to account for the presence of permanent towns, a chiefdom level of social organization, temporary federations of chiefdoms under centralized leadership, and long distance trade networks. The chiefdoms were characterized by dual features of political organization and an emphasis on matrilineal succession. . . . I strongly suspect that the Guale inhabitants were scattering in order to avoid contact with the missionaries, whom they refused to listen to or accept. Significant factors in their resistance would have been the practice of forced tribute payment in maize to the Santa Elena garrison and the epidemic of 1569–1570, which was blamed on the priests. Sedeño's letter read as if they were intentionally exaggerating the "misery" of the land and the recalcitrance of the pagans, perhaps in order to procure a transfer. Rogel's letter is clearly an apology for his abandonment of the mission, placing the blame for his failure on the intransigent natives and the policies of the secular authorities. . . . The Jesuit portrait of a highly mobile, dispersed population with insufficient maize to last the year and a weakly developed political system does not conform with the earlier French reports or with subsequent documentation. . . . The Jesuit reports were exaggerated and misleading [Jones 1978:179, 191].

Jones's reinterpretation suggests another way of viewing Guale subsistence, its settlement pattern, and sociopolitical organization. Perhaps relevant here is recent research on the Calusa of southern Florida, clearly a powerful nonagricultural chiefdom with far-reaching political clout, fully capable of repelling Spanish advances (Marquardt 1986, 1987; Widmer 1988; Zubillaga 1946; see also Milanich, this volume).

Conflicting evidence aside, there can be no question that the Spanish imposed a sedentary agricultural economy on the Guale and other Indians of La Florida, keeping people in place to promote Christianity, make allies, and generate stable supply lines (Milanich 1978:82; see also Bushnell, this volume). Such nucleation may have been so successful that it changed primary economic practices (Larson 1978:132). But if such modifications occurred, they stand in marked contrast to patterns to the south, where Deagan (1978:89, 113) found a remarkable continuity in eastern Timucuan subsistence and settlement patterns—even though the Spanish encouraged horticulture by introducing new techniques and European technology (see below).

Although reliable evidence about Guale settlements is difficult to obtain from the documentary sources, perhaps the following account of an Orista town in 1666 can be applied to the Guale as well: "The Ttowne is scituate on the side or rather in the skirts of a faire forrest, in which at several distances are diverse fields of maiz with many little houses stragglingly amongst them for the habitations of the particular families" (Sandford 1911). This and similar descriptions suggest a "dispersed town" settlement pattern, with horticultural plots and residences scattered in the vicinity of the town center.

Relatively little is known about the specific locations of Guale communities, although the available evidence strongly suggests that they existed in a wide variety of microenvironments. Such settlements were probably located along the banks of major rivers, extending beyond the bounds of estuarine saline water and into the pine barrens proper. Maize plots were located behind the town center itself, opposite the river or creek banks. Local differences in the productivity of shellfishing, hunting, and horticulture may also have fostered some degree of economic specialization and created a greater need for an organized system of intercommunity exchange. Although most Guale apparently maintained permanent residence in a single community, some may have shifted their winter residence to be near areas of hunting, fishing, or shellfish collection.

Such Guale "towns" were not so much specific places as a discrete groups of people governed by consensus, fully capable of changing locality, building new shelters, and planting fields in one place after another. The town of Santa Catalina de Guale, the onetime capital of Guale Province, is a case in point. Bushnell (1990) has recently traced this town to at least seven known sites between 1564 and 1728.

Guale Sociopolitical Organization. During the contact period, the Guale were aligned into a number of well-organized, politically stratified chiefdoms. Although the boundaries and membership of these chiefdoms shifted in response to changing external politics, three principal chiefdoms existed throughout the period between initial European contact and the early seventeenth century (Figure 24-2). Each chiefdom had two principal towns in which the leader and some family members and retainers lived. The town centers included a large, round, community building (the *buhío*) in which periodic councils and intercommunity feasts were held. The ritual chunkey game, common to many Southeastern aboriginal groups, was performed with poles and a disk-shaped stone in a playing ground adjacent to the community buildings (Hudson 1976; San Miguel 1902; Sandford 1911).

The primary leadership of each chiefdom was rotated between the two principal towns. The principal leader of a chiefdom was known as the mico. Some Spanish reports define another office, the mico mayor, suggesting that these

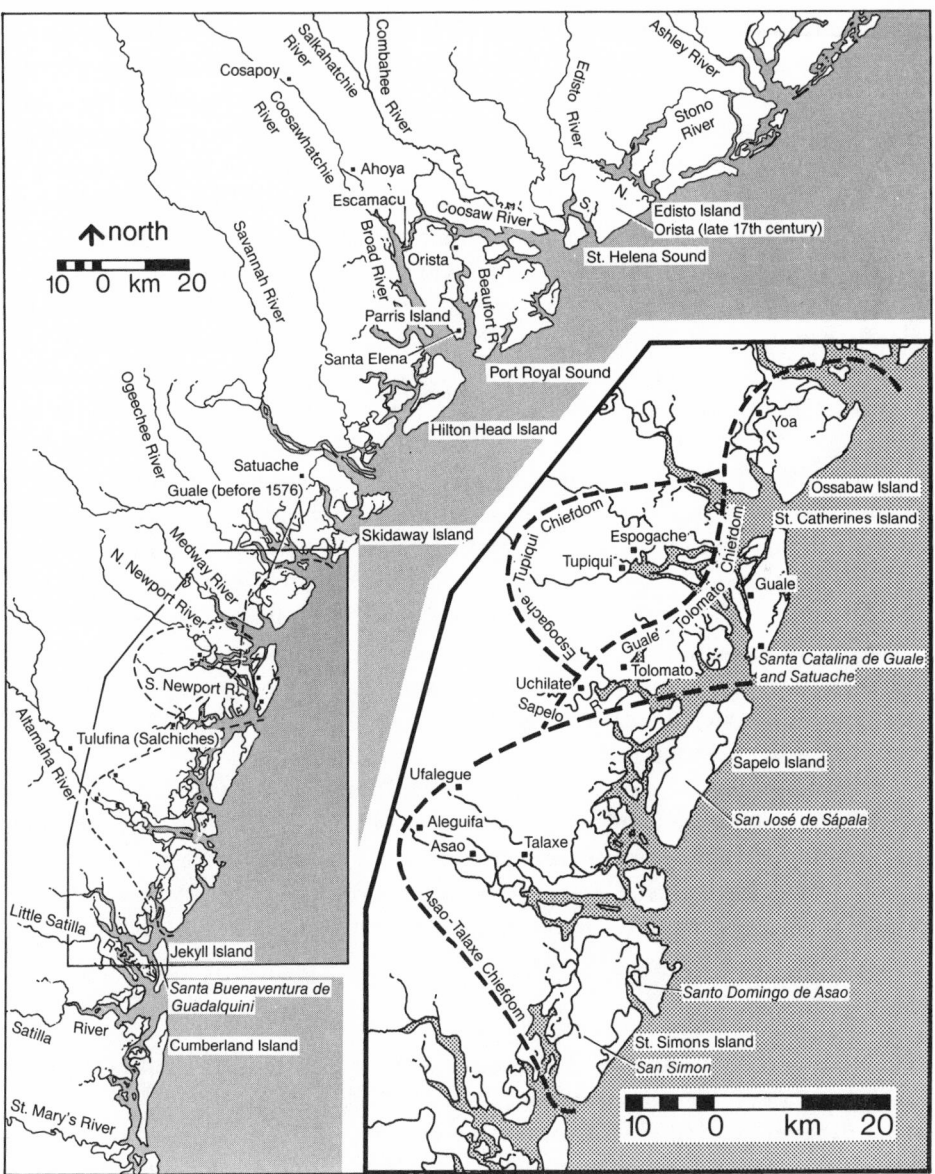

Figure 24-2. Approximate locations of Spanish period towns and settlements along the sixteenth- and seventeenth-century Georgia coast. Dashed line denotes approximate boundaries of southern chiefdoms (after Jones 1978:Figure 17).

were two hierarchically related officers, each of whom lived in one of the two principal towns. A leadership council consisted of the two primary individuals, plus a number of leaders of secondary importance (often termed *caciques* and *principales* in the Spanish sources). Micos were commonly accompanied by other important, titled leaders (variously termed *mandador*, *aliagita*, *tunaque*, and *heredero* [or heir to the mico]). The roles and duties of the latter are poorly known, although they may have also resided in the principal towns.

The principal Guale leaders were probably the heads of clans, in which descent was traced matrilineally. Positions of authority were commonly inherited by one's younger brother, sister's son, or (in later years) by a sister's daughter. During the seventeenth century, female leaders became increasingly common, perhaps because of depopulation due to the effects of repeated epidemics, limited participation by males in mission communities, and Spanish policies stipulating that men were to serve in various labor projects, in St. Augustine and elsewhere. At times, Franciscans opposed the principle of matrilineal succession, but they were more vocal about their opposition to the common practice of polygyny. Male leaders often had several wives, each of whom resided in a separate house; the wives were sometimes sisters. As discussed below, the friars' attempt to abolish polygyny and disrupt traditional lines of succession were major factors in the revolt of 1597 (García 1902).

Because the Guale settlement pattern fostered some degree of economic specialization among communities, chiefdoms became a primary mechanism for integrating the regional economy, chiefs serving as collectors and redistributors of food and other products. The most common mode of redistribution was the periodic ritual feast, in which items such as maize, fish, oysters, and acorns were lavished on guests. Early French sources suggest that chiefs either owned substantial agricultural land, or at least maintained authority to collect tribute of maize for their own use, as well as for future distribution in the community feasts (Bennett 1975). Chiefs also compensated their supporters in military activities with valued items such as deerskins, shell money, and metal tools received in exchange with Europeans.

Archaeological evidence suggests that the Guale participated in an active, long-distance trade network with inland peoples (Larson 1980). The exchange involved mostly elite or nonessential goods, indicating that the Guale political hierarchy may have played a central role in regional as well as local trade. Unfortunately, the implications of such long-distance exchange are largely unknown.

The Timucua

When the French established Fort Caroline (near Jacksonville, Florida) in 1564, the Timucua occupied the northern third of the Florida peninsula (plus a little of southeastern Georgia). The Timucua were composed of a number of separate tribes who spoke the same language. The western groups lived primarily in the pine and oak forests of north-central Florida, and the eastern Timucua derived their subsistence from the rivers, swamps, lagoons, and barrier islands. The key sources addressing the Timucuan lifeway in the precontact and contact period include Deagan (1978, 1979), Ehrmann (1940), Milanich (1978), Milanich and Sturtevant (1972), Spellman (1948), and Swanton (1922:320–387); see also Milanich and Fairbanks (1980:216–227), and Swanton (1929).

Early French and Spanish accounts provide considerable information about the Timucua, although they concentrate almost exclusively on the Saturiwa, who lived from St. Augustine northward to the mouth of the St. Marys River (Hakluyt 1903a, 1903b; Ribault 1964; see also Figure 24-1). The renowned Le Moyne illustrations are also based largely on the Saturiwa (Le Moyne 1875; Lorant 1946; see also Sturtevant 1977). These 42 sketches were prepared by Jacques Le Moyne, a cartographer who accompanied Ribault at Fort Caroline (near modern Jacksonville), then converted to engravings by Theodore De Bry in 1591. Although the depictions provide numerous details of the Timucuan lifeway—and are often used by prehistorians to reconstruct the precontact lifeways—they are marred by numerous inaccuracies, and must be used with care. Sauer (1971:207–208) concludes that Le Moyne could not have personally witnessed several of the scenes portrayed, and points out the engravings are remarkably similar to those prepared by De Bry a year earlier recording sixteenth-century Brazilian Indians. The Le Moyne drawings can be trusted only when independent verification is available (Milanich and Sturtevant 1972:4; Sturtevant 1977).

The linguistic affiliation of the Timucuan language remains unresolved. Using largely geographic evidence, early investigators (such as Gatschet 1878) assigned the Timucuan-speakers to the Muskhogean stock; but more recently Haas (1958, 1971, 1978) and Swadesh (1964) have suggested an affiliation with Siouan or Arawakan. Granberry (1971) has suggested ties with the Warau language of the northeastern coast of Venezuela (see also Crawford 1975; Granberry 1987).

Precontact population levels in the Timucuan province have likewise been the subject of considerable debate. Henry Dobyns (1983) has examined depopulation among the Timucua as a test case, deriving a number of highly controversial population estimates (1983:204–208, 293–294), which would place the precontact population level for Timucua at 722,000. On the assumption that 95 percent of this population perished during the first century after exposure to European diseases, Dobyns computed a total of only 36,450 Timucuan survivors in 1617. Several reviewers have heavily criticized these estimates (e.g., Henige 1986), arguing that Dobyns was naive in his evaluation of the source materials and overenthusiastic in estimating the degree of population loss.

The Timucuans were divided into eastern and western divisions (Deagan 1978; Milanich 1978; see also Figure 24-2). The Western Timucua—the Potano, Ocale, Utina, and Yustega—lived in the pine-oak forests of north-central Florida west of the St. Johns River. To the east, the other Timucuan tribes lived along the riverine and coastal environments to the east of the St. Johns River. The economy of all tribes was based on limited cultivation of maize, beans, squash, tobacco, and other cultigens, heavily supplemented by the exploitation of terrestrial and estuarine resources (see the chapters by Reitz and Ruhl, this volume). They farmed and lived in permanent villages from the spring through the fall, then dispersed into smaller groups to hunt, fish, and collect specific resources (such as acorns, hickory nuts, blueberries, and roots).

Each tribe comprised 5 to 20 villages (Milanich and Sturtevant 1972:3), and accounts from the contact period suggest that major Timucuan villages consisted of roughly two dozen dwellings, housing perhaps 200 Indians. Le Moyne's sketches show that villages were sometimes palisaded, and that they were located near freshwater streams or lakes. The palm-thatched houses were circular, and public granaries were erected. Each village had a large, round council house and open ceremonial plazas. Like most Southeastern Indians, the Timucua based their sociopolitical organization on matrilineal, exogamous named clans. Whereas early French accounts mention one chief having 40 villages under his control, such centralized authority rapidly disappeared with European contact. Priests commonly attempted to work through the traditional village chiefs, since the conversion of a single cacique could rapidly lead to the adoption of Christianity by an entire village. The later writings of Fr. Francisco Pareja (Milanich and Sturtevant 1972), stationed at San Juan del Puerto, suggest that each village had its own chief, each under the jurisdiction of a head chief who exacted tribute, in the form of produce, which was stored in a central warehouse.

Timucuan beliefs and ritual practices are well recorded in the Pareja *Confessionario* of 1613 (Milanich and Sturtevant 1972). Shamans used a variety of techniques for curing the sick, including prayer, herbal concoctions, and ritual fires. Before they adopted Christian customs, the Timucua used to bury their dead in mounds, important individuals often accompanied by their shell cups, used for the consumption of cassina. The bodies of lesser individuals were sometimes stored in charnel houses, then interred in the mounds en masse. Even under the supervision of priests, the Timucua continued to place grave goods as offerings inside burial shrouds (Milanich and Fairbanks 1980:224).

By 1700, the precontact Timucuan lifeway had been extensively modified, in part because of depopulation and also because of the inevitable blending that resulted from diverse Christian Indian groups flocking to the protective walls of St. Augustine.

The Apalachee

The Apalachee controlled the territory between the Aucilla River and a little west of the Ochlockonee River, from the Gulf coast northward to the Georgia state border, or a little farther. They formed a distinctive political and cultural group, recognized as such by themselves and by other Indian groups to the south. The Apalachee are descendants of the precontact Fort Walton culture. This Mississippian people lived in multiple- and single-mound villages and encircling farmsteads. They had the highest population density and horticultural productivity of the mission Indians. The most important sources addressing the Apalachee lifeway of the precontact and contact period include Boyd et al. (1951), Hann (1988), and Swanton (1922, 1946); see also Covington (1972), Hann (1986), Milanich and Fairbanks (1980:227–230).

Like many other Southeastern tribes, the Apalachee spoke a Muskhogean language. Milanich and Fairbanks (1980:228) think Apalachee was probably a dialect of the Hitchiti spoken by a number of tribes living to the north of Apalachee territory during the historic period (see also Haas 1978; Swanton 1922:11, 130). A single example of the Apalachee language has survived, a 1688 letter from the chiefs of Apalachee to the Spanish king (Hann 1988:118); the only other source of linguistic information is a few isolated Apalachee words, many of them glossed in Father Paiva's impassioned 1676 manuscript describing the ball game (translated in Hann 1988: Appendix 2).

The Guale and Apalachee languages belong to the general Muskhogean family and they share a number of words whose form remained substantially intact from Proto-Muskhogean. Still, these two languages were not mutually intelligible, and in 1673, two friars spoke of the need in St. Augustine for missionaries capable of mastering the three major mission languages: Guale, Timucuan, and Apalachee (Hann 1988:120). Only rarely could an interpreter be relied upon to handle more than one native language.

Population levels in Apalachee are not accurately known. Milanich and Fairbanks (1980:230) and Hann (1988:163) suggest that 25,000 people lived in Apalachee during the early seventeenth century, rejecting Swanton's (1946:91) earlier estimate of only 5,000 Apalachee for the year 1676. Just before Moore's raid of 1704, the Apalachee population had dropped to perhaps 6,400 Indians (following Hann 1988:169).

Apalachee Subsistence. During precontact times, the Apalachee were a sedentary, agricultural people, who relied on fish, game, acorns, and other wild plant foods to supplement and enhance their diet. Although Spanish accounts emphasized the mobile nature of the coastal groups, no mention is made of such mobility for the Apalachee, making them (in Spanish eyes at least) excellent candidates for missionization.

The Apalachee were renowned as the most intensive cultivators of maize in Florida during Mississippian times (Larson 1980:191–192, 214), and this fabled productivity ultimately spurred Spain into launching the intensive mission effort there in 1633. When de Soto overwintered in Apalachee, he was impressed with the expansive fields of agricultural products and the ample supplies of foodstuffs cached for the winter. A century and a half later, Calderón described Apalachee agricultural practices primarily as slash-and-burn, with planting undertaken in April (Wenhold 1937). During the Mission period, the Apalachee also began cultivating European wheat, planted in October and harvested in June.

Apalachee Sociopolitical Structure. Dobyns (1983) and Fairbanks (1985) have argued that the Spanish entrada into Apalachee and elsewhere resulted in a massive reorganization of the culture and major population reduction. While in the Apalachee area in 1540, de Soto clearly encountered a complex chiefdom-level organization. But later Spanish missionaries found little evidence of organization above the village level (Fairbanks 1985:133–134). Although some ritual patterns were retained, mound building had stopped by the time the missionaries arrived and Southern cult paraphernalia were totally lacking from these mission sites. The scattered Apalachee villages of the Mission period apparently held migrants from the west and the north, probably refugees from similar depopulations. Combined with the loss of redistributive chiefdomship organization during the mid-sixteenth and early seventeenth centuries, this change shattered traditional lifeways throughout the Southeast. In fact, Fairbanks attributes the failure of Spanish Florida to an underestimation of how depopulated the Southeast had become owing to the excesses of the de Soto expedition (1985:139).

Although some Mississippian traits are found among the Timucua and the Guale, only the Apalachee participated fully in the Mississippian cultural pattern (as defined by Milanich, this volume). Accordingly, Bushnell (this volume) argues that the link between sedentism and the sacraments meant that true missionization occurred only among the most sedentary groups, particularly the Apalachee.

Like all chiefdoms, the Apalachee had a permanent hierarchy of political offices filled by those selected through social ranking ascribed by birth. Whereas some chiefdoms were "simple," with a single level of chiefly authority, others, like the Apalachee, were considerably more complex and were based on an intricate system of paramount and subordinate chiefs.

Although almost no documentation exists about the pre-mission Apalachee, we do know that, like most Southeastern groups, they were matrilineal, with positions of authority passing not to the son of the deceased, but rather to his nephew, the son of his eldest sister. Despite Spanish grumbling about this practice, the custom survived intact until the destruction of the Apalachee villages in 1704. Under this system, responsibility for the custody, education, and discipline of children rested with the family of the mother; the father was not involved. But there is no documentary indication that Apalachee women ever succeeded to leadership posts, as was the case among the Timucua and Guale (Hann 1988:70).

During the early sixteenth century, two large villages—Ivitachuco and Anhaica Apalache—seem to have anchored either end of this densely settled area, with numerous smaller villages scattered almost in arcs around these eastern and western termini (Hann 1988:96). These two polities seem to have been separated by the kind of no-man's-land corridor de Soto noted in the chiefdoms to the north. The site of Ivitachuco, discovered and partly excavated in 1968, overlooks Lake Iamonia (Jones and Shapiro, this volume) and Anhaica has now been firmly identified in downtown Tallahassee (Ewen, this volume).

Documentary evidence from the Mission period suggests that the two chieftains of Ivitachuco and San Luis (probable successor to Anhaica) seem to have enjoyed a higher status than the leaders of the other villages (Hann 1988:98), but the relative status between the two rulers is unclear. At the height of the Mission period, during the second half of the seventeenth century, the political structure in Apalachee consisted of 11 largely independent and territorially distinct villages, each also serving as a nucleus for missionary outreach. Each Apalachee village, whether a major community or satellite settlement, was controlled by a hereditary chief who was the highest-ranking native official. Certain material privileges, such as the accumulation of bearskins, gifts from the Crown, captured booty, and exemption from labor tribute, accompanied such offices. In precontact days, this chief probably exerted a measure of priestly as well as political leverage.

This social order is evident in the discord that arose over the Spanish practice of using Apalachee as pack animals to transport tribute between their homeland and the St. Augustine colony (see Gannon, this volume). Particularly offensive was the threat of conscripting members of the Apalachee elite, who had always been exempt from manual labor, into service as burden-bearers. Although the Franciscans attempted to enlighten the governors on the nature of Apalachee social structure—arguing that chiefs were equivalent to Spanish lords—the secular leadership ignored the warnings, and rebellion was often the result (Bushnell 1989:141; see also Bushnell, this volume).

The Apalachee Ball Game. Perhaps the best-known feature of Apalachee life is the sports complex, involving at least three different ball games. The Western Timucua shared the ball game, although the coastal Timucuans may have followed somewhat different rules. Considerable information survives about the nature of this sport, which also contained non-Christian religious symbolism and rituals (Bushnell 1978; Hann 1988:92). Contemporary accounts emphasize the brutality and destructiveness involved, one observer commenting, "When this pileup begins to become untangled, they are accustomed to find four or five stretched out like tuna; over them are others gasping for breath, because, inasmuch as some are wont to swallow the ball, they are made to vomit it up by squeezing their windpipe or by kicks to the stomach. Over there lie others with an arm or a leg broken" (Hann 1988:76). Deaths were apparently not uncommon, with two fatalities reported in the plaza of San Luis. Although the ball game may have been discouraged during the first half of the seventeenth century, it was not until 1657 that Governor Rebolledo explicitly forbade this native sport.

History of European Involvement

Evangelization during the Entrada

Men of the cloth accompanied the conquistadors from the earliest European penetration of La Florida. Some priests were needed to administer to the religious needs of the explorers, but other were enlisted specifically to scout out possibilities for ecclesiastical outreach among the native populations.[2]

The earliest entrada, Ponce de León's voyage of discovery in 1513, lacked a missionary component; he was simply to search for and settle the rumored island of Bimini. But while planning for his second voyage, Juan Ponce was specifically directed by the Spanish king, Ferdinand V, to "Treat [the Indians] as best you can, seeking in every possible way to convert them to our Holy Catholic Faith." Accordingly, the 1521 expedition included several secular and regular priests. But the campaign foundered when Ponce de León's landing party was repelled by a storm of Calusa arrows (Davis 1935). Badly injured, Ponce de León returned to Cuba, where he died of his wounds. So ended the initial missionary effort in La Florida.

A more formidable missionary endeavor was spearheaded by Lucas Vásquez de Ayllón, judge (*Oidor*) of the Royal Audiencia of Santo Domingo, descendant of a distinguished Mozarabic family in Toledo, a veteran of the political struggles of early Hispaniola, and a wealthy sugar planter, rancher, and slave trader. In 1523, Ayllón obtained a contract to explore and eventually settle the new land. This pact stipulated that Ayllón was to sponsor an initial voyage along the southeastern coast of the present United States in 1525 and then personally attempt to plant a full-blown colony—including women, black slaves, and missionaries—somewhere along the coast.

Ayllón was to finance this entire settlement expedition himself, except for religious expenses, which were to be repaid to him from revenues, if any, derived from the new colony. Departing Hispaniola in July 1526, Ayllón's party of 500 included two priests and one lay brother of the Order of St. Dominic. Ayllón first landed at the Jordan River (Santee River), but abandoned that site when no Indians were found in the vicinity. Using information derived from two exploratory voyages made southward along the coast during the weeks spent on the banks of the Jordan, Ayllón moved his colony southward to San Miguel de Gualdape in September 1526 (Oviedo 1851). But inadequate supplies, the winter cold, numerous deaths, and dissension within the colony doomed the potential missionary effort at San Miguel. Ayllón himself died in the arms of one of the Dominican priests. The 150 survivors gave up and fled home to Santo Domingo. The whereabouts of San Miguel remains unknown, although Hoffman (1984) has recently argued that this colonial and mission complex may be in the vicinity of Sapelo Sound (Georgia). If so, then Ayllón's missionaries were preaching to the Guale Indians.

Spanish merchandise introduced to the Indians by the Ayllón colony was carried far inland by Indian traders, and was discovered there by members of the 1540 de Soto expedition (Elvas 1907). The Ayllón colony doubtless also introduced the fateful European diseases that shattered some of the interior groups encountered by de Soto (Varner and Varner 1951).

Similar failures attended the early missionary and exploratory ventures of Pánfilo de Narváez in 1527, whose expedition included five Franciscan friars and a number of secular priests (see the chapters by Milanich and by Marrinan et al., this volume).

The more proficient de Soto expedition of 1539–1540 was regulated by a cedula from King Charles I, stipulating that he take "priests who shall be appointed by us for the instruction of the natives of that province in our holy Catholic Faith, to whom you are to give and pay the passage, stores, and the other necessary subsistence for them according to our condition." But these lofty goals were quickly undermined by the callous and cold-blooded methods of de Soto and his followers (as detailed in several chapters in Part 1 of this volume). Although eight secular and four regular priests accompanied the de Soto expedition, the ecclesiastical impact was minimal.

Subsequent evangelical crusades by Cancér (1549) and Tristán de Luna (1559–1561) were equally ineffective (Bolton 1921:121–128; Gannon 1965; Lowery 1905). Despite royal orders to convert the Indians of La Florida to Christianity, the explorers too often perceived them as chattel, suitable only to serve as slaves, bearers, food provisioners, and guides. Finally, acting on advice from Spain's most accomplished naval commander, Pedro Menéndez de Avilés, King Philip II in 1561 formally abandoned plans to colonize and missionize this area. Crown and clergy alike acknowledged that four decades of exploration had left La Florida unconquered, unsettled, unexploited, and decidedly unchristian (Matter 1972:30).

Menéndez Colonizes and Missionizes La Florida

But Philip II quickly changed his mind when French Huguenot explorers under René de Goulaine de Laudonnière and Jean Ribault expropriated the Florida coastline and began building military fortifications (Bennett 1975; Conner 1927). Not only did these settlements undermine Spanish claims to La Florida, but the French presence directly threatened the gold-laden Spanish fleets passing through the Straits of Florida. Alarmed, the Crown prevailed upon Menéndez de Avilés, already captain-general of the Indies Fleet, to accept the office of *Adelantado de la Florida*—the contractual conqueror—with orders to purge the French threat to Spanish interests.

Inextricably intertwined with the aims of conquest and colonization, religious conversion of the nonbelieving native was a critical consideration in the royal contract of March 15, 1565 (Lyon 1976:43, 47). Menéndez was compelled by the Crown to supervise—at his own expense—a sweeping program to missionize Spanish Florida, to be carried out in peace, friendship, and Christianity. More than a dozen missionaries were to accompany Menéndez, four padres supplied by the Society of Jesus, the remainder to be selected by any other religious order satisfactory to the adelantado (Zubillaga 1941). Despite such provisions, only a few secular priests and no regular clergy actually sailed with Menéndez in 1565.

Menéndez de Avilés expeditiously discharged his military responsibility by cold-bloodedly eradicating the French threat within two months of landing in La Florida (Lyon 1976:100–130; 1988). Shortly after scrambling ashore at St. Augustine, Menéndez and his men named the site of their landing Nombre de Dios, the name still in use today (Deagan 1983). Exactly when the mission was established there is unknown (Hann 1989), but Nombre de Dios was to serve as homeland to the Spanish missionary efforts for two centuries, and St. Augustine was to become the southern stronghold. Pressing northward, Menéndez quickly positioned his colonial headquarters at Santa Elena, on Parris Island in South Carolina (Lyon 1976:156–157; see also Chatelain 1941 and South, this volume). Despite the early flush of military success, Menéndez soon realized that the local terrain and native people would vastly complicate his second task, the missionization of La Florida.

Late in 1566, Menéndez launched his first large-scale missionary expedition, ordering Captain Juan Pardo to explore and fortify the territory west of Santa

Elena, and to announce to the various caciques that the Spaniards carried the news of the gospel of salvation from afar. Pardo's initial expedition traveled more than 500 miles, reaching the foot of the Appalachian Mountains (DePratter and Smith 1980; DePratter et al. 1983). The next fall, Pardo returned to tour his previously established garrisons and reached far beyond into Alabama. Pardo was accompanied by a chaplain, Fr. Sebastian Montero, who apparently enjoyed some success in his mission efforts at the settlement of Guatari (Gannon 1965:30–31; Lowery 1905:276; Zubillaga 1946:317–328). But this interior outpost was abandoned when Montero withdrew in 1572.

Jesuits Enter La Florida

After a year of bureaucratic postponements, the first Jesuits finally sailed to join Menéndez in June 1566, to establish the first Jesuit mission to Spanish America. Although Fr. Pedro Martínez, the superior, was killed near the mouth of the St. Johns River, Menéndez personally escorted Father Juan Rogel and Brother Francisco Villareal to their stations in south Florida. But the short-lived outposts among the Calusa and Tequesta Indians were soon abandoned and both Jesuits returned to St. Augustine. Given the failures to the south, and current state of rebellion among the Indians living near St. Augustine, the Jesuits trained their evangelical sights northward, toward the provinces of Guale and Orista.

Recognizing the degree to which soldiers drained Indian food supplies, and deploring the unchristian examples set by garrison behavior, Father Segura attempted to isolate the missions of Guale from Spanish settlements and forts. Simultaneously, Father Rogel labored to the north in Orista, making a determined effort to learn the local language. Although initially encouraging, Rogel's struggles were once again undermined when 40 Spanish soldiers descended upon his mission looking for food, enhancing already growing Indian resentment against the Spanish. Rogel and Segura finally conceded defeat and returned to Santa Elena.

Undaunted, in 1570 Father Segura led a small party far to the north to establish Ajacán, a mission in the Chesapeake Bay region, probably not far from the later English settlement at Jamestown, Virginia (Lewis and Loomie 1953; Zubillaga 1946:471–479). But this enterprise ended in disaster when all the priests were killed, less than five months after their arrival. Jesuit blood spilled in the Chesapeake was the final straw, and the Society of Jesus quit La Florida altogether in 1572. In four years, Jesuit missionaries had baptized only six Indians, including four children—all at the point of death.

Rogel rationalized the failures by complaining that the Indians were on the whole unsuited to Christianity, in large measure because of their migratory settlement patterns. He also grumbled that the deportment of Spanish soldiers— demanding food, beating and killing the natives, and abusing their women— outraged the Indians (Zubillaga 1946). As discussed earlier, Rogel's dour assessments still play a key, if controversial role in our understanding of precontact coastal agriculture and economy (e.g., Jones 1978; Larson 1969, 1980; Thomas 1987; see also Bushnell, this volume).

Matter (1972:60) suggests that the Jesuits failed because of lukewarm support from the Jesuit hierarchy, intransigent attitudes on the part of Rogel and his colleagues (especially with regard to Native American customs of plural marriage and worship), dissension between religious and secular officials in La Florida (exacerbated by the prolonged absence of Menéndez), and the wretched conditions in the support colonies at Santa Elena and St. Augustine. The Jesuits thoroughly alienated native populations by their association with the Spanish garrison, which demanded heavy payments by the Indians in cultivated foodstuffs. The Guale also blamed the missionaries for instigating the massive epidemic of 1569 and 1570 (Vargas Ugarte 1935; Zubillaga 1941, 1946).

Similarly, Eugene Lyon attributes the Jesuit setbacks to the short-sighted Spanish outlook toward Native Americans:

> What Juan Rogel could not see . . . was that the strict inculcation of Christian doctrine also posed a threat to the Indian cultures. Under the influence of the charisma of Pedro Menéndez' driving personality and exposed to the power and technology of European civilization, the Indians had taken the first steps to Christianization. The insistence on exclusive acceptance of Catholicism by the Indians would not be lightly imposed, however. Elimination of the old rites, ceremonies, and beliefs would imply a thoroughgoing change in Indian life. As they sensed, it, in fact, would mean the total alteration of their culture. The enforcement of such change would be accomplished only through heavy and consistent pressure by the Spanish over a period of time [Lyon 1976:205].

Franciscans Supersede the Jesuits

Thinking that another religious order might be more effective, Pedro Menéndez turned for help to the Franciscan Fathers (Barrientos 1965). Although the Crown ordered that a dozen Franciscans be dispatched in early 1563, only by 1573 is there definite evidence of a Franciscan presence in La Florida (Barcía 1951; Hann 1989). Over the next several years, the number of friars in Spanish Florida fluctuated somewhat, and for a time, even St. Augustine was left without the services of a priest. Records from 1578 show that only two friars were stationed in La Florida, one each in St. Augustine and Santa Elena. Six years later, only four Franciscan friars were stationed in all of La Florida, and they too spent their time attending to Spanish needs at the sister cites of St. Augustine and Santa Elena, with little time for missionizing the Guale and Timucua.

These early Franciscan undertakings seemed as ill-fated as the Jesuit attempts. The Indians of La Florida particularly resented the continual ecclesiastical meddling in political matters. Continued demands by the Spanish authorities for food-tribute payments and a general pattern of Spanish military harassment did much to harden Indian resistance to the mission effort. This challenge took the form of open rebellion against the town of Santa Elena in 1576. Anti-Spanish hostility continued through early 1579, when the Spanish retaliated by burning 20 towns, killing many Indians, and destroying much of the stored maize in Guale communities. That this destruction covered a coastal distance of 45 leagues indicates the widespread degree of native discontent. The missions were then abandoned by the Franciscans, and the rebellion intensified from 1580 through 1582. The uneasy northern frontier was permanently lost in 1587 with the abandonment of Santa Elena, and the capital of La Florida permanently moved southward to St. Augustine (Geiger 1937; Lanning 1935; Lyon 1984; South 1988).

The religious picture brightened somewhat in October 1587, when Father Reinoso arrived in St. Augustine with a dozen other Franciscans in tow. Governor Menéndez Marquez assigned friars to the pioneer mission at Nombre de Dios and to other primary Indian towns scattered throughout Timucua and Guale; they also established a number of visitas, which lacked a resident missionary. Non-Christian visitors became a reservoir of potential converts, and by 1595 Spanish officials estimated that 1,500 Christian Indians lived in La Florida. Spain now enjoyed effective control of the coastline from Cape Canaveral northward to St. Catherines Island (Georgia), and missionaries looked forward to extending the rim of Christendom inland.

The Guale Rebellion of 1597

By 1597, six friars had been allocated to the Guale coast, and they reported some initial successes (Geiger 1937:87). But the rosy Franciscan outlook mutated almost overnight when a new rebellion threatened the entire missionary enterprise in La Florida.

The immediate cause of the 1597 revolt was one priest's actions in the chiefdom encompassing the towns of Guale and Tolomato. Friar Pedro de Corpa had admonished an Indian named Don Juanillo for practicing polygyny—a common practice among the precontact Guale—and had accordingly attempted to deprive him of his rights to inherit a position of leadership (García 1902; Geiger 1937:88; Lanning 1935:82–83; Oré 1936; see also Harkins, this volume). Five of the six friars serving Guale were quickly killed and numerous doctrinas torched as Juanillo's discontent spread up and down the Georgia coast. The sole priestly survivor, Francisco de Avila, was taken by the rebels to an interior community, where he was tortured and humiliated until his release the following year.

While the uprising lasted, the Christian Timucuans of San Pedro de Mocamo (on Cumberland Island) moved southward to the protection of San Juan, and Governor Méndez de Canzo created a regional famine, demolishing stored harvests up and down the Georgia coast. Some authorities argued that La Florida should be abandoned altogether: To facilitate easier access to the interior, and to its 1,200 Christianized Indians, the surviving friars advised the Crown to move the presidio from St. Augustine northward to Guale (Arnade 1959).

Some historians view the 1597 uprising as an unanticipated, tragic turn of events, particularly because only three months earlier several Guale leaders had dutifully traveled to render obedience to the new governor, Gonzalo Méndez de Canzo, who bedecked them with gifts. From his perspective as church historian, Maynard Geiger (1937:88–89) concluded:

The Indian revolt of Guale was a desperate attempt to wipe out the Christian culture that had just taken root. Christian morality faced a hand-to-hand conflict with inveterate pagan custom. The attempt of the friars to replace simultaneous polygamy by Christian monogamy was to be accompanied by the shedding of blood. . . . If the heir to the caciquedom was to go on in open defiance of a fundamental Christian law, he would nullify to a great extent whatever efforts the missionaries made in behalf of Christianity.

A more contemporary Franciscan expression of this viewpoint is voiced by Fr. Conrad Harkins (this volume), who reviews recent steps by the Catholic Church to canonize the five Franciscans martyred in the 1597 rebellion.

From his ethnohistorical purview, Jones (1978:183–184) argues that the 1597 rebellion was not a single case of discontent with the actions of the priesthood, but rather an insurrection climaxing 27 years of nearly uninterrupted rebellion against excessive and repeated Spanish demands for food and continued military harassment (see also San Miguel 1902; Sturtevant 1962). Furthermore, documentary evidence suggests that the revolt was conducted by a well-integrated federation of chiefdoms; the strength of the rebel leaders was broken only by a particularly vicious series of Spanish reprisals in 1598. By 1601, these leaders were driven underground some distance inland, among Indian allies known as Salchiches. Under the leadership of the Spanish, the coastal chiefdoms led a massive attack upon the fugitive rebels. This attack, like the rebellion of 1597, suggests the existence of a federation of nearly all the Indians along the Guale coast. In this view, Indian hostility ran much deeper than the ill-feelings of a single malcontent, which suggests that Christianity had barely taken root at all.

La Florida Missions during the Seventeenth Century

Immediate causes aside, the 1597 rebellion shook La Florida to its core. The resulting anarchy disrupted the momentum of the ongoing Franciscan crusade, creating a breeding ground for the later, weakening of the mission system of La Florida, and exacerbating the quarrels between secular and church officials. When Philip III learned of the insurrection, he seriously considered abandoning the colony altogether. But upon further investigation, the Crown decided to continue its support, and the peaceful political reorganization of the Guale coast began in 1603 (Pearson 1974; Ross 1926; Serrano y Sanz 1912). Undaunted by their previous misfortunes, Franciscan missionaries returned to the coast in 1605.

The Franciscan mission effort hit full stride when Bishop Juan de las Cabezas de Altamirano arrived in St. Augustine on March 15, 1606. This consequential visitation sparked a religious revival throughout La Florida, the friars exhorting the now-contrite Guale to cooperate with the church and state in reestablishing a peaceful frontier (Geiger 1937; Wenhold 1937). Governor Pedro de Ybarra directed the Indians of Asao (in the Altamaha drainage) to "erect crosses along their roads similar to the one they have at the landing place. The Cross is the perfect symbol of a Christian" (Geiger 1937:174–175). The missionaries urged the remaining mainland settlements in Guale to relocate onto the barrier islands, and established (or reestablished) mission settlements on Jekyll Island (Guadalquini), Sapelo Island (San José de Sápala), St. Simons Island (Santo Domingo de Asao), and St. Catherines Island (Santa Catalina de Guale). Still, mission population declined steadily throughout the seventeenth century, as a result of continuing epidemics, the removal of some people to St. Augustine for forced labor programs, increasing attacks against the coastal missions by English-supported interior Indians, and an endless trickle of Guale defectors to the interior. In most cases, single mission towns in the seventeenth century were the amalgam of several earlier towns.

But more critical to the success of the Franciscan venture was the ambitious expansion westward, beyond coastal Guale and Timucua into the interior, reaching the Potano and Utina in the early 1600s, then the western province of Apalachee, and eventually into distant Apalachicola (Figure 24-3). After the first exploratory contacts by de Soto and others, the Spanish made no attempt to missionize the Apalachee until 1608, when friars began visiting the easternmost villages. But owing to the lack of manpower and the considerable distance from St. Augustine, formal evangelization did not begin until 1633, when the first permanent missionaries were assigned to Apalachee, the religious vanguard that would establish a major Spanish presence for decades to come. Soldiers followed friars about five years later, lingering in Apalachee until 1651, when they were temporarily withdrawn at the insistence of the missionaries (Hann 1988:14).

The key problem facing the westward-looking colonists was that supplies, tribute, and trade goods had to be sent via a long overland route from St. Augustine to the garrisons and missions of Apalachee. The situation eased somewhat in 1639, when a port was established at St. Marks, enabling frigates to run between St. Augustine and the Apalachee coast in fewer than 13 days. Although the agricultural abundance of Apalachee could now more readily reach Spanish consumers in St. Augustine, these ships were also maneuvered by the missionaries to establish commercial trade of their own, which intensified the already bitter feelings between sacred and secular factions (Hann 1988:15–16).

The mission effort at Apalachee expanded dramatically in the 1640s, when more than 40 principal chiefs converted to Christianity and allowed doctrinas to be established in their villages (Hann 1988:16). As in Guale a half-century before, Apalachee Indian followers accepted, at least superficially, the stipulations of Hispanic Christianity. But as native populations dwindled in Guale and Timucua, the Spanish increased their labor demands upon the Apalachee. The Apalachee became increasingly anxious as their Spanish rulers gradually diminished the supply of gifts and favors to new converts, and the Apalachee leadership particularly objected to performing personal services for Spanish soldiers. This smoldering hostility burst forth in the animated assault of 1647, when rebellious non-Christian Apalachee assassinated three of the eight Franciscans stationed in the province, dismantling the seven principal missions in Apalachee and suspending all missionary work there.

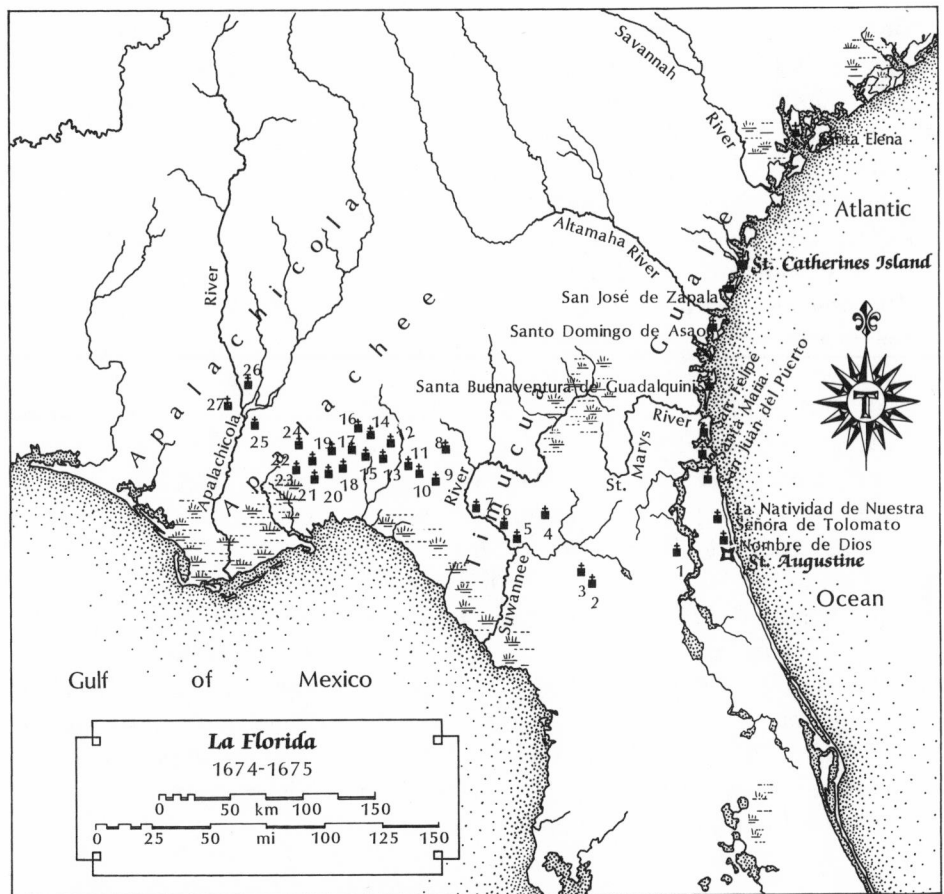

Figure 24-3. The mission system throughout La Florida at the time of Bishop Calderón's visitation, 1674–1675 (after Gannon 1965:64, facing): (1) San Diego de Salamototo, (2) San Francisco de Potano, (3) Santa Fé de Toloca, (4) Santa Catalina de Afuerica, (5) Santa Cruz de Ajohica, (6) Santa Cruz de Tarihica, (7) San Juan Guarcara, (8) Santa Elena de Machaba, (9) San Pedro de Potohiriba, (10) San Mateo, (11) San Miguel de Asile, (12) San Lorenzo de Ivitachuco, (13) La Concepción de Ayubale, (14) San Francisco de Oconi, (15) San Juan de Aspalaga, (16) San José de Ocuya, (17) San Pedro de Patali, (18) San Antonio de Bacuqua, (19) San Damian de Cupahica (also called Escambi), (20) San Luis de Talimali, (21) San Martín de Tomoli, (22) La Purificación de Tama, (23) Santa Cruz de Capoli, (24) Asunción del Puerto, (25) La Encarnación a la Santa Cruz de Sábacola, (26) San Carlos, (27) San Nicholás.

When peace was restored, Franciscans and Indians alike contended that the Spanish had provoked the revolt and criticized the overly severe retaliation visited upon the dissidents. The official postmortem exploring the causes of the 1547 rebellion further amplified the friction between the friars and the officials of St. Augustine, ultimately leading to the dismissal of Governor Rebolledo (Gannon, this volume).

At midcentury—the pinnacle of the so-called Golden Age—the Franciscans boasted that 26,000 Christianized Indians lived in La Florida, with 70 friars operating nearly 40 principal missions (Matter 1972:88, 106). But these figures are probably optimistic exaggerations produced by church officials (Boyd 1939:256; Geiger 1940:125–126; Serrano y Sanz 1912:132–133; Spellman 1965:361). Although 70 Franciscans were indeed authorized for La Florida by the Crown—and these are the numbers commonly cited in secondary sources—only a single document, a 1655 report by Díaz de la Calle, claims that such a large number actually served there at any one time (Lanning 1935:213, 264, n. 17; see also Matter 1972:345). A more realistic number would seem to range between 34 and 50 actually serving in La Florida at any single time.

The precarious peace was soon shattered by an eight-month rebellion that began in Timucua in 1656, but apparently did not spread to Apalachee (Gannon 1965:57–58; Hann 1988:22; Lanning 1935:169, 204–208; Matter 1972:107, 346; Sweett and Sheppy 1940:42). Missions were sacked and six friars fleeing Apalachee for Havana were drowned, thereby depriving La Florida of all missionaries acquainted with the Apalachee language. Many of the remaining Franciscans embarked upon a program of civil disobedience against the governor and refused to discipline the rebellious Indians.

La Florida received its second and long-awaited episcopal visitation when Bishop Don Gabriel Díaz Vara Calderón arrived in St. Augustine in August 1674. Calderón's record of his 10-month inspection tour is an unparalleled account of Spanish Florida in its prime (Wenhold 1937; see also Figure 24-3). He visited 36 major mission stations, locating each of the major missions with reasonable accuracy (Boyd 1948; Hann 1989). Like the visitation by Bishop Altamirano nearly seven decades earlier, Calderón's generated an uplifting sense of optimism throughout the mission communities.

Spanish–British Conflicts

But Spanish hegemony in La Florida was soon to be challenged by the English, who in 1670 had founded a settlement at Charles Town (South Carolina). The territory from there south to St. Augustine became a region of conflict and contention between England and Spain until 1763 and was regarded as a "debatable land" (Bolton and Ross 1925).

Spanish missions on the barrier islands of coastal Georgia were the first victims of this basically European conflict. In 1670 the English and Spanish agreed, through the Treaty of Madrid, that Britain might forever hold the areas in America and the West Indies that were already regarded to be in her possession. The British inferred that actual possession meant ownership, but the Spanish interpreted this agreement to mean that the line of the southern boundary of English lands was drawn at Port Royal in Carolina.

Spain's immediate response to the new British settlement was to launch an expedition to attack and destroy Charles Town. Although the expedition did destroy Port Royal, the Spanish fleet was disrupted by storms and forced to retreat southward without even threatening Charles Town. In 1671, the Spanish governor ordered that a 25-man garrison be established on St. Catherines Island. But the detachment did not long remain at that level, falling to 13 in 1672 and to 9 by 1675 (Matter 1972:192–195). At this point, the border towns became uneasy, and numerous Indian groups took to the road, many Yamassees taking up residence in long-abandoned Timucua. Some lingered in the Guale towns, speaking the Guale language and being considered relatives. Of 50 Indians sent from Guale to perform labor service at St. Augustine in 1673, fewer than 10 were Christian (Matter 1972:273–274).

The year 1680 was a turning point as the English began a steady push down the coast and across the interior toward the Mississippi. "For a decade the English cloud hovered over Santa Catalina, guardian of the Guale border. . . . The Guale missions were a menace, and their neophytes would make good slaves on Carolina plantations" (Bolton and Ross 1925:35). That year, a band of Chiscas, Creeks, and Cherokees armed by the English attacked Mission Santiago de Ocone (on Jekyll Island) and were thrown back. A few days later, they reappeared 300 strong at Santa Catalina. The lieutenant there was Capt. Francisco de Fuentes, housed with his five soldiers in the convento. Five of the six Indian guards were killed. Fuentes organized a defense with the 40 remaining warriors, 16 of whom possessed firearms. Fighting all day, they held off the enemy, withstanding siege in the fortified mission church for more than a day (Bolton and Ross 1925:36).

The defense of Santa Catalina seems to have been well planned and executed, although Fuentes took the almost unprecedented risk of placing firearms into the hands of Guale Indians (Lanning 1935:215–216). When Governor Salazar heard of this attack, he dispatched reinforcements from St. Augustine, but this force arrived after Santa Catalina had been abandoned. Father Juan de Uzeda, priest of the Indian parish of San José de Zápala (on Sapelo Island) gave a cool welcome to the refugees from Santa Catalina, and he was outraged when Fuentes requisitioned his and the church's private stores of corn earmarked for those erecting a fort there.

Considerable discussion ensued about how to get the people of Santa Catalina to return home, for the fields of St. Catherines were viewed as the breadbasket of St. Augustine. For some time, St. Catherines Island continued to be called "the frontier with the enemy," an empty title since the Guale refused to live there. Although 100 Canary Island families were assigned to move to St. Catherines Island, they never appeared. Nor would the Yamassee Indians living on Amelia Island agree to defend and farm the Spanish frontier.

As English attacks along the coast increased, the Spanish abandoned the coast from Cumberland Island northward. By 1683, the mission towns had been evacuated; those Guale Indians who did not choose to defect to the Carolina settlements or to hostile interior native groups were deposited in communities on or near Amelia/Fort George Island, and near St. Augustine. The Indians of Santa Catalina de Guale experienced peace at Santa María during the 1680s and 1690s, but they found neither the time nor the resources to complete the stockade for their own protection (Bushnell 1986:6–11). In 1702, Santa María was overrun by a detachment of Carolinians, Indians, and blacks from the invading army of James Moore. Captain Fuentes oversaw a second evacuation, ferrying church ornaments, women, and children over to San Juan del Puerto. But the Indians refused to stay with Fuentes, and those not fleeing into the woods eventually made their way to St. Augustine. During this period, other Guale Indians were also moved to several settlements near St. Augustine, where they could be drawn upon as laborers.

In six short years, Spain lost the entire province of Guale, after offering surprisingly little resistance. Although the governors of La Florida had been charged with the defense of the colony, the Crown had systematically failed to supply them with the tools necessary to the task.

English attacks were not restricted to the northern frontier of La Florida. Beginning in 1685, the British began attacking mission towns in Apalachee and Timucua. In 1701, the War of Spanish Succession fractured the uneasy peace between England and Spain. The next year, this conflict spilled into the New World (to be known in America as Queen Anne's War), dismantling the mission system throughout La Florida. The Floridian portion of Queen Anne's War commenced on May 20, 1702, when a band of Apalachicola Indians, apparently at the instigation of Governor Moore of South Carolina, burned the Christian town of Santa Fé in Timucua. Later that month, Governor Moore himself laid siege by land and sea to St. Augustine, destroying most of the town. Although Moore's land forces swept across the missions north of the St. Johns River, he failed to breach the sturdy coquina walls of the Castillo de San Marcos.

In early 1704, still smarting over his failure to purge the Spanish foothold at St. Augustine, Moore led a column of 50 whites and 1,000 Indians in attacking the missions of Apalachee. Afraid to leave St. Augustine defenseless, the Spanish governor refused to dispatch a relief column to Apalachee, and Moore ruthlessly dismantled the Apalachee missions.

During these repeated raids across Apalachee between 1701 and 1704, an estimated 3,000 Spanish Indians were killed, leaving only 200 Apalachee scattered across four villages. Hann (1988:227–236) isolates several factors beyond the obviously superior firepower of Moore's party to explain the ease with which these Englishmen and native allies could so thoroughly eradicate Spain's extensive mission system: irrational and ineffective leadership by the deputy the governor assigned to defend Apalachee, the increased demands of the labor repartimiento on the Apalachee Indians, disruptive influences of Spanish ranching and other commercial activities, alienation and demoralization resulting from unresolved promises for better treatment of the local Indians, and conflicts between the Apalachee and their Indian neighbors.

Apalachee Province remained abandoned until peace temporarily returned to La Florida in 1714. The province of Timucua, between Apalachee and St. Augustine, shared a similar fate when Carolinian Indians devastated the few remaining Timucuan missions in 1706. The once-extensive mission chain was reduced to a few sparsely populated settlements clinging about the base of Castillo San Marcos at St. Augustine (see Deagan, this volume).

When La Florida was ceded to England in 1763, even the sparse remnants of mission life had vanished. Although the Spanish flag flew over St. Augustine once again (from 1783 to 1821) the missions of La Florida were never successfully revitalized (Siebert 1940).

Hispanic Designs for La Florida's Missions

Like all Hispanic settlements in the New World, the missions of La Florida were viewed as an extension of idealized Iberian design, codified in 1573 when Philip II issued a comprehensive compilation of 148 ordinances dealing with all aspects of site selection, city planning, and political organization (Bushnell 1981:43; Crouch et al. 1982). Designed to remove town planning from the hands of military captains, the Laws of the Indies defined an urban tradition and spatial configuration that were repeated throughout the era of Spanish colonization.

The preferred Hispanic plan was a direct attempt to transplant a "civilized" lifeway upon a wilderness highly "frontier" in character. Clearly much of urban St. Augustine conformed with the ordinances (Deagan 1983:185–191). The sixteenth-century layout followed the standardized grid plan, the town lots corresponding almost exactly to the Spanish *pie* dimension (13.4 × 26.8 m), just as stipulated in the ordinances. But, as expected, the degree to which these a priori rules were actually translated into architectural reality varied considerably. In St. Augustine, the central plaza—hallmark of Spanish urban planning and a mainstay of the ordinances—may not have been constructed; moreover, the first church appears to have been built at the north end of sixteenth-century St. Augustine, in direct contradiction to the ordinance stipulating that the church be located closer to the coast. The founders of St. Augustine also gridded their town plan to conform to local patterns of drainage and microtopography; following the rigid urban plan set out in Philip II's decrees would have required a centralized plaza, usurping the residentially most desirable high ground. The public buildings of St. Augustine were similarly grouped on the better drained ridges at the northern end of town, rather than downtown.

What the Missions of La Florida Actually Looked Like

Although these royal decrees theoretically applied only to permanent civic settlements—not to temporary missions or military encampments—in practice there was little distinction between the two types of settlement in North America. The familiar ordinances were applied equally to urban centers and mission outposts (Bolton 1917:44; Crouch et al. 1982:28). In the strict sense, these missions incorporated an entire settlement—not just the religious edifices—defining a space in which tribal economies were reorganized, new crops and European methods of cultivation were introduced, and scattered native American groups were nucleated ("reduced") into new settlements where instruction included music, reading, and writing (Kubler 1940:6–7).

In La Florida, the combined environmental, political, and architectural realities conspired against the Southeastern missions—not a single shred of mission architecture today survives above-ground anywhere in Spanish Florida. Until very recently, our knowledge about the physical appearance of these mission complexes was derived almost exclusively from documentary evidence:

> The Spanish missions of Florida did not conform to the romantic notion of clois-
> tered lush gardens, tolling missions bells, handsome, striking churches set in
> peaceful, idyllic villages surrounded by bountiful fields and orchards and content-
> edly grazing livestock. . . . The chief impression gained from the few available
> documents . . . is one of stark realism, revealing crude buildings and few tools,
> poverty as well as plenty, war, discord, martyrdom, and toil by a handful of
> Spanish Franciscans, their Indian converts, and a few soldiers in a primitive wil-
> derness [Matter 1972:123–124].

Although Robert Matter's disenchanting account of Florida missions remains to
some degree valid, more recent archival and especially archaeological investigations suggest that mission architecture and town planning cannot be readily dismissed as simply "stark" and "crude." Today, the best information regarding
mission layout and town plan comes from the intensive archaeological investigations of mission sites such as Santa Catalina de Guale (Thomas 1987, 1988a,
1988b; see also Saunders, this volume) and San Luis de Talimali, the Spanish
administrative headquarters in Apalachee, home of one of the most important
Indian chiefs of the province, and the largest of the Apalachee missions (Boyd
et al. 1951; Hann 1988:194–226; Shapiro 1987; see also the chapters by Jones, Shapiro, Hann, this volume). Our present knowledge regarding mission architecture in La Florida is summarized in a subsequent paper by Saunders. Despite
a flurry of archaeological activity during the past decade, she correctly emphasizes the limited scope of most excavations, the need for finer chronological control, and the overall paucity of reliable architectural data. For most missions in
Spanish Florida, architectural reconstruction still unfortunately relies heavily on
informed conjecture and analogy to better-known examples from the western
borderlands or Latin America. The true degree of architectural standardization
and variability remains anybody's guess at this point.

Hann (1988:212–217) and Bushnell (1990) have discussed the church furnishings of La Florida. Although their accounts differ in some specifics, it is clear
that despite the sometimes impoverished frontier setting, the churches of the
late seventeenth century in La Florida were well endowed with the fixtures and
provisions required for proper worship.

Aside from the church and convento complex, the most striking feature of the
La Florida mission was the council house (or *buhío*), a traditional Southeastern
architectural construction without parallel elsewhere in the borderlands. In his
1674–1675 visitation, Bishop Calderón described the "typical" council house as
round, constructed of wood, covered with straw, and open at the top: "Most
of them can accommodate from 2,000 to 3,000 persons." Calderón's remarkable
characterization was viewed with skepticism by most Southeastern scholars. But
the recent discovery and excavation of the council house at San Luis have erased
all doubt because the archaeological remains of this *buhío* are fully 36 meters in
diameter—easily approximating Calderón's estimate. The compelling excavations of the San Luis council house are discussed by Shapiro and Hann (this
volume).

Bishop Calderón described the native dwellings in Apalachee as round in
form, "of straw, without a window and with a door and a *vara* high and a half

a *vara* wide. On one side is a granary supported by 12 beams, which they call a *garita*, where they store the wheat, corn and other things they harvest" (Wenhold 1938:12–13). The public granary at San Luis in the mid-1680s has been briefly described:

> Once [the] produce is collected, it is to be placed in the community storehouse, of which the principal cacique is to have one key and the other, the elder whom the lieutenant of this province names; and its distribution is to be in assistance of the poor orphans and widows, who do not plant a field for themselves and in order to feed the soldiers who go on the service of His Majesty; and in order to buy some ornaments for the church as well as to purchase hoes and hatchets for the service of the council houses and the work of the said field [Joaquin de Fiorencía, translated by Hann 1988:209].

Cemeteries were also a conspicuous feature of mission life, reflecting the importance attached by the friars to proper Christian burials as an outward sign of true conversion. The resulting mortuary patterning is thus highly informative about conditions in the missions of La Florida, and recent archaeological excavations are providing new data regarding the remarkable variability in mortuary practices within Spanish Florida (Thomas 1988b:110–114; see also Marrinan 1985; Shapiro and Jones, this volume). Today, our information derives from roughly half a dozen mission cemeteries—places in which Christian Indians were interred—plus data from Nuestra Señora de la Soledad (in downtown St. Augustine), an urban baseline showing how colonial Spaniards buried one another in La Florida.

During the seventeenth century, the Soledad cemetery was located near one of the primary parishes of St. Augustine, with some graves apparently excavated into the church floor, and others concentrated in a *campo santo* adjacent to the church (Koch 1980, 1983). The mission cemeteries were likewise closely associated with churches, but the pattern varies surprisingly from mission to mission. In our excavations at Mission Santa Catalina (Larsen 1990; Thomas 1987, 1988a), 400 to 450 Indians were found buried beneath the church, and no graves are known from anywhere else in the mission compound (although excavations are continuing). Burials were also placed inside the church at Patale, with some of the interments apparently made after the building had collapsed. The remaining known cemeteries throughout the Apalachee and Timucuan missions consisted of a distinctive *campo santo*, sometimes enclosed by an open structure and commonly spaced 15 to 30 m from the church (see the chapters by Saunders and Jones and Shapiro, this volume).

Likewise, orientation and burial posture seem consistent between the St. Augustine cemetery and its mission outposts. Citizens of St. Augustine usually buried their dead with head oriented to the east, and arms crossed on the chest (Koch 1983:203), a characteristic "Christian" posture recognized at all the known mission cemeteries throughout La Florida. The exact orientation varies somewhat, but most such graves were positioned parallel to the primary mission axis; the observed variability in grave orientation probably reflects only different site orientations rather than deviations from mortuary practices per se.

The burials of Spaniards in St. Augustine were highly standardized. The corpse was wrapped in a simple shroud, without grave goods, although occasionally an embellished coffin was used. Only one of the First Spanish period (pre-1763) graves at Soledad contained any grave goods at all; Burial 16 was accompanied by a silver crucifix and a rosary, and Koch (1983:224) properly speculates that this individual was a parish priest. These simple pauperlike burials reflect the Hispanic Catholic customs prevalent in the sixteenth and seventeenth centuries (Foster 1960:144).

The same is true for some of the mission cemeteries (Thomas 1988b). Grave goods were absent or rare in many of the *campos santos* of Apalachee and Timucua, and the more than 100 burials excavated at Nombre de Dios were also accompanied by relatively few artifacts. But some mission cemeteries contained large and impressive grave assemblages. An extraordinarily rich inventory was found associated with graves beneath the church at Mission Santa Catalina, and numerous artifacts were also recovered at Patale I and San Damian de Escambi; very limited test excavations in the mission cemetery at San Luis suggest that at least some neophytes were buried with considerable grave goods.

Although the Catholic continuities are readily understood, we are at present unable to account for the extreme variability in mortuary practices between the urban context at St. Augustine and the various satellite missions. Doubtless part of this diversity is due to the differential sample sizes involved, and in no case has a single cemetery been adequately excavated to disclose the overall mortuary pattern.

At Mission Santa Catalina, we found that the highest-quality grave goods were clustered near the altar, with the value of specific items trailing off as distance from the altar increased (Thomas 1988b). This pattern certainly suggests variability due to status differentiation, but one must avoid the overly simplistic "high-status/low-status" dichotomy to explain such patterning. A rigid status hierarchy pervaded all aspects of life in La Florida, where "people differentiate themselves wherever there are disparities of background or belongings to be envied or flaunted" (Bushnell 1981:15). In St. Augustine, status was conditioned by wealth, social position, race, and place of birth, among other factors (Deagan 1983:30).

The cemeteries of La Florida also undoubtedly reflect one's perceived "status" relative to God. Some cemeteries were divided into districts for the holy and the unholy (Koch 1983:220), with placement inside the church conditioned by dichotomies such as clergy–lay person, blessed–unblessed, single–married, child–adult, and poor–affluent. Speaking of burial practices in St. Augustine, Bushnell (1981:26) noted that "even after death there were class distinctions. The hidalgo was buried in a private crypt. . . . Other plots of consecrated earth were priced at three or four ducats. A slave's final resting place cost one ducat, and a pauper was laid away free."

We are only now beginning to appreciate the multiplicity of factors reflected in mortuary variability throughout the cemeteries of La Florida. Research in this important direction has just begun.

Hispanic Strategies of Conversion and Coercion

Hispanic designs are likewise reflected in their modified "reduction" strategy for the Indians of La Florida. In missions throughout the New World, the friars commonly "reduced" the Indian community, congregating scattered and sometimes seasonally nomadic native populations into mission centers, where the aboriginal spiritual needs could be attended year-round. Although relatively little is known about precontact village patterning of La Florida, apparently the friars working in this province accommodated more to the existing aboriginal pattern, setting up their doctrinas in or near the principal village of the district, and from there reaching outlying groups in nearby subordinate villages (Hann 1986). But once the primary mission had been established, and a nucleus of Christian Indians converted, the missionaries began exerting pressure not only to keep converted Indians within the mission proper, but also to move new Indian groups into the doctrina.

Bushnell (this volume) argues that in La Florida, such qualified reduction transcended indisputable economic considerations. While it is true that increased sedentism would indeed establish the foundation for intensifying agricultural productivity, the rationale for restricting mobility was to induce a "deeper cultural command": the necessity for all Catholics to live within physical reach of the sacraments, "like rational beings." The so-called sacramental imperative—the pledge to attend weekly Mass and obligatory feast days—hence prescribed that Christianized Indians live in fixed settlements within earshot of the all-important church bell.

Probably because of the marked social stratification of precontact societies in La Florida, such centralized administration of Indian towns fared somewhat better than equivalent attempts in the Caribbean (Deagan 1978:298, 1985). In Spanish Florida, both missionaries and secular officials attempted, where possible, to work through the existing aboriginal political structure. In fact, the failure to do so contributed directly to the 1597 rebellion in Guale (see above), and also the 1656 rebellion in the western Timucuan area (Boyd et al. 1951; Bushnell 1979). Converting caciques to Christianity was considered the utmost priority. Especially during the sixteenth century, priests performed marriages between Spanish soldiers and high-ranking Indian women, Pedro Menéndez de Avilés himself taking on an Indian consort (implying that such intermarriage was itself viewed as a viable means of spreading Hispanic hegemony; see also references cited in Deagan 1978:299).

Bushnell (1989) suggests a provocative mechanism for such control. She argues that seventeenth-century La Florida should be viewed as two symbiotic republics: the Republic of Spaniards and a separate, separately administered Republic of Indians (see also McAlister 1984:391–395). According to Crown dictum, the two republics were to be united only in allegiance to the Crown and obedience to the true faith. Otherwise, they were to be strictly separated, spatially, socially, and bureaucratically.

The Republic of Indians, less centralized than the Spanish counterpart, consisted of cacique and headmen (considered by the Spanish to be a town council). The formal means of communication was the annual *visita*, or tour of inspection, by the governor or a representative, with notaries dutifully transcribing the proceedings (e.g., Pearson 1974). It is clear that the caciques wielded real power, as they had the authority to have secular officials and even friars reassigned (Bushnell 1989:139). Like their Spanish counterparts the hidalgos, caciques and headmen were to be exempt from taxation, manual labor, and corporal punishment, and were permitted to carry swords and ride horses. Such Indian officials were supported by the communal planting of specifically designated, communally tended fields. In effect, the governor ensured authority, and the cacique delivered labor.

Economic Realities in the Florida Missions

The enterprise of La Florida never achieved self-sufficiency, and considerable financial and logistic support was required from the Spanish Crown. Beginning in 1570, a regular annual royal subsidy, termed the *situado*, was created to support the Florida colony. Initially, this obligation was paid from Panama and later Havana, but the burden was shifted to the royal treasury of Mexico City in 1592 (Bushnell 1981:64). A persistent theme running through the seventeenth-century administrative texts in La Florida is the failure of the annual situado to arrive in time, and in adequate amounts (Bushnell 1981; Matter 1973:22; see also Loucks 1979; Reitz and Scarry 1985). Officially, the situado was allocated to cover the pay, subsistence, and clothing of the soldiers and friars, plus the salary of the royal officials and governors. This annual subsidy from Mexico also contributed gifts and rewards for elite Indian leaders; "they accepted this bounty as no more than their due, and when presents were delayed, loyalty faltered" (Bushnell 1989:137).[3]

Complaining bitterly about the poor soil conditions around St. Augustine and elsewhere, the Spanish nevertheless depended heavily upon Indian-supplied agricultural products, particularly maize (and in Apalachee, to some degree, wheat). Jonathan Dickinson commented on how many Indians kept hogs and chickens (Andrews and Andrews 1975). Several chapters in this section (particularly those by Larsen et al., Reitz, and Ruhl) summarize the growing archaeological and biocultural evidence available regarding subsistence at these missions.

Within the mission villages, Indians were expected to sow separate fields as support for the priesthood, and to help purchase the necessities of proper worship. Other fields were tilled to support the widowed and poor, and the military. Spaniards viewed local Indian populations as a ready labor pool, to be exploited in exchange for defense, Christianity, and other alleged advantages of Iberian society. Owing largely to their productivity and inaccessibility by direct water routes, much of this burden fell upon the Apalachee people, particularly as the native populations of Guale and Timucua wasted away. Participation in such labor repartimiento not only took men away from their families for prolonged periods of time, but created a serious health risk because it exposed the Apalachee to new diseases in St. Augustine—to say nothing of the physical abuse resulting from carrying heavy loads on their backs for 200 miles. Debate over such abuses further strained the relations between civil and church authorities.

A prosperous livestock industry blossomed in the western provinces during fairly early mission times. Apalachee-raised hogs were marketed at relatively low prices in St. Augustine in the 1670s, although when Spaniards forcefully cornered the hog market, prices inflated rapidly (Hann 1988:136). Meat was supplied to St. Augustine from cattle ranches in Timucua; hides and tallow from Apalachee were exported to Havana. In 1681, one Havana-bound ship, loaded at the Apalachee port of St. Marks, contained 700 cow hides; In 1685, another carried 100 chickens, 110 hams, 35 jars of lard, 300 deerskins, 44 bushels of corn, and 60 arrobas of pine tar (Hann 1988:137). Although Spanish officials directed that duties be collected on visiting ships to Apalachee, there is little evidence that such taxes were actually collected (Bushnell 1981:81–82).

La Florida in the seventeenth century clearly failed to live up to the expectations of Pedro Menéndez de Avilés, who had envisioned a flourishing land of precious metals, pearls, wine, cattle, and grain. Although there can be no question that the mission enterprise suffered at times from lack of support, there is evidence that Franciscan missions sometimes became relatively prosperous. In the late 1600s, Governor Diego de Quiroga y Losada complained to the king about unfair competition from the friars (Matter 1972:156), who refused to sell corn to the infantry stationed in Apalachee. The governor emphasized some of the Franciscan advantages in commerce: The Indians tilled the soil at no cost to the friars; a good share of the tobacco, swine, chickens, and vegetables raised by the Indians were sold at market in St. Augustine (the profit going into the friars' coffers); the friars even bartered this merchandise of unpaid Indian labor with ships that came to port in Apalachee. Although the Franciscans responded that such commerce was required to supply the necessary church furnishings, the governor insisted that the corn be supplied to support the local garrison. Matter (1973:37) felt that "the evidence suggests that the missionaries, living among and dominating or greatly influencing their Christian converts, perhaps generally ate better than most other Spaniards in Florida." Examination of the limited archaeological remains available to date from Florida's missions seems to support Matter's suspicions (Reitz, this volume; Thomas 1988b).

Primarily through the mission system, the Europeans intensified Indian farming by introducing new crops and techniques. Recent biocultural research has demonstrated the increased intensity of maize agriculture during the Mission period. Mortuary samples from coastal Georgia strongly suggest that prehistoric populations adopted a mixed economy, based at least in part on maize agriculture. The evidence currently available likewise indicates that a maize diet exacts a physical toll, significantly reducing the quality of life among the Indians of La Florida (Larsen 1982, 1984, 1990; see also Larsen et al., this volume). Skeletal infections increased dramatically. People—especially women—became shorter. Both deciduous and permanent teeth became smaller. Bones became more fragile (and could not withstand as much bending and torsional stress). Teeth—especially those of women—started to decay. About the only improvement occurred at the joints; people suffered less degeneration of the elbow and knee, and of the upper and lower back. The Mission period Guale Indians were, without question, subjected to a series of biological stresses, including (but not limited to) epidemics, food shortages, and military action by both Spanish and British forces. Some degree of increased sedentism and demographic nucleation, coupled with intensification of horticulture undoubtedly resulted in related disease and nutritional stresses.

The dramatic changes wrought by the introduction of corn growing can be traced back well into the precontact period, but conditions were made considerably worse upon the arrival of the missionaries, particularly because of the periodic food shortages, reduced dietary diversity, co-opting of stored foodstuffs to feed the European colonists, demographic decline due to European diseases, and an increased work load demanded as tribute to support Spanish colonists.

Sacred vs. Secular in Spanish La Florida

Throughout the so-called Golden Age, relations between civil and church authorities were marred by discord and disorder (Matter 1972; Gannon, this volume). The governors, as military men, felt that the colony's first priority was defense; accordingly, a greater proportion of the annual situado should be withheld from the missions, to be applied to defense-related expenditures. Conflict also arose over the number of troops needed to defend the frontier mission towns. Many such disagreements reflected the long-standing friction regarding the appropriate friar/soldier ratio. For bureaucratic purposes, Franciscans were listed on the military roles, and the friars were supposed to receive soldiers' pay from the situado. The governors hence viewed these noncombatants as "taking up" soldiers' spaces in La Florida. But the friars apparently enjoyed more success in persuading the Crown of their needs, since the Franciscan strength generally increased whereas the number of effective soldiers remained static or declined.

Such financial and logistical skirmishes raged throughout the seventeenth century. Ill will also arose regarding the details of jurisdiction and authority over mission Indians. The most important of these early jurisdictional confrontations involved charges and countercharges stemming from the Guale rebellion of 1597 (Geiger 1937:104–105, 122–123; Matter 1972:207; Sweett and Sheppy 1940:28, 31–32). In 1598, Governor Gonzalo Menéndez de Canzo informed the Crown that the Franciscans had been martyred largely because the friars had attempted to usurp civil jurisdiction over local Indian factions; Canzo also argued that only he, not the friars, should communicate directly with the Crown regarding affairs of state. The Franciscans countered that they, too, deserved direct access to the Crown, and blamed the governor's inexperience for escalating the rebellion. The pope, they claimed, had granted them the right to invest mission Indians with positions of authority; in effect, they considered themselves both governor and bishop of their parishes, answerable only to the religious superiors of their order (Geiger 1937:189–193). This, and similar disputes convinced Robert Matter that "the jurisdictional conflict underlay all or most of the church–state dissension in Florida. Strong, dedicated, zealous, and jealous men on both sides, acutely aware of their own powers, and sensitive to any real or imagined infringement on them, were unable to subordinate personal animosities, prejudices, and ambitions to compromise on the practical exercise of power and authority over the subjected aboriginies [sic]" (1972:245).

Friars also bickered with civil authorities over the treatment and exploitation of the Christian Indian populations, particularly by troops assigned to mission duty. Even before the arrival of the Franciscans, Governor Pedro Menéndez de Avilés clashed with the Jesuit superior over his policy of stationing troops to defend the missions. But despite Jesuit and Franciscan attempts to shield the Indians from colonial and military abuses, the situation had nearly reversed in the late seventeenth century, with governors and subordinates defending the Indians against the excesses of the missionaries. Such disputes over military and religious priorities reflected deep-seated differences in perception about the true role of the mission system: as strictly agent of the Church or as an ingredient of a presidio system designed to conquer and safeguard new frontiers.

The role of the third constituent in this equation—the Native Americans of La Florida—although only dimly reflected in the surviving documentary record, remains a most worthwhile topic for archaeological and ethnohistorical consideration in the future.

Acknowledgments

I gratefully acknowledge the welcome and necessary assistance of Margot Dembo, Todd Himstead, and Lorann S. A. Pendleton. I also thank Amy Turner Bushnell, Eugene Lyon, and Jerald T. Milanich for comments on this manuscript.

Notes

1. Hispanic jurisdiction over La Florida divides into two periods. The First Spanish period begins with the founding of St. Augustine in 1565 and ends in 1763 with the Treaty of Paris, when Florida was ceded to England. A Second Spanish period, which arose in 1783 when East Florida was ceded back to Spain, lasted until 1821, at which time Florida was transferred to the United States.

2. We distinguish here between *secular* and *regular* priests. "Secular" clergy work in geographically defined parishes, under the jurisdiction of a bishop. "Regular" priests, so called because they are subject to a Rule, or "regula," belong to a religious order (such as Jesuit or Franciscan) and are assigned to special duty, particularly missionization. Only "regular" priests take vows of poverty, chastity, and obedience (Gannon 1965:xiv; see also Harkins, this volume).

3. Until recently, the economic picture of Spanish Florida was surmised from so-called literary accounts, verbal rather than enumerative reports, such as administrative correspondence, reports of investigations, and so forth, in which statistical data appear only incidentally (Sluiter 1985:1, n. 4). Such qualitative, judgmental documents created a widely held opinion that the annual subsidy (the *situado*) was erratic, often left unpaid for years on end (e.g., Chatelain

1941:21). But significant primary documentation that has recently surfaced suggests that the situado was indeed paid with considerable regularity (Hoffman 1973; Sluiter 1985). Spanish treasury accounts, now available for the period 1571–1651, show that the only significant disruption in the situado took place between 1636 through 1648, when the internal Mexican economy faltered. Sluiter does not, however, examine other fiscal disruptions such as the costs of loss and leakage, bribes, prolonged per diems and lawsuits, sequestration, malfeasance, piracy, shipwrecks, debased coinage, or interest, including the discounting of wage certificates (Amy Turner Bushnell, personal communication).

Chronology: Key Dates in the History of the La Florida Missions

1521	Priests accompany Ponce de León.
1526	Lucas Vásquez de Ayllón attempts to establish missions with Dominican priests.
1527	Pánfilo de Narváez expedition includes five Franciscan friars and a number of secular priests.
1539–1540	De Soto expedition includes eight secular and four regular priests, but ecclesiastical impact is minimal.
1566	Jesuits establish missions among the Calusa and Tequesta Indians in South Florida.
1566–1567	Juan Pardo, in the company of Jesuits, attempts missionization west of Santa Elena; these interior outposts abandoned in 1572.
1570	Father Segura establishes the Ajacán mission in the Chesapeake Bay region; all priests killed less than five months after arrival.
1572	Society of Jesus quits La Florida, and Pedro Menéndez turns to the Franciscan order.
1595	Spanish officials estimate that 1,500 Christian Indians are living in La Florida.
1597	Rebellion breaks out in Guale and five Franciscans are killed; Phillip III considers abandoning La Florida.
1605	Franciscan missionaries return to Guale coast and Bishop makes visitation in 1606.
1607	Some of the Apalachee ask Spaniards to send missionaries.
1608	The first Franciscans welcomed at Ivitachuco (Apalachee).
1612	Spanish authorities reject the Apalachee's request for a permanent mission.
1633	First two friars arrive to establish a permanent mission presence among the Apalachee.
1647	Rebellion in Apalachee.
1650	Franciscans boast that 26,000 Christianized Indians live in La Florida, with 70 friars operating nearly 40 principal missions; rebellion in Timucua.
1670	British establish colony at Charles Town (South Carolina).
1674–1675	Long-awaited episcopal visitation by Bishop Don Gabriel Díaz Vara Calderón, who visits 36 major mission stations and favorably reports on conditions in La Florida.

1675	Garrison established on St. Catherines Island.
1680	British launch unsuccessful attack on Mission Santiago de Ocone, then attack and force abandonment of Mission Santa Catalina de Guale.
1685	British begin attacking mission towns in Apalachee and Timucua.
1702	Moore's forces attack Christian town of Santa Fé in Timucua, then lay siege to St. Augustine, but fail to breach Castillo de San Marcos.
1704	Moore leads 50 whites and 1,000 Indians in an attack on the missions of Apalachee, thoroughly eradicating the mission system of La Florida.
1763	La Florida ceded to England.

References

Andrews, Evangeline W., and Charles McL. Andrews (editors)
 1975   *Jonathan Dickinson's Journal or God's Protecting Providence.* Valentine Books, Stuart, Florida.
Arnade, Charles W.
 1959   *Florida on Trial, 1593–1602.* University of Miami Press, Coral Gables.
Barcía, Andrés González de
 1951   *Barcía's Chronological History of the Continent of Florida*, translated by Anthony Kerrigan. University of Florida Press, Gainesville.
Barrientos, Bartolomé
 1965   *Pedro Menéndez de Avilés, Founder of Florida*, translated by Anthony Kerrigan. University of Florida Press, Gainesville.
Bennett, Charles E. (editor)
 1975   *Three Voyages, René Laudonnière.* University Presses of Florida, Gainesville.
Bolton, Herbert E.
 1917   The Mission as a Frontier Institution in the Spanish-American Colonies. *American Historical Review* 23:42–61.
 1921   *The Spanish Borderlands: A Chronicle of Old Florida and the Southwest.* Yale University Press, New Haven.
Bolton, Herbert E., and Mary Ross
 1925   *The Debatable Land.* University of California Press, Berkeley.
Boyd, Mark F.
 1939   Spanish Mission Sites in Florida. *Florida Historical Quarterly* 17:254–280.
 1948   Enumeration of Florida Spanish Missions in 1675. *Florida Historical Quarterly* 27(2):181–188.
Boyd, Mark F., Hale G. Smith, and John W. Griffin
 1951   *Here They Once Stood: The Tragic End of the Apalachee Missions.* University of Florida Press, Gainesville.
Brinton, Daniel G.
 1969   [1859] *Notes on the Floridian Peninsula, Its Literary History, Indian Tribes and Antiquities.* Joseph Sabin, Philadelphia.
Bushnell, Amy
 1978   That Demonic Game: The Campaign to Stop Indian Pelota Playing in Spanish Florida, 1675–1684. *The Americas* 35:1–19.
 1979   Patricio de Hinachuba: Defender of the Word of God, the Crown of the King, and the Little Children of Ivitachuco. *American Indian Culture and Research Journal* 3:1–21.
 1981   *The King's Coffer: Proprietors of the Spanish Florida Treasury 1565–1702.* University of Florida Press, Gainesville.
 1986   *Santa María in the Written Record.* Florida State Museum Department of Anthropology Miscellaneous Project Report Series No. 21. Gainesville.

1989   Ruling "the Republic of Indians" in Seventeenth-century Florida. In *Powhatan's Mantle: Indians in the Colonial Southeast*, edited by Peter H. Wood, Gregory A. Waselkov, and M. Thomas Hatley, pp. 134–150. University of Nebraska Press, Lincoln.

1990   *The Archaeology of Mission Santa Catalina de Guale: 2. The Support and Supplying of the Seventeenth-Century Doctrina.* Anthropological Papers of the American Museum of Natural History, in press.

Chatelain, Verne E.

1941   *The Defenses of Spanish Florida, 1565 to 1763.* Carnegie Institution of Washington Publication No. 511.

Conner, Jeanette Thurber (editor)

1927   *Jean Ribault, The Whole and True Discovery of Terra Florida.* Florida State Historical Society, Deland.

Covington, James W.

1972   Apalachee Indians, 1704–1763. *Florida Historical Quarterly* 50:366–384.

Crawford, James M.

1975   Southeastern Indian Languages. In *Studies in Southeastern Indian Languages*, edited by James M. Crawford, pp. 1–120. University of Georgia Press, Athens.

Crook, Morgan R., Jr.

1986   *Mississippi Period Archaeology of the Georgia Coastal Zone.* University of Georgia Laboratory of Archaeology Series Report No. 23. Athens.

Crouch, Dora P., Daniel J. Garr, and Axel I. Mundigo

1982   *Spanish City Planning in North America.* MIT Press, Cambridge.

Davis, T. Frederick

1935   Juan Ponce de León's Voyages to Florida. *Florida Historical Quarterly* 14:3–70.

Deagan, Kathleen

1978   Cultures in Transition: Fusion and Assimilation among the Eastern Timucua. In *Tacachale: Essays on the Indians of Florida and Southeastern Georgia during the Historic Period*, edited by Jerald Milanich and Samuel Proctor, pp. 89–119. University Presses of Florida, Gainesville.

1979   *Timucua 1580: Research and Exhibit Plan for a 1580 Timucua Village near St. Augustine, Florida Reconstruction ca. 1580.* St. Augustine Restoration Foundation, St. Augustine.

1983   *Spanish St. Augustine: The Archaeology of a Colonial Creole Community.* Academic Press, New York.

1985   Spanish-Indian Interaction in Sixteenth-century Florida and Hispaniola. In *Cultures in Contact: The European Impact on Native Cultural Institutions in Eastern North America, A.D. 1000–1800*, edited by William W. Fitzhugh, pp. 281–318. Smithsonian Institution Press, Washington, D.C.

DePratter, Chester B., C. M. Hudson, and M. T. Smith

1983   The Route of Juan Pardo's Explorations in the Interior Southeast, 1566–1568. *Florida Historical Quarterly* 62(2):125–158.

DePratter, Chester B., and Marvin T. Smith

1980   Sixteenth Century European Trade in the Southeastern United States: Evidence from the Juan Pardo Expeditions (1566–1568). In *Spanish Colonial Frontier Research*, edited by Henry F. Dobyns, pp. 67–77. Center for Anthropological Studies, Albuquerque.

Dobyns, Henry F.

1983   *Their Number Become Thinned: Native American Population Dynamics in Eastern North America.* University of Tennessee Press, Knoxville.

Ehrmann, W. W.

1940   The Timucuan Indians of Sixteenth-century Florida. *Florida Historical Quarterly* 18:168–191.

Elvas, Gentleman of

1907   The Narrative of the Expedition of Hernando De Soto, by the Gentleman of Elvas.

In *Spanish Explorers in the Southern United States, 1528–1543. Original Narratives of Early American History*. Charles Scribner's Sons, New York.

Fairbanks, Charles H.
1985　From Exploration to Settlement: Spanish Strategies for Colonization. In *Alabama and the Borderlands: From Prehistory to Statehood*, edited by R. Reid Badger and Lawrence A. Clayton, pp. 128–139. University of Alabama Press, University.

Fernandez de Oviedo y Valdés, Gonzalo
1851　*History of the Indies*. Madrid.

Foster, George M.
1960　*Culture and Conquest: America's Spanish Heritage*. Viking Fund Publications in Anthropology No. 27. Wenner-Gren Foundation for Anthropological Research, New York.

Gannon, Michael V.
1965　*The Cross in the Sand: The Early Catholic Church in Florida*. University of Florida Press, Gainesville.

García, Genaro
1902　*Dos Antiguas Relaciones de la Florida*. J. Aguilar Vera y Compania, Mexico.

Gatschet, Albert S.
1878　The Timucua Language. *Proceedings of the American Philosophical Society* 17:490–504.

Geiger, Maynard
1937　The Franciscan Conquest of Florida. *Studies in Hispanic-American History 1*. Catholic University of America, Washington, D.C.
1940　*Biographical Dictionary of the Franciscans in Spanish Florida and Cuba (1528–1841)*. Franciscan Studies 21.

Goggin, John M., and William C. Sturtevant
1964　The Calusa: A Stratified, Nonagricultural Society (with notes on sibling marriage). In *Explorations in Cultural Anthropology: Essays in Honor of George Peter Murdock*, edited by Ward H. Goodenough, pp. 197–219. McGraw-Hill, New York.

Granberry, Julian
1971　Final Collation of Texts, Vocabularly Lists, Grammar, of Timucua for Publication. *American Philosophical Society, Yearbook 1970*, pp. 606–607.
1987　*A Grammar and Dictionary of the Timucuan Language*. Anthropological Notes 1. Horseshoe Beach, Florida.

Haas, Mary R.
1958　A New Linguistic Relationship in North America: Algonkian and the Gulf Languages. *Southwestern Journal of Anthropology* 14:231–264.
1971　Southeastern Indian Linguistics. In *Red, White, and Black: Symposium on Indians in the Old South*, edited by Charles Hudson, pp. 44–54. University of Georgia Press, Athens.
1978　The Position of Apalachee in the Muskogean Family. In *Language, Culture, and History: Essays by Mary R. Haas*. Stanford University Press, Palo Alto.

Hakluyt, Richard
1903a　*The Principal Navigations, Voyages, Traffiques and Discoveries of the English Nation, Made by Sea or Overland to the Remote Furthest Quarters of the Earth*, vol. 8 (1600). James MacLehose, Glasgow.
1903b　*The Principal Navigations, Voyages, Traffiques and Discoveries of the English Nation*, vol. 9 (1600). James MacLehose, Glasgow.

Hann, John H.
1986　Demographic Patterns and Changes in Mid-seventeenth Century Timucua and Apalachee. *Florida Historical Quarterly* 64:371–392.
1988　*Apalachee: The Land between the Rivers*. University of Florida Press, Gainesville.
1989　Summary Guide to Spanish Florida Missions and Visitas with Churches in the Sixteenth and Seventeenth Centuries. *The Americas*, in press.

Henige, David
1986   Primary Source by Primary Source? On the Role of Epidemics in New World Depopulation. *Ethnohistory* 33:293–312.

Hilton, W.
1911   A Relation of a Discovery by William Hilton [1664]. In *Original Narratives of Early
American History*, edited by A. S. Salley, vol. 15, pp. 37–61. Charles Scribner's Sons,
New York.

Hoffman, Paul E.
1973   A Study of Florida Defense Costs, 1565–1585: A Quantification of Florida History.
Florida Historical Quarterly 51:401–422.
1984   The Chicora Legend and Franco-Spanish Rivalry in La Florida. *Florida Historical
Quarterly* 62:419–438.

Hudson, Charles
1976   *The Southeastern Indians*. University of Tennessee Press, Knoxville.

Jones, Charles Colcock, Jr.
1873   *Antiquities of the Southern Indians, Particularly of the Georgia Tribes*. D. Appleton,
New York.

Jones, Grant
1978   The Ethnohistory of the Guale Coast through 1684. In *The Anthropology of St. Catherines Island: 1. Natural and Cultural History*, edited by David Hurst Thomas et al.
Anthropological Papers of the American Museum of Natural History 55(2):178–210.
1980   Guale Indians of the Southeastern United States Coast. In *Georgia Geological Survey, Department of Natural Resources, Guidebook*, edited by James D. Howard, Chester
B. DePratter, and Robert W. Frey, pp. 215–224. Athens.

Koch, Joan K.
1980   *Nuestra Señora de la Soledad: A Study of a Church and Hospital Site in Colonial St. Augustine*. Unpublished Master's thesis, Florida State University. Tallahassee.
1983   Mortuary Behavior Patterning and Physical Anthropology in Colonial St. Augustine. In *Spanish St. Augustine: The Archaeology of a Colonial Creole Community* by Kathleen Deagan, pp. 187–227. Academic Press, New York.

Kubler, George
1940   *The Religious Architecture of New Mexico*. Taylor Museum, Colorado Springs.

Lanning, John Tate
1935   *The Spanish Missions of Georgia*. University of North Carolina Press, Chapel Hill.

Larsen, Clark Spencer
1982   *The Anthropology of St. Catherines Island: 3. Prehistoric Human Biological Adaptation*.
Anthropological Papers of the American Museum of Natural History 57(3):155–270.
1984   Health and Disease in Prehistoric Georgia: The Transition to Agriculture. In *Paleopathology at the Origins of Agriculture*, edited by Mark N. Cohen and George J.
Armelagos, pp. 367–392. Academic Press, New York.

Larsen, Clark Spencer (editor)
1990   *The Archaeology of Mission Santa Catalina de Guale: 2. Biocultural Interpretations of a
Population in Transition*. Anthropological Papers of the American Museum of Natural
History, in press.

Larson, Lewis H.
1969   Aboriginal Subsistence Technology on the Southeastern Coastal Plain during the
Late Prehistoric Period. Unpublished Ph.D. dissertation, Department of Anthropol-
ogy, University of Michigan, Ann Arbor.
1978   Historic Guale Indians of the Georgia Coast and the Impact of the Spanish Mission
Effort. In *Tacachale: Essays on the Indians of Florida and Southeastern Georgia during the
Historic Period*, edited by Jerald Milanich and Samuel Proctor, pp. 120–140. University
Presses of Florida, Gainesville.

1980   *Aboriginal Subsistence Technology on the Southeastern Coastal Plain during the Late Pre-historic Period*. University of Florida Press, Gainesville.

Le Moyne, Jacques
1875   *Narrative of Le Moyne, an Artist Who Accompanied the French Expedition to Florida under Laudonnière, 1564*. Translated from the Latin of De Bry. Osgood, Boston.

Lewis, Clifford M., and Albert J. Loomie
1953   *The Spanish Jesuit Mission in Virginia 1570–1572*. University of North Carolina Press, Chapel Hill.

Lorant, Stefan (editor)
1946   *The New World: The First Pictures of America*. Duell, Sloan and Pearce, New York.

Loucks, Lana Jill
1979   Political and Economic Interactions between Spaniards and Indians: Archaeological and Ethnohistorical Perspectives of the Mission System in Florida. Unpublished Ph.D. dissertation, Department of Anthropology, University of Florida, Gainesville.

Lowery, Woodbury
1905   *The Spanish Settlements within the Present Limits of the United States: Florida 1562–1574*. G. P. Putnam, New York.

Lyon, Eugene
1976   *The Enterprise of Florida: Pedro Menéndez de Avilés and the Spanish Conquest of 1565–1568*. University Presses of Florida, Gainesville.
1984   *Santa Elena: A Brief History of the Colony, 1566–1587*. South Carolina Institute of Archaeology and Anthropology Research Manuscript Series 193. Columbia.
1988   Pedro Menéndez's Strategic Plan for the Florida Peninsula. *Florida Historical Quarterly* 67:1–14.

McAlister, Lyle N.
1984   *Spain and Portugal in the New World, 1492–1700*. University of Minnesota Press, Minneapolis.

Marquardt, William H.
1986   The Development of Cultural Complexity in Southwest Florida: Elements of a Critique. *Southeastern Archaeology* 5(1):63–70.
1987   The Calusa Social Formation in Protohistoric South Florida. In *Power Relations and State Formations*, edited by Thomas C. Patterson and Christine W. Gailey, pp. 98–116. American Anthropological Association, Washington, D.C.

Marrinan, Rochelle
1985   *The Archaeology of the Spanish Missions of Florida: 1565–1704*. Florida Journal of Anthropology Special Publication No. 4, pp. 241–252.

Matter, Robert Allen
1972   The Spanish Missions of Florida: The Friars versus the Governors in the "Golden Age," 1606–1690. Unpublished Ph.D. dissertation, Department of History, University of Washington, Seattle.
1973   Economic Basis of the Seventeenth-century Florida Missions. *Florida Historical Quarterly* 52:18–38.

Milanich, Jerald T.
1978   The Western Timucua: Patterns of Acculturation and Change. In *Tacachale: Essays of the Indians of Florida and Southeastern Georgia during the Historic Period*, edited by Jerald Milanich and Samuel Proctor, pp. 59–88. University Presses of Florida, Gainesville.

Milanich, Jerald T., and Charles H. Fairbanks
1980   *Florida Archaeology*. Academic Press, New York.

Milanich, Jerald T., and William C. Sturtevant
1972   *Francisco Pareja's 1613 Confessionario: A Documentary Source for Timucuan Ethnography*. Florida Division of Archives, History, and Records, Tallahassee.

Oré, Luís Gerónimo de
   1936   The Martyrs of Florida (1513–1616), translated and edited by Maynard Geiger. *Franciscan Studies* 19, iii–xx, 1–145. Joseph W. Wagner, New York.
Pearson, Fred Lamar, Jr.
   1974   Spanish Indian Relations in Florida, 1602–1675: Some Aspects of Selected Visitas. *Florida Historical Quarterly* 52(3):261–273.
Reitz, Elizabeth J., and C. Margaret Scarry
   1985   *Reconstructing Historic Subsistence with an Example from Sixteenth-century Spanish Florida*. Society of Historical Archaeology Special Publication Series 3. Ann Arbor, Michigan.
Ribault, Jean
   1964   *The Whole and True Discouerye of Terra Florida*. University of Florida Press, Gainesville.
Ross, Mary
   1926   The Restoration of the Spanish Missions in Georgia, 1598–1606. *Georgia Historical Quarterly* 10(3):171–199.
Sandford, R.
   1911   A Relation of a Voyage on the Coast of the Province of Carolina [1666]. In *Narratives of Early Carolina, 1650–1708. Original Narratives of Early American History*, edited by A. S. Salley, vol. 15, pp. 82–108. Charles Scribner's Sons, New York.
San Miguel, Fray Andrés de
   1902   Relación de las Trabajos que la Gente de una nao llamada Nra Señora de la Merced Padeció y de algunas Cosas que en Aquella Flota Sucedieron. In *Dos Antiquas Relaciones de la Florida*, edited by Genaro García, pp. 153–226. J. Aguilar Vera y Compania, Mexico.
Sauer, Carl
   1971   *Sixteenth Century America*. University of California Press, Berkeley.
Serrano y Sanz, M. (editor)
   1912   *Documentos Históricos de la Florida y la Luisiana. Siglos XVI al XVIII: Biblioteca de los Americanistas, Madrid*, Librería General de Victoriano Suarez, Madrid.
Shapiro, Gary
   1987   Archaeology at San Luis: Broad-Scale Testing, 1984–1985. *Florida Archaeology* 3:1–271.
Siebert, Wilbur
   1940   The Departure of the Spaniards and Other Groups from East Florida, 1763–1764. *Florida Historical Quarterly* 19(2)145–154.
Sluiter, Engel
   1985   *The Florida Situado: Quantifying the First Eighty Years, 1571–1651*. University of Florida Libraries, Gainesville.
Smith, Hale G.
   1956   *The European and the Indian: European–Indian Contacts in Georgia and Florida*. Florida Anthropological Society Publication 4. Gainesville.
Smith, Hale G., and Mark Gottlob
   1978   Spanish–Indian Relationships: Synoptic History and Archeological Evidence, 1500–1763. In *Tacachale: Essays on the Indians of Florida and Southeastern Georgia during the Historic Period*, edited by Jerald Milanich and Samuel Proctor, pp. 1–18. University Presses of Florida, Gainesville.
South, Stanley
   1988   Santa Elena: Threshold of Conquest. In *The Recovery of Meaning: Historical Archaeology in the Eastern United States*, edited by Mark P. Leone and Parker B. Potter, Jr., pp. 27–72. Smithsonian Institution Press, Washington, D.C.
Spellman, Charles W.
   1948   The Agriculture of the Early North Florida Indians. *Florida Anthropologist* 1:37–48.

1965   The "Golden Age" of the Florida Missions, 1632–1674. *Catholic Historical Review* 51:354–372.

Sturtevant, William C.
1962   Spanish-Indian Relations in Southeastern North America. *Ethnohistory* 9(1):41–94.
1977   The Ethnological Evaluation of the Le Moyne-De Bry Illustrations. In *The Work of Jacques Le Moyne de Morgues: A Huguenot Artist in France, Florida, and England*, vol. 1, edited by Paul Hulton, pp. 69–74. British Museum Publications, London.
1978   The Last of the South Florida Aborigines. In *Tacachale: Essays of the Indians of Florida and Southeastern Georgia during the Historic Period*, edited by Jerald Milanich and Samuel Proctor, pp. 141–162. University of Florida Press, Gainesville.

Swadesh, Morris
1964   Linguistic Overview. In *Prehistoric Man in the New World*, edited by Jesse D. Jennings and Edward Norbeck, pp. 527–556. Chicago: University of Chicago Press.

Swanton, John R.
1922   *Early History of the Creek Indians and Their Neighbors*. Bureau of American Ethnology Bulletin No. 73. Washington, D.C.
1929   The Tawasa Language. *American Anthropologist* 31:435–453.
1946   *The Indians of the Southeastern United States*. Bureau of American Ethnology Bulletin No. 137. Washington, D.C.

Sweett, Zelia, and Mary H. Sheppy
1940   *The Spanish Missions of Florida*. St. Augustine.

Thomas, David Hurst
1987   *The Archaeology of Mission Santa Catalina de Guale: 1. Search and Discovery*. Anthropological Papers of the American Museum of Natural History 63(2):47–161.
1988a *St. Catherines: An Island in Time*. Georgia History and Culture Series. Georgia Endowment for the Humanities, Atlanta.
1988b Saints and Soldiers at Santa Catalina: Hispanic Designs for Colonial America. In *The Recovery of Meaning in Historical Archaeology*, edited by Mark P. Leone and Parker B. Potter, pp. 73–140. Smithsonian Institution Press, Washington, D.C.

Vargas Ugarte, Ruben
1935   The First Jesuit Mission in Florida. *Historical Records and Studies*, vol. 25. U. S. Catholic Historical Society, New York.

Varner, J. G., and J. J. Varner
1951   *The Florida of the Inca. Written by the Inca, Garcilaso de la Vega*. University of Texas Press, Austin.

Wenhold, Lucy L. (translator and editor)
1937   *A 17th century Letter of Gabriel Díaz Vara Calderón, Bishop of Cuba, Describing the Indians and Indian Missions of Florida*. Smithsonian Miscellaneous Collections 95(16). Publication 3398.

Widmer, Randolph
1988   *The Evolution of the Calusa. A Nonagricultural Chiefdom on the Southwest Florida Coast*. University of Alabama Press, Tuscaloosa.

Zubillaga, Felix
1941   La Florida: La misión jesuítica (1566–1572) y la colonización española. *Bibliotheca Instituti Historici S.I.*, vol. 1. Institutum Historicum S.I., Rome.
1946   Monumenta antiquae Floridae (1566–1572). *Monumenta Historica Societatis Iesu*, vol. 69. Monumenta Missionum Societatis Iesu, vol. 3. Missiones occidentales, Rome.

Chapter 25 ■

John W. Griffin

Changing Perspectives on the Spanish Missions of La Florida

During the past century romantics, historians, and archaeologists have focused some of their attention on the Spanish missions of the present southeastern United States. These strands have met and intertwined to the extent that all three must be examined if we are to understand how the missions of La Florida have been viewed through time.

Nearly a century ago the planning and publicity for the 400th anniversary of the Columbian encounter stimulated interest in things Spanish in the United States. The following headline in the *New York Herald* of March 4, 1894, was a likely result:

MAY BE AMERICA'S
OLDEST BUILDING
Picturesque Ruins of a Venerable
and Mysterious Structure
in South Florida
Was it Erected by Columbus?

The structure in question was a coquina stone ruin at New Smyrna, Florida, which a local minister had pointed out as an ancient religious edifice. The article suggested that the building was a church or mission in a now-forgotten settlement dating from the second voyage of Columbus (Luther 1987:18).

Historians were not slow to reply to this flight of fancy. Almost immediately Florida historian George Fairbanks penned "a conclusive refutation" stating that the mysterious ruin was in fact a sugar mill of the late eighteenth century. Woodbury Lowery added that the offending newspaper article "chiefly consists of purely gratuitous assumptions concerning questions which have never even been in dispute" (Lowery 1901–1905 1:433–434).

In the highly unlikely event that any archaeologist was interested enough to have issued a comment, it was not recorded. It would be another four decades before archaeologists would consider such disputes as touching upon their discipline.

At the turn of the century, the history of Spanish La Florida was incompletely known, in part because it was difficult to gain access to the manuscript sources, both physically and linguistically, and just as importantly because of the ethnocentrism of English-speaking writers and the persistence of the Black Legend. Scholars such as Buckingham Smith, Edward Gaylord Bourne, and Woodbury Lowery had researched and written on Spain in North America, but had primarily concentrated on the adventurous period of discovery and conquest.

Church-oriented authors had also begun to narrate the story of the Spanish missions. John Gilmary Shea's *The Catholic Church in Colonial Days* (1886) contained a chapter on the church in Spanish Florida that devoted a few pages to the mission efforts, concentrating on the early part of the story and the Guale rebellion of 1597.

In the Southwest and in California—where sources were richer and more readily available, where the mission past was recent, and where structures remained in view—much more was known and published. However, historian Herbert Bolton said that this work was most often

> chronicles of the deeds of the Fathers, polemic discussions by sectarian partisans, or sentimental effusions with literary, edifying, or financial intent. . . . [L]ittle has been said of these missions in relation to the general Spanish colonial system, of which they were an integral and a most important part [Bannon 1964:188].

The scholarly books of Franciscan Father Zephyrin Engelhardt were notable exceptions, Bolton noted, but were closely confined to California. In fact, Father Engelhardt had published a series of articles in the *Franciscan Herald* in 1913 and 1914 on the Franciscans in Florida (Engelhardt 1913–1914). Although this is the best account of Florida mission activities from that period, it remained relatively unknown to other historians.

Bolton's role in developing and spreading the concept of the significance of the Spanish Borderlands in New World history, and his insistence that the mission was a vital part of the borderland story, is well known and widely appreciated. His part in advocating and demonstrating a less ethnocentric approach to our national history is obvious. He did not, however, fully adopt what might be considered an anthropological viewpoint concerning the subjects of the mission endeavors, the Indians.

Bolton's *The Spanish Borderlands* (1921) discussed the period of the exploration and conquest of Florida in some detail, but became very sketchy after leaving the sixteenth century. He mentioned, but did not describe or place, the "mute but eloquent ruins scattered here and there along the Atlantic coast" (Bolton 1921:160).

Several years later Bolton (1925) published *Arredondo's Historical Proof of Spain's Title to Georgia*, which makes no textual reference to mission ruins, but carries as its frontispiece a photograph of the tabby ruins near St. Marys, Georgia, labeled, "Ruins of Santa Maria Mission near St. Marys, Georgia."

The 1920s also saw the collection of photostats of many documents from the Spanish archives by the Florida State Historical Society, under the sponsorship of John B. Stetson. Some of this collection was translated and published, but the promising program of research was cut short by the Depression of 1929.

Despite the waves of anti-Catholicism that were sweeping the South, romantic ideas of Spanish architecture and Spanish culture were emerging to become important elements of the feverish land boom of the 1920s. It was this Spanish mystique, meshed with some uncritical applications of history, that spread the idea that certain ruins along the Georgia and Florida coasts were those of Spanish missions.

Although the proposed Columbian connection suggested in 1894 for the ruins at New Smyrna was soon discarded, the mission myth was not. A wealthy New Yorker, Washington E. Connor, purchased these ruins, and in 1914 he gave the "mission" ruins as a birthday present to his new bride, Jeanette Thurber Connor. Mrs. Connor, who is best known for an ambitious program of translation and publication of Spanish documents from the Stetson collection, unfortunately also became the central figure in the identification of tabby and coquina ruins in Georgia and Florida as Spanish mission sites.

Marmaduke Floyd in his rebuttal to the mission myth recalls that beginning about 1914 Mrs. Connor's enthusiastic visits to the Georgia coast fueled earlier sparks into flame. "The idea that the several tabby sugar works in Georgia might really have been Spanish missions infected those who did not know of their origin" (Floyd 1937:167). Here was a historian, Mrs. Connor, albeit not a professionally trained one, whose credits over the next few years would include a definitive biography of Pedro Menéndez de Avilés and two volumes of translations of the colonial records of Spanish Florida. She said these were missions, and many believed her, but she never produced a published analysis or argument to support the assertion, nor did anyone else.

The supporting "evidence" consisted of such statements as, one could see "in the fitted coquina blocks and the fine lines of the arches something more than the construction of a sugar mill" (Connor 1926:n.p.).

This argument based on the quality and size of the ruins was supported further only by general statements that the ruins were found approximately at the proper number of leagues from St. Augustine to match documentary locations of missions. Despite the transparency of these claims there were few challenges. However, Marmaduke Floyd (1937) of Georgia was a major critic, and in Florida a booklet debunking the New Smyrna ruins was published by Charles Coe (1941). Interestingly, neither of these critics was a professional historian.

Most professional historians of that era had little interest in pursuing questions of a specific topographic or geographic nature. Bolton (1921:viii), who did considerable trail following in the West, apparently did not think of questioning the local wisdom when he spoke of mission ruins "scattered all the way from Georgia to San Francisco." Nor did he mention the discrepancy between his own statement (Bolton 1925:1) that "most of the Spanish establishments in Guale were on the islands," and the map in the same book that showed a number of them on the mainland. One suspects the influence of his student and colleague Mary Ross, who was a supporter of the sugar-mill mission claims.

The lack of critical judgment on this issue is explained by a scholarly void. In an unpublished lecture, historian E. M. Coulter (1932:n.p.) of the University of Georgia made and defended the startling statement that,

> In no history of Georgia ever written down to the present year 1932, has the Spanish occupation of Georgia ever been described or even alluded to. If we are to depend on our histories of Georgia, the only Spaniards who ever strode across the Georgia landscape were De Soto and a few other small explorers.

Coulter supported his claim with citations from a number of volumes of state history. He mentioned (1932:n.p.) that "certain specialists, writing for restricted purposes," such as Shea and Lowery, should have awakened the professional historians, but they had not. For Coulter, the "noonday sun" arrived with Bolton's *Spanish Borderlands*, and with the advent into the South of Bolton students Johnson (1923), Ross (1926), and Lanning (1935). He noted the persistent question about the old coastal ruins: Who built them, planters or Spanish missionaries? He called for investigations by historians, architects, and archaeologists as the only way to settle the issue, and this may be the first serious suggestion that archaeologists had a role to play in the understanding of the Spanish mission period in the Southeast.

Archaeological projects had already begun on Spanish mission sites in California, the Southwest, and Texas as part of depression-spawned relief programs. Often these investigations were of the now-suspect foundation-chasing type of excavation pursued for architectural and restoration ends, but at least it was the beginning of professional involvement.

In Georgia, a large acreage containing the Elizafield ruins, the purported mission of Santo Domingo de Talaxe, was offered to the state if it would restore the mission. The land was accepted as a state park, but state officials thought it might be a good idea to authenticate the ruins. Archaeologist James A. Ford was working at Ocmulgee and was assigned to the project, which was carried out in 1934. Ford (1937) found no evidence of Spanish artifacts in his excavations, noted that all dimensions were standard English, and that all evidence pointed to early nineteenth-century construction. In the process of his study he also visited other purported mission ruins and was able to point out their similarity to the disproved Elizafield structure. Archaeology had entered the mission–mill controversy with a vengeance, causing a last-minute shift of emphasis in the planned formal dinner accepting the ruins of the mission of Santo Domingo.

Today, we see Ford's Elizafield work not only as the beginning of Spanish mission archaeology in the Southeast, albeit with negative results, but also as the forerunner of investigations into the plantation archaeology of the area, and thus a pioneer work of historical archaeology (Joseph 1989:55).

This rebuttal of the cherished mission myth was not immediately accepted by everyone. At the very time that Ford was in the field, the eminent James A. Robertson, executive secretary of the Florida State Historical Society, wrote that the ruin at St. Marys was "beyond all doubt a Spanish mission," as was the one at New Smyrna. He regarded the two as the "finest Spanish mission ruins . . . beyond all doubt . . . in all of Georgia and Florida" (Floyd 1937:188). This attitude was to linger for decades.

In addition to the Floyd and Ford contributions (Coulter 1937), the late prewar years saw Lanning's (1935) documentary study of the Georgia missions, Boyd's (1939) first paper on the location of Florida missions, and Geiger's (1937, 1940) volumes on the Franciscans of Florida. Before the interruption of the Second World War, the documentary base for mission studies was greatly improved, and archaeology and history had jointly approached a problem—Elizafield— with positive results.

Following the war, in 1946, Hale G. Smith and I began work in Florida. We were both interested in the direct historical approach, and in problems of culture change and acculturation. Hence, we seized every opportunity to look at sites and situations of the contact period. In Tallahassee we found the retired internationally known malariologist and epidemiologist, Mark F. Boyd, joyfully pursuing his hobby of history, for a dollar a year. He turned our interest to the mission sites of Apalachee, and Smith had soon excavated a part of one of the missions and I had tested the site of San Luis. As far as I know, these two test excavations were the first in the Southeastern missions, although San Luis had been visited by Gordon Willey in 1940. We gained some idea of the character of a mission site and its associated artifact assemblage. Boyd's translations and his constant consultation were invaluable. This working relationship culminated in a book, *Here They Once Stood* (Boyd et al. 1951).

With these insights into the structures and artifacts of the missions, we turned our attention to the coquina ruins of the Florida coast, where the mission myth still lingered. We soon established to our own satisfaction, and that of most others, that all of them dated from the early nineteenth century, and were associated with plantations of the Second Spanish and Territorial periods. At the New Smyrna ruins, where "the mythical yarn . . . apparently began spinning" (Floyd 1937:189), we found no aboriginal remains and no Spanish artifacts. The "chapel" exactly matched the machinery house at the nearby Bulow plantation, which had been visited by John James Audubon while it was under construction. All documents pointed in the same direction.

Yet, such tales die hard. I had convinced even the people who had erected the bronze marker on the New Smyrna site that it was erroneous, when our boss, the chairman of the State Park Board, himself the editor of the *Miami Herald*, told a reporter, in effect, that his archaeologists were probably correct, but that the legend was much more attractive. Nevertheless, the coquina and tabby sugar mills of Florida and Georgia had been removed from scholarly concern as possible Spanish mission sites, and had been properly placed in the context of nineteenth-century plantation studies.

Within the next few years Smith, now at Florida State University, continued to survey and test mission sites in the Tallahassee area. John Goggin entered the field at the University of Florida and developed a strong and consuming interest in historical archaeology. He worked at a number of Mission period sites, and secured the material for his definitive monographs on Spanish olive jars and majolica (Goggin 1960, 1968). Ripley Bullen and I located a mission site on Amelia Island, and I also tested the site of San Juan del Puerto on Fort George Island.

Meanwhile, Sheila Kelly Caldwell (1953, 1954) had been excavating mission sites on the Georgia coast and Lewis Larson had carried out a mission site survey along that same coast.

The archaeological work between the end of World War II and 1960 was primarily directed toward locating documented Spanish mission sites and determining their architectural and artifactual complexes. It was basically a period of survey and testing. Statements such as, "the period is a fertile one for the social scientist interested in the dynamics of culture change, and the present paper can do no more than suggest the problem" (Boyd et al. 1951:156), indicated broader concerns that could not be addressed by the data at hand.

Historians in the meantime continued to add to the corpus of available sources. An English translation of the 1722 chronological history of Florida by Barcia (1951) was published. The more than 100,000 photostat pages of the Stetson collection, which had lain dormant since the early 1930s, were transferred to the University of Florida where they were calendared. Both of these projects were sponsored by the St. Augustine Historical Society.

The following decade of the 1960s, viewed by many as a critical turning point in American archaeology, was relatively quiet on the front of mission archaeology in La Florida. Goggin's (1960, 1968) monographs on Olive Jars and majolica appeared, but one looks in vain for major site-oriented publications on the missions. Some things were going on, but they were minor. Lewis Larson and I separately visited the site of Santa Catalina on St. Catherines Island. Hale Smith, John Goggin, and Charles Fairbanks, and their students, were certainly not idle, but their efforts were not concentrated on mission archaeology at that time. Toward the end of the decade the Florida Division of Archives and History began a Spanish mission survey project, most of the results of which appeared in the following decade.

In the 1960s, the ethnohistory project at the University of Florida extracted notes from the extensive documentary collections available (Fairbanks and Fleener 1964), providing a useful tool for mission research. Spanish–Indian relations were discussed in an important paper by Sturtevant (1962). The decade was even richer in historical contributions with TePaske's (1964) book on the governorship of Spanish Florida, Spellman's (1965) article on the Golden Age of the missions, Gannon's (1965) *The Cross in the Sand*, and Pearson's (1968) detailed dissertation on two *visitas* to the missions.

In 1966 the state of Florida had authorized a study of the Spanish missions, but the lack of funding delayed fieldwork until 1968 (Jones 1970). During the next four years a number of sites were located and tested and several publications resulted (Jones 1972, 1973; Morrell and Jones 1970).

The 1970s were an extremely productive decade for historical archaeology on Spanish sites of the Southeast. Faculty and students at the University of Florida and Florida State University were active in this period; we need only mention the names of Charles Fairbanks, Jerald Milanich, and Kathleen Deagan in support of this statement. Although Spanish St. Augustine and other historic sites received more attention than the missions, feedback from this work enriched and illuminated the mission archaeology. In 1977, as part of a long-range project on St. Catherines Island, Georgia, Thomas (1987) began the successful search for and investigation of the mission of Santa Catalina. At the end of the decade an excellent, but unpublished, doctoral dissertation by Jill Loucks (1979) summarized the state of our knowledge of the Florida missions and developed a number of testable hypotheses.

Likewise, the historians and ethnohistorians had not been idle. Matter (1972) produced a dissertation on the seventeenth-century Spanish missions of Florida, in which he challenged Bolton's claim that the mission was a successful agent of borderland control. Eugene Lyon's (1976) significant study of the Menéndez era appeared. The volume entitled *Tacachale* (Milanich and Proctor 1978) contained chapters by a number of anthropologists summarizing the aboriginal situation of the contact period in the mission areas of Florida and Georgia. Milanich and Sturtevant (1972) annotated a translation of Father Pareja's 1613 *Confessionario*. An excellent thesis by Boniface (1971), entitled *A Historical Geography of Spanish Florida, circa 1700*, brought the somewhat different viewpoints and insights of the cultural geographer to bear on this area of concern.

All of us who are archaeologists know that historians were slow to recognize the possible contributions of archaeology to their studies. As I have indicated, some of us who were archaeologists in the 1940s and 50s were eager to work with historians, and did in fact strike up some fruitful partnerships.

It was in the 1960s that significant numbers of historical archaeologists began to disparage the relevance of documentary sources to their understanding of archaeological sites and materials. I know that more than once I heard "all history is a lie" seriously espoused by some of my colleagues. It is certainly true that many questions that archaeologists would like historians to answer are not ones that seem pertinent to the historian, and vice versa (Deagan and Scardaville 1985). But as more and more historians have been exposed to anthropology, and have followed developments in their own discipline in such areas as social and cultural history, it has become easier for them to understand our concerns, if not necessarily to adopt them. I also get the impression that more archaeologists are understanding the stance of the historian, appreciating the real potential of documentary context for archaeology, and perhaps even coming to enjoy narrative history for its own sake. Certainly we are seeing far more communication between historians and archaeologists, and this seems to be even more pronounced in the geographical areas of the Spanish Borderlands.

When historian Scardaville (1985:195) says, "Historians must admit the limitation of their sources and realize that historical archaeology is essential where documentation is weak or absent," and when archaeologist Deagan (1983:263) says that when the patterns revealed by archaeology "are integrated with the data of social history and anthropology, we learn things that could not have been studied through any one of those disciplines alone," there is hope for both disciplines.

We have reached the present decade, a period of unprecedented activity. It is a period in which, as never before, numerous disciplines and subdisciplines are involved, far beyond the old duo of archaeology and history. The papers that make up this volume are concerned with recent field and analytical results, and reflect the multifaceted approaches current today, written by persons who, if space permitted, should be individually acknowledged. In themselves, these papers will best illustrate the present perspectives on the Spanish missions of La Florida.

References

Bannon, John Francis
  1964 *Bolton and the Spanish Borderlands*. University of Oklahoma Press, Norman.
Barcia, Andres Gonzales
  1951 *Barcia's Chronological History of the Continent of Florida*. Translated by Anthony Kerrigan. University of Florida Press, Gainesville.
Bolton, Herbert E.
  1921 *The Spanish Borderlands*. Yale University Press, New Haven.
  1925 *Arredondo's Historical Proof of Spain's Title to Georgia*. University of California Press, Berkeley.
Boniface, Brian George
  1971 *A Historical Geography of Spanish Florida, circa 1700*. Unpublished Master's thesis, University of Georgia, Athens.
Boyd, Mark F.
  1939 Spanish Mission Sites in Florida. *Florida Historical Quarterly* 17:254–280.
Boyd, Mark F., Hale G. Smith, and John W. Griffin
  1951 *Here They Once Stood: The Tragic End of the Apalachee Missions*. University of Florida Press, Gainesville.
Caldwell, Sheila K.
  1953 Excavations at a Spanish Mission Site in Georgia. *Southeastern Archaeological Conference Newsletter* 3(3):31–32.
  1954 A Spanish Mission House near Darien. *Early Georgia* 1(3):13–17.
Coe, Charles H.
  1941 *Debunking the So-called Spanish Mission near New Smyrna Beach, Volusia County, Florida*. Fitzgerald, Daytona Beach, Florida.
Connor, Jeanette Thurber
  1926 Portion of Address Given at the Unveiling of the Mission Tablet February 26, 1926. Ms. on file, private library of John W. Griffin.

Coulter, E. Merton
  1932   The Spanish Missions in Georgia. Ms. on file, St. Augustine Historical Society. St. Augustine, Florida.
  1937   *Georgia's Disputed Ruins*. University of North Carolina Press, Chapel Hill.
Deagan, Kathleen
  1983   *Spanish St. Augustine*. Academic Press, New York.
Deagan, Kathleen, and Michael Scardaville
  1985   Archaeology and History on Historic Hispanic Sites: Impediments and Solutions. *Historical Archaeology* 19:32–37.
Engelhardt, Fr. Zephyrin, O.F.M.
  1913–1914 Missionary Labors of the Franciscans among Indians of the Early Days (Florida). *Franciscan Herald*, Vols. 1 and 2 [WPA transcript, P. K. Yonge Library, University of Florida, Gainesville].
Fairbanks, Charles H., and Charles J. Fleener
  1964   The Trial Ethnohistory Project at the University of Florida. *Florida Anthropologist* 17:110–112.
Floyd, Marmaduke
  1937   Certain Tabby Ruins on the Georgia Coast. In *Georgia's Disputed Ruins*, edited by E. Merton Coulter, pp. 3–189. University of North Carolina Press, Chapel Hill.
Ford, James A.
  1937   An Archaeological Report on the Elizafield Ruins. In *Georgia's Disputed Ruins*, edited by E. Merton Coulter, pp. 193–225. University of North Carolina Press, Chapel Hill.
Gannon, Michael V.
  1965   *The Cross in the Sand: The Early Catholic Church in Florida, 1513–1870*. University of Florida Press, Gainesville.
Geiger, Maynard
  1937   *The Franciscan Conquest of Florida (1573–1618)*. Catholic University of America, Washington, D.C.
  1940   *Biographical Dictionary of the Franciscans in Spanish Florida and Cuba (1528–1841)*. Franciscan Studies 21. St. Anthony Guild Press, Paterson, New Jersey.
Goggin, John M.
  1960   *The Spanish Olive Jar: An Introductory Study*. Yale University Publications in Anthropology 62. New Haven.
  1968   *Spanish Majolica in the New World*. Yale University Publications in Anthropology 72. New Haven.
Johnson, James Guyton
  1923   The Spanish Period of Georgia and South Carolina, 1566–1702. *Bulletin of the University of Georgia*, Athens.
Jones, B. Calvin
  1970   Missions Reveal State's Spanish-Indian Heritage. *Archives and History News* 1(2).
  1972   Spanish Mission Sites Located and Test Excavated. *Archives and History News* 3(6)1–2.
  1973   A Semi-subterranean Structure at Mission San Joseph de Ocuya, Jefferson County, Florida. *Bureau of Historic Sites and Properties Bulletin* 3:1–50. Department of State, Tallahassee.
Joseph, J. W.
  1989   Pattern and Processes in the Plantation Archaeology of the Lowcountry of Georgia and South Carolina. *Historical Archaeology* 23:55–68.
Lanning, John Tate
  1935   *The Spanish Missions of Georgia*. University of North Carolina Press, Chapel Hill.
Loucks, Lana Jill
  1979   *Political and Economic Interactions between Spaniards and Indians: Archaeological and*

Ethnohistorical Perspectives of the Mission System in Florida. Unpublished Ph.D. dissertation, Department of Anthropology, University of Florida, Gainesville.

Lowery, Woodbury
1901–1905 *The Spanish Settlements within the Limits of the United States.* 2 vols. Putnam, New York.

Luther, Gary
1987 *History of New Smyrna, East Florida, with Illustrations.* Gary Luther, New Smyrna Beach, Florida.

Lyon, Eugene
1976 *The Enterprise of Florida: Pedro Menéndez de Avilés and the Conquest of 1565–1568.* University of Florida Presses, Gainesville.

Matter, Robert Allen
1972 *The Spanish Missions of Florida: The Friars Versus the Governors in the "Golden Age,"* 1606–1690. Unpublished Ph.D. dissertation, University of Washington, Seattle.

Milanich, Jerald T., and Samuel Proctor (editors)
1978 *Tacachale: Essays on the Indians of Florida and Southeastern Georgia during the Historic Period.* University Presses of Florida, Gainesville.

Milanich, Jerald T., and William C. Sturtevant
1972 *Francisco Pareja's 1613 Confessionario: A Documentary Source for Timucuan Ethnography.* Translated by Emilio F. Moran. Department of State, Tallahassee.

Morrell, L. Ross, and B. Calvin Jones
1970 San Juan de Aspalaga: A Preliminary Architectural Study. *Bureau of Historic Sites and Properties Bulletin* 1:25–43. Department of State, Tallahassee.

Pearson, Fred Lamar, Jr.
1968 *Spanish Indian Relations in Florida. A Study of Two Visitas, 1657–1678.* Unpublished Ph.D. dissertation, University of Alabama.

Ross, Mary
1926 The Restoration of the Spanish Missions in Gerogia, 1598–1606. *Georgia Historical Quarterly* 10:171–199.

Scardaville, Michael C.
1985 Approaches to the Study of the Southeastern Borderlands. In *Alabama and the Borderlands: From Prehistory to Statehood,* edited by R. Reid Badger and Lawrence A. Clayton, pp. 162–196. University of Alabama Press, University.

Shea, John Gilmary
1886 *The Catholic Church in Colonial Days.* John G. Shea, New York.

Spellman, Charles W.
1965 The Golden Age of the Florida Missions. *Catholic Historical Review* 51:354–372.

Sturtevant, William C.
1962 Spanish–Indian Relations in Southeastern North America. *Ethnohistory* 9:41–94.

TePaske, John Jay
1964 *The Governorship of Spanish Florida: 1700–1763.* Duke University Press, Durham, North Carolina.

Thomas, David Hurst
1987 *The Archaeology of Mission Santa Catalina de Guale: 1.* Search and Discovery. Anthropological Papers of the American Museum of Natural History 63(2):47–161.

Thomas, David Hurst, Grant D. Jones, Roger S. Durham, and Clark S. Larsen
1978 The Anthropology of St. Catherines Island: 1. Natural and Cultural History. *Anthropological Papers of the American Museum of Natural History* 55(2)178–210.

Chapter 26 ∎

Clark Spencer Larsen, Margaret J. Schoeninger,
Dale L. Hutchinson, Katherine F. Russell,
and Christopher B. Ruff

Beyond Demographic Collapse: Biological Adaptation and Change in Native Populations of La Florida

Perhaps the most discussed issue regarding the biological consequences for native populations of the arrival of Europeans to the New World is the dramatic loss of life in the former (e.g., Cook 1981; Crosby 1986; Sauer 1966; Thornton 1987). This scholarly concern for largely demographic questions—especially as these questions relate to epidemic disease—by anthropologists and historians alike is certainly evident for the Southeastern borderlands in particular (e.g., Dobyns 1983; Milner 1980; Ramenofsky 1987; Smith 1987). We begin our discussion here by stating that the catastrophic effects of the of Old World pathogens on native populations should be viewed as one facet of a multifaceted problem. Equally important for understanding the consequences of contact are questions relating to how native populations responded and adapted to great social, dietary, and behavioral changes representing in some instances relatively long periods of time.

To be sure, some native populations underwent sudden extinction, at times within a generation or two. And these extinctions were likely due to the profound effects of Old World diseases for which native populations had no acquired immunities. On the other hand, in some regions, including La Florida, generations of survivors continued to respond to new and novel challenges brought about by the arrival of Europeans despite truly dismal circumstances.

This chapter is concerned primarily with the contributions of the study of human skeletal remains to a comprehensive understanding of population biology in the missions of La Florida. These data help to underscore one dimension of the diversity of native responses to a variety of demands during the Mission period. The discussion focuses on two general themes: (1) the quality of life, and (2) physical behavior and life-style. The former details the negative consequences of the arrival of Europeans, including dietary change and decrease in resource diversity, nucleation of population, and disease. The latter provides information on the role of changing work patterns, behavior, and activity level.

The Populations of La Florida

Missionization in La Florida occurred among four primary tribal groups, including the Timucua, Apalachee, and Apalachicola to the west, and the Guale along the Atlantic coast north of the St. Marys River (see Thomas, this volume). The earliest missions were established among the Guale, who were some of the first native populations to be encountered by Europeans north of Mexico (Jones 1978; Thomas 1987). In order to document biological adaptation of these populations via the evidence provided from the study of human remains, it is essential that large series of these materials be available for study. A number of mission cemeteries have been excavated throughout La Florida (see below). Only for the contact period Guale, however, are existing skeletal samples of sufficient size for a population level of study. Moreover, large precontact series have been studied for this tribal region only (Larsen 1982, 1984). These precontact skeletal samples provide a baseline from which we can assess biological changes subsequent to the arrival of Europeans. Given the scope and breadth of both the precontact and contact Guale skeletal series, we focus most of our discussion on this region. We then examine aspects of human biology in other regions of La Florida.

The Archaeological and Ethnohistorical Context

Native inhabitants of the Georgia coast were undoubtedly quite attracted to the region because of the diversity of estuarine and marine resources that were available for exploitation (Reitz 1988, this volume; Reitz and Scarry 1985; Ruhl, this volume; Thomas et al. 1978). Archaeological evidence indicates that for most of the prehistoric occupation of the region, subsistence economy was focused on the collection, gathering, and hunting of wild resources. The time during which plant domesticates—especially maize—entered into the diet and its importance relative to other resources has been the subject of considerable debate (see reviews in Jones 1978; Larsen 1982; Thomas 1987). The botanical evidence is meager on this point, but the appearance of densely populated, nucleated settlements and the concomitant increase in complexity of social organization that is characteristic of the Mississippian fluorescence during the last few centuries of prehistory in the eastern United States is consistent with a dietary reconstruction involving the use of maize agriculture (Smith 1986; Steponaitis 1986). Thus, by the twelfth century, maize was an important food source (Larsen 1982, 1984). Reitz (1988) has argued, however, that it was unlikely that plant domesticates replaced marine resources during this time. Rather, marine resources continued to contribute substantially to diet.

With the establishment of missions in Guale, how did subsistence economy and lifeway in general change? From a reading of the sixteenth-century and seventeenth-century archaeological evidence and historical records, it appears that maize continued to be relied upon by native populations associated with missions. Maize and other crops took on additional importance because they were grown in order to support the mission clergy and military personnel, and for export to St. Augustine (Bushnell 1987). Wild plants and animals continued to contribute to the subsistence economy (e.g., Duncan 1987; Reitz 1988, this volume; Ruhl, this volume), and marine resources were also heavily utilized (Reitz 1988). Archaeological and historical evidence alone does not make clear the relative importance of marine resources and terrestrial animals and plants (including maize). We address this issue later in this chapter.

Native labor represented an important part of the economic interests that the Spanish had in the region. Indians associated with the missions provided the primary source of labor that was necessary for the planting and raising of crops, fortification and other construction projects, woodcutting, cargo bearing, military service, and other activities. With regard to food production, Governor Canzo remarked, "but with all this and the grain from maize, the labor that they endure in the many cultivations is great, and, if it were not for the help of the Indians . . . , it would not be possible to sow any grain" (unpublished translation provided by John H. Hann).

To the west, in Apalachee, Hann (1988) notes that natives carried heavy burdens over long distances. The cost in human resources is illustrated by the account given by Fray Alonso Moral:

> All of the natives of those provinces suffer great servitude, injuries, and vexations from the fact that the governors, lieutenants, and soldiers oblige them to carry loads on their shoulders to the Province of Apalachee and to other regions to the fort of St. Augustine. . . . Each year from Apalachee alone more than three hundred are brought to the fort at the time of the planting of the corn, carrying their food and the merchandise of the soldiers on their shoulders for more than eighty leagues with the result that some of them die and those who survive do not return to their homes because the governor and the other officials detain them in the fort so they may serve them. . . . This is the reason according to the commonly held opinion that they are being annihilated at such a rate [Hann 1988:140–141].

In an effort to control native populations and provide an accessible labor pool for the aforementioned activities, they were centralized into a limited number of areas usually associated with missions. Thus, the pattern of settlement involving population nucleation that had begun before the arrival of Europeans continued into the contact period. These manipulations of native populations resulted in a number of negative consequences for the mission neophytes. For example, the Guale suffered periodic harassment from the military and demands for food (Jones 1978). A direct response to this harassment and other infringements was a series of native uprisings that resulted in brutal retaliations by the Spanish in the form of the burning of towns, crops, and stored foods, the latter of which were essential for supporting the populations through the winter months. Many Indians lost their lives either during these confrontations with the Spanish military or as a result of the sickness and food shortages that followed.

Other consequences of the arrival of Europeans and the establishment of missions resulted from the disease baggage carried into the New World from the Old. Contrary to the assertions of some scholars (e.g., Dobyns 1983), the New World was not a disease-free haven prior to contact. Indeed, abundant skeletal evidence indicates that various infectious diseases were present among native populations (e.g., Baker and Armelagos 1988; Powell 1988), including the precontact Guale (Larsen 1982; Powell 1989). Needless to say, however, devastation was brought about by the new diseases (Jones 1978; Larsen 1989). The concentration of populations around mission centers undoubtedly exacerbated the situation by providing circumstances conducive to the maintenance and spread of both existing infectious diseases (e.g., treponematosis and tuberculosis) and newly introduced infectious diseases (e.g., smallpox and measles).

In addition, the missions established on the Georgia coast served as a buffer between the English-occupied Carolina colony and Spanish-occupied La Florida. However, mounting pressure from British concerns and the use of force by British troops and their Indian allies resulted in the abandonment in 1680 of the principal Spanish outpost on the Georgia coast—Santa Catalina de Guale—and its eventual reestablishment on Amelia Island in 1686. Continued problems and harassments by the British, Indian allies, and occasional pirate raids forced yet another abandonment and relocation of this mission (Santa Catalina de Guale de Santa María) in 1702 to St. Augustine.

In the following discussion we examine diachronic trends in environmental stress and life-style during the precontact and contact periods in Guale. Four time periods are examined: precontact preagricultural (pre-A.D. 1150); precontact agricultural (A.D. 1150–1550); early contact (A.D. 1607–1680); and late contact (A.D. 1686–1702). The human remains examined from the precontact preagricultural period are largely from the Late Woodland period (A.D. 700–1150) sites on the Georgia coast. The precontact agricultural period is represented by remains from the Georgia coast. Most of these remains are from the Irene Mound site, a large Mississippian period (A.D. 1150–1450) ceremonial-habitation complex at the mouth of the Savannah River on the north Georgia coast. The early contact period is represented by human remains from Santa Catalina de Guale on St. Catherines Island, and the late contact period is represented by human remains from the descendant Santa Catalina de Guale de Santa María on Amelia Island. Because we are reporting on an investigation still in progress, some of the interperiod variable comparisons involving all four periods are not yet available. Where appropriate, we indicate which of the specific periods are included in our observations.

Stress

It is quite clear that native populations of La Florida and Guale were subject to a general increase in environmental stress that resulted from the arrival of Europeans and establishment of mission centers. The concept of stress has become an increasingly important tool for understanding the consequences of disruptive events (e.g., starvation, disease), and it is central to the study of adaptation in archaeological populations from this and other regions (see Goodman et al. 1988). The time depth provided by the well-documented archaeological series from the region offers a context for the identification of failures and successes subsequent to the arrival of Europeans. By examining markers of stress in these human remains, it is possible to associate them with general and specific stressors (environmental insults that have the potential of causing physiological disruption) or groups of stressors and their role in adaptation. For purposes of the present discussion, we follow the definition of stress provided by Huss-Ashmore and her coworkers of stress as "the physiological disruption of an organism resulting from environmental perturbation" (1982:396).

Our discussion of stress takes into account (1) diet quality (bone chemistry and dental caries) and resource diversity; (2) growth disruption (enamel defects); (3) iron-deficiency anemia (porotic hyperostosis); and (4) demography.

Diet: Bone Chemistry

Past foodways and patterns of dietary change can shed light on resource diversity and nutritional quality. With regard to precontact and contact Guale, our current knowledge about the relative proportion of dietary items and change through time is poor, in part because of the vagaries of archaeological evidence. However, the recent investigation of carbon and nitrogen stable isotope ratios in human bone collagen samples from four time periods—precontact preagricultural, precontact agricultural, early contact, and late contact—by Schoeninger and her coworkers (1989, unpublished), has provided information on the contribution of maize and marine animals to the Guale diet.

The $\delta^{13}C$ value (a measure of the ratio $^{13}C/^{12}C$) has been shown to measure consumption of two major dietary categories, including (1) C4 plants (e.g., maize) versus C3 plants (most leafy plants); and (2) marine versus terrestrial foods. The former has been important to the documentation of the introduction and intensification of maize agriculture in interior areas of the eastern United States (e.g., Buikstra et al. 1987; Keegan 1987), and the latter has been valuable in identifying the use of marine foods in areas not using C4 plants (e.g., Schoeninger et al. 1983; Tauber 1981). For regions where both C4 plants and marine resources were utilized, their contribution is difficult to assess because of the overlap of the chemical signatures of carbon isotope ratios in them (Schoeninger et al. 1989). The analysis of $\delta^{15}N$ (a measure of the ratio $^{15}N/^{14}N$), however, has been successfully used to estimate the amount of marine resources in diet regardless of whether C4 plants were consumed. Study of both $\delta^{13}C$ and $\delta^{15}N$ has shown that it is possible to look simultaneously at the contribution of C4 plants and marine resources in diet.

Comparisons of values for both carbon and nitrogen indicate a general increase in $\delta^{13}C$ values (means: precontact preagricultural, -14.5; precontact agricultural, -13.0; early contact, -11.5; late contact, -11.5) and a decrease in $\delta^{15}N$ values (means: precontact preagricultural, 12.8; precontact agricultural, 10.3; early contact, 9.4; late contact, 10.1). These changing isotope values reflect a general decrease in the use of marine foods (molluscs and fish) and an increase in dependence on terrestrial foods, especially maize (Schoeninger et al. 1989). These data indicate, however, that although maize becomes a significant part of precontact and contact Guale diet, it does not replace the use of marine resources. Marine resources continue to be important in subsistence, but to a reduced extent.

Diet: Dental Caries

Dental caries is an age-progressive disease process that is characterized by the focal demineralization of dental hard tissues by organic acids that are produced by bacterial fermentation of dietary carbohydrates, especially sugars. Maize contains a simple sugar (sucrose) that is more readily metabolized by oral bacteria than other, more complex carbohydrates (Larsen 1987; Powell 1985). Because sugar is known to promote caries (Newbrun 1982), the introduction and increased consumption of maize should result in an increased prevalence of cariogenic activity from the early to late periods in the samples studied here.

The frequency of dental carious lesions is available for all four subsamples (Larsen et al. 1989). The percentage of carious teeth in each period is as follows: precontact preagricultural, 1.3; precontact agricultural, 11.4; early contact, 8.0; late contact, 34.2. Therefore, there is an increase in dental decay after the adoption of maize agriculture, a slight drop in frequency during the early mission period, and a dramatic increase during the late contact period. The overall pattern shown in these comparisons reveals a clear increase in the prevalence of dental caries. The slight decline in the early contact period was not expected, especially in the light of the dietary reconstruction based on bone chemistry. However, it is important to point out that the early contact skeletal series is considerably less well preserved than the other samples. Indeed, many teeth in the sample were missing, in large part because of poor preservation. It seems likely that a carious tooth would preserve even less well than a noncarious tooth. More important, however, is a fourfold increase in frequency of carious teeth in the late contact series. There is no evidence—historical or archaeological—that would indicate that sugar was introduced to native populations during the late contact period. Therefore, the findings based on change in frequency of carious lesions indicate that maize took on a much more significant role in diet during the late seventeenth century.

In sum, taken together, the change in $\delta^{13}C$ and $\delta^{15}N$ values and in the increase in frequency of dental carious lesions shows a reorientation of subsistence. The greater emphasis on maize coupled with the decrease in use of marine foods suggests that there was decline in dietary breadth, and hence, a decrease in nutritional quality. This development began prior to the arrival of Europeans in the region, and it reached its most pronounced form in the late contact period.

Growth Disruption: Enamel Defects

Another important marker of stress in past populations is a condition known as enamel hypoplasia. Hypoplasias are circumferential lines or pits on tooth crowns that represent incompletely formed enamel arising from a disruption of cells—ameloblasts—that are responsible for its formation (Huss-Ashmore et al. 1982; Larsen 1987). Disruption that occurs during the formation of enamel is caused by a variety of factors, including disease or dietary stresses, or both (Huss-Ashmore et al. 1982; Larsen 1987). Because of the nonspecific nature of enamel hypoplasia, it is considered a marker of generalized systemic disruption (Kreshover 1960). Enamel does not remodel in life. Observation of hypoplasias, therefore, provides a permanent, retrospective history of stress events that are left as indelible markers on the tooth crowns.

Enamel forms in a layer-like fashion beginning at the tip of the tooth crown and finishing at the cementoenamel junction. Therefore, a hypoplasia that is relatively wide from top to bottom represents a stress event of longer duration than a hypoplasia that is relatively narrow (Blakey and Armelagos 1985; Hutchinson and Larsen 1988). Experimental evidence suggests that wider hypoplasias may also be related to severity of the stress episode (Suckling et al. 1986).

A comparison of precontact preagricultural, precontact agricultural, and early contact period teeth shows a general increase in hypoplasia width through time (Hutchinson and Larsen 1988, 1989). Eight tooth types were examined: maxillary and mandibular first and second incisors, canines, and first molars. The tooth crowns of these teeth begin forming during the first six months following birth and are completely formed by the sixth year (Ubelaker 1984). Findings based on the study of widths of hypoplasias in these teeth therefore indicate that stress episodes associated with the first six years of life increase in duration or severity in both precontact agricultural and early contact Guale. These findings are consistent with an increase in frequency of individuals affected by hypoplastic activity from the precontact to contact period. That is, 21 percent more individuals are affected by enamel hypoplasias in the contact period compared with the populations prior to contact (Hutchinson and Larsen 1988).

In order to assess how missionization may have contributed to an increase in stress in the contact period, hypoplasia widths in a nonmission skeletal series from the nearby early contact Pine Harbor site on the Georgia mainland were compared with the early contact mission sample from Santa Catalina de Guale on St. Catherines Island (Hutchinson and Larsen 1988). Interestingly, the Pine Harbor dental series exhibited narrower hypoplastic bands than the Santa Catalina dental series. Because the Pine Harbor population was not associated with a mission, it most likely enjoyed a more traditional lifeway without the negative aspects of mission life. The narrower hypoplasias in the Pine Harbor series suggest, then, that this population may have experienced a relatively reduced stress load than the contemporary mission population in the region.

Because of the nonspecific nature of hypoplasias, we are not able to link specific stressors to either the increase in widths of enamel hypoplasias or the greater widths in early contact mission populations relative to nonmission populations. However, these findings provide support for a model of decaying environmental conditions both in late prehistory and in the contact period. Most likely, it was a combination of a variety of stressors that was responsible for increase in growth disruption in later populations in the region.

Iron Deficiency Anemia: Porotic Hyperostosis

Porotic hyperostosis is a pathological skeletal condition characterized by the presence of porous, sievelike alterations of compact bone in the roof areas of the eye orbits, the flat bones of the cranium, and to a lesser extent, other cranial bones. Porotic hyperostosis has been related to a variety of stress contexts (e.g., nutritional deprivation, parasitism, infection), but regardless of ultimate cause, the skeletal changes arise from increased demand for red blood cells stimulated by any anemia (Martin et al. 1985; Ortner and Putschar 1985). The bony changes occur during childhood anemia episodes, and like hypoplasias, are interpreted best in the light of stress events associated with this period of life (Stuart-Macadam 1985).

Observations on porotic hyperostosis in the Guale series have been made for two of the four periods, namely the precontact agricultural and the late contact periods. The former is represented by a subsample consisting of the Irene Mound population studied by Larsen (1982) and Powell (1989). In the Irene Mound crania, Powell (1989) has reported a low frequency of 8 percent with porotic hyperostosis. She suggests that despite the consumption of iron-poor foods (e.g., maize) and the occupation of a restricted village area conducive to the exchange of endemic pathogens and contamination by fecal wastes, chronic hemolytic anemia was not a major problem prior to European contact.

It is possible that we may be looking at diets of elite individuals from the Irene Mound site. Perhaps, nonelite individuals are interred outside of this ceremonial-habitation complex. If so, elite individuals may have enjoyed a diet that is not conducive to the development of iron deficiency anemia. However, examination of other late prehistoric human remains from the Georgia coast shows a very low frequency of porotic hyperostosis (Larsen, personal observation). In our estimation, therefore, it seems unlikely that social status and differential diet alone can explain the pattern of this pathological condition for this time period.

An alternative model for explaining the low prevalence of porotic hyperostosis in the Irene Mound series is suggested by a closer examination of diet. Layrisse and his coworkers (1968) have provided experimental evidence that demonstrates that iron absorption in individuals fed maize is quite low. However, diet supplemented with fish increases iron absorption by 300 percent. As discussed above, archaeological and stable isotope ratio evidence indicates that marine resources remained an important component of diet, even after the adoption of maize agriculture. The consumption of marine foods may have served to buffer these populations from iron deficiency.

Our study of late contact period crania provides a very different profile of prevalence of porotic hyperostosis from that observed in the precontact Irene Mound crania. Of the 93 late contact period crania examined, 27 percent exhibited skeletal manifestations of anemia. When the sample is subdivided into two age groups—15 years or less, and older than 15 years—we find 73 percent with lesions in the younger age group and 13 percent with lesions in the older age group. This frequency change in porotic hyperostosis indicates an increase in anemic episodes in contact period juveniles. If the consumption of marine resources was responsible for reducing anemia in the precontact agriculturalist Irene Mound population, then the increase in porotic hyperostosis found in the late contact period suggests that there was a reduction in their use after contact. Thus, with an increase in the consumption of maize, a very iron-poor food, and a decline in the use of marine resources, anemia became a major health problem during the contact period.

Demography

Demographic patterns in past human populations have been used in the investigation of quality of life under different dietary and other environmental circumstances (see discussions in Acsádi and Nemeskéri 1970; Buikstra and Mielke 1985; Lovejoy et al 1977). Our study of age-at-death in the precontact (preagricultural and agricultural) and contact (early and late) periods in Guale has provided preliminary evidence of changing profiles of mortality and fertility that are consistent with a picture of population decline provided by the historical record.

A comparison of the percentage of individuals dying (d_x) in five-year age classes indicates that the precontact agricultural series has a younger mortality peak and younger mean age-at-death than the precontact preagricultural series (Larsen 1982). Although this trend has been documented in other areas of the eastern United States and has been interpreted as representing a population undergoing a decline in life expectancy (Lallo et al. 1980), Johansson and Horowitz (1986) have indicated that the pattern more likely reflects an increase in fertility rather than an increase in mortality.

Buikstra and her coworkers (1986, 1987) have suggested that the proportion of D_{30+} (number of individuals older than 30) to D_{5+} (number of individuals older than 5) can be used to estimate birth rate in archaeological skeletal series. They argue that on the basis of the inverse relationship between the proportion and birth rate, an increase in the proportion represents a decrease in birth rate, and conversely, a decrease in the proportion represents an increase in birth rate (Buikstra et al. 1986). A comparison of the proportion D_{30+}/D_{5+} for the precontact preagricultural and agricultural periods shows a decrease (from 0.4222 to 0.1667). This decrease, therefore, suggests that the shift to an agricultural lifeway saw an increase in the birth rate.

The contact period skeletal series are represented by decidedly older individuals than the precontact skeletal series (Larsen and Russell 1989). Mortality in the late contact period is high during the first five years, low during the 5- to 35-year period, and again high after age 40. Over one-fifth (22.9 percent) of the individuals in the sample are older than 45. The trend of increase in mean age-at-death and later adult mortality may reflect a population undergoing a demographic revival despite the aforementioned deteriorating conditions. Alternatively, this trend could represent a population experiencing decline, especially decline related to a decrease in birth rate. Indeed, a calculation of the proportion D_{30}/D_5 for the early contact period (0.2642) and late contact period (0.7263) suggests a decrease in birth rate. We conclude that decline in birth rate coupled with an increase in mortality contributed to a reduction in population size during the early and late contact periods.

That the Guale were experiencing a population decline in the seventeenth century is strongly supported by the early written records by missionaries and other Europeans at the time. For example, there is a marked reduction in the number of native settlements and populations occupying these settlements. By 1675 there were altogether no more than seven settlements with fewer than five hundred natives associated with missions in the area north of Cumberland Island (Jones 1978). By 1686, no mission populations are known to have occupied this region. Although this dramatic reduction was due in part to migrations southward, other factors—especially disease—contributed to the decline. Governor Rebolledo had observed considerable losses of Indians in this regard in Guale and Timucua "because they have been wiped out with the sickness of the plague and small-pox which have overtaken them in the past years" (quoted in Hann 1986:378).

Estimates of population size from historical accounts and from cemetery data indicate that only about 200 Indians were in the area of Santa Catalina de Guale de Santa María by the close of the seventeenth century. With regard to historical sources, in his visit to Amelia Island in 1700, Governor Zúñiga y Cerda reported that the whole of the island could not have been occupied by more than 200 natives (Bushnell 1986). This figure is somewhat less than, but certainly on the order of, an estimate of 216 individuals derived from the population size formula provided by Ubelaker (1984:96) as it is applied to cemetery data from the mission (Larsen and Russell 1989).

Zúñiga y Cerda's reference to the local population as a "miserable, low-spirited people" (quoted in Bushnell 1986:11) takes on much more meaning when viewed in the context of the conditions of the time. Although there are no references to birth rate in native populations, the evidence for change in mortality profiles provided from the study of age-at-death suggests that a reduction in birth rate may have also contributed to the reduction in population size that is documented in written and skeletal records.

Life-Style: Work Load and Behavioral Inference

As noted above, the arrival of Europeans in La Florida had profound implications for life-style in general and work behavior in particular. Undoubtedly, however, work behavior had changed prior to the European contact with the shift from a subsistence economy based exclusively on wild plants and animals to one based at least in part on maize agriculture. Two areas of investigation have provided important data on the impact of the shift from hunting and gathering to a mixed economy as well as the later arrival of Europeans and the establishment of mission centers in the sixteenth and seventeenth centuries. These areas of investigation include (1) osteoarthritis, and (2) cross-sectional geometric properties of long bones.

Osteoarthritis

Osteoarthritis (also known as degenerative joint disease) is an age-related disorder involving degenerative changes of articular joints of the skeleton. Manifestations of the disorder on the joints include either a buildup of bone on joint margins or the erosion and loss of bone on joint surfaces, or both (Larsen 1987). The etiology of osteoarthritis is multifactorial and includes the cumulative effects of metabolic, immunologic, genetic, and mechanical stimuli (cf. Aegerter and Kirkpatrick 1975; DeRousseau 1988; Jurmain 1977). Jurmain (1977, 1980), Merbs (1983), and others have provided evidence from archaeological contexts that lifestyle and especially level and type of mechanical demand figures prominently in its interpretation. Therefore, for purposes of our discussion, we examine osteoarthritis patterning in the context of mechanically related influences.

Data on three subseries of the Guale precontact and contact populations are available, including precontact preagricultural, precontact agricultural, and late contact. A comparison of the frequency of osteoarthritis in the two precontact samples revealed a marked decline in frequency in the agriculturalists relative to the preagriculturalists. The reduction in frequency was especially marked in vertebral, elbow, and knee articular joints (Larsen 1982, 1984). Because the level of mechanical stress is in all likelihood related to relative degree of work load, it appears that the shift to a lifeway involving the use of maize occasioned a decline in mechanical demand.

In sharp contrast to the trend of decline in frequency of osteoarthritis in the precontact populations, there is a marked increase in the late contact period. The increases are especially noteworthy in vertebral, elbow, wrist, and foot joints (Griffin and Larsen 1989). Undoubtedly, some of the difference in frequency between the precontact and contact series is related to the older age composition in the latter. However, the great increase in frequency cannot be explained entirely by age factors (Griffin and Larsen 1989). Therefore, it would seem that the establishment of missions in this region of La Florida and the resultant change in life-style saw a dramatic increase in mechanical demand. We suggest that the written documentation regarding the demands placed on natives as a labor source is reflected by the increase in osteoarthritis in the late contact period.

A comparison of females and males shows a decline in gender differences of osteoarthritis frequency, especially in the vertebral articular joints, from the precontact to the contact periods. These findings suggest that although both females and males saw a reduction and then an increase in the frequency of osteo-arthritis for the respective precontact agriculturalist and late contact periods, the types of physical behaviors that influence the development of the disorder throughout life became more similar between the sexes in the mission popula-tion. It may be that mission adults, regardless of gender, experienced the same level of demand with regard to work activity in the contact period.

Cross-sectional Geometric Properties

Throughout life, bones are subject to a variety of forces that result from walking, running, and other activities. Acting in different combinations, these forces in-clude tension, compression, shear, bending, and torsion. The size, shape, and geometric configuration of bones contribute to their integrity under these differ-ent loading modes. Therefore, an understanding of changes in work demand and behavior in general is provided by the study of mechanical factors and how they influence bone structure.

Using biomechanical beam theory developed by civil and mechanical engi-neers (see Timoshenko and Gere 1972), it is possible to interpret the complex nature of cross-sectional shapes of long bones in the light of several properties. In a mechanical beam model, the strength of a long bone (rigidity) is determined by two primary cross-sectional geometric properties, including (1) area, and (2) second moments of area of bone in a cross section. The cross-sectional area is proportional to strength in compression and tension applied noneccentrically (not off the longitudinal axis of the bone diaphysis), and the second moments of area are proportional to strength in torsion (twisting) and bending along the bone diaphysis (Ruff and Hayes 1983). Simply stated, a decline in these proper-ties represents a decline in bone strength, and by inference, a decline in mechan-ical demand.

Long bones from the lower and upper limbs—femur and humerus, respectively—representative of the precontact preagricultural and agricultural and early contact Guale were analyzed (Larsen and Ruff 1989; Ruff et al. 1984). A comparison of cross-sectional properties between the two precontact groups shows a clear decline in bone strength in the femur and humerus. In the contact period, there is a reversal of this trend.

Looking at these data by gender for both skeletal elements, one sees that the bone strength of females and males decline prior to contact. In the contact per-iod, however, whereas males show an increase in bone strength in the lower and upper limbs, females show an increase in the lower limb, but a continued decrease in the upper limb. These results suggest that the shift from hunting and gathering to agriculture saw a decline in mechanical stress, a finding that is consistent with the aforementioned change in osteoarthritis frequency. In con-trast, behavioral changes associated with increased labor demands on native populations resulted in a general increase in mechanical demand, except in the female upper limb.

A comparison between left and right humeri in the three subsamples shows a dominance of the right limb, a pattern that is typical of human populations in general. The degree of right over left dominance does not remain uniform, but rather shows a decline over time in the Guale series (Fresia et al. 1989). The decline is most marked in the comparison of the two precontact groups, and is less marked between the precontact agricultural and early contact groups. Although both sexes show a decline in right limb dominance, the decline is especially pronounced in females. Females show very strong differences between left and right sides prior to contact. During the contact period, however, asymmetry is reduced to minimal levels. Therefore, sexual dimorphism in use of the upper limbs was most dissimilar in the earliest period and most similar in the contact period. In a study of populations worldwide, Ruff (1987) has suggested that the intensity of the reliance on agriculture resulted in a reduction in the division of labor by gender. The findings reported here lend further support to this hypothesis.

These findings based on change in frequency of osteoarthritis and cross-sectional geometric properties during the contact period suggest that both males and females were subject to increased work loads. It may have been more difficult for females to care for newborn and young children under increasing labor demands. We speculate, therefore, that the period of time between births for individual women may have increased, thereby contributing to a decline in the birth rate.

Other Regions of La Florida

As is clear from the above discussion, skeletal evidence indicates that at least one group of native peoples in La Florida were profoundly affected by the establishment of missions. What does the study of human skeletal remains from mission sites reveal about the other regions of La Florida? Unfortunately, very little is known about human biology either before or after the arrival of Europeans in Timucua, Apalachee, or Apalachicola. Other mission skeletal samples have been recovered (see review in Larsen 1989; Thomas 1987), but, with few exceptions, most have been either reinterred (e.g., San Damian de Escambi, 143 burials), or are otherwise unsuitable for study owing to many years of exposure in an open-air museum (Nombre de Díos, ca. 100 burials). We are currently investigating two additional Amelia Island skeletal series. One is from an ossuary containing mostly disarticulated remains (n=59 individuals; Simmons et al. 1989) and the other includes remains (ca. 120 individuals) recovered from Santa María de Yamassee.

The study of human remains from Apalachee missions provides some information on human health during this time period. Storey (1986) has examined a series of 58 burials from San Pedro de Patale and compared them with a late prehistoric period sample from the nearby Lake Jackson site (n=24). Among other findings, she observed a decrease in hypoplasia frequency. Although the size of the samples is limited, these data suggest that this mission population may have enjoyed relatively good health in comparison with their precontact ancestors.

Preliminary test excavations at San Luis de Talimali by Gary Shapiro produced several dozen teeth in secondary contexts from the mission cemetery. Because the sample is small and most of these teeth are from preadults, it is impossible to draw conclusions regarding reconstruction of lifeway (see Larsen 1988). However, the cemetery appears to be quite large and its excavation would undoubtedly provide a substantial data base.

An especially intriguing aspect of the study of Mission period human biology is the development and rise of the mission system in Apalachee that occurred during the decline of Guale and Timucua. By 1672, Santa Catalina de Guale was less than a decade away from collapse and abandonment, whereas the mission system in Apalachee had built up from one mission to 11 missions serving 8,000 to 9,000 Indians (Hann 1988). Bishop Calderón's census of 1675 indicates that 13,152 Christianized Indians occupied all of La Florida (Wenhold 1936). If these figures are accurate, the Apalachee were clearly the chief players in Indian–Spanish relations. Of the missions of Apalachee, San Luis de Talimali was occupied by the largest resident native population of some 1,400 natives (Hann 1988). Thus, while Guale was experiencing sharp declines in population size, Apalachee was thriving. If more skeletal remains become available from Apalachee, the next step in the study of biological adaptation and change in La Florida will be to compare patterns of health and life-style between Apalachee and Guale. These data will play a key role in providing biological details of success in one system and failure in another.

Other Regions of the Spanish Borderlands

There has been only a limited amount of research done on contact period human remains from other regions of the Spanish Borderlands (Larsen 1989). One notable exception has been the preliminary work completed on human remains from Mission La Purísima by Walker and his coworkers (1989). It is possible to provide some simple comparisons between the Georgia/Florida and California series.

An analysis of stable isotope ratios from the California mission shows that marine resources and maize were of relatively little importance in the diet there, in contrast to the Georgia and Florida coasts. These data, as well as those provided by the analysis of animal and plant food remains suggest, rather, that the La Purísima population focused on terrestrial resources. Moreover, while the California series showed no increase in hypoplasias, comparisons of precontact and contact teeth from Guale indicate increases, at least with respect to number of individuals affected. Despite these differences, however, the missions of both California and La Florida experienced a decline in the diversity of food resources (see Walker et al. 1989) that almost certainly had negative consequences for the health of these populations. Both mission systems experienced dramatic reduction in population size, and these reductions are well documented in the written records. Quite clearly, more research is needed on skeletal samples from other regions of the Spanish Borderlands in order to provide a more complete picture of biocultural change.

Conclusions

Beginning several centuries prior to European contact, native populations occupying what became known as La Florida experienced a population increase, greater social complexity, and a shift to a more sedentary lifeway concomitant with a reorientation of diet from one based on hunting and gathering to one based partly on maize agriculture. These changes saw a reduction in the quality of life and a reduction in mechanical demand. With the arrival of the Europeans and the founding of mission centers during the late sixteenth century in Guale, the addition of new stressors—periodic food shortages, reduced dietary diversity, loss of valuable stored foods, European-introduced diseases, increased work demand, retaliation by the military following native uprisings, and pressure from the English-occupied regions to the north—resulted in the decline and eventual extinction of these populations.

The historical record indicates that there was a shift in focus of the mission system from Guale and Timucua to Apalachee. Population figures available for Apalachee indicate a certain degree of success, but until larger skeletal samples are made available from this region, we can only guess at the biological implications. For now, we have to rely exclusively on archaeological and historical evidence for our understanding of adaptation in this region.

A decade ago, Milner (1980) advocated the integration of cultural and biological data derived from mortuary contexts from the Southeastern United States as a means of developing a better understanding of postcontact native demographic change in the region. This chapter has demonstrated the rich record that human skeletal remains has to offer for both demographic interpretation and dietary and behavioral inference. This multifactorial approach is the only one that can explain fully the multifaceted biological consequences of contact as they relate to the missions of La Florida in the eastern Spanish Borderlands.

Acknowledgments

The discussion presented in this chapter is based on a long-term study of biocultural adaptation of prehistoric and contact period coastal Georgia and northeastern Florida native populations. We wish to thank David Hurst Thomas (American Museum of Natural History) and Jerald T. Milanich (Florida Museum of Natural History) for their cooperation in the excavation and study of human remains from St. Catherines Island and Amelia Island. The recovery of human remains from Santa Catalina de Guale was made possible only by the diligent efforts of field crews under the direction of Clark Spencer Larsen on St. Catherines Island during the years 1982–1986. The combined efforts of archaeological crews from Northern Illinois University, the University of Florida, Williams College, and the University of North Florida, and cooperating institutions on Amelia Island under the able supervision of Rebecca Saunders (University of Florida) is also gratefully acknowledged. Funding for fieldwork on St. Catherines Island came primarily from the St. Catherines Island and Edward John

Noble foundations. The recovery of human remains from sites on Amelia Island would not have come about had it not been for generous funding from Dr. and Mrs. George H. Dorion. The study of the human remains from both localities was funded by the National Science Foundation (grant awards BNS-8406773, BNS-8703849, and BNS-8747309 to CSL). Mark C. Griffin, Susan Simmons, Rebecca Shavit, and Joanna E. Lambert gave invaluable assistance in many aspects of the project.

References

Acsádi, Gy., and J. Nemeskéri
  1970 *History of Human Life Span and Mortality*. Akadémiai Kiadó, Budapest.
Aegerter, E. E., and J. A. Kirkpatrick
  1975 *Orthopedic Diseases: Physiology, Pathology, Radiology*. Saunders, Philadelphia.
Baker, Brenda J., and George J. Armelagos
  1988 The Origin and Antiquity of Syphilis. *Current Anthropology* 29:703–737.
Blakey, Michael L., and George J. Armelagos
  1985 Deciduous Enamel Defects in Prehistoric Americans from Dickson Mounds: Prenatal and Postnatal Stress. *American Journal of Physical Anthropology* 66:371–380.
Buikstra, Jane E., and James H. Mielke
  1985 Demography, Diet, and Health. In *The Analysis of Prehistoric Diets*, edited by Robert I. Gilbert Jr. and James H. Mielke, pp. 362–422. Academic Press, Orlando.
Buikstra, Jane E., Jill Bullington, Douglas K. Charles, Della C. Cook, Susan R. Frankenberg, Lyle W. Konigsberg, Joseph B. Lambert, and Liang Xue
  1987 Diet, Demography, and the Development of Horticulture. In *Emergent Horticultural Economies of the Eastern Woodlands*, edited by William F. Keegan, pp. 67–85. Occasional Paper No. 7. Southern Illinois University at Carbondale Center for Archaeological Investigations.
Buikstra, Jane E., Lyle W. Konigsberg, and Jill Bullington
  1986 Fertility and the Development of Agriculture in the Prehistoric Midwest. *American Antiquity* 51:528–546.
Bushnell, Amy Turner
  1986 *Santa Maria in the Written Record*. Miscellaneous Project Report Series No. 21. Department of Anthropology, Florida Museum of Natural History, Gainesville.
  1987 Displacement and Sequent Relocation of the Santa Catalina de Guale Mission Indians. Paper presented at the meetings of the Society for Historical Archaeology, Savannah.
Cook, Noble David
  1981 *Demographic Collapse: Indian Peru, 1520–1620*. Cambridge University Press, New York.
Crosby, Alfred W.
  1986 *Ecological Imperialism: The Biological Expansion of Europe, 900–1900*. Cambridge University Press, New York.
DeRousseau, C. Jean
  1988 *Osteoarthritis in Rhesus Monkeys and Gibbons*. Contributions to Primatology, Vol. 25. Karger, Basel.
Dobyns, Henry F.
  1983 *Their Number Become Thinned: Native Population Dynamics in Eastern North America*. University of Tennessee Press, Knoxville.
Duncan, Gwyneth A.
  1987 Faunal Remains and Subsistence at the Mission Santa Catalina de Guale, St. Ca-

therines Island, Georgia. Paper presented at the meetings of the Southeastern Archaeological Conference, Charleston.

Fresia, Anne E., Christopher B. Ruff, and Clark Spencer Larsen
1989 Temporal Decline in Bilateral Asymmetry of the Upper Limb on the Georgia Coast. In *The Archaeology of Mission Santa Catalina de Guale: Biocultural Interpretations of a Population in Transition*, edited by Clark Spencer Larsen. Anthropological Papers of the American Museum of Natural History, in preparation.

Goodman, Alan H., R. Brooke Thomas, Alan C. Swedlund, and George J. Armelagos
1988 Biocultural Perspectives on Stress in Prehistoric, Historical, and Contemporary Population Research. *Yearbook of Physical Anthropology* 31:169–202.

Griffin, Mark C., and Clark Spencer Larsen
1989 Patterns in Osteoarthritis: A Case Study from the Prehistoric and Historic Southeastern U.S. Atlantic Coast. Poster presented at the meetings of the American Association of Physical Anthropologists, San Diego.

Hann, John H.
1986 Demographic Patterns and Changes in Mid-Seventeenth Century Timucua and Apalachee. *Florida Historical Quarterly* 64:371–392.
1988 *Apalachee: The Land between the Rivers*. University Presses of Florida, Gainesville.

Huss-Ashmore, Rebecca, Alan H. Goodman, and George J. Armelagos
1982 Nutritional Inference from Paleopathology. In *Advances in Archaeological Method and Theory*, Vol. 5, edited by Michael B. Schiffer, pp. 395–473. Academic Press, New York.

Hutchinson, Dale L., and Clark Spencer Larsen
1988 Determination of Stress Episode Duration from Linear Enamel Hypoplasias. *Human Biology* 60:93–110.
1989 Stress and Lifeway Change: The Evidence from Enamel Hypoplasias. In *The Archaeology of Mission Santa Catalina de Guale: Biocultural Interpretations of a Population in Transition*, edited by Clark Spencer Larsen. Anthropological Papers of the American Museum of Natural History, in preparation.

Johansson, S. Ryan, and S. Horowitz
1986 Estimating Mortality in Skeletal Populations: Influence of the Growth Rate on the Interpretation of Levels and Trends during the Transition to Agriculture. *American Journal of Physical Anthropology* 71:233–250.

Jones, Grant D.
1978 The Ethnohistory of the Guale Coast through 1684. In *The Anthropology of St. Catherines Island: 1. Natural and Cultural History*, by David Hurst Thomas, Grant D. Jones, Roger S. Durham, and Clark Spencer Larsen. Anthropological Papers of the American Museum of Natural History 55:178–210.

Jurmain, Robert D.
1977 Stress and Etiology of Osteoarthritis. *American Journal of Physical Anthropology* 46:353–366.
1980 The Pattern of Involvement of Appendicular Degenerative Joint Disease. *American Journal of Physical Anthropology* 53:143–150.

Keegan, William F.
1987 Diffusion of Maize from South America: The Antillean Connection Reconstructed. In *Emergent Horticultural Economies of the Eastern Woodlands*, edited by William F. Keegan, pp. 329–344. Occasional Paper No. 7. Carbondale Center for Archaeological Investigations, Southern Illinois University.

Kreshover, Seymour J.
1960 Metabolic Disturbances in Tooth Formation. *Annals of the New York Academy of Sciences* 85:161–167.

Lallo, John W., George J. Armelagos, and Robert P. Mensforth
1980 The Role of Diet, Disease, and Physiology in the Origins of Porotic Hyperostosis. *Human Biology* 49:471–483.

Larsen, Clark Spencer
  1982 *The Anthropology of St. Catherines Island: 3. Prehistoric Human Biological Adaptation.* Anthropological Papers of the American Museum of Natural History 57:155–270.
  1984 Health and Disease in Prehistoric Georgia: The Transition to Agriculture. In *Paleopathology at the Origins of Agriculture*, edited by Mark N. Cohen and George J. Armelagos, pp. 367–392. Academic Press, Orlando.
  1987 Bioarchaeological Interpretations of Subsistence Economy and Behavior from Human Skeletal Remains. In *Advances in Archaeological Method and Theory*, Vol. 10, edited by Michael B. Schiffer, pp. 339–445. Academic Press, San Diego.
  1988 *Human Remains from Mission San Luis de Talimali.* Submitted to San Luis Archaeological and Historic Site. Copies available from B. McEwan, Director of Archaeology, San Luis Archaeological and Historic Site, Tallahassee, Florida.
  1989 Biocultural Interpretation and the Context for Contact. In *The Archaeology of Mission Santa Catalina de Guale: Biocultural Interpretations of a Population in Transition*, edited by Clark Spencer Larsen. Anthropological Papers of the American Museum of Natural History, in preparation.
Larsen, Clark Spencer, and Christopher B. Ruff
  1989 Biomechanical Adaptation and Behavior on the Prehistoric Georgia Coast. In *Southeastern Bioarchaeology: A Regional Perspective on the Dynamic Integration of Physical Anthropology and Archaeology*, edited by Mary Lucas Powell, Patricia S. Bridges, and Ann Marie Mires. University of Alabama Press, Tuscaloosa, in press.
Larsen, Clark Spencer, and Katherine F. Russell
  1989 Patterns in Mortality at Contact: Paleodemography of Mission Santa Catalina de Guale de Santa María. Paper presented at the meetings of the American Association of Physical Anthropologists, San Diego.
Larsen, Clark Spencer, Margaret J. Schoeninger, Rebecca Shavit, and Katherine F. Russell
  1989 Dietary and Demographic Transitions on the Southeastern U.S. Atlantic Coast. Unpublished Ms.
Layrisse, M., C. Martinez-Torres, and M. Roche
  1968 Effect of Interaction of Various Foods on Iron Absorption. *American Journal of Clinical Nutrition* 21:1175–1183.
Lovejoy, C. Owen, Richard S. Meindl, Thomas R. Pryzbeck, Thomas S. Barton, Kingsbury Heiple, and David Kotting
  1977 Paleodemography of the Libben Site, Ottawa County, Ohio. *Science* 198:291–293.
Martin, Debra L., Alan H. Goodman, and George J. Armelagos
  1985 Skeletal Pathologies as Indicators of Quality and Quantity of Diet. In *The Analysis of Prehistoric Diets*, edited by Robert I. Gilbert Jr. and James H. Mielke, pp. 227–279. Academic Press, Orlando.
Merbs, Charles F.
  1983 *Patterns of Activity-Induced Pathology in a Canadian Inuit Population.* National Museum of Man Mercury Series, Archaeological Survey of Canada Paper No. 119. Ottawa.
Milner, George R.
  1980 Epidemic Disease in the Postcontact Southeast: A Reappraisal. *Mid-Continental Journal of Archaeology* 5:39–56.
Newbrun, Ernest
  1982 Sugar and Dental Caries: A Review of Human Studies. *Science* 217:418–423.
Ortner, Donald J., and Walter G. J. Putschar
  1985 *Identification of Pathological Conditions in Human Skeletal Remains.* Smithsonian Contributions to Anthropology No. 28.
Powell, Mary Lucas
  1985 The Analysis of Dental Wear and Caries for Dietary Reconstruction. In *The Analysis of Prehistoric Diets*, edited by Robert I. Gilbert Jr. and James H. Mielke, pp. 307–338. Academic Press, Orlando.

1988   *Status and Health in Prehistory: A Case Study of the Moundville Chiefdom*. Smithsonian Institution Press, Washington, D.C.

1989   On the Eve of Conquest: Life and Death at Irene Mound, Georgia. In *The Archaeology of Mission Santa Catalina de Guale: Biocultural Interpretations of a Population in Transition*, edited by Clark Spencer Larsen. Anthropological Papers of the American Museum of Natural History, in preparation.

Ramenofsky, Ann F.

1987   *Vectors of Death: The Archaeology of European Contact*. University of New Mexico Press, Albuquerque.

Reitz, Elizabeth J.

1988   Evidence for Coastal Adaptations in Georgia and South Carolina. *Archaeology of Eastern North America* 16:137–158.

Reitz, Elizabeth J., and C. Margaret Scarry

1985   *Reconstructing Historic Subsistence, with an Example from Sixteenth-Century Spanish Florida*. Special Publication Series No. 3. Society for Historical Archaeology.

Ruff, Christopher B.

1987   Sexual Dimorphism in Human Lower Limb Bone Structure: Relationship to Subsistence Strategy and Sexual Division of Labor. *Journal of Human Evolution* 16:391–416.

Ruff, Christopher B., and Wilson C. Hayes

1983   Cross-Sectional Geometry of Pecos Pueblo Femora and Tibiae—A Biomechanical Investigation: I. Method and General Patterns of Variation. *American Journal of Physical Anthropology* 60:359–381.

Ruff, Christopher B., and Clark Spencer Larsen

1989   Postcranial Biomechanical Adaptations to Subsistence Strategy Changes on the Georgia Coast. In *The Archaeology of Mission Santa Catalina de Guale: Biocultural Interpretations of a Population in Transition*, edited by Clark Spencer Larsen. Anthropological Papers of the American Museum of Natural History, in preparation.

Ruff, Christopher B., Clark Spencer Larsen, and Wilson C. Hayes

1984   Structural Changes in the Femur with the Transition to Agriculture on the Georgia Coast. *American Journal of Physical Anthropology* 64:125–136.

Sauer, Carl Ortwin

1966   *The Early Spanish Main*. University of California Press, Berkeley.

Schoeninger, Margaret J., Michael J. DeNiro, and Henrik Tauber

1983   Stable Nitrogen Isotope Ratios of Bone Collagen Reflect Marine and Terrestrial Components of Prehistoric Human Diet. *Nature* 220:1381–1383.

Schoeninger, Margaret J., Nikolaas J. van der Merwe, Katherine Moore, Julia Lee -Thorp, and Clark Spencer Larsen

1989   Decrease in Diet Quality between the Prehistoric and Contact Periods on St. Catherines Island, Georgia. In *The Archaeology of Mission Santa Catalina de Guale: Biocultural Interpretations of a Population in Transition*, edited by Clark Spencer Larsen. Anthropological Papers of the American Museum of Natural History, in preparation.

Simmons, S., C.S. Larsen, and K.F. Russell

1989   Demographic Interpretations from Ossuary Remains during the Late Contact Period in Northern Spanish Florida. *American Journal of Physical Anthropology* 78:302.

Smith, Bruce D.

1986   The Archaeology of the Southeastern United States: from Dalton to de Soto, 10,500–500 B.P. In *Advances in World Archaeology*, Vol. 5, edited by Fred Wendorf and Angela E. Close, pp. 1–92. Academic Press, Orlando.

Smith, Marvin T.

1987   *Archaeology of Aboriginal Culture Change in the Interior Southeast*. University Presses of Florida, Gainesville.

Steponaitis, Vincas P.

1986   Prehistoric Archaeology in the Southeastern United States, 1970–1985. *Annual Reviews of Anthropology* 15:363–404.

Storey, Rebecca
  1986   Diet and Health Comparisons between Pre- and Post-Columbian Native Americans in North Florida. Paper presented at the meetings of the American Association of Physical Anthropologists, Albuquerque.
Stuart-Macadam, Patty
  1985   Porotic Hyperostosis: Representative of a Childhood Condition. *American Journal of Physical Anthropology* 66:391–398.
Suckling, Grace, D. C. Elliott, and D. C. Thurley
  1986   The Macroscopic Appearance and Associated Histological Changes in the Enamel Organ of Hypoplastic Lesions of Sheep Incisor Teeth Resulting from Induced Parasitism. *Archives of Oral Biology* 31:427–439.
Tauber, Henrik
  1981 ^{13}C Evidence for Dietary Habits of Prehistoric Man in Denmark. *Nature* 292:332–333.
Thomas, David Hurst
  1987   *The Archaeology of Mission Santa Catalina de Guale: 1. Search and Discovery.* Anthropological Papers of the American Museum of Natural History 63:47–161.
Thomas, David Hurst, Grant D. Jones, Roger S. Durham, and Clark Spencer Larsen
  1978   *The Anthropology of St. Catherines Island: 1. Natural and Cultural History.* Anthropological Papers of the American Museum of Natural History 55:155–248.
Thornton, Russell
  1987   *American Indian Holocaust and Survival.* University of Oklahoma Press, Norman.
Timoshenko, S. P., and J. M. Gere
  1972   *Mechanics of Materials.* Van Nostrand Reinhold, New York.
Ubelaker, Douglas H.
  1984   *Human Skeletal Remains: Excavation, Analysis, Interpretation.* Taraxacum, Washington, D.C.
Walker, Phillip L., Patricia Lambert, and Michael J. DeNiro
  1989   The Effect of European Contact on the Health of Alta California Indians. In *Columbian Consequences. Vol. 1: Archaeological and Historical Perspectives on the Spanish Borderlands West*, edited by David Hurst Thomas, pp. 349–364. Smithsonian Institution Press, Washington, D. C.
Wenhold, Lucy L.
  1936   A 17th Century Letter of Gabriel Diaz Vara Calderón, Bishop of Cuba, Describing the Indians and Indian Missions of Florida. *Smithsonian Miscellaneous Collections* 95(16):1–14.

Chapter 27 ■

David J. Weber

Blood of Martyrs, Blood of Indians: Toward a More Balanced View of Spanish Missions in Seventeenth-Century North America

In 1573, following a failed Jesuit attempt, Franciscans began to preach in Spanish Florida. During the first three decades they made little headway, but then progressed rapidly. By the mid-1600s, Christian churches stood in villages of Guales and Timucuans along the Atlantic coast from the Carolinas south to St. Augustine. Westward from St. Augustine an inland mission trail ran through Timucuan territory to the Apalachee country around present-day Talahassee. By 1675, a century after they had begun, Franciscan evangelists had extended that inland trail still farther west into what is today southwestern Georgia and southeastern Alabama. There, over 250 miles west of the main base at St. Augustine, Franciscans briefly insinuated themselves into villages of Chacatos and Apalachicolas—peoples the English would later call Choctaws and Lower Creeks.

Meanwhile, more than halfway across the continent, Franciscans enjoyed similar success at planting missions among Pueblos in New Mexico. Arriving in 1598 with Juan de Oñate, friars began to build permanent missions in New Mexico later than they did in Florida. In just over three decades, however, they established themselves in every substantial Pueblo community, from the Piro pueblo of Socorro in the south to the Tiwa pueblo of Taos some 200 miles to the north, and along an east-west axis that ran nearly 300 miles from the Hopi villages in the west to Pecos and Abó to the east (Gannon 1965).[1]

On the southern fringes of North America, then, a small number of Spanish preachers made rapid inroads into the communal and individual lives of large numbers of natives in the seventeenth century.[2] It was a remarkable achievement. Alone, or with the aid of a single companion and a small military escort, a Franciscan moved into an Indian community and persuaded its residents to construct a temple to an alien god. Among peoples whose largest enclosed public spaces had been, in the main, circular *kivas*, or circular council houses, the friars oversaw the construction of small, rectangular churches. These *conquistadores* of the spirit seldom numbered more than 50 at a time in either seventeenth-century Florida or New Mexico; they wore no armor and carried neither gun nor sword (Matter 1972).[3] Nonetheless, they persuaded numerous Indians to participate in Christian rituals and, at the very least, to take on some of the external attributes of Spanish Christians.

Historians' Explanations

How have historians explained the rapid thrust of these opening salvos in the Spanish Franciscans' two-and-a-half-century offensive against what they called paganism in North America? The answer has varied over time. Through much of this century, historians interpreted the Franciscans' penetration of Indians' worlds largely in Franciscan terms. Few historians attributed missionary expansion to divine providence, as friars often did in the 1600s, but historians generally adopted the Franciscans' view that the priests' own hard work, self-sacrifice, skill, and energy overcame the resistance of obdurate, slothful, and ungrateful savages. Just as historians retold the friars' story of their own success, so too did historians emulate Franciscans by not lingering over disturbing questions about the morality of evangelism.[4]

A passage from the writing of Maynard Geiger, a Franciscan historian who in the late 1930s chronicled his confrères' achievements in seventeenth-century Florida, succinctly suggests the dominant motif. Geiger portrayed the Franciscans as hardy "pioneers."

> Urged on by apostolic zeal, imbued with love for the least progressive of their fellow-men, at times even thirsting for martyrdom, they left the cultural ties of their homeland for manly toil on a cheerless frontier. Often they met scenes dismal and disheartening; people barbaric or savage; primitive agriculture and housing; undeveloped intelligence; a crass morality. The situation was faced with laudable fortitude. True religion was taught, and Christian morality instilled; the wilderness was cleared; homes and houses of worship were built, and schools established; domestic animals were introduced, and agriculture was begun or improved. The missionaries studied the native languages and cultures . . . in order to endear themselves to their rude neophytes [Geiger 1940:1, 1937].

No murky cultural relativism clouded Geiger's vision—or that of most other North Americans interested in missions in his day. As a Franciscan, Geiger might, of course, be expected to laud the achievements of his predecessors, but his views also fitted comfortably into the mainstream of mission historiography.

Dominating that mainstream was the first generation of historians of the so-called Borderlands school, inspired by Berkeley historian Herbert Eugene Bolton (whose disciples included two influential Jesuits, Peter Masten Dunne and John Francis Bannon; for a full list of Bolton-trained doctors, see Bannon 1978:Appendix). In their effort to break down negative stereotypes of Spaniards, the early Boltonians exalted and romanticized Spaniards in general and missionaries in particular. Paradoxically, the same Boltonians who sought to rehabilitate the reputations of Spaniards, failed to question stereotypical views that portrayed Indians as benighted, if not bedeviled and malevolent "untamed savages" (Bolton 1915:19).[5]

Notwithstanding his own foray into Indian history and his sympathy for the subject, Bolton himself set the tone in his classic essay, "The Mission as a Frontier Institution in the Spanish American Colonies," published in 1917. He made the important point that the mission, previously viewed solely as a religious institution, had the fundamental secular goal of advancing, defending and, as he put it, "civilizing" Spanish frontiers in the Americas. While acknowledging that "the missions did not, in every respect, represent a twentieth-century ideal," and noting that "sometimes, and to some degree, they failed, as has every human institution," Bolton judged the missions a great success—"a conspicuous feature of Spain's frontiering genius" (Bannon 1964:211).

Prior to the mid-1960s, the theme of Christophilic triumphalism dominated the abundant American scholarship on North American missions. Historians such as Carlos Castañeda retold stories of how the padres carried "the light of Christianity and the comforts of civilization to the untutored children of the forest" (Castañeda 1945:289; see also Barth 1950:376). The padres, historian John Tate Lanning claimed, brought "comfort and the most softening influence" to the "miserable life" of the "American aborigine." In praise of the padres, Lanning noted (with no hint of sarcasm) that "the toleration shown by them is a marvel. . . . [T]hey permitted the Indians to wear long hair" (Lanning 1935:73–74). The results of the Franciscans' tolerant efforts, these historians asserted, were a "triumph" (Gannon 1965:37) and a "success" (Espinosa 1944:84).

In the pages of these Eurocentric histories, treacherous Indians often failed to appreciate the padres' triumph and behaved badly. As historian J. Manuel Espinosa put it, "missionary success was . . . paid for with the blood of martyrs" (Espinosa 1944:84). But even when natives rebelled and made martyrs of the padres, pro-missionary historians refused to acknowledge missionary efforts as failures. "In mission history every page written with the blood of martyrs is glorious," one Jesuit historian has explained, and "would attract the blessings of heaven for the conversion of natives" (Zubillaga 1941:430). Historians who have issued such pious assessments of the value of the blood of missionary martyrs often seem to place little value on the blood of Indians.

In the late 1970s, Jesuit historian John Francis Bannon, a former student of Bolton's, reviewed the historical literature on Spanish missions in the Borderlands that had been published over the six decades since Bolton's famous essay first appeared. Some scholars, Bannon noted, had challenged the mission's impact "as a beneficent force," but Bolton's general viewpoint, Bannon argued, remained intact. Whatever the mission's failure, it "may still have been one of the more humane approaches of a conquering people" (Bannon 1979:305, 320). Bannon's interpretation of the literature put a gloss on a profound shift that had begun to accelerate in the late 1960s; historians had already begun to take a more critical and balanced view of the Spanish missionary process.

Influenced by anthropologists and ethnohistorians and unburdened by the task of whitewashing the Black Legend, a growing number of historians had begun to examine missions from Indian viewpoints, and to question the criteria for measuring Franciscan successes. Some scholars had begun this reassessment long before, and represented a strong minority tradition,[6] but certainly from the mid-1960s on, the critics' voices grew louder. For seventeenth-century Florida, for example, Michael V. Gannon, writing under the name of Rev. Charles W. Spellman, articulated the new interpretive thrust. Decrying the conventional notion that there was an idyllic "Golden Age" of the Florida missions, Gannon/ Spellman wrote:

> The so-called "Golden Age" was a time of unrelieved poverty and hardship for the friars, of hunger and want and near-slavery for the Indians, of acrimonious disputes between missionaries and officials, of violent Indian revolts, and of equally violent civil suppressions. . . . The "Golden Age" was rather a "Time of Troubles" [Spellman 1965:355].[7]

By the 1980s, a one-sided view of the missionary process seems to have fallen from fashion—even among present-day Catholic missionaries (Luzbetak 1985:512–519).

Some historians, of course, resisted the new current and sought to weigh the good intentions of the padres against their dolorous impact on native communities. Historian Francis Guest, for example, explained the mentalité of the friars with the skill of an ethnographer and urged us to judge the padres by the standards of their day (Guest 1979:1–77, 1985:1–66). Although it is valuable to understand the worldview of Franciscans of the early modern era, it is also important to remember that natives did not share that worldview and did not invite the padres to impose it on them.[8] As late as 1986, ethnohistorian Bernard Fontana chided historians for forgetting that the missionization process "takes place between two parties: the missionaries and those who are missionized. To know one without knowing all we can about the other," Fontana argued, "may provide us with a lot of knowledge but not with much understanding" (Fontana 1986:55).

An inquiry into the dynamics of Franciscan missionization in seventeenth-century North America exemplifies how knowledge of "those who are missionized" can increase our understanding of the entire missionary process. The object of such an inquiry should not be to achieve a more balanced view by seeing Indians merely as victims. Rather, we must also try to understand the role that natives played in determining the scope, shape, and ultimate success or failure of the Franciscans' missionary program.

To understand missionized people is, of course, to raise the elusive "question of the other" that has intrigued our colleagues in literary studies, or the question of how to write the history of a "people without history," that has bedeviled anthropologists and historians alike.[9] For seventeenth-century North America, these questions seem especially intractable because extant sources restrict our vision of this world almost entirely to the hegemonic discourse of the colonizers. Few voices of the missionized have endured in printed form; we have no North American counterpart to the eloquent counterhegemonic discourse of seventeenth-century native writers of Mesoamerica or South America, such as Felipe Gauman Poma de Ayala in Peru (for other examples, see Adorno 1986:146, n.5). Of necessity, then, the reconstruction of Indian–Spanish relations in the seventeenth-century missions of Florida and New Mexico must rely largely on insights gained from Spanish sources and anthropological and archaeological evidence—augmented by conjecture and tempered by a strong resistance to the creation of anachronisms.

Natives' Viewpoints

It seems clear that whatever skill, resources, and force the Franciscans brought to their struggle to extend Christianity to natives in Florida and New Mexico, they did not succeed unless Indians cooperated, and Indians cooperated only when they believed they had something to gain from the new religion and the tangible benefits that accompanied it, or too much to lose from resisting it.

Some natives welcomed missionaries, calculating that friendly relationships with friars would bring material benefits, such as gifts and access to Spanish trade goods.[10] Others saw the Franciscans as a key to defense against predatory Indian neighbors or predatory Spaniards. Natives often regarded priests as useful intermediaries between themselves and the potentially hostile Spanish soldiers. Viceroy Antonio de Mendoza made the telling remark that Indians, "welcome the friars, and where they flee from us like deer . . . they come to them" (Hammond and Rey 1960:161; see also Axtell 1982:37; Sanz de Lezaún 1937:3:47). Some natives saw an alliance with the friars as a way to shift the balance of power against enemies from other tribes. In the early stages of Franciscan missionary work in New Mexico, for example, growing pressure from Apaches appears to have driven a number of Pueblos to the friars—just as pressure from Comanches would later drive Apaches to seek missionaries.[11] Thus, natives sought to manipulate missionaries to promote their own security much as the Spanish Crown tried to utilize missionaries to secure its frontiers from natives and imperial rivals. When conditions were right, the natives' tactics worked and enabled some of their societies to survive (see, e.g., Axtell 1982:37; Cushing 1979:182; Hu-DeHart 1981:3).

Initially, at least, submission to the foreign priests also seemed to offer natives access to awesome spiritual power. To some Indians, Franciscans may have appeared to be "powerful witches" who needed to be appeased, or powerful shamans with whom it seemed wise to cooperate (Shipek 1985:485).[12] Like Christians, many North American Indians believed that priests and ceremonies had power to mediate between man and nature (Dozier 1970:50; Loucks 1979:28–31). Franciscans claimed such power as they conjured cures, rain, and good harvests. From the first, several signs of the friars' power were readily evident to Indians. Armed Spanish soldiers and splendidly attired government officials prostrated themselves before the unarmed, plain-robed priests. Franciscans introduced and controlled domestic animals, larger than the natives had previously known, and could thereby provide a steady supply of meat without hunting (Gutiérrez 1987:18; Polzer 1976:48).[13] Strange diseases that took the lives of Indians spared Europeans who followed the Christian god. At first, then, natives had reason to believe that the foreign preachers possessed life-saving powers. The specter of death from mysterious maladies probably persuaded some tribes to request missionaries and some Indian mothers to seek baptism for their children (Dobyns 1981:54; Reff 1985:14, 264, 322–324; Smith 1987:126).

The extent to which Indians saw themselves as beneficiaries of relationships with missionaries was, in part, specific to the values of each native society. When Franciscans brought gifts to Pueblos, for example, they put the Pueblos in their debt. In the Pueblo world, the acceptance of gifts implied reciprocity (Gutiérrez 1987:6–10, 34–38). Franciscan celibacy, to cite another example, may have seemed unremarkable to some natives, but probably awed the Pueblos for whom, as historian Ramón Gutiérrez has put it, "sexuality was the very project of the cosmos." Pueblo males believed that by abstaining from sexual activity for several days they achieved greater strength for the hunt, for curing, or for conjuring rain. What power might accrue to those friars who practiced life-long sexual abstinence (Gutiérrez 1987:20)![14]

Economic and environmental conditions also figured into the natives' calculations of costs and benefits. It seems no coincidence that nomads and seminomads, such as Apaches in the Southwest or Chiscos in the Southeast, succeeded at retaining their spiritual and physical independence for they could move beyond the Spanish sphere and leave behind little of value at traditional hunting or gathering places (for attempts to convert Apachees and other nomads in the 1600s, see Forbes 1960:116–120, 128–129, 158, 159–160; John 1975:76). Conversely, Franciscans in Florida and New Mexico made their earliest conversions among town-dwelling agriculturalists, who had the most to lose if antagonized Spaniards burned their villages and trampled their crops—the more so perhaps in arid New Mexico, which offered few ecological niches to which Pueblo farmers might escape. Of course, some town-dwellers, protected from reprisal by distance or natural barriers, managed to retain a high degree of spiritual independence and physical freedom. Hopis, for example, submitted to missionaries in 1629, but regained their independence in 1680 and refused thereafter to permit a missionary to remain among them. "The religion of the Moqui [Hopi] today is the same as before they heard about the Gospel," lamented one Franciscan who visited their isolated mesa-top villages in 1775 (Fray Silvestre Vélez de Escalante's diary, quoted in Adams 1963:136).

Natives who decided to accept missions after weighing their apparent benefits and liabilities also determined which aspects of Christianity and European culture they would embrace and which they would reject. As a rule, those native societies that had not been vitiated by war or disease adopted from the friars what they perceived was both useful and compatible with their essential values and institutions. Ideally, they sought to add the new without discarding the old, or to replace elements in their culture with parallel elements from the new—as they had done long before the arrival of Europeans.[15] In the religious sphere, for example, many natives simply added the Christian deity to their pantheons and welcomed the Franciscan as another shaman into their community. Guales who previously had carried offerings of food to mortuary temples now brought those offerings on the Day of the Dead; in place of shell gorgets, Guales wore religious medals (Larson 1978:135; Thomas 1988:119). Some Pueblos seem to have incorporated Franciscans, and perhaps even Jesus, into their cosmography as Kachinas, or representatives of mythological beings (Gutiérrez 1987:52).[16] In the area of material culture, to take other examples, neophytes added foods to their diet without discarding the old, added metal to the tips of their hoes yet retained their way of farming, and used metal tools for carpentry but did not change radically the method of constructing their own buildings (Deagan 1978:113–114; Dozier 1970:65–67; Hann 1988:239, 241, 243; Super 1988:88).

However selective neophytes might have been in adopting aspects of Christianity and Spanish culture, their decision to accept missionaries began to transform their cultures—often in ways that neither they nor the missionaries intended. Adoption of items of European material culture usually brought about profound transformations.[17] By cultivating certain European crops and raising European domestic animals, for example, natives often enriched their diet, lengthened the growing season, deemphasized hunting in favor of agriculture, and made it possible for their villages to support denser populations. Their prosperity also made them more attractive targets for raids by nomads, and forced them to devote more resources to defense.[18] To take another example, the political structures and religious systems of some Indian communities fractured as leaders became bitterly divided between those who converted and those who did not. On occasions, factionalism (doubtless a feature of precontact Indian societies) become so bitter that it led to bloodshed (for an example in Florida, see Covington 1963:130–131; in New Mexico, Cordell 1984:354–355). Thus, in ways too numerous to enumerate and that varied greatly among Indian peoples, acceptance of missionaries and European material goods transformed native economies, polities, social structures, and family life. Native groups who accepted missionaries and who had previously enjoyed independence found themselves reduced from the status of sovereign peoples to subject populations. They came to occupy one of the lowest rungs on the socioeconomic ladder of the new social order.

Notwithstanding the direct and indirect transformations effected by the missionary process, it appears that natives, more often than not, successfully resisted the friars' efforts to eradicate or significantly transform their religious beliefs or cultural values. Although they made superficial adjustments to please the friars or to win the favor of the Christian god, such as participating in Catholic rituals or changing burial customs, neophytes on the seventeenth-century Spanish frontier apparently retained the integrity of their religions (for changes in burial customs, see, e.g., Deagan 1978:114; Larson 1978:134). Some natives probably underwent sincere conversions, and other individuals probably found a way to synthesize old and new religions—much as Christians in Spain blended elements of pagan and Catholic belief and ritual. More commonly, however, it appears that mission Indians practiced both the old and the new religions simultaneously. Mission Indians did not survive long enough in Spanish Florida to testify to the depth or manner of their conversions, but Pueblos did. To this day, many simultaneously practice Catholicism through the intermediary of a Catholic priest, and indigenous religious traditions through native priests—compartmentalizing each religion rather than synthesizing the two.[19]

One can imagine many reasons why neophytes did not succumb so completely to the blandishments of the new religion that they rejected the old. One reason, it seems likely, was that the bright future that Franciscans offered at the outset of the courtship quickly lost its luster. Indeed, the terms of exchange had shifted against the mission Indians in the seventeenth century. Along with the padres' gifts and access to trade goods had come demands for labor and resources, and those demands on individual neophytes increased as Indian populations declined. Obedience to the Franciscans and their god did not stop the spread of diseases strange to the natives. The worlds of the natives continued to collapse. By 1680, the Pueblo population had fallen by at least half, to some 17,000, since the Franciscans' arrival.[20] In Florida, the eastern Timucuans had nearly disappeared by 1680; a Spanish census of 1675 reported that only 1370 remained, most of them west of the Suwannee River. Florida, as one historian has put it, "had become a hollow peninsula" (Bushnell 1978:4; see also Deagan 1978:89–90, 95; Milanich 1978:59–88). The Apalachees had declined from about 25,000, from their first contact with missionaries early in the 1600s, to some 10,000 by about 1680 (Hann 1988:163–166). Enemy raids, desertions, movement into colonists' communities, and forced labor also diminished the numbers of Indians in missions, but epidemics of smallpox, measles, and other difficult-to-identify diseases appear to have been the principal cause of these rapid population declines (see, e.g., Dozier 1970:63; Hann 1988:175–178, 180).

The prayers of the padres did not shield the natives from European diseases or from other natural or man-made disasters. In the semiarid Southwest, years passed when little rain fell upon the land. Crops failed, hunger increased, and the surviving crops and livestock proved tempting targets for Apache raiders. In the Southeast, a skilled Indian labor force at the Spanish missions proved irresistible to English slave hunters by the late seventeenth century.

In such troubled times it must have seemed to Indian neophytes that Franciscan shamans had lost their magic, or that the Christian god did not have the strength of the old gods (Gutiérrez 1987:42). A story handed down among the Pueblos, originating perhaps at Zuni, tells of a struggle between the Christians' "God" and Poshaiyanyi, a Pueblo deity to whom the Pueblos would turn when they launched a full-scale offensive against the Spaniards in 1680.

God and Poshaiyanyi were going to have a contest to see which one had the most power. They were going to shoot at a tree. God shot at it with a gun and cut a gash in the bark. Poshaiyanyi struck it with a bolt of lightning and split the trunk in half. Next they were going to see which one had the best things to eat. God had a table with lots of good things on it. Poshaiyanyi ate on the ground; he had some fat deer meat and some tortillas. God watched Poshaiyanyi eat for a while, then he got down on the ground and ate with him [Chávez 1967:115].[21]

To control the forces of the cosmos, which seemed to have deserted them, mission Indians turned more openly to traditional gods, such as Poshaiyanyi, and to prayers, ceremonies, and priests that had proved efficacious in the past (for evidence of this among the Pueblos, see Dozier 1970:50; Scholes 1942:16). The friars, however, condemned those traditional religious practices as idolatrous, and forcibly denied the natives freedom of worship. Thus, natives learned to their sorrow that Christianity was incompatible with some of their most cherished values and institutions, and that their decision to accept baptism was irrevocable in the eyes of the friars.

With the aid of soldiers, some Franciscans quashed non-Catholic public religious ceremonies, and intruded into the most private aspects of natives' lives. In every province where they established missions in the seventeenth century— among Pueblos, Timucuans, Guales, Apalachees, and Apalachicolas—some of the friars attempted to end polygamy and to impose indissoluble monogamy on natives. In so doing, the friars often enraged and humiliated native males who lacked the Christian arithmetic that one wife was better than two or three. Timucuans, who explained to one priest that "they enjoyed their vice and therefore it must not be evil but good and just," received an unsympathetic hearing (Covington 1963:133; see also Hann 1988:12–13; Matter 1972:74; Oré 1936:101). Among the Pueblos, where sexuality and sanctity were closely linked, the affront to their dignity must have been especially deep (Foote and Schackel 1986:26–29; Gutiérrez 1987:22). Perhaps, too, the hypocrisy of those Christians (including some of the friars) who themselves engaged in sexual practices prohibited by their church, did not go unnoticed by natives (for evidence of such conduct among priests in New Mexico, see Scholes 1942:188).

Oppressed in body and in spirit, many mission Indians sought ways to extricate themselves from the loving embrace of the sons of St. Francis. Strategies varied. Some individuals fled, as did entire communities on a few occasions. Others tried to rid themselves of individual priests by making their lives unpleasant (Pueblos at Taos served their padre tortillas with urine and mouse meat), or by murdering them.[22] Neophytes also rebelled. Mission Indians revolted on a large scale at least once in each of the four mission provinces of Florida, before finally contributing to the complete collapse of the Florida missions between 1680 and 1706. And on a number of occasions Pueblos revolted in New Mexico before their successful rebellion of 1680 drove all Spaniards out of the province. Friars often understood these revolts as the work of the "devil," or as a sign of native ingratitude (Oré 1936:73). The actions of natives, however, who killed Franciscans, mocked Christianity, and desecrated the friars' sacred objects and shrines, make it clear, at least in retrospect, that freedom of religious and cultural expression stood high on the agenda of rebellious mission Indians. Natives rebelled against the Spanish colonial system for many reasons, of course, including excessive demands for labor and tribute imposed on them by private parties and ecclesiastical and civil officials (see, e.g., Boyd et al. 1951:6–8, 19; Bushnell 1979:6; Hann 1988:260–261; also, for New Mexico, Hackett 1941).

Frontier Failures

An attempt to understand missions from the viewpoints of the missionized and of those Indians who eluded missionization implicitly undermines the conventional wisdom that missions represented a triumph or a success. A more balanced view compels the question: success for whom?

The Spanish Franciscans who contended with native religions on the seventeenth-century frontiers of North America succeeded when they measured their achievement by the number of mission communities where natives worshiped as Catholics and lived as Spaniards, or the number of souls sent heavenward through baptism. By this latter standard, the deaths of neophytes from European diseases did not diminish the padres' achievements. Franciscans not only regarded the deaths of Indians and non-Indians as a manifestation of God's will, but, as one historian has noted, "missionaries would have philosophically preferred dead Christians to live pagans" (Archibald 1978:180; John 1975: 189–190). At a less transcendental but more demonstrable level, the friars may also have succeeded, as they and many latter-day historians have argued, in saving natives from extinction at the hands of Spanish settlers and soldiers (see, e.g., Bolton 1917:211; Cushing 1979:182; Gómez Canedo 1977:143; Hu-DeHart 1981:3; Kelsey 1985:511).

Whatever they accomplished, the Franciscans recognized that they fell short of their goal of weakening the indigenous religions and replacing them with their own. After 80 years of missionary efforts among the Pueblos, for example, one Spaniard complained that "most" of them "have never forsaken idolatry, and they appear to be Christians more by force than to be Indians who are reduced to the Holy Faith" (Luís de Quintana, in Forbes 1960:177; see also Dozier 1970:50). A true synthesis of the belief systems of the natives and the Spanish intruders did not occur in the seventeenth century. Rather, religions and values remained in lively contention with one another. To the extent that the militant Franciscans persecuted native religious leaders and tried to impose religious orthodoxy by force, they drove true believers into secret worship and provoked violent resistance (Dozier 1970:55). Critics of the missions have compared them to penal institutions and Indian neophytes to inmates, who suffered from pestilence, oppression, brutality, and "near-slavery" (Spellman 1965:355; see also Bowden 1981:xvi; Dozier 1970:55; Heizer 1978:121–139; Matter 1981:402 [on conditions in California, see Costo and Costo 1987; Meighan 1987:187–201; Sandos 1988:1253–1269]). Critics have questioned the right of missionaries "to invade the most sacred inner precincts of another man's being" (Matson and Fontana 1977:31), and have charged the Franciscans with "religious persecution" (Ortiz 1983:281).

The friars also failed to achieve fully their goal of Hispanicizing the Indians—a goal that some scholars have found neither laudable nor possible (see Fontana 1986:58). It seems clear in retrospect that the missionaries could not have transmitted cultural values effectively in an institution that, in practice, isolated Indians from the larger Hispanic community and in which members of the recipient culture, apparently as dedicated to their own values as Spaniards were to theirs, so vastly outnumbered the missionaries who represented the donor culture.[23]

Finally, missions failed to serve the defensive function that the Crown imagined they would. In Florida and New Mexico, native rebellions proved especially costly. They destroyed not only the missions but rolled back the entire Spanish frontier. As one historian has argued, Spain's "fantasy" of relying on missionaries for Indian control had "helped to divert it from establishing realistic defenses" (Matter 1975:36; see also Matter 1975:32, n.48; 37, n.67; Arnade 1960:277).

Whatever their spiritual successes, then, missionaries failed to advance permanently, defend effectively, or Hispanicize deeply Spain's North American frontiers of the seventeenth century. Although Franciscans succeeded initially in pushing the edges of Christendom into parts of North America, natives pushed them back. Despite new safeguards that the Spanish Crown had built into the system in the late sixteenth century, friars and natives in seventeenth-century North America repeated a cycle that had played itself out a century before in other regions of Spanish America where natives' initial acceptance of missionaries had turned to disillusion, estrangement, and finally to resistance in its many forms, including rebellion (see Farriss 1984:68–79; Gibson 1964:111–112; Korth 1968:51–52, 60, 81; MacLeod 1973:120–142; Stern 1982:51–79). In seventeenth-century North America, then, the mission did not fit Bolton's model of a successful "frontier institution." In many respects, it represented a frontier failure, and it failed in large part because Indians did not wish it to succeed.

In the eighteenth century, when the Crown abandoned its excessive dependence on missionaries, and relied more on soldiers to advance and hold its North American frontiers, the mission-presidio complex may have made greater inroads among those natives who either could not or would not resist the increased force that Spain brought to bear upon them. That, however, is another story.[24]

Acknowledgments

Work on this essay was facilitated by support from the Andrew W. Mellon Foundation, the Center for Advanced Study in the Behavioral Sciences at Stanford, and my own institution, Southern Methodist University. Jane Lenz Elder, research assistant par excellence, aided in numerous ways and prepared the final manuscript for publication. I am also grateful to several generous and astute colleagues who read the manuscript and offered advice that I have invariably valued even if I did not always accept it: Amy Turner Bushnell, the University of South Alabama; Olive Patricia Dickason, the University of Alberta; R. David

Edmunds, Texas Christian University; Ramón Gutiérrez, the University of California, San Diego; John L. Kessell, the University of New Mexico; Peter Onuf,
Southern Methodist University; and David Hurst Thomas. I am also grateful to
Professor Gutiérrez for granting me permission to quote from and to cite his
provocative essay: "When Padre Jesus Came, the Corn Mothers Went Away: The
1680 Pueblo Revolt Reconsidered."

Notes

1. The most accessible narration of these events, and a convenient guide to sources,
is Gannon (1965). There is no specialized overview of the Franciscan missions in
seventeenth-century New Mexico, but two works by anthropologists serve as the best
points of departure: Spicer (1962), and Dozier (1970).

2. I am following the common usage of defining North America as that part of the
continent north of Mexico.

3. The Crown apparently authorized as many as 70 friars for Florida, but the actual
number usually stayed below 50 (see Matter 1972:417–418, Table 3). In New Mexico, 66
was apparently the highest number authorized in the 1600s, but usually fell short of that
(Scholes 1942:9).

4. In saying the Franciscans did not linger over such questions, I do not mean to
imply that they did not raise them. See, for example, Phelan (1970:9–10), and
MacCormack (1985:443–466), with its fine discussion of the theological questions surrounding the Christian tension between authority and reason.

5. A number of writers have commented on this Eurocentrism of the early
Boltonians. See Weber (1988:60–62). Bolton paradoxically did pioneering work in Indian
history and tried to steer some of his students in that direction (John 1988:193–194).

6. Perhaps the most outspoken critic of the missions was Sherburne F. Cook, whose
monographs, *The Indian versus the Spanish Mission* and *The Physical and Demographic Reaction of the Nonmission Indians in Colonial and Provincial California*, appeared in 1943, and
were reprinted in Cook (1976).

7. Spellman's grim picture stands in sharp contrast to the interpretation in Gannon
(1965), which affirmed the existence of the "Golden Age." What is remarkable, and certainly a historiographical rarity, is that Spellman's and Gannon's work, both appearing
in 1965, were written by the same person. As Gannon explained the story to me in a
telephone conversation (June 12, 1989), Spellman had begun a study of the seventeenth
century for a special issue of the *Catholic Historical Review*, but had completed just a bare
outline when he died. Gannon decided to finish the article, writing it in Spellman's name
as a memorial to him. As Gannon looked more deeply into the seventeenth century, his
own views on the "Golden Age" began to shift, representing, as he explained to me,
"a maturation of my understanding of what actually happened." Gannon's own manuscript on the Florida missions, *The Cross in the Sand*, presented a rosier picture, but was
then in press and could not be changed. Gannon had remained silent about his author-
ship of the Spellman article until the spring of 1989, when he was provoked into coming
to Spellman's defense. Gannon continues to subscribe to the argument that he advanced
in the article that he wrote under Spellman's name, and his more "mature" view seems
to have become the dominant one in Florida historiography, if the work of Robert Allen
Matter is an indication. See, for example, Matter (1972, 1981:402).

Earlier historians of seventeenth-century New Mexico also claimed to have found
a "Golden Age" in the first decades of expansion. See, for example, Espinosa (1944:84)
and Lynch (1954:xx). Perhaps, however, because Pueblos repudiated the missionary program so thoroughly in rebellions in 1680 and 1696, New Mexico historians had been less
inclined to romanticize the missions. See, for example, Scholes (1937). More recent dis-

cussions of Franciscan activity in seventeenth-century New Mexico have continued to be critical. See, for example, Forbes (1960) and John (1975).

8. That some Franciscans used coercive means, including force and the threat of force, to eradicate native religions and replace them with their own, seems to me well established. Not all friars agreed with the use of coercion, but those who argued for coexistence and gradual change generally lost out to those who saw native religions as the handiwork of the devil and who advocated their rapid and violent eradication. There is a large literature on this subject. See, for example, Clendinnen (1982), Guest (1979), Kamen (1988), MacCormack (1985).

9. In the study of colonial Spanish America, Tzvetan Todorov (1982) brought "the question of the other" into greater prominence. On the "People without History," a phrase given currency by Eric Wolf, see Sheridan (1988a), who provides an interesting case study and a fine introduction to this question.

10. Most authorities, and most Franciscans of the time, took the view that gifts and trade goods were powerful inducements. See, for example, Hann (1988:123–133).

11. John (1975:56) suggests this possibility for the years 1607–1608, when the Franciscans reported an unusual number of baptisms. See, too, ibid., 258–303.

12. Shipek offers a delightful reconstruction of how Kumeyaay Indians probably responded to Franciscans. Native responses can only be reconstructed through an informed imagination, but on the points in these paragraphs, anthropologists and historians seem to agree. See, for example, Gutiérrez (1987:16–18, 42).

13. I do not mean to suggest that Indians preferred raising livestock to hunting, but only to suggest that the relative efficiency of keeping large animals contained may have impressed natives.

14. For attempts to convert Apaches and other nomads in the 1600s, see, for example, Forbes (1960:116–120, 128–29, 158, 159–60). See, too, the episode recounted in John (1975:76).

15. This is, of course, a universal tendency, and there is widespread agreement among scholars that a syncretic religion developed among most natives in Spanish America. See, for example, Barth (1950:339), and Gibson (1964:100–101, 134). For Spanish North America see Deagan (1978:112–114), Spicer (1962:506–508, 567–572), and Schroeder (1979:239). This was also true in English America (Axtell 1982:39).

16. For a modern reference to Jesus as a Kachina, see Fergusson (1931:33). Among the Hopis, who resisted Christianity more staunchly than other Pueblos, Frederick J. Dockstader found no case of a Kachina "taken over from white culture" (Dockstader 1985:11).

17. See, for example, Dozier (1970:65), who probably understates the impact of material culture, but who notes that "the most tangible changes . . . affected the economy." For Florida, see the wide-ranging essay by Hilton (1983:249–270). Hann (1988:237–263) devotes a chapter to "Indian and Spanish Interaction and Acculturation," much of which represented missionary and Indian interaction. For a contrary view on the impact of material culture, see Reff (1985:325).

18. For an especially cogent discussion of the indirect impact of the acceptance of European domestic animals and winter wheat on the Pimas, see Sheridan (1988b:157–160). See, too, John (1975:67), Larson (1978:133), and Ford (1987:73–91). Reff (1985:316–321) dismisses the importance of European "innovations" including livestock, but I believe that he overstates his case. Archaeological evidence suggests that Spanish trade goods were not abundant, especially in comparison with those available through the French and English. See, for example, Larson (1978:135–138), but the few trade goods that Spaniards did offer, together with those animals and plants that reproduced themselves, seem to me to be of great significance.

19. Pueblo practice has been termed a "dual tradition," or "compartmentalization" (Dozier 1961:94). I am drawing the distinction between this, and a syncretic religion.

Scholes (1942:16) argues that in societies like those of the Pueblos, where "religion, village government, and social institutions were so closely interrelated . . . it was impossible to abolish any part without destroying the whole." For an extraordinary example of a Pueblo individual who publicly professed Catholicism, but who privately continued traditional practices, see Kessell (1980–1981:16–17). Matter (1981:418–420) provides a brief and balanced assessment of this question for Florida. For elements of syncretism in Spain, see Christian (1972, 1981).

20. The rate and percentage of decline of the Pueblo population over the course of the seventeenth century cannot be stated with accuracy because estimates of the base population as of 1600 vary wildly. See Schroeder (1983:254). The decline of numbers of Pueblos and their towns may have occurred quite early in the century. See Forbes (1960:139, 175) and Fray Juan de Pardo to the Viceroy, Mexico, September 26, 1638, who estimated the Pueblos had declined from 60,000 to 40,000 due to smallpox "and the sickness that the Mexicans call *cocolitzli*" (Hackett 1923–1937:3:108).

21. Part of a folk tale from Santo Domingo, that apparently originated at Zuni. Chávez identifies this figure as *Pohé-Yemo*. In Tewa, the correct name is *P'ose yemu*—"he who scatters mist before him" (Ortiz 1980–1981:21).

22. For an example of the flight of a village, see the case of a Guale village cited in Gannon (1983:232). Benavides (1916:97) told of the urine and mousemeat at Taos (he reported this as a murder attempt, but Taoseños certainly would have used more lethal substances if they intended to kill the priest), and of the death of a priest at the Hopi Pueblo of Awatovi from what he believed to be poison (1916:77). Both Florida and New Mexico had a substantial number of martyrs, some of whom died rather mysteriously.

23. Polzer (1976:53–54, 58) suggested that missionaries did not fail in this task, but rather that the racially stratified non-Indian world beyond the mission was "probably incapable of preparing and accepting Indians into the more advanced forms of frontier society" (1976:55). His position, however, seems to beg the question. For the other viewpoint, see Ricard (1966:153–154, 288–295).

24. Naylor and Polzer (1986:9) comment on the tendency of Borderlands historians to generalize about the presidio, on the basis of the more abundant sources of the eighteenth century. The same question might be raised about historical treatment of missions. The change in emphasis in New Mexico, the one area of North America where missions survived from the seventeenth to eighteenth centuries, was recently limned with clarity and grace by Kessell (1989:127–138).

References

Adams, Eleanor B.
  1963   Fray Silvestre and the Obstinate Hopi. *New Mexico Historical Review* 38:97–138.
Adorno, Rolena
  1986   *Gauman Poma: Writings and Resistance in Colonial Peru*. University of Texas, Austin.
Archibald, Robert
  1978   Indian Labor at the California Missions: Slavery or Salvation? *Journal of San Diego History* 24:172–182.
Arnade, Charles W.
  1960   The Failure of Spanish Florida. *Florida Historical Quarterly* 16:271–281.
Axtell, James
  1982   Some Thoughts on the Ethnohistory of Missions. *Ethnohistory* 29:35–41.
Bannon, John Francis
  1978   *Herbert Eugene Bolton: The Historian and the Man*. University of Arizona, Tucson.
  1979   The Mission as a Frontier Institution: Sixty Years of Interest and Research. *Western Historical Quarterly* 10:303–322.

Bannon, John Francis (editor)
1964 *Bolton and the Spanish Borderlands.* University of Oklahoma Press, Norman.

Barth, Pious
1950 *Franciscan Education and the Social Order in North America, 1502–1821.* Chicago.

Benavides, Alonso de
1916 *The Memorial of Fray Alonso de Benavides, 1630,* edited by Frederick Webb Hodge and Charles Fletcher Lummis. Translated by Mrs. Edward E. Ayer. Privately printed, Chicago.

Bolton, Herbert Eugene
1915 *Texas in the Middle Eighteenth Century: Studies in Spanish Colonial History and Administration.* University of California Press, Berkeley.
1917 The Mission as a Frontier Institution in the Spanish American Colonies. In *Bolton and the Spanish Borderlands,* edited by John Francis Bannon, pp. 187–225. University of Oklahoma Press, Norman. Originally published in 1917.

Bowden, Henry Warner
1981 *American Indians and Christian Missions: Studies in Cultural Conflict.* University of Chicago Press, Chicago.

Boyd, Mark F., Hale G. Smith, and John W. Griffin
1951 *Here They Once Stood: The Tragic End of the Apalachee Missions.* University of Florida Press, Gainesville.

Bushnell, Amy T.
1978 "That Demonic Game": The Campaign to Stop Indian Pelota Playing in Spanish Florida, 1675–1684. *The Americas* 35:1–19.
1979 Patricio de Hinachuba: Defender of the Word of God, the Crown of the King, and the Little Children of Ivitachuco. *American Indian Culture and Research Journal* 3:1–21.

Castañeda, Carlos E.
1945 The Sons of St. Francis in Texas. *The Americas* 1:289–302.

Chávez, Angélico
1967 Pohé-Yemo's Representative. *New Mexico Historical Review* 42:85–126.

Christian, William A., Jr.
1972 *Person and God in a Spanish Village.* Seminar Press, New York.
1981 *Local Religion in Sixteenth-Century Spain.* Princeton University Press, Princeton.

Clendinnen, Inga
1982 Disciplining the Indians: Franciscan Ideology and Missionary Violence in Sixteenth-Century Yucatan. *Past and Present* 94:27–48.

Cook, Sherburne F.
1976 *The Conflict between the California Indian and White Civilization.* Reprinted. University of California Press, Berkeley. Originally published 1943, as *The Indian versus the Spanish Mission* and *The Physical and Demographic Reaction of the Nonmission Indians in Colonial and Provincial California.*

Cordell, Linda S.
1984 *Prehistory of the Southwest.* Academic Press, Orlando, Florida.

Costo, Rupert, and Jeannette Henry Costo (editors)
1987 *The Missions of California: A Legacy of Genocide.* Indian Historian Press, San Francisco.

Covington, James W. (editor)
1963 *Pirates, Indians and Spaniards: Father Escobedo's "La Florida."* Great Outdoors, St. Petersburg.

Cushing, Frank Hamilton
1979 Zuni and the Missionaries: Keeping the Old Ways. In *Selected Writings of Frank Hamilton Cushing,* edited by Jesse Green, pp. 176–184. University of Nebraska, Lincoln.

Deagan, Kathleen A.
1978   Culture in Transition: Fusion and Assimilation among the Eastern Timucua. In *Tacachale: Essays on the Indians of Florida and Southeastern Georgia during the Historical Period*, edited by Jerald Milanich and Samuel Proctor, pp. 89–119. University of Florida, Gainesville.

Dobyns, Henry F.
1981   *From Fire to Flood: Historic Human Destruction of Sonoran Desert Riverine Oases.* Ballena Press, Socorro, New Mexico.

Dockstader, Frederick J.
1985   *The Kachina and the White Man: The Influence of White Culture on the Hopi Kachina Cult.* Revised. University of New Mexico, Albuquerque. Originally published 1954.

Dozier, Edward P.
1961   Rio Grande Pueblos. In *Perspectives in American Indian Culture Change*, edited by Edward H. Spicer, pp. 94–186. University of Chicago Press, Chicago.
1970   *The Pueblo Indians of North America.* Holt, Rinehart and Winston, New York.

Espinosa, J. Manuel
1944   Our Debt to the Franciscan Missionaries of New Mexico. *Americas* 1:79–87.

Farriss, Nancy M.
1984   *Maya Society under Colonial Rule: The Collective Enterprise of Survival.* Princeton University Press, Princeton.

Ferguson, Erna
1931   *Dancing Gods: Indian Ceremonials of New Mexico and Arizona.* University of New Mexico, Albuquerque.

Fontana, Bernard L.
1986   Indians and Missionaries of the Southwest during the Spanish Years: Cross Cultural Perceptions and Misperceptions. *Proceedings of the 1984 and 1985 San Antonio Missions Research Conferences*, pp. 55–59. LEBCO Graphics, San Antonio.

Foote, Cheryl J., and Sandra K. Schackel
1986   Indian Women of New Mexico, 1535–1680. In *New Mexico Women: Intercultural Perspectives*, edited by Joan M. Jensen and Darlis A. Miller, pp. 17–40. University of New Mexico, Albuquerque.

Forbes, Jack D.
1960   *Apache, Navaho, and Spaniard.* University of Oklahoma Press, Norman.

Ford, Richard I.
1987   The New Pueblo Economy. In *When Cultures Meet: Remembering San Gabriel del Yunge Oweenge*, pp. 73–91. Sunstone Press, Santa Fe.

Gannon, Michael V.
1965   *The Cross in the Sand: The Early Catholic Church in Florida, 1513–1870.* University of Florida Press, Gainesville.
1983   Conflicto entre iglesia y estado en Florida: La Administración del Gobernador don Juan Márquez Cabrera, 1680–1687. In *La influencia de España en el Caribe, la Florida, y la Luisiana, 1500–1800*, edited by Antonio Acosta and Juan Marchena, pp. 211–234. Insituto de Cooperación Iberoamericana, Madrid.

Geiger, Maynard
1937   *The Franciscan Conquest of Florida (1573–1618).* Catholic University of America, Washington, D.C.
1940   *Biographical Dictionary of Franciscans in Spanish Florida and Cuba, 1528–1841, Franciscan Studies*, vol. 21. St. Anthony Guild Press, Paterson, New Jersey.

Gibson, Charles
1964   *The Aztecs under Spanish Rule: A History of the Indians of the Valley of Mexico, 1519–1810.* Stanford University Press, Stanford.

Gómez Canedo, Lino
1977   *Evangelización y Conquista: Experiencia Franciscana en Hispanoamérica.* Editorial Porrúa, Mexico.

Guest, Francis F.

1979 An Examination of the Thesis of S. F. Cook on the Forced Conversion of Indians in the California Missions. *Southern California Quarterly* 59:1–77.

1985 Cultural Perspectives on California Mission Life. *Southern California Quarterly* 65:1–65.

Gutiérrez, Ramón

1987 When Padre Jesus Came, The Corn Mothers Went Away: The 1680 Pueblo Revolt Reconsidered. Unpublished manuscript.

Hackett, Charles Wilson (editor)

1923–37 *Historical Documents Relating to New Mexico, Nueva Vizcaya, and Approaches Thereto.* 3 vols. Carnegie Institution, Washington, D.C.

1941 *Revolt of the Pueblo Indians and Otermín's Attempted Reconquest, 1680–1682.* 2 vols. Translated by Charmion Clair Shelby. University of New Mexico Press, Albuquerque.

Hammond, George P., and Agapito Rey (editors and translators)

1940 *Narratives of the Coronado Expedition, 1540–1542.* University of New Mexico, Albuquerque.

Hann, John H.

1988 *Apalachee: The Land between the Rivers.* University of Florida Press/Florida State Museum, Gainesville.

Heizer, Robert

1978 Impact on Colonization of the Native California Societies. *Journal of San Diego History* 24:121–139.

Hilton, Sylvia-Lyn

1983 El Impacto Español en La Florida, Siglos XVII y XVII. In *La Influencia de España en el Caribe, la Florida, y la Luisiana, 1500–1800,* edited by Antonio Acosta and Juan Marchena, pp. 249–270. Instituto de Cooperación Iberoamericana, Madrid.

Hu-DeHart, Evelyn

1981 *Missionaries, Miners, & Indians: Spanish Contact with the Yaqui Nationa of Northwestern New Spain, 1533–1820.* University of Arizona, Tucson.

John, Elizabeth A. H.

1975 *Storms Brewed in Other Men's Worlds: The Confrontation of Indians, Spanish, and French in the Southwest, 1540–1795.* Texas A&M University Press, College Station.

1988 Crusading in the Spanish Borderlands: An Essay Review. *Journal of the Southwest* 30:190–199.

Kamen, Henry

1988 Toleration and Dissent in Sixteenth-Century Spain: The Alternative Tradition. *The Sixteenth Century Journal* 19:3–23.

Kelsey, Harry

1985 European Impact on the California Indians. *The Americas* 41:494–511.

Kessell, John L.

1980–81 Esteban Clemente: Precursor of the Pueblo Revolt. *El Palacio* 86:16–17.

1989 Spaniards and Pueblos: From Crusading Intolerance to Pragmatic Accommodation. In *Columbian Consequences. Vol. 1: Archaeological and Historical Perspectives on the Spanish Borderlands West,* edited by David Hurst Thomas, pp. 127–138. Smithsonian Institution Press, Washington, D.C.

Korth, Eugene H., S. J.

1968 *Spanish Policy in Colonial Chile: The Struggle for Social Justice, 1535–1700.* Stanford University Press, Stanford.

Lanning, John Tate

1935 *The Spanish Missions of Georgia.* University of North Carolina Press, Chapel Hill.

Larson, Lewis H., Jr.

1978 Historic Guale Indians of the Georgia Coast and the Impact of the Spanish Mission Effort. In *Tacachale: Essays on the Indians in Florida and Southeastern Georgia during the*

Historic Period, edited by Jerald Milanich and Samuel Proctor, pp. 120–140. University of Florida, Gainesville.

Loucks, L. Jill
1979 *Political and Economic Interactions between Spaniards and Indians: Archaeology and Ethnohistorical Perspectives of the Mission System in Florida*. Unpublished Ph.D. dissertation, University of Florida, Gainesville.

Luzbetak, Louis J.
1985 If Junípero Serra Were Alive: Missiological-Anthropological Theory Today. *The Americas* 41:512–519.

Lynch, Cyprian J.
1954 Introduction. In *Benavides' Memorial of 1630*, translated by Peter P. Forrestal, pp. i–xxv. Academy of American Franciscan History, Washington, D.C.

MacCormack, Sabine
1985 "The Heart Has Its Reasons": Predicaments of Missionary Christianity in Early Colonial Peru. *Hispanic American Historical Review* 65:443–466.

MacLeod, Murdo J.
1973 *Spanish Central America: A Socioeconomic History, 1520–1720*. University of California Press, Berkeley.

Matson, Daniel S., and Bernard L. Fontana (editors and translators)
1977 *Friar Bringas Reports to the King: Methods of Indoctrination on the Frontier of New Spain, 1796–97*. University of Arizona Press, Tucson.

Matter, Robert Allen
1972 *The Spanish Missions of Florida: The Friars versus the Governors in the "Golden Age," 1606–1690*. Unpublished Ph.D. dissertation, University of Washington, Seattle.
1975 Missions in the Defense of Spanish Florida, 1566–1710. *Florida Historical Quarterly* 54:18–38.
1981 Mission Life in Seventeenth-Century Florida. *Catholic Historical Review* 67:401–420.

Meighan, Clement W.
1987 Indians and California Missions. *Southern California Quarterly* 69:187–201.

Milanich, Jerald T.
1978 The Western Timucua: Patterns of Acculturation and Change. In *Tacachale: Essays on the Indians of Florida and Southeastern Georgia during the Historical Period*, edited by Jerald T. Milanich and Samuel Proctor, pp. 59–88. University Presses of Florida, Gainesville.

Naylor, Thomas H., and Charles W. Polzer (editors)
1986 *The Presidio and Militia on the Northern Frontier of New Spain. A Documentary History. Vol. 1: 1570–1700*. University of Arizona Press, Tucson.

Oré, Luis Gerónimo de
1936 *The Martyrs of Florida, 1513–1616*. Edited and translated by Maynard Geiger. Joseph F. Wagner, New York.

Ortiz, Alfonso
1980–1981 Popay's Leadership: A Pueblo Perspective. *El Palacio* 86:18–22.
1983 San Juan. In *Southwest*, edited by Alfonso Ortiz, pp. 278–295. Handbook of North American Indians, William C. Sturtevant, general editor. Smithsonian Institution, Washington, D.C.

Phelan, John Leddy
1970 *The Millennial Kingdom of the Franciscans*. University of California Press, Berkeley. Originally published 1956.

Polzer, Charles W.
1976 *Rules and Precepts of the Jesuit Missions of Northwestern New Spain*. University of Arizona Press, Tucson.

Reff, Daniel T.
1985 *Demographic and Cultural Consequences of Old World Diseases in the Greater Southwest, 1520–1660*. Unpublished Ph.D. dissertation, University of Oklahoma, Norman.

Ricard, Robert
 1966   *The Spiritual Conquest of Mexico: An Essay on the Apostolate and the Evangelizing Methods of the Mendicant Orders in New Spain: 1523–1572*. Translated by Lesley Byrd Simpson. University of California Press, Berkeley.
Sandos, James A.
 1988   Junípero Serra's Canonization and the Historical Record. *American Historical Review* 93:1253–1269.
Sanz de Lezaún, Juan
 1937   Account of Lamentable Happenings in New Mexico [November 14, 1760]. In *Historical Documents Relating to New Mexico, Nueva Vizcaya, and Approaches Thereto*, vol. 3, edited by Charles Wilson Hackett, pp. 468–479. Carnegie Institution, Washington, D.C.
Scholes, France V.
 1937   *Church and State in New Mexico, 1610–1650*. Historical Society of New Mexico, Publications in History, vol. 7. University of New Mexico Press, Albuquerque.
 1942   *Troublous Times in New Mexico, 1659–1670*. Historical Society of New Mexico, Publications in History, Vol. 11. University of New Mexico Press, Albuquerque.
Schroeder, Albert H.
 1979   Shifting of Survival in the Spanish Southwest. In *New Spain's Far Northern Frontier*, edited by David J. Weber, pp. 237–256. University of New Mexico Press, Albuquerque.
 1983   Pueblos Abandoned in Historic Times. In *Southwest*, edited by Alfonso Ortiz, pp. 236–254. Handbook of North American Indians, vol. 9, William C. Sturtevant, general editor. Smithsonian Institution, Washington D.C.
Sheridan, Thomas E.
 1988a How to Tell the Story of a "People without History." *Journal of the Southwest* 30:168–189.
 1988b Kino's Unforseen Legacy: the Material Consequences of Missionization among the Piman Indians of Arizona and Sonora. *Smoke Signal*, 49 & 50:151–167.
Shipek, Florence C.
 1985   California Indian Reactions to the Franciscans. *The Americas* 41:480–493.
Smith, Marvin T.
 1987   *Archaeology of Aboriginal Culture Change in the Interior Southeast: Depopulation during the Early Historic Period*. University of Florida, Gainesville.
Spellman, Charles W.
 1965   The "Golden Age" of the Florida Missions, 1632–1674. *Catholic Historical Review* 51:354–372.
 1962   *Cycles of Conquest: The Impact of Spain, Mexico, and the United States on the Indians of the Southwest, 1533–1960*. University of Arizona Press, Tucson.
Stern, Steve J.
 1982   *Peru's Indian Peoples and the Challenge of Spanish Conquest: Huamanga to 1640*. University of Wisconsin Press, Madison.
Super, John
 1988   *Food, Conquest, and Colonization in Sixteenth-Century Spanish America*. University of New Mexico Press, Albuquerque.
Todorov, Tzvetan
 1982   *The Conquest of America: The Question of the Other*. Translated by Richard Howard. Harper & Row, New York.
Thomas, David Hurst
 1988   Saints and Soldiers at Santa Catalina: Hispanic Designs for Colonial America. In *The Recovery of Meaning: Historical Archaeology in the Eastern United States*, edited by Mark P. Leone and Parker B. Potter, Jr., pp. 73–140. Smithsonian Institution Press, Washington, D.C.

Weber, David J.
    1988   John Francis Bannon and the Historiography of the Spanish Borderlands: Retrospect and Prospect. In *Myth and the History of the Spanish Southwest: Essays by David J. Weber*, pp. 55–88. University of New Mexico, Albuquerque.
Zubillaga, Félix
    1941   *La Florida: La Misión Jesuítica (1566–1572) y la colonización española*. Institutum Historicum S.I., Rome.

Chapter 28 ■

Michael V. Gannon

Defense of Native American and Franciscan Rights in the Florida Missions

In 1595 the Order of Friars Minor, or Franciscans, launched a full-scale, concerted effort to convert the native populations of La Florida to the Church. Eighty years later, at the time of the visitation to Florida and present-day Georgia of Bishop Gabriel Díaz Vara Calderón (1674–1675), perhaps as many as 25,000 natives had been baptized, catechized, and, as the friars would have seen it, civilized. Writing in 1937, American Franciscan historian Maynard Geiger described the period of the sixteenth-century successes as the "Golden Age" of the Florida missions. More recent study of the documents for the period discloses that except for the quantitative gains, the "Golden Age" never quite happened: despite the geographic expansion of the mission system itself and the increasing numbers of natives "reduced" to Christianity, as the Spaniards were wont to put it, the so-called "Golden Age" was a time of unrelieved poverty and hardship for the friars, of hunger and near-slavery for the converts, of acrimonious disputes between missionaries and officials, of violent Indian revolts, and of equally violent civil suppressions. The idyllic picture of Indians living in harmony and prosperity under the sound of mission bells does not emerge at many points in the records of seventeenth-century Spanish Florida.

One continuous thread of unassailable good that does emerge, however, is the Franciscans' defense of the human, civil, and religious rights of the indigenous peoples and also of their own rights against the depradations of the provincial governors. In two notable instances, during the governorships of Diego de Rebolledo (1655–1659) and of Juan Márquez Cabrera (1680–1687), they denounced outrages committed by the two governors with such effect that both officials were removed from office.

The first indications of trouble between the mission natives and the governors at St. Augustine came in 1638 when several tribes of Apalachee (around present-day Tallahassee) revolted against their Spanish masters. With a small force the governors quickly put down the rebellion and "humbled" the natives' pride. Many of the Apalachees, together with troublesome Timucuans near St. Augustine, were conscripted to forced labor on the fortifications at the Spanish capital.

In 1647 the Christian Apalachees revolted again, and this time their indignation toward all persons and things Spanish embraced the friars (three of whom were killed), most of the mission churches and chapels in the province (which were destroyed), and many of the sacred vessels and liturgical objects (which were despoiled or stolen). When Governor Pedro Menéndez Márquez first sent soldiers against the rebels, they suffered embarrassing defeat, but a second concentrated assault overcame the rebels and the governor inflicted terrible reprisals, executing 12 ringleaders and sentencing 26 others to labor on the fortifications. To the remainder he gave pardon on the condition that they would be required to send additional men as needed to the works at St. Augustine.

Native Floridian and Franciscan alike resented the forced labor program, the friars seeing it as a violation of the natives' basic human rights. New outrages followed in 1648 when the governor, the royal officials, and common soldiers impressed natives under forced labor conditions to cultivate the private gardens of their homes. The Franciscans complained to the Crown that so pernicious was this practice even married men were being seized from the *doctrinas* and forced to work apart from their wives and children for periods over a year in length. Some of the men had died from their exertions.

Seven years later, in 1655, these provocations reached such a state that, as the friars reported again to the Crown, even the friars and their new religion had not escaped identification with the oppressive and manipulative officialdom at St. Augustine. Furthermore, they wrote, under the current Governor Diego de Rebolledo, Timucuan and Apalachee males were being impressed to carry food from their own inadequate supplies to St. Augustine under conditions that were harsh and totally unjust. It was time, they said, to take a stand for native rights and to reject tyranny.

Typical was the voice of Fray Juan Gómez de Engraba, 46-year veteran of the mission fields, who complained to authorities in Spain that the Apalachees were being loaded down like pack animals and forced to transport corn the 100 leagues to the presidio. Even the nobles among them, who had always been exempt from manual labor, were being made to serve as *cargadores*. This was particularly offensive to the natives, the friar pointed out, because under Spanish law and custom the nobles were considered *hidalgos* and *cavalleros* who were employed as counselors. Fray Gómez wrote that when Rebolledo sent notice to the nobles that they, too, would have to serve as burden-bearers, they replied with a letter of their own to "that creole governor of Cartegena"—an insult no doubt contrived with the aid of the friars—that they refused to serve because they were chiefs and had vassals subject to them. Some of the natives expressed their fear that they would be killed by Rebolledo once they reached the presidio, assuming that they survived the march: They remembered that under Rebolledo's predecessor, Governor ad interim Pedro Benedít Ruytiner, only 10 out of 200 natives who carried burdens to St. Augustine returned alive to their homes, the rest having died of hunger on the way.

Not surprising to the friars, a revolt took shape beginning with the *cacique* (chief) of Tarihica (Mission Santa Cruz de Tarihica) in Timucua. He circularized the other caciques of Timucua with notice of his intention not to comply with the governor's demands and of his resolve to use force if necessary to oppose him. Tarihica's stand rallied the other Timucuan chiefs to the same cause, which greatly annoyed Rebolledo ("man of little experience that he was," as Fray Gómez put it), who responded by issuing another call for the chiefs to send their nobles for service. Offended by the insensitive actions of the governor, the caciques of the Timucuan missions (San Martín de Tomoli, Santa Fe de Toloca, San Francisco de Potano, San Pedro de Potohiriba, Santa Elena de Machaba, San Francisco de Chuaquin, and Santa Cruz de Tarihica), assisted by caciques in other missions, but none in Apalachee, organized an armed rebellion. When Rebolledo sent soldiers to put down the rebels by direct military action, he was unsuccessful. The native forces had constructed wood forts that were formidable enough to withstand the kinds of weapons that Rebolledo's men had taken into the hinterland. Although there was some fighting with casualties on both sides, the result was inconclusive. Withdrawing the soldiers, Rebolledo decided to subvert the revolt by capturing and executing the caciques one by one. Sixty men under Sergeant Major Adrian de Canizares succeeded in seizing 11 of the rebel leaders in Timucua and Apalachee, all of whom they garroted. The executions enraged the natives, who took out their wrath on the closest Spanish symbols at hand, which were the primitive mission compounds, many of which were destroyed to their foundations. Six missionary friars then serving in Apalachee boarded a vessel on the Gulf coast to take refuge in Havana. It is not clear from the documents whether they left in fear of their lives or in disgust at the practices of the governor; tragically, all six drowned in the crossing.

In a joint report to Spain, the Franciscans who remained in Florida charged that Rebolledo's violations of native rights and dignity had brought about the revolt. They especially condemned the slaughter of the caciques. There were other abuses that needed correction, they said: The presence of soldiers in and near the mission compounds not only was intimidating to the converts, it also was a cause of bad moral example to the Christian neophytes. The governor himself possessed a hacienda at Asyle on the Timucua-Apalachee border, where he enriched himself by means of servile native labor. These practices were both insensitive to the work of the friars and abusive of the dignity of natives who, despite every royal directive to the contrary, were being treated as slaves. It was not for this that the natives had been "reduced" to Christianity, the friars argued, but so that they might have the Gospel preached to them.

Rebolledo wrote his own letter to the Crown defending his actions in the interior and stating his intention to continue the labor program. As for the petitions of the friars, their only real reason for objecting to the presence of soldiers, he said, was the fact that without their presence the friars would be the sole and absolute masters of the natives. With some plausibility, he argued that with only 300 *arrobas* [25-pound units] of maize in the royal stores, his garrison was ill-prepared to meet an English attack on his colony, rumors of which had been communicated to him only recently by the Crown itself (April 12, 1656). Thus, he argued, he had no choice but to issue the detested orders to the caciques.

In Spain the Council of the Indies was exasperated by the constant flow of complaints about Rebolledo's administration from the friars. Even granting the need for emergency food measures as explained by the governor, and recognizing that in a province as isolated and nonproductive as Florida certain irregularities were to be expected, the council decided that Rebolledo had exceeded Spanish law and Christian justice in his treatment of the natives. It therefore came down hard on the side of the Franciscan defense of native rights and sent orders for the immediate arrest of Rebolledo and for his detention under guard in Havana until transportation could be arranged to bring him before formal criminal proceedings in Spain. Rebolledo died before these orders could be carried out.

After the conclusion of this church–state battle and the restoration of peace among the rebellious tribes of the interior, the Franciscans returned to most of their previous posts to pick up the pieces. Although church-state relations would continue to be tense, there was no similar outright rupture until the administration (1680–1687) of Governor Juan Márquez Cabrera, lately governor of the province of Honduras, and now captain-general and governor of St. Augustine and of the provinces of Florida. At the date of his appointment, Márquez had behind him 29 years of military service in Spain, Italy, and the Caribbean, during which he rose in rank from common soldier to that of sergeant-major. When his residencia was taken in 1671–1672, at the conclusion of a six-year term as governor of Honduras, he received high marks for the quality of his administration from the 24 witnesses who were examined, as well as from the caciques of the Indian villages who came forward to testify to his honesty and integrity. On all sides he was acclaimed for the manner in which he maintained justice and peace; helped poor widows in their distress; personally carried food and money to the needy in times of pestilence; protected the natives from being molested; built churches, convents, and missions; reminded the *doctrineros* (missionaries) of their obligation to educate and to care for the natives; and personally taught the natives how to plant and irrigate their maize fields. Márquez was so outstanding a soldier, statesman, and Christian, his successor as governor, Don Pedro de Godoy Ponce de León, recommended him to the Crown as worthy to occupy any position to which the king might choose to appoint him. Eight years later the king chose Florida in *América del Norte*.

One should have thought that when this apparent warrior-saint undertook his new responsibilities in Florida he would have exhibited the same success in war, the same concern for justice and peace, the same charity toward widows and the needy, and the same personal solicitude for the native populations in the *doctrinas*, mission villages, for which he had been recognized so singularly in Honduras. As the evidence overwhelmingly demonstrates, just the reverse occurred. Although Márquez displayed many of the expected attributes of a military commander, bringing to near completion, for example, the new stone fortress at St. Augustine, the Castillo de San Marcos, he was driven back on almost all active military fronts by native forces, many of them former inhabitants of the Spanish doctrinas, under the leadership of English officers and adventurers. Márquez's fortunes in this respect may have been due to historic forces and circumstances over which he had little control, but he rationalized his failure, on true grounds or not, by blaming those losses on the doctrineros of the missions that were overrun.

Not only did Márquez never personally instruct or assist the natives in the missions of Florida, as he had done in those of Honduras, it is not recorded in the hundreds of documents that survive from his administration that he ever once so much as visited a mission in Florida, except those that he happened to encounter on his journey overland from Apalachee in the northwest corner of the peninsula, where his ship landed on first arriving in Florida, to the capital city of St. Augustine in the east. Later claims, made in writing to the king, that he had made a formal visita to the Apalachee missions (about which the king's *Consejo de Indias* [Council of the Indies] made repeated requests for a detailed report), were denounced as lies by the Franciscans who knew that Márquez had merely "passed through."

As for his reputation from Honduras for maintaining justice and peace, it must be said that no governor of Florida in the seventeenth century, even including the much-criticized Rebolledo, was so resented in his time for having been the cause of injustice and discord. When, after six years, he finally left St. Augustine, the population gathered joyfully in the streets to share the heady air of peace and freedom. And as for widows, Márquez's only recorded action on their behalf was to evict one of them, Ana Ruíz de Valverde ("thrown onto the beach," as she said), and to requisition her house for his own, because he liked it better than the governor's appointed residence. If one were to identify the needy of Florida, besides the Indians who always lived on a bare subsistence level, the list would include the Franciscans in the mission fields, the *criollos* (St. Augustine-born residents of Spanish descent), and the unfortunate Indian conscripts, black slaves, Mexican and Cuban ne'er-do-wells, and the convicts, who served on the labor force of the castillo then under construction. Márquez, as befitted his office, had no direct relations with the laborers; neither did he take any initiative on their behalf. To the Franciscans and the criollos he showed outright contempt. In word and in deed he seems to have chosen every available chance over six years' time to castigate, ridicule, and demoralize the friars and the non-Spanish born vecinos of his presidio. In his documented relationships with these two groups he revealed himself to be bigoted, arrogant, boorish, profane, and, surprisingly for all his experience in statecraft, tactless.

What is most remarkable is that in the end this proud and noble warrior deserted his post and sailed ingloriously to Havana. Knowing full well that he was abdicating command at a time when the provinces under his charge were threatened on all sides by active military forces of the English and French, Márquez nonetheless boarded ship in the harbor and threw his baton into the sea, crying, "There's where you can go for your government in this filthy place!" Why did he do it? The reason that Márquez gave (in a letter to the king dated April 13, 1687), if it was not the only reason, no doubt was the principal one: He had been driven out of St. Augustine by the Franciscan friars and by the secular clergy of the city. How had they done this? The friars, headed by el Reverendo Padre fray Pedro de Luna, minister provincial of the Franciscan *Provincia de Santa de la Florida* (province of St. Helen of Florida, which included Cuba), headquartered in St. Augustine, and the three secular clergy of the city, led by the chaplain of the garrison and former ecclesiastical judge and *vicario* (pastor) of the *iglesia parroquial* (parish church), the licenciado Joseph Pérez de la Mota, had entered into a collusion for the purpose of denying Márquez the sacraments of the church. Specifically, Márquez charged, the religiosos and the clérgios had refused to hear his confession and to give him absolution. It being the Easter season, when every Catholic Christian was bound by Church law to receive the sacraments for the salvation of his soul, Márquez had no alternative but to go to Havana in order to have his sins confessed and absolved. He further advised the king that, once this was done, he would return to his post. When Márquez did return, on June 6, he was arrested, on the grounds of deserting his post, by the acting governor, who had assumed command in his absence, was imprisoned, and eventually sent to Spain for trial.

A basic problem between Márquez and the church was one of jurisdiction. Not unlike many previous governors in Florida, and for that matter other governors and royal officers of the king throughout the New World, Márquez fell into the institutional quicksand called the *Patronato Real de las Indias*, by which the king and his councils not only nominated candidates for every ecclesiastical office but also directed, often in the minutest details, every activity of the church in the New World, whether it be in the bishoprics, the parishes, the convents, or the missions of the religious orders in the hinterlands. This papal-mandated union of altar and throne was recognized and honored throughout the Spanish Florida experience. What was disputed by the Franciscans in Florida in the seventeenth century was not the royal privilege, but the presumption of the governors that they shared in the exercise of the patronato real as royal vice-patrons of the church. The Franciscans contended that the patronato real did not extend to the governors who, they argued, represented the king in temporal matters only. Many bitter clashes between the religiosos and the governors occurred on this point during the administrations of Governors Gonzalo Méndez de Canzo (1596–1603), Pedro de Ybarra (1603–1609), Andrés Rodríguez de Villegas (1630–1631), and Rebolledo. Compounding the problem was the fact that Florida was a royal colony subject directly to the Crown, without being under any intermediary authority such as the vice-royalty of New Spain or the Audiencia of Santo Domingo. The question was properly resolved by the Crown: When during the Rebolledo administration the Madrid government issued a cédula that tightened royal control over ecclesiastical appointments, the Franciscans in Florida, concerned about interference of the civil government in their affairs, managed to secure an exemption from the provisions of the cédula. Not unexpectedly, the provincials at St. Augustine employed the exemption in the widest latitudes of interpretation. By allowing the question of jurisdiction to remain moot in Florida, Crown officials created a situation that, already well before Márquez's time, invited discord and weakened the bonds of social union. With all this quicksand before him, well advertised in the archives of his Gobierno, Márquez should have been aware and cautious. Instead, he reacted to contrary opinion from the friars as though he had never heard of such behavior before, and his reaction to it was as impetuous as it was condemnatory. The early battles belonged to Márquez; it was the friars who would win the war.

In the decade prior to Márquez's administration the missionary work of the sons of St. Francis reached what may well be described as its zenith. The total number of friars reached 51 and the number of doctrinas reached 33: There were 7 north of St. Augustine along the Guale islands (in present-day Georgia), 13 in the Timucua country of the north central peninsula, and 13 in by far the most populous district, that of Apalachee in the northwest corner of the peninsula. The friars claimed more than 13,000 baptized natives living in and around the mission compounds, although their numbers were declining—owing to diseases imported by the Spaniards and to the blandishments of English agents—and those who remained wore a thin veneer of Christianity and Western culture over persistent aboriginal customs and beliefs. The Florida missions were never an unqualified success, but they probably were seen at their best in 1674–1675 when the Bishop of Santiago de Cuba, Gabriel Diaz Vara Calderón, studied every doctrina on an official visita and endorsed what he saw with enthusiasm. The historian is surprised to find that only one decade later the doctrineros are squabbling with the military, the natives are languishing or going over wholesale to the English, and the doctrinas as well as the populations are declining rapidly in number. Márquez is making the Franciscans scapegoats for his failures, the Franciscans are fastening responsibility for their troubles on the governor, and, it must be added, the Sons of St. Francis are exhibiting an indisputable collapse of spiritual zeal and dedication.

Hundreds of pages of documentation record the imbroglio, and it appears that almost the entire war was conducted on paper, with each side forwarding its selected materials to the king. Only rarely did Márquez and his Franciscan adversaries confront each other personally. The climax of the drama was played out in San Agustín, where leadership of the religious resistance movement took an unusual turn. Until 1684 the doctrineros in the field and the minister provincial, with his definidores, in the city had been the sole voices raised against Máquez's contumely. In that year a new voice and a new leader emerged in the person of a secular clérgio, mentioned earlier in our narrative, the licenciado Joseph Pérez de la Mota, proprietary chaplain of the castillo and infantry forces. It is safe to say that by this date, if there was anyone whom Márquez detested more than a Franciscan friar it was Pérez de la Mota. And Márquez's scorn was returned in kind.

The first major strike directly at Márquez took place on July 7, 1684, when Pérez threatened the governor with excommunication *latae sententiae* and a fine of 200 silver ducados for having placed too tight a guard around the three churches of the city and environs where an escaped black slave might seek asylum. Márquez rejected the vicario's threat as unfounded, and nothing came of it. Threats of excommunication were not enough. The decisive moment came when Pérez gained the cooperation of the other secular clergy and of the entire Franciscan administrative staff in the city in a massive sanction against Márquez. All clergy, secular and regular, would refuse to grant sacramental absolution to the governor. Fray Antonio de la Crúz was the first to make the refusal. He was soon followed by the outgoing vicario Marcos González at the parish church, who similarly refused. Márquez then returned to the convent where Fray Juan Chrysosthomos refused him. Then it was back to the parish church where surely the incoming new vicario Alonso de Leturiondo would hear his confession and absolve him, but to Márquez's surprise and frustration, he, too, refused. Still another return to the convent, to the confessional of Fray Joseph de la Barrera, yielded the same result. What grounds had the churchmen devised for their action? There were three grounds, one general and two particular.

The general complaint was that Márquez simply was not contrite. For absolution to be valid it was required that the penitent show true contrition for his sins, and firm purpose of amendment. This Márquez had not done; as Leturiondo put it, "He only pretends contrition." The two particular grounds for denying the sacrament involved restitution for individual offenses. The first case was that of the widow Ana Ruíz de Valverde, mentioned earlier. She had been "violently and tyrannically thrown into the street," said Leturiondo, and her house, a *casa de posadas* (inn), was requisitioned by the governor, even though he already had houses in which to live. "Is this justice?" Leturiondo asked. And then he made his point: No absolution would be given Márquez unless he first made a commitment of restitution, that is, unless he began the process of restoring the widow to her home and of paying her back rents and damages. The second restitution case was less concrete. While Pérez de la Mota was vicario ad interim, Leturiondo reported, the governor routinely treated him in public with disrespect and contempt. Márquez called him such names as *curilla* (little pastor), *falsario* (liar), and *cabeza de motín* (leader of mutiny). "He would even speak this way in church while Pérez de la Mota was vesting for Mass." Leturiondo asked, "Does not this great scandal require restitution?" What it called for, specifically, was a public apology.

Márquez showed no sign that he was willing to make either restitution. He claimed simply that no priest would hear his confession. Leturiondo, to whom we are indebted for the particulars of this incident, replied that the governor's claim was a sham. Márquez could receive the sacrament any time he wished: All he had to do was give adequate sign of contrition and make restitution in the two specific cases described. When no sign of compliance came from Márquez, Leturiondo wrote the governor in a spirit of what he called "love and understanding" to suggest that all the clergy of the city, secular and religious, meet with Márquez in his home "to clear the path so that he would be freely able to confess." Márquez, however, twice sent the letter back unread. A few weeks later, he threw his baton into the sea, and sailed to Havana—cause for him to be arrested for deserting his post.

In recounting these barest details of the sorry affair, one cannot excuse the decline of missionary zeal that characterizes the Florida Franciscans in the period. Yet one wonders to what extent that decline was the result of constant pressure on the friars to defend themselves and their native charges against the constant vituperative stream of obloquy and contempt that was directed their way by the governor. The rights and dignity of the missions, which means the rights and dignity of the native peoples, were placed at ruinous discount. The result had to be demoralizing for friar and native alike. No doubt the friars acted on their own behalf by participating in the ouster of Márquez through the powerful sacramental means employed. But in the end they were also acting for their life commitments: the welfare of their converts. The defense of native rights does not stand out quite as selflessly here as in the case of friars vs. Rebolledo. But it does stand out.

References

Gannon, Michael V. [pseudonym Charles W. Spellman]
  1965   The "Golden Age" of the Florida Missions, 1632–1674. *Catholic Historical Review* 51(3):354–372.
  1983   Conflictos entre Iglesia y Estado en Florida: la administratión del Gobernador Don Juan Márquez Cabrera, 1680–1687. *La Influencia de España en el Caribe, al Florida y la Luisiana, 1500–1800*, pp. 211–234. Instituto de Cooperación Iberoamericana, Madrid.
Hann, John H.
  1988   *Apalachee: The Land between the Rivers*. University of Florida Press, Gainesville.
Pearson, Fred Lamar, Jr.
  1983   Timucuan Rebellion of 1656: The Rebolledo Investigation and the Civil-Religious Controversy. *Florida Historical Quarterly* 61(3):260–280.
Stetson Collection, 17th Century Documents from the Archivo General de Indias, Sevilla; P.K. Yonge Library of Florida History, University of Florida: *Santo Domingo* 70, 141, 151, 225, 226, 227, 234, 235, 230, 834, 856, 864.

Chapter 29 ■

Conrad Harkins, O.F.M.

On Franciscans, Archaeology, and Old Missions

Historians, archaeologists, and the general public have shown considerable interest in the remains of the several Franciscan missions unearthed in this decade in Florida and Georgia. The discovery of Mission Santa Catalina de Guale on St. Catherines Island by David Hurst Thomas in 1981; the opening to the public of the San Luis de Talimali Archaeological Site in Tallahassee in 1985; the discovery, also in 1985, of Mission Santa María or Santa Catalina on Amelia Island; the location of Mission San Martin in Ichetucknee Springs State Park and of Mission Santa Fe de Toloca in Alachua County in 1987; the excavations at St. Francis Barracks, the State Arsenal, in St. Augustine in 1988; and the publication in that year of John H. Hann's masterful study, *Apalachee: The Land between the Rivers*—are significant steps in the readjustment of the lens with which we view the importance of the Spanish colony of La Florida. When Americans think of the Spanish missions, their thoughts no longer run exclusively to the Southwest, but include also the more extensive chain that branched north toward the Chesapeake and west to the Apalachicola.

This recent excavation and research has been followed with casual interest by the spiritual descendants of those Christians, ecclesiastical and secular, who strove to impart the Gospel to the populace of the New World. The demographic movement has created a new Catholic population in the South. This factor, together with the increase in the Hispanic-American population, and the approach of the Columbian Quincentenary are all reasons for specifically Catholic interest in the rediscovered missions of the Southeast, but all people with religious commitment cannot but have an interest in the enormous program of evangelization, adorned with its achievements and marked by its failures, that the Spanish mission system represented.

General Franciscan Interest in Archaeology

Among those who share this interest are the spiritual brothers of the friars who worked, suffered, and died among the chiggers and ticks, gnats and mosquitoes, snakes and alligators, to bring Christianity to the native populations of Florida, Georgia, and South Carolina. Today, only some 25 members of the Order of Friars Minor, the Franciscans who built the approximately one hundred doctrinas and mission outposts that once dotted the Southeast, are engaged in ministry in this area.[1] While their predecessors were of Spanish blood and were members of the St. Augustine-based province of Santa Elena, their modern counterparts are members of the New York-based Holy Name Province, whose origins lie in the flight of German friars from the nineteenth-century *Kulturkampf* of Bismarck. The American friars of today are concerned about evangelization of a secularist society and ministry to the alienated and disaffected. As such, they combine curiosity about findings in southern sands and admiration for the zeal and heroism of their Spanish predecessors with impatience and indignation with the report of anything savoring of injustice to the Native American populations of the past.

Franciscan interest in the excavations has moved at various levels. There is the general interest that every group has in its past. The discovery of a Franciscan mission on the Georgia coast through the use of a proton magnetometer (Thomas 1988:26), the uncovering of a mission cemetery while clearing land for a house (Milanich and Saunders 1986:8), the finding that part of an eighteenth-century Franciscan friary remains intact, although encapsuled in a military arsenal[2]—all these events capture the imagination. For the historian, the interest is more serious. Histories of religious communities are usually written from an analysis of constitutions and statutes, documents that tell how religious life was supposed to be lived. At times chronicles provide insights into the lived reality. But it is rare that one has the opportunity to study the physical evidence of a community. Buried under the southern sands of Georgia and Florida are the dimensions of the friars' church, of their convento, of their cells. In the midden is the evidence of how well they ate, and whether they ate better than the soldiers and the Indians. In the goods found buried with the Indians at St. Catherines, perhaps, is even an indication of a willingness on the part of the friars to accept the customs of their congregations. Although one does not wish to endorse the depredations of Governor Moore for bringing the missions to such a sudden and violent end, he has given us on a minor scale a Franciscan Pompeii and Herculaneum.

Interest in Georgia Martyrs

Religious interest has focused particularly upon the excavations at St. Catherines Island in Georgia and at the Florida State Arsenal in St. Augustine, because of the relationship of these sites to the tragic death of five friars at the hands of rebellious Indians in September 1597. On September 13, Fray Pedro de Corpa died at Mission Nuestra Señora de Guadalupe in the village of Tolomato, near Darien, Georgia. Fray Blas de Rodríguez died at Mission Santa Clara at Tupiqui near modern Eulonia on September 16. A day later, on September 17, which marked the Feast of the Stigmata of St. Francis, the two friars at Santa Catalina de Guale, Fray Miguel de Auñón and Fran Antonio de Badajoz, met their violent end. Finally, Fray Francisco de Beráscola was killed at Mission Santo Domingo de Asao on St. Simon's Island, probably on September 18.[3] The bodies of Fray Miguel and Fray Antonio were recovered by faithful Christian Indians and buried at the foot of the mission cross on St. Catherines. On the arrival of Spanish soldiers, the remains were exhumed. Their condition was such that they could not be transported, and thus they were reburied in a marked grave.[4] Years later, they were reinterred at the friary chapel in St. Augustine,[5] possibly with the remains of Fray Blas, whose body had also been found.[6]

The identification of the deaths of the five friars as a case of martyrdom was swift. *La Florida*, the epic poem of Fray Alonso de Escobedo, dated 1606–1609, already terms them "martyrs." Francisco de Beráscola, for example, is "the martyr saint from Basque whom the Province of Biscaya invokes as Patron" (Pou y Martí 1927:48–60; Escobedo 1963:30). On October 16, 1612, the fifteenth anniversary of Fray Blas's death at Tupiqui, the Custody of Santa Elena, as the Franciscan entity in Florida was then known, wrote to Philip III of Spain, clearly setting forth the claim (AGI:232; Omaechevarría 1955:367). The representation to the king was made, it has been noticed, "with the awareness that his Catholic Majesty, by virtue of his *Patronato Real* over the territories of the New World, granted by successive papal bulls, was in effect the Vicar of the Pope in matters ecclesiastical" (Wyse 1985:31). Franciscan martyrologies after 1638 include the five friars.[7]

However auspicious the early interest in the martyrs, their case was destined to lie dormant for four centuries. With the virtual extinction of the Franciscan presence in Florida in 1763, the martyrs were all but forgotten. In 1941, however, they were included in an unsuccessful petition of the American hierarchy to the Sacred Congregation of Rites for the beatification of 118 missionaries who gave their lives for the faith in the territory of the United States in the period 1542–1886. Although the breadth and depth of this petition doomed it, the research already done on the Georgia martyrs convinced Franciscan authorities that here was a bona fide and provable case of martyrdom that should not be neglected. Considerable activity both in historical research and in popularizing the cause occurred in the 30 years after 1950, until the cause was formally opened on February 22, 1984 (Wyse 1985:30–35).

Canonization Procedures

Current laws governing canonization cases were promulgated by Pope John Paul II on January 25, 1983, and later supplemented by Norms issued by the Sacred Congregation for the Causes of the Saints (Sarno 1983; specific references are given in the text in parentheses). Cases begin before the bishop of the diocese in which the candidates, called Servants of God, died. In the case of the Georgia martyrs, the responsible prelate is Bishop Raymond W. Lessard of Savannah. It is his task to inquire about the life, the virtues or the martyrdom, the reputation for sanctity or martyrdom, alleged miracles, and the antiquity of the cult. The diocesan investigation extends to the life of the Servant of God, writings, relevant documents, witnesses, and miracles, and results in a transcript sent to the congregation in Rome.

The cause usually comes to the attention of the bishop through a petitioner, in this case the Holy Name Province of the Order of Friars Minor. The petitioner, with the permission of the bishop, appoints a postulator, whose prime responsibility is to investigate the reputation of the Servant of God for sanctity and the importance of the cause to the church. The postulator for the Georgia martyrs is Fr. Alexander Wyse, O.F.M., church historian and former director of the Academy of American Franciscan History in Washington, D.C. The cause is formally initiated only after the bishop receives the petition and its accompanying documentation.

In the light of recent criticism of the cause of Fr. Junípero Serra (Sandos 1988:1253–1269), it may be beneficial to note some cautions built into the law. The first documentation required is "an accurate, chronologically arranged report on the life and deeds of the Servant of God, on his virtues or martyrdom, on his reputation of sanctity and for performing wonders." The norms themselves pointedly state: "Nor should all those things be omitted which seem to be contrary or less favorable to the cause itself" (10 a). A similar caution in the norms occurs in the statement made regarding the testimony of living witnesses: "Those with opposite opinions must also be included" (10 c). Should the bishop receive information that would constitute an obstacle to the cause, and if the postulator cannot overcome that obstacle, the bishop may judge that the cause should not be admitted (12).

As the cause goes forward, the postulator is assisted by a historical commission, which is particularly important in causes going as far back as that of the Georgia martyrs. The commission has the responsibility to present a report on the facts of the case, to document the case, and to give a judgment on the authenticity and value of the documents (14). Ultimately, its members will be called as witnesses to testify under oath "that they gathered all those things which pertain to the cause" and "that they neither falsified nor changed any document or text" (21). Chairman of the historical commission for the cause of the Georgia martyrs is Fray Francisco Morales, O.F.M., former vice-director of the Academy of American Franciscan History; the other members are Edward J. Cashin, chairman of the Department of History, Political Science, and Philosophy at Augusta College, Georgia, and F. Lamar Pearson, professor of history at Valdosta State College, Georgia. The commission is at present preparing its report.

The postulator's antagonist—the law never describes him as such—is the promoter of justice, who is required to be expert in theological, canonical, and, if the case calls for it, historical matters. Once the historical commission, and the theological commission if there are writings to be considered, make their report, the promoter of justice formulates "interrogatories." These are described as "most effective in searching out and finding the truth about the life of the Servant of God, his virtues or martyrdom, his reputation of holiness or martyrdom" (15). The promoter of justice is present at the examination of witnesses, who must respond to his "interrogatories" (16). When all is done, he once again inspects the acts and documents to formulate whatever additional inquiries he finds necessary (27b). Finally, those interested in the cause are told to refrain from acts that might deceive the faithful into thinking that the mere completion of the episcopal inquiry guarantees eventual canonization (36).

When the case goes to Rome, it is still a long way from completion. In the Congregation for the Causes of Saints, an officer called the "relator" prepares the "position" on virtues or martyrdom. This document is subjected to the scrutiny of historical and theological consultors, and of the promoter of the faith, all of whose comments accompany it to a judgment by the cardinals and bishops of the Congregation. The "sentences" of the cardinals and bishops are presented to the pope for the final decision.

Historical Sources

The sources for the history of the Georgia martyrs are first and foremost the documents emanating from the Spanish civil and ecclesiastical officials in Florida, dated from January 12, 1598, to October 16, 1612. These documents from the *Archivo General de las Indias, Audiencia de Santo Domingo*, have been published by Ignacio Omaechevarría in a modern Spanish edition (1955:12:291–370). Narrative descriptions of the martyrdom include the account by Fray Luis Geronimo de Oré, *Relación de los mártires que ha habido en las Provincias de la Florida*, written in 1617–1620, existing in a modern edition of Atanásio López (1931–1933) and translated into English by Maynard Geiger (Oré 1936). Of less value is the epic poem of Fray Alonso de Escobedo, *La Florida*, probably written between 1606 and 1609, of which parts pertaining to the martyrdom have been published by Jose Pou y Martí, and by López, and translated into English by A. F. Falcones (Escobedo 1963). We cite the translation and give the manuscript reference in brackets. Barcía's *Ensayo cronológico para la historia general de La Florida*, although far removed in time (1723), also mentions the martyrdom (Barcía 1951).

Historical Data

The facts of the deaths of the five Franciscans are as follows. The single most difficult moral obligation imposed by the friars on converts to Christianity was monogamy. In 1597, Juanillo, a baptized Christian and son and heir of the principal cacique of Guale, after taking a second wife, was reprimanded by Fray Pedro de Corpa, the resident priest of Mission Nuestra Señora de Guadalupe in the village of Tolomato. Corpa, in conjunction with Fray Blas Rodríguez, who was the regional superior of the friars and lived at Mission Santa Clara at Tupiqui, also deprived Juanillo of his presumptive right to succeed as head mico (Lanning 1935:82–83). Such a succession would have doomed the Christian effort to establish monogamy.

Without saying anything and without obtaining the customary permission to leave the mission, Juanillo departed for the interior. He stole back a few nights later with followers painted like himself for violence. They broke down the door of Fray Pedro's house and dispatched him with a blow of the macana (Barcía 1951:81; Oré 1936:73).[8] There followed an orgy of release from the sexual restraint that Christian morality had imposed. Corpa's body, thrown into the woods, was never recovered. Barcía relates a long harangue by Juanillo in which he argues that having killed one, they would suffer no greater punishment for killing all the friars. This decided, Pedro's head was placed on a pike in the harbor as a victory trophy (Barcía 1951:181–182).[9]

The death of Fray Blas de Rodríguez followed three days later. With the element of surprise gone, the insurgents trod with more reserve. Fray Blas, informed of his inescapable death, was allowed time to offer Mass, distribute his personal possessions, and even essay to turn his captors from their purpose. According to Oré, that gained him two days to prepare for death while witnessing the desecration of the church, before his skull was crushed with the macana. That may have been too generous an estimate. Lucas, the Indian executed for complicity in Fray Blas's death, testified that he had only two hours' warning in which to offer Mass and take his leave (Oré 1936:74–75; López 1933:2:22).

The situation was perhaps more delicate at Mission Santa Catalina de Guale where the Christian cacique was determined to save the priest, Fray Miguel de Auñón, and his lay assistant, Fray Antonio de Badajoz. Embarrassed to deal with Fray Miguel, the cacique dealt with Fray Antonio, offering boat and guides to reach San Pedro (Cumberland Island). Incredibly, Fray Antonio did nothing, even after a second day's warning. On the third day, his own life threatened, the cacique told Miguel that he was now powerless to save them. The two friars celebrated Mass and spent four hours in prayer. If Lanning is right and it was September 17, it was also the Feast of the Stigmata of St. Francis. The Gospel contained the words: "If a man wishes to come after me, he must deny his very self, take up his cross, and begin to follow in my footsteps" (Matthew 16:24). Sacking the convento, Juanillo's band first encountered Antonio, who was dispatched quickly with the macana. There was hesitation and opposition to the killing of Miguel after he had been stunned by a blow, but a second blow muted the debate (Oré 1936:74–75; Barcía 1951:182). Escobedo (1963:31 [155b]—page citation is for translation; the ms. reference appears in brackets) dwells in fantasy. Shortly thereafter, Francisco de Beráscola, in charge of Mission Santo Domingo de Asao on St. Simon's Island, disembarking on his return from St. Augustine, was seized from behind and killed with blows from the macana (Oré 1936:93; Barcía 1951:182).[10]

A Case of Martyrdom?

Such then is the raw material on the basis of which the Bishop of Savannah, the bishops and cardinals of the Congregation for the Causes of Saints, and ultimately the pope will make a judgment of sanctity. But unlike the case of Junípero Serra, the judgment here is not about a heroic practice of virtue over a lifetime, but about the achievement of martyrdom. "Death for the sake of Christian faith or Christian morals" is the definition offered by a contemporary Catholic theological work (Rahner and Vorgrimler 1981:293).

Do we have a true case of martyrdom in the deaths of Pedro de Corpa and his companions? All of the captured Indians interrogated in January of 1598 and the later narrative accounts agree that the friars were killed because of the Christian manner of life they promoted and enforced among the Christian Indians. Lucas testified concerning the death of Fray Blas de Rodríguez that the micos and caciques ordered his death "because he was a scoundrel and prohibited their sorceries and their taking more than one wife."[11] Of the death of Pedro de Corpa, the Indian Francisco said the cause was "Don Juan, the heir of Tolomato, because he censured his evil deeds and scolded him."[12] The other four Indians who gave reasons for the killings—Bartolomé, Buenaventura, Alonso, and Pedro—all mentioned the friars' prohibiting their having more than one wife. Two mentioned also the scolding by the friars, and two, the abrogation of the Indian law (López 1933:2:19–21).[13] It is clear, then, that the cause that stood out above all others was the insistence of the friars that Christian Indians maintain monogamous unions.

The Georgia martyrs were martyrs for monogamy, for marriage, for morality, and only indirectly for faith. No less a theologian than the great Dominican doctor, St. Thomas Aquinas, provided the theological basis for the claim of martyrdom:

> The work of any virtue, insofar as it is referred to God, constitutes a certain protestation of faith, through which it is known to us that God requires such a work from us and rewards us for it. In this way it can be the cause of martyrdom. Whence we celebrate in the Church the martyrdom of blessed John the Baptist, who underwent death not in a matter of denying the faith but for the reprehension of adultery [*Summa theologiae* 1899:40].

In their 1612 letter to the king reporting on the state of the faith in Florida since the death of the friars, the Definitory of Santa Elena Custody offers that very argument of Aquinas:

> In the beginning we endured many trials and many threats of death. They tried to kill us on many occasions, as in fact they did in the province of Guale, martyring five religious, taking others prisoner. And although they did not martyr them for their faith, they certainly martyred them for the law of God and our commandments which they taught them and which were very contrary to their lives and traditions, particularly because we did not consent to married Christians having more than one wife. This was the reason the Baptist was beheaded when he reprimanded Herod. This is the reason that the Indians gave and give today, recognizing their sin in martyring them [AGI 1598:232; Omaechevarría 1955:367].

To qualify for martyrdom, however, the Georgia friars would also have had to die willingly. What is to be said of Pedro de Corpa when three Indians reported that he was sleeping when he was killed, or of Francisco de Beráscola, who may have been clubbed from behind? The Indian Lucas testified that only Fray Blas knew in advance the hour of his death, although Lucas may not have known of the warning afforded Fray Miguel and Fray Antonio on St. Catherines.[14]

The truth is that the friars were schooled in a spirituality that recognized in the desire to so imitate Christ as to die with him in a proclamation of the Gospel, the highest form of Christian perfection. It was a spirituality of martyrdom grounded in the Rule of St. Francis, which ended with a chapter devoted to those who "by divine inspiration want to go among the Saracens and other infidels." The classic commentary on the Rule, attributed to St. Bonaventure, spoke of this chapter as one that "opens a door to those thirsting for martyrdom" (Bonaventure 1889:8:431b, 436). When the friars stepped on board ship in Havana for the Florida coast, they knew that death to which they were opening themselves. Theirs was the will to martyrdom long before it was realized in their flesh.

Fray Miguel de Auñón is a case in point. A nobleman turned friar, famous for his beautiful singing voice and preaching ability, he was summoned back from Florida shortly before his death to preach in Havana. Unable to make headway around Cape Canaveral, he gave it up and returned to Florida. Oré (1936:68) quotes him:

> God did not send me to the city of Havana, but to this land to instruct the Indians; here I intend to remain until death, because I have to receive therein some great favor from God; thus I believe that my inability to proceed farther with the journey has not been in vain.

Subsidiary Questions

Evangelization

Although it would seem that a convincing case can thus be made for the Georgia martyrs, a number of subsidiary questions remain. We would like to know what degree of evangelization the Indians had received. We would like to know the degree of discipline that was enforced among the Christian Indians. We would like to know more about the attitude of the friars toward the native culture. The answers to these questions would help us to see the act of martyrdom in a broader perspective.

How evangelized were the Indians at the time of the martyrdom? The evangelizers were certainly capable and committed. Pedro de Corpa was priest and confessor of the Franciscan province of Castile, had spent 10 years in Florida, and knew the language of Guale well (Oré 1936:71). Blas de Rodríguez, priest and confessor of the Franciscan province of San Gabriel in Spain, had spent 17 years in Florida and was also well versed in the Indian language (Oré 1936:71). Miguel de Auñón, trained in the Classics, respected theologian and preacher, was much loved by the Indians, but in his less than two years in Florida, he could not have known the language well (Oré 1936:68; Escobedo 1963:19 [137b]). Fray Antonio, his lay companion, had received a quick course in theology and evangelical methods in Florida and wore the clerical tonsure to profit from whatever respect it earned from the Indians. He had 10 years of experience in Florida and spoke the language well (Escobedo 1963:32–22 [159–159b]). Fray Francisco de Beráscola is described by Escobedo as "kindly and learned" (1963:19 [138b]).

A few passing remarks by chroniclers give some insight into evangelical methods. Escobedo comments on the instructions given by the commissary to Fray Antonio in "the proper manner of teaching the Divine Law to the idolatrous Indian." He says, "It would be some time after instruction that the Indian would decide for himself whether to believe in Jesus Christ or not and if he should enter the Church by means of baptism, the water which gives life to the soul that is dead." These instructions give some assurance that conversions were not rushed or forced (Escobedo 1963:33 [159b]).

Fray Francisco de Beráscola's methods may have been more controversial, although they show an effort to adapt to the Indian culture. Escobedo (1963:21 [140b]) says that he "was able to win many Indians into the faith by wrestling with them and throwing the iron spear a great distance." His strength was legendary among Spanish and Indians alike. On an expedition to Tama earlier in 1597, he had functioned as a bodyguard to Fray Pedro Fernández de Chozas, walking to his right because "he was a brave man and his strength was such that he could conquer the most ferocious giant." But strength may stir resentment instead of respect. According to Barcía (1951:182), Beráscola "badly frightened the Indians." Further, while plotting his death, and having learned of his absence, they lamented, "for they felt that had accomplished nothing if Fray Francisco were left alive." Barcía is a late source, but one must ask if this is a hint of physical repression against delinquent Indians.

Punishment

Because the question of physical force or punishment of the Indians in the missions has become an issue (see Sandos 1988:1253–1269), it is worth noting here that none of the Indians interrogated concerning the martyrs mentioned such punishment. Fray Francisco de Avila, the heroic friar, wounded, captured, and enslaved for 10 months by the revolting Indians, but not one of the martyrs, did in fact pay for the severity of his classroom discipline. Several times the boys nearly killed him "in view of the fact that when the religious had taught them Christian doctrine, he had sometimes struck them" (Oré 1936:77). It is probably safe to say Fray Avila was not the only friar to employ such methods, whether on Indian, Spaniard, or American.

In the wake of the Juanillo revolt, the five surviving friars emerged as champions of Spanish law and order among the Indian population. During the investigation conducted by Fernándo Valdés, son of Don Pedro Valdés, governor of Cuba, in September 1602, the friars in formal depositions to the king, laid the blame for the revolt squarely at the feet of Governor Mendez Canzo (López 1933:2:25–33; Arnade 1959:60–70). Fr. Pedro Ruíz, who in 1609 would become superior of the Franciscans of Cuba and Florida, testified that what was needed was "the gallows and the knife." Because of the laxity of the governor in administering justice, Indians believed that after becoming Christians they could engage with impunity in conduct that would not go unpunished by their own caciques. This state of affairs demoralized the Christian caciques, who, being subject to Spanish authority, had to tolerate what they would have punished. The friars, Ruíz complained, instead of being able to champion the Indians with the governor in matters of justice and mercy, had become the accusers of the Indians before the governor, who ignored the friars and protected the Indians (López 1933:2:23–24; Arnade 1959:64–69).

Fray Pedro Ruíz had reason to be severe. He wrote on the fifth anniversary of the death of Fray Blas de Rodríguez that he had come to Florida with Corpa, Auñón, and Beráscola, and Guale was still unsafe for the friars to return to. The thought of the governor sitting safely in St. Augustine with his garrison of soldiers, not enforcing law and order in the missions and not supporting the friars in their attempt to do so, they being alone, separated by several leagues of swamps, waterways, and bad roads, must have seemed intolerable. His criticism of the governor was most direct, but the letters of the other friars constituted a united front, and on November 19, 1602, Governor Canzo was recalled.

Attitude to Native Culture

It is difficult to know for certain the attitude of the friars toward the native culture of the Indians. Escobedo (1963:132 [327b]) writes in broad black strokes:

> They are rabid enemies of the Christian. They are fond of women, a serious evil, and every Indian must have as many as he wishes. His glory is sin, and because of sin the Indian suffers and dies. Moral abuses are practiced; hence they are transgressors of natural law and traitors to Spain . . . they are inveterate liars.

Seeing so many elements of Indian culture at odds with Christian practice, Escobedo found it difficult to see the good. The friars' love for the Indians moved them to want to change the Indians' ways. The friars believed that the teachings of Jesus were intended for every nation, and obviously for the peoples who accepted the Gospel, those elements of a culture not in conformity with those teachings would be changed. Among Christian neophytes the ways of war must yield to the ways of peace, Indian sorcerers must yield to Christian priests, and most difficult for the Indians of Guale to accept, the practice of polygamy must yield to monogamy.

How difficult the marriage situation was for Indians and their evangelizers is shown by the poignant experience of Fray Juan de Guadalupe on St. Catherines and of Fray Estevan de San Andrés at Mission Santo Domingo at Talaxe. During the revolt, the Indians had taken as wives women other than or in addition to the one previously recognized in the church as the legitimate wife. The Indian could not abandon the second woman and her children, who would perish without the food and fuel that the father provided, and since the second wife was often the only one, the male Indian himself feared starvation without a woman to prepare the meal.

A problem again arose with the principal cacique in Guale who had taken his sister-in-law as second wife. For a while the friars temporized and let him keep the sister-in-law in his house while abstaining from relations with her. But because of scandal, the friars eventually said he would have to send her away. The cacique's solution was to put her in a separate hut, but this too gave rise to scandal because the pagan Indians kept their several wives in separate huts. Even when the cacique's first wife died, the friars would not let him enter the house of his sister-in-law.[15]

It is a difficult passage to read. It is obvious that the friars were beside themselves in their desire to be faithful to the teaching of Jesus and in their compassion for the Indians. The solution that time offered was simply death. Oré (1936:101) writes:

> The religious were not able to solve the situation by any remedy, for it was grave and onerous, so they were discouraged. They turned to God in prayer and besought Him to remedy the affair. He favored them so that gradually He brought them back and on His part evened out the difficulty, taking some of them out of this world to the other. Thus the partners became free of their former alliance and were able to contract anew.

Oré relates that the Indian, in tears, pleaded that he had no relatives and would die of hunger without someone to prepare his meal, as would his children if he could not bring them food and fuel. The friars offered to raise the children themselves in return for his abandoning sin. The sad case ended with the sister-in-law dying and the Indian calling on the people to take warning from his case (Oré 1936:101). One thing is certain: If the suffering of the evangelizers bore witness to Christian faith, equally so did the suffering of the evangelized Indian.

Some Concluding Comments

This discussion of the interest of modern Franciscans in the missionary activity of their confreres in the province of Santa Elena has focused on the martyrs of 1597. It would be an exaggeration to claim that Franciscans generally have any great interest in this period. Not every Franciscan is historian, archivist, or archaeologist. The Order of Friars Minor is a fraternity of men who have come together for the purpose of living the Gospel today, and not every aspect of the past is transparently relevant to the end of the twentieth century. There is scarcely a parallel between the Christian evangelist of today confronting other cultures and the civilized Spanish friar encountering the naked Indian of the Florida coast.

The modern friar tends to adopt the culture of a people, to look for connections between its values and the values of the Gospel, and to interpret Christian values in that culture. To adopt the culture of the primitive Florida Indians, the friars would have had to go naked, and the rebellious Indians seemed but too willing to adopt the clothing of the murdered friars—that is, to adopt elements of the Spanish culture. The modern friar tends to live in the present, to be open to the future, but to be willing to learn from the past. As a case in point, the heroic example of Pedro de Corpa and his confreres in giving their lives for the teachings of the Gospel is clearly meaningful and inspiring.

The contemporary Franciscan, because he is both contemporary and Franciscan, wants to know the truth about Pedro de Corpa and anything else that pertains to history. What he is about is the kingdom of God, which is built upon truth, the whole truth, and nothing but the truth. He believes that only the truth will set humanity free (John 8:32). The archaeologist and the historian within the principles and limits of their respective sciences discover this truth. Their trowels, proton magnetometers, and word processors are today's instruments of God's peace. The words of Cicero quoted by Pope Leo XIII in 1883 when he opened the Vatican Archives and again by Pius XII when he addressed the Congress of Historical Sciences in 1955, seem appropriate: "The first law of history is not to dare to say anything false; and then not to dare to leave out anything of the truth; that there be no suspicion of favor in writing and no simulation."[16] This is a law for historians, for archaeologists, and for ecclesiastics.

Acknowledgments

I gratefully acknowledge the editorial assistance provided by Margot Dembo, American Museum of Natural History.

Notes

1. A whole family of Franciscan religious orders traces origins to St. Francis of Assisi, 1182–1226, and many members of these communities minister in the South. The reform group to which the Spanish missionaries belonged merged with others to form the Order of Friars Minor in 1897. Today, the Friars Minor Conventual staff the parish in Darien, Georgia, near the place where Pedro de Corpa was martyred in 1597.

2. The existence of an intact portion of the convento, well known to historians, was mentioned in an article by Julie Crum in the *Florida Times-Union/Jacksonville Journal*, Sunday, May 8, 1988.

3. The dating of the individual deaths was fixed by John Tate Lanning (1935:82–110).

4. The bodies of Fray Miguel and Fray Antonio were found by the Spanish soldiers under Alonso Díaz, sergeant major, on November 4. The remains being untransportable,

the head and eight small bones of Fray Miguel were taken to Governor Canzo, who turned them over to Fray Blas de Montes, who had been commissioned to investigate the death of his confreres (Omaechevarría 1955:309).

5. "The Christian Indians buried the body [of Fray Miguel] at the foot of a very high cross which he himself had erected. Six years afterwards when [the Spaniards] came to look for his bones, they found them at the foot of the cross, as the Indians had told them" (Oré 1936:75). This would date the removal of the remains to St. Augustine in 1603. Barcía dates the removal to St. Augustine in 1605, writing under that date: "The Franciscan Fathers, who had returned to catechize the Indians of Guale, removed the venerable bodies of Fray Miguel de Auñon and Fray Antonio de Badajoz from the sepulchre given them by the Indians at the foot of the Cross which Fray Miguel had erected, and interred them in a suitable place" (Barcía 1951:188–189). In 1635, Fray Francisco de Ocana referred to miracles worked by the Lord "con sus cuerpos, que están en el combento de San Francisco del Pueblo de San Augustín con grande concurso así de españoles como de yndios." Although he speaks of seven martyrs of 1602, the reference must be to the Guale martyrs of 1597 (Pou y Martí 1927:85).

6. Oré (1617–1620) asserted that the body of Fray Blas de Rodríguez was not recovered (Oré 1936:76), but Díaz had reported finding it on November 5, 1597, the head split into three or four parts, and reinterring it at Tupiqui (AGI, 224; Omaechevarría 1955:310). It is reasonable to assume that the remains were later transported to St. Augustine with those of Fray Miguel and Fray Antonio.

7. "In Florida, Natalis Beatorum Martyrum Michaelis ab Occania, Petri de Corpa, Petri a Velasco, Blasii Roderici et Antonii, qui ob Christianam Religionem, ab Apostatis Indis, telis sunt confixi." Septembris VIII (Arturus a Monasterio 1638:412).

8. Escobedo gives a rather fanciful account in which, after the death of Beráscola and Auñón, Corpa was tortured, hanged, and only when the rope broke in three places (!), was his head smashed (1963:32 [157b]). According to three of the Indians who gave testimony on July 20, 1598, Corpa was asleep in his cell when he was killed with a macana. Lucas, subsequently executed for his role in the death of Blas de Rodríguez, said Corpa was killed by the cacique of Ufalague and Sufalete (AFI, Patronato 19, in López 1933:2:17). Under torture on July 27, Lucas testified that he was not present at the death of Pedro de Corpa. But he also said that of the five martyrs only Fray Blas knew the hour of his death. On July 28, he gave the time of Fray Pedro's death as "al quarto del alba" (López 1933:2:22). Francisco, the second Indian, testified on the 20th that he was from Tolomato and had known Pedro de Corpa a long time. He denied being present at his death, which he had heard was ordered by the mico of Tolomato and Don Juan, his heir. The act itself he attributed to a principal cacique of the Salchiches. An Indian named Buenaventura, also from Tolomato, testified that Corpa was sleeping when killed (López 1933:2:18–19).

9. The head being so displayed, perhaps it was not smashed. A skull in the Fort King George Museum is sometimes said to have been that of Pedro de Corpa (see Wyse 1985:35).

10. Escobedo's account (1963:29–30 [149–152b]) can only be exaggerated.

11. "Porque era vellaco y les quitaba sus hichicerias y que no tubiesen mas de una muger" (López 1933:2:17).

12. "Dixo que la cause fue don Juan eredero de Tolomato, porque le rreprehendia sus bellaquerias y le rrenia" (López 1933:2:18).

13. The rejection of Juanillo's aspirations to the position of cacique at Tolomato was not a reason given by the captured Indians as a cause of the murders. This is the equivalent of saying that the political involvement of Pedro de Corpa and Blas de Rodríguez against Juanillo in itself was not a significant factor in their martyrdom. Indeed, the political significance of Juanillo's rejection is limited by the consideration that succession was not absolutely hereditary and was in this case otherwise contested. Furthermore, since Tolomato was already Christian and subject to Spain, it is arguable that the Spanish

enculturation that had already taken place justified the intervention against Juanillo. The friars were not imposing monogamy on pagan Indians but insisting that Christian Indians ruling over other Christian Indians give good example. What loomed large for the Indians was not Juanillo's political future but the difficulties of monogamous marriage (see Lanning 1935:82–83).

14. See note 8 above. On the will to martyrdom, St. Bonaventure wrote: "Dicendum, quod ad martyrium completum duo concurrunt, scilicet iusta voluntas et iusta cause" (IV Sent., Dub. 1 in Opera omnia [1889:4: 116a]).

15. Before the Catholic Church's revision of Canon Law in 1983, an invalidating marriage impediment existed between those who, during a lawful marriage, committed adultery with a promise of marriage or an attempted marriage (see 1917 Code, Canon 1075, 1. Oré 1936:100–103).

16. Cicero, *De oratore* 1.2.15, cited by Pope Leo XIII (1884) and by Pius XII (1955).

References

Archivo General de Indias (AGI)
1598   Información jurídica sobre los sucesos de la provincia de Guale (San Augustín, 12 de enero de 1598). *Audiencia de Santo Domingo 224.* [See infra Omaechevarria, Ignacio]

Arnade, Charles W.
1959   *Florida on Trial: 1593–1602.* Hispanic American Studies No. 16. University of Miami Press, Coral Gables, Florida.

Arturus a Monasterio
1638   *Martyrologium franciscanum. Parisiis.*

Barcía [Carballido y Zúñiga, Andrés González de]
1951   *Barcías Chronological History of the Continent of Florida,* translated by Anthony Kerrigan (*Ensayo cronológico para la historia general de la Florida*). University of Florida Press, Gainesville. Originally published in 1723.

Bonaventure, St.
1889   *Expositio super Regulam Fratrum Minorum,* x:1 and xii:1, in *Opera Omnia (Ad Claras Aquas).*

Covington, James W. (editor) and A. F. Falcones (translator)
1963   *Pirates, Indians and Spaniards: Father Escobedo's "La Florida."* Great Outdoors, St. Petersburg, Florida.

Escobedo, Fray Alonso Gregorio de
1963   *La Florida* in translation see infra, Covington and Falcones. Published also in part in Spanish, see infra, Pou y Martí, 1927; Omaecheverría, 1955; and López, ed., vol. 1, 1931.

Hann, John H.
1988   *Apalachee: The Land between the Rivers.* Ripley P. Bullen Monographs in Anthropology and History No. 7. University Presses of Florida, Gainesville.

Lanning, John Tate
1935   *The Spanish Missions of Georgia.* University of North Carolina Press, Chapel Hill.

Leo XIII (Pope)
1884   Saepenumero considerantes, August 18, 1883. *Leo XIII P.M., Acta* 3:268. Rome.

López, Atanásio, O.F.M., (editor)
1931–1933 *Relación histórica de la Florida escrita en el siglo XVII por el P. Fr. Jeronimo de Oré* (the account of Father Luis Gerónimo de Oré), 2 vols. Madrid.

Milanich, Jerald T., and Rebecca Saunders
1986   *The Spanish Castillo and the Franciscan Doctrina of Santa Catalina, at Santa Maria, Amelia Island, Florida (8–Na-41).* Miscellaneous Project Report Series No. 20. Florida State Museum, Gainesville.

Omaechevarría, Ignacio, O.F.M.
  1955   Martires franciscanos de Georgia. *Missionalia hispánica* XII:12–35, 291–370.
Oré, Luis Gerónimo de, O.F.M.
  1936   *The Martyrs of Florida*. Translated and edited by Maynard Geiger, O.F.M. Franciscan Studies 18. Joseph F. Wagner, New York.
Pius XII (Pope)
  1955   Address to 10th International Congress of Historical Sciences, September 7, 1955. *Acta Apostolicae Sedis* 47:682.
Pou y Martí, José M.
  1927   Estado de la orden franciscana y de sus misiones en América y Extremo Oriente en el año de 1635. *Archivo Ibero-Americano* 28.
Rahner, Karl, and Herbert Vorgrimler
  1981   *Dictionary of Theology*. 2nd ed. Crossroad, New York.
Sandos, James A.
  1988   Junípero Serra's Canonization and the Historical Record. *American Historical Review* 93:1253–1269.
Sarno, Robert J. (translator)
  1983   *The Sacred Congregation for the Causes of the Saints, New Laws for the Causes of the Saints*. Rome.
Summa theologiae
  1899   Summa theologiae, II, IIae, Q. CXXIV, Art. 5 in *Opera omnia*. Rome.
Thomas, David Hurst
  1988   *St. Catherines: An Island in Time*. Georgia Endowment for the Humanities, Atlanta.
Wyse, Alexander, F.F.M.
  1985   The Five Franciscan Martyrs of Georgia. *Provincial Annals* 34. Franciscan Province of the Most Holy Name of Jesus, New York.

Chapter 30 ■

Amy Turner Bushnell

The Sacramental Imperative: Catholic Ritual and Indian Sedentism in the Provinces of Florida

The Spanish determination to see all Indians settled for life in villages is well known. "People of reason" (*gente de razón*), it was understood, lived *políticamente*, and the polity was municipal. If in the New World many Spaniards fell short of this norm,[1] they continued to believe in it and to apply it to natives.

Historians of colonial Spanish America have identified three kinds of directed settlement. *Población*, according to contemporary usage, signified the populating of new lands, often done by founding and subsidizing new pueblos of Indian settlers. *Congregación* referred to congregating the inhabitants of remote or depopulated settlements in fewer, more accessible places. *Reducción* had the same meaning as congregación, except when it referred to the "people lacking in reason" (*gente sín razón*), who lived "without known habitation." Wild people were said to be "reduced" to civilization when they accepted fixed settlement in closely supervised "reductions," where they could be trained in useful habits and spared the sin of going idle and doing as they pleased.[2]

It is easy to infer that all Spanish-directed settlement, wherever encountered and whatever the form taken, had the same goal: the exploitation of native labor in a plural society dominated by Spaniards. The principal useful habit expected of male and female commoners in Spain, obviously, was to farm productively, satisfying an array of liens on peasant agriculture. Should commoners in the Indies not similarly produce above the subsistence level and surrender the difference to their betters in the form of tithes, tribute, and taxes? The Church, the Crown, and the descendants of conquerors all agreed that they should.

Yet on the mission frontier the primacy of the economic motive in directed settlement is not readily demonstrable. The Crown laid out alms for missionary travel and maintenance in regions where there was little hope of recouping the royal investment (Bushnell 1989b; Gómez Canedo 1977:35).

The missionaries, in turn, urged sedentism upon their neophytes long before there was a population of Spanish settlers to exploit them, and thereafter did their best to keep the Republic of Spaniards separate from the Republic of Indians. The rationale for fixed settlement on the peripheries of empire must be sought elsewhere than in the profit motive. As Francis Guest points out, the "specific reason why the Spanish . . . require[d] converted Indians to make their residence at the missions still needs to be investigated" (Guest 1979:60).

One of the sixteenth-century apostles to New Spain, Fray Toribio de Benavente (better known as Motolinía), advised Emperor Charles V that the Indians would have to be gathered into villages, like the peasants of Spain, so they could be civilized and evangelized (Ricard 1966:135–136). Iberian civilization and Roman Catholicism were two sides of the same coin. Population, congregation, and reduction were institutions for advancing civilization; mission and *doctrina* were their counterparts for the advancement of religion. On the one side, the product was a peasant; on the other, a Catholic Christian.[3]

Yet on a remote frontier, increases in agricultural production were likely to come about as by-products of induced settlement. When a seasonally nomadic, foraging population was reduced, it became, in effect, place-bound, restricted to the environs of a single location. The usual foods in season were suddenly unavailable; it was a sin, no less, to leave one's doctrina long enough to go and harvest them. The common way in which a calorie deficit created by fixed settlement was overcome was by increasing the percentage of cultivated foods in the diet. If the result was intensified agriculture, this was incidental to a deeper cultural command.

Just as a civilized person by definition lived under authority in a town, a Catholic was constrained to live within reach of the sacraments. This was the sacramental imperative: the obligation to be present in church on set days to observe set rituals, and the related obligation to stay within the beat of an itinerant priest. These two unyielding, enforceable obligations prescribed fixed settlement to the Indian convert. The importance of this imperative in shaping the course of Spanish and Indian interaction has not been widely appreciated.

The Florida Pacifications

In the mission provinces of Florida, far from the centers of colonial wealth and power, the operation of the sacramental imperative can be seen plainly. Florida, like Cuba, was one of the later "islands" of the Indies to be colonized, partly because it evinced no riches, and partly because its inhabitants were exceptional warriors. Juan Ponce de León, Pánfilo de Narváez, and Hernando de Soto were only three in a long line of unsuccessful conquistadors.

What some historians call the "High Conquest" ended formally in 1573 with Philip II's Ordinances of Pacification. For some time beforehand, Spanish expansion had been gradually changing character to become more deliberate, more selective, and, despite notorious lapses, more peaceful. An *adelantado*, or contractual conqueror, might secure the first foothold, but for subsequent advances, even strategic ones, the Crown (which as patron of the Church had the missionizing orders at its disposal) relied on soldiers of the cross.

The missionizing orders, in turn, directed their immediate attention to the "people of reason" with whom they experienced the best results, or, for want of these to the "docile people" (Prado and Menéndez Márques 1667), prepared to leave off wandering in the woods to live lives of order regimented by the sound of church bells. It was the roving, often marauding, people who put the cap on Spanish expansion. Referred to in Florida as "Chichimecos" or as "Caribs," depending on whether they made their entrance by land or by sea, these free-ranging natives were virtually impossible to subdue by force and could be reduced to agrarian settlements only by the promise of gifts or the necessity of asylum. They made fickle subjects and wayward converts. Unless their habitat possessed unusual attractions or was a base of international outlawry, they were generally left to themselves.

What little the Spanish had learned about the natives of Florida during the High Conquest was discouraging. Father José de Acosta placed the majority of them, along with Brazilian Indians and Pacific Islanders, in his third and last category of barbarians, that of savages. Savages lived without law, king, pacts, magistrates, or republic. They shifted their habitations or holed up in caves and dens more like wild beasts than humans (Gómez Canedo 1977:xiv–xvi). They were inescapably ignoble.

Notwithstanding Acosta's secondhand impressions, when adelantado Pedro Menéndez de Avilés arrived in Florida in 1565 he encountered a wide variety of Indian societies on whom to practice the developing principle of pacification. The powerful, seagoing Calusas of South Florida, guarding the narrow waters that led out of the Caribbean, were nonhorticultural, basing their sedentism squarely on marine resources. Despite Menéndez's efforts and those of his successors for 130 years, the Calusas were never Christianized. Perhaps their naval power made them too great a challenge; perhaps it was merely that their boats made them unacceptably mobile. On the Atlantic coast south of St. Augustine, assorted groups of seasonal nomads with a level of social stratification far below that of the Calusas also resisted conversion.

The Oristas (Cusabos) of coastal South Carolina and the Guales of coastal Georgia depended heavily on hunting, fishing, and foraging. They followed an annual round that took them in the fall to oak groves, in the winter to estuaries, in the spring to scattered clearings for swidden agriculture, and in the summer back to the estuaries, where their chiefs maintained centers of information and redistribution (Crook 1988; cf. Reitz 1988). The eastern Timucuans inhabiting the barrier islands and coastal marshes east of the St. Johns River had an essentially similar life-style.

After varying periods of resistance, the Guales and eastern Timucuans by and large accepted Christianity and were persuaded to devote more time to squash, beans, and corn. West of the St. Johns, the more horticultural western Timucuans, whose territory ran from the St. Johns west to the marshes of the Gulf, were also Christianized.

Neither the Guales nor the Timucuans, eastern or western, surrendered their traditional right to secede at will, an option that they exercised communally in uprisings and individually by fugitivism. Between these practices and the epidemics that struck Florida during the first half of the seventeenth century, the mission provinces of Timucua and Guale were virtually depopulated by 1675 (Bushnell 1978b:3–5).

Apalachee Province, around present-day Tallahassee, was characterized by the richest farmlands and the most intensive agriculture in all of Florida (Hann 1988). During the demographic crisis of the seventeenth century, a shortage of Christian inhabitants in the other provinces had severe consequences. Guale Province declined to three towns; the "old fields" of the doctrinas in Timucua Province gave way to ranches; and hundreds of Indian refugees, set in motion by the shock waves of English settlement to the north, poured into the peninsula to occupy the ruins of missions. Only in highly agricultural Apalachee was population comparatively constant (Bushnell 1978a, 1986, 1989b; Deagan 1985; Hann 1986b, 1988:160–169; Zúñiga y Cerda 1702).

If there were such a thing as a social laboratory, the varying responses of the Indians of Florida would suggest a positive correlation between the degree of agrarian sedentism and the ability to conform to Catholicism. The Florida-based Jesuit Juan Rogel, like many missionaries before and after him, was conscious of the relationship. In 1570 he made this often-quoted statement about the natives of Orista to his patron Pedro Menéndez:

> The main obstacle to their conversion is their wandering scattered nine months a year. If we are to gather fruit, the Indians must join and live in settlements and cultivate the soil, raising sustenance for the whole year and once they are firmly fixed in one place preaching may begin. As this is not done we have had no results these four years, and would not for fifty.
>
> To unite them in this manner will be difficult and will take a long time to do it lawfully and not by compulsion or armed force. For they have been accustomed to living in this way for many thousands of years, and to want to take them from it would be like death to them. And even if they were willing, the land will not produce, being poor and miserable, and exhausting itself very quickly, and thus they themselves say that this is the reason they go about so scattered, moving from so many places [Rogel 1570].

As Father Rogel predicted, the Oristas rejected conversion. Shortly afterward the Jesuits moved their ministry to the more promising Chesapeake, leaving Florida to the mendicant order of the sons of St. Francis.

Unlike some orders, Franciscans did not relocate their neophytes as a means of helping them to break with the past. Instead, they attempted to place their friaries, or *conventos*, in existing settlements, preferably in the largest community. From the mission compound in the head town a missionary went out with his portable altar and visual aids to tend a circuit of satellite *visitas* in the smaller towns. The whole eventually formed an Indian doctrina, with the resident Franciscan as *doctrinero* (Gómez Canedo 1977:48).

Once installed in an Indian community, the Franciscan began a dedicated assault on unacceptable native beliefs and practices. Florida's rare ethnographic sources testify to these campaigns. Fray Francisco Pareja's attempts to stamp out heathenism and hedonism in eastern Timucua led to his Timucuan–Spanish *Confessionario* containing explicit questions about sexuality and superstitions (Milanich and Sturtevant 1972). Fray Juan de Paiva, with native research assistants, recorded the myths and magic associated with a ball game played in western Timucua and Apalachee (Bushnell 1978b; Hann 1988:70–95, 328–353).

In the early years of a conversion, adults and children attended classes daily to recite the prayers, be drilled in the doctrine, and learn music. After 10 years or longer—time for the children to grow up—the "live conversion" matured into an Indian parish or doctrina liable to tithes, while its civic counterpart, the congregation or reduction, became an Indian pueblo subject to tribute. Full "secularization" was generally postponed for lack of secular clergy, and the regular clergy continued as parish priests (Gómez Canedo 1977:51–52).

Despite their well-tested methods, the Franciscans were not wholly satisfied with the progress of conversions in Florida. After the Guale Rebellion of 1597, they and the other Spaniards paused to take stock of the 1,200 Christians who remained (Arnade 1959; Méndez de Canzo 1602). According to Fray Francisco Pareja (1602), the "bad and willful" ones went "inland to pueblos of heathen, where they remain[ed] for one year and two without hearing Mass." His colleague Fray Pedro Bermejo (1602) suggested that the ones living in "hamlets of three and four and five houses" be reduced to the head towns, to "help one another in their labors," and to "be better indoctrinated," and to make it easier for their friars to "visit them in their necessities and infirmities." A few years later Pareja and a third friar reported that the Indians were still reluctant to reduce themselves to "regular towns" and continued to "wander off to their relatives" (Peñaranda and Pareja 1607).

In 1612, in a periodic report on the state of the missions, four friars advised the Crown that they had little to show for 20 years in Florida.

> All our doctrine seemed to convert itself into hatred and abhorrence against us, the service of Your Majesty, and Spaniards in general, and against the livestock we tried to introduce, [the Indians] killing and exterminating them like vermin, and they did the same to the trees and seeds, wishing to leave no trace or smell of us [Franciscans of Florida 1612].

It was a waste of effort to make war on people without "buildings or inheritances" in their pueblos, the friars continued candidly. People for whom "moving from one place to another ten leagues away" was "like nothing," who were accustomed to living in the woods "as free as deer," could always do more damage to Spaniards than Spaniards could do to them. They were never likely to be conquered "like those of New Spain, who are much more subdued and have houses and properties to lose, and these people nothing at all." But the friars saw signs that things in Florida were beginning to change. The hand of God was at work. Chiefs from the more orderly interior were starting to raise crosses, build churches, and ask for friars.

Teresa Martín, an Indian woman from the interior long married to a Spanish soldier, testified in St. Augustine that the people of her land were different.

> They are not fickle and deceitful like the people of this land. In this land all they do is pick up their quivers and their trash and go from one island to another and from one swamp to another to hunt and gather shellfish, without any place of their own.

Her people, she said, were "people of settlements and established neighborhoods, surrounded by their children and grandchildren and great- grandchildren" (Martín 1600).

The "Heathen in the Woods"

The Franciscans, acting much like agricultural extension agents, introduced their converts to iron tools and more intensive farming techniques. This allowed a more sedentary agricultural economy to develop in areas of Timucua where the soils were suitable (Deagan 1985:302–303), and on the islands of Guale (Bushnell 1989b). Yet years after the hand of God fell heavy upon Florida, the Indians were still halfhearted farmers. In 1646 the doctrineros allegedly had to urge their parishioners repeatedly to plant and cultivate enough corn for their needs (Pérez n.d.). In 1681, new doctrineros exhorted a new generation in the same words to raise corn, "their only grain and staple." Full granaries were a requisite if the friars were going to "aggregate and keep them together," the better to "instill, indoctrinate, teach, and administer to them the holy sacraments," they claimed, for such was the natives' "uselessness, weakness and natural indolence" that "they would not have been preserved to live socially and rationally in settlements," otherwise, but would be living in their old manner, "like wild animals of the forest" (Franciscans of Florida 1681).

Indians were "content with little," protested their ministers, members of a mendicant order. "For something of this world that will cost them some work they aren't ones to kill themselves." As a result, the natives often ran short of corn and had to "go into the woods to maintain themselves with plants and roots." It was what they were used to, and knowing no better, they thought it "a good life" (Franciscans of Florida 1681). A diet of acorns, dates, and roots from the lagoons was inadequate, Fray Francisco Pérez told them. Between the poor food and the mosquitoes and the discomforts of being always on the move, he thought it no wonder that they sickened and died (Pérez n.d.).

Despite their spiritual fathers' disapproval, Timucuan and Guale Christians persisted in their own ideas of the good life and took frequent, unauthorized leave from their doctrinas. Forsaking the missions en masse was equivalent to launching an uprising; the best-known example is the 1597 Guale Rebellion. In that instance, the Spanish went north on several campaigns, eventually got the Indians themselves to defeat the rebels, and then re-reduced the Guales to a chain of restored doctrinas (Geiger 1937). What is not generally known is that there was another Guale insurrection in 1645 (Menéndez Márques and Horruytiner 1647; Ruíz de Salazar Vallecilla 1645), and in the early 1680s a third, after which the province was deserted for good (Auto on Governor Márques Cabrera [1688?]; Hita Salazar 1683; Luna [1688?]; Quiroga y Losada 1688). Fugitivism by individuals was insurrection on a small scale.

The friars had two reasons to discourage the Indians from foraging in family or lineage groups. First, it made them "remiss in Christian obligation on those days" when they were "supposed to be in church" (Luna n.d.). Second, the doctrinero who wanted to say Mass for any of his parishioners, or minister to them, or keep them from "taking up with heathen in the woods," was forced to choose one group and follow, at great personal inconvenience (Pérez n.d.).

Pursuing one's parishioners presented difficulties. The rituals of Roman Catholicism were ancient and complicated, ill suited for transfer to any frontier, much less to one where the sites of worship themselves were evanescent. In order to say the simplest Mass in the poorest chapel, a priest had to assemble and preserve from sacrilege 35 separate items, one of them a stone altar (Bushnell 1989b; Durand 1896:facing 40).

A permanent church with a resident minister possessed a heavier, more elaborate set of the basic ornaments, vessels, and fittings, plus the paraphernalia needed to perform marriages, baptisms, and burials with decency. The least one of the Indian doctrinas had, in addition, a supply of portable crosses and processional lanterns, disciplinary whips and stocks, leather-bound recordbooks with ornate clasps, large bells to call the children to catechism and the adults to Mass and evening prayers, riveting pictures of heaven and hell, and above all, *santos*—wooden or plaster images of the saints, Christ, and the Virgin, colorfully painted and richly adorned (Hann 1986a).

The material trappings of Catholicism may have presented a transportation problem, yet they were undeniably attractive. In 1681, Francisco and Matheo, chiefs of a newly formed Yamassee mission at Mayaca, brought suit through Domingo de Leturiondo, official defender of the Indians, against their most recent minister, Fray Bartolomé Quiñones. That he had abandoned them they did not seem to mind, but he had carried off the ornaments and the two bells that the king had "given to their town and no other." They conjectured that Fray Bartolomé had taken it "ill that they let heathen come and mix with Christians," but, they said, "they could not dismiss them or refuse to receive them, being one and alike their vassals" (Leturiondo [1682?]).

It was a familiar story. Mayaca, on the upper reaches of the St. Johns River, was a place that could not keep a mission. According to the officials of the Florida treasury, the Indians of the area spent most of their time in the countryside looking for roots. As they would not reduce themselves to farming or form pueblos, had no friar, and paid no tribute, the officials wrote them off as unproductive. At Mayaca, people would not "live like Christians." The place itself was "irreduceable" (Menéndez Márques and la Rocha n.d.). According to a brother Franciscan, Fray Bartolomé had made himself sick "wandering in the woods" after the Yamassees, "an indomitable, unreasonable nation" who would "by no means settle down, much less plant for their sustenance, or be found ever in a designated place" (Chrisóstomo 1688).

Mayaca lay in the *Rinconada*, the great expanse of marshlands south of the Cabo de Cañaveral (Zúñiga y Cerda 1701). Long before, Governor Gonzalo Méndez de Canzo (1602) had dismissed the Indians between the St. Johns River and the coast below St. Augustine as "a miserable people" who sustained themselves on fish and the "roots of the swamps and forests." They had no cities or towns, he said, their chiefs were little respected, there was great diversity of languages, and they were all "as poor as can be."

The Rinconada was "full of idolaters and gentiles," reported the Franciscans in 1693. Most of them did not "work in fields," but sustained themselves "with the fish they catch in abundance and some wild fruits." Perhaps gifts of iron hoes would "induce them to plantings and to live like rationals" (Franciscans of Florida 1693). Once again, however, the Indians left the conversions and retired to "miry woods and labyrinths of sawgrass." The king's advisers suspected ill treatment, for surely Indians would never "absent themselves and retire to the woods unless they were provoked by some vexation" of Spaniards (Zúñiga y Cerda 1701).

They were confusing the Rinconada with Apalachee, where Spanish ranches were encroaching upon Indian fields and the Indians were reacting with fugitivism. Antonio Ponce de León, local defender of the Indians, addressed the king about that problem directly: "It is not right that when Your Majesty is spending his royal patrimony solely to reduce souls to the holy faith, that they should be lost in the woods because of the interests of private persons" (1702). But in the Rinconada case, Governor Joseph de Zúñiga y Cerda assured the Crown that the natives had gone off "for no reason, . . . moved solely by their obstinacy and ignorance, like the sons of the woods that they are" (1701).

In 1728 the Franciscans were still trying to convert various groups of Rinconada Indians, with small success. The Jororos would "neither sow nor cultivate, but only wander about the whole year, men and women alike, searching the seashore for something to eat, killing alligators and other unclean animals, which for them is delectable sustenance," while the Costas, "by nature vile," were "an utterly useless nation," who "when they take a notion . . . leave their huts and go off to eat dates" (Bullones 1728).

Like the Rinconada Indians, unknown numbers of Guales, Timucuans and Apalachees managed to avoid conversion and to live unchaperoned within the Pale. These rarely mentioned "heathen in the woods" resisted the divisive power of the gospel to stay in contact with their Christian kinsmen and commensals. Still other groups of non-Christians washed into the provinces from time to time through the permeable borders. In 1639, Governor Damián de Vega Castro y Pardo wrote:

A great number of Indians called Chiscas, people who pride themselves on their fierceness, wander at will through these provinces. . . . I have been trying to collect them somewhere by themselves, assigning them a place to settle . . . [so they] may calm down and earn their living by hunting and trying to work and cultivate the land, with the object of making them vassals of Your Majesty and converting them. . . . They will be useful to track down and return those fugitive Indians who absent themselves from their doctrinas . . . [to] wander about idly and associate with heathen and fall into the danger of apostasy [Vega Castro y Pardo 1639].

Things did not work out as the governor intended. The Chiscas opted to "live without known settlements in the woods and threaten the Christians into joining them and leaving the law of God" or they would "kill them all" (Menéndez Márques and Horruytiner 1647).

The Law of God

The "law of God" was the sum of Christian obligations, the "yoke of the holy evangel" (Prado and Menéndez Márques 1668), which at the time of baptism an individual took on himself or laid on one of his children. While a coerced conversion, like a coerced marriage, was invalid, a promise to obey the law of God, like a marriage vow, could be enforced. It was a contract and the power of civil authority stood behind it.

Spanish civil control over Hispanized Indians, or what Spaniards called the Republic of Indians, was channeled through the chiefs (Bushnell 1989a). A native group with a mild form of social stratification was apt to find conversion accompanied by some gain in chiefly power at the expense of commoner autonomy. As one St. Augustine treasury official reported:

Indians are required to have licenses to go from pueblo to pueblo and to advise of it, because these barbarians went around freely without informing their chiefs and no one ever knew who was in town and who wasn't, [which was] bad for teaching and conversions [Argüelles 1600].

The four Franciscans who signed the report on the state of the missions in 1612 said that Apalachee was not yet ready for conversions because "some of the Indians obey[ed] their chiefs poorly." The king should send more soldiers, they thought, so that "the chiefs with the favor and aid of Your Majesty could subdue their Indians" (Franciscans of Florida 1612).

A Christian chief was expected to keep close track of his vassals. In 1701 Governor Zúñiga y Cerda instructed a council of chiefs in the telescoped province of Guale to have their vassals "live like Christians, attending Mass the days of precept, and the children going to doctrina daily, and keeping crosses and images of saints in their houses with all decency and reverence." The people should not "dance the forbidden dances," and if they saw one of their number "delinquent in Christian observance or practicing some heathen rite or ceremony," they should denounce him so the offense to God could be corrected (Caciques of Guale 1701).

The chiefs of Apalachee and Timucua were similarly instructed not to let their vassals "play ball or make use of lascivious heathen dances." They were to report all "scandals and concubinages," Indians "curing in the heathen manner," and women "aborting with medicines and herbs." Their vassals, too, were to have "crosses decently treated in their houses (a large cross at the door of the house, and inside at the head of their beds other small ones) and to recite the Ave María and say their rosaries daily before these crosses," and furthermore, to "venerate and assist their friar, planting corn and wheat in his field and that of the youths who help at the convent," and finally, to "attend church all the days of obligation," not "missing Mass on feastdays or skipping doctrina" (Bushnell 1989b; Florencia 1694–1695).

Of the seven sacraments through which a Catholic could receive Grace, baptism alone was indispensable. The hapless infant who expired before baptism was barred from the presence of God forever. The friars were troubled on this account in 1656 when the Timucuans rose in rebellion and returned to living like heathen, "paying attention only to their dances and matters of war." Indian husbands were "wandering with their wives out in the woods"; children would be born and "die without benefit of the holy sacrament of baptism" (Franciscans of Florida 1657). In another instance a friar advanced as an argument against the practice of using Indian men to carry burdens that if it became too oppressive, women would refuse to raise male children and would secretly drown and bury them out in the fields, unbaptized (Moreno Ponce de León n.d.)

Baptism, representing a change in status from pagan to Christian, placed an individual under new obligations and made him capable of new sins. This is why the rite was restricted to three categories of candidates: persons who had successfully completed a course of indoctrination lasting as long as four years (López 1602), infants whose parents could be counted on to raise them as Christians, and anybody on a deathbed who could repent and believe. Five years of epidemics in eastern Timucua before 1617 produced thousands of deathbed conversions (Bushnell 1981:13, 98). The tired priests, hurrying from one scene of sorrow to another, reminded themselves that they were reaping a bountiful harvest of souls.

The baptized person who survived to sin again could become freshly acceptable to God by means of the sacrament of penance, which called for confession, contrition, and absolution. In the form of last rites, penance gave comfort to the dying. A "good death" allowed a person time to confess and be shriven; in a "bad death," confession was somehow prevented, as when a person dropped dead, was stricken mute, or was murdered.

During the epidemic, or *peste*, the Franciscans went about "with great labors day and night" (Franciscans of Florida 1617a), bearing their kits for sick calls: two books, a crucifix, a stole, and miniature containers for holy oils, holy water, consecrated wafers and salt (Durand 1896:facing 88, 137). The "great mortalities among the Indians" left in their wake "some hamlets of small consideration and very few Indians—ten or eight houses, and in other places few or none." It was decided to congregate them, because the Indians could not be indoctrinated at such a distance and were Christians in name only. By the time a friar received word that one of his flock in a distant visita was sick and went out to "sacrament" him, the person was usually dead (Franciscans of Florida 1617a).

Indian souls were especially at risk during the building of the Castillo de San Marcos in St. Augustine. Queen Regent Mariana, informed of numerous deaths in the labor camps outside the capital—the natives being "weak and unused to hard work and short rations"—made provision for them to have friars who spoke the Timucuan, Apalachee, and Guale languages, believing that the person "who comes to the extreme of life without a priest to understand his language places his salvation in grave doubt" (Somoza 1673).

The law of God required every baptized Catholic to confess once a year, a practice known as "complying with the Church." In Florida, the Franciscans' count of the natives who complied with the Church during Lent in the various doctrinas, including the subordinate visitas, functioned as a provincial census and was the basis for the labor levy (Leturiondo 1687; Florencia 1694–1695; Luengo 1676).

In a time when laymen rarely took communion, Franciscans reserved the Eucharist for natives of advanced understanding and proven devotion who had just confessed (Pareja 1602; Ricard 1966:122–124). All Catholics, however, were required under pain of mortal sin to attend Mass on Sundays and feastdays of obligation (Leturiondo 1697). The friars whipped Indians, male and female, chief and commoner, for the sin of missing Mass as they did for concubinage, adultery, and other "offenses to God" (Franciscans of Florida 1681; Fuentes 1681; Márques Cabrera 1681; [Arias de Servantes] 1682).

The women who spent a few days gathering nuts in the forest were not simply laying in a year's supply of nut oil; in the Spanish view, they were "wandering about in the woods" without spiritual guidance, "committing a thousand mortal sins" ([Fuentes] 1682). If the friars did not "remedy offenses" of this nature, the natives took "advantage, as ignorant people will, of the freedom" they were given "to lose respect for the *religiosos* and speak to them without deference," and "wander as fugitives in the woods" and, in the end, "die there as barbarians" (Franciscans of Florida 1617b).

A doctrinero could be more strict about enforcing the law of God than the priest of a Spanish parish—a compelling reason to keep Indians isolated from Spaniards. Soldiers especially set a "noxious and scandalous example" to those new in the faith, for when it came to soldiers, "those who want to hear Mass do, and those who don't, don't, nor do they confess or comply with the things that Christians must" (Franciscans of Florida 1664; 1617b). Settlers presented an extra problem. When creole merchants and ranchers moved into San Luis, capital of Apalachee, they reportedly displaced the Indians from the center of town, pushing them so far out that to get to Mass some of them had to walk for a league (Ponce de León 1702).

A town with a one-league radius would have been a dispersed settlement. The ideal settlement pattern, as far as the Spanish were concerned, was not dispersed but nucleated, the Indians living "reduce[d] beneath the bell of their doctrinas and the hand of their doctrineros" (Auto on Governor Márques Cabrera [1688?]), as they did in New Spain, within a charmed circle 560 yards in radius measuring from the church campanile (Wolf 1959:164). The ideal, in other words, was Mediterranean campanilism.

Many Apalaches built their houses by choice in the midst of their fields, living scattered out instead of close together (Hann 1988:25, 174, 179–180). Judging from a 1687 request for friars, the same pattern held for other provinces. Every doctrina, whether in Apalachee, Timucua, or Guale, needed its own minister because "the dwelling places [were] spread out and the Indians' houses distant from the church," the natives being "unable to reduce themselves to regular towns because of their plantings" (Auto on the Need for Friars 1687). If this was true, then nowhere in Florida were the Indians disposed to realize, in full, a Spanish settlement pattern.

The Import of the Imperative

To assume that an intent to exploit lay behind the Florida conversions and their precondition, sedentism, would be to reason from effect to cause. When the Indians' mobility was restricted, the amount of food contributed to the diet by normal hunting and gathering declined, the shortage was made up by increased farming, and an agricultural surplus was the exploitable result.

It is true that governors and creoles, chiefs and friars, all discovered ways to profit from the surplus value of native labor once a provisioning trade developed between Havana and the Gulf coast provinces, but this happened two-thirds of a century after the first conversions. As late as 1630, an incoming governor commented that Florida was an economic backwater "without *encomiendas*, workshops, or mines," where the natives died inexplicably, being "the least worked and the best treated in the Indies" (Rodríguez de Villegas 1630).

The reason for restricting native mobility in the first place was the duty of a Christian to live within reach of the sacraments. It was impossible for a "son of the woods" to obey the law of God. Father Rogel could not have put it more plainly: "If we are to gather fruit, the Indians must join and live in settlements and cultivate the soil" (1570). Only as a peasant, "reduced beneath the bell of his doctrina and the hand of his doctrinero," could an Indian fulfill the sacramental imperative.

The link between sedentism and the sacraments inhibited the conversion of all but the sedentary. As interpreted by the missionaries, Roman Catholic ritual was incapable of adapting to any environment beyond the town-centered kind in which it had developed. Other environments had to adapt to it, and they seldom did. Out on the peripheries of empire, in the remote places "without encomiendas, workshops, or mines," it was the refusal or the inability of nomadic and semisedentary Indians to abide by the sacramental imperative and live in fixed settlements that determined the territorial limits of conversions and thereby set the effective bounds of Spanish sovereignty.

Acknowledgments

Research for this study was conducted in 1986–1987 while the author was a Rockefeller fellow with the Program in Atlantic History, Culture, and Society at the Johns Hopkins University. Earlier versions have been presented at meetings of the American Historical Association (Washington, D.C., December 1987) and the Society for American Archaeology (Atlanta, April 1989).

Notes

1. Richard M. Morse speaks of the "dissolvent effect" of the American natural resources, soil and subsoil, on both the "communitarian traditions of rural, seignorial Europe" and the "metropolitan institutions of urban, imperial Europe" (1962:333).

2. When early English colonists spoke of "reducing" Indians, it was in the sense of humbling them (Axtell 1985:131–178).

3. L. N. McAlister has called *congregación* and *doctrina* "the most exclusively American of all the institutions employed by Spain in the Indies" (1984:170).

References

Argüelles, Bartolomé de
  1600   Letter to the Crown, 2-20-1600. SD 229/32.
[Arias de Servantes, Juan]
  1682   Letter to unnamed superior, 8-10-1682, San Joseph de Ocuya. With Juan Márques Cabrera, 6-28-1683, SD 226/105.
Arnade, Charles W.
  1959   *Florida on Trial, 1593–1602*. University of Miami Press, Coral Gables, Florida.
Auto on the Ecclesiastical Visita
  1688   Depositions, 3-29-1688. SD 864/10B.
Auto on the Friars
  1683   Depositions, 6-28-1683. SD 226/105.
Auto on Governor Márques Cabrera
  1681   Depositions, 5-30-1681. SD 226.
  [1688?] Depositions, [3–29–1688?], Havana. SD 864/8.
Auto on Mayaca and Enacape
  1682   Depositions, before 3-11-1682 to 10-1682. With Juan Márques Cabrera, 10-7-1682, SD 226/95.
Auto on the Need for Friars
  1687   Depositions, 2-22-1687. SD 864/5.
Axtell, James
  1985   *The Invasion Within: The Contest of Cultures in Colonial North America*. Oxford University Press, New York.
Bermejo, Pedro
  1602   Declaration. In Franciscans of Florida, 1602.
Bullones, Joseph
  1728   Letter to Gerónimo Valdés, Bishop of Cuba, 8-13-1728, Havana. With Joseph Bullones, 10-5-1728, SD 865.
Bushnell, Amy Turner
  1978a The Menéndez Márques Cattle Barony at La Chua and the Determinants of Economic Expansion in Seventeenth-Century Florida. *Florida Historical Quarterly* 56:407–431.

1978b That Demonic Game: The Campaign to Stop Indian Pelota Playing in Spanish Florida, 1675–1684. *Americas* 35:1–19.

1981 *The King's Coffer: Proprietors of the Spanish Florida Treasury, 1565–1702.* University Presses of Florida, Gainesville, Florida.

1986 Santa María in the Written Record. Miscellaneous Project Report Series 21. Florida State Museum Department of Anthropology, Gainesville, Florida.

1989a Ruling the Republic of Indians in Seventeenth-Century Florida. In *Powhatan's Mantle: Ethnohistory of Indians in the Colonial Southeast*, edited by Peter Wood, M. Thomas Hatley, and Gregory A. Waselkov, pp. 134–150. University of Nebraska Press, Lincoln.

1989b *The Archaeology of Mission Santa Catalina de Guale: The Support and Supplying of the Florida Conversions.* American Museum of Natural History, Anthropological Papers. New York, forthcoming.

Caciques of Guale
1701 Council at Santa María, 2-11-1701. With Zúñiga y Cerda Residencia, SD 858, cuaderno 4.

Chrisóstomo, Juan
1688 Declaration. In Auto on the Ecclesiastical Visita, 1688.

Crook, Morgan R., Jr.
1988 An Ecological Model for the Proto-Historic Guale. In *Land and Sea*, edited by J. L. Peacock and J. C. Sabella, pp. 122–139. Proceedings of the Southern Anthropology Society No. 21.

Deagan, Kathleen A.
1985 Spanish-Indian Interaction in Sixteenth-Century Florida and Hispaniola. In *Cultures in Contact: The Impact of European Contacts on Native American Cultural Institutions A.D. 1000–1800*, edited by William W. Fitzhugh, pp. 281–318. Smithsonian Institution Press, Washington, D.C.

Durand, Abbé
1896 *Catholic Ceremonies and Explanation of the Ecclesiastical Year.* Benziger Bros., New York.

Florencia, Joachín de
1694–1695 Visita of Apalachee and Timucua. With Torres y Ayala. Residencia, EC 157.

Franciscans of Florida
1602 Depositions before Pedro de Valdés, 9-14-1602 to 9-16-1602. SD 235/10.
1612 Letter to the Crown, 10-16-1612. SD 232/61.
1617a Triennial report to the Crown, 1-14-1617. SD 235/18.
1617b Report to the Crown, 1-17-1617. SD 235.
1657 Report to the Crown, 9-10-1657. SD 235.
1664 Report to the Crown, 6-16-1664. SD 233.
1681 Letters to Governor Márques Cabrera, 5-19-1681 to 5-30-0681. In Auto on Governor Márques Cabrera, 1681.
1693 Report to the Crown, 12-5-1693. SD 235/134.

Fuentes, Francisco de
1681 Letter to Governor Márques Cabrera, 10-30-1681, Sápala. In Auto on the Friars, 1683.
1682 [Fuentes, Francisco de]. Letter to the Friar [of San Luís], 11-27-1682, San Luís. With Juan Márques Cabrera, 6-28-1683, SD 226/105.

Geiger, Maynard, O.F.M.
1937 *The Franciscan Conquest of Florida (1573–1618).* Catholic University of America, Washington, D.C.

Gómez Canedo, Lino
1977 *Evangelización y Conquista: Experiencia Franciscana en Hispanoamérica.* Editorial Porrúa, México, D.F.

Guest, Francis F.
   1979   An Examination of the Thesis of S. F. Cook on the Forced Conversion of Indians in the California Missions. *Southern California Quarterly* 41:1–77.
Hann, John H.
   1986a Church Furnishings, Sacred Vessels and Vestments Held by the Missions of Florida: Translation of Two Inventories. *Florida Archaeologist* 2:147–164.
   1986b Demographic Patterns and Changes in Mid-Seventeenth Century Timucua and Apalachee. *Florida Historical Quarterly* 64:371–392.
   1988   *Apalachee: The Land between the Rivers*. University Presses of Florida, Gainesville.
Hita Salazar, Pablo de
   1683   Letter to the Crown, 5-20-1683, SD 226.
Leturiondo, Alonso de
   1687   Letter to the Crown, 4-18-1687. SD 234/75.
   1697   Letter to the Crown, 4-29-1697. SD 235/143.
Leturiondo, Domingo de
   [1682?] Petition on behalf of Francisco and Matheo, caciques of Mayaca, [4-1682?]. In Auto on Mayaca and Enacape, 1682.
López, Baltasar
   1602   In Franciscans of Florida, 1602.
Luengo, Juan
   1676   Letter to the Crown, 11-30-1676. With Alonso del Moral, n.d. [summary on 11-5-1676], SD 235/104.
Luna, Pedro de
   n.d.   Letter to the Crown, n.d. [summary seen in Council of the Indies, 3-4-1682]. SD 235/115.
   [1688?] Letter to the Crown, [3-29-1688?]. SD 864/9.
McAlister, L. N.
   1984   *Spain and Portugal in the New World, 1492–1700*. University of Minnesota Press, Minneapolis.
Márques Cabrera, Juan
   1681   Letter to the Crown, 6-14-1681. SD 226 and SD 839/67.
Martín, Teresa
   1600   Declaration. With Relation of La Tama, 2-4-1600, SD 224/32.
Méndez de Canzo, Gonzalo
   1602   Letter to the Crown, 9-22-1602. SD 224.
Menéndez Márques, Antonio, and Francisco de la Rocha
   n.d.   Letter to the Crown, [before 3-11-1682]. In Auto on Mayaca and Enacape, 1682.
Menéndez Márques, Francisco, and Pedro Benedit Horruytiner
   1647   Letter to the Crown, 3-18-1647. SD 229.
Milanich, Jerald T., and William C. Sturtevant (editors)
   1972   *Francisco Pareja's 1613 "Confessionario": A Documentary Source for Timucuan Ethnography*. Translation by Emilio F. Moran. Florida Department of State, Tallahassee.
Moreno Ponce de León, Pedro
   n.d.   Letter to the Crown, [summarized on 10-26-1651]. SD 235/67.
Morse, Richard M.
   1962   Some Characteristics of Latin American Urban History. *American Historical Review* 67(2):317–338.
Pareja, Francisco
   1602   Declaration. In Franciscans of Florida, 1602.
Peñaranda, Alonso de, and Francisco Pareja
   1607   Letter to the Crown, 11-20-1607. SD 224/84.
Pérez, Francisco
   n.d.   Memorial. N.p., [summary seen in Council of the Indies on 7–28–1646]. SD 235.

Ponce de León, Antonio
    1702   Letter to the Crown, 1-29-1702. SD 863/43.
Prado, Joseph de, and Juan Menéndez Márques
    1667   Letter to the Crown, 9-22-1667. SD 847/4.
    1668   Letter to the Crown, 6-30-1668. SD 229/134.
Quiroga y Losada, Diego de
    1688   Letter to the Crown, 4-1-1688. SD 839/119.
Reitz, Elizabeth J.
    1988   Evidence for Coastal Adaptations in Georgia and South Carolina. *Archaeology of Eastern North America* 16:137–158.
Ricard, Robert
    1966   *The Spiritual Conquest of Mexico: An Essay on the Apostolate and the Evangelizing Methods of the Mendicant Orders in New Spain, 1523–1572.* Translated by Lesley Byrd Simpson. University of California Press, Berkeley.
Rodríguez de Villegas, Andrés
    1630   Letter to the Crown, 12-27-1630. SD 225/30.
Rogel, Juan
    1570   Letter to Pedro Menéndez de Avilés, 12-9-1570, Havana. In Eugenio Ruidíaz y Caravia, *La Florida: Su conquista y colonización por Pedro Menéndez de Avilés*, vol. 2:301–308. Madrid, 1893–1894.
Ruíz de Salazar Vallecilla, Benito
    1645   Letter to the Crown, 4-16-1645 [summary]. SD 225.
Somoza, Antonio de
    1673   Letter to the Crown, 5-2-1673. SD 235/97.
Vega Castro y Pardo, Damián de
    1639   Letter to the Crown, 8-22-1639. SD 225.
Wolf, Eric
    1959   *Sons of the Shaking Earth.* University of Chicago Press, Chicago.
Zúñiga y Cerda, Joseph de
    1701   Letter to the Crown, 3-10-1701. SD 840/4.
    1702   Letter to the Crown, 11-5-1702. Zúñiga y Cerda Residencia, SD 858/B-241.

Chapter 31 ■

B. Calvin Jones and Gary N. Shapiro

Nine Mission Sites in Apalachee

From at least the time of de Soto until 1704, the north Florida province of Apalachee was bounded by the Aucilla and Ochlockonee rivers. This 30-mile (50 km) wide territory may have held more than 30,000 inhabitants in 1528, but its Christian Indian population was closer to 10,000 throughout the seventeenth-century Mission period (Hann 1986a).

Apalachee was famous among Florida's Indians as a wealthy province. Narváez and de Soto traveled there in haste in the hope of finding gold, but Apalachee's true wealth lay in its produce. The province included some of the best corn-growing lands in Florida, and this was the magnet that eventually attracted Spanish interests and Spanish missions a century after de Soto passed through it.

Florida's earliest missions were concentrated on the Atlantic coast and inland near St. Augustine. By the mid-seventeenth century, epidemics, harsh treatment, and native unrest had greatly diminished the ability of nearby Timucua Indians to provide food for St. Augustine. But to the west, leaders of the populous and fertile Apalachee province began asking for missionaries early in the seventeenth century. A formal mission effort was launched in 1633 in the hope that Apalachee's produce could help support St. Augustine. Apalachee included 14 principal missions and more than 40 satellite villages in 1675. The province was brought to ruin by Creek Indian and British attacks in 1704.

The Spanish Mission Project

In 1968, what is now the Florida Division of Historical Resources began a project to locate and excavate Apalachee mission sites. Three mission sites had been located in previous decades. These were San Luis de Talimali (8Le4), whose location was known to Tallahassee's earliest settlers; the Scott Miller site (8Je1); and the Pine Tuft size (8Je2). The last two were discovered and tested by Mark Boyd and Hale Smith (Boyd et al. 1951:104–189). Beginning in 1968, we used the existing historical and archaeological evidence to predict the locations of additional mission sites. Within four years, another six mission sites were discovered by Calvin Jones (1972:32) between the Aucilla and Ochlockonee rivers.

Historical Evidence

Historical evidence for mission locations was provided by visitation records. These documents report on visits to the missions by secular and religious officials. In some of these, distances of the missions from St. Augustine, or their distances relative to one another, were recorded. The known location of San Luis provided a baseline from which to measure mission distances within the province. Although other available documents were also consulted (Boyd 1937, 1953; Swanton 1922), the survey relied primarily on the 1674–1675 Calderón visitation (Boyd 1939, 1948; Wenhold 1936). The Calderón document provides two lists of the missions and their distances from one another. One of the lists, submitted by Calderón himself, provides distances rounded off to the nearest league, and the second, submitted by Florencia, provides distances rounded to the half-league (Table 31-1).

For survey purposes, the league was considered to equal 2.6 miles (4.2 km). Although straight-line distances along the presumed east-west mission corridor were the basis for the initial survey, there was no assurance that this was the intention of Calderón or Florencia. Instead, distances provided by historical documents may reflect estimates based on winding trails or may in fact be in error. The area eventually given high priority in the survey encompassed a radius of about one mile (1.6 km) surrounding the straight-line distance estimates.

John Hann (1986a, 1986c) recently published new translations and analyses of additional visitation records. It is now clear that a number of mission sites were relocated during the Apalachee Mission period (1633–1704). These new data should not only lead to discoveries of additional mission sites, but should also help us determine whether known archaeological sites correctly match their historical names.

Maps were another useful source of historical information. There are two known maps that show Apalachee mission locations. The first may have been drawn in 1683 by Manuel Solana (Figure 31-1). Drafted at a very small scale,

Table 31-1. Location of Apalachee Mission Sites Based on 1674–1675 Historical Records

Mission Sites, from San Luis	Leagues between Missions		Actual Distance, Air Miles[a]	
	Calderón	Florencia	Miles	2.6 mi.
San Luis de Talimali (8Le4)				
San Damian de Escambe (8Le120)	1	1	2.16	0.83
San Pedro de Patale (8Le152)	4	4	10.56	4.06
San Pedro de Patale (8Le157), second location	?	?	3.2	1.3
San Joseph de Ocuya (8Je72)	4	4	5.82	2.23
San Juan de Aspalaga (8Je1)	2	1.5	2.96	1.12
San Francisco de Oconel (8Je2)	1	1	3.68	1.4
San Lorenzo de Ivitachuco (8Je100)	2	2	5.2	2.0
San Miguel de Asile (8Je106)	2	1.5	3.2	1.3

[a]Air miles or map distances do not reflect actual distances between missions along the Camino Real because of curves in the Spanish trail around lowlands and elevational differences that added distance.

this map shows the general shape of the entire Franciscan mission trail. The second map was drawn during the reconnaissance of Admiral Landeche in 1705, a year after its complete destruction and abandonment (Figure 31-2). The Landeche map shows a bird's-eye view north from the port of San Marcos. Among the four missions shown, a sketch of San Luis, the provincial capital, appears in the upper right.

Archaeological Evidence

At the beginning of this study, the three known mission sites provided basically three kinds of archaeological information: (1) environmental characteristics of the site location, (2) characteristics of mission artifact assemblages, and (3) architectural and site plan characteristics (Boyd et al. 1951).

San Luis, Scott Miller, and Pine Tuft had several environmental characteristics in common. First, all were located in the Tallahassee Hills physiographic region, whose Orangeburg soils are among the best in Florida for growing crops. All were located on hills, at elevations greater than 55 m above mean sea level. Finally, each site overlooked a nearby permanent water source, either a spring, stream, or lake. These characteristics enabled Jones to fine-tune his survey methods, and to target specific areas as potential Mission sites.

To be confirmed as a mission, the site had to contain the appropriate mission period artifacts, but this was not enough. Mission period assemblages, which Hale Smith had termed "Leon-Jefferson," may also be found at contemporaneous nonmission sites, such as ranchos or outlying Spanish farmsteads. The second prerequisite was mission-style architecture, and importantly, the church or cemetery (see also Saunders, this volume). Major buildings at San Luis, Scott Miller, and Pine Tuft all had wattle and daub construction (Griffin 1951; Morrell and Jones 1970; Boyd et al. 1951). Church excavations at the latter two sites revealed prepared clay floors. All buildings were characterized by wrought iron

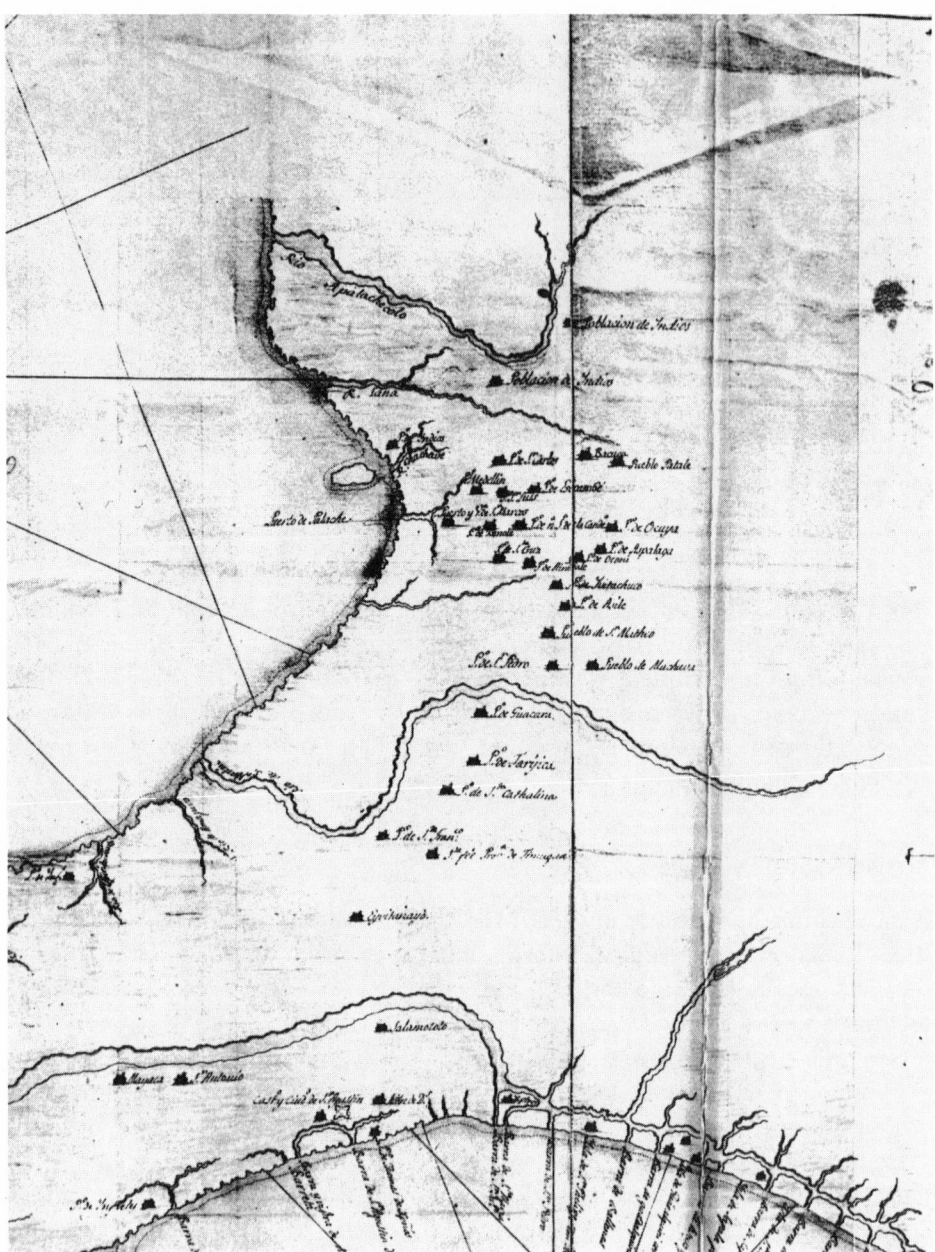

Figure 31-1. Map of Spanish missions, attributed to Manual Solana, ca. 1683 (after Chatelain 1941:Map 7).

nails or spikes. Although there was no archaeological or historical evidence for cemeteries at Apalachee missions, such features were anticipated on the basis of historically documented Catholic practice (see Koch 1983:218–227).

These characteristics provide a contrast with what little is known about late prehistoric sites in this area. Rectangular floor plans, prepared clay floors, ceme-

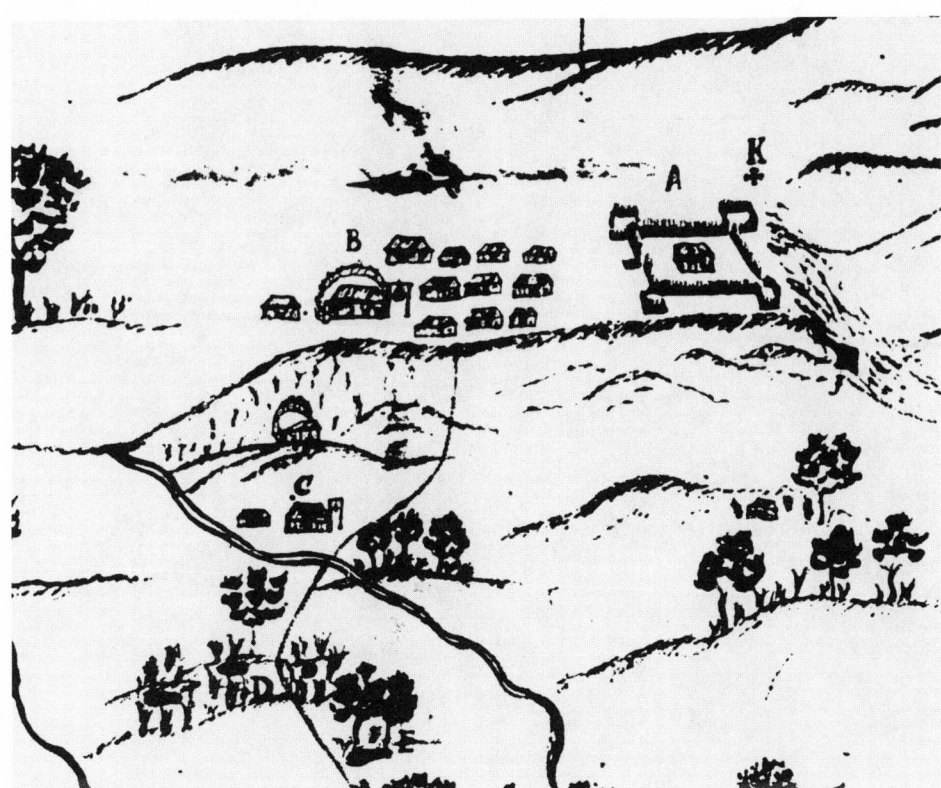

Figure 31-2. Part of a map drawn during the reconnaissance of Admiral Landeche in August 1705. The map legend indicates: A. Fort of San Luis, B. Convent of the Fathers of Saint Francis, C. village of the Chinosa, K. site where the bells were buried. See Boyd et al. (1951:Plate 1) for a reproduction of the entire map and legend.

tery burials (extended and aligned with one another), and imported Spanish artifacts together provide a signature for mission sites.

Survey

Survey areas were prioritized on the basis of the available environmental, archaeological, and documentary information. Each potential location was then visited and test-excavated to determine whether Spanish artifacts were present. If so, more intensive excavations were conducted to reveal the architectural and site plan attributes necessary for positive identification of a mission site. Armed with this model to locate and identify missions, Jones added six sites to the list of known missions. Excavations were also conducted at the Pine Tuft site, which was previously known. A brief account of the discovery and investigation of each site follows. Figures 31-3 and 31-4 show the location and archaeological plan of each site.

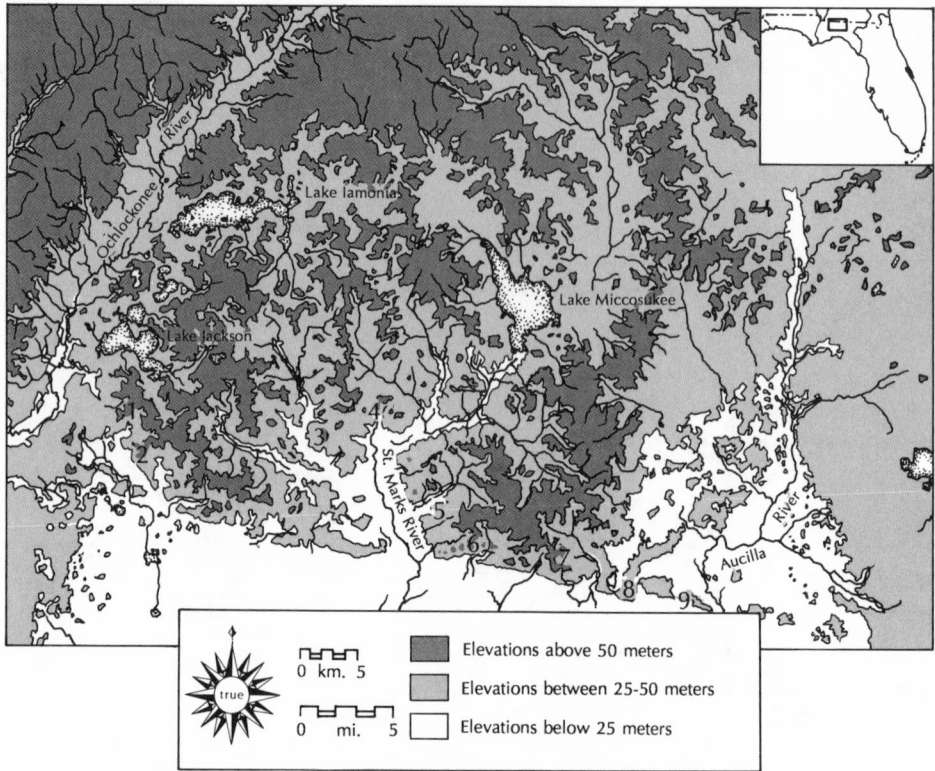

Figure 31-3. Simplified topographic map of Apalachee's uplands with locations of nine known mission sites: (1) Escambe (8Ler120), (2) San Luis (8Le4), (3) Patale I (8LE1521), (4) Turkey Roost/Patale II (8LE157), (5) Ocuya (8Le72), (6) Aspalaga (8Je2), (7) Scott Miller/Allyubale (8Je1), (8) Ivitachuco (8Je100), (9) Asile (8Je106).

Nine Mission Sites

Escambe (8Le120)

Site 8Le120 is thought to be the mission of San Damian de Escambe. Discovered in June 1968, the site is located on a level area near the west edge of a hill, at an elevation of 64 m (210 ft.). It overlooks a series of springs that lie to the northwest. Excavations there in 1969 and 1970 revealed the church and cemetery. Three additional buidings are suspected within an area of 0.4 ha (Jones 1970a, 1970b).

The cemetery was oriented northwest to southeast and contained 143 burials arranged in rows. A gridded array of about 65 postmolds defined the limits of the cemetery on the northeast, southwest, and northwest sides—an area measuring 9.75 × 30.5 m. The posts, measuring from 10 to 30 cm in diameter, were placed about 2.50 m apart. Burials extended a few meters beyond the post pattern to the southeast. It is unclear whether these posts are the remains of an open structure or some kind of cemetery markers. This was the first mission

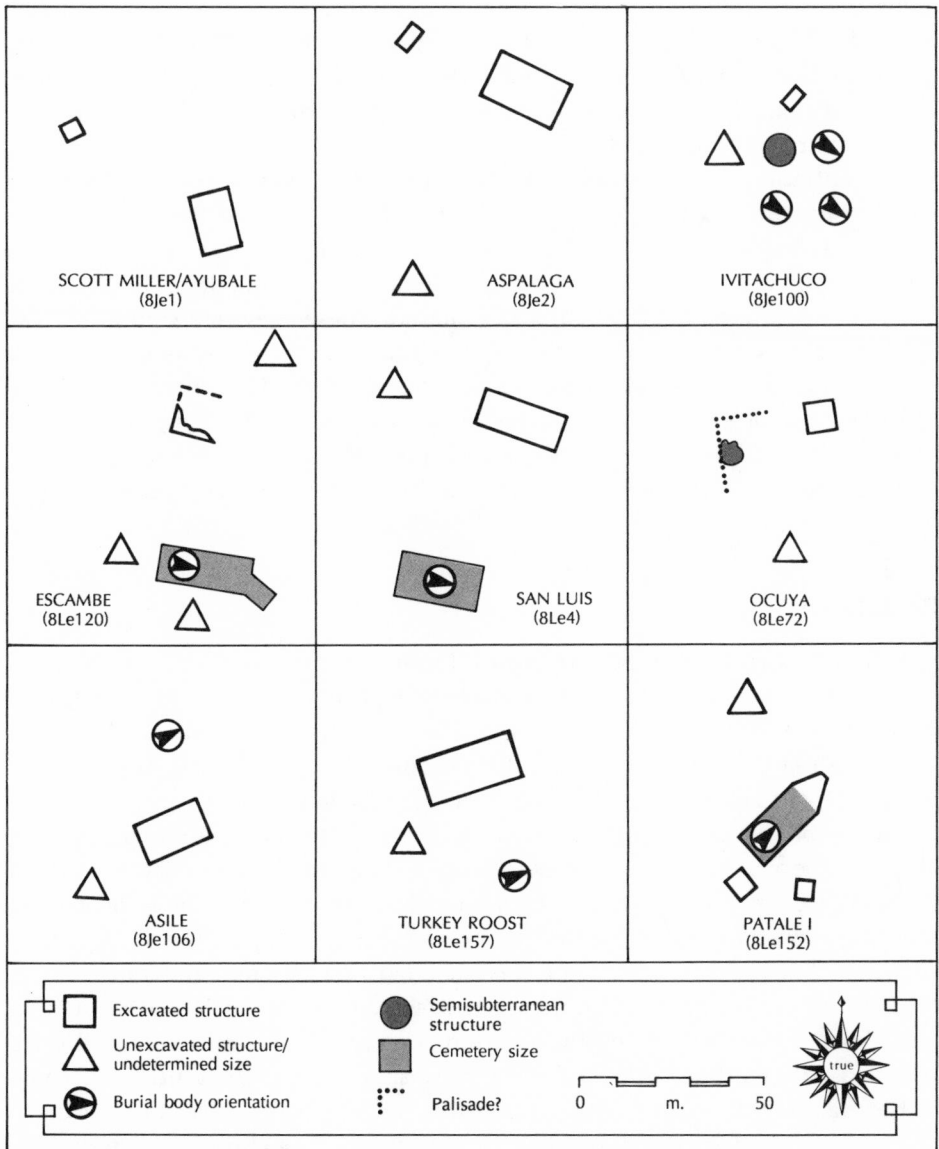

Figure 31-4. Archaeological features of church complexes at nine Apalachee mission sites.

cemetery discovered in Apalachee. Only 42 of the burial pits were excavated. With the exception of one flexed child, all burials were extended supine, with heads toward the southeast and feet to the northwest. Three individuals—two adults and one child—were buried in wooden coffins.

The poorly preserved remains of a building that may have been the church were located 28 m northeast of the cemetery. The long axis of this building, which had burned, shared the cemetery's northwest to southeast alignment. Only two of the church walls could be observed. These meager remains suggest a building with board walls rather than wattle and daub. Daub was present along the two walls, but it apparently was only used as chinking at the base. The suspected church measured 10 m in width and at least 12 m in length, but its complete dimensions could not be determined. A large heavy iron door latch recovered from the vicinity of the east end of this structure indicates substantially constructed doors and a probable southeast facade.

Concentrations of wrought iron nails, spikes, and Spanish pottery suggest a smaller structure about 10 m northeast of the church. Between this area and the suspected church walls, several gun parts, brass bell fragments, an iron vise, cannon ball, iron grenades, a Soligen-made rapier and dirk, hand drills, lead musket shot, gun flints, and brass stirrups were found. These suggest a smithing area.

About 30 m southwest of the church and adjacent to the west end and south sides of the cemetery, concentrations of nails and Spanish pottery indicate a third and probable fourth poorly preserved structure. All buildings at this site appear to have had compact sterile sand floors and board walls. Daub chinking was not found with the smaller structures. Perhaps one of these buildings was the convento.

Patale I (8Le152)

Site 8Le152 is thought to be the earliest location of San Pedro y San Pablo de Patale. The site was discovered in 1968, and partly excavated in 1971 (Jones 1971). It is located near the west edge of a hill, at an elevation of 57.9 m (190 ft.) above sea level. A ravine immediately downslope and to the north that is dry at present was probably a spring during mission times.

Excavations revealed four wattle and daub buildings within an area of 0.4 ha. Three of these were completely excavated, while a fourth had been bulldozed after its discovery. The church, which measured 10.5 × 26 m, has a constricted sanctuary like those in the Southwest and was oriented on a southwest to northeast axis. The prepared clay floor was intruded upon by numerous burial pits that shared the building's alignment. There were 67 individuals, most of whom were buried in extended, supine position. Except for one individual, all were oriented with their heads toward the northeast and feet to the southwest. Some of the graves apparently were dug after the building was no longer standing.

A second structure stood about 5.5 m southwest of the church/cemetery. This wattle and daub building, measuring 6.4 × 5.6 m, is thought to have been the convento. A third building was located southeast from the center of the church. It measured about 5.5 × 4.6 m. This clay-floored building may have been the kitchen, but its orientation differs somewhat from the other buildings.

This probable short-lived mission site contains a significant pre-Mission Fort Walton occupation. Since 1984 this site has been the subject of extensive research directed by Rochelle Marrinan of Florida State University (see Marrinan 1985). She has excavated the remains of a probable pre-Mission Fort Walton council house and other features associated with the Mission period. Her work in areas also outside the mission complex should lead to important new information about mission life.

Turkey Roost/Patale II (8Le157)

The Turkey Roost site (8Le157) may be a post-1647 location of Patale. It was discovered and tested during the summer of 1969 by Jones. The site, which overlooks a major headwater of the St. Marks River, is on the southwest slope of
a hill at an elevation of 35 m (115 ft.) above sea level. A spring is located
downslope, to the immediate northwest.

About half of the well-preserved church was excavated and its entire perimeter was outlined by predicting and exposing the regularly spaced deep outer
wall posts. The church, of wattle and daub construction, measured 12 × 23.5
m and was oriented from southwest to northeast. The cemetery location was
discovered approximately 25 or 35 m southeast of the church, but it has not been
excavated and its size is unknown. A smaller daub concentration about 10 m
southwest of the church is the suspected convento location, but it also remains
to be tested. As at other mission sites, the Spanish buildings and cemetery appear to be located within a 0.4-ha area. Rochelle Marrinan has recently initiated
a program of systematic posthole testing at Turkey Roost (Marrinan and Bryne
1987). Her project should yield broad-scale data directly comparable to those
from San Luis and Patale I (8Le152).

Ocuya (8Je72)

The site of San Joseph de Ocuya (8Le72) was discovered in the summer of 1968.
It is located on the northwest edge of a relatively low hill at an elevation of 38
m (125 ft.) above sea level. The site overlooks the spring-fed Burnt Mill Creek,
which is immediately northwest. Excavations were conducted that fall in a feature that has been interpreted as a semisubterranean structure, or pit house
(Jones 1973). A second excavation, in the spring of 1972, revealed what was
likely the convento. The pit house, with walls and roof of wattle and daub, had
an irregular shape, measuring about 6.4 × 5.9 m. Its undulating floor was at
a maximum depth of 146 cm below surface. The depression had been completely
filled with Mission period garbage by the time a wall trench, perhaps part of
a palisade, intruded through its fill.

The suspected convento was located about 10 m southeast of the pit house.
It was of wattle and daub construction, and measured about 9.4 × 10.4 m. A
series of internal posts indicate the building was partitioned into two rooms of
equal size. The suspected church location, 10 to 30 m southwest of the convento,
has not been tested.

Pine Tuft/Aspalaga (8Je2)

The Pine Tuft site (8Je2) was discovered in the late 1930s by Mark Boyd, who
suggested it was the site of San Juan de Aspalaga (Boyd 1939:273). It is located
near the southwest edge of a hill at 55 m (180 ft.) above sea level. A natural lake,
measuring about 3 ha, lies immediately southwest of the site.

Hale Smith excavated at Pine Tuft in the early 1950s, exposing a portion of the church. The site was revisited in 1968 by L. Ross Morrell and B. Calvin Jones, who located and excavated the convento and completely exposed the church structure that had been partly exposed by Smith (Morrell and Jones 1970). Architectural remains were remarkably well preserved, owing to the in situ carbonization of numerous planks and timbers.

Both structures had prepared clay floors. Although both buildings were oriented along a northwest to southeast axis, their exact alignments varied by a few degrees. The church, with its several interior partitions, was enclosed by a wattle and daub wall measuring 22.3 × 12.6 m. Although wattle and daub was the predominant wall construction technique, charred remains of two other types of wooden wall construction were observed. The convento measured roughly 5 × 6 m, and was located 19.5 m northwest of the church. One or more buildings appear, on the basis of surface indications, to have been located about 30 m south of the church. These have not been excavated.

Scott Miller/Ayubale (8Je1)

The Scott Miller site (8Je1) is located near the western edge of a high hill at an elevation of 67 m (220 ft.) above sea level. A spring is located on the western slope below the site. Like Pine Tuft, the Scott Miller site was discovered by Mark Boyd (1939), who suggested it was the San Francisco de Oconee mission site.

Boyd conducted excavations at the site in 1940 and Hale Smith in 1947 (Boyd et al. 1951:107–136). In view of new archaeological data and a reconsideration of historic evidence, Morrell and Jones (1970:26) suggested that Scott Miller was the site of La Concepción de Ayubale rather than the Oconee mission. The site's historical identity remains unclear. In any event, Smith's excavations there uncovered the remains of two buildings and a large borrow pit filled with seventeenth-century refuse.

The large building was interpreted as the church. Like the church at Pine Tuft, the larger building at Scott Miller had interior partitions. Smith suggests that the building actually represents two adjoining structures with a walled enclosure. The enclosure measured 17.8 × 12.0 m, was oriented from north northwest to south-southeast. A second building, measuring 6.0 × 4.9 m, was located about 35 m northwest of the church. Both buildings had clay floors and wattle and daub walls. The borrow pit, located only a few meters north of the church, measured about 15 m in diameter and extended to a maximum depth of 254 cm below surface.

Ivitachuco (8Je100)

San Lorenzo de Ivitachuco is identified with site 8Je100, and was discovered and partly excavated in 1972. The site occupies the northwest edge of a hilltop at an elevation of 64 m (210 ft.) above sea level. Springs located downslope to the northwest and southeast undoubtedly were the water source of the settlement. The site overlooks Lake Iamonia, also to the northwest.

Excavations revealed a structure, presumably the convento, measuring 4.7 ×

6.4 m. The building was apparently constructed of wood, and its dimensions were indicated by the distribution of ash-colored soil and wrought nails. A large pit was encountered approximately 10 m southwest of the convento. A test trench through this feature indicates it was 7.9 m in diameter and extended to a depth of 112 cm below surface. Jones interprets this feature, which contained Spanish pottery, as a semisubterranean structure. The cemetery was immediately east and southeast of the convento. Although only partly excavated, the cemetery was apparently L-shaped, measured 30 m on a side, and contained 300 to 600 burials. Burials were oriented from northwest to southeast, with heads to the southeast.

Unlike the other mission sites, Ivitachuco showed no evidence of wattle and daub or prepared clay floors. An area containing large spikes northwest of the cemetery is the suspected church location. The mission complex appears confined to a 60 × 60 m section of the site.

Asile (8Je106)

Site 8Je106 was discovered and tested in the spring of 1972. It occupies a hilltop at 36 m (120 ft.) above sea level. A small sinkhole, located about 33 m southeast of the site, was probably the water source for the settlement. Although it is on the west side of the Aucilla River, and therefore within the historically described boundaries of Apalachee, the site has been identified as one of the locations for San Miguel de Asile, usually considered the westernmost Timucua mission. This identification is based on its distance from other known sites in 1674–1675. Another important factor is the ambiguity in historic documents as to whether Asile was part of Apalachee or Timucua. The 1657 Rebolledo visitation includes Asile within Apalachee, and in later years, Asile is known to have had an Apalachee chief (Hann 1986b). Its location on the west site of the Aucilla River may account for this historical confusion, which haunts Asile's archaeological identification even to this day.

The church at Asile had wattle and daub walls and was built on a prepared clay platform. It was oriented from southwest to northeast and measured 10.5 × 18.5 m. The cemetery was located about 15 m north of the church. Excavations in the cemetery consisted of a single 10-ft. square in which 10 individual burials and a single mass burial were uncovered. An area 18 m southwest of the church is suspected on the basis of surface indications (daub and wrought iron nails) to be the convento location.

San Luis (8Je4)

The site of San Luis de Talimali (8Je4) is the only mission whose identity cannot be disputed. Local Indians preserved knowledge of the site after its abandonment, and its ruins were observed by the earliest American surveyors in 1823. San Luis is situated on a broad, flat hilltop at 63 m (200 ft.) above sea level. Three or four springs seep from the wall of a steep ravine on the hill's northeast side. These provided water for the settlement.

Because it was in private ownership, San Luis was not visited during the Spanish Mission Project of the late 1960s. It was, however, the subject of archaeological excavations on three separate occasions prior to 1968. In the late 1940s, excavations in the area of the San Luis fort were conducted by John Griffin (1951:139–160), and in 1950 by Hale Smith. In 1956 and 1957 Charles Fairbanks conducted a third excavation in the fort area. L. Ross Morell conducted salvage excavations when Ocala road was built along the site's east boundary in 1967.

In 1983, the site was purchased by the State of Florida for development as a center for mission research and public interpretation (see also Shapiro and Hann, this volume). Although several distinct parts of the settlement have been tentatively identified on the basis of broad-scale surveys, the town plaza, council house, fort, church, and cemetery were located in 1985–1988 with the aid of the organizational model developed in previous mission work (see Shapiro 1985).

The church measured 9.5 m × 22 m and was oriented slightly south of east. It had a clay floor and wattle and daub walls. Massive amounts of daub indicate a substantially constructed building. Although extensive previous potholing had occurred within its ruins, significant data relating to its size and construction were found inact. This structure, which was 70 percent excavated, is suspected of having a southeastern facade.

Confirmation of the cemetery, based on an anticipated location of 30 m south of the church, was made though a series 1 × 4 m test units placed in that area. The edge of the cemetery's actual location was 33.5 m. The excavation and augering of a 4 m² unit in the cemetery revealed a 12 × 22 m cemetery, which is suspected of containing about 250 individuals. Orientation of the cemetery is parallel to the church and the 10 or more individuals in the excavated unit were extended with their heads toward the southeast. Intrusive burials were common and glass trade beads were found with several individuals. Children found in this unit, near the west end of the cemetery, may indicate a separate section for their placement, as previously found at the Escambe and Ivitachuco missions.

Insights from New Data

Data recovered between 1968 and 1972 point to several patterns in site location and plan, but they also indicate variability. It is important to recognize both the similarities and differences among sites.

First, the environmental model used to predict site locations was largely supported by the discovery of additional sites. Six of the nine known missions are located on hills between elevations of 55 and 67 m above sea level, near a permanent water source, and near abundant Orangeburg soils. There are three important exceptions, however. The Asile, Ocuya, and Turkey Roost (post-1647 Patale) sites are located between the 35- and 38-m topographic contours. Turkey Roost is especially anomalous in this regard, for it is located on a shoulder slope at an elevation of 35 m. We suggest the unusual settings of Turkey Roost, Ocuya, and Asile are best understood at a regional scale of analysis.

Regional Considerations

Figure 31-3 shows a simplified topographic map of Apalachee's uplands, which, because of its excellent soils, held the vast majority of Apalachee's inhabitants. Each known mission site is indicated by a number. The sharp break between the uplands and the sandy coastal plain to the south is called the Cody Scarp, indicated here by the 25-m contour line. The hills are also bounded by the Aucilla River on the east and by the Ochlockonee River on the west. These natural features are the historical boundaries of Apalachee.

Near the center of the province, the St. Marks River Valley effectively divides Apalachee's uplands (and its best farming soils) into two large territories. There is some historical archaeological evidence to suggest that this ecological division may parallel an east-west political and demographic subdivision of the province (Shapiro 1986). The existence of an eastern and western uplands also helps explain aspects of the seventeenth-century road that connected Apalachee missions with one another. This in turn helps to explain the unusual location of the Turkey Roost site.

Beginning at the Aucilla River and continuing west, the mission road followed close to the Cody Scarp until it reached the St. Marks valley. The St. Marks probably did not form a complete barrier to travel, but its swampy terrain could be avoided by skirting around the drainage to the north. Turkey Roost, thought to be a post-1647 Patale site, was located at the headwaters of the St. Marks drainage. From here the mission road split into a northern and southern circuit from which missions in the western highlands could be reached. On the basis of historic documents, John Hann (1986e) suggests Patale was a crossroads for travel within the province and an entrepoint for contact with other Indian groups north of Apalachee. This fits well with Turkey Roost's geographic position at the top of the drainage that divides Apalachee's uplands into eastern and western segments. Villages in both upland areas could be reached directly from Patale.

There is another important pattern in the regional distribution of known mission sites. Six of the nine missions are located where the productive upland soils are close to creeks that were probably navigable by canoe to the coast. The net result is that missions were located at the southern extreme of the Tallahassee hills. This provides a contrast with the eight sites thought to have been important late prehistoric centers in Apalachee. The Mississippian mound and village sites are generally located several kilometers north of the Cody Scarp, and are adjacent to lakes rather than navigable streams (but some missions are also adjacent to lakes).

This pattern reflects the economic basis for Apalachee's mission system. The Spanish Crown supported missionization of the Apalachee in part to provide food for St. Augustine. Corn and hides from Apalachee were shipped by canoe to the Gulf coast. From there they were transported south to the Suwannee River, upstream to a loading station on the Santa Fe River, and finally overland to St. Augustine (Hann 1988:149). The southerly location of the missions and their proximity to navigable streams reflect the economic basis of Apalachee's missions and may help explain the generally lower topographic settings of the Turkey Roost, Ocuya, and Asile sites.

Mission Layout

Figure 31-4 shows the schematized plan and layout of the church complex at the nine sites for which archaeological data are available. Structures revealed archaeologically are shown as shaded rectangles, or in the case of two pit houses, as hatchured areas of circular or irregular shape. Buildings whose locations are suspected on the basis of surface finds or limited testing are indicated by a triangle. A circle indicates cemetery excavations. The arrow shows the orientation and direction of burials. Interments are placed with heads in the direction of the arrow and feet toward the circle.

A church complex consists of a least two buildings, usually interpreted as the church and convento. The church, which is the larger of the two, is usually rectangular in plan, while the convento is roughly square. The long axes of churches vary in size from 17.8 to 26 m in length. Church widths are more consistent, ranging from 11 to 12.6 m. In terms of area, church sizes range from 195 to 280 m^2 (2100–3000 ft.^{2}).

Convento sizes range from 30 to 92 m^2 (315–1020 ft.^{2}). At sites for which data are available, these buildings are separated from the churches by distances of 4 to 30 m. The convento location appears to be related to the church orientation. If the long axis and facade of the church was oriented to the southwest, as at the two Patale sites (8Le152 and 8Le157), then the convento was located in front of the church, but to one side. Presumably this was to avoid obstructing the facade. If the church was oriented toward the southeast, as at Scott Miller and Pine Tuft (8Je1 and 8Je2), the convento was apparently located in back of the church and either aligned with it or to one side.

At some sites, a third building was revealed as part of the church complex. Like the convento, this building is roughly square and smaller than the church. At Asile and Pine Tuft, the third building was located to one side of the church, and at a greater distance from the church than was the convento. In such cases, the three buildings form a right triangle, allowing for an open space or courtyard to complete a quadrangle. At Escambe a probable fourth building was used to complete this arrangement. Buidings may have been connected by a picket that also enclosed the courtyard. Such an arrangement is suggested by historic documents that hint at the fortified nature of church compounds (Boyd et al. 1951:44, Plate 1) and may be indicated archaeologically at Pine Tuft.

Semisubterranean pit houses were identified at two sites (Ocuya and Ivitachuco). Jones (1973) suggests these may indicate the incorporation of a native religious structure within the mission complex, paralling the incorporation of kivas within the Franciscan missions of seventeenth-century New Mexico.

The church complex at each site—including church, cemetery, and convento—probably was limited to an area of 0.25 to 0.5 ha. These features are invariably aligned with one another, but orientations differ from one site to the next. Figure 31-5 shows the orientations of nine mission complexes. The arrow in Figure 31-4 indicates the long axis of the church, if that information was available. If not, the arrow indicates the alignment of burials. Burial alignments are identical to the long axes of the churches in the four cases where both features are present. At Ocuya, neither feature was uncovered, and here the arrow indicates alignment of the convento.

Despite considerable variation, there is some pattern to the mission orientations. In eight out of nine cases, missions are oriented between 45 and 81 degrees east or west of north. The exception is 8Je2, the Scott Miller site. This suggests that a roughly east-west, rather than north-south, orientation was the preferred alignment for churches.

Five of the six cemeteries discovered are located to one side of the church, at distances ranging from about 15 to 33.5 m. At Ivitachuco the children's part of the cemetery (northwest) is within 3 m of the presumed convento. Burials were found within the church only at Patale (8Le152). At Escambe and

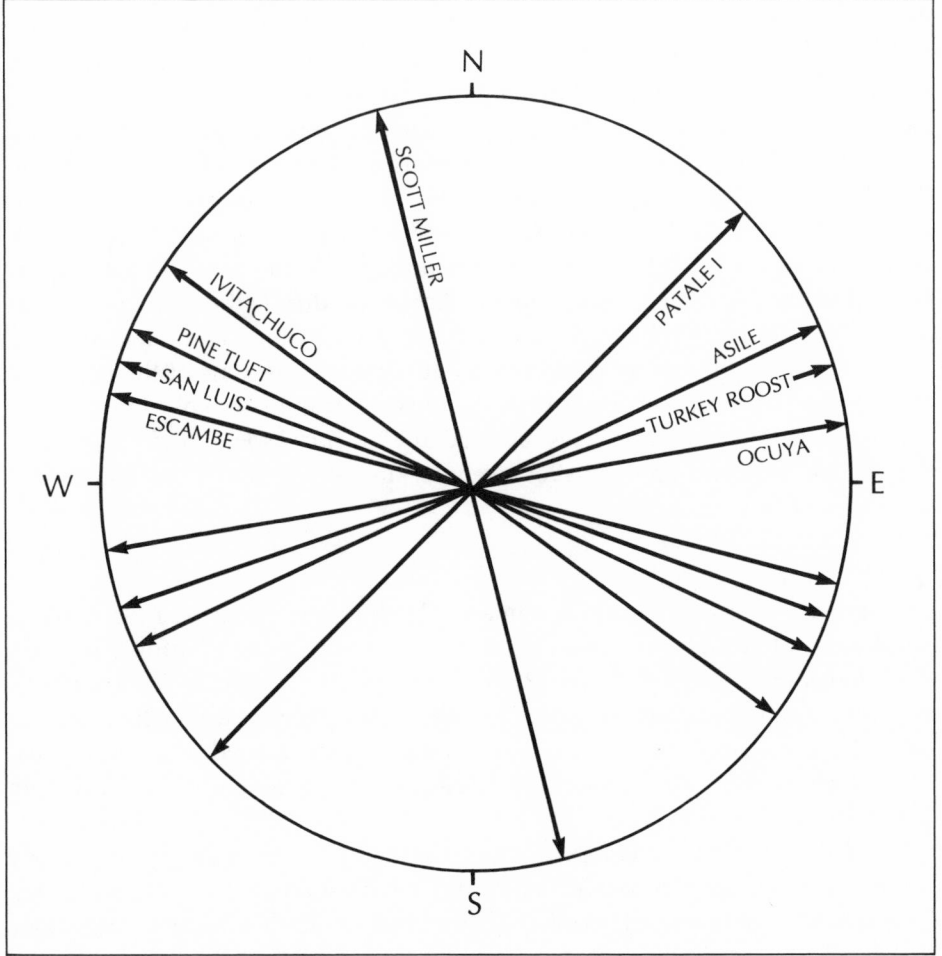

Figure 31-5. Orientation of church complexes at nine Apalachee mission sites.

Ivitachuco, postmold patterns within the cemetery suggest some kind of open structures, but their form and function remain unknown.

The number of burials at each cemetery is variable, perhaps reflecting the size of each doctrina's population or the duration of site occupancy. Only two cemeteries were completely exposed. The Patale (8Le152) cemetery contained 67 individuals, while Escambe contained 143. Although they were not completely excavated, the sampled parts of San Luis's cemetery suggest it contains 250 interments, and Ivitachuco, 300 to 600 interments.

Grave goods, while extremely scarce, were best represented at Patale (8Le152). About 15 percent of the burials there were accompanied by glass or rolled copper beads. Similar grave goods were also found at Escambe, Patale (8Le157), and San Luis. Thus they appear to have been more common at these late seventeenth-century missions, but more complete excavations will be needed to verify this assumption. Trade goods were apparently much more common throughout the century in coastal provinces like that of Guale, where supplies were more easily obtained (see Thomas 1987).

Architecture

There is also some architectural variability in the church complexes. Patale (8Le152) is the only mission to date that has a constricted sanctuary, which is similar to early seventeenth-century missions of the Southwest (Kubler 1940). This form, associated with one of the early seventeenth-century Apalachee missions, including interior church burials, and a Southwest facade suggests that at least some of the architectural variability among the mission may reflect broader cultural and religious changes in Apalachee during the seventeenth century. Although most mission buildings had walls of wattle and daub, those at Ivitachuco were apparently constructed entirely of wood. One of the buildings at Escambe had board walls with daub chinking at the base. A wide range of wall construction techniques was revealed at Pine Tuft (Morrell and Jones 1970). Clay floors, common on most sites, were lacking at Ivitachuco and Escambe.

Artifacts

Quantified artifact data are at present available for four Apalachee mission sites. These are Scott Miller, San Luis, Ocuya, and Patale I (8Le152) (Griffin 1951; Jones 1973; Jones et al. 1986; Shapiro 1986; Boyd et al. 1951). Recent analyses have added little to the basic inventory of Leon-Jefferson artifacts originally compiled by Smith and Griffin (Boyd et al. 1951). What we *have* learned, however, is that the frequencies of artifact types vary widely—not only among sites, but within sites as well.

San Luis provides a good example of variability within a single site. Thirty percent of the pottery recovered by Griffin's excavations in the fort area of San Luis consisted of imported Spanish types (Griffin 1951:150). Recent excavations in other parts of the site show Spanish pottery contributed about 15 percent of the pottery from suspected Hispanic village and church complex. Excavations in the San Luis council house, and test pits in other suspected village areas yielded less than 2.5 percent Spanish ceramics (Shapiro 1986).

Artifact frequencies vary widely among sites even when specific site contexts are comparable. For example, Smith found that Spanish pottery contributed 31.7 percent of ceramics from the church complex at Scott Miller (Griffin 1951:154). This provides a striking contrast with data from the church complex at Patale I, where Spanish pottery represented only 1 percent of the total (Jones et al. 1986). The variability in these assemblages is critical to an understanding of the Apalachee mission system. Although a number of explanations of this variability have been suggested (see, e.g., Shapiro and Marrinan 1986), their evaluation must await detailed studies of collections from the remaining five known sites.

Lacunae

Although we recognize that more is known about the missions of Apalachee than any other province of La Florida, we are struck by the inadequacy of our data. Even though excavations have been conducted in the church complexes of these nine sites, no single church complex has been excavated in its entirety. Only since 1984 have we begun to investigate the parts of missions outside the church complex. Recent, ongoing projects at San Luis, Patale I, and Turkey Roost show great promise, but are in their beginning stages. For example, we have yet to uncover large areas in domestic contexts, although such excavations are at present under way at San Luis.

On a regional scale, we recognize that a considerable number of Apalachee mission sites have yet to be located. A greater shortcoming is our poor knowledge of contemporary nonmission sites. Although we know from historic documents and limited archaeological survey that there were literally thousands of scattered farmsteads, only one Apalachee homestead has been excavated (Bierce-Gedris 1981). Our knowledge of Spanish ranchos and outliers is similarly deficient. An integrated regional site survey along the line of that recently conducted by Bryne (1986) is badly needed.

We do not bemoan the gaps in our data, as these provide the framework for our research agenda. Our spirits are kept buoyant by the resurgence of interest in the missions of La Florida shown by the general public and by our academic colleagues. We are greatly in debt to both groups.

References

Bierce-Gedris, Katharine
    1981   *Apalachee Hill: The Archaeological Investigation of an Indian Site of the Spanish Mission Period in Northwest Florida*. Unpublished Master's thesis, Department of Anthropology, Florida State University, Tallahassee.
Boyd, Mark F.
    1937   The Expedition of Marcos Delgado from Apalachee to the Upper Creek County in 1686. *Florida Historical Quarterly* 16(1):2–32.
    1939   Spanish Mission Sites in Florida. *Florida Historical Quarterly* 17(4):254–380.

1948 Enumeration of Florida Spanish Missions in 1675. *Florida Historical Quarterly* 27(2):181–188.
1953 Further Consideration of the Apalachee Missions. *The Americas* 9(4):459–479.
Boyd, Mark F., Hale Smith, and John Griffin
1951 *Here They Once Stood.* University of Florida Press, Gainesville.
Bryne, Stephen C.
1986 *Apalachee Settlement Patterns.* Unpublished Master's thesis, Department of Anthropology, Florida State Unifersity, Tallahassee.
Chatelain, Verne E.
1941 *The Defense of Spanish Florida, 1565 to 1763.* Carnegie Institute of Washington Publication 511.
Griffin, John W.
1951 Excavations at the Site of San Luis. In *Here They Once Stood*, edited by Mark F. Boyd, Hale G. Smith, and John W. Griffin, pp. 139–162. University Presses of Florida, Gainesville.
Hann, John H.
1986a Demographic Patterns and Changes in Mid-Seventeenth Century Timucua and Apalachee. *Florida Historical Quarterly* 64:371–392.
1986b Translation of Governor Rebolledo's 1657 Visitation of Three Florida Provinces and Related Documents. *Florida Archaeology* 2:81–145, Florida Bureau of Archaeological Research, Tallahassee.
1986c Historical Documentation for the Patale Site. In *San Pedro de Patale, A Seventeenth Century Spanish Mission in Leon County, Florida*, by Jones et al., in preparation.
1988 *Apalachee, The Land between the Rivers.* University Presses of Florida, Gainesville.
Jones, B. Calvin
1970a Missions Reveal State's Spanish-Indian Heritage. *Archives and History News* 1(2):1–3. Department of State, Tallahassee.
1970b 17th Century Spanish Mission Cemetery Is Discovered near Tallahassee. *Archives and History News* 1(4):1–2. Department of State, Tallahassee.
1971 State Archaeologists Unearth Spanish Mission Ruins. *Archives and History News* 2(4):2. Department of State, Tallahassee.
1972 Spanish Mission Sites Located and Test Excavated. *Archives and History News* 3(6):1–2. Department of State, Tallahassee.
1973 A Semi-Subterranean Structure at Mission San Joseph de Ocuya, Jefferson County, Florida. *Bureau of Historic Sites and Properties Bulletin* 3:1–50. Department of State, Tallahassee.
Jones, B. Calvin, John H. Hann, and John Scarry
1986 *San Pedro de Patale, A Seventeenth Century Spanish Mission in Leon County, Florida.* Florida Bureau of Archaeological Research, Tallahassee, in press.
Koch, Joan K.
1983 Mortuary Behavior Patterning and Physical Anthropology in Colonial St. Augustine. In *Spanish Augustine: The Archaeology of a Colonial Creole Community* (by Kathleen A. Deagan) 9:187–227.
Kubler, George
1940 *The Religious Architecture of New Mexico.* Taylor Museum, Colorado Springs.
Loucks, Lana Jill
1979 *Political and Economic Interactions between Spaniards and Indians: Archaeological and Enthnohistorical Perspectives on the Mission System in Florida.* Unpublished Ph.D. dissertation, Department of Anthropology, University of Florida. University Microfilms, Ann Arbor.
Marrinan, Rochelle A.
1985 The Archaeology of the Spanish Missions of Florida. In *Indians, Colonists, and Slaves: Essays in Memory of Charles H. Fairbanks*, edited by Kenneth W. Johnson, Jona-

than M. Leader, and Robert C. Wilson, pp. 241–252. Florida Journal of Anthropology Special Publication No. 4. Gainesville.

Marrinan, Rochelle A., and Stephen C. Bryne
  1987   San Pedro y San Pablo de Patale: An Outlying Seventeenth Century Apalachee Mission. Paper presented at the Society for Historical Archaeology, Savannah.

Morrell, L. Ross, and B. Calvin Jones
  1970   San Juan de Aspalaga: A Preliminary Architectural Study. *Bureau of Historic Sites and Properties Bulletin* 1:25–43, Florida Department of State, Tallahassee.

Shapiro, Gary
  1985   The Apalachee Council House at Seventeenth Century San Luis. Paper presented at the Southeastern Archaeological Conference, Birmingham.

  1986   *Archaeology at San Luis: 1984–1985 Broad-Scale Testing.* Florida Archaeology 3. Florida Bureau of Archaeological Research, Tallahassee, in press.

Shapiro, Gary, and Rochelle Marrinan
  1986   Two Seventeenth Century Spanish Missions in Florida's Apalachee Province. Paper presented at the Society for Historical Archaeology, Sacramento.

Swanton, John R.
  1922   *Early History of the Creek Indians and Their Neighbors.* Smithsonian Institution, Bureau of American Ethnology Bulletin No. 73. Washington, D.C.

Thomas, David Hurst
  1987   *The Archaeology of Mission Santa Catalina: 1. Search and Discovery.* Anthropological Papers of the American Museum of Natural History, 63(2):47–161.

Wenhold, Lucy L.
  1936   *A 17th Century Letter of Gabrial Diaz Vara Calderon, Bishop of Cuba, Describing the Indians and Indian Missions of Florida.* Smithsonian Miscellaneous Collections 95(16):1–15. Washington, D.C.

Chapter 32 ■

Gary N. Shapiro and John H. Hann

The Documentary Image of the Council Houses of Spanish Florida Tested by Excavations at the Mission of San Luis de Talimali

If one were transported back in time to the main plaza of a seventeenth-century mission of Spanish Florida, the most impressive structure to immediately catch the eye would not be the church, as one might expect. Rather, it would be a huge round building that the Spaniards referred to as *la casa concejil* or *el buhío grande* or *principal*, or, at times, simply *el buhío*. We call it the council or town house, or great or principal lodge. In the mission provinces of Apalachee, Guale, and Timucua the council house appears to have functioned year round as the seat of native government, general meeting place for the natives, locus for dealing with Spanish authorities, place of refreshment and entertainment, inn for visitors, and stage for various native rituals and the display of newly taken scalps. The frequent mention of the council house, the one structure for which we have detailed descriptions, and its survival through the mission era, reflect its importance and ubiquity.

Descriptions of Southeastern Council Houses

Bishop Gabriel Díaz Vara Calderón, who visited all the mission provinces in 1675, provided the best general description of this structure in that region:

All of the places have a council house that they call the great lodge which is of wood covered with straw (*paxa*), round in form with a very large opening (*claraboya*) in the top, and the most able to hold from two and three thousand persons, furnished all around the interior area with niches, which they call *barbacoas*,[1] and they serve as beds and seats for the caciques and leading men and as lodging for the soldiers and travelers. They hold the dances and celebrations in it around a great bonfire, which they make in the middle of it. The religious pastor attends [them] in order to prevent what is indecent and lewd and they last until they sound *las ánimas*[2] [Díaz Vara Calderón 1675].

Other observers have provided additional details about the size of council houses and their embellishments, describing specific structures at times. In the 1690s Jonathan Dickinson portrayed the council house at the Guale mission of Santa María on Amelia Island as a round structure about 81 feet (24.69 m) in diameter "with 32 squares, in each square a cabin[3] about 8 foot long of a good height, being painted and well matted. The center of this building is a quadrangle of 20 foot being open at the top of the house" (Dickinson 1981:67). The council house of a smaller Mocaman mission, Santa Cruz de Guadalquini, was about half the size of the one at Santa María; it was 50 feet (15.24 m) in diameter and contained only 16 painted cabins or compartments around the inside of its outer wall. Each of its cubicles could hold two people. Fires were prepared near those compartments in addition to the one at the center of the quadrangle. Dickinson recorded that, after evening church services, the friar and many of the Indian men and women repaired to the council house for the traditional native dance held in the open area at the structure's center. Dickinson (1981:65–67) used the term "warhouse" in alluding to these structures, suggesting the building's strong identification with the warrior element.

In some part of Timucua at least, council house walls were covered with murals. A Florida-born Spaniard wrote of a place in Timucua "where the Indians extract very fine and light powders of all colors, which they use to make pigments, and with them they paint their council houses and churches, their battles and histories with great naturalness" (Hann 1986a: 201). Neither Dickinson nor the Spaniard said anything more specific about that painting, but some of it may have been analogous to that alluded to by David I. Bushnell and William Bartram.

Bushnell (1919:80) noted that the custom of whitewashing various buildings was "evidently quite general among the southern Indians, and several materials were used, including decayed shells, white clay, and in later days lime was prepared by burning oyster and clam shells." He did not know "To what extent the houses were otherwise decorated," noting that "it was done among the Creeks and probably followed to some degree by the other tribes of the region." Bushnell went on to note Bartram's observations on paintings that he had seen among the Creek, "particularly on the walls of the houses comprising the Public Square." Bartram had remarked that "the walls are plastered very smooth with red clay, then the figures or symbols are drawn with white clay, paste, or chalk; and if the walls are plastered with clay of a whitish or stone color, then the figures are drawn with red, brown, or bluish chalk or paste. . . . [The] drawings represented many forms of animal and plant life."

A young shipwrecked Spaniard, who landed on the Georgia coast near the mouth of the Altamaha in 1595, described a structure different from those portrayed by Dickinson and the bishop. The young Spaniard and his shipmates were lodged in a

> big *jacal*,[4] round in form, made of entire pine trees, which lacked only their branches; and, poorly stripped of their bark, they had their base fixed in the ground and extremities all joined together at the top like a pavilion-style tent or like the rods of a parasol. Three hundred men could sleep in it. Within it, it had a continuous [bed] all around the wall, each couch or bed well fitted for many men to rest or sleep on it. And as there was no other bedding except for some straw, which they throw underneath [one]. The door of the *jacal* was so small, made thus on purpose against the cold, that, in order to enter into it, we had to stoop down. . . . And in order not to feel the cold at night and to sweat without clothes, it sufficed to close the door made of straw, which they kept there for this [García 1902:195).

That structure was in a Guale village along the Altamaha that was subordinate to Asao's chief. It predates the establishment of the mission at Asao and differs obviously from the Guale lodge described a century later by Dickinson.

After the shipwreck survivors had spent two days in this village, the head chief at Asao insisted that they come upriver to his nearby village for the rest of the time that they were to stay in his domain. On arriving, the Spaniards "found the head chief and his leading men, who were many, in a big and clean plaza, at the door of a *jacal* similar in every respect to the first, but larger" (García 1902:195). After the leading men had staged a lengthy game of chunkey on the plaza, the young Spaniard recorded,

> We all entered into the *jacal* together and each of us sat down, Spaniards, chiefs, and leading men, on the bed, which was raised more than a yard from the ground. In the *jacal* and close to the door on the right side of it there was an idol or badly carved human figure. For ears it had those of a coyote and for a tail that of the coyote as well; the rest of the body was painted with red ochre. Close to the feet of the idol there was a wide-mouthed jar (*tinaja*) full of a beverage that they call *cacina* and around the jar and the idol there was a great number of two-liter pots (*ollas de a dos asumbres*) also full of *cacina* [García 1902:196].

The Spaniard then described a black drink ritual held in the council house in which the players consumed copious amounts of cacina "until their bellies became like a drum." He noted that eventually on their opening their mouths "with very great calmness each one began ejecting a great stream of water as clear as it was when they drank it, and others on their knees on the ground, with their hands went about spreading the water that they regurgitated to one side and the other" (García 1902:196).

When the survivors reached the Salt-Water Timucua mission of San Pedro

Mocama on Cumberland Island, the inhabitants brought them to the *jacal*, which the young Spaniard described as larger still than the two he had seen among the Guale and as "open at the top with a skylight (*claraboya*) such as can be made in a *jacal* round in shape and made of whole pine trees" (García 1902:199).

The mention of the skylight here implies that it was lacking the heat-retention qualities attributed to the Gualean house. That the Gualean lodge held out the cold so well suggests that the poles that formed the roof were covered with sheets of bark or matting, which may have been covered in their turn with earth, or that the structure was akin to the earth-lodge at the Ocmulgee National Monument.

In 1663 William Hilton described the council house at Santa Elena, which still had a cross before it at that late date: "A fair house builded in the shape of a dovehouse, round, two hundred foot at least compleatly covered with Palmeta-leaves, the wal-plate being twelve foot high or thereabouts, within lodging rooms and forms: two pillars at the entrance of a high Seat above all the rest" (Swanton 1922:62).

That "high Seat" with the pillared entrance was undoubtedly the bench reserved for the principal cacique, who is alluded to elsewhere as having a special bench or *barbacoa* reserved to him. In 1695, at Apalachee's Santa Cruz de Capoli, the visitor installed the heir to that chieftainship, which had been withheld until then for an unspecified reason. It was recorded that the visitor "gave him possession of the chieftainship at once, on learning that it was his rightfully, and in token of this, he seated him on the principal bench (*barbacoa*) of the council house of this place and ordered all of its inhabitants to obey and respect him as principal cacique" (Florencia 1695:67). In Calusa in the 1560s the chief was similarly spoken of as "seated on his bench or platform (*banco o estrado*)" (Zubillaga 1946:284).

As a sign of respect, the Indians made "the salute (*salba*) to the chief seated on his bench in the council house" (Méndez de Canzo 1602). René Laudonnière described the ceremony among the Timucua, noting that the leading natives met each morning in the council house where the king sits on a seat "higher than all the others. There each, one after the other, comes and salutes him. The older ones begin the salutation by raising both hands on a level with their faces, saying, "Ha, he, ya, ha, ha." The others respond, "ha, ho." In this way they all salute and take seats" (Bennett 1975:14). This ceremony may have been tendered to the chief in part in his character as priest, as it is much like the reverence the *usinulo*[5] made to the Apalachee ball pole, which Fray Juan de Paiva interpreted as idolatry (Hann 1988:339).

Among the Guale, another seat was reserved for the chief's nephew-heir, who bore the title, *tunaque* (Argüelles 1677:527). It is probable that rank or the favor of the chief determined occupancy of the benches closest to that of the chief and that some of those benches also stood higher than ones assigned to lesser gentry. For the Cherokee's rotunda, Bartram noted that all around the inside "betwixt the second range of pillars and the wall, is a range of cabins or sophas, consisting of two or three steps, one above or behind the other, in theatrical order, where the assembly sit or lean down" (Bartram 1973:367).

Roundness characterized council houses of the mission provinces of Spanish Florida. The Creek and even the Iroquoian Cherokee also had round council houses, known aptly as "the rotunda" (Bartram 1973:366; Bushnell 1919:74). A possible exception is a long narrow structure described by Oviedo, which Bushnell placed on the Guale coast. Bushnell was unsure about the structure's function, remarking, "Whether this was in reality a great communal dwelling, as among the Iroquois, or served the purpose of the large, circular town house of later generations, may never be known" (Bushnell 1919:83). Bushnell probably erred in locating those long, rectangular structures in Guale rather than north of Santa Elena in territory inhabited by Siouian or Iroquoian peoples. Oviedo's sources were survivors of the Ayllón settlement of San Miguel de Gualdape. Indeed, the nature of this structure may well be evidence that Gualdape lay beyond the territory of Muskhogean peoples such as the Guale and Cusabo.

Oviedo described the edifice as follows.

> There are some principal houses along the coast, each one of which among that people must be considered as a settlement, because they are very large, and are made from tall and handsome pines. And in the top portion they leave the branches and the leaves. And afterward, they make a row (*hilera*) or line (*rengle*) of pines as a wall and another for the other side, with a width of fifteen or thirty feet remaining in the middle from one row to the other, and, in length, a good three hundred or more feet. They join the branches together at the top, and thus, there is no need for a roof (*texado*) or cover. Nevertheless, they cover all the top with very well placed mats inserted into the empty spaces. . . . And within, there are other pines crosswise with the surface of the first ones, which doubles the thickness of the wall. Thus the mud-wall (*tapia*) becomes thick and strong becauses the pieces of lumber are together. And two hundred men could very well be or fit in each such house of these, and live in them, as the Indians do [Fernández de Oviedo y Valdés 1851:3:631].

Oviedo's last statement seems to indicate that the structure was a communal dwelling rather than a council house per se.

Of the accounts of de Soto's passage through Timucua and Apalachee, only that of Ranjel mentioned council houses. Ranjel noted that Uriutina had "a very large council house (*buhío*) in it, in the middle of which there was a large open space (*patio*)." At Napituca, Ranjel recorded that 300 hostile captives were put into a lodge (*buhío*) (Fernández de Oviedo y Valdés 1851:1:552, 553).

Symbol of Community Bond

In mission times—and earlier times as well, no doubt—the council house symbolized and enshrined the bond of community and, among less sedentary coastal peoples, was the one sign of community. Control over the council house and over the order of service to those who frequented it was a source of the chief's power and prestige. Among the Guale and probably among other coastal peoples as well, the council house was primarily the property of the chief and a symbol of the political bond that held the people together. In 1602 St.

Augustine's governor remarked that those coastal settlements did not merit being designated "organized villages," let alone cities or towns, because they amounted to nothing more than each cacique's "having a community house where the Indians come together to hold their dances and assemblies and to drink a brew of *cacina*, which cannot be done in any other place except in the said house of the aforesaid cacique." The people's houses, the governor noted, were "scattered about at intervals on the edges of the woods" (Méndez de Canzo 1602). In 1677 a visitor to Guale and Mocama characterized the council houses as places "where it is the custom to hold the assemblies and hearings (*audiencias*)[6] for those who recognize they are united (*agregados*) to the said council houses" (Argüelles 1677:525). The same sense of citizenship in a council house is conveyed in a complaint by Santa Catalina de Guale's cacique "that the Indians of this place were passing from one council house to another with slight cause, something that it is ordered that they are not to do, as a means of good government since the time of the *mico* don Alonso." In response, the visitor ordered that the Indians "should remain in their own state (*estado*)" (Argüelles 1677:526v.).

The above allusion to *cacina* implies clearly that the franchise, as it were, for the distribution of *cacina* was restricted to the council house and its proprietor, the principal cacique. The survival of this custom three-quarters of a century later was illustrated during the 1678 visitation at Salamototo. A chieftainness from that district, where the Spanish trail crossed the St. Johns River, who was usually kept in bed by chronic illness, asked permission to prepare *cacina* in her house, as it was forbidden among them to make this beverage inside a private dwelling. The visitor granted her request, but stipulated that *cacina* thus prepared was to be served only to her and that she was not to have anyone else in the house on such occasions (Leturiondo 1678).

The continued importance of the council house and the chief's proprietorship of it was reflected a generation later at Guadalquini. The visitor reminded the Mocaman inhabitants that the preceding governor had ordered them to move to the more secure island settlement of San Juan del Puerto and asked why they had not done so. The cacique replied that he had done his best to persuade his villagers to move, going so far as to build a council house for them at San Juan (Pueyo 1695:134).

Activities in the Council House

In Apalachee, as among the Cherokee, the council house was the stage for dances and other prescribed rituals associated with those peoples' ball games (see Bartram 1973:367–368; Hann 1988:78, 80, 340–341). Fray Paiva described one aspect of the Apalachee ceremonies thus:

> At the setting sun or later they gathered in the *bujio*, which is to say, the houses of their government. They place benches for the players. And they are low, some logs hollowed out underneath, without legs. And they are to put them in front of

the place with which they are playing. They give me to understand that, if the place lies to the north, they place the benches toward the south so that they will come to have their faces toward the north. And the dancers have to go out by the south side, letting out whoops, and indicating the direction with their arm extended. And the drummer and he of the *marua'* and the women, all must be facing toward the place with whom they are to play, because, they say, if they were to turn their backs, it was a sign they had to lose. Accordingly, they place the fasting chief behind these benches of the players. And they placed fires between the chief and the players, which had to be new. And the latter was not to be used except by the chief for inhaling tobacco [Hann 1988:340–341].

On the night before the raising of a new ball post, the Apalachee council house witnessed a less decorous dance than the one alluded to above. For that evening the usual sexual taboos were suspended. Paiva described this feature of the ceremony thus. "As a guarantee of good luck for the season, any man had carte-blanche to touch, fondle, etc. any of the women who came, whether they were married or single." The headman went about urging the women not to defend themselves against those advances lest the village lose all the games it played under that pole (Hann 1988:80).

As is evident from the above and earlier references, council houses, in the missionized provinces at least, were not always a male sanctum, in contrast to those of the later Creek. Dickinson noted the presence of men and women at the evening dance at Santa Cruz (Bartram 1973:448; Dickinson 1981:66). During the 1694–1695 visitations of Apalachee, Timucua, and Guale settlements, women attended the public meetings with the visitor in the council houses (Florencia 1695:*passim*; Pueyo 1695:*passim*)

Other important activities are documented as having taken place in the council house. Among them was the plotting of war preparations, the display of scalps consequent on such activity, and the celebration of the successful warriors' feats. One source recorded that scalps were carried "to the council house on a pine branch as an indication of their victory. There they hang [them] up and they dance the war dance for many days" (Fernández de Florencia 1678; García 1695; Hann 1986a:199). Evidence abounds that the council house served as an inn for newly arrived soldiers and for travelers in general (Hann 1986b:*passim*). The practice and restrictions on it are highlighted by a regulation issued by the visitor in western Timucua in 1694. He ordered the governor's deputy there not to allow "any Spaniard, Black, or Mulatto [to] sleep anywhere except in the principal council house, nor that they remain more than three days in the place" under a penalty of 10 ducats for Spaniards and 50 lashes for blacks and mulattos (Florencia 1695:105).

Such regulations were posted routinely in the council houses. That the edicts did not always receive the utmost respect is reflected in an injunction against graffiti by a Guale visitor, charging that no one among the natives "be so bold as to smear paint on or scribble on these orders that remain posted in the villages" (Pueyo 1695:137).

Archaeological Evidence from San Luis

It is time to see what elements of this documentary image were confirmed by the excavations at the San Luis de Talimali site and what information not reflected in the documents was added by the excavations. Of course, not all the elements alluded to in the preceding pages would leave an easily recognizable signature. Some would probably not leave any at all.

Excavations on the council house site occurred during the 1985 and 1986 field seasons. Detailed topographic and auger surveys of most of the site in 1984 permitted tentative identification of the council house site and other major town components such as the church, convent, main plaza, and "higher and lower status" portions of the settlement. The suspected location of the fort had been confirmed in 1949 by John W. Griffin.

Two remarkable surface features were particularly important in locating the council house. The first, a low earthen embankment surrounding an extensive level depression, which measures 125 m across, outlines the central town plaza. The embankment, 30 cm high, is reminiscent of the Indian ball fields described by eighteenth-century writers. The second feature was a flat, elevated platform at the southeast end of the "Great Circle," the name given to the embankment surrounding the plaza. The platform, surrounded by depressions believed to be borrow pits, was later discovered to have been raised artificially to provide a level floor for the council house. On that flat platform the auger survey showed a near absence of pottery, but a large quantity of burned clay that roughly followed the platform edges. Whether by accident or by design, this council house stood directly across the plaza from the church, where the *cabildo*, or town hall, would usually be found in a Spanish or mixed community in the New World.

The platform's diameter of almost 40 m ruled out block excavation. To narrow the investigation further, we used soil-resistivity and soil coring tests. The coring survey revealed a doughnutlike pattern that fit neatly on the platform surface. This could have been interpreted as the ruins of a circular, clay-walled building, a rectangular one, or a series of smaller rectangular buildings surrounding an open courtyard. The excavation was begun on the northeast section, where the burned clay distribution seemed best preserved. For more details on this testing, see Shapiro (1987).

First Year of Excavation

The four-month excavation of a 104-m² area during the 1985 field season revealed that the burned clay did not derive from daub walls, but from a scorched clay floor that occupied most of the excavation. The very few wrought nails present suggested the structure was not Spanish in style. We mapped, sectioned, and completely excavated 45 postmolds, numerous postholes, and 19 cob-filled smudge pits. The smudge pits were intriguing in their regularity. Each measured about 20 cm in diameter, and the cobs burned usually at depths of 30 to 50 cm below surface.

The arrangement of these features suggested an outer ring of wall posts of a circular structure 36 m in diameter containing concentric rings of less substantial posts, believed to be supports for benches or cabins lining the interior of the outside wall. Under the benches were two concentric rings of smudge pits. In addition, there were two interior rows of substantial posts accompanied by another ring of smudge pits. Finally, one additional post stood out from the rest. It measured 50 cm in diameter and extended to a depth of 167 cm below surface. This enormous post was believed to be one of a series of large interior supports for rafters extending from the outer wall toward the building's center.

With these data, it was possible to create a hypothetical floor plan of the entire structure. The arc of the cob pit suggested a structure 36 m in diameter. It was assumed the building was perfectly circular and that the features seen in our 10 percent sample of the platform were repeated continuously around its perimeter. In addition to hundreds of wall posts, bench supports, and cob pits, eight major interior supports were predicted (including the single sample from 1985). Although we had no window to the building's center, we suspected a central quadrangle of four enormous supports would have surrounded a central hearth and framed the opening in the roof. This hypothetical floor plan was to be a general guide for the 1986 excavations. None of us were prepared for the degree to which it proved correct.

Second Year of Excavation

The first endeavor in 1986 was to confirm the eight major interior supports. The first to be located was immediately south of our 1985 excavation. Like its 1985 counterpart, this post held a distinctive soft black fill. To find the third one, we used the coring device to pinpoint the black fill and then opened a 2-m excavation to reveal the post. Intoxicated by these early successes, we skipped all the way across the platform to find a fourth post, whose actual center was only 80 cm away from its predicted center. The coring tool alone found the other four.

Finding those eight major supports confirmed the identity of the council house. This freed us to begin seeking answers to particular questions about the structure. Among these were both architectural and behavioral questions such as: Did the interior posts and cob pits represent an earlier, smaller council house or an inner tier of benches? Were there four additional support posts within the circle of eight? Was there a central hearth and what was its form? Was the platform an intentional creation? How often was the structure rebuilt or repaired? What specific activities could be inferred from features and artifacts found? What access did the natives have to Spanish tools, weaponry, and pottery?

To answer some of these questions, we opened three units to reveal major support posts. We extended a 1-m-wide trench across the building to learn about platform construction and to reveal the hearth. We enlarged the 1985 excavation to provide a window to the interior and a larger contiguous area in which to map artifact distributions. Field observations in 1985 suggested that most artifacts would be found near the interior walls, so we placed several units along the building perimeter to check the locations of outer wall posts and to test the notion that certain artifact types may have been unequally distributed, according to the status or identity of the building's regular occupants.

The perimeter units encountered wall supports precisely along the predicted arc. In 1985 spacing between wall posts had not been calculated precisely. It proved to be 2.8 m from center to center. Although it was not recognized at the time, this spacing was present in the 1985 excavation, but obscured by rebuilding.

The perimeter excavations and the eight major support posts highlighted the structure's enormous size and the precision with which it was laid out and built. The outer wall posts form a circle 37 m in diameter. This size conforms to the general image projected by Bishop Calderón, namely that these structures could hold 2,000 to 3,000 people, but the San Luis council house is considerably larger than any of the specific circular structures described in other documents for Spanish Florida and for the neighboring areas. It is three times the size of the prehistoric Apalachee council houses found to date by B. Calvin Jones and Rochelle Marrinan. Their council houses were 12 m in diameter (Jones, Marrinan, personal communication 1988). To date the sole rival to the San Luis structure seems to be the rotunda at the Irene Mound site, which also had a diameter of about 37 m (Caldwell and McCann 1941:30).

The precision of its construction is equally impressive. The building is perfectly circular. Further testimony of the builders' skill came from the excavation of a second major support post. The one revealed in 1985 extended 168 cm below surface. We sectioned a second one to see whether the 1985 example was representative. It was, but our cross section of the post taught us much more. The posthole dug to erect the post extended 205 cm below surface, deeper apparently than the architects had intended. They backfilled the posthole to raise its base 32 cm before setting the huge pine post in place. The absolute elevation of its flat base was, remarkably, only 2 cm lower than that of the major support post sectioned in 1985. The 2-cm difference could as easily be our measurement error as theirs.

With this single measurement, we learned three things about the council house in addition to its precision. *First*, the builders must have cut the major support posts to a desired length prior to setting them in the ground. Postholes were backfilled to the correct depth so the posts would all be raised to the same height. *Second*, the concern with raising all the posts to the same height seems to indicate that the tops of these posts were connected by a beam or wall-plate that bore most of the weight of the rafters that thrust up from the outer walls. *Finally*, it appears likely that the council house was entirely rebuilt, at least once, rather than simply repaired. If only a single support was replaced at any given time, it seems unlikely that a replacement post would have been cut to the same length and buried the same depth as the original posts nearby.

The 1-m-wide trench across the building from east to west revealed the "clay floor" to be a clay cap, measuring up to 20 cm in thickness, present only in the east half of the building. The west half floor is of sandy texture, difficult to distinguish within the natural transition from sandy topsoil to orange sandy-clay subsoil. It could be either the natural level of the surface there or could be blown in or built up by sandy topsoil removed from the plaza. It is worthy of note that Jones's prehistoric council house had a packed clay floor and that six or seven flexed burials had been dug through that floor (Jones, personal communication 1988).

That east-west trench also showed the central hearth to have been so thin and close to the surface that it would have been lost had that part of the site ever been plowed. The hearth was apparently a surface fire that had no well-prepared basin, rim, or pedestal. It did, however, contain much pottery, chert flakes and charcoal of hickory-shell fragments, and pine (Scarry, personal communication 1988).

The two innermost circles of posts proved to be contemporary with the large structure, rather than the outer wall and bench supports of an earlier structure. Because the inner posts were associated with cob pits, the archaeologists believe they were supports for an inner tier of benches and that their substantial size indicates that they also served as structural supports to prevent sagging of the wall plate that linked the eight major posts and bore much of the weight of the enormous rafters.

Pressed for time, we were unable to expand the excavation in the center to establish whether four central supports existed. Intensive probing with a coring tool showed no other support posts within the circle of eight. This suggests an extremely large opening in the roof, which may have been as large as 15 m, or 40 percent of the building's diameter. Dickinson's 50-foot-wide lodge had a roof opening measuring 15 feet, or 30 percent of the building's diameter. That finding is consistent with historical accounts such as Calderón's, which indicate that council houses had "a very large opening in the top."

Summary

The model suggested by the combined results of the 1985 and 1986 excavations shows two concentric rings of benches or cabins and a central hearth (see Figure 32-1). The dance ground surrounding the fire was 20 m in diameter. One of the most impressive statistics is the predicted number of support posts, which comes to 136. This is a massive amount of wood (all of it pine), and does not include any elements of the superstructure. It must have required a massive effort to harvest and transport these timbers, especially in the light of archaeological evidence that the feat was performed perhaps three times between 1656 and 1704.

With reference to indications of the building's use, besides fragments of burned clay, pottery was by far the most abundant type of material recovered and it was almost totally native in origin. Of the 6,561 analyzed sherds, only 106, or 1.6 percent, were imported Spanish or Oriental types, a very low percentage in comparison with the fort, church complex, and the village area east of the plaza. Nearly all the sherds date to the Mission period occupation, 1656–1704. Although prehistoric Fort Walton and Middle Woodland components are well represented on other parts of the site, only 13 potsherds from the coun-

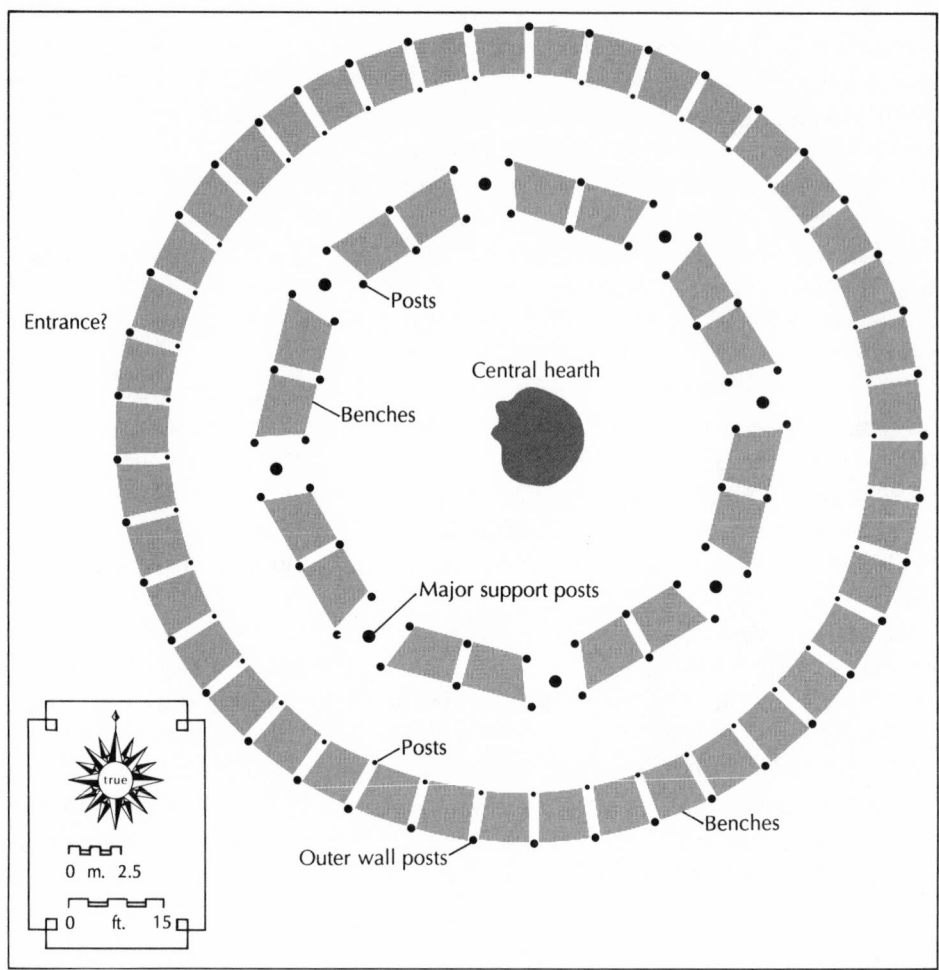

Figure 32-1. Reconstructed floor plan of the council house at San Luis.

cil house could be associated with late prehistoric Fort Walton period and may have been brought in with the fill. None could definitely be assigned to the Woodland period.

We recovered 162 glass beads, 2 glass pendants, and 1 cut crystal bead. We consider this a large quantity considering the nonburial context and the usual screen size of ¼-inch mesh. A single small brass medallion was the only Christian religious object found. Its condition was too poor to identify the individuals depicted.

Sixteen partial or complete Itchetucknee points were recovered that were strikingly uniform in material and manufacture. We were surprised to find a small point made of quartz and a triangular arrowhead of pale green glass. Both are nonlocal materials. More than 1,500 chert flakes were recovered. Most were of the same honey-colored chert as the points. The flakes were by-products of the final stages in the making of Itchetucknee points.

With reference to firearms, we recovered five pieces of lead shot, the pan and cover of a matchlock, one prism-style gunflint of European manufacture, and four locally produced gunflints.

The distribution of the artifacts in the council house clearly reveals concentrations of pottery along the interior wall and in the hearth. In absolute terms, there is a greater density of pottery on the east side of the building than on the west. This could be attributed to the regular sweeping of the floor recorded for some Creek council houses or to more intensive use of the east side of the building (Van Doren 1955:357). Nancy Washer's chemical analysis of soil samples also indicates more intensive use of the east side. The scarcity of pottery on the west side was paralleled by an absence of heavily scorched patches of soil near the west-side benches. The most intensively burned parts of the floor are directly in front of the benches that line the east side of the interior wall. They may be the result of numerous informal surface fires made by occupants of individual benches for cooking, light, and heat.

On the whole, excavation of the council house at San Luis has shown that it conforms in most respects to the documentary portrayals of council houses in Spanish Florida and to the references to activities occurring therein that are liable to have left detectable evidence. A notable exception is the absence of daub walls on the San Luis structure. Somewhat of a surprise as well is the huge size of that structure, despite the assertion to that effect by Bishop Calderón. No round structure approaching that size seems to have been recorded elsewhere in the East. The great size of the opening at the top was also unexpected, although it was suggested in the documents. The material and labor invested in the structure are witness to the importance attached to it as the center for many vital aspects of the community's life. Despite the importance of this institution controlled by the chief, there is no evidence that Florida's *buhío*, in mission times at least, played the political and economic role Mary Helms attributed to the chiefly *buhío* of early sixteenth-century Panama, except for its function as a "metaphor for communal solidarity and for the strength and support of the chiefship" (Helms 1979:9–10, 40–69). At contact, however, it is conceivable that the *buhío* played such a role in Florida and in the Southeast in general.

In its turn, the San Luis excavation rendered information not even hinted at in the documents. Revelation of the existence and number of the smudge pits is one of its striking contributions. The precision with which the plan was traced by the architects and followed by the builders was another surprise. It is to be hoped that the resurgence of mission excavations occurring in Spanish Florida at present and the current search for de Soto sites will uncover the remains of additional council houses and thereby throw more light on the role of this most important institution among the natives of the southeastern United States in the sixteenth and seventeenth centuries.

Acknowledgments

Although John Hann is responsible for this article's final form, the section on the excavation at San Luis was extracted almost totally from Gary Shapiro's paper, "Inside the Apalachee Council House at San Luis," presented at the 1987

Southeastern Archaeological Conference in Charleston. Part of the historical portion as well is derived from Shapiro's paper, but some of my translations were the ultimate source of that portion of his paper. Bonnie McEwan and Richard Vernon made helpful comments on several points that were unresolved when Shapiro prepared his paper. I undertook the task with the conviction that the ideas Gary elaborated in that paper should not go unpublished because of his passing and that their publication would be a fitting memorial to his work at San Luis.

Notes

1. Velázquez et al. (1960:97) define *barbacoa* thus: "(Amer.) 1. Barbecue, meat roasted in a pit in the earth. 2. A framework suspended from forked sticks." In Florida, however, the contexts in which *barbacoa* was used suggest that the word's primary meaning there was an open, raised, lattice-work or grill-like platform that might serve as a seat or bed or device for roasting or smoking, or drying meat, fish, or other food.

2. Generally this term has the sense of sunset, when bells were rung to remind the living to pray for the souls or *animas* of the faithful departed who might still be in purgatory. But there is evidence that the dances lasted beyond sunset, as one might expect.

3. This term was used to describe these compartments in the council houses that served as a seat and a sleeping platform.

4. *Jacal* is probably of Mexican origin. The young Spaniard went on to become a famous Carmelite friar in Mexico. The term probably meant Indian hut or wigwam. Kessell (1979:105) used the term for the temporary structure built by the Pecos to serve as the first church at the mission of Cicuye.

5. This title means "beloved son." There is a suggestion in the Apalachee ball game manuscript that, in the absence of a son of the chief to fill that post, it might be filled by a daughter.

6. The Spanish term used here connotes a legal proceeding. Dealing with matters of justice was a principal function of the audiencia.

7. The *marua* is probably some sort of rattle.

References

Argüelles, Antonio de
    1677   Record of the visitation of the Province of Guale and Mocama, 1677–1678. AGI EC, leg. 156B, SC.
Bartram, William
    1973   *Travels through North and South Carolina, Georgia, East and West Florida.* Facsimile of the 1792 London edition. Beehive Press, Savannah, Georgia.
Bennett, Charles (translator)
    1975   *Three Voyages.* University of Florida Press, Gainesville.
Bushnell, David I.
    1919   *Native Villages and Village Sites East of the Mississippi.* Bureau of American Ethnology Bulletin No. 69. Smithsonian Institution, Washington, D.C.
Caldwell, Joseph, and Catherine McCann
    1941   *Irene Mound Site, Chatham County, Georgia.* University of Georgia Press, Athens.
Díaz Vara Calderón, Bishop Gabriel
    1675   Relación de lo que está descubierto en todo el distrito de la florida y expecificación de los naturales de cada parte y inclinaziones, 1675. AGI SD 151.

Dickinson, Jonathan
1981 *Jonathan Dickinson's Journal or, God's Protecting Providence.* Edited by Evangeline Walker Andrews and Charles McLean Andrews. Florida Classics Library, Stuart.
Fernández de Florencia, Juan
1678 Letter to Governor Pablo de Hita Salazar, San Luis de Talimali, August 30, 1678. Report that the principal leaders who went to make war on the Chiscas . . . made in the presence of Captain Juan Fernández de Florencia. . . . In Hita Salazar, 1678, q.v. Translation by John H. Hann on file at FBA.
Fernández de Oviedo y Valdés, Gonzalo
1851 *Historia General y Natural de las Indias, y Tierra-Firme del Mar Oceano.* 5 vols. Imprenta de la Real Academia de la Historia, Madrid.
Florencia, Joaquín de
1695 General Inspection that the Captain Joaquín de Florencia made of the Provinces of Apalachee and Timucua . . . 1694–1695. AGI EC leg. 157A, cuaderno I, folios 44–205, SC. Translation by John H. Hann, FBA.
García, Andrés
1695 *Autos* made officially by the adjutant, Andrés García, Lieutenant of the Provinces of Timucua, against Santiago, native to the village of San Pedro. Year of 1695. AGI EC leg. 157A, cuaderno I, folios 172ff., SC. Translation by John H. Hann FBA.
García, Genaro
1902 *Dos Antiguas Relaciones de la Florida.* Tip. y Lit. de J. Aguilar, Mexico.
Griffin, John W.
1951 Excavations at the Site of San Luis. In *Here They Once Stood*, by Mark Boyd, Hale Smith, and John Griffin, pp. 139–160. University of Florida Press, Gainesville.
Hann, John H.
1986a Translation of Alonso de Leturiondo's Memorial to the King of Spain. *Florida Archaeology* 2:165–225.
1986b Translation of Governor Rebolledo's 1657 Visitation of Three Florida Provinces and Related Documents. *Florida Archaeology* 2:81–145.
1988 *Apalachee: The Land between the Rivers.* University Presses of Florida, Gainesville.
Helms, Mary W.
1979 *Ancient Panama Chiefs in Search of Power.* University of Texas Press, Austin.
Hita Salazar, Pablo de
1678 Letter to the king, St. Augustine, November 10, 1678. AGI SD 220, SC.
Kessell, John L.
1979 *Kiva, Cross, and Crown: The Pecos Indians and New Mexico 1540–1840.* U.S. Department of the Interior, National Park Service, Washington, D.C.
Leturiondo, Domingo de
1678 Inspection of the Provinces of Apalachee and Timucua, 1677–1678. AGI EC leg. 156B, folios 519–616, SC. Translation by John H. Hann, FBA.
Méndez de Canzo, Gonzalo
1602 Letter to the king, St. Augustine, September 22, 1602, AGI SD 224, Jeannette Thurber Connor Collection, reel 2 of the copy held by the P. K. Yonge Library of Florida History.
Pueyo, Juan de
1695 General visitation of the Provinces of Guale and Mocama made by the Captain Don Juan de Pueyo. . . . AGI EC leg. 157A, cuaderno I, folios 109–140, SC. Translation by John H. Hann, FBA.
Shapiro, Gary
1987 Archaeology at San Luis: Broad-scale testing, 1984–1985. *Florida Archaeology* 3:1–271.
Swanton, John R.
1922 *Early History of the Creek Indians and Their Neighbors.* Bureau of American Ethnology Bulletin No. 73. Smithsonian Institution, Washington, D.C.

Van Doren, Mark (editor)
  1955   *Travels of William Bartram.* Dover Press, New York.
Velázquez de la Cadena et al., Mariano
  1960   *New Revised Velázquez Spanish and English Dictionary.* Follett, Chicago.
Zubillaga, S. J., Felix
  1946   *Monumenta Antiquae Floridae.* Monumenta Historica Societatis Iesu, Rome.

Chapter 33 ■

Rebecca Saunders

Ideal and Innovation: Spanish Mission Architecture in the Southeast

According to Kubler (1948:269), the construction of a mission compound in Mexico followed a prescribed course. A rudimentary church was set up first, probably an open chapel. Then streets were laid out around a central plaza, lots assigned, and a convento was built. Only then was a more substantial church constructed. In Mexico, this monastery church was often reserved for Spanish use and the open chapel continued to be used for mass for the Indians (McAndrew 1965:341). In the Yucatan and Tlaxcala, two areas distinguished by poverty and predominantly Indian congregations, the open chapel was the only religious edifice.

A great deal of variability in the construction of early missions is evident in the attempts to standardize form. In 1548, Philip II issued several edicts ordering monasteries to conform to a standard scheme; in 1569 the Franciscan Order sent a standardized plan to all those of the order about to build (McAndrew 1965:124–125). Within these standards, Kubler (1948:54–55) noted "a multitude of variant solutions to the problem of building had to be devised for the many different cultural environments." Nevertheless, the study of Mexican monastic establishments has defined a set of commonalities between missions that represent the distillation of the ideal monastery.

A representative mission compound in New Spain (Kubler 1948; Ricard 1966) was established in a strategic location, often on high ground. Site preparation often included ambitious leveling and filling (Kubler 1948:177). The compound itself consisted of a masonry single-nave church with a sanctuary and altar, choiry, and a baptismal font (McAndrew 1965:133). After the Council of Trent (1545–1563), east-west orientation of the nave was rejected; in Mexico, preference for the east-west orientation survived until about 1600, after which orientation became unimportant (Kubler 1948; McAndrew 1965:504). Where churches were oriented east-west, the altar was to the east.

Kubler (1948:24 n.) stated that the size of the church was determined by the projected size of the burial population, although this is difficult to reconcile with the fact that burials were also placed in the atrio (see below). Proportionally speaking, the ratio of width to length of a single-nave church was about 1:4 (Kubler 1948:242). The sanctuary was set off from the nave by elevation and by a reduction in width. The sanctuary was most commonly trapezoidal, but both its shape and proportions varied. Sacristies were most often subsumed into the volume of the *convento*. A baptistry was often set near the entrance on the same side of the church as the sacristy.

Kubler (1948:249) described four doors for the church, each prescribed by custom and recorded in the *Instrucciones fabricae* compiled by Cardinal Borromeo around 1580. In addition to the west entrance, another door led to the sanctuary from the convento; another led directly onto the cloister. A north door leading to the atrio was associated with neophytes and was "invariably present" (Kubler 1948:251).

"The Franciscans were alone in postulating a conscious ideal of conventual poverty" (Kubler 1948:344). According to the statutes of the province, conventos could have no more than six cells 8 feet wide and 9 feet long. The garden walk was to be 5 feet wide and the cloister 7 (Kubler 1948:344 fn). Since the Spanish foot is 88 percent of the English (Manucy 1985:48), the convento without cloister would have been no longer than 14 × 16 m. Kubler added that the Franciscans rarely observed these restrictions, except in small communities and in border provinces.

In Mexico, the convento abutted the church to the north or south of the main door, with no significance attached to the specific location (Kubler 1948:342). The convento usually consisted of two stories, with cells on the upper floor, and the *de Profundis* (the anteroom where the Profundis was recited), refectory, and kitchen on the ground floor.

A large walled courtyard (*atrio*), often artificially leveled or raised, extended in front of the church. The area enclosed was determined by the size of the community (Kubler 1948:316). Although the atrio originally functioned as a reservoir for the overflow of converts attending mass at the small mission churches, it also served as a place for religious instruction (Ricard 1966:165), and as a center for administrative, fiscal, and social occasions. It was the site of processesions by *cofradios* and could also be used for burial. The most desirable locations for burial in the atrio would be near the church and sanctuary (Kubler 1948:319).

Several authors have discussed the Native American contribution to Mexican architecture. McAndrew (1965:237) believed the atrio was suggested to the Spanish by the courtyard that typically surrounded the *teocalli* (the pyramidal base and summit shrine of Aztec and Maya religious architecture), and Kubler (1948:422) thought the open chapel, in addition to being practical, might be a concession to the Indian custom of outdoor worship in that courtyard. On the whole, however, both Kubler (1948) and Foster (1960) believed that most elements of Mexican religious architecture were either generic to urban communities or Spanish. Kubler (1948:102) found that Aztec building practices were retained only when they agreed with Spanish principles. The degree of agreement was serendipitous to say the least. The Aztec were skilled stonemasons and their Precolumbian architectural standards included the planned towns with grid layouts and plazas typical of Spanish Renaissance plans.

Missions in La Florida: Aspects of Variability

The simple wattle and daub, thatch, or board mission buildings of La Florida were a far cry from the sophisticated stonemasonry of the Mexican missions. Neverthless, the construction of missions in La Florida also involved a convergence of materials and techniques. Southeastern Indian town plans included the placement of civic and religious buildings on a central plaza. The Southeastern Indian also shared some building materials and techniques with the Spanish peasant, including post construction of simple rectangular one-celled dwellings with outbuildings. Both the Guale Indian and the Spanish peasant used wattle and daub for walls. There is no evidence of wattle and daub construction prehistorically for the Apalachee or Timucua, although these peoples were no doubt familiar with the technique. Wood was not used in construction in Precolumbian times except for support members; vertical board siding was introduced by the Spanish. Requiring expensive nails and lumber, such structures were restricted to the elite in St. Augustine (Manucy 1985:43).

As in Mexico, there probably were some attempts to standardize this melange (e.g., Thomas 1988a:109). Such standardization may be evident in the one primary map that remains for a mission in La Florida (Figure 33-1). Drawn up in 1691, the legend indicates that the map represents the Mission Santa Catalina on Amelia Island, Florida. Because of the similarity of this plan to the archaeologically exposed layout of the Santa Catalina mission on St. Catherines Island, Georgia, constructed at least 90 years before the map was drawn up, it has been suggested that the 1691 "map" is more of a plan depicting an ideal mission compound (Thomas 1988a:96).

Church dimensions on the 1691 map are 26 × 13.5 m; the width is almost exactly half the length, not the 1:4 described for Mexican churches. The shape remains rectangular. The friary is 13.5 × 7.5 m (within the Mexican guidelines); the detached kitchen is 12 × 7 m. The relationship between the length and the width of these two buildings, like the church, is slightly greater than 0.5. Although depicted, a garrison house has not been identified archaeologically in

Figure 33-1. Plan view (1691) of Mission Santa Catalina de Guale, located on Amelia Island, Florida (after Thomas 1987, Figure 7; courtesy of the P. K. Yonge Library of Florida History, University of Florida).

a mission compound in La Florida. This "quadrangle" plan, then, consisted of a church, convento, and kitchen arranged around a courtyard (15 x 7 m on the 1691 map), with the buildings tied together by a covered walkway.

This layout has been hypothesized for a number of missions in Guale, Timucua, and Apalachee. The presumed prevelance of this plan is interesting because it has no precedent in Spanish religious architecture. However, quadrangles composed of three or four rectangular buildings arranged around a courtyard did characterize the secular domestic architecture of both St. Augustine, at the de la Cruz site (Deagan 1983), and at Santa Elena (South et al. 1988). Deagan (1985:13) has referred to the layout at the de la Cruz site as an attempt to "transplant an idealized Iberian spatial template to the wilderness of Florida." The mission quadrangle may represent another example. In addition, the use of the quadrangle plan may be an indication of the lack of formal architectural training of the friars (Kubler 1948:105–128), who, perforce, used a secular architectural plan with which they were familiar. Finally, recognizing the convergence of many Spanish and Southeastern Indian architectural traits, it must be added that in the Creek towns of Bartram's time a quadrangle plan was also used in both sacred and secular architecture (Swanton 1946:392), although it is not known whether this plan existed within the confines of La Florida prehistorically.

Despite attempts to prescribe a standard form, a great deal of variability between mission layout and construction can be expected for a number of reasons. Principal among these would be whether or not the mission was established in an extant village, in which case the friar would be forced to adapt his ideal to existing features and site topography. The examples of Tlaxcala and Yucatan indicate that local economies influenced mission architecture. Local economies, in turn, should reflect the availability of materials, either naturally present or readily available because of proximity to St. Augustine or other ports. The size of the labor force would have an effect on the size of projects, and the location of the mission in terms of its strategic importance might also influence the money available for building the mission.

The time period in which the mission in question was constructed would also seem to be a crucial factor in determining its architectural characteristics. The destruction of social systems due to population loss made the native population more tractable in later years. However, the labor force became smaller (Hann 1986a, 1986b; Manucy 1962). Although never good, systems of supply did get better through time with the establishment and maintenance of the mission road and the establishment of a port in Apalachee in 1647. Locally available supplies, such as wood, became scarcer (Hann 1986a; Saunders 1987).

The political circumstances at the time a mission was built were another factor. For instance, Governor Canzo personally supervised the construction of a most "imposing" church at San Pedro de Mocamo in 1603 because that community had remained loyal to the Spanish during the Guale rebellion (Ross 1926:177). Once missions became prevalent, buildings might be expected to become more elaborate, as friars consciously promoted competition between villages in the construction of elaborate buildings (Geiger 1936:104; Ross 1926:177; for Mexico, see Kubler 1948; Ricard 1966).

Environment, politics, economics, and the date of construction must all be considered as causes of variability between missions. At a lower level, the architectural and managerial expertise of the friars supervising construction at each mission must also be considered. It is at this level that differences in footings or framings for wall bases or different techniques for column stabilization might be explained. The endless problems of improvised construction should generate a great deal of architectural variability.

Some problems and biases in our data base made it difficult to detail and explain the differences between missions by the interplay of these factors. First, the constant movement of missions in response to soil exhaustion and the depletion of local resources make it difficult to associate sites with specific missions and the dates of site occupation hard to establish. Without a secure period of occupation, questions about the adaptation of mission architecture to changing social and environmental conditions cannot be answered.

In addition, our data recovery is probably skewed toward the more archaeologically visible missions—those with burned wattle and daub structures. There are actually two biases here. The first is toward the later missions, those extant between 1702 and 1704, most of which were burned in the campaign Carolina Governor James Moore waged against Spanish Florida during those years. These burned missions are more visible archaeologically than earlier ones abandoned to decay. The other bias is toward the overrepresentation of wattle and daub, which is more visible than either burned or decayed wooden structures. On the other hand, in rereading site reports, we often questioned whether the material described was daub (clay tempered with vegetable fibers) or burned clay present as flooring, or for some other architectural purpose. So-called daub construction may also be overrepresented in our samples because of this misidentification.

Missions in Apalachee

A settlement plan and architectural pattern for Apalachee missions has been modeled by Jones and Shapiro (1987; this volume). Most of the data on which this model was based came from the inspired but limited excavations conducted by the Bureau of History and Records during the late 1960s and early 1970s. In these excavations structure function was sometimes inferred rather than demonstrated. Often the larger structure was routinely identified as the church, regardless of interior architecture or the artifacts recovered. Certainly the interior architecture of the "churches" at Ayubale (8Je1; Smith 1951) and Aspalaga (8Je2; Morrell and Jones 1970) is difficult to reconcile with that of a single-nave church, the predominant form used by the Mendicant missionaries in Mexico. Architectural characteristics and artifacts recovered might also indicate that these two structures were conventos. If they were churches, it should be recognized that most of the congregation would have had to hear mass outside. In view of this and other discrepancies, the Apalachee model is best treated as a hypothesis to be tested.

The data do suggest that in Apalachee there may be a variation of the idealized mission plan. Where three buildings have been located, they form a right triangle, with a courtyard completing the quadrangle (Jones and Shapiro, this volume). If accurate, this represents a departure from the more rectangular configuration at Santa Catalina. Fences are hypothesized to have enclosed the mission compound.

If, as in Mexico, church size was based on the size of the population it served, there would be little expectation that churches would be of similar sizes in Apalachee. Jones and Shapiro found, however, that length varied only about 5 m, from 17.8 to 23.5 m. Width remained fairly constant, between 11 and 12.6 m. These data suggest that the size of the church has little to do with the size of the congregation (perhaps because in many areas the congregation heard mass from an open chapel?).

At San Luis, evidence in the form of two postmolds set 2.5 m inside the south wall near the altar end of the church suggest that the sanctuary was set off from the interior by another wall. Architecture at Aspalaga suggests a similar technique (field notes of Calvin Jones). At Patale I (8Le152), a polygonal sanctuary similar to those of Mexico and the southwest is unique in La Florida. The San Luis church may have had a north door in addition to the main entrance (Shapiro and Vernon 1989).

Convento sizes varied widely, from 30 to 92 m² (Jones and Shapiro, this volume). The distance from the church also varied from 4 to 30 m; location with respect to the church seems to vary with the orientation of the church. Some of these discrepancies, however, may be due to the misidentification of feature function. For instance, Marrinan (personal communication, March 1989) believes that the feature 5 m from the door of the church at Patale I, previously identified as the convento, was part of a prepared clay surface on which the church was built.

Burials in Apalachee were either within the church (perhaps only at the earliest sites) or in cemeteries 15 to 35 m from the church. There is some indication that light structures covered some outdoor cemeteries. Nothing is known of the third building, presumably the kitchen.

Most identified mission buildings were built of wattle and daub, a technique that may have been introduced into Apalachee by the Spanish. In some cases the daub was whitewashed, which presupposes that lime was either imported or produced on site. Construction at Ivitachuco (8Je100) and Escambe (8Le120) was of wood; construction at Aspalaga entailed both wattle and daub and wood. Why these missions were constructed differently is unknown; there is simply not enough documentary or archaeological information about the period of occupation, mission populations, availability of resources, or other variables to attempt to interpret these differences. However, as in St. Augustine, board construction may imply some elite economic status.

Site reports indicate that other techniques used in the construction of buildings were variable. For instance, construction at Aspalaga was quite sophisticated. Wattles for daub walls were set in soft clay held in plank forms, much like modern cement wall footings (Morrell and Jones 1970:36). In the vertical board construction, boards were attached to major supports by means of a wall shoe. Major support posts were not buried, but erected on the subfloor surface (Morrell and Jones 1970:36). At Ocuya (8Le72; Jones 1972), rectangular wall stud bases were embedded in clay-filled postholes, whereas at Ayubale wall trenches were used, with clay banked up around support posts. At San Luis, support posts were set in postholes and clay was packed around the base of the wattling in the walls (Shapiro and Vernon 1989:11). Most of these techniques would seem to be attempts to prevent water or insect damage to the structural members and wall bases. Since posts in St. Augustine only lasted an average of five years (Manucy 1985:40), techniques that would reduce the frequency of repair must have been constantly sought.

In Apalachee, only the testing programs at San Luis and Patale I have been extensive enough to investigate the relationship of the mission compound and aboriginal town (Shapiro 1987; Shapiro and Marrinan 1986). At San Luis, there is clear evidence of the incorporation of the religious settlement into a traditional Apalachee town plan (Shapiro 1987). Unfortunately, at Patale a late prehistoric occupation at the site obscures the colonial relationships (Marrinan, personal communication March 1989). However, enough comparable data are available from these two missions to suggest that the greater artifact diversity and the more formalized settlement plan at San Luis were related to the more urban character of that mission (Marrinan 1985; Shapiro and Marrinan 1986). In addition, a formal settlement pattern was possible at San Luis because it was a new foundation, whereas Patale I *may* have been established in an extant town.

Missions in Timucua

Jones (1972:2) commented that the Spanish buildings and community plan in western Timucua were "essentially identical to those found in the Apalachee provinces." Recent excavations indicate more variability. Architectural information is available for San Pedro de Protohiriba, ca. 1617–1704; San Miguel de Asile, established in 1609–1655, destroyed in 1704; Baptizing Springs, 1587–1611; Fig Springs (San Martín), 1608–1656; Santa Fe, 1606–1704; and the Richardson site, 1600–1630.

Information from San Pedro is limited to the identification of a wooden structure 11.6 m², identified as the convento, and the presence of a cemetery 61 m northeast of the structure (Jones 1972:4). Support posts for the convento were set on prepared clay foundations (*Madison County Carrier* 1972). At San Miguel de Asile, an 11.9 × 19.5 m wattle and daub structure with a prepared clay foundation has been located; a cemetery was found 15.2 m north of this structure. The structure at Asile was identified as a church, and the dimensions and relationship with the cemetery conform to the Apalachee model. However, the building was said to have three horizontal rows of interior support posts (Jones 1972:2). These posts would congest the nave area and block the view of the altar, suggesting that either this was not a congregational church (and an open chapel was available for Indian worship) or that the structure had a different function.

The site at Baptizing Springs (Loucks 1979) is the only possible visita excavated to date. Two Spanish structures were located. A sleeper (a wall foundation placed on ground surface rather than in a subsurface trench) of packed clay appears to have been constructed for the wall base of both structures. The larger of the two buildings, Structure B, was 8 × 10 m, and had a clay floor. Charred posts remained on only three sides. Loucks suggested that Structure B was the church or a residence for a priest. In fact, the three-walled construction suggests that it may have been an open chapel.

The smaller Structure A, 30 m north-northwest of B was 7 × 7.5 m. There was no evidence of a clay floor. A large hearth occupied the center of this structure. Although there was not enough systematic testing at Baptizing Springs to verify this hypothesis, a 30-m courtyard area may have existed between Structure A and B. The lack of alignment between the two structures and the possible open chapel may be a signature for the less formal plan of visitas.

Structures A and B were described as wattle and daub buildings, and daub processing pits were associated with both of them. However, these pits may have been used to prepare clay for the floor and sleepers, as the deposition of the material (Loucks 1979:132) suggests that it was burned clay rather than daub. Donna Ruhl (personal communication, March 1989) has looked at what little of this material can be found at the Florida Museum of Natural History and concurs that it is not daub.

Construction techniques and associated artifacts distinguished two aboriginal structures from those of the Spanish. Although the size and configuration of both aboriginal structures were obscure, posts were clearly set in individual pits; there was no evidence of wall sleepers or clay floors. With the exception of the features at the Fountain of Youth site (Chaney 1987; Merritt 1983) and the Richardson site (Milanich 1972), these are the only aboriginal structures excavated in mission contexts. Despite the fact that the resident Indians had no doubt constructed the Spanish buildings, there was no evidence of acculturation in the construction of their own dwellings at any of these three sites.

Extensive and intensive testing at San Martín has elucidated the mission compound and associated aboriginal village. Like the Baptizing Springs site, San Martín appears to have had an open chapel. Weisman (1988) has found evidence that the chapel area was filled and leveled and then a sanctuary was constructed of vertical wall boards set in shallow grooves in the ground. Clay was used as chinking between these boards. The sanctuary floor was elevated and perhaps covered with wood. Major support posts for a thatched roof were not set in the ground, but on prepared pads of clay. The roof extended beyond the sanctuary over a clay floor laid in an L-shape to the north and west of the sanctuary and a dirt floor on the south side. Total covered area was about 10.5 × 8.5 m (Weisman, personal communication, April 1989).

Artifact distributions indicate that the location of the convento was 24 m north of the church, with the intervening area serving as a courtyard. To date, however, only a single post and remnants of a disturbed packed floor have been found in this location. Construction materials are thought to have been board or thatch. A cemetery occupied the northeastern end of the compound.

The only area on the eroded hilltop that might have contained the kitchen is not on the courtyard, but in the village area at the southwestern end of the village plaza. In contrast to the church and convento, the kitchen appears to have been constructed of wattle and daub. It also had remnants of a prepared clay floor.

Excavations are under way in the village area of San Martín, south of the mission compound. A 30-m-diameter aboriginal structure, possibly a council house, stands opposite the church across a 40-m-wide plaza. The absence of daub suggests that it was a thatched structure, with large interior support posts.

At Santa Fe, remnants of the mission compound are scattered over an acre on top of a knoll (Ken Johnson, personal communication, 1989). Three buildings have been identified to date; none have been excavated. The buildings appear to have been arranged in a triangle around a courtyard, a configuration like that modeled for Apalachee. A cemetery was to the northeast. All three structures located on the knoll were built predominantly of wood; over 300 nails and spikes have been mapped at the site. Vertical board construction of large structures and the concomitant abundant nails indicate a substantial economic investment at the site. Such investment is consistent with Santa Fe's position as the leading Timucuan mission (Milanich and Johnson 1989:4). This position may have been attained because the site was near the junction of two major roads, it may have received more regular supplies, or there may have been more opportunities for trade. In addition, majolicas from the compound area of the site indicate that it is an early occupation; wood may have been more plentiful.

Two coastal Timucuan mission sites have been investigated. The Fountain of Youth site north of St. Augustine was the location of the mission Nombre de Dios. Even as late as 1700, this mission was the only stone (coquina—a naturally occuring limestone composed of fragments of shell and coral) structure in St. Augustine except for the blockhouse in the castillo (Manucy 1962:21). No doubt the mission's proximity to the coquina quarries on Anastasia and to the economic and political center of St. Augustine accounts for the stonework. Results of the excavations in the village area have been mentioned.

San Juan del Puerto, on Fort George Island, Florida, was established among the Timucua by 1595. Tacatacuru were settled at the site after 1597 (McMurray 1973:73), and Yamassee Indians sometime after 1675. Two possible mission compound locations have been identified. W. Jones's (1967) excavations revealed a serpentine palisade in the extreme southeastern part of the site that Jones believed to be a stockade containing three buildings—"flimsy structures that had been built and rebuilt many times"—arranged in a quadrangle plan (W. Jones 1967:14, 17). There was no evidence of daub construction in the area Jones tested.

Dickinson and Wayne (1985) place the mission compound of San Juan del Puerto 100 m north and west of Jones's excavations. Resistivity indicated several rectangular structures; the one tested may have been constructed of wattle and daub. These structures may have been arranged around a courtyard or work area. The only whole structure thus defined appears to be about 12 m long and 6 m wide. A cemetery, possibly associated with a light structure, lay some 25 m to the southeast of this complex. An oval area lacking shell (but not pottery) could define a plaza southeast of the compound (Dickinson and Wayne 1985:Figure B-1). The salient data here are the possible locations of two compounds, one constructed of board or thatch and the other of wattle and daub. Majolicas recovered from the two hypothetical compounds suggest that the southern one was earlier, but some later types were recovered from the south, and earlier types were present in the north.

Missions in Guale

Two long-term excavations are currently being conducted on Guale missions. Both excavations concern the Mission Santa Catalina de Guale. The American Museum of Natural History has explored the earlier location of the mission on St. Catherines Island, Georgia, while the Florida Museum of Natural History has conducted research on Amelia Island, Florida, where the mission was reestablished in 1686.

The Santa Catalina de Guale mission was established on St. Catherines Island by the late 1580s. The formal arrangement of the Santa Catalina mission has been mentioned. Completely destroyed by fire in the Guale rebellion in 1579, the mission was rebuilt in the early 1600s, apparently in exactly the same location and with the same ground plan. This indicates that the quadrangle plan was extant prior to 1597.

The post-rebellion church was a single-nave structure, 20 m long by 11 m wide (Thomas 1988a:96, 1988b:31–35, 1987). Two types of building materials were used. Wattle and daub construction was used for the facade and nave; for this section, posts were set in shell-lined postholes. Vertical wall boarding formed the sanctuary. The use of vertical wall boarding for the sanctuary may reflect its "high status," as does the fact that the sanctuary was elevated above the nave. A sacristy was on the left side of the altar. The Santa Catalina church is the only church excavated to date with evidence of a formal atrio. This was a 15 m^2 area surrounded by a low wall. The interior of the atrio was surfaced with water-rolled shell.

Few details are available for the early church. There is more information on the similarities and differences in the construction of the early and the later convento. Interpretations presented here should be considered preliminary, however, as excavation and analysis are incomplete.

Both conventos were built of wattle and daub. The early structure, defined by relatively large postholes with clean fill, was at least 10×20 m, as large as most churches. All of this structure may not have been enclosed with daub walls; however, site preparation for construction of the late convento has destroyed the evidence for this. The early convento was divided into three rooms measuring 10 6 m and one measuring 10×4 m.

The later structure had wattle and daub walls enclosing a 9.5-$\times$-8.5-m area. Porches may have been attached to the southern and western exposures. The interior of the later convento was divided into two rooms, one of which contained a clay font. A third room, not walled with wattle and daub, may have extended south past the wattle and daub wall fall. In the southeastern corner of the structure, attached to the possible porch on the south side, is an area of wall trenches that may describe storage areas.

Twenty meters to the northwest of the late convento was the kitchen, measuring 4.5 × 6 m. This structure was constructed of wattle and daub, but walled on only three sides. The convento and kitchen may have been connected by a covered walkway, which would also have covered the well located between the two structures. Palisade postholes have been uncovered north of the kitchen but the extent and configuration of the palisade remain undefined.

Interpretation of the mission plan of Santa Catalina on Amelia Island is less secure. The site itself housed two missions: Santa María, occupied by Yamassee Indians sometime before 1675 and abandoned in 1683; and Santa Catalina, removed to Amelia Island in 1686 and destroyed in Moore's raid of 1702. The distinguishing characteristic of the two Amelia Island missions is the presence of shell sleepers for the outer walls. The function of these sleepers was probably to raise the walls above the surface and thus protect them from damp and insects.

Only the church has been located for the Santa María component. It was built of wood. One hundred and eighteen burials (about half the original burial population) were excavated from inside the church, contradicting the hypothesis that burial inside a church was an early trait. In addition, several of the burials were intruded on by construction features of the church, suggesting that Christian burials were interred before the structure was completed. The presence of raw clay in the burial pits may suggest that the structure was floored. Raw clay was absent in the matrix and burial pits of the northernmost section of the church; if this was the sanctuary area, a different kind of flooring may have been used.

The locations of the church and kitchen for the Santa Catalina mission on Amelia Island have not been identified with certainty. The convento has been located and excavated. It was a small wattle and daub structure, 12 × 7 m, divided into two rooms. A roof extended over porches on the north and south sides of the building; a storage room may have been constructed on the south porch. Like Santa María, the walls rested on thin shell footers. Unlike anything at Santa María, a wide shell "sidewalk" extended around the north and east side of the convent. The framing of the north porch by the sidewalk suggests that it may have functioned as a loggia. However, its location on the north side deviates from the location of the loggia in the St. Augustine plan, in which the porch is always on the south or east side of the structure to catch the sun (Manucy 1962).

Large postholes in various alignments over the site suggest fencing and/or palisades; documentary evidence from 1700 indicates that a stockade was begun at the site but never finished (Saunders 1987). Indians cited the lack of labor and the scarcity of wood as reasons for not completing the project (Hann 1986a). This emphasizes that the period of construction was a major factor in the outcome of mission construction.

Summary

This review of the available data indicates that a combination of formal plans and informal construction techniques were used at the missions in La Florida. At those sites where extensive, systematic testing programs were implemented, the data indicate that the missions were laid out on some variant of the quadrangle plan (which may be derived from secular domestic architectural designs). The exception is San Martín. Evidence from San Luis, San Martín, and San Juan del Puerto indicates that the mission quadrangle was commonly located on a large plaza typical of both Renaissance-inspired Spanish town planning and traditional Southeastern Indian towns.

If the mission was established in an extant town, the configuration of the compound may have had to be adapted to extant site features. The formality of the town plan may also be related to the time of establishment, as suggested by the results from San Martín, and/or site function, as the Baptizing Springs visita suggests. Poor site visibility for both early missions and visitas will continue to hamper research into these aspects of variability. The construction materials used and the scope of projects completed may have been affected by a depletion of local resources as the evidence from Amelia Island demonstrates.

The economic and political importance of the site would also have affected site plan and architecture. For instance, Santa Catalina on St. Catherines Island was an early foundation, but from its inception it appears to have had large buildings in a formal layout. This was possible because the town was new (Hann 1989a:23–24). At the same time, the mission's economic status as a breadbasket for St. Augustine and its political function as a stronghold against British and French encroachment also contributed to its apparent stability and prosperity. Similarly, San Luis and Patale were at least partly contemporaneous, but the importance of San Luis is seen in its formal town plan and artifact diversity; the formal plan was possible because San Luis was a new town. The location of the mission with respect to resources and roads was also a factor, as in the case of Santa Fe and Nombre de Dios.

The architectural characteristics can be summarized as follows. Site preparation included filling and leveling and, at Patale I, the laying of a broad clay pad extending beyond the walls of the church. Church sizes were standard within about 5 meters. Proportions were also regular, with the width varying between 0.5 and 0.6 times the length. Like their more elaborate Mexican counterparts, sanctuaries were emphasized by elevation and a reduction in width, usually within a rectangular mass; flooring may also have differed from that of the nave. Conventos varied more freely, due to both the number of permanent friars, and, perhaps, the commitment to poverty of the friar in charge. Kitchens are poorly known. The only completely exposed structure to date is at Santa Catalina on St. Catherine's Island; it was a open structure, perhaps similar, at least in principle, to that illustrated by Manucy (1962:122–123).

In 1675, Calderón (Wenhold 1936) described the churches of Apalachee, Timucua, and Guale as being built of wood. This contrasts with Bullones's (Hann 1989:11) statement that even before Moore's raids, only churches of straw were possible. Calderón may have been citing an ideal—an ideal perhaps reiterated in the use of wood in the sanctuary of Santa Catalina. Bullones's comments appeared in a letter arguing against secularization of the missions, in which it might have been expedient to emphasize the meanness of the churches of the time. The two contradictory reports probably reflect Spanish views about appropriate and inappropriate building materials more than the actual situation in the late seventeenth century.

Archaeological evidence indicates that a heterogeneous mix of building materials was used, probably because of the types of resources available, and the size of the labor pool. There is some evidence that building materials varied with the ethnic composition of the mission population (ethnically homogeneous Timucuan missions may not have been constructed of wattle and daub); however, this is difficult to establish because of the movement of peoples throughout the Mission period. A number of different construction techniques were used, many of which appear to have been efforts to extend the life of posts and wall bases.

One of the problems encountered in this study was the lack of data needed to make useful comparisons of mission architecture along temporal lines. We need more documentary evidence and finer chronological control from artifact assemblages to date occupation sequences. In addition, sites need to be tested more extensively and structures more intensively to learn enough about village layout and building construction to answer questions about ideals and innovations in both Spanish and Indian architecture of La Florida.

Acknowledgments

I would like to thank all of the archaeologists of La Florida for their graciousness in sharing their data, some of which had literally just been uncovered as this article was being written. Discussions with Rochelle Marrinan, Bonnie McEwen, Brent Weisman, and Ken Johnson helped to hone my understanding of Mission period architecture. And of course, without Jerald T. Milanich, many of us would not have had the inspiration (or money) to dig with.

References

Chaney, E.
  1987   The Sixteenth Century Spanish Occupation at the Fountain of Youth Park Site. Paper presented at the Annual Meeting of the Florida Anthropological Society Meetings, Clearwater.
Deagan, K.
  1983   The Mestizo Minority: Archaeological Patterns of Intermarriage. In *Spanish St. Augustine: The Archaeology of a Colonial Creole Community*. Academic Press, New York.
  1985   The Archaeology of Sixteenth Century St. Augustine. *Florida Anthropologist* 38(1–2):6–33.
Dickinson, M. F., and L. B. Wayne
  1985   Archaeological Testing of the San Juan del Puerto Mission Site (8Du53), Fort George Island, Florida. Report prepared for Fairfield Communities, Jacksonville, Florida.
Foster, G. M.
  1960   *Culture and Conquest: America's Spanish Heritage*. Quadrangle Books, Chicago.
Geiger, M. J.
  1936   *The Early Franciscans in Florida and Their Relation to Spain's Colonial Effort*. George Washington University Press, Washington, D. C.

Hann, J.

1986a General Visitation of the Provinces of Guale and Mocama Made by the Capt. Don Juan de Pueyo. Paper on file, San Luis Archaeological and Historical Site, Tallahassee, Florida.

1986b Demographic Patterns and Changes in Mid-Seventeenth Century Timucua and Apalachee. *Florida Historical Quarterly* 64:371–392.

1989a Summary Guide to Spanish Florida Missions and Visitas with Churches in the Sixteenth and Seventeenth Centuries. Manuscript on file, Bureau of Archaeological Research, Tallahassee.

1989b Fray Bullones 1728 Report on the Missions. Paper on file, San Luis Archaeological and Historical Site, Tallahassee, Florida.

Jones, B. C.

1972 Spanish Mission Sites Located and Test Excavated. *Archives and History News* 3(6):1–2.

Jones, B. C., and G. N. Shapiro

1987 Nine Mission Sites in Apalachee. Paper presented at the 1987 Meeting of the Society for Historical Archaeology, Savannah.

Jones, W. M.

1967 A Report on the Site of San Juan del Puerto, a Spanish Mission, Fort George Island, Duval County, Florida. Xerox on file at the Florida Museum of Natural History, Gainesville.

Kubler, G.

1948 *Mexican Architecture of the Sixteenth Century*. Yale University Press, New Haven.

Loucks, L. J.

1979 *Political and Economic Interactions between Spaniards and Indians: Archaeological and Ethnohistorical Perspectives of the Mission System in Florida*. Unpublished Ph.D. dissertation, Department of Anthropology, University of Florida, Gainesville.

McAndrew, J.

1965 *The Open-Air Churches of Sixteenth-Century Mexico: Atrios, Posas, Open Chapels, and Other Studies*. Harvard University Press, Cambridge, Massachusetts.

McMurray, J. A.

1973 The Definition of the Ceramic Complex at San Juan del Puerto. Unpublished Master's thesis, Department of Anthropology, University of Florida, Gainesville.

Madison County Carrier

1972 State Sponsored Archaeological and Historical Research at the San Pedro Mission Site, Madison County, Florida. *Madison County Carrier*, edited by Tommy Greene. Section B, pp. 1–8. June 15.

Manucy, A.

1962 *The House of St. Augustine: Notes on the Architecture from 1565–1821*. St. Augustine Historical Society.

1985 The Physical Setting of Sixteenth Century St. Augustine. *Florida Anthropologist* 38(1–2):34–53.

Marrinan, R. A.

1985 The Archaeology of the Spanish Missions of Florida: 1565–1704. In *Indians, Colonists, and Slaves: Essays in Memory of Charles H. Fairbanks*, edited by K. W. Johnson, J. M. Leader, and R. C. Wilson, pp. 241–252. *Florida Journal of Anthropology* Special Publication No. 4.

Merritt, J. D.

1983 Beyond the Town Walls: The Indian Element in Colonial St. Augustine. In *Spanish St. Augustine: The Archaeology of a Colonial Creole Community*, edited by K. Deagan, pp. 125–150. Academic Press, New York.

Milanich, J. T.

1972 Excavations at the Richardson site, Alachua County, Florida: An Early 17th Century Potano Indian Village (With Notes on Potano Culture Change). *Bureau of Historic Sites and Properties Bulletin* 2:35–61.

Milanich, J. T., and K. W. Johnson
1989 *Santa Fe: A Name out of Time.* Miscellaneous Project Report Series No. 41. Florida Museum of Natural History, Gainesville.

Morrell, L. R., and B. C. Jones
1970 San Juan de Aspalaga: A Preliminary Architectural Study. *Bureau of Historic Sites and Properties Bulletin* 1:25–43.

Ricard, R.
1966 *The Spiritual Conquest of Mexico: An Essay on the Apostolate and the Evangelizing Methods of the Mendicant Orders in New Spain, 1523–1572.* University of California Press, Berkeley.

Ross, M.
1926 The Restoration of the Spanish Missions in Georgia, 1598–1606. *Georgia Historical Quarterly* 10(3):171–199.

Saunders, R.
1987 *Excavations at 8Na41: Two Mission Period Sites on Amelia Island, Florida.* Miscellaneous Project Report Series No. 35. Florida Museum of Natural History, Gainesville.

Shapiro, G. N.
1987 The Anthropology of Town Plan at San Luis. Paper presented at the 1987 Meeting of the Society for Historical Archaeology, Savannah.

Shapiro, G. N., and R. A. Marrinan
1986 Two Seventeenth Century Spanish Missions in Florida's Apalachee Province. Paper presented at the 1986 Meetings of the Society for Historical Archaeology, Sacramento.

Shapiro, G. N., and R. Vernon
1989 The 17th Century Mission Church and Cemetery at San Luis. Paper presented at the 1989 Meetings of the Society for Historical Archaeology, Baltimore.

South, S., R. K. Skowronek, and R. E. Johnson
1988 *Spanish Artifacts from Santa Elena.* Anthropological Studies No. 7. Occasional Papers of the South Carolina Institute of Archaeology and Anthropology, Columbia.

Smith, H. G.
1951 A Spanish Mission Site in Jefferson County, Florida. In *Here They Once Stood: The Tragic End of the Apalachee Missions*, by M. F. Boyd, H. G. Smith, and J. W. Griffin, pp. 107–138. University of Florida Press, Gainesville.

Swanton, J. R.
1946 *The Indians of the Southeastern United States.* Smithsonian Institution Bureau of American Ethnology Bulletin No. 137. Smithsonian Institution Press, Washington, D. C.

Thomas, D. H.
1987 *St. Catherines: An Island in Time.* Georgia History and Culture Series. Georgia Endowment for the Humanities, Atlanta.
1988a Saints and Soldiers at Santa Catalina: Hispanic Designs for Colonial America. In *The Recovery of Meaning: Historical Archaeology in the Eastern United States*, edited by M. P. Leone and P. B. Potter, Jr., pp. 73–140. Smithsonian Institution Press, Washington, D. C.
1988b *The Archaeology of Mission Santa Catalina de Guale: 1. Search and Discovery*, Vol. 63: Part 2. Anthropological Papers of the American Museum of Natural History, New York.

Weisman, B. R.
1988 *Excavations at Fig Springs (8Col): Season 2, July–December, 1988.* Florida Archaeological Reports 4. Tallahassee.

Wenhold, L. L.
1936 *A 17th Century Letter of Gabriel Diaz Vara Calderón, Bishop of Cuba, Describing the Indians and Indian Missions of Florida.* Smithsonian Miscellaneous Collections 95(16).

Chapter 34 ■

Elizabeth J. Reitz

Zooarchaeological Evidence for Subsistence at La Florida Missions

There is a tendency to concentrate on responses to the natural environment when discussing human adaptations, especially those that pertain to subsistence, even though adaptations may also be responses to the social environment. Since changes in the natural environment (e.g., climatic changes) are less common than are changes in the social environment, we can expect the archaeological record to reflect many responses to social changes. One of the Columbian consequences was that many previously unacquainted cultures were forced to develop new cultural patterns as they encountered and made sense of one another. The process of culture change that occurs in such instances has been termed acculturation. Acculturation includes "those phenomena which result when groups of individuals having different cultures come into continuous first-hand contact, with subsequent changes in the original cultural patterns of either or both groups" (Redfield et al. 1936:149). Behavioral change is presumed to flow from the dominant to the subordinate group (Foster 1960:7–9), although it is more likely that changes must occur in both groups.

In the case of La Florida, we can identify two reasons why there should be change on both sides. On the one hand, Indians and Spaniards were faced with new social, political, and economic demands to which they had to respond. In addition, Spaniards were faced with a natural environment unlike any they had previously encountered (Reitz and Scarry 1985:33, 35, 40). Although Spain planned to make missions its primary tool for changing Indian institutions into Spanish ones, Spaniards based at missions were a long way from home and had to make accommodations of their own to their new surroundings. Under such conditions, acculturative responses must have been made by both Indians and Spaniards.

Food remains would be a good source of information about cultural behavior and change. The acquisition of food is central to a group's economic, political, and ideological life. Changes in these parts of a cultural system should be reflected in subsistence behavior. If you have ever tried to change your own diet, you know that changes in food habits are not easily accepted. On the other hand, the acquisition of food is a daily problem. If sufficient amounts of one's usual foods cannot be obtained because of conflicts in schedules or local availability, changes must be made quickly.

One way that Spaniards dealt with their need for food was to alter their subsistence strategy to include foods acquired from Indians. Spaniards expected to receive food as gifts, in trade, as alms, or as tribute payments. The foods that went from Indians to Spaniards probably were at first native foods rather than Spanish ones. Initially the Spanish colonial diet might have been very similar to Indian diets, especially if a large part of it was provided by Indians. At missions Spaniards might attempt to alter Indian habits to increase their access to preferred European foods. In that case, native foods might be replaced by European ones. On the other hand, we might find that Indian food patterns did not become European ones. The Indian diet might remain as it had been before contact or might emphasize a different complex of resources. In either case, the Spanish colonial diet would be neither European nor Indian.

Food was commonly overlooked in sixteenth- and seventeenth-century accounts, unless to claim there was not enough of it. There are glimpses of Indian foodways in the Spanish accounts, often in the context of some type of petitions for support or the redress of a grievance involving food (e.g., Boyd et al. 1951:25, 31, 41). These accounts provide hints that changes in Indian food habits occurred at missions, but the reports are neither objective nor detailed. We know, for example, that there were horses, pigs, cows, and chickens at missions, but we do not know how abundant these animals were, to what extent domestic animals replaced wild animals, whether access to domestic animals was restricted to one social or ethnic group, or what spatial or temporal differences might have existed among missions.

Archaeological evidence is one of the few sources of information about these acculturative processes. For studies of acculturation we need evidence of subsistence activities from pre-missionized Indians living in the general vicinity of a specific mission, as well as data for both mission Spaniards and Indians. Although there have been decades of archaeological work at missions in La Florida, in no case do we have evidence of animal use from all three cultural contexts. This problem is compounded by the fact that the western mission chain traverses a region in which the soils are highly acidic and the preservation of animal bone is very poor. We are unlikely ever to have data from the western chain of missions similar to those from the northern chain.

Nonetheless, archaeological evidence of animal use is available from several sixteenth- and seventeenth-century missions in La Florida. The evidence summarized here was collected from archaeological sites and studied using zooarchaeological methods (Wing and Brown 1979). Excavated vertebrate bones were compared with modern vertebrate skeletons in order to identify the animals recovered from each site. Quantification of the results of these identifications provides an estimate of relative abundances of animals used at the site. The most standard quantification is an estimate of the Minimum Number of Individuals (MNI) in an assemblage. MNI is estimated by considering the evidence for symmetry, age, and sex for each species identified and calculating the number of individuals necessary to explain the elements identified. The percentages of one group of animals may then be compared with other groups for subsistence information.

Among the many biases in archaeological data, two are particularly important here. Recovery techniques, especially the screen size used to retrieve animal remains from archaeological sites, profoundly influences one's interpretation of the subsistence activity being studied (Reitz and Quitmyer 1988). If ¼-inch mesh screens are used to recover animal remains, bones from small animals, such as most fishes, are easily lost. The evidence for heavy use of mammals such as deer, pigs, and cows is enhanced proportionately. If ⅛-inch mesh or flotation techniques are used to recover animal remains, the percentage of fishes recovered from the site usually increases and our understanding of the subsistence pattern being studied changes. It is very difficult to compare samples recovered with different screen sizes because of this bias. The second bias is associated with small samples (Grayson 1984). Larger samples probably more accurately reflect the richness of a subsistence practice than do small ones. Whenever there is disagreement between small samples recovered with ¼-inch mesh and large samples recovered using ⅛-inch mesh or flotation, the larger, more throughly recovered samples are considered more accurate than the smaller, less throughly recovered ones.

The Western Mission Chain

The western mission chain extended from St. Augustine, Florida, across the northern part of the Florida peninsula to present-day Tallahassee and beyond. Little zooarchaeological evidence is available from this area in large part because soil conditions are very poor for bone preservation. The remains of cow, pig, horse, and several wild animals are reported from San Francisco de Oconee, San Luis de Talamali, and Fig Springs (Boyd et al. 1951:175; Deagan 1972; Smith 1956:49), but these are not reported in detail. Unless the few animal bones that are preserved are identified and quantified, it is difficult to determine whether

European domestic animals replaced wild mammals, turtles, and fishes, or whether domestic animals were incorporated into an otherwise pre-Hispanic strategy.

Study of the only quantified zooarchaeological data from the western mission chain suggests that European animals did not replace wild animals in the subsistence strategy, but instead were incorporated into a strategy that continued to make use of locally available wild foods. These data are from excavations conducted by L. Jill Loucks (1979) at a seventeenth-century north-central Florida mission site adjacent to Baptizing Spring (8Su65). The identity of the mission is unknown. The Baptizing Spring materials were recovered using a variety of techniques. Loucks examined acculturation in subsistence and social patterns combining floral, faunal, and inorganic materials. In samples from Indian contexts, she showed that native prestige goods maintained their symbolic significance and that similar European goods provided Spanish reinforcement of aboriginal roles and status. Although Indians had access to European plants and animals, this access may have been restricted to high-status individuals. Pigs and cows were the only domestic animals identified from the Spanish deposits; each contributed 8 percent of the estimated individuals in a sample of 13 individuals (Loucks 1979:226). Deer accounted for 31 percent of the individuals. The terrestrial gopher tortoise constituted 46 percent of the individuals identified from the Spanish area of the site. No fish were identified in the Spanish deposits at the mission. Pigs and cows identified in the Indian village associated with the mission contributed an estimated 8 percent of the individuals in a sample of 35 individuals. The remains of at least 12 deer were identified. A squirrel, a raccoon, alligators, gopher tortoises, pond turtles, box turtles, and a mullet were also identified in the village.

These data provide an interesting glimpse into differences between subsistence at St. Augustine and at one of the western missions, but the Baptizing Spring sample is small and but one example out of many possible ones. Excavations are currently being conducted at San Luis de Talamali (8Le4), San Pedro y San Pablo de Patali (8Le152), and Fig Springs mission (8Co1) so it can be hoped that more will be known about subsistence activities at the western missions in the near future, in spite of the poor preservation usually encountered.

The Northern Mission Chain

The northern mission chain extended from St. Augustine at least to Santa Elena, the early capital of La Florida, located on the coast of what is now South Carolina. This northern chain followed a large continental embayment known as the Georgia Bight (Reitz 1988a). The chief physiographic feature of the Georgia Bight is a series of marsh and barrier islands, which lie in front of an extensive estuarine system. Most of the missions were placed on these islands. The animals of the islands, estuaries, and adjacent mainland were similar along the entire coastal stretch from the town of St. Augustine to Santa Elena.

Zooarchaeological evidence from the northern mission chain is far more abundant than from the western chain. Excavations at the Fountain of Youth site

(8SJ31), just north of St. Augustine, have provided data from a pre-Hispanic occupation as well as from an Indian village associated with the Nombre de Dios mission. The pre-Hispanic St. Johns IIc deposits are probably those of Chief Seloy's village. Mission data from Fountain of Youth are from a late sixteenth–early seventeenth-century Timucuan village (Reitz 1988b). The Timucuan materials were recovered using flotation techniques (see Scarry and Reitz, this volume, for additional discussion).

Extensive excavations at the Kings Bay site (9Cam171), on the Kings Bay Naval Submarine Base in Camden County, Georgia, have produced information about pre-Hispanic animal use in the Kings Bay area and some evidence for the historic period. The pre-Hispanic data used here are from the Savannah and the St. Johns II periods (Smith et al. 1981:512–514, 592). The Savannah deposits at Kings Bay dated between A.D. 700 and 1526 (Smith et al. 1981:940). The St. Johns II period is dated from A.D. 800 until contact (Milanich and Fairbanks 1980:23). The postcontact Indian data are from contexts that contained San Marcos ceramics and Spanish majolicas (Smith et al. 1981:508–509, 515, 601). As the nearest mission was probably San Pedro de Mocama on Cumberland Island (Milanich 1972), these deposits do not appear to have been associated with a mission. This postcontact Indian occupation at the Kings Bay site is referred to as San Marcos (Smith et al. 1981:601). The Savannah and St. Johns materials were excavated using ⅛-inch mesh for recovery. San Marcos materials were recovered from zone deposits with ¼-inch screen and from column samples with a ⅛-inch mesh.

Additional data from the northern mission chain are available from pre-Hispanic Indian, historic Indian, and Spanish mission deposits on St. Catherines Island, Georgia. The Irene period on St. Catherines Island dates between A.D. 1300 and 1550 (DePratter 1979:111). Data from the preceding Savannah period, A.D. 1150–1300 (DePratter 1979:111), are presented as well. Fallen Tree, a historic Indian village located immediately adjacent to the Santa Catalina de Guale mission and Spanish deposits from inside the mission provide evidence of the precontact situation. The Savannah and Irene data are composites from 51 sites sampled during a transect survey of the island conducted before excavation of Santa Catalina de Guale began, and all data presented here were collected during the survey rather than from recent excavations (Reitz 1989; Thomas 1987). A ¼-inch screen was used to recover the pre-Hispanic materials and a ¹¹⁄₃₂-inch screen to recover the Fallen Tree and some mission remains from St. Catherines Island.

Although much is known about pre-Hispanic Indian animal use in the area covered by the northern mission chain (Reitz 1988a), these data are not perfect. It would be desirable to compare evidence for pre-Hispanic subsistence from the Kings Bay area with pre-Hispanic data from the vicinity of Santa Catalina de Guale and Nombre de Dios in order to establish a pre-Hispanic base line against which to compare postcontact subsistence strategies. Ideally, this would involve a comparison of Savannah period or St. Johns period data at all three locations. Unfortunately, it is not possible to compare Savannah or St. Johns data from all areas because the distribution of these cultures overlaps only in the Kings

Bay locality. Therefore, the St. Johns II data from the Fountain of Youth site are compared with the St. Johns II data from the Kings Bay site and the Savannah data from the St. Catherines Island survey are compared with the Savannah data from the Kings Bay site (Table 34-1).

A comparison of the large Fountain of Youth sample and the smaller Kings Bay sample suggests that estuarine resources were heavily used by pre-Hispanic Indians. Deer, other wild mammals, birds, and turtles were apparently used in low numbers. Sharks, rays, and fishes constitute the largest group in both collections. The list of estuarine animals used is too long to summarize here, but the variety suggests a complex and sophisticated use of estuarine resources. The most common estuarine components in both collections were sea catfishes, drums, and mullets. Many of these were very small. The commensal category includes animals that are found in the vicinity of human habitations and so could have been nonfood items. It is also possible that some or all of these animals were eaten. Commensal animals in this case were a mole, a Hispid cotton rat, snakes, and amphibians. In every respect these St. Johns II data are similar to those from most pre-Hispanic sites on the Georgia/Florida coast (Reitz 1988a). It is clear that the primary strategy for vertebrate use was to take advantage of the abundant resources in the estuarine waters.

Caution should be exercised in comparing the Savannah period data (Table 34-1) since the St. Catherines' Island survey data were recovered with ¼-inch screen, which is known to reduce the recovery of fish, and the collection is quite small. This caution is especially important since the pre-Hispanic sample from St. Catherines sharply contrasts with the larger sample from the Kings Bay site, which was recovered using ⅛-inch. The Kings Bay sample is more in keeping with what is found routinely elsewhere along the Georgia Bight when fine-screen recovery methods are employed than are the St. Catherines' data. Al-

Table 34-1. Savannah and St. Johns II Faunal Summaries

Faunal Groups	Savannah, St. Catherines		Savannah, Kings Bay		St. Johns, Kings Bay		St. Johns, Fountain of Youth	
	MNI	Percent	MNI	Percent	MNI	Percent	MNI	Percent
Domestic mammals								
Domestic birds								
Deer	8	25.8	3	1.2	1	2.3	3	1.4
Other mammals	9	29.0	2	0.8	2	4.7	1	0.5
Wild birds	1	3.2	2	0.8	1	2.3	1	0.5
Turtles/alligators	4	12.9	10	3.9	1	2.3	2	0.9
Sharks/rays/fishes	7	22.6	228	88.7	36	83.7	204	93.6
Commensal taxa	2	6.5	12	4.7	2	4.7	7	3.2
Total	31		257		43		218	

Note: St. Catherines Island data were recovered with ¼-inch screen (Reitz 1989); Kings Bay data with ⅛-inch (Smith et al. 1981:512–514); and Fountain of Youth data with flotation techniques (Reitz 1988b).

though there are no substantive differences in the types of animals identified, the percentages of individuals estimated for two collections differ considerably. The most striking contrast is in the high percentage of deer and other mammals found in the St. Catherines' collection. This difference is at least in part attributable to the ¼-inch screen used to recover the St. Catherines' materials and to the small sample size, but it also may indicate that different subsistence strategies were practiced on St. Catherines Island and in the Kings Bay area.

Examination of the San Marcos data from the Kings Bay site suggests that Indian subsistence during the Mission period, but away from the immediate vicinity of a mission, did not change markedly (Table 34-2). The Kings Bay site San Marcos data are presented both as a large ¼-inch sample and a small ⅛-inch sample in order to demonstrate again the effect of recovery method on vertebrate samples. The loss of small animals associated with larger screen sizes is clear in the ¼-inch samples. Nonetheless, in both ¼-inch and ⅛-inch samples it appears likely that the subsistence pattern observed in the St. Johns II samples continued into the historic period. Deer are the most prominent mammal in the ¼-inch sample, but one of the least common animals in the ⅛-inch sample. Fish included primarily sea catfish and drums, although a wide variety of other sharks, rays, and fish were identified. The St. Johns II and San Marcos samples suggest stability in animal use after contact rather than pronounced change. This possibility needs to be tested further.

Interestingly, this may also have been the case at some mission sites (Table 34-3). The Timucuan data from the Fountain of Youth site are similar to those from the St. Johns II component at the site as well as to the San Marcos data from the Kings Bay site (Table 34-1). There were no domestic animals in the Timucuan sample and only one deer. The only other mammals identified were a rabbit and a dolphin. The fish identified were primarily sea catfish and drums, although the collection contained the usual range of sharks, rays, and other fish. One change that may be significant is an increase in the estimated percentage

Table 34-2. Mission Period: San Marcos Faunal Summaries

| | Kings Bay Site | | | |
| | ¼-inch | | ⅛-inch | |
Faunal Groups	MNI	Percent	MNI	Percent
Domestic mammals				
Domestic birds				
Deer	13	6.3	1	2.0
Other mammals	22	10.7	1	2.0
Wild birds	8	3.9	2	4.0
Turtles/alligators	27	13.2	2	4.0
Sharks/rays/fishes	127	62.0	43	86.0
Commensal taxa	8	3.9	1	2.0
Total	205		50	

Source: Smith et al. (1981:508, 515).

Table 34-3. Mission Period: Mission Indian Faunal Summaries

| Faunal Groups | Fountain of Youth, Timucua | | St. Catherines Island Irene | | Fallen Tree | |
	MNI	Percent	MNI	Percent	MNI	Percent
Domestic mammals					1	2.0
Domestic birds					1	2.0
Deer	1	0.8	44	23.9	27	54.0
Other mammals	2	1.6	25	13.6	10	20.0
Wild birds	1	0.8	3	1.6	2	4.0
Turtles/alligators	2	1.6	39	21.2	2	4.0
Sharks/rays/fishes	115	89.1	67	36.4	6	12.0
Commensal taxa	8	6.2	6	3.3	1	2.0
Total	129		184		50	

Note: Fountain of Youth data were recovered by flotation (Reitz 1988b). St. Catherines Island Irene data were recovered using ¼-inch mesh and the Fallen Tree data using ¹¹⁄₁₃-inch mesh (Reitz 1986).

of commensal animals. One of the commensal animals identified from the Timucuan village was an Old World House mouse.

However, when the Fallen Tree data are compared with those from the preceding Savannah (Table 34-1) and Irene components (Table 34-3) subsistence changes at some missions may be indicated. Between the Savannah and Irene periods there may have been a decrease in the use of mammals and turtles, with a corresponding increase in fishes. This shift is not as dramatic as that which is found in the Fallen Tree and Savannah/Irene collections. With allowances for the small sample size from the Fallen Tree village and the use of a ¹¹⁄₃₂-inch screen, these data may suggest a change in the role of vertebrates in the subsistence strategy of Indians living near the Santa Catalina de Guale mission. One of these changes is indicated by the presence of pig and chicken in the village. Another possible change is an increase in deer and other wild mammals, with a corresponding decline in the use of turtles and fish. These data suggest that the interaction with the Santa Catalina de Guale mission altered the Indian diet in ways that did not occur near the Nombre de Dios mission. Striking as the contrast is, a sample recovered using large-meshed screens and containing the remains of only 50 individuals should not be used as proof of a major change in mission Indian subsistence. Development of this idea and its implications must await study of additional Fallen Tree samples recovered with finer-meshed screens and corroborative evidence from other mission villages.

When the Nombre de Dios Indian collection from Fountain of Youth is compared with that from Fallen Tree (Table 34-4), it appears that there may have been distinct Indian responses at the two missions. There does not appear to have been a substantial break with traditional use of animal resources by Indians living at Nombre de Dios. The Santa Catalina evidence, however, suggests a departure from pre-Hispanic subsistence habits by Indians living at Fallen Tree.

Although these differences may be due to both recovery method and sample size, they raise a number of interesting questions concerning the behavioral factors that may also be involved.

Not only is it possible that different subsistence strategies were practiced in the mission Indian villages associated with Nombre de Dios and Santa Catalina de Guale, but there were apparently differences in the Spanish diet at the two places as well (Table 34-4). Data are not available from the Spanish occupation at Nombre de Dios, but they are available from sixteenth-century deposits in nearby St. Augustine. (For a more extensive discussion of sixteenth-century Spanish subsistence, see Scarry and Reitz, this volume.) When the large Spanish St. Augustine collection is compared with the currently limited data available from Spanish deposits inside Santa Catalina de Guale, there is some suggestion of a substantial difference in the vertebrate foods being used at the two locations. In this case, recovery technique and sample size may be factors. If the Santa Catalina data are an accurate reflection of Spanish diet at the mission, it is apparent that fewer European domestic animals and deer were utilized at St. Augustine than at the mission. At St. Augustine pigs appear to have made up 4 percent of the individuals, cows 1 percent, and deer 3 percent. The Spanish diet at St. Augustine changed substantially as locally available wild foods were incorporated into a strategy in which the use of domestic animals was not common. At the same time, Spaniards living in the mission compound had a diet that was altered to include locally available wild foods, but in percentages unlike those experienced by their compatriots at St. Augustine. In the Santa Catalina sample, pigs may have accounted for 8 percent of the individuals and deer 35 percent. These data seem to indicate that Spaniards at the mission enjoyed greater access to domestic animals, as well as greater access to venison, than did Spaniards back in town. The diet that they enjoyed, however, was neither Spanish nor Indian, but made use of animals in a completely new fashion. Addi-

Table 34-4. Mission Period: Spanish Faunal Summaries

Faunal Groups	St. Augustine		Santa Catalina	
	MNI	Percent	MNI	Percent
Domestic mammals	54	4.8	2	7.7
Domestic birds	45	4.0		
Deer	31	2.8	9	34.6
Other mammals	44	3.9	4	15.4
Wild birds	71	6.3	3	11.5
Turtles/alligators	61	5.4	1	3.8
Sharks/rays/fishes	767	68.1	6	23.1
Commensal taxa	53	4.7	1	3.8
Total	1126		26	

Note: St. Augustine and Santa Catalina de Guale collections were recovered using ¼-inch mesh (Reitz 1989; Reitz and Scarry 1985).

tional samples from Santa Catalina are currently being examined, so it will not be long before this possibility can be tested using larger samples.

Discussion

The assumption is often made that Indian subsistence changed dramatically after contact with Spaniards, and that European colonial subsistence practices were unmodified by native ones. Contrary to this expectation, a study of archaeological food remains from a few La Florida missions suggests that through a process of fusion, Indian and Spanish techniques were combined to create a new system and that there was not a homogeneous response.

This summary of pre-Hispanic Indian, mission Indian, and Spanish zooarchaeological evidence suggests that all three groups practiced subsistence strategies based on the use of a number of terrestrial, riverine, and estuarine animals, with only limited use of domestic animals in the historic period. Although sample sizes are highly variable and recovery methods not uniform, the zooarchaeological evidence suggests that some Indian and all Spanish diets changed in response to the colonial setting and that these responses were highly variable. At Nombre de Dios mission, Indians may have continued to practice a pre-Hispanic strategy apparently little changed by the mission experience. Spaniards at St. Augustine, however, substantially altered their diet by adopting many Indian foods. On St. Catherines Island both Indians and Spaniards altered their subsistence strategy. Mission Indians living at Fallen Tree began husbanding domestic animals. The Spanish diet in the mission incorporated many of the same animals used by pre-Hispanic and mission Indians, but in proportions unlike those used either by Indians or by Spaniards at St. Augustine. They also managed to have access to more domestic animals than either Indians or Spaniards at St. Augustine.

Much more work needs to be done both at pre-Hispanic sites and at missions to assess the full richness of the human response to the colonial setting, but it is apparent that both Indians and Spaniards felt the consequences of the Columbian experience and responded in a variety of ways.

Acknowledgments

I wish to thank Kathleen A. Deagan, David H. Thomas, Robin L. Smith, and Edward E. Chaney for access to their excavated faunal materials and financial support. Gwyneth Duncan, Jennifer Freer, Marc S. Frank, David J. Varricchio, Timothy S. Young, and Karen G. Wood, as well as Lori Taylor and Emmett Walsh, assisted with the identifications, which were done using the comparative collections at the Zooarchaeology Laboratory of the Florida Museum of Natural History and the Zooarchaeology Laboratory of the University of Georgia's Museum of Natural History. Funding was provided by the Edward John Noble Foundation, the U.S. Department of the Navy (contract N00025–79–0013), the Florida Board of Regents STAR Grant Program, the Florida State University

COFRS Summer Faculty Research Program, the Colonial Dames of America, the National Endowment for the Humanities (grant RO 32437–78–1425), the Historic St. Augustine Preservation Board, and the St. Augustine Restoration Foundation.

References

Boyd, Mark F., Hale G. Smith, and John W. Griffin
  1951   *Here They Once Stood: The Tragic End of the Apalachee Missions*. University of Florida Press, Gainesville.
Deagan, Kathleen A.
  1972   Fig Springs: The Mid-Seventeenth Century in North-Central Florida. *Historical Archaeology* 6:23–46.
DePratter, Chester B.
  1979   Ceramics. In *The Anthropology of St. Catherines Island 2. The Refuge-Deptford Ceramic Complex*, by D. H. Thomas and C. S. Larsen, pp. 109–132. Anthropological Papers of the American Museum of Natural History 56(1).
Foster, George M.
  1960   *Culture and Conquest*. Quadrangle Books, Chicago.
Grayson, Donald K.
  1984   *Quantitative Zooarchaeology*. Academic Press, Orlando.
Loucks, Lana Jill
  1979   *Political and Economic Interactions between Spaniards and Indians: Archaeological and Ethnohistorical Perspectives of the Mission System in Florida*. Unpublished Ph.D. dissertation, University of Florida, Gainesville. University Microfilms, Ann Arbor.
Milanich, Jerald T.
  1972   Tacatacuru and the San Pedro de Ocama Mission. *Florida Historical Quarterly* 50(3):283–291.
Milanich, Jerald T., and Charles H. Fairbanks
  1980   *Florida Archaeology*. Academic Press, New York.
Redfield, Robert, R. Linton, and M. Herskovitz
  1936   Memorandum for the Study of Acculturation. *American Anthropologist* 38:149–152.
Reitz, Elizabeth J.
  1988a Evidence for Coastal Adaptations in Georgia and South Carolina. *Archaeology of Eastern North America* 16:137–158.
  1988b Faunal Remains from the Fountain of Youth Park Site (8-SJ-31). Ms. on file, Department of Anthropology, University of Georgia, Athens.
  1989   Faunal Remains from the St. Catherines Island Transect Survey. Ms. on file, Department of Anthropology, University of Georgia, Athens.
Reitz, Elizabeth J., and Irvy R. Quitmyer
  1988   Faunal Remains from Two Coastal Georgia Swift Creek Sites. *Southeastern Archaeology* 7(2):95–108.
Reitz, Elizabeth J., and C. Margaret Scarry
  1985   *Reconstructing Historic Subsistence with an Example from Sixteenth Century Spanish Florida*. Society for Historical Archaeology Special Publication No. 3.
Smith, Hale G.
  1956   *The European and the Indian*. Florida Anthropological Society Publication 4.
Smith, Robin L., Chad O. Braley, Nina T. Borremans, and Elizabeth J. Reitz
  1981   *Coastal Adaptations in Southeast Georgia: Ten Archaeological Sites at Kings Bay*. Department of Anthropology, University of Florida. Submitted to U.S. Department of Navy, Contract No. N00025-79-C-0013.

Thomas, David Hurst
  1987   *The Archaeology of Mission Santa Catalina de Guale: 1. Search and Discovery.* Anthropological Papers of the American Museum of Natural History 63(2).
Wing, Elizabeth S., and Antoinette Brown
  1979   *Paleonutrition: Method and Theory in Prehistoric Foodways.* Academic Press, New York.

Chapter 35 ■

Donna L. Ruhl

Spanish Mission Paleoethnobotany and Culture Change: A Survey of the Archaeobotanical Data and Some Speculations on Aboriginal and Spanish Agrarian Interactions in La Florida

> The repertory of Spanish-introduced crops rapidly revolutionized native food plant production across the continent from Florida to California. The Spanish taught the Indians new techniques for raising these and traditional domesticates. Gardens, orchards, and plow agriculture were employed to assure a successful harvest [Ford 1985:360].

Over 400 years have passed since the first Spanish settlements in La Florida were established. First as explorers and conquerors, and later as colonists, the Spaniards had a profound impact upon the aboriginal populations they encountered. Mission Indians, like other Southeastern Indians, were not always complacent about the injustices they incurred under Spanish contacts, as evidenced by martyred and rebuffed Jesuit and Franciscan friars, rebellions (e.g., Guale 1576, 1580, 1582, 1597; Timucua 1656; Apalachee 1647; Jororo 1696), and accounts of intractable Indians (e.g., Boyd et al. 1951; Gannon 1967; Lanning 1935; Oré 1936; Solís de Merás 1964). Their expansionistic manner and Iberian purview led them to induce Hispanicization, in part, through catechization and agrarianization of the aboriginal populations they encountered and sought to convert, control, and/or exploit.

The evangelizing friars and settlers, with their new activities and lifeways (e.g., plants, animals, irrigation, plows and other farm tools, grazing pastures), altered La Florida's ecology, as they did elsewhere in the New World (e.g., Clewell 1980; Crosby 1972; Eliott 1987; Florescano 1987; McAlister 1984; Macleod 1987; Ross 1975; Sauer 1966; Smith and Rice 1989; West 1989). Both natural and cultural responses to the directed changes imposed (e.g., Foster 1960; Linton 1940; Spicer 1961) were to induce variable results in the cornucopia of the New World cultures and environments that the Spaniards confronted.

In La Florida, some Old World plants adapted to the new environments readily, while others did not. Some agrarian practices and livestock ranches worked, while others failed. In part, this had to do with the variable ecological communities and terrain that existed throughout the territory; but also with the infringement upon Indian rights to fields, gathering areas, and hunting regions (e.g., Bushnell 1978; Hann 1986a, 1988; Ross 1975). Even though there was an awareness on the part of the friars to maintain a balance of power between themselves and between the various caciques, as they recognized the political and hierarchical status within and between the Indian tribes of La Florida, they were not always able to do so (Bushnell 1989; Deagan 1987). And while the *encomienda* (assignment of services and/or tributes) was not in practice in La Florida, the *repartimiento* (an obligatory labor service) took its toll on the Indians (e.g., exploited their labor; took them away from their homes, fields, and families for extended periods; was deemed humiliating as well as debilitating; e.g., Bushnell 1979, 1981).

Conversion and salvation of the Indian soul was the moral goal and justification for the hard labors expected of the Indians, who were to work the land and grow foodstuffs for the presidio, the friars, church goods, as well as themselves. Although the presidio, the pueblos, and missions were a part of the Indian acculturation, conversion was the strong force behind the former, while intermarriage was the mediating factor for Spanish acculturation (Deagan 1983:268). The immediate incorporation of native American foodstuffs into the Spanish diet and households abbetted the success of the first settlers and presumably the criollo population that followed (e.g., Deagan 1973, 1978, 1983). Missionaries were the major link between the Europeans and the Indians and it was essential for them to make accommodations to Indian foods and shelter if they were to survive (Hann n.d.).

Indian customs toward Spanish foodways are not well understood, although the initial acceptance and additive integration (Spicer 1961) of certain plant foods was rapid (e.g., Bartram 1958; Blake 1981; Reitz and Scarry 1985; Ruhl 1988a, n.d.; Sheldon 1978; Smith 1987; Swanton 1946). The rapid acceptance of certain European goods and not others raises a number of issues, for instance, availability and accessibility (i.e., did the Indians have equal access to all European goods or only those that were locally successful and/or that the Spanish chose to offer or make available?). Peaches and watermelon were found at interior sites before Spaniards ever reached the areas. Yet, access and subsequent acceptance and/or adaptation to preferred but limited goods has not yet been assessed. The friars' zeal for conversion and religious training and the proper goods (e.g., sacramental oils, wheat for hosts, grapes for sacramental wine; linen, wax, incense) and needs (e.g., horses or mules) for this training and conversion was omnipresent (Bushnell 1981, 1987; Hann 1988; Marrinan 1985). Eventually this would impinge upon the Indians' labor as they would be required to sow additional fields to purchase church goods. However, the Crown also wanted its share of the produce.

While the ideal ecclesiastical objective was conversion, with subsequent plans to support the missions, this was not the typical pattern expected by the mother country for its colonies in the New World: "Colonies are structured by those who rule them to benefit the mother country and its ruling classes. . . . They are, at least in part, organized economically to send out to others significant portions of their most valuable or profitable raw materials and products." (Macleod 1987:315). Because of its strategic position, La Florida was supported by the Crown (through the Mexican situado), even though its material benefits were less rewarding than its other possessions, such as the Peruvian silver mines at Potosi or its monocrop (e.g., sugarcane, wheat, grapes) plantation/haciendas of Central and South America. By the seventeenth century, Spain's internal affairs were in turmoil, which probably helped the colonies move toward agricultural self-sufficiency (e.g., in La Florida the colonists started cattle ranches and wheat farms, and experimented with hybrid corn).

Eventually, the fertile lands of north and northwest Florida offered enough goods for the missions and some food for the garrison in St. Augustine. Documentary evidence suggests that toward the second half of the seventeenth century missions were able to provide not only the New World crops that the Spanish and Indians relied upon as their staples, but possibly both Old and New World grains, which were economically valued and exploitable. Religious motivation played an important and ever-present hand in the manipulation of the southeastern Indians' way of life; yet, "it would appear that it was the essentially non-religiously-motivated elements of the missions and the larger administrative structure of which they were a part that most profoundly affected the southeastern Indians under their influence, and led to their ultimate disappearance" (Deagan 1987:1).

Forcing agricultural practices upon a preexisting sedentary agricultural, horticultural, or semisedentary horticultural group versus a more transhumant or semisedentary group of hunters-fisherfolk-gatherers is a difference of kind not of degree, which was met by rejection, admixture, and/or acceptance (e.g., Connor 1926; Deagan 1978; Hann 1988, 1990; Jones 1978; Larson 1978; Milanich 1978; Sweett 1938; Sweett and Sheppy 1940). The degree of "success" or persuasion was met with various responses, which in part have been associated with traditional Indian practices, personalities (e.g., see Bushnell's [1978] account of the Indian chief Don Patricia de Hinachuba), arable land, land rights, and the extant political, economic, and religious systems (e.g., Crook 1978; Deagan 1978, 1987; Hann 1988, 1989; Marquardt 1987; Milanich 1978; Swanton 1922, 1946; Widmer 1988).

Unfortunately, much of the research at mission sites is still in progress, so that my comments should be considered only preliminary. In addition, it has only been in the last few years that archaeobotanical studies have been undertaken at historic or prehistoric sites in the southeastern part of La Florida. Consequently, many of our hypotheses concerning prehistoric horticultural or agricultural practices are based on historical materials and indirect archaeological evidence (e.g., cob-marked pottery; see Borremans 1985; Crook 1978; Larson 1978, 1980; Milanich 1978; Milanich and Fairbanks 1980; Widmer 1988).

Before going any further, it is important to make two observations: (1) the sampling strategies (random excavations and planned research designs, soil sample size, screen size) and processing methods (mechanical or flotation) vary from one site to another; and (2) we need to define the terms "cultivation," "horticulture," and "agriculture." These terms are often used interchangeably and, yet, they differ in meaning or emphasis of degree and kind. Cultivation is the deliberate intervention by humans in a particular plant's breeding cycle, through acts such as tilling, harvesting, and the selection of seed or rootcrops for future planting. Agriculture and horticulture appear to be at opposite ends of a subsistence/cultivation continuum and, to a certain extent, are a matter of degree rather than kind, but if the various types of water harvesting methods are included, we have a difference of kind involving production and distribution, and ultimately affecting consumption. Farrington and Urry (1985) have suggested that *horticulture* is a small-scale garden with an array of plant crops, but only a few of each type are grown, whereas *agriculture* is a large-scale system in which one or a few plant crops are grown extensively in large quantities. Agriculture and the existence of a staple crop(s) are often interlinked; yet the differential preservation of archaeobotanical remains tends to complicate our understanding and interpretations of subsistence/cultivation systems. Although the emphasis in agriculture is on foodcrop/staples, animal husbandry may also be a part of the system (e.g., pig herding, cattle raising).

To consider, in part, culture change and/or continuity as reflected in the archaeobotanical record, we need to know what the practices were before as well as during the Mission period, and ideally even afterward in each of the different areas in question. Similarly, to assess the process of acculturation versus, for example, adaptation or accommodation, we must have available the various pieces to that puzzle (i.e., in this instance, both the Spanish as well as the Indian data). Archaeobotanically, this is really many years down the road and many hours of research away from where we stand at the present. Nevertheless, some direct data do exist that may shed some light on this avenue of research, and may generate more.

Spanish mission archaeology has been investigated on and off since the turn of the century; however, it has only been in the last 5 to 10 years that any serious attention has been given to the input and significance of paleoethnobotanical research. Overall, archaeological and ethnohistorical studies of Spanish missions have tended to examine Iberian material culture by working primarily in the Spanish domiciles, forts, and mission complexes. With this renewed interest in mission site archaeology and early contact studies, in the past few years attempts to understand culture change through adaptation, adoption, accommodation, acculturation, deculturation, and other mechanisms have begun to include the Native American populations that were affected by the change. At the same time, the archaeobotanical record also reflects the Spanish lifeways more than the aboriginal populations, as the majority of plant remains come from Spanish settlements. Consequently, I looked to the available prehistoric record to provide some insights to aboriginal subsistence/cultivation systems.

In the remainder of this paper we examine the role of cultivation, horticulture, and agriculture from prehistoric to Mission periods within the confines of the southeastern part of the Spanish Borderlands (i.e., coastal Georgia and westward toward Florida's panhandle). The objective is to evaluate whether European agricultural innovations had an effect on the preexisting aboriginal subsistence/cultivation economy and overall plant utilization. Some of the underlying questions include: (1) What do we know about Indian plant use and practice during the Mission period? (2) What paleoethnobotanical data exist for Spanish missions in La Florida? and (3) What were the effects of the Spaniards upon the missionized Indians (i.e., can we glean some partial insights about the processes of culture change from the archaeobotanical remains)?

Indian and Spanish Subsistence/Cultivation and Plant Use

Maize, beans, and squash have been reported as the staple foodstuffs of the Southeastern Indians for decades; yet this triad is far from the total inventory of plants utilized by prehistoric and historic populations. Limited archaeological information exists concerning Indian plant use and practices (e.g., horticulture) during the protohistoric and the subsequent Mission period (e.g., Alexander 1984; Deagan 1973; Hally 1981; Hann 1986a, 1986b, 1988; Hudson 1979; Larson 1980; Newsom 1986, 1987; Reitz and Scarry 1985; Ruhl 1988a, 1988b, 1989, n.d.; Scarry 1984, 1985a, 1985b, 1986, 1987, 1988). Some accounts suggest the types of foodstuffs that were used, but few offer us useful information concerning other plant uses (e.g., dyes, medicines, clothes, buildings, implements; see Hariot 1971; Speck 1909; Swanton 1922, 1946; Ulmer and Beck 1951) or the techniques for producing the types and quantities of foods shared, taken, or demanded by the first explorers and later settlers (e.g., Cabeza de Vaca 1871; Dickenson 1975; Fontaneda 1945; Laudonnière 1975; Ranjel 1922; Ribaut 1964; Rogel in Larson 1980). As the subtitle to this section suggests, two basic topics of plant exploitation are considered here—a survey of the prehistoric and historic evidence for subsistence/cultivation strategy in the primary territories affected by the Spaniards: Guale (coastal Georgia), eastern and western Timucua (east, central, and north-central Florida), and Apalachee (north and northwest Florida), as well as a few other missions to the south of these regions (i.e., the Jororo and Calusa). When possible, the available data on plants other than corn, beans, and squash, and their uses will be included. An underlying objective here is to determine whether the impact was a matter of degree or of kind and, if so, its effects upon understanding better some of the processes of culture change in these regions.

Coastal Georgia

Guale. Direct horticultural evidence for coastal Georgia is slim, and although it has received lip service for many years as well as being the basis for hypotheses for and against its significance (Crook 1978; Larson 1978, 1980; Reitz 1988; Smith et al. 1981; Walker 1985; Wallace 1975), there are relatively few analyses of systematically collected and analyzed plant remains for this area (Ruhl 1987, 1988b, 1989, n.d.; Scarry 1984, 1985a, 1985b).

Indirect evidence for prehistoric maize cultivation comes from bioanthropological analyses of skeletal remains. Populations dating from the twelfth century A.D. reflect maize in the diet, followed by an apparent increase in sedentism (Larsen 1987:5; Larsen et al., this volume). Also, morphological changes on the bone tend to reflect a change in life-styles from hunters-fisherfolk-gatherers to cultivators through time (Larsen 1987; Larsen and Saunders 1987; Larsen et al. this volume). Nitrogen analyses of pre- and postcontact groups indicate an increase in maize after contact, which is collaborated, in part, by the large amount of cobs, cupules, and kernels recovered from late seventeenth-century Guale mission sites on St. Catherines and Amelia islands (Ruhl 1989).

Even though there are virtually no corn, beans, squash, or other cultigens for either prehistoric or protohistoric sites (see the many column samples from the Kings Bay Project; e.g., DesJean 1985:147, 150, 194; Saunders 1985:121–122; 164–165; Walker 1985:254), the early historic accounts and documents indicate a surplus (of corn and other goods), which was shared with the French and Spaniards. In addition, depictions and accounts of granaries suggest that the preservability and storage of maize reflect sedentary communities practicing an intensive form of subsistence cultivation.

Two notions concerning historic Guale settlement patterns and horticultural practices and their significance have been deduced from the available archaeological data and historical materials (see Jones 1978:179, 187–194; Larson 1980:206–209; Thomas, this volume). In both Larson's (1980) and Jones's (1978) scenarios, the presence of corn alone is not the problem; the importance of corn and other plants in the diet of the coastal Guale is. Further, when the shift(s) is from corn holding a lesser or different economic status (e.g., supplement, religious) to a greater one (e.g., food staple, fuel, fodder, ceremonial, commercial), it is significant. Larson's bioanthropological data would indicate that the agrarian practices had been around for a few centuries by the time of European contact and that the early stages of incipient horticulture on the coast were more problematic than they were after contact. This latter transition was more a matter of degree than of kind and is said to have been stimulated by the onset of new technologies and worldviews (e.g. hatchets to assist in felling forests and clearing fields more rapidly; metal hoes to prepare the land; new hybrid seed stock from elsewhere in the New World and possibly La Florida; fertilizer(s)?; irrigation strategies; monocropping; arboriculture-orchards; work ethics, religious zeal).

Archaeologically, Larson (1953, 1980) has recovered some corncobs and cupules along with some possible beans in a coastal midden at Pine Harbor. Associated with these finds was an assemblage consisting of chenopod, poke, persimmon, grape, and cherry that suggested to Yarnell and Larson that local cultivation did occur. They further concluded that these plant remains reflect weed and common pioneer communities typical of abandoned or old fallow fields (1980:206). I wonder if it might reflect intentionally sown or non-manipulated plants, once they appeared.

Each of the above has some type of economic value (e.g., as foodstuffs, dyes, cordage), even if they are traditionally considered "weeds" in our contemporary folk nomenclature. Is it feasible to conjecture that these other plant remains—and not only the corn and possible beans—were planted or allowed to grow in the field together? Our conception of corn fields is usually one of large expanses of land with a single plant type—the monocrop syndrome. Hariot (1588) has described not only the volume of goods produced, but also the diversity of plants (all of which are grown in a single field). Maize (*pagatowr*), beans (*okindgier*), and squash (*macocqwer*) were growing; but also, melons, gourds (*macocqwer*), peas/beans (*wickonzowr*) herbs (e.g., *melden*), spices (e.g., *orach*— a salt–producing plant), and marigold/sunflower (*planta solis*), and tobacco (*uppowoc*), which were apparently grown side by side. "All the commodities I have described are planted sometime separately, but more often mixed together in one plot" (Hariot in Lorant 1946:244).

Plant cultivation in the Guale area and further north was most intensive in the coastal region, yet the cultivators were small, widely dispersed family units (Larson 1980:218). Early Jesuit accounts indicate that the Guale had little interest in growing corn, even when hoes and grains were provided (e.g., Jones 1978; Lyon 1984; Rogel in Larson 1978:123; 1980:206–209). Also, they were not as tractable as the missionaries had thought or hoped, which may reflect semi-sedentary hunters-fisherfolk-gatherers along with a horticultural base of subsistence.

Attempts at Santa Elena to grow European and Indian cultigens were accomplished (Gardner 1980, 1981; Lyon 1984; Reitz and Scarry 1985; Scarry 1983, 1984; Scarry and Retiz, this volume; South et al. 1988). The sixteenth-century town settlements established primarily for garrisons and millitary strongholds are not directly comparable to seventeenth-century missions. Although similar practices and customs may have been enforced, the labor source, goals, and objectives were not the same.

The role of the friars in the seventeenth century, compounded by disease and the depopulation that this created in Guale sociopolitical organization, cannot be minimized in our attempts to understand the subsequent shift that occurred in maize cultivation along the Georgia coast. We have documentary materials from the seventeenth century (and archaeobotanical data) referring to agricultural endeavors along the Guale coast. By this time, many diseases and influenzas had attacked the various coastal and mainland survivors (e.g., Hann 1987).

Apparently these farmers are the ones who worked the lands and produced the bounty that was so valued in St. Augustine. In particular, Santa Catalina de Guale on St. Catherines was deemed the "bread basket," and the Governor of St. Augustine in the late 1600s wanted the Guale, then on Amelia Island, to return to St. Catherines to produce grain for the coffers (Bushnell 1981, 1986, 1987; Hann 1986c, 1987, n.d.).

Both Dunlop (1929) and Dickenson (1975) describe extensive fields on St. Catherines Island during their travels along the Georgia coast. Dickenson (1975:70) notes, "We got to the place called St. Catelena, where hath been a great settlement of Indians, for the land hath been cleared for planting, for some miles distant." Archaeobotanically we are beginning to see the probable produce from these fields and gardens. Corn (*Zea mays*), wheat (*Triticum* sp.), squash (*Cucurbita pepo*), watermelon (*Citrullus vulgaris*), gourd (*Lagenaria vulgaris*), beans (*Phaseolus vulgaris*), peas (*Pisum sativum*), and cantaloupe (*Cucumis melo*) are being recovered from both dry and wet (well) components dating to the seventeenth century (Ruhl 1988b, 1989, n.d.). Other plant remains include a number of wild nut and fruit tree remains: hazelnut (*Corylus* sp.), acorns (*Quercus virginiana, Quercus alba, Quercus* sp.), hickory (*Carya* sp.), walnut (*Juglans* sp.), persimmon (*Diosperus virginiana*), plum/cherry (*Prunus* sp.), as well as the domesticated peach (*Prunus persica*) and numerous commensals (e.g., species of the grass family (Poaceae), bean family (Fabaceae), knotweed family (Polygonaceae), amaranth (pigweed, *Amaranthus* sp.), and goosefoot (Chenopodium sp.)

Although the data are sketchy, it appears that there were at least two, if not more, shifts or phases in the subsistence/cultivation continuums along the Georgia coast, from incipient horticulture to intensive agriculture. With the preexisting horticulturists in place by contact, the next shift was a matter of degree and not kind, and this directed agrarian cultural change was possibly more a matter of substitution and/or addition than replacement.

East and Central Florida (Eastern Timucua and Jororo)

Eastern Timucua. Moving further south along Florida's coast and inland waterways, cultivation was deemed most important around the lower regions of the St. Johns river. Yet, it was never really of primary importance to the diet (Deagan 1978; Larson 1980:218; Russo 1988). Larson (1980:209) has suggested that, like the Guale to the north, the Timucua, who did have corn in their villages, "practiced shifting agriculture." Apparently, subsistence patterns changed little from early contact to as late as 1728, as documents still indicated that the Indians were semihorticulturists leaving for the forests whenever they desired (Deagan 1978:113; see also Reitz and Scarry 1985; Scarry and Reitz, this volume). Archaeological data indicate the presence of cultigens at some early sites as well as the introduction of European hoes and agrarian practices. Even though all of the friars encouraged intensive agriculture, they did not seem to have been as effective as in Guale, western Timucua, and Apalachee.

Mestizaje, infertile soils, the situado, disease, and the repartimiento may have had an effect on horticultural practices here (e.g., Deagan 1973, 1983). Close contact with the Spaniards increased the chances of disease, and the Timucua succumbed to many of the plagues and other European diseases (e.g., Connor 1926; Deagan 1978; Dobyns 1983; Hann 1988; n.d.), as a result of which the remaining Indians experienced cultural changes. Spanish recognition of the poor soils and the Spaniards' proximity to incoming supplies, albeit variable (as Bushnell has noted, the supply of goods was not as critical as was the distribution) may have played a role in the accessibility of food and other supplies. This might have increased the need for more intensive cultivation by the resident Timucua groups. Their labor, however, may have been considered more valuable at the presidio as evidenced in the later documents, which note that the repartimiento spread into the western part of La Florida as coastal Indians became exhausted (e.g., Bushnell 1979, 1981; Hann 1988).

At best, our archaeobotanical and historical data indicate limited horticultural subsistence in prehistoric times, which was probably related to the poor soils and climatic conditions in this region (e.g., Fitzhugh 1985). Confronted with environmental obstacles, and stifled by political and military strategies, innovations met with limited success (agrarian practices were apparently a secondary consideration). The directed change imposed here was of a different nature, as many of these Indians changed from being the primary producers to the recipients and consumers.

Jororo. An attempt was made to convert the Indians and introduce agrarian practices in the areas to the south of St. Augustine intermittently over the centuries of Spanish intervention. As late as the 1690s, missions were being built in the areas of the lower and middle regions of the St. Johns. Groups living in these areas are thought to have been hunters-fisherfolk-gatherers and nonhorticulturists (e.g., Larson 1980; Russo 1988). Although research is under way in this area, Newsom's excellent analysis of two column samples from Hontoon Island is virtually our only empirical data base for the St. Johns. Her archaeobotanical research in this multicomponented wet site indicates that prehistoric populations were intensively gathering from the aquatic environment (i.e., cabbage palm [*Sabal palmetto*], amaranth [*Amaranthus* sp.], Amaranthaceae, bristlegrass [*Setaria* sp.], nut sedge [*Cyperus* sp.], huckleberry [*Gaylussacia* sp.], blueberry [*Vaccinium* sp.], pokeweed [*Phytolacca americana*], Chenopodiaceae, groundcherry [*Physalis* sp.], and elderberry [*Sambucus canadensis*]; see Newsom 1986:52–54 for a complete botanical inventory). Although both bottlegourds (*Lagenaria siceraria*) and squash (*Cucurbita pepo*) were present in the earlier levels, this does not necessarily reflect intentional cultivation, as these species can occur as camp followers without tending.

Only within the historic levels of the column samples have cultigens (corn and squash) been recovered, which Newsom suggests may have been introduced by the Spanish at Hontoon or the Mt. Royal site (European artifacts and corn have been recovered from this site on the west bank across from Hontoon Island (Jones in Newsom 1987:79). These latter two sites are thought to be the Mission of San Salvadore de Mayaca (Newsom 1986:18–22; see also Connor 1926; Hann 1989; Mexía 1951 [1602]; Mitchem 1989; Newsom 1987; Solís de Merás 1964;

Sweett 1938; Sweett and Sheppy 1940). Apparently, in this area neither the early ethnographic accounts nor the archaeobotanical data suggest the possibility of horticulture in prehistoric or protohistoric times. The migration of Spaniards and/or southward moving Indians, ideas (agricultural techniques), and goods (e.g., hoes, cultigens) is conceivably the basis for the shift from an emphasis on aquatic/wetlands species to terrestrial species, both cultigens and an intensity of wild species, during the historic period.

Recent work along the St. Johns has produced preliminary evidence of another Mission period site. To date it has produced small fragments of acorns and corn in the phase 1 testing excavations (M. Russo, personal communication, 1989). Apparently, mission attempts south of St. Augustine in the last decade of the seventeenth century were prompted by English and aboriginal encroachment to the north (Connor 1926; Hann 1989; Sweett and Sheppy 1940). Requests for hoes and axes by these friars were filled promptly and generously by the Crown, perhaps in an effort to establish more strategic locations along its southern extent and thus maintain its hegemony. It may be that the semisedentary hunters-fisherfolk-gatherers rebelled (1696) not only because of the Crown's attempt to convert them and introduce Spanish customs, but, also, because of its attempts to turn them into agriculturists.

Southeast (Tequesta) and Southwest (Calusa) Florida

Along Florida's more southerly reaches only two systematically collected, floated, and analyzed archaeobotanical samples (primarily prehistoric sites—1 southeast and 6 southwest) are available (Scarry 1985; Scarry and Newsom 1989). The assemblages reflect nonhorticultural communities that exhibited a fruit-procurement strategy including cabbage palm (*Sabal palmetto*), cocoplum (*Chrysobalanus icaco*), mastic (*Mastichodendron foetidissimum*), saw palmetto (*Serenoa repens*), sea grape (*Cocoloba* sp.), and hogplum (*Ximenia americana*).

Early Spanish chroniclers and later missionaries (e.g., 1566–1569, 1697) to these areas indicated that these groups were nonhorticultural. Some controversy has ensued over the past few years concerning this point among the Calusa and prehistoric groups around the Okeechobee Basin on the basis of various types of indirect evidence (e.g., population size, sedentism, levels of sociopolitical complexity, corn pollen, wooden mortars and pestles; see Dobyns 1983; Fontaneda 1945; Goggin and Sturtevant 1964; Hann 1990; Marquardt 1987; McGoun 1989; Milanich 1987; Sears 1982; Scarry and Newsom 1989). The omission of maize from early reports would tend to support the nonhorticulture faction; however, the intensive use of root crop(s) (e.g., coontie- *Zamia* sp.) cannot be overlooked (Ruhl 1985; Scarry and Newsom 1989). Even though there are ethnohistorical hints that a bread was made from roots (e.g., Connor 1925:60; Fontaneda 1945:27–28), its absence from the archaeobotanical record, collected in traditional fashion, should not be surprising in this subtropical environment where preservation is limited. Although a shift from a fruit procurement strategy and, possibly, even an intensive root-harvesting strategy was a matter of kind compared to an agricultural strategy, missionary attempts in these areas failed, in part, because of the location and terrain as much as the power and cunning of its people.

North and North Central Florida

Western Timucua. Here, too, there is little direct archaeological (historic or pre-historic) evidence for cultivation, even though this is a more diverse region both edaphically and environmentally than the pine flatwoods of the coast. Both wet-land and terrestrial habitats can be found in this region, including areas that are suitable for agrarian pursuits. Direct archaeobotanical data from prehistoric sites are meager. Cumbaa (1975) has suggested an intensive harvest in this re-gion during the first few centuries A.D. on the basis of the botanical inventory of hickory (*Carya tomentosa*), acorns (*Quercus* sp.), pine cones (*Pinus elliottii*), cherry laurel (*Prunus caroliniana*), and legumes (Leguminosae-wild or cultigen not determined). Hickory, oak, and palm berries (*Sabal palmetto*) have been re-covered from later (Alachua tradition) sites; while the corn evidence is indirect (e.g., cob-marked ceramics, increased village size, hoes, grinding tools; Milanich 1971, 1978; Milanich and Fairbanks 1980). Although the prehistoric evidence for this region is slim, we have its onset centuries before European introductions.

Using measurements from cob-marked pottery fragments, Kohler (1979a, 1979b) observed an apparent increase in kernel thickness between A.D. 700 and A.D. 1600. Apparently, the precontact measurements suggest a slower rate of change than exhibited in the postcontact materials analyzed (Kohler 1979a:4). If this supposition is correct, the rate of change suggested may reflect: (1) an intensification of an already existing crop, which was advanced by technological innovations and was accompanied by political, social, and economic change; and (2) introduced varieties of maize (Kohler 1979a:5; Lyon 1984). Milanich (1978:81) has hypothesized that the short-term occupation at a few mission and mission-related sites in this region may have been a response to the intensive horticultural practices imposed, which depleted the soils and forced relocation.

Data from sites with Spanish and Indian components consist of a handful of sites in north central Florida. Remains from the Indian village areas of two sites (Richardson—possibly the Francisco de Potano visita and the Zetrouer site) con-tained charred corn and indicated short-term occupations (see also Fox Pond, possible mission of San Francisco de Potano; Symes and Stephens 1965). Charred kernels of corn were recovered from Richardson (Milanich 1972) and may suggest storage of a partly processed foodstuff, while the 50 or so corncobs recovered from two small concentrations at Zetrouer (Seaberg 1955:14) appear to have represented a secondary use of this plant (e.g., as fuel, for insect control (smudge pit?). Overexploitation of the soils, coupled with competition for land (cattle ranches were begun in this region to supply St. Augustine with meat and cattle by-products around the middle of the seventeenth century), may have been significant factors in aboriginal movements. At the Baptizing Spring site, however, Loucks (1979) excavated some Spanish and Indian structures. Archaeobotanical data were recovered only from the Indian buildings. These consisted of both Old and New World species of wild and domesticated plants (i.e., corncobs, a possible pea (*Pisum* sp.?), peach (*Prunus persica*), and hickory). The absence of any plant remains from Spanish structures was thought to reflect differences in Spanish and Indian discard patterns. It may also reflect the extent of the Spanish occupation, the function, and use(s) of the living space. The limited direct evidence for Spanish influence at this site vis-à-vis the plant inventory suggested to Loucks that the Spaniards may not have attempted to change the cultivation strategy of the Indians, as they had at other missions.

Some further questions that arise here are What was the nature of this "mission"? Who was processing and preparing the foodstuffs? Does the combination of plant goods reflect rare and/or cherished commodities or abundant and/or utilitarian goods? For example, the presence of hickory nuts may indicate that the Spaniards only saw the by-products and thus the Indians are the presumed laborers who prepared foodstuffs as well as its gatherers.

Discard patterns may relate to the type of foodstuff, availability, and size or quantity of item in question. For instance, hickory shells, like peach stones, are or tend to be ubiquitous at sites, presumably because of their accessibility, abundant use, and preservability. The former tend to be found in hearths and pits in concentration. Peaches, however, are often single deposits, which seem to suggest a random versus a restricted discard pattern. Caches of materials, on the other hand, may indicate intentional storing of seeds for planting or for preserving goods, as in the case of the 3,200 persimmon pits from one structure (Chapman and Shea 1981) and the bushel or more of seeds from Fig Springs (Deagan 1972). If so, this may be an indication of prehistoric arboricultural practices.

Orchard growing is presumably a practice introduced from the Old World, yet the practice of trees being grown intentionally may have occurred in Precolumbian times (e.g., Ford 1985). There is some evidence that the Indians practiced some form of arboriculture and/or silviculture (cf. Bourne 1922; Cowan 1985; Watson 1988). If that is the case, the presence of peaches at an Indian dwelling and site may reflect not only the rapid integration (Spicer 1961) of the fruit, but also that the planting of a tree, which takes years to reach maturity, is a substitutive process (e.g., Smith 1987:123–126; White 1975:159–160). Arboriculture versus annual cropping may be seen as a difference of kind rather than of degree.

From 1949 to 1952 John Goggin collected materials from the springs near the head of the Itchetucknee River, which were then thought to be the site of the Santa Catalina de Afuerica Mission (Deagan 1972). Plant remains along with thousands of other Indian and Spanish artifacts were recovered. The charred corncobs, hickory nuts, and gourd fragments along with hundreds of uncharred peach stones that were retrieved suggest local agricultural endeavors (e.g., peach orchards, annual cropping of corn, and possibly squash cultivation as well as the gathering of wild nuts). An iron hoe also lends some support to this picture of agriculturists in north-central Florida.

Recent documentary research has indicated that the Fig Springs site is actually the mission of San Martín, one of the earliest missions in western Timucua, which dates to the early seventeenth century (Hann 1989). Recent excavations at this site (Weisman 1988, 1989) have unearthed wild and domesticated plant species as well as Old and New World species such as palm berries, hickory nuts, corn, and peaches from a closed context feature in the village area (Lee Newsom, personal communication). As the earlier unprovenienced finds have indicated, there is evidence of the gathering of wild fruits and nuts along with a subsistence strategy of cropping and the raising of fruit trees.

Northwest Florida (Apalachee)

De Soto chroniclers and subsequent mission accounts refer to maize and other plants from Cale to the Santa Fe, but it is in the province of Apalachee that densely populated areas and horticultural productivity abound (e.g., Bourne 1922:82; Wenhold 1936). It is in this northern region, as well, that more prehistoric sites are known with vegetal remains, especially corn, than in the other areas.

Weeden Island. Along the Apalachicola and Chattahoochee River drainages some of the earliest evidence of corn and other vegetable remains (wild fruits [*Prunus americana*] and nuts [walnut, hickory, and acorn]) were recovered from the Sycamore site, a ninth-century Weeden Island household. Milanich (1974:32) suggested that these people were hunters, fisherfolk, and gatherers as well as horticulturists occupying the ravines around the Apalachicola River, who also apparently cultivated their crop(s) to the north where the land was flat and fertile.

Fort Walton. By this period (circa A.D. 1000–1550) corn is seemingly commonplace, as evidenced by the increased number of charred corncobs and kernels in the archaeobotanical record (13 sites; see Alexander 1984:2, 3, Table 1). However, there is also evidence for supplemental plant gathering (e.g., acorns, hickory, persimmon, maypop) at Fort Walton sites (Alexander 1984:2–3, 8, 12, 16), as there was to the east in the north central region. Data from this pivotal time tend to suggest a transition in the degree to which horitculture and gathering play a role in the overall subsistence economy, with the increasing presence of corn (e.g., Alexander 1984).

At a site (J5 or 8Ja8) 7 km north of the Curlee site (White 1982) on the Apalachicola River, Bullen (1958:344, 349–350) recovered corn from what he suggested was a ceremonial context. Recent research has indicated that the onset and development of corn may have had a religious and ideological foundation in the Southeast (see Johannessen 1988; Scarry 1989). A large corn mass from Structure 1, Mound 3, at the Lake Jackson site was found in the center of the premound floor and may also reflect ceremonial activities (Alexander 1984:17; Jones 1982:9).

Alexander's (1984) work at three Fort Walton sites (High Ridge, Lake Jackson, and Velda) has increased the species list for utilized plants. Two additional cultigens (bean [*Phaseolus vulgaris*] and sunflower [*Helianthus annuus*]) were recovered through the use of flotation techniques. Persimmon, acorn, and hickory were also recovered along with other noncultigens (chinquapin [*Castanea* sp.], maypop [*Passiflora incarnata*], saw palmetto [*Serenoa repens*], cabbage palm [*Sabal palmetto*], plum/cherry [*Prunus* sp.], and the bean family [*Fabaceae*]). What is of interest at these three Ft. Walton sites is the percentage of corn by weight in relation to the other species present, especially acorn and hickory. Between 55 and 98 percent of the plant species recovered consisted of corn at all three Fort Walton sites. Although comparability is tenuous because of the variability in recovery strategies, contexts, and so on, these percentages suggest a relative shift from hunting-fishing-gathering groups of earlier times, where hickory and acorn dominate our samples, to the later period, where corn increases. In addition to the dietary cultigens (corn, bean, sunflower, and presumably squash), the Apalachees' ancestors cultivated tobacco (e.g., Hann 1988:127) in prehistoric times.

Apalachee. Both Hann's (1988:126–159) seminal work on the Apalachee and Larson's (1980:210–220) research on aboriginal subsistence have served to integrate the historical materials and archaeological data from this region. Hann (1988:126) has noted that the Apalachee were "a sedentary people, depending primarily on agriculture for their food supply but also relying on fish, game, and wild fruit and nuts to supplement what they grew" when the Spaniards first entered Apalachee (see also Milanich and Fairbanks 1980:227–231). In contrast to the coastal peoples, who were less sedentary, the accommodations made by the Apalachee in regard to agricultural pursuits were seemingly not much different. They were already tilling the land intensively and were centrally based; their land was fertile and crops productive. The European effort to introduce plants, animals, and metal hoes (iron mattocklike instruments) was still being met with varying degrees of acceptance. For instance, cattle ranches seemed to be a major disruption in the balancing of powers (Bushnell 1979) between Spaniard and Indian as it affected aboriginal land use.

Most of the archaeobotanical data for the Apalachee missions come from three sites: (1) the church at the Pine Tuft sites—possibly San Juan de Aspalaga (8Je1); (2) the church at the Scott Miller site—possibly San Francisco de Oconee or Nuestra Senora de le Purissima (8Je2); (3) and San Luis de Talamali (8Le4), in particular, the council house (Hann 1988, Jones 1972; Morrell and Jones 1970; Scarry 1986; Shapiro 1985, 1987a, 1987b; Shapiro and Hann, this volume; Shapiro and Vernon 1989; Smith 1951). These sites contained grains, seeds, and fruit stones that indicate the storage of whole or processed plants; cobs used as smudge pits; and seeds indicative of ceremonial uses, rather than the more typical assemblages from refuse deposits that reflect the by-products of food preparation.

Archaeobotanically, there is evidence for Old World domesticates (watermelon [*Citrullus vulgaris*], peach [*Prunus persica*], hazelnut [*Corylus avellana*], and wheat [*Triticum* sp.]) from Apalachee mission sites along with New World cultigens (corn, beans, squash [*Cucurbita pepo, Cuccurbita* sp.-rind, peduncles, and seeds], and sunflower). The wild taxa include such supplemental foods as hickory and oak; wild fruits include maypop, persimmon, cabbage palm, and bramble (*Rubus* sp.), and a handful of commensals have been identified, as well as a few seeds of the yaupon (*Ilex vomitoria*) (Scarry 1986, 1987, 1988).

Religious and/or ceremonial uses of plants may be hypothesized for the Spaniards as well as the Indians. Although wheat grains may have been stored for seed stock, it is also reasonable to hypothesize that it was stored for use in the manufacturing of the Holy Eucharist (host) in the Catholic ritual of communion. It is probable that this crop played a sacred and secular role in the Spaniards and missionized Indians' customs. However, the Indians did not seem to prefer this as a staple, but rather grew it for alms for the missionaries and to feed it to their elderly (Bushnell 1979). The growing and use of this crop tends to reflect the accommodations, adaptations, and beginning stages of acculturation in food and other customs that were being exchanged between the missionaries and their converts.

The Indian use of yaupon leaves to make the famed black drink is known throughout the southeast (Hudson 1979). The presence of its seeds from the council house floor at San Luis suggests its probable ceremonial use. Yet the presence of Old World cultigens (watermelon and wheat) on the council house floor reflect possible Indian accommodations/adaptations in this traditional setting. Seeds from these three species also indicate the possibility of special processing and/or preparation within the council house, and thus suggest that different types of activities and/or rituals occurred therein (Scarry 1988).

Historical documents offer descriptions of plants being used for other beverages besides the black drink (*tolocano*, which included dried blueberries, persimmons, ground nuts, and corn; hickory milk); for vegetable oils (acorn and hickory), along with animal fats (hogs and cattle) that presumably replaced the labor-intensive vegetable oils, although native bear oil has been recorded by later chroniclers and naturalists); starchy roots (e.g., ache, pinoco, and zebaca); medicinal herbs (itamo and chitabexatica-used to heal wounds; *muy cordial*—a blackberry tonic or syrup; and other oils and extracts from an array of plants (Hann 1986a:91–102, 1988:126–159; Larson 1980:209–220; Leturiondo in Hann (1986b) [1700]:196–203).

Information concerning Indian preparation of the land, the implements and techniques employed, and laborers utilized is scanty. In one seventeenth-century document, Bishop Calderón speaks of a slash-and-burn technique being employed by the Apalachee: "During January they burn the grass and weeds from the fields preparatory to cultivation" (Calderón 1675 in Wenhold 1936:13). It appears that the fields in question were left fallow from the previous season(s) as the vegetation burned ("grass and weeds" and not trees and shrubs) signals the seral stages of secondary succession (Clewell 1980). Intentional burning may have been for fertilizing as well as clearing the fields.

Spellman (1948) suggested that digging sticks and hoelike devices of wood and shell were used to work the land. Communal practices for the plowing and sowing of the fields are suggested for the aboriginal populations during the Mission period. Accounts of males being away from the missions to partake in the obligatory repartimiento imposed by the Crown for work to, from, and at the presidio in St. Augustine as well as independent work at the increasing number of ranches, suggest that the burden may have fallen more heavily upon the remaining Indians at the reduced mission (women, children, and the elderly). "All in common cultivate and sow the lands of the cacique. As alms for the missionaries and the needy widows, they sow wheat in October and harvest it in June. This is a crop of excellent quality in the province of Apalachee, and so abundant that it produces seventy fanegas from one fenega sown" (Calderón 1675 in Wenhold 1936:13).

Archaeobotanically, this latter Old World crop is beginning to appear in greater quantities in the seventeenth-century record than in sixteenth century remains. Wheat grains have been identified from coastal and interior sites (San Luis, 8Je1; 8Je2; Santa Catalina de Guale on Amelia Island, Florida and Santa Catalina de Guale on St. Catherines Island, Georgia). This may reflect the relative success of the wheat farms and the cattle ranches, as wheat cropping usually requires careful manuring (Braudel 1981). These ventures were begun in the mid-1600s and continued in subsequent decades (e.g., Bushnell 1978, 1981; Hann 1988; Rebolledo 1657; Ross 1975). Botanically, however, corn was the mainstay here, as elsewhere in the northern reaches of La Florida.

Variability in kernel shape and attributes of cobs provide clues to the varietal differences in corn (Nickerson 1953). Corn kernels, cupules, and cobs recovered from Apalachee sites suggest that there may be introduced cultivars present or a hybrid between a local and nonlocal cultivar (Scarry 1986:6, 1988:10, 24). Presumably such hybrids were used by both Spaniards and Indians, but not necessarily in the same way (e.g., Hann 1988:127; Scarry 1988). Nevertheless, the majority of corn remains found here, as at other mission sites, is Northern Flint (eastern 8–10 row maize), which is a reliable variety in these regions.

Summary

To date the archaeobotanical data from Spanish mission sites have generated information on Old World cultigens, New World cultigens (both local and exotic), indigenous wild fruits and nuts, and commensals. Preliminary comparisons suggest that the diets of the sixteenth-century settlers and military and that of the friars were similar, although documents indicate that they were often without traditional sumptuary supplies. Aboriginal diets suggest a variety of subsistence/cultivation systems with different levels of emphasis on hunting, fishing, gathering, and/or cultivating the land (horticultural and/or agricultural practices).

Comparisons between the coastal Guale, eastern and western Timucua, and interior Apalachee populations prior to contact and during the Spanish mission efforts in the southeastern Spanish Borderlands indicates that we are just beginning to understand the complexity of the economic changes that occurred within and between these populations.

Hypotheses involving the Spanish impact on aboriginal subsistence strategies, land use practices, the indigenous vegetation, and other forms of plant utilization are only beginning to emerge from the archaeobotanical data base. Through analysis of the prehistoric and historic archaeobotanical record, we have a way

Table 35-1. Hypothesized Impact of Spanish Agricultural Practices upon Aboriginal Subsistence Strategies in the Lower Southeast

Geographical Regions and Tribal Areas in the Lower Southeast	Condition of Mobility[a]			Subsistence Strategies[b]						Hypothesized Levels of Integration[c]
	N	SS	S	H-F-G	I-C	S-H	H	A	AA	
East and Central—Jororo	X—X			X	S?					Kind
E. Timucua	X			S		X—?—X				Degree— ?
Coastal Georgia—Guale	X			S		X—?—X				Degree
Southeast—Tequesta	X			X		S?	(root crop?)			Kind
Southwest—Calusa		X		X		S?	(corn/root crop?)			Kind
North and North-Central—W. Timucua	X—X			S			X?			Degree
Northwest—Apalachee		X		S				X		Degree
Spain		X		S					X	Degree

[a]Condition of mobility: nomadic (N); semisedentary (SS); and sedentary (S). Presumed type at time of contact.
[b]Subsistence Strategy: hunters-fisherfolk-gatherers (H–F–G); incipient horticulturists (IC); semihorticulturists (S-H); horticulturists (H); agriculturists (A); agriculturists—plants and animals (AA). S (supplemental) and X (primary) refer to the emphasis on each type of subsistence strategy.
[c]The hypothesized level or type of impact is considered in differences of degree and of kind.

(albeit limited) to observe the reactions, accommodations, and adaptations to European agrarian introductions. It appears that those groups who exhibited a cultivation/subsistence economy before missionization (e.g., Apalachee) may have been more receptive, whereas those populations whose archaeobotanical and historical record reflected a limited cultivation strategy or who were nonhorticulturist (e.g., Jororo), would be far less likely to readily accept an agricultural strategy. These differences were probably ones of degree and of kind, respectively, with various levels or gradations within the subsistence/cultivation system (Table 35-1).

References

Alexander, M.
  1984 Analysis of Plant Materials from Three Fort Walton Sites: High Ridge, Velda, and Lake Jackson. Paper presented at the 41st Annual Meeting of the Southeastern Archaeological Conference, Pensacola, Florida.
Bartram, W.
  1958 *The Travels of William Bartram*, edited by F. Harper. Yale University Press, New Haven.
Blake, L.
  1981 Early Acceptance of Watermelon by Indians of the United States. *Journal of Ethnobiology* 1(2):193–199.
Borremans, N.
  1985 Archaeology of the Devil's Walkingstick Site: A Diachronic Perspective of Aboriginal Life on a Tidal River in Southeast Georgia. Unpublished Master's thesis, Department of Anthropology, University of Florida, Gainesville, Florida.
Bourne, G.
  1922 *Narratives of the Career of Hernando de Soto*, Vol. 1. Allerton, New York.

Boyd, M., H. G. Smith, and J. Griffin
  1951   *Here They Once Stood*. University of Florida Press, Gainesville.
Braudel, F.
  1981   *The Structures of Everyday Life: Civilization and Capitalism 15th-18th Century*, Vol. 1. Harper and Row, New York.
Bullen, R.
  1958   Six Sites Near the Chattahoochee River in the Jim Woodruff Reservoir Area. In *Florida River Basin Surveys Papers* No. 14, edited by F. Roberts, pp. 316–358. Bureau of American Ethnology Bulletin 169. Smithsonian Institution, Washington D.C.
Bushnell, A.
  1978   The Menendez Marquez Cattle Barony at La Chua and the Determinants of Economic Expansion in Seventeenth-Century Florida. *Florida Historical Quarterly* 55(4):407–431.
  1979   Patricia de Hinachuba: Defender of the King and the Little Children of Ivitachuco. *American Indian Culture and Research Journal* 3:1–21.
  1981   *The King's Coffer*. University Press of Florida, Gainesville.
  1986   *Santa Maria in the Written Record*. Miscellaneous Project Report Series No. 21. Florida State Museum, Department of Anthropology.
  1987   The Supplies for the Sacraments. Ms. on file at the American Museum of Natural History, Department of Anthropology, New York.
Cabeza de Vaca, A.
  1871   *Relation of Álvar Núñez Cabeza de Vaca*. B. Smith, translator. J. Munsell, New York.
Chapman, J., and A. Shea
  1981   The Archaeobotanical Record: Early Archaic Period to Contact in the Lower Little Tennessee River Valley. *Tennessee Anthropologist* 6(1):61–84.
Clewell, A.
  1980   The Vegetation of Leon County, Florida. In *The Leon County Bicentennial Survey Report: An Archaeological Survey of Selected Portions of Leon County, Florida*, by L. Tesar, pp. 386–440. Miscellaneous Project Report Series No. 49. Bureau of Historic Sites and Properties, Division of Archives, History, and Records Management, Department of State, Tallahassee.
Connor, J. (editor and translator)
  1925   *Colonial Records of Spanish Florida. Vol. 1:1570–1577*. Florida State Historical Society, Deland.
Connor, J.
  1926   The Florida Missions of the Franciscan Friars and Their Mission for the Jororo Indians of New Smyrna. Ms. on file at the P. K. Yonge Library of Florida History, University of Florida, Gainesville.
Cowan, C.
  1985   Understanding the Evolution of Plant Husbandry in Eastern North America: Lessons from Botany, Ethnography, and Archaeology. In *Prehistoric Food Production in North America*, edited by R. I. Ford, pp. 205–244. Anthropological Papers No. 75. Museum of Anthropology, University of Michigan, Ann Arbor.
Crook, R.
  1978   *Mississippian Period Community Organizations on the Georgia Coast*. Ph.D. dissertation, Department of Anthropology, University of Florida. University Microfilms, Ann Arbor.
Crosby, A.
  1972   *The Columbian Exchange: Biological and Cultural Consequences of 1492*. Greenwood Press, West Port, Connecticut.
Cumbaa, S.
  1975   *Patterns of Resource Use and Cross-cultural Change in the Spanish Colonial Period*. Ph.D. dissertation, University of Florida. University Microfilms, Ann Arbor.

Deagan, K.
  1972 Fig Springs: The Mid-Seventeenth Century in North-Central Florida. *Historical Archaeology* 6:23–46.
  1973 *Mestizaje* in Colonial St. Augustine. *Ethnohistory* 20:55–65.
  1978 Cultures in Transition: Fusion and Assimilation among the Eastern Timucua. In *Tacachale: Essays on the Indians of Florida and Southeastern Georgia during the Historic Period*, edited by J. T. Milanich and S. Proctor, pp. 89–119. University of Florida Presses, Gainesville.
  1983 *Spanish St. Augustine: The Archaeology of a Colonial Creole Community*. Academic Press, New York.
  1987 Accommodations, Conflict, and Removal: The Impact of the Spanish Missions on Southeastern Indian Life. Paper presented at Native Peoples of the Southeastern United States. March 6, Tallahassee, Florida.

DesJean, T.
  1985 Descriptive Archaeology of the Devils Walking Stick Site (9CAM77), The South Bunker Area. In *Aboriginal Subsistence and Settlement Archaeology of the Kings Bay Locality*, Vol. 1, edited by W. Adams, pp. 125–151. Reports of Investigations No. 1. Department of Anthropology, University of Florida, Gainesville.

Dickenson, J.
  1975 *Jonathan Dickenson's Journal or God's Protecting Providences*, edited by E. Andrews and C. Andrews. Valentine Books, Stuart, Florida.

Dobyns, H.
  1983 *Their Number Become Thinned: Native American Population Dynamics in Eastern North America*. University of Tennessee Press, Knoxville.

Dunlop, Captain
  1929 Capt. Dunlop's Voyage to the Southward 1687. In *The South Carolina Historical and Genealogical Magazine*.

Elliott, J.
  1987 Spain and America before 1700. In *Colonial Spanish America*, edited by L. Bethell, pp. 59–112. Cambridge University Press, Cambridge.

Farrington, I., and J. Urry
  1985 Food and the Early History of Cultivation. *Journal of Ethnobiology* 5(2):143–157.

Fitzhugh, W. (editor)
  1985 *Cultures and Contact*. Smithsonian Institution Press, Washington, D.C.

Florescano, E.
  1987 The Hacienda in New Spain. In *Colonial Spanish America*, edited by L. Bethell, pp. 250–285. Cambridge University Press, Cambridge.

Fontaneda, Do d'Escalante
  1945 *Memoir of Do d'Escalante Fontaneda Respecting Florida, Written in Spain about the Year 1575*, edited by D. O. True and translated by B. Smith. Glade House, Coral Gables, Florida.

Ford, R. (editor)
  1985 Patterns of Prehistoric Food Production in North America. In *Prehistoric Food Production in North America*, edited by R. Ford, pp. 341–364. Anthropological Papers No. 75. Museum of Anthropology, University of Michigan, Ann Arbor.

Foster, G.
  1960 *Culture and Conquest*. Viking Fund Publications in Anthropology No. 27. Wenner-Gren Foundation, New York.

Gannon, M.
  1967 *The Cross in the Sand: The Early Catholic Church in Florida, 1513–1870*. University of Florida Press, Gainesville.

Gardner, P.
  1980 Appendix C: Analysis of the Santa Elena Flotation Samples. In *Discovery of Santa*

Elena, edited by S. South, pp. 106–107. Research Manuscript Series No. 165. University of South Carolina Institute of Archaeology and Anthropology, Columbia.

1981 Appendix IV: Plant Remains from Features 117 and 141, Santa Elena, South Carolina. In *Exploring Santa Elena 1981,* by S. South, pp. 165–170. Research Manuscript Series No. 184. University of South Carolina Institute of Archaeology and Anthropology, Columbia.

Goggin, J., and W. Sturtevant

1964 The Calusa: A Stratified Non-agricultural Society (with Notes on Sibling Marriage). In *Explorations in Cultural Anthropology: Essays in Honor of George P. Murdock,* edited by W. Goodenough, pp. 179–219. McGraw-Hill, New York.

Hally, D.

1981 Plant Preservation and the Content of Paleobotanical Samples: A Case Study. *American Antiquity* 46(4):723–742.

Hann, J.

1986a The Use and Processing of Plants by Indians of Spanish Florida. *Southeastern Archaeology* 5(2):91–102.

1986b Translation of Alonso de Leturiondo's Memorial to the King of Spain. *Florida Archaeology* 2:165–225. Florida Bureau of Archaeological Research, Tallahassee.

1986c General Visitation of the Provinces of Guale and Mocamo made by The Capt. Don Juan Peyo. Ms. on file San Luis Archaeological and Historic Site, Tallahassee.

1987 Twilight of the Mocamo and the Guale as portrayed in the 1695 Visitation. *Florida Historical Quarterly* 461:1–24.

1988 *Apalachee: The Land between the Rivers.* University Presses of Florida, Gainesville.

1989 Summary Guide to Spanish Florida Missions and Visitas with Churches in the Sixteenth and Seventeenth Centuries. Ms. on file at the Bureau of Archaeological Research, Tallahassee, Florida.

1990 Mission to the Calusa. Introduction by William H. Marquardt, translations by J. Hann. Ms. on file; Department of Anthropology, Florida Museum of Natural History, Gainesville, Florida.

n.d. Letters of Fray Baltazar Lopez, Fray Francisco Pareja and Fray Pedro Ruiz about the State of the conversion of the Indians of Florida. Ms. on file San Luis Archaeological and Historic Site, Tallahassee, Florida.

Hariot, T.

1971 A Report of the New Found Land in Virginia. In *The New World, The First Pictures of America,* compiled by S. Lorant. Duell, Sloan, and Pease, New York. Originally published 1588.

Hudson, C. (editor)

1979 *Black Drink: A Native American Tea.* University of Georgia Press, Athens.

Johannesson, S.

1988 The Farmers of the Late Woodland. Paper presented at the 50th Annual Meeting of the Southeastern Archaeological Conference, New Orleans.

Jones, C.

1972 Colonel James Moore and the Destruction of the Apalachee Missions in 1704. *Florida Bureau of Historic Sites and Properties Bulletin* 3:1–50.

1982 Southern Cult Manifestations at the Lake Jackson Site, Leon County, Florida: Salvage Excavation of Mound 3. *Midcontinental Journal of Archaeology* 7(1)3–44.

Jones, G.

1978 The Ethnohistory of the Guale Coast through 1684. In *The Anthropology of St. Catherines Island: 1. Natural and Cultural History.* Anthropological Papers of the American Museum of Natural History 55(2), New York.

Kohler, T.

1979a Corn, Indians, and Spaniards in North-Central Florida: A Technique for Measuring Evolutionary Changes in Corn. *Florida Anthropologist* 32(1)1–7.

1979b Analysis of Corncobs from the Baptizing Springs Site, Florida. In *Political and*

Economic Interactions between Spaniards and Indians: Archaeological and Ethnohistorical Perspectives of the Mission System in Florida, by L. Loucks, pp. 340–349. Unpublished Ph.D. dissertation, Department of Anthropology, University of Florida, Gainesville.

Lanning, J.
1935 *The Spanish Missions of Georgia.* University of North Carolina Press, Chapel Hill.

Larsen, C.
1987 Stress and Adaptation at Santa Catalina de Guale: Analysis of Human Remains. Paper presented at the Society for Historical Archaeology, Savannah, Georgia.

Larsen, C., and R. Saunders
1987 The Two Santa Catalina Cemeteries. Paper presented at the Annual Meeting of the Southeastern Archaeological Conference, Charleston, South Carolina.

Larson, L.
1953 Coastal Mission Survey. Unpublished manuscript. Copy on file, Florida Museum of Natural History.
1978 Historic Guale Indians of the Georgia Coast and the Impact of the Spanish Mission Effort. In *Tacachale: Essays on the Historic Indians of Florida and Southeastern Georgia during the Historic Period,* edited by J. T. Milanich and S. Proctor, pp. 121–140. University Presses of Florida, Gainesville.
1980 *Aboriginal Subsistence Technology on the Southeastern Coastal Plain during the Late Prehistoric Period.* University Presses of Florida, Gainesville.

Laudonnière, René de
1975 *Three Voyages.* Translated and edited by C. E. Bennett. University Presses of Florida, Gainesville.

Leturiondo, Alonso de
1986 Translation of Alonso de Leturiondo's Memorial to the King of Spain, translated by J. Hann. *Florida Archaeology* 2:165–225. Florida Bureau of Archaeological Research, Tallahassee. Originally published [1700].

Linton, R.
1940 *Acculturation in Seven American Indian Tribes.* D. Appleton-Century, New York.

Loucks, J.
1979 *Political and Economic Interactions between Spaniards and Indians: Archaeological and Ethnohistorical Perspectives of the Mission System in Florida.* Unpublished Ph.D. dissertation, Department of Anthropology, University of Florida, Gainesville.

Lyon, E.
1976 *The Enterprise of Florida.* University Presses of Florida, Gainesville.
1984 *Santa Elena: A Brief History of the Colony, 1566–1587.* Research Manuscript Series No. 193. University of South Carolina Institute of Archaeology and Anthropology, Columbia.

McAllister, L.
1984 *Spain and Portugal in the New World, 1492–1700.* University of Minnesota Press, Minneapolis.

McGoun, W.
1989 *Prehistoric Peoples of South Florida.* Unpublished Ph.D. dissertation. Department of Anthropology, University of Florida, Gainesville.

Macleod, M.
1987 Aspects of the Internal Economy. In *Colonial Spanish America,* edited by L. Bethell, pp. 315–360. Cambridge University Press, Cambridge.

Marquardt, W.
1987 South Floridian Contacts with the Bahamas: A Review and Some Speculations. Paper presented at the Symposium, Bahamas 1492: Its People and Environment, Freeport, Bahamas.

Marrinnan, R.
1985 The Archaeology of the Spanish Missions of Florida: 1565–1704. *Florida Journal of Anthropology,* Special Publication No. 4:241–252.

Méxia, A.
1951 Useful and Convenient Directions Giving Faithfully the Rivers, Channels, Lagoons, Woodlands, Settlements, Embarcartion, and Landing Places, and Hamlets, Encountered from the City of St. Augustine to the Bar of Ais [1602]. In *A Survey of the Indian River Archaeology, Florida*. Yale University Publications in Anthropology No. 44. Yale University Press, New Haven.

Milanich, J. T.
1971 *The Alachua Tradition of North Central Florida*. Contributions of the Florida State Museum, Anthropology and History, No. 17.

1972 *Excavations at the Richardson site, Alachua County, Florida: an Early 17th Century Potano Indian Village*. Bulletin of Historic Sites and Properties, No. 2. Division of Archives, History, and Records Management, Tallahassee.

1974 *Life in a 9th Century Indian Household, A Weeden Island Fall-Winter Site on the Upper Apalachicola River, Florida*. Bureau of Historic Sites and Properties Division of Archives, History, and Records Management Bulletin No. 4, pp. 1–44. Florida Department of State, Tallahassee.

1978 The Western Timucua: Patterns of Acculturation and Change. In *Tacachale: Essays on the Indians of Florida and Southeastern Georgia during the Historic Period*, edited by J. T. Milanich and S. Proctor, pp. 59–88. University Presses of Florida, Gainesville.

1987 Corn and Calusa: DeSoto and Demography. In *Coasts, Plains and Deserts: Essays in Honor of Reynold J. Ruppe*, edited by S. Gaines, pp. 173–184. Anthropological Research Papers No. 38. Arizona State University, Tempe.

Milanich, J., and C. Fairbanks
1980 *Florida Archaeology*. Academic Press, New York.

Mitchem, J.
1989 Florida Indians after 1492: The Question of Archaeological Evidence for Antillean-Florida Migrations. *American Anthropologist* 91(3):762–765.

Morell, R., and C. Jones
1970 *San Juan de Aspalaga (a Preliminary Architectural Study)*. Bureau of Historic Sites and Properties Bulletin 1:25–43. Florida Department of State, Tallahassee.

Newsom, L.
1986 Plants, Human Subsistence, and Environment: A Case Study from Hontoon Island (8-Vo-201), Florida. Unpublished Master's thesis, Department of Anthropology, University of Florida, Gainesville.

1987 Analysis of Botanical Remains from Hontoon Island (8Vo202), Florida: 1980–1985 Excavations. *Florida Anthropologist* 40(1):47–84.

Nickerson, N.
1953 Variation in Cob Morphology among Certain Archaeological and Ethnological Races of Maize. *Annals of the Missouri Botanical Garden* 40:79–111.

Oré, L.
1936 *The Martyrs of Florida (1513–1616)*. Translated by M. Geiger. Joseph Wagner, New York.

Ranjel, R.
1922 Narrative of Hernando de Soto Mission of 1539. In *Narratives of the Career of Hernando de Soto in the Conquest of Florida, II*, edited by E. Bourne, pp. 43–150. Allerton, New York.

Rebolledo, Diego de
1657 Translation of Governor Rebolledo's 1657 Visitation of Three Florida Provinces and Related Provinces and Related Documents, translated by J. Hann. *Florida Archaeology* 2:81–146. Florida Bureau of Archaeological Research, Tallahassee.

Reitz, E.
1988 Evidence for Coastal Adaptations in Georgia and South Carolina. *Archaeology of Eastern North America* 16:137–158.

Reitz, E., and C. M. Scarry
1985 *Reconstructing Historic Subsistence with an Example from Sixteenth Century Spanish Florida.* Special Publication Series No. 3. Society for Historical Archaeology, Ann Arbor.

Ribaut, J.
1964 *The Whole and True Discouerye of Terra Florida.* Reprinted. University of Florida Press, Gainesville. Originally published 1563, London.

Ross, J.
1975 Appendix A: 1651 Description of a Florida Wheat and Cattle Farm. In *Patterns of Resource Use and Cross-cultural Dietary Change in the Spanish Colonial Period*, by S. Cumbaa. Ph.D. dissertation, Department of Anthropology, University of Florida. University Microfilms, Ann Arbor.

Ruhl, D.
1985 Seminole Plant Use, Coonti-Hateka. *Withlacoochee River Archaeological Council Newsletter* 2(2):4–5, 10–11.
1987 Preliminary Findings of an Archaeobotanical Sample of Grains from St. Catherines Island, SCDG Quad IV-STR-1; S-99-B (W)58. Ms. on file, American Museum of Natural History.
1988a The Introduction and Archaeological Significance of *Prunus persica*, (L.) Batsch into *La Florida*: An Overview and some Speculations. Paper Presented at the 40th Annual Florida Anthropological Society, Winter Park, Florida.
1988b Old Customs and Traditions in New Terrain: A Look at the Sixteenth and Seventeenth Century Paleoethnobotanical Data from *La Florida*. Paper presented at the 50th annual Southeastern Archaeological Conference, October 20–22, New Orleans.
1989 Palaeoethnobotany at the Two Santa Catalina de Guale Missions: A Preliminary View of the Subsistence and Non-subsistence Botanical Remains. Paper presented at the First Joint Archaeological Congress (SHA), January, Baltimore.
n.d. Corn, Wheat, and Hispanic/Aboriginal Interaction: A Paleoethnobotanical Study of Two Coastal Guale/Spanish Mission Sites in La Florida. Files of the author.

Russo, M.
1988 Coastal Adaptations in Eastern Florida: Models and Methods. *Archaeology of Eastern North America* 16:159–176.

Sauer, C.
1966 *The Early Spanish Main.* University of California Press, Berkeley.

Saunders, R.
1985 Descriptive Archaeology of the Devils Walking Stick Site (9CAM177), North Bunker Area and the Fiber Tempered Area. In *Aboriginal Subsistence and Settlement Archaeology of the Kings Bay Locality*, Vol. 1, edited by W. Adams, pp. 105–124, 152–168. Department of Anthropology Reports of Investigations 1. University of Florida, Gainesville.

Scarry, C. M.
1983 Appendix 11: Analysis of the Floral Remains from the 1982 Santa Elena (38Bu162) Excavations. In *Revealing Santa Elena 1982*, by S. South, pp. 113–143. Research Manuscript Series 188. University of South Carolina Institute of Archaeology and Anthropology, Columbia.
1984 Appendix XII: Analysis of Floral Remains from the 1983 Fort San Felipe (38BU162G) Excavations. In *Testing Archaeological Sampling Methods at Fort San Felipe 1983*, by S. South, pp. 179–200. Research Manuscript Series 190. University of South Carolina Institute of Archaeology and Anthropology, Columbia.
1985a The Use of Plant Foods in Sixteenth Century St. Augustine. *Florida Anthropologist* 38(1–2):70–80.
1985b Paleoethnobotany of the Granada Site. In *Excavations at the Granada Site*, by J. Griffin, pp. 181–248. Florida Division of Archives, History, and Records Management, Tallahassee.

1986 A Descriptive Report on Plant Remains from the Mission Sites 8JE1 and 8JE2. Unpublished paper on file at the Florida Bureau of Archaeological Research, Tallahassee.

1987 A Preliminary Examination of Plant Remains from Test Excavations at San Luis. In *Archaeology at San Luis: 1984–1985 Broad Scale Testing*, by G. Shapiro, pp. 249–256. In *Florida Archaeology*, No. 3. Florida Bureau of Archaeological Research, Tallahassee.

1988 Plant Remains from the San Luis Council House. Ms. on file at the Florida Bureau of Archaeological Research, Tallahassee.

1989 Variability in Mississippian Corn Production. In Forager, Farmer, Indian Chief: Plant Production and Social Relations in the Prehistoric Eastern Woodland, edited by C. Scarry. Ms. for University Presses of Florida, Gainesville.

Scarry, C., and L. Newsom

1990 *Archaeobotanical Research in the Calusa Heartland.* In *Culture and Environment in the Domain of the Calusa*, edited by W. Marquardt. Institute of Archaeology and Paleoenvironmental Studies, University of Florida, Monograph 1. Gainesville, Florida, in press.

Seaberg, L.

1955 The Zetrouer Site: Indian and Spanish in Central Florida. Unpublished Master's thesis, Department of Anthropology, University of Florida.

Sears, W.

1982 *Fort Center.* University Presses of Florida, Gainesville.

Shapiro, G.

1985 The Apalachee Council House at Seventeenth Century San Luis. Paper presented at the 1985 Southeastern Archaeological Conference, Birmingham, Alabama.

1987a *Archaeology at San Luis: 1984–1985 Broad-Scale Testing.* Florida Archaeology Number 3. Florida Bureau of Archaeological Research: Tallahassee, Florida.

1987b Inside the Council House at San Luis. Paper Presented at the 1987 Annual Southeastern Archaeological Conference, Charleston, South Carolina.

Shapiro, G., and R. Vernon

1989 The 17th Century Mission Church and Cemetery at San Luis. Paper presented at the Society for Historical Archaeology, Baltimore.

Sheldon, E.

1978 Childersburg: Evidence of European Contact Demonstrated by Archaeological Plant Remains. *Southeastern Archaeological Conference Special Publication* 5:28–29.

Smith, G., and P. Rice

1989 Acculturation and Trade in the Colonial Wine Industry of Peru, Some preliminary Observations. Paper presented at the First Joint Archaeological Congress (SHA), January, Baltimore.

Smith, H.

1951 A Spanish Mission Site in Jefferson County, Florida. In *Here They Once Stood*, by M. Boyd, J. Griffin, and H. Smith, pp. 107–138. University of Florida Press, Gainesville.

Smith, M.

1987 *Archaeology of Aboriginal Culture Change in the Interior Southeast: Depopulation during the Early Historic Period.* University Presses of Florida, Gainesville.

Smith, R., C. Bradley, N. Borremans, and E. Reitz

1981 Coastal Adaptations in Southeast Georgia: Ten Archaeological Sites at Kings Bay. Report submitted to the U.S. Department of the Navy by the Department of Anthropology. University of Florida, Gainesville.

Solís de Méras, Gonzalo

1964 *Pedro Menendez de Aviles*, translated by J. Thurber Connor. University of Florida Press, Gainesville.

South, S., R. Skowronek, and R. Johnson
  1988   *Spanish Artifacts from Santa Elena*. Anthropological Studies No. 7. University of
    South Carolina Institute of Archaeology and Anthropology, Columbia.
Speck, F.
  1909   *Ethnology of the Yuchi Indians*. Anthropological Publications 1(1). University Mu-
    seum, University of Pennsylvania.
Spellman, C.
  1948   The Agriculture of the Early North Florida Indians. *Florida Anthropologist* 1(3-4):
    37–48.
Spicer, E.
  1961   Types of Contact and Processes of Change. In *Perspectives in American Culture
    Change*, edited by E. Spicer, pp. 517–544. University of Chicago Press, Chicago.
Swanton, J. R.
  1922   *Early History of the Creek Indians and Their Neighbors*. Government Printing Office,
    Washington, D. C.
  1946   *The Indians of Southeastern United States*. Bureau of American Ethnology Bulletin
    No. 137. Washington, D. C.
Sweett, Z.
  1938   Early Spanish Missions of Florida, 1600–1769. Typewritten manuscript on file with
    the P. K. Yonge Library of Florida History, University of Florida, Gainesville.
Sweett, Z., and M. Sheppy
  1940   *The Spanish Missions of Florida*. Writers Program, Works Projects Administration,
    State of Florida Federal Works Agency.
Symes, M., and M. Stephens
  1965   A-272: The Fox Pond Site. *Florida Anthropologist* 18:65–72.
Ulmer, M., and S. Beck (editors)
  1951   *Cherokee Cookery*. Museum of the Cherokee Indians, Cherokee, North Carolina.
Walker, K.
  1985   The Protohistoric and Historic Indian Occupation at Kings Bay: An Overview. In
    *Aboriginal Subsistence and Settlement Archaeology of the Kings Bay Locality. Vol. 1: The
    Kings Bay and Devils Walking Stick Sites*, edited by W. Adams, pp. 55–73. Department
    of Anthropology, University of Florida, Gainesville.
Wallace, R.
  1975   *An Archaeological, Ethnohistoric, and Biochemical Investigation of the Guale Aborigines
    of the Georgia Coastal Strand*. Ph.D. dissertation, Department of Anthropology, Uni-
    versity of Florida. University Microfilms, Ann Arbor.
Watson, P.
  1976   In Pursuit of Prehistoric Subsistence: A Comparative Account of Some Contem-
    porary Flotation Techniques. *Midcontinental Journal of Archaeology* 1:77–100.
  1989   Early Plant Cultivation in the Eastern Woodlands of North America. In *Foraging
    and Farming: The Evolution of Plant Exploitation*, edited by D. Harris and G. Hillman.
    London.
Weisman, B.
  1988   Archaeological Investigations at the Fig Springs (8Co-1) Mission. Ms. on file
    Florida Division of Recreation and Parks.
  1989   Excavation Summary. Fig Springs Mission Project, April 3, 1989. Ms. on file
    Florida Division of Historical Resources.
Wenhold, L.
  1936   *A 17th Century Letter of Gabriel Diaz Vara Calderon, Bishop of Cuba, Describing the
    Indians and Indian Missions of Florida*. Smithsonian Miscellaneous Collections,
    95(16). Smithsonian Institution, Washington, D. C.
West, G. J.
  1989   Early Historic Vegetation Change in Alta California: The Fossil Evidence. In
    Columbian Consequences. Vol. 1: Archaeological and Historical Perspectives on the Spanish

Borderlands West, edited by David H. Thomas, pp. 333–348. Smithsonian Institution Press, Washington, D.C.

White, J.

1975   Historic Contact Sites as Laboratories for the Study of Culture Change. *The Conference on Historic Site Archaeology Papers 1974* 9:153–163.

White, N.

1982   The Curlee Site and Fort Walton Development in the Upper Apalachicola-Lower Chattahoochee Valley. Unpublished Ph.D. dissertation, Department of Anthropology, Case Western Reserve University.

Widmer, R.

1988   *The Evolution of the Calusa: A Nonagricultural Chiefdom on the Southwest Florida Coast.* University of Alabama Press, Tuscaloosa.

Contributors

Amy Turner Bushnell is research associate in anthropology at the American Museum of Natural History, assistant professor of history at the University of South Alabama, and former historian for the museum of San Agustín Antiguo. Author of *The King's Coffer* and several articles dealing with provincial Florida, she has recently completed a monograph about the support and supplying of seventeenth-century missions. Her field is the Hispanic American peripheries.

José Maria Cruxent is professor of archaeology and ceramics at the University of Falcon (Venezuela) and is currently directing the archaeological program at the site of La Isabela in the Dominican Republic. Originally from Catalonia (Spain), he has worked for more than five decades in the prehistoric and historical archaeology of Latin America and the Caribbean. He carried out pioneering research in the historical archaeology of this region, collaborating widely with North American scholars. His work, including hundreds of publications, has won numerous awards, most recently the prestigious Venezuelan National Prize.

Caleb Curren is director of archaeology at the Alabama-Tombigbee Regional Commission and a research associate at Pensacola Junior College. His general research interests include the archaeology of the Gulf Coastal Plain. He has participated in investigations in the southeast United States, Yucatan, central Mexico, and Brazil. Ethnohistorical research of the conquest period in the southeast United States is currently his main research emphasis.

Kathleen A. Deagan is curator of historical archaeology and chairperson of the department of anthropology at the Florida Museum of Natural History, University of Florida. Her field and collections research have concentrated on the Spanish occupation of Florida and the Caribbean, and major excavation projects include 17 years in St. Augustine (Florida) and 9 years in Haiti and the Dominican Republic. Other related work has been undertaken in Spain, Peru, Honduras, and throughout the Caribbean.

Chester B. DePratter is a research professor at the South Carolina Institute of Archaeology and Anthropology. He has conducted extensive research on the contact period of the southeastern United States, and he has coauthored papers on the Hernando de Soto, Juan Pardo, and Tristán de Luna expeditions. He serves on the regional De Soto Trail Commission and is chairman of the South Carolina Columbus Quincentenary Commission.

David H. Dye is assistant professor of anthropology at Memphis State University. He has specialized in the archaeology and ethnohistory of the Southeast. His long-term research interests including various aspects of prehistoric technology, protohistoric acculturation, and the anthropology of nineteenth-century Native Americans.

Charles R. Ewen received his Ph.D. from the University of Florida and at present directs the Sponsored Research Program at the Arkansas Archaeological Survey. His primary research interest is the Spanish colonial period, and he has directed excavations in Florida and Haiti.

Michael V. Gannon is professor of history and director of the Institute for Early Contact Period Studies at the University of Florida. His research and writing has been devoted primarily to the southeastern Spanish Borderlands with an emphasis on the Franciscan missions. Through the institute, he assists historical, archaeological, and archival projects directed toward the Columbus Quincentenary.

Manuel García-Arevalo has carried out archaeological research throughout the Dominican Republic and Haiti for two decades. He has published extensively on both prehistoric and contact period Taino art and archaeology, and serves on the Dominican National Commission for the Observation of the Quincentenary. He also curates the García-Arevalo Foundation Archaeological Museum, which includes some of the world's finest collections of Taino art. He is president of the García-Arevalo Foundation in Santo Domingo, which supports considerable research and publication, and has been an important force in the archaeology of the Dominican Republic and Caribbean.

John W. Griffin is currently a consulting archaeologist residing in St. Augustine, Florida. He was previously chief of the Southeast Archaeological Center, National Park Service, and directed several agency programs for the state of Florida. His research in the archaeology of the Spanish Borderlands began immediately after World War II, and has continued alongside work in other historical periods and in prehistoric sites in the Southeast.

David J. Hally is associate professor of anthropology at the University of Georgia. He has focused his research and writing on the late prehistoric cultures of the Southeast, particularly in Georgia. His long-term research interests include pottery vessel form and function, the archaeology of households, and the spatial organization of chiefdoms.

John H. Hann is historian and translator for the San Luis Archaeological and Historical Site, Tallahassee, administered by the Florida Bureau of Archaeological Research in the Division of Historical Resources under the secretary of state. He has taught Latin American history at Florida State University and New Mexico State University. He has published articles and translations on the Indians and Spanish missions of the Southeast in anthropological, archaeological, and historical journals and a monograph on the Apalachee.

Conrad Harkins, O.F.M., holds a doctorate in medieval studies and previously served as director of the Franciscan Institute, St. Bonaventure (New York), and editor of *Franciscan Studies*. He has been actively researching the Cause of the Georgia Martyrs and has firsthand archaeological experience at Franciscan mission sites in Georgia and Florida.

Charles Hudson is professor of anthropology and history at the University of Georgia. He is the author and editor of several books on the history and culture of the Indians of the southeastern United States.

Dale L. Hutchinson is a doctoral candidate in anthropology at the University of Illinois at Champaign-Urbana. His major research interests are human health and biocultural adaptation, human osteology and paleopathology, and the archaeology of the Americas.

B. Calvin Jones is an archaeologist for the Florida Division of Historical Resources. He is best known for his mission explorations in Florida, and he has also excavated in Texas, Oklahoma, and New Mexico.

Jane Landers is a visiting assistant professor of history at the University of Florida (Gainesville), and director of the History Teaching Alliance. Her primary research interest is race relations in colonial Spanish America and she is the historian for the ongoing archaeological investigations at Fort Mose (Florida), site of the first free black town in the United States.

James B. Langford, Jr. is an independent researcher with a focused interest on Late Mississippian cultures in the southeastern United States. He is founder and president of the Coosawattee Foundation, a nonprofit archaeological research and educational organization; he also serves as chairman of the Georgia De Soto Trail Commission.

Clark Spencer Larsen is associate professor of anthropology at Purdue University, West Lafayette (Indiana), and a research associate in anthropology at the American Museum of Natural History (New York). He has worked extensively with archaeological human remains and currently focuses his research on biocultural adaptation in native New World populations, including the postcontact period in the southeastern United States.

Janet E. Levy is associate professor of anthropology in the Department of Sociology, Anthropology, and Social Work at the University of North Carolina at Charlotte. Her research interests include the development of complex societies in the eastern United States and in Western Europe.

Keith J. Little is a research associate at both the Alabama-Tombigbee Regional Commission and Pensacola Junior College. He has been actively involved with conquest archaeology research in the southeastern United States for the past 12 years.

Eugene Lyon is director of the Center for Historic Research, St. Augustine Foundation at Flagler College (St. Augustine, Florida). He is a specialist in the sixteenth-century

Spanish presence in North America, with particular interest in the Menéndez period in Spanish Florida. The center holds a substantial body of primary documents from a variety of Spanish and American archives, from which a database of sixteenth-century materials has been organized. He has collaborated with several archaeologists in the study of colonial Puerto Real, Santa Elena, Santa Catalina, and St. Augustine. He located a précis of the *Relación* of Fray Sebastián de Cañate, a fifth de Soto narrative, and found in the Archives of the Indies (Seville) material descriptive of Columbus's caravel *Niña*.

Rhonda L. Majors is a candidate for the Master of Arts degree in the Department of Anthropology, Florida State University, and currently a trainee with the U.S. Forest Service.

Rochelle A. Marrinan is assistant professor of anthropology at Florida State University. Her research interests include the historical archaeology of the Southeastern United States and the Caribbean, with fieldwork in Haiti and Florida.

J. Alan May is director of the Schiele Museum of Natural History Archaeology Program and adjunct professor of anthropology at the University of North Carolina at Charlotte. He specializes in the prehistory of the North Carolina piedmont, with an emphasis on late prehistoric and protohistoric periods. His long-term research interests include coastal Georgia prehistory and remote sensing.

Jerald T. Milanich is curator of archaeology at the Florida Museum of Natural History, where he was a member of the team responsible for the traveling exhibit "First Encounters: Spanish Explorations in the Caribbean and United States, 1492–1570." He has carried out archaeological and ethnohistorical research on the native peoples of the Southeast United States, especially Florida and Georgia. Recent work has focused on the events and peoples of the sixteenth and seventeenth centuries.

Jeffrey M. Mitchem received a Ph.D. in anthropology from the University of Florida. He is currently assistant professor of anthropology, Louisiana State University. His major research interests include the archaeology of early sixteenth-century sites in the Southeast, ceramic technology, ethnohistory, and mortuary practices. He has conducted archaeological research in the Southeast and the Great Basin. He is the author of several scholarly papers on the archaeology of Florida and early Spanish–Native American contact.

David G. Moore is the staff archaeologist for the western office of the North Carolina Division of Archives and History, in Asheville, North Carolina. His interests include the archaeology of the southern Appalachian Mountains, Cherokee archaeology, and complex societies in the southeastern United States. He is currently studying the late prehistoric and protohistoric periods in the Catawba River Valley in North Carolina.

Dan F. Morse is the Northeast Arkansas station archaeologist for the Arkansas Archaeological Survey. Since 1967, he has concentrated on the archaeology of northeast Arkansas and the Mid-South, publishing extensively on this region, most notably the *Archaeology of the Central Mississippi Valley*. His major research interests include Paleo-Indian, lithic technology, the development of Mississippian societies, and the protohistoric contact period.

Phyllis A. Morse is a research associate with the Arkansas Archaeological Survey. She has conducted considerable research on the protohistoric and historic periods of northeast Arkansas. She wrote *Parkin*, the first specific associated with the de Soto expedition into Arkansas, and she co-authored *Archaeology of the Central Mississippi Valley* with Dan F. Morse.

Ann F. Ramenofsky is an associate professor of archaeology at the University of New Mexico. As suggested by her recent book, *Vectors of Death: The Archaeology of European Contact*, she is interested in demography, epidemiology, archaeological method, and theory of the contact period. Her recent fieldwork has centered on the late prehistory of Louisiana.

Elizabeth J. Reitz is associate professor of anthropology in the Department of Anthropology at the University of Georgia (Athens). Her research interests include human use of coastal resources in both pre-Hispanic and historic periods. She has conducted zooarchaeological analysis of faunal materials from sixteenth-century sites in South Carolina, Georgia, Florida, and the Caribbean.

Christopher B. Ruff is associate professor of anatomy at Johns Hopkins University, Baltimore (Maryland). He uses biomechanics theory to study the interface between behavior and skeletal morphology in a number of North American skeletal samples, living human and nonhuman primates, and early hominid and hominoid remains from East Africa.

Donna L. Ruhl is a doctoral candidate in anthropology at the University of Florida, and a graduate research assistant at the Florida Museum of Natural History. Her research is focused on the archaeobotanical remains from southeastern sites and she is currently working on the paleoethnobotany of two Spanish missions in La Florida.

Katherine F. Russell is a Ph.D. student in the biological anthropology program at Kent State University (Ohio) and anatomy instructor at the Case Western Research University School of Medicine. Her interests include human identification, paleodemography, hominoid anatomy, and biocultural adaptation.

Rebecca Saunders is a doctoral candidate in anthropology at the University of Florida, and a graduate research assistant at the Florida Museum of Natural History. She has conducted archaeological research throughout the American Southeast, and is currently attempting to define the aboriginal ceramic complexes at two Spanish mission sites in northern La Florida.

C. Margaret Scarry is an adjunct instructor in anthropology at Florida State University, a research associate of the Florida Museum of Natural History, and an archaeobotanical consultant. Her primary interest is in the articulation between subsistence economies and others aspects of social systems. Most of her research has dealt with the late prehistoric and early historic cultures of the southeastern United States. Besides working on plant remains from sixteenth-century Spanish Florida, she has directed excavations at the Moundville site (Alabama) and analyzed archaeobotanical collections from Alabama, Florida, Maryland, Mississippi, and New York.

John F. Scarry is supervisor of the archaeological research section of the Florida Bureau of Archaeological Research, and adjunct lecturer in the Department of Anthropology, Florida State University. His research interests include chiefdoms and the emergence of organizational complexity, quantification of archaeological analysis, and the impact of European societies on the native peoples of North America. Specializing in the archaeology of the late prehistoric and early historic Southeast, he has studied Mississippian sixteenth-century European contact and seventeenth-century mission sites in northwestern Florida.

Margaret J. Schoeninger is associate professor of anthropology at the University of Wisconsin, Madison. Her research is concerned with the complex nature of diet and its role in adaptation in past human populations. She has done extensive research on chemical signatures of diet in archaeological human remains. She has worked on North America, Africa, and Europe.

Gary N. Shapiro, before his untimely death in 1988, served as director of archaeology at San Luis Archaeological and Historical Site in Tallahassee for the Florida Division of Historical Resources. During his five-year tenure he established the foundation and course of the archaeological research program focusing on seventeenth-century Spanish-Indian relations in Florida's mission period. His research interests included late prehistoric chiefdoms of the Southeast, and he published in a number of archaeological journals. Shapiro was a founding member of the Lamar Institute and served as editor of its newsletter, *Lamar Briefs*.

Marvin T. Smith is visiting assistant professor at the University of Georgia. A specialist in the contact period in the Southeast, his research interests include the effects of early European exploration and colonization on the Indians of the interior Southeast, and the material culture of European-Indian trade.

Stanley South is an archaeologist and research professor at the South Carolina Institute of Archaeology and Anthropology, University of South Carolina. Founder of the *Conference on Historic Site Archaeology*, South has written dozens of research papers and monographs. In 1977, he published the influential book *Method and Theory in Historical Archeology* and edited *Research Strategies in Historical Archeology*. He has excavated extensively throughout the American Southeast, most recently at Santa Elena (South Carolina). In 1987, he received the J. C. Harrington Medal in Historical Archaeology.

David Hurst Thomas, a member of the National Academy of Sciences, is at present curator of anthropology at the American Museum of Natural History (New York). He has specialized in North American archaeology, conducting extensive research in the Great Basin and the American Southeast, including the discovery and 10-year excavation of sixteenth- and seventeenth-century *Mission Santa Catalina de Guale* (St. Catherines Island, Georgia). He has published four archaeology textbooks, written several dozen monographs and scientific articles dealing with archaeological method and theory, and served as general editor for *The North American Indian* (21 volumes) and *The Spanish Borderlands Sourcebooks* (30 volumes).

David J. Weber, Robert and Nancy Dedman Professor of History at Southern Methodist University, is author or editor of fourteen books, including: *The Taos Trappers: The Fur Trade in the Far Southwest, 1540–1846; Foreigners in Their Native Land: Historical Roots of the Mexican Americans; New Spain's Far Northern Frontier . . . 1540–1821; The Mexican Frontier, 1821–1846: The American Southwest under Mexico; Richard H. Kern: Expeditionary Artist in the Far Southwest, 1848–1853;* and *Myth and History of the Hispanic Southwest*. He is currently working on a history of the borderlands, "The Spanish Frontier in North America, 1513–1821."

John Worth is a doctoral student in anthropology at the University of Florida. His current research interests include the archaeology and ethnohistory of early historic period Indians in the Spanish missions of north-central Florida.